Essays on Ayn Rand's
Atlas Shrugged

Essays on Ayn Rand's
Atlas Shrugged

Edited by Robert Mayhew

LEXINGTON BOOKS

A division of
ROWMAN & LITTLEFIELD PUBLISHERS, INC.
Lanham • Boulder • New York • Toronto • Plymouth, UK

LEXINGTON BOOKS

A division of Rowman & Littlefield Publishers, Inc.
A wholly owned subsidiary of The Rowman & Littlefield Publishing Group, Inc.
4501 Forbes Boulevard, Suite 200
Lanham, MD 20706

Estover Road
Plymouth PL6 7PY
United Kingdom

British Library Cataloguing in Publication Information Available

Library of Congress Cataloging-in-Publication Data

Essays on Ayn Rand's Atlas Shrugged / edited by Robert Mayhew.
    p. cm.
    Includes bibliographical references and index.
    ISBN 978-0-7391-2779-7 (alk. paper) — ISBN 978-0-7391-2780-3 (pbk. : alk.
paper) — ISBN 978-0-7391-3636-2 (ebook)
    1. Rand, Ayn. Atlas shrugged. I. Mayhew, Robert.
PS3535.A547A9434 2009
813'.52—dc22   2009008838

Printed in the United States of America

∞™ The paper used in this publication meets the minimum requirements of
American National Standard for Information Sciences—Permanence of Paper
for Printed Library Materials, ANSI/NISO Z39.48-1992.

Contents

Preface

Atlas Shrugged is Ayn Rand's *magnum opus*. Not only is it her fullest presentation of her philosophy, it is the one novel, she said, that is "completely my sense of life, without reservations." (This quote, and those that follow, are from the biographical interviews [Ayn Rand Archives].) She explained:

> the form of literature in which I feel . . . most at home, which represents my literary sense of life, would be where *everything* is made by me—everything except the metaphysical human abstractions. In other words, it has to be things as they *might* be, but from then on I want them to be as they *ought* to be—as I want to make them. . . . I want to be in my own universe of my own abstractions, so that even the villains are stylized by me.

Atlas Shrugged, she says, "was completely my kind of universe" for two main reasons: (1) It has "a very strong plot gimmick," that is, "it is built on an unusual plot device which is not naturalistic in any sense; it's not even realistic." (2) It is "completely detached from any journalistic reality." By contrast, *We the Living* (which is set in 1920s Soviet Russia) is not "fully" her "kind of writing, because it's too historical." Similarly, *The Fountainhead* is "a little too realistic," because it mentions "specific years and specific facts, like the Depression." The story is "tied to a particular period. In *Atlas* I felt completely as if I'm building the whole universe."

The present collection of essays is a guide through and exploration of this universe and its creation.

I had originally intended to organize this volume into three parts: the history of *Atlas Shrugged*, *Atlas Shrugged* as literature, and *Atlas Shrugged* as philosophy. But I found that too many essays, in fundamental ways, did not fit well or exclusively under any such headings. (This is clear, for example, in the case of chapters 2–4, which cover the history of the novel as well as issues in literary esthetics.) So I have dispensed with the division into parts, though the chapters are roughly organized so that the more historical pieces are placed at the beginning, and the more philosophical (beyond esthetics) come at the end. An exception is the opening chapter.

In chapter 1, "The Part and Chapter Headings of *Atlas Shrugged*," Onkar Ghate writes that these headings "serve as guideposts to direct our attention to central issues that must be understood and central contradictions that must be resolved in order to grasp both the mystery and the logic of *Atlas Shrugged*." Ghate serves as a guide through these issues, and these contradictions and their resolution. The result is a detailed and extremely useful aid to the study of the novel, and an excellent overview with which to begin this collection.

The two essays that follow, Shoshana Milgram's "Who *Was* John Galt? The Creation of Ayn Rand's Ultimate Ideal Man" and "The Spirit of Francisco d'Anconia: The Development of His Characterization," explain in great detail what the early notes and drafts of *Atlas Shrugged* tell us about the creation of two of the novel's major heroes. Complementing the second of these essays is Tore Boeckmann's "A Note on Francisco's Ancestry," which describes the influence that the eponymous character from Schiller's *Fiesco* (a play Rand admired) had on her creation of Francisco d'Anconia.

The next three essays describe the history of *Atlas Shrugged*, from its completion to its publication and initial reception. Mary Ann Sures's "Working for Ayn Rand" is an excerpt from *Facets of Ayn Rand: Memoirs by Mary Ann Sures and Charles Sures*, and includes (among other "facets") a firsthand account of the day Ayn Rand finished the novel. Richard Ralston's "Publishing *Atlas Shrugged*" describes not the story of Rand's struggle to find a publisher (which was central to the publication histories of her earlier novels) but the criteria according to which she selected Random House from among the many publishers vying for the next novel from the author of *The Fountainhead*. Michael S. Berliner's "The *Atlas Shrugged* Reviews" describes the generally hostile nature of the reviews the novel received, and underscores that this hostility came as much from the Right as it did from the Left. He gives special attention to the worst of all the reviews, that of religious conservative and ex-communist Whittaker Chambers in the *National Review*. Following Berliner's essay, and published here for the first time, is the devastating critique that Leonard Peikoff wrote in a letter to the *National Review* in response to Chambers's dishonest treatment of *Atlas Shrugged*.

With Tore Boeckmann's "*Atlas Shrugged* and the Metaphysics of Values," we move from history to esthetics. Boeckmann describes the values—and especially the extrathematic values—that make an Ayn Rand novel an Ayn Rand novel. Receiving special attention are good-versus-good conflicts, romantic tests of strength, the spiritual nobility of material production, and the glory of America. The next two essays discuss *Atlas Shrugged* in connection with other famous novels. Andrew Bernstein's "*Atlas Shrugged* as the Culmination of the Romantic Novel" compares it to two nineteenth century novels that Ayn Rand admired: Victor Hugo's *Les Misérables* and Fyodor Dostoyevsky's *The Brothers Karamazov*. Harry Binswanger's "A Tale of Two Novels" provides a brief contrast between *Atlas Shrugged* and James Joyce's *Ulysses* that supports his conviction that "one of these novels is a stylistic masterpiece, and the other is trash."

Ever since its publication in 1957, there has been talk of adapting *Atlas Shrugged* into a film or (later) into a television mini-series. But no such film or series has yet been realized. Relying on Ayn Rand's writings on esthetics, her comments on filming *Atlas Shrugged*, and her own work on a screenplay for a proposed nine-hour mini-series, Jeff Britting's "Adapting *Atlas Shrugged* to Film" lays out principles that should guide any proper film adaptation of the novel.

Ayn Rand wrote that the theme of *Atlas Shrugged* is "the role of the mind in man's existence." In "*Atlas Shrugged* on the Role of the Mind in Man's Existence," Gregory Salmieri describes in detail what the novel has to say about this role. In doing so, he presents some of the essentials of Rand's view of man, and introduces some of the ethical content of the novel, thus offering an excellent transition to the two essays in the present collection that focus on Rand's moral philosophy. In "Ayn Rand's Ethics: From *The Fountainhead* to *Atlas Shrugged*," Darryl Wright explains how and why, contrary to Rand's initial expectations, *Atlas Shrugged* presents "a more detailed, more complex, more systematic, more fully validated—and, in some ways, different—view of ethics from *The Fountainhead*." Tara Smith's "No Tributes to Caesar: Good or Evil in *Atlas Shrugged*" examines the novel's presentation of the choice between good and evil, and the ultimate either-or nature, and life-or-death consequences, of that choice.

The next three essays present us with prime examples of good and evil in *Atlas Shrugged*. Two focus on its presentation of businessmen as heroes, which makes this novel virtually unique in the history of literature. Ayn Rand described the plot-theme of *Atlas* as "The men of the mind going on strike against an altruist-collectivist society." In "The Businessmen's Crucial Role: Material Men of the Mind," Debi Ghate discusses the intellectual and spiritual nature and value of businessmen, and explains why, given the novel's plot-theme, its heroes *had* to include businessmen. Edwin Locke's "The Traits of Business Heroes in *Altas Shrugged*" underscores the fact that the businessmen in *Atlas* are *moral* heroes by focusing on the virtues (e.g., rationality, independence, justice) that they embody. Tara Smith's "'Humanity's Darkest Evil': The Lethal Destructiveness of Non-Objective Law"—covering issues in ethics, political philosophy, and philosophy of law—takes us from the good presented in the novel to a primary evil, and demonstrates (among other things) how destructive non-objective law is for businessmen.

There follow two essays on Galt's speech—of which Ayn Rand once wrote: "This is the philosophy of Objectivism." In "The Role of Galt's Speech in *Atlas Shrugged*," Onkar Ghate demonstrates the integral role the speech plays in the action and story of the novel, and how the speech contributes to the novel's theme. Taking off from Ghate's essay, Allan Gotthelf's "Galt's Speech in Five Sentences (and Forty Questions)" offers readers interested in exploring in detail the speech's structure and content some methods for doing so, and some of the results of Gotthelf's own application of these methods. These two essays provide an eagle's-eye view of the speech, and a proper understanding of its place in the novel.

The penultimate essay is Gregory Salmieri's "Discovering Atlantis: *Atlas Shrugged*'s Demonstration of a New Moral Philosophy," a tour de force rich in discussion of philosophical issues, many not dealt with elsewhere in the collection. Salmieri describes in great detail—focusing on the characters Hank Rearden and Dagny Taggart—the means by which the philosophical (and especially the ethical) truths of the novel are induced. The volume ends with an excellent complement to Salmieri's "Discovering Atlantis" and its discussion of Dagny: Allan Gotthelf's "A Note on Dagny's 'Final Choice,'" which explains why John Galt (and not Fransisco or Rearden) is her "final, irreplaceable, choice."

Completing the volume are two appendixes, each consisting of an outline created by Salmieri: one of the action of the entire novel, and the other of Galt's speech.

The preparation of this collection began, and some of the essays in it were written, in 2007, the year marking the fiftieth anniversary of the publication of *Atlas Shrugged*. Since its publication, the novel has never been out of print, and in the first decade of the twenty-first century it still averages sales of well over 100,000 copies a year. As Richard Ralston states in his publishing history of the novel: "At this writing total sales exceed 6,250,000 copies—a remarkable total for a lengthy, serious, intellectual novel that enshrined businessmen and industrialists as the unacknowledged heroic leaders of human progress, and directly challenged the traditional moral and philosophical pretensions of modern society." The present collection represents a small tribute to this magnificent novel.

Robert Mayhew
Seton Hall University
November 2008

Acknowledgments

I wish to thank Leonard Peikoff (Executor of the Estate of Ayn Rand) for permission to use previously unpublished material of Ayn Rand, and Jeff Britting (Archivist of the Ayn Rand Archives) for his assistance in accessing this material. Thanks also to Lynda Phung and the staff at Lexington Books for their work on this volume, and to Neil Erian for preparing the index. Special thanks are due to Tore Boeckmann, who read through and commented on the proofs of the entire work. I am grateful to Seton Hall University for its continued support of my research, including a sabbatical leave in the last part of which I began my work on this volume. Finally, many thanks to both the Ayn Rand Institute and the Anthem Foundation for Objectivist Scholarship for grants that supported this project.

Bibliographical Note

Unless otherwise indicated, quotes from *Atlas Shrugged* will be followed by page number(s) in parentheses in the text and not by an endnote. Pagination refers to the original hardback edition (New York: Random House, 1957), which has the same pagination as the 1999 Plume quality paperback edition (which includes Leonard Peikoff's introduction to the thirty-fifth anniversary edition).

In some chapters, the author quotes from, and refers to information contained in, a series of biographical interviews that Ayn Rand gave in 1960–1961, the tapes and transcripts of which are in the Ayn Rand Archives. References will appear in the endnotes as: Biographical interviews (Ayn Rand Archives).

1

The Part and Chapter Headings of *Atlas Shrugged*

Onkar Ghate

At over a thousand pages long and dealing with the fate of a civilization, *Atlas Shrugged* is a story of incredible scope and complexity. Its theme is the role of man's reasoning mind in achieving all the values of his existence. Its plot is driven by a central question, a seeming contradiction: If the men of the mind are the creators and sustainers of man's life, why do they continually lose their battles and witness their achievements siphoned off and destroyed by men who have abandoned their minds? The story focuses on how the men of the mind learn to ask and to answer this question, thereby putting a stop to their own exploitation.

To resolve the apparent contradiction demands of the heroes a ruthless commitment to logic: to identify the problem, learn its fundamental cause, and grasp the path to its solution. To liberate themselves, the men of the mind must discover, understand, and then practice a new set of philosophical principles. And for we as readers to really appreciate the story's progression, the same exacting logical focus is demanded of us. The names of the three parts of *Atlas Shrugged* are certainly a tribute to Aristotle and his discovery of the laws of logic (as Ayn Rand herself describes the three parts in the afterword to *Atlas Shrugged*, "About the Author"). But they are more than this. They name the fundamental logical issue that the events of that part of the story are (and that we as readers should be) focused on. They, in conjunction with the individual chapter headings, serve as guideposts to direct our attention to central issues that must be understood and central contradictions that must be resolved in order to grasp both the mystery and the logic of *Atlas Shrugged*.

Let us explore how this is so.

I will discuss each of the parts and chapters of *Atlas Shrugged* in their chronological order, but I will not be recapping their events. This is not meant to be an exhaustive summary. Think of it more as a study guide. I am assuming familiarity with the events of each part and each chapter: Given that familiarity, I am trying to highlight how the part and chapter headings help integrate those events and thus enable us to gain a deeper understanding of the story and its meaning. (All quotations will be from the part or chapter under discussion, unless otherwise indicated.)

PART I: NON-CONTRADICTION

Part I of *Atlas Shrugged* begins with Eddie Willers' attempt to convince James Taggart, President of Taggart Transcontinental Railroad, to face the considerable problems on its Rio Norte Line. This line provides service to the last booming area of the United States, the state of Colorado. Part I ends with Ellis Wyatt, the most productive of Colorado's industrialists, setting fire to his oil fields and vanishing.

The main sequence of action in part I is the destruction of the only reliable rail line servicing Colorado, the Phoenix-Durango, and Hank Rearden's and Dagny Taggart's relentless effort to construct a replacement, the John Galt Line, a replacement fully worthy of the explosion of productivity taking place in Colorado. The principal paradox of part I is why Hank and Dagny face such tremendous opposition, from every corner of society, to their attempt to save Colorado, and why, when their desperate struggle eventually succeeds, their achievement and Colorado's are nevertheless so easily, effortlessly destroyed.

As this main line of action unfolds, a multitude of other mysteries and seeming contradictions surface. Why, for instance, does an institution devoted to science, the State Science Institute, denounce the scientific achievement that is Rearden Metal? Why does Jim destroy the Phoenix-Durango, even though this jeopardizes the existence of his own railroad? Why won't Owen Kellogg take the better job that Dagny offers him? Why is the philosopher Hugh Akston working as a cook in a diner? Why did Francisco d'Anconia, who possessed the promise of becoming one of the world's great industrialists, turn into a playboy? Why has Wyatt abandoned his greatest love, his oil fields? Why, in a civilized world, is there a pirate roaming the oceans? Why does it seem like there is a fifth Halley Concerto, one of joy and deliverance, when Richard Halley composed only four? Why was the incomparable achievement of the motor abandoned as though it were worthless scrap? Who is John Galt?

Even wider questions arise. Pitted against the received views on these issues, the events of part I raise questions about who actually are the exploited and the exploiters in society, what really determines who rises to the top and who sinks to the bottom, and what actually is the relation between the spiritual and the material.

Only when Hank and Dagny learn to resolve, in parts II and III, all these questions and apparent contradictions will they understand the fate of the

John Galt Line—that is, why, despite Hank and Dagny's enormous life-giving power, their achievement *had* to meet the end it did.

Chapter I: The Theme

Atlas Shrugged is a mystery story, but it contains no false clues or leads. To unravel its mystery requires only philosophical acumen. Indeed, everything essential that is to be discovered is contained in preliminary form here, in the first chapter. As its title suggests, this chapter presages the destruction—and the rebirth—to come.

We get a glimpse, as Eddie Willers walks through the streets of New York City, of decay: bums asking for money, skyscrapers covered in grime, a prosperous street now consisting of one where only a fourth of its shops are out of business. Willers' mood sets the tone. His apprehensive feeling that "your days are numbered" is accurate—this, he and we will later learn, is the consequence of Galt's strike (12). By Galt withdrawing the men of the mind, the world's days *are* numbered. Willers' memory of the oak tree from childhood—his feeling of safety from its enormous vitality and strength, and his feeling of betrayal upon discovering it to be an "empty shell," its "heart . . . rotted away long ago"—is not a causeless memory (5). The oak tree is what Taggart Transcontinental represents to the adult Eddie Willers; its great building gives him a "sense of security"; he thinks it will always stand (6). But its heart—the mind that rules it—has also rotted away. Its president is James Taggart—and we see what that means as Jim evades the problems on the Rio Norte Line and seeks to avoid the responsibility of decision.

The decision maker, the only reason Taggart Transcontinental still has a heartbeat, is Dagny. But though everyone knows that she's the one who runs things, she is never officially given that recognition or sanction: she is Vice-President in Charge of Operation while Jim is president. Nevertheless, it is Dagny who, by her own admission, saves Taggart Transcontinental from the disasters created by Jim and the Board, such as Mexico's imminent nationalization of Taggart Transcontinental's San Sebastián Line.

But Dagny's job is growing more and more difficult, because good men are now "so strangely hard to find" (17). And yet when she does find one, when she tries to promote to superintendent Owen Kellogg, a young engineer who loves his work, he refuses her offer—for no discernible reason.

What we are actually seeing here is the central conflict of the story: the parasite Jim, trying to exist off the achievements of the mind; Dagny, willing to carry him along in the name of her love for her railroad and for all of existence; and another mind, Kellogg, no longer willing to do penance for that love. And we witness the first effects of the strike on New York City; the strike will have succeeded when the lights of the city go out completely. We even get a glimpse of the fact that Dagny is the strikers' most dangerous enemy; most dangerous in body, of course, because she is the one propping up the looters;

but also most dangerous in spirit, because she is the only one who has the capacity to see the strikers for what they are: it is she who spots the young brakeman whistling Halley's Fifth Concerto.

And we glimpse the causes of the conflict. Willers and Dagny are motivated by the right, but do not have the words to name it. Willers does not even know fully what is right—he learns this from Dagny—but like her his motive is to do "whatever is right" and to "always reach for the best within us" (6). The young girl looking down the railroad track, planning one day to run Taggart Transcontinental, knows what is the best within her. But even in adulthood, Dagny is unable fully to name why this is morally right and, especially, to understand the importance of so naming it. This leaves her vulnerable. It is her brother who seizes the realm of morality and so the moral high ground. Jim declares that it is only he that is moved by moral considerations and feelings; she is concerned with the "selfish greed for profit" while Jim is concerned with higher, more important things, like the whole nation and "the human element" (22, 20).

More deeply, we see that Dagny, who is unable fully to put into words even her own approach to existence (Halley's Fifth Concerto gives her an emotional experience of it), cannot fathom her brother's. She does not and has never accepted his view of morality; she senses that there is something not stupid but monstrous at the root of his moral slogans and motivation, but she cannot identify or even believe it. "She wondered why he resented the necessity of dealing with Rearden, and why his resentment had such an odd, evasive quality. . . . If she were insane, thought Dagny, she would conclude that her bother hated to deal with Rearden because Rearden did his job with superlative efficiency; but she could not conclude it, because she thought that such a feeling was not within the humanly possible" (19).

Even more deeply, we glimpse the source of their two opposing approaches to existence: James evades the responsibility of consciousness, Dagny embraces it. When we first meet Jim, he declares to the world outside his door, "Don't bother me, don't bother me, don't bother me" (7). When we first meet Dagny, she has not slept for two days because "she could not permit herself to sleep; she had too many problems to consider and not much time" (14). In their first meeting in the book, Jim struggles to escape the responsibility of judgment, that is, to judge how to save the Rio Norte Line and whether to use Rearden Metal, while Dagny eagerly accepts it.

Thus all the central questions of the story are raised here, in the first chapter. And the answers, for Dagny as for the reader, are all to be found by answering the question with which the chapter begins—and mysteriously ends: "Who is John Galt?"

Chapter II: The Chain

This chapter's title obviously derives from the bracelet made from the first pouring of Rearden Metal. At a gathering that includes the Rearden family and

Paul Larkin, Hank Rearden's wife, Lillian, refers to it as "the chain by which he [Hank] holds us all in bondage" (43). Expressing the prevailing moral attitude that the successful seek to oppress the less successful, she asks rhetorically: "What would happen to Henry's vanity if he didn't have us to throw alms to? What would become of his strength if he didn't have weaker people to dominate? What would he do with himself if he didn't keep us around as dependents?" (43)

But the contradiction is that Lillian's description does not seem to match either Hank's attitude and actions—or those of his family.

His family does not cower in his presence; on the contrary, it is they who berate and make demands on him. And Hank has spent the last ten years of his life not in domination of weaker individuals, but in pursuit of a metal superior to steel. Through prodigious thought and effort, he has finally succeeded. He desperately wants to celebrate, but the only salute he receives is a wordless grin of understanding from one of his workers. Indifferent to his family, he does not want to face them tonight, because they won't understand. "He had never asked anything of them," he thinks to himself; "it was they who wished to hold him, they who pressed a claim on him—and the claim seemed to have the form of affection, but it was a form which he found harder to endure than any sort of hatred. . . . They professed to love him for some unknown reason and they ignored all the things for which he could wish to be loved" (37).

The chain seems to run in the other direction. As a reflection of his own tremendous life-giving power, Hank is enormously benevolent. He views others as like himself; when he walks home from the mills, he feels "certain that every living being wished him well tonight" (32). Once home, however, he starts to wonder if his family actually does; but he reproaches himself: their insulting comments must be their form of expressing solicitude and affection. He struggles to understand them, but can't. He certainly does not share their standards and does not feel guilty at their accusations; he smiles when Lillian tries to trap him because he forgot their wedding anniversary. He senses that they are radically unlike him, that they are disappointed that Lillian's trap didn't induce guilt and are "wounded by the mere fact of his being" (37). But then he tells himself, don't "start imagining the insane" (37). His sense of justice does not permit him to "condemn without understanding, and he could not understand" (38). He will not impose his standards on them; even if he loathes their goals, their goals must mean to them what his mills and metal mean to him. They're simply "bewildered, unhappy children"—and even if he cannot understand what they wish to achieve, he can help them achieve it; he can grant Lillian her anniversary party and Philip his funding for Friends of Global Progress (40).

In fact, Hank does not apply his standards fully even across his business. Larkin warns him not to announce his views too publicly—that they're Hank's mills and that his goal is to make steel and money; people regard his standards as antisocial. But Hank doesn't "give a damn what they think" (39). Yet despite his incredible devotion to his business and its profits, he cannot bring himself to examine one area of his operations too closely: his man in Washington. Though he knows he needs one, "he could not quite convince himself that it was necessary. An inexplicable kind of distaste, part fastidiousness, part boredom, stopped him whenever he considered it" (40).

The deepest question this chapter raises is: What *are* Hank's standards—and what would happen if he named and consistently applied them? His is a career of relentless effort to build his business, to earn, to grow, to achieve and to deserve ever greater achievements. Yet when he looks back on his life, something is missing. Standing straight, "as if before a bench of judgment," he thinks of signs lighted against the darkness: "Rearden Ore—Rearden Coal—Rearden Limestone"; he wishes he could light a sign above them all, "Rearden Life" (32). This is an eloquent expression of his need for full self-esteem: he is efficacious, but does any standard exist under which his actions and entire life would be evaluated as moral? This is the deepest contradiction of the chapter: on the night of his greatest triumph, we see a lonely figure, desperate to celebrate, wondering "why happiness could hurt" (30).

Chapter III: The Top and the Bottom

This chapter opens with a meeting atop a skyscraper and closes with a meeting underground. But the top doesn't seem like a top, and the bottom doesn't seem like a bottom.

In a windowless, cellar-like room built on the roof of a skyscraper, Jim, Orren Boyle, Larkin, and Wesley Mouch meet in New York's most expensive barroom. Using language that is at once conventionally moral and public-spirited sounding, and also vague and almost indecipherable, men of no particular achievement—Boyle's start in business was through a two-hundred-million-dollar loan from the government and "nobody ever paid any attention" to Mouch—negotiate a deal (45). With their mysterious deal concluded, they discuss their attempt to cash in on the San Sebastián Mines. These do not seem like men fit to run anything. Why are they at the top of the world?

On the other hand, in the underground employees' cafeteria of Taggart Transcontinental, in a sparkling room with "a sense of light and space," Willers and a railroad worker—John Galt—discuss real problems (62). In language that is simple and clear, Willers outlines what Dagny, with his help, will do to save the railroad: build the Rio Norte Line, using McNamara as the contractor to lay the rail. These two employees appear competent men, the kind who can get things done. Why are they at the bottom?

The intervening part of the chapter provides clues to the answer. We witness Dagny's rise through Taggart Transcontinental, her worship of ability, her brushing aside of accusations of conceit and selfishness, her embrace of responsibility as others seek to avoid it. But we also see her relation to Jim, as he rises through Taggart Transcontinental. She cannot understand his motives but she doesn't think he is "smart enough to harm the railroad too much" (52). Like Hank, she cannot bring herself to examine Jim's "Washington ability" too closely: "there were many kinds of work which were offensive, yet necessary, like cleaning sewers" (52). And in any event, she would always be there to fix any damage he caused.

Unable to understand Jim, it is she who makes his continued actions possible. His first project as president of Taggart Transcontinental is the San Sebastián Line, a project that bleeds losses for the railroad and undermines the Rio Norte Line. Because of that project, Dagny considers, for the first time, quitting, but shakes her head in angry denial: "she told herself that Taggart Transcontinental would now need her more than ever" (55). Because of Jim's plan, two Directors and the Vice-President in Charge of Operation resign. "She never understood why the Board of Directors voted unanimously to make her Vice-President in Charge of Operation" (56). But the answer is contained in the novel's next sentence. "It was she who finally gave them their San Sebastián Line" (56). After three years of their failures, she completes the line in a year. It is only because of her that Jim can remain at the top of Taggart Transcontinental.

Dagny, we see in this chapter, longs for her radiant kind of world, a world ruled not by ineptitude but by ability—an ability worth matching or beating. But that world remains hidden from her, in the underground of Taggart Transcontinental, because of her own contradiction: she longs for that world but constantly props up the ineptitude that is her brother. Even though Dagny does not realize it yet, her sanction elevates James and his ilk to the top and relegates Galt to the bottom.

Chapter IV: The Immovable Movers

The end of the previous chapter hinted at the supreme importance of motive power—it is the world's motive power that Galt must stop—and this chapter highlights its importance.

Its central event is the National Alliance of Railroads' passage of the Anti-dog-eat-dog-Rule, whose effect will be to destroy in nine months the best rail line to Colorado, Dan Conway's Phoenix-Durango. The rule's passage was part of the deal negotiated in the cellar barroom.

Dagny urges Conway to fight the injustice, knowing also that the rule will actually make her job in Colorado more difficult. But Conway's motor has stopped. He who built an obscure railroad into a successful enterprise, no longer wants to fight. Why? Because he's lost the conviction that he is in the right. The Alliance "had the right to do it," he tells Dagny; "the world's in a terrible state right now. . . . Men have to get together. . . . I suppose somebody's got to be sacrificed. . . . I have no right to complain. The right's on their side." Deep down, he senses that the sacrifice of the best railroad to its inferior competition is "damn unjust!" But to fight it "would be wrong. I'm just selfish."

"Oh, damn that rotten tripe!" Dagny tells him. "You know better than that!" Conway answers: "I don't know what is right any more. . . . I don't think I care." Wordlessly, Dagny knows that "Conway would never be a man of action again." She wonders what has defeated him (77–79).

Conway has relinquished precisely what Dagny won't. In the name of her own existence, she is dedicated to that which she sees to be right: *she* has always been "the motive power of her own happiness" (65). This conviction is why she is indignant about the Anti-dog-eat-dog-Rule. It is this conviction that makes Dagny (and those like her) an immovable mover: she originates motion in pursuit of the right and will not allow herself to be moved or deflected from her chosen path precisely because it is right.

In complete contrast to Conway and Dagny are Jim and Betty Pope. Theirs is the contradictory spectacle of conscious motion without purpose. "Here's another day," Pope declares, "and nothing to do" (70). Jim stumbles into the living room of his apartment, unable to remember why he's there. He can't be bothered to figure out why he does the things he does: the two of them slept together because that's what people do. The only times he has the semblance of purposeful motion is when he can undermine Dagny, and more generally, achievement: he relishes the opportunity to put the skids under Dagny at the Board meeting and gloats over the destruction of Conway.

Dagny will have to learn that Jim's motivation is the opposite of hers: not pursuit of the right, but pursuit of the right's destruction. Dagny senses that Jim's gloating over both Conway and her contains "a secret she had never suspected, and it was crucially important that she learn to understand it. But the thought flashed and vanished" (76). What moves men like Jim?

The question at once seems important and unimportant. In Dagny's kind of world, in the presence of immovable individuals like her and Hank Rearden, the issue seems unreal. "Don't waste time trying to figure him out," Hank tells her. "Let him spit. He's no danger to anyone. People like Jim Taggart just clutter up the world" (85). He and Dagny will "save the country from the consequences of their actions" and then go on to greater achievements; the lunacy of people like Jim is "demented, so it has to defeat itself" (84). Within the minds of Hank and Dagny, there is room for only a single field of concern: concern for their vision of what Rearden Metal will create—a single-minded concern for movement toward that which they know to be right.

And yet, in contradiction to Hank and Dagny's attitude, some seemingly immovable movers are disappearing. Taggart Transcontinental's and the nation's best contractor, McNamara, abruptly quits and vanishes, walking out on "a pile of contracts . . . worth a fortune"; Richard Halley gave up composing at the height of his success; and Francisco d'Anconia, who retains "the smile of a man who is able to see, to know and to create the glory of existence," has become an aimless chaser of women (65, 69). Have they all been defeated, like Conway? (Or have they learned a new conception of the right?) And what will happen to Ellis Wyatt? Like Dagny, he is outraged by the Anti-dog-eat-dog-Rule—he who will be its next sacrificial victim. Wyatt knows he is in the grips of evil, and he is affected by its presence in a way that Hank is not: "You expect to feed off me while you can," Wyatt tells Dagny (thinking she is like Jim), "and to find another carcass to pick dry after you have finished mine. That is the policy of most of mankind today." In the name of what he knows to be right, Wyatt will not fade away like Conway. He will remain a man of action: "I may have to go; but if I go, I'll make sure that I take all the rest of you along with me" (82).

This is not Hank's attitude, but is there a crack in Hank's motive power? Does he know that his course of action is right? "We're a couple of black-guards, aren't we?" he declares to Dagny in a strange tone of dispassionate wonder. But when he looks at his mills, there is "no guilt in his face, no doubt, nothing but the calm of an inviolate self-confidence"—self-confidence, without full self-esteem (88).

Chapter V: The Climax of the d'Anconias

This chapter's name has an obvious derivation: because of his incredible mind, the childhood Francisco held the promise to become "the climax of the d'Anconias" (94). The chapter's full effect is only to deepen the contradiction that is the adult Francisco.

Relentlessly purposeful, dedicated to d'Anconia Copper, admiring of money-making and of productive work as "the only system of morality that's on a gold standard," intensely passionate about Dagny—given what Francisco was, what could cause him to become what he has become? (100) And what *has* he become? Has he given up, like Conway? But then why take, Dagny wonders, "the ugliest way of escape"—an intelligence drowned in throwing parties and chasing women? (116). Moreover, when Dagny meets Francisco in his hotel room to discuss the San Sebastián mines, he does not seem like a man who has given up—and doubt is even cast on whether he chases women.

Clues to the answer are contained in Francisco's childhood. Jim is resentful of Francisco's ability, and Dagny senses that there is something dangerous in men like her brother, but Francisco dismisses her. "Good God, Dagny! Do you expect me to be afraid of an object like James?" (99). Francisco's attitude slowly begins to change, however, in college; he tells Dagny that they are "teaching a lot of drivel nowadays" (99). And from college Jim acquires "a tone of aggressive self-righteousness"; it is "as if he had found a new weapon" (99). Dagny sees the first crack in Francisco's seeming invulnerability shortly after college, when he's working as head of the New York office of d'Anconia Copper. Looking out the window of his office for a long time, his face tight with "an emotion she had never believed possible to him: of bitter, helpless anger," he says to her: "'There's something wrong in the world. There's always been. Something no one has ever named or explained'" (111).

A few years after this episode, Francisco asks her whether she could give up Taggart Transcontinental, pleads with her to help him remain, and warns her that "I will have a reason for the things I'll do. But I can't tell you the reason and you will be right to damn me" (115).

The "things I'll do" begin to emerge with the San Sebastian disaster. Francisco, it appears, has done it on purpose. Jim and his gang wanted to ride on Francisco's coattails, so that knowledge on their part would be unnecessary. Why should Francisco have to exist in some different way? Why are they outraged when he does not prevent the nationalization of the mines, since this act is supposed to be good? Why is the People's State of Mexico accusing *him* of defrauding *them* when his looted mines prove worthless?

When Dagny tells Francisco that he of all people should be fighting the looters, he answers that it is she whom he must fight. What amuses him most is that the San Sebastian disaster has helped destroy the Phoenix-Durango and will, he thinks, destroy Wyatt and then Taggart Transcontinental. She regards this as blasphemy to Sebastian d'Anconia—but he named those mines in tribute to his great ancestor.

Like Dagny, we are left to wonder: Could it be that in some inconceivable way Francisco has actually become what he promised to be: the climax of the d'Anconias?

Chapter VI: The Non-Commercial

What is the relation between the material and the spiritual? The conventional view is that either you are a spiritual person, who is therefore unconcerned with the material world, or you are a materialist, who is therefore preoccupied with money and devoid of any spiritual concern. The events of this chapter seem to contradict both notions.

The guests Lillian invited to celebrate her wedding anniversary are regarded as the spiritualists: the philosopher Dr. Simon Pritchett, the author Balph Eubank, the composer Mort Liddy, the magazine editor Bertram Scudder, the philanthropist Claude Slagenhop. Supposedly, their spiritual concerns are too lofty for the material world. But it is difficult to say just what those spiritual concerns *are*. It is clear what these men are against—Pritchett is against logic and man's delusions of grandeur; Eubank is against free will, plot, happy endings, and stories that portray man as heroic; Liddy is against melody; Scudder is against property rights; and Slagenhop is against all ideas. But what are these men for? Whenever they speak of that, it always concerns controlling those who deal with the material world. Pritchett wants to reduce men to instinct and *force* them to be free, claiming that this isn't a contradiction "in the higher philosophical sense"; Eubank wants to limit "the sale of any book to ten thousand copies"; Scudder and Slagenhop want to seize industrialists' property (134–35). They all support the Equalization of Opportunity Bill, which would break up Hank's business empire.

Hank is the materialist. And he certainly *is* intensely concerned with conquering the material realm by creating new products, like Rearden Metal, and building a business empire. But it doesn't seem accurate to characterize Hank as devoid of spiritual concern. On the contrary, he seems a profoundly spiritual person, moved by the essence of spiritual motivation: the desire to do what is *right*. The reason he sits troubled and paralyzed in his dressing room, unable to finish getting ready for his anniversary party even though he believes he owes Lillian his presence there, is that for the first time in his life the knowledge of what is right is losing its power to move him. "The impossible conflict of feeling reluctance to do that which was right," he thinks to himself, "wasn't it the basic formula of moral corruption?" (131). All the while, he is haunted by his desire for Dagny, a desire he must struggle against and silence—a passionate desire to do what is wrong.

But even if Hank is spiritual, he doesn't identify himself as such: the only terms he has are those of his society. "'You don't care for anything but business.' He had heard it all his life, pronounced as a verdict of damnation. . . . He had never held that creed, but he had accepted it as natural that his family should hold it. He took it for granted—wordlessly, in the manner of a feeling absorbed in childhood, left unquestioned and unnamed—that he had dedicated himself, like a martyr of some dark religion, to the service of a faith which was his passionate love, but which made him an outcast among men, whose sympathy he was not to expect." He thinks it his duty to provide Lillian with "some form of existence unrelated to business. But he had never found the capacity to do it or even to experience a sense of guilt" (127–28).

But though he doesn't provide Lillian an existence unrelated to business, he does leave the spiritual realm to Lillian and her friends, thinking his world is unaffected by their prattle. But it isn't. It is they who are pushing the Equalization of Opportunity Bill. The bill is a product of their irrational ideas—which is the reason why Hank cannot even take the bill seriously. "Having dealt with the clean reality of metals, technology, production all his life, he had acquired the conviction that one had to concern oneself with the rational, not the insane" (130).

Even more devastating than this, it is Lillian who has turned his sexual desire into his enemy. Just as she tries to make him feel guilty for his devotion to his mills—at the anniversary party she deliberately makes the bracelet of Rearden Metal look ugly on her arm—so she tries the same in regard to his sexual desire. She has degraded the act of sex and helped him conclude that his desire is materialistic, low, animalistic. But his desire remains, and he now thinks it's his duty to struggle against it. Lillian did not succeed in regard to his work—he does not accept her evaluation of his mills. Why? Because he knows firsthand their actual meaning (though he does not yet have the words to fully name that meaning). But she does succeed in regard to his sexual desire, because he has no firsthand experience of its true spiritual significance, much less the words to name that significance.

It is this split between the spiritual and material that Dagny won't accept. She longs for spiritual celebration of her material achievement and bemoans the fact that her world has nothing to offer, unable to understand why it doesn't. Wandering the streets of New York (in "The Immovable Movers"), Dagny had looked for spiritual fuel—only to be met with the products of Lillian's cocktail-party crowd, like "The Vulture is Molting." Francisco names what she feels at the party, among men who actually have nothing to celebrate: "what a magnificent waste!" (154). She desires a man worthy of her—unbeknownst to her, she came to the party only because Hank would be there—but finds no one in the world. Her desperate desire to have the bracelet of Rearden Metal comes from her struggle to preserve her view of the world, where the material and spiritual form an inseparable union. The bracelet is the material symbol of a supreme spiritual accomplishment.

So this chapter leaves us with the question of the actual relation between the spiritual and the material. The spiritual people, the intellectuals, artists and cultural spokesmen, the self-described "non-commercial," don't seem spiritual. They don't seem motivated by the desire to do what is right, and they seem intensely preoccupied with the material realm. What are they after? What is their purpose? What does Lillian want? The supreme materialist, by contrast, seems the most spiritual figure, intensely concerned with doing what is right. But he dismisses the spiritual and moral realms, content to leave them to men who could not even be sweepers in his mills. Why? And why, more widely, is the world bereft of true spiritual grandeur? Why can't Dagny find her equal?

Chapter VII: The Exploiters and the Exploited

Who are the exploiters and who the exploited?

The view that men like Hank, Dagny, and Wyatt have heard all their lives is that they exploit the Ben Nealy's of the world. But isn't this a contradiction? What does Nealy *have* to exploit? He can't even do his job properly without the minds of Dagny and Wyatt to guide him. Dagny and Wyatt are not oppressors standing in his way; he is an obstacle standing in their way: Nealy simply quits the job as the denunciations of Rearden Metal escalate. Men like Wyatt do not seek to exploit the Nealy's of the world, they seek to be free of such obstacles, which is one reason they have fled to Colorado.

The real exploiters are selfless, "public-spirited" men like Jim, Wesley Mouch, and Dr. Robert Stadler—and the exploited are individuals like Dagny, Hank, and Wyatt. In the name of the public interest, Jim has killed the Phoenix-Durango and now tries to loot the corpse. Jim constantly seeks to position himself so that Dagny sustains Taggart Transcontinental while he remains on top, doing nothing. After the crash of Taggart Transcontinental's stock (a consequence of Jim killing the Phoenix-Durango), it is Dagny who must build the Rio Norte Line and save Taggart Transcontinental, risking her career, while he remains unaffected. "Nothing will change," Dagny tells him, "except the kind of show you will put on for your friends . . . and the fact that it will be a little harder for me" (194). Mouch, similarly, has been on Rearden's payroll, using it to advance up the ladder of power in Washington; Mouch then helps pass the Equalization of Opportunity Bill. And through the State Science Institute, Stadler forces all "the greedy ruffians who run our industries" to pay for his theoretical research. And to maintain the State Science Institute's prestige, he also tries to keep Rearden Metal off the market. (How will the "greedy ruffian" Hank then fund Stadler's research? This is one of the contradictions Stadler refuses to face.) More widely, the looters in Washington and New York are exploiting the last bastion of productivity, Colorado, a fact Dagny senses in the cab ride with Jim, seeing through the cab's window all the products flowing into the city from the industries of Colorado.

Why do the exploited permit their exploitation? They don't—when they can grasp the moral issue and the evil involved. Dagny stops the cab and leaps out when she learns that she is supposed to debate Bertram Scudder on whether Rearden Metal is a lethal product of greed. "You goddamn fool," she declares to Jim, "do you think I consider the question debatable?" (175). Hank refuses the State Science Institute's demand that he keep Rearden Metal off the market (or sell it to them, so that they can use it but keep it off the market). "Would you tell me," Dr. Potter asks him, "just between us, it's only my personal curiosity—why are you doing this?" Hank answers: "I'll tell you. You won't understand. You see, it's because Rearden Metal is *good*" (182). Hank also refuses his mother's demand to give a job to his brother Philip. He realizes that if he gave a job to Philip, he would be betraying his mills. "What are they, your mills—a holy temple of some kind?" his mother asks. "'Why . . . yes,' he said softly, astonished at the thought." "Don't you ever think of people," his mother responds, "and of your moral duties?" "I don't know what it is that you choose to call morality," Hank answers. "No, I don't think of people—except that if I gave a job to Philip, I wouldn't be able to face any competent man who needed work and deserved it" (209).

But more often, they cannot understand the nature of the evil they face. Dagny is cautious around both Jim and Stadler, but cannot grasp their level of moral corruption. And because of her passionate love for her railroad, she will pay any price for it. She will leave Taggart Transcontinental and her position of Vice-President, perhaps never to return, in order to build the John Galt Line; she will agree to Jim's terms; and she will go see Stadler about the State Science Institute's statement on Rearden Metal. She accepts that Jim and the others will erect obstacles in front of her, but hopes they'll leave her and Hank alone long enough to complete the John Galt Line; indeed, the one condition she imposes on Jim is: "keep your Washington boys off" (197).

Hank too cannot yet understand them: he cannot understand what motivates them and he doesn't want to descend into their filth to find out. When his mother tells him her conception of morality is that "virtue is the giving of the underserved" Hank replies: "Mother, you don't know what you're saying. I'm not able ever to despise you enough to believe that you mean it" (209). When the Equalization of Opportunity Bill passes, Hank thinks to himself: "There is

an obscenity of evil which contaminates the observer. There is a limit to what
it is proper for a man to see. He must not think of this, or look within, or try
to learn the nature of its roots" (215). And like Dagny, Hank too will pay any
price for the love of his mills. Indeed, he barely has time to notice the price. The
Equalization of Opportunity Bill and its evil fade from his mind as he thinks of
a new type of bridge design, one combining a truss and an arch.

We see here again the question of the relation between the spiritual and
the material. Dagny and Hank apply the right spiritual standard to the material realm when they see the issue—she refuses to appear on Scudder's radio
program and Hank refuses to hire Philip. But Dagny and Hank cannot understand the corruption of the mystics who split the spiritual from the material
nor understand what these people are after in the material world. This leaves
Dagny and Hank vulnerable to exploitation. For what the mystics seek is to be
freed from the need to consider such issues as the true, the good, the earned,
and the deserved when it comes to the "low," "grubby" material world. Stadler
wants to pursue his theoretical physics, unconcerned with whether his material means of doing so are deserved. Jim wants to be the President of Taggart
Transcontinental, unconcerned with the need to earn his position. Hank's
mother wants Hank to give Philip a job he doesn't deserve and to make it look
like Philip is doing *Hank* a favor. What we see here is that the spiritual-material split is a way to escape justice—or better, to invert it, to insist that spiritual
grandeur comes from inverting the requirements of the material world. Virtue,
according to Hank's mother, is the giving of the undeserved.

And so when Dagny goes to see Stadler to tell him that there is only one
reason he must speak out in defense of Rearden Metal, "you must say it, because it is true"—she is actually sanctioning his evil and his exploitation of
individuals like her (189). She is acting as if he is, like her, dedicated to the
truth as an absolute.

Dagny herself doesn't accept a split between the spiritual and the material,
but she also doesn't have the words to identify fully their union, and her vision of their actual relation is eroding. When the bum in the diner laments
that there's "no spirit involved in manufacturing or sex" and that morality is
"judgment to distinguish right and wrong, vision to see the truth, courage to
act upon it, dedication to that which is good, integrity to stand by the good at
any price. But where does one find it?"—the joke, of course, is on him (177).
He could find it if he looked straight at the woman sitting in front of him. But
Dagny's vision of the ideal is also slipping: she has stopped expecting to find
people dedicated to the true and the good and has stopped expecting to find
spiritual grandeur and celebration in the world. She doesn't even realize that
she's attracted to Hank for precisely this need and desire.

We're left to wonder: Is a person's choice then either to become an exploiter
of others, or to be exploited by an evil he cannot understand and thereby
slowly lose his vision of the good? We do get glimpses of another possibility:
men who are resigning and vanishing, men who refuse to be exploited but

who do not themselves become exploiters. Is Francisco one of them? Dagny places Francisco on the side of the looters, but is he? This much we know: he will not help Dagny build the John Galt Line—and he tells her that John Galt will come to claim it.

Chapter VIII: The John Galt Line

In contrast to the previous two chapters, which dealt with the split between the spiritual and the material, this chapter showcases their unity. The longing and loneliness that Dagny feels, alone in her office of the John Galt Line, is the despair that her spiritual values will not be brought into material form, that the man at the end of the rails, and the love she would feel for him and him for her, will remain only "her own thought of what life could be like" (220). The spiritual should be made real. This is the meaning of the achievement that is the John Galt Line.

"It was a strange foreshortening between sight and touch," Dagny thinks to herself as she sits in the fireman's chair on the first run of the John Galt Line, "between wish and fulfillment, between—the words clicked sharply in her mind after a startled stop—between spirit and body. First, the vision—then the physical shape to express it. First, the thought—then the purposeful motion down the straight line of a single track to a chosen goal. Could one have any meaning without the other? Wasn't it evil to wish without moving—or to move without aim? Whose malevolence was it that crept through the world, struggling to break the two apart and set them against each other?" (240–41). Looking through the cab, she wonders:

> Who made it possible for four dials and three levers in front of Pat Logan to hold the incredible power of the sixteen motors behind them and deliver it to the effortless control of one man's hand? These things and the capacity from which they came—was this the pursuit men regarded as evil? Was this what they called an ignoble concern with the physical world? Was this the state of being enslaved by matter? Was this the surrender of man's spirit to his body? She shook her head, as if she wished she could toss the subject out of the window and let it get shattered somewhere along the track. She looked at the sun on the summer fields. She did not have to think, because these questions were only details of a truth she knew and had always known. (241)

This unity of spirit and matter, of a disciplined intelligence devoted to its life on earth, is the meaning of the John Galt Line. And this is what Dagny and Hank celebrate when they sleep together. She knows it, he doesn't.

If we turn from Dagny and Hank's creation of the John Galt Line to the world's reaction, we see that their achievement is granted no moral recognition or spiritual significance. Eddie Willers senses the danger of this. "Why does she have to hide?" he asks the Taggart Transcontinental worker. "Why are they torturing her in return for saving their lives? . . . There's something

about it all that I can't define, and it's something evil. That's why I'm afraid"
(218). The presence of this evil is also the source of Wyatt's rebellious anger,
when he thinks that the John Galt Line will soon be destroyed. "To the world
as it seems to be right now!" he shouts, and then throws the champagne glass
across the room (250).

Why is the achievement that is the John Galt Line in such danger? The danger comes from divorcing the material from the spiritual—from Dagny and
Hank creating the John Galt Line but not demanding the spiritual and moral
recognition that is their due.

By contrast, it is precisely this divorce of matter from spirit that Galt won't
permit himself. He is in love with Dagny and wants to go to her, when he sees
her alone, slumped across the desk of her office, thinking of him (though she
doesn't know it). Dagny is not ready to strike, and his action of entering her
office would betray his vision of what he knows the world can be and in the
name of which he is on strike.

Chapter IX: The Sacred and the Profane

If anything is regarded as sacred by the world, it is the moral sentiments Jim
voices. He declares that the pursuit of profit is not a noble motive but working for others is, that building a rail line for prosperous industrialists when
poor people need transportation is wrong, that inventing a new metal when
numerous nations still go without iron is evil, that pride is the worst sin and
selflessness the greatest virtue, that there are higher things in life than material
products like rails and bridges, and that these higher spiritual things cannot be
identified or measured. Jim's relationship with Cherryl too would be regarded
as noble, an act of charity toward her.

Yet Jim's actual sentiments and actions seem to contradict this evaluation:
far from being sacred, they seem profane. His moral slogans serve as weapons
to discredit Dagny and Hank and to hold his own nonachievement as superior to their achievements. With the success of the John Galt Line, however,
his self-deception is more difficult to maintain; he finds himself wishing they
had failed, yet frightened by what this would reveal about himself if he faced
it. Cherryl is the one person he wants to see after the success of the John Galt
Line, because her misdirected hero worship at once props himself up in his
own eyes—it is as though he were actually good—and also allows him to recapture a sense of superiority—by being able to successfully defraud her. Their
encounter serves as "his revenge upon every person who had stood cheering
along the three-hundred-mile track of the John Galt Line" (267).

And what in fact seems sacred, Dagny and Hank's desire for each other,
Hank, echoing the world's standards, damns as profane. Hank has accepted
one aspect of the spirit-matter split. As Jim denounces production as materialistic, so Hank denounces sex as animalistic; as Jim declares suffering the
proof of virtue, so Hank declares pleasure the proof of vice. Yet his evaluation

of their affair contradicts his actual experience: he is finding for the first time joy and serenity in his personal life. He's starting to glimpse that his desire for Dagny and hers for him comes from the core of their beings: he asks Dagny to wear the bracelet made from the first pouring of Rearden Metal, the symbol of his productive ability, the symbol of his virtue.

More widely, the spirit-matter dichotomy is accepted by the world, and so what it should regard as sacred, it treats as insignificant or profane. Hank attends a banquet held in his honor because he thinks that his opponents have at last learned to appreciate the value of Rearden Metal—and for that, he would forgive anyone anything. But what he learns about them is that they don't value anything, that they are merely going through motions copied from a better age. Both the John Galt Line and the productive explosion in Colorado should be regarded with reverence; Hank thinks it's now "clear track ahead" and that after giving the world the demonstration he and Dagny gave it with the first run of the John Galt Line, the Equalization of Opportunity Bill will be scrapped (277). But that's not the popular attitude, as expressed by Mr. Mowen.

Mowen thinks he has a right to live as he has always lived, his routine undisturbed. He does not look with reverence at Hank's and Dagny's or Colorado's achievements. He seeks protection from them. There ought to be a law, he says, against businesses moving to Colorado. He should be protected from the dog-eat-dog competition of the Stockton Foundry—and Taggart Transcontinental should face more competition in Colorado. Hank shouldn't be able to manufacture so much Rearden Metal that he disrupts other people's markets— but Mowen should be able to get as much Rearden Metal as he wants. Wyatt's output should be capped to "leave the little people a chance"—but something ought to be done about the shortage of oil in the city (272). Mowen wants a material existence that requires no thought or logical consistently—and he expects Washington, somehow, to make this possible. "Steps are being taken," he tells Kellogg. "Constructive steps. The Legislature has passed a Bill giving wider powers to the Bureau of Economic Planning and National Resources" (273).

The nation should value industry (along with the ambition and greed that creates it), but as Dagny and Hank discover on their vacation, industry is disappearing from vast stretches of America. This fact is crystallized by the desecration of the motor. It was an invention that would have revolutionized the world, abandoned in a defunct factory. And even when the factory itself was looted, its most valuable treasure passed unnoticed, probably stripped for parts so that someone's diapers could hang "on a clothesline made of the motor's missing wires" (291).

In such a world, what can be the fate of the John Galt Line and Colorado?

Chapter X: Wyatt's Torch

In one of its meanings, a "torch" refers to something that serves to illuminate, enlighten, or guide. Dagny and Hank are on two quests for which they need illumination and guidance: to find the inventor of the motor and to save Colorado.

The superlative achievement that is the motor has been abandoned, its promise unfulfilled and its inventor and his fate, unknown. How is this possible? Who invented it? What has happened to him? Even more desperately, the looters are threatening to destroy Colorado. But how can Hank and Dagny stop the looters? Hank knows of "no weapons but to pay for what he wanted, to give value for value, to ask nothing of nature without trading his effort in return, to ask nothing of men without trading the product of his effort. What were the weapons . . . if values were not a weapon any longer?" (303). Similarly, Dagny can see "no way of fighting, no rules of battle, no weapons" (298). What action could she take "against the men of undefined thought, of unnamed motives, of unstated purposes, of unspecified morality. . . . What were the weapons . . . in a realm where reason was not a weapon any longer?" (300).

Dagny senses that these two quests are linked, because the mind that could invent the motor would know how to fight the looters.

Wyatt's burning oil fields—and that which caused him to light them—do illuminate both quests, but Hank and Dagny must learn to see this for themselves. They must learn that Wyatt's act was not an act of rebellious despair but in fact the only way for Wyatt to fight the looters. They must learn to view their own achievements with full pride and to grasp that to fight evil, there cannot be even one act of cooperation, material or spiritual, with it.

Hank in particular is disarmed by guilt. In accepting an aspect of the spiritual-material dichotomy, he has damned as sin his joyous affair with Dagny. His sense of guilt now undercuts the righteousness he needs to fight the looters. "He did not know—as he sat slumped at his desk, thinking of the honesty he could claim no longer, of the sense of justice he had lost—that it was his rigid honesty and ruthless sense of justice that were now knocking his only weapon out of his hands. He would fight the looters, but the wrath and fire were gone" (303).

But Hank must also grasp the fundamental motive of his enemies. He now senses that there is something monstrous about his family; but at this point he still cannot believe that they mean what they're saying. Yet he is beginning to see that the issue is crucially important. "Lillian," he asks her, no longer on the defensive in their conversation, "what purpose do you live for?" When she answers that perhaps spiritual, enlightened people don't attempt to do anything, and that they certainly don't spend their time on the grimy job of manufacturing plumbing pipes, Hank answers: "'I know that you feel contempt for the plumbing pipes. You've made that clear long ago. Your contempt means nothing to me. Why keep repeating it?' He wondered why this hit her; he did not know in what manner, but he knew that it did. He wondered why he felt with absolute certainty that *that* had been the right thing to say" (308).

Dagny too is catching glimpses of the nature of the evil she faces. In the course of searching for the inventor of the motor, she comes across many variations of evil: Mayor Bascom, Eugene Lawson, Lee Hunsacker, the Starnes heirs. When Ivy Starnes tells her of the noble, spiritual plan they imposed at the Twentieth Century Motor Company—only to see it defeated by the selfish, base, materialistic nature of men—"Dagny heard a cold, implacable voice saying somewhere within her: Remember it—remember it well—it is not often that one can see pure evil—look at it—remember—and some day you'll find the words to name its essence" (323). This *is* the essence she must grasp. She must grasp that Eric Starnes—"the man who gives his life for malice"—is the essence of evil (321). She must identify what she has now but sensed about Jim: that self-interest is not his motive.

If she could identify their motive, she would see that Wyatt's fate—"Ellis Wyatt being choked, with his own bright energy turned against him as the noose"—*must* be the fate of all the life-bringers in the looters' system (335). And then she would see that the actions of Midas Mulligan, of Judge Narangansett, of William Hastings, of the engineers at the Twentieth Century Motor Company, and of Ellis Wyatt are the only way to fight the looters—that in saving Jim's neck, as she admits she has done, she is only tightening the noose around hers.

Her quest would then be over, for she will have solved the secret Galt solved and that involves, in Hugh Akston's words, "something greater—much greater—than the invention of a motor run by atmospheric electricity" (331).

PART II: EITHER-OR

Part I focused on achievement: the creation of a rail line made of a new metal superior to steel, in order to provide service to the booming state of Colorado. It dealt with the obstacles Dagny and Hank faced in building the John Galt Line—both the men of ability disappearing and the looters like Jim, Mouch, Boyle, and Stadler attacking Rearden Metal, destroying the Phoenix-Durango and passing the Equalization of Opportunity Bill. It showed how Dagny and Hank succeeded nevertheless—and then how easily their achievement was destroyed by the looters' directives.

Part II contains no comparable act of achievement. Colorado rapidly disintegrates and Dagny and Hank are left trying to tread water, hoping that they can somehow prevent the whole country from going under. The only thing that gives meaning to the future for Hank and Dagny, a future where achievement would once again be possible, is the quest to find the inventor of the motor and learn why his invention was left abandoned in a factory.

They must learn that it is either-or. Either the world is such that an inventor of a new power source is admired, or it is a world where achievement disappears. Either it is a world where the productive state of Colorado is protected and not looted, or it is a world that descends into a thousand Starnesvilles. There is no stable middle ground, only a downward spiral. The appearance of a firm middle ground came only from the fact that there always seemed to be another victim to loot. But as more and more industrialists vanish, from Colorado and elsewhere, new victims are more difficult to find.

In a last stab to find a stable middle ground, the looters attempt to freeze the nation and the economy by issuing Directive 10-289. Under the directive, they know, there will be no new achievement, but also, they hope, no further decay because everyone will be tied to their jobs, performing the same routine over and over. But by outlawing achievement and its source, the thinking mind, the looters simply hasten the nation's disintegration.

The Taggart tunnel disaster illustrates how the nation descends from the shining productivity that was Colorado to the fate of Starnesville. As a result of Directive 10-289, there are few thinking men left on Taggart Transcontinental. They've been replaced by individuals who seek to exist without judgment, without having to decide whether something is either A or non-A. In reality, either it is safe to send a coal-burning engine into the tunnel or it is not safe. But no one at Taggart Transcontinental will officially declare that it is safe or not safe. They seek to exist in some indefinite, nebulous middle. The passengers too seek to exist in the middle. They accept and echo all the ideas and slogans of the looters, yet still expect there to be functioning trains and a functioning industrial civilization. They discover otherwise; their last sight on earth is Wyatt's torch.

Looking at it another way, what destroyed the Twentieth Century Motor Company and led to Starnesville is precisely what the whole nation is now trying to implement: the special tax imposed on Colorado was morally justified by noting that Colorado was "the state best able to assist the needier states to bear the brunt of the national emergency" (part I, 334). The results of this morality have to be the same.

This is what the Twentieth Century Motor Company's young engineer grasps. He realizes that it is either-or. Either you are on the side of the mind and achievement or you are on the side of the world's corrupt moral ideal—and only the sanction of the victims has obscured this fact. When he hears the Starnes' plan, John Galt promises to stop the motor of the world.

What he has learned is what Hank and Dagny must discover. Both are caught in the middle. Hank senses the freedom that would come from quitting—he laughs at Wyatt's act of destruction and later at the crash of d'Anconia Copper's stock, and he wants to laugh when Ragnar tells him no one will be permitted to manufacture Rearden Metal. But he stops himself because he cannot desert his mills—nor blame Ragnar for the course of action Ragnar has chosen.

Hank is beginning to discover with Francisco's help, however, that he is in the middle: he hasn't been fighting the looters, he's been propping them up through his moral sanction. But Hank thinks he can withdraw his sanction, as he does at his trial, and still remain in the world fighting the looters.

Dagny does quit after Directive 10-289 is passed, but she doesn't know how to go on after that. She feels caught in a world without shape or identity. "It seems monstrously wrong to surrender the world to the looters," she says, "and monstrously wrong to live under their rule. I can neither give up nor go back. I can neither exist without work nor work as a serf" (618). But she rushes back to the world after the tunnel disaster, unable to abandon her love to its complete destruction.

Both Hank and Dagny must learn that their battle is either-or: that they are either on the side of the strikers or on the side of the looters, either on the side of the mind or on the side of the mindless.

Chapter I: The Man Who Belonged on Earth

The title of this chapter refers to Hank—and to Stadler. Both men have a spirit-matter split. Hank is a man who belongs on earth, or more exactly, Dagny thinks to herself, "a man to whom the earth belongs"; but he is only beginning to discover this fact (370). Stadler, by contrast, is the man to whom the earth could have belonged, but he's renounced it.

When Hank walks to Dagny's apartment from the conference with the doomed copper producers, he is filled with loathing for the world. "If what he saw around him was the world in which he lived, then he did not want to touch any part of it, he did not want to fight it, he was an outsider with nothing at stake and no concern for remaining alive much longer" (374). But Hank does not succumb to the loathing; he sees and chooses to hold on to the possibility of another mode of existence, of men whose purpose is to rise and to build, to create metals and motors; "so long as he knew that there existed one man with the bright courage of a new thought, could he give up the world to those others? . . . the men who invented motors did exist, he would never doubt their reality, it was his vision of them that had made the contrast unbearable, so that even the loathing was a tribute of his loyalty to them and to the world which was theirs and his" (377).

Hank is a this-worldly idealist: he wants to make the ideal, real. This has always been his motivation in business, to build in the image of his vision of what could be—to erect mills and produce steel and invent a metal superior to steel. He's now *beginning* to see that this union of the spiritual and the material should pervade his whole life—that he should not leave his capacity to love Dagny unexpressed, confined to the hopeless longings of paintings and museums—that the pleasure of luxuries are real when infused with spiritual significance, as they are between him and Dagny—that his desire for her and hers for him are expressions and celebrations of their desire to live—"that that which he had called her depravity" in Wyatt's house "was her highest virtue—this capacity of hers to feel the joy of being, as he felt it" (378).

As a this-worldly idealist, Hank won't surrender the world to evil. He would not, for instance, sell Rearden Metal to the State Science Institute without knowing what Project X is. And he is now beginning to see how to fight his enemies. They depend on some kind of sanction from their victims—the traffic cop from the State Science Institute needed Rearden to pretend that the transaction would be a friendly sale, just as Stadler needed Dagny to pretend that his was still a mind devoted to intelligence and truth, not to their destruction.

But can you remain in the looters' world without sanctioning their evil? Hank senses the answer, when he laughs in triumph and deliverance at Wyatt's burning oil fields, but he then pulls back, "now condemned to constant vigilance against himself" (363). He wants to remain in the world, with his mills and his metal, and still fight the looters. He'll discover it's either-or.

Stadler too feels loathing for the world as it is, but for him the loathing has become a constant emotion. Why? Because rather than fighting for his kind of world and for any man with the courage of a new thought, as Hank resolves to do, Stadler declares the fight futile—what can you do when you have to deal with people? Instead of fighting, he chooses to make terms with evil by divorcing spirit from matter. He seeks as a refuge a pure world of theory and intellect. He renounces the material world as low and unworthy—a realm in which intelligence is unneeded. The only possible function of its inhabitants is to serve him; he commands—he needs a research laboratory or more heating at the Institute—and they should obey. He thereby helps deliver the world to the mindless and so, eventually, to the brute.

And this is precisely what we begin to see springing up everywhere: rule by the non-mind, from the State Science Institute "successfully" reclaiming Wyatt's oil fields without producing a drop of oil—to Jim claiming that Taggart Transcontinental is at its most profitable because unearned money is flowing in from Washington—to the Wet Nurse becoming the Deputy Director of Distribution for Rearden Metal. It is this fact that Floyd Ferris's book, *Why Do You Think You Think?* drives home to Stadler and which he must evade: Stadler has placed his name and intellect in the service of the anti-mind. Stadler desperately longs for men of intelligence—while promoting the idea that men are irrational and that intelligence is unnecessary to live in the world. He wants above all to see Galt, but has to hope Galt is dead, because Galt's is the voice that would blast away Stadler's evasions and reveal Stadler's actual motivation.

For Stadler too it is either-or: either he acknowledges the inescapable fact that life on earth demands intelligence, and like Hank resolves to fight for these men instead of making them his victims—or he holds that the material world does not demand intelligence. But then what do its keepers need Stadler for? This is his great fear: rather than the Floyd Ferrises of the world—the valets of science—ministering to him, they won't need him any longer.

Chapter II: The Aristocracy of Pull

As Francisco remarks, the aristocracy of pull has replaced the aristocracy of money. The people now running the country, we see in this chapter, trade not in money but in men. They therefore must hold something over the men whom they trade.

It is a precarious form of existence: even within the world of the looters, none can be certain his blackmails will work. Jim had Mouch in his pocket because of written evidence documenting how Mouch double-crossed Rearden. But Mouch is getting to be so influential in Washington that even such an ugly scandal would not derail him; Jim's hold on Mouch is slipping: Mouch doesn't even bother to show up for Jim's wedding.

But as these men jockey for the power to loot, their schemes require that there still exist men who make money. They believe there will always be producers continuing to produce, whom they can exploit. The power-seekers at Jim's wedding are all counting on Francisco to make d'Anconia Copper wildly profitable. They are, in Francisco's words, "the men of the double standard . . . the men who are the hitchhikers of virtue." But what if Francisco removes the pillar holding them up, by deliberately choosing not to produce? With the news of d'Anconia Copper's impending crash, we see the looters for what they are: "These men had become a pile of rubble, clattering in the wind of panic, the rubble left of a structure when its key pillar has been cut" (422).

But three pillars remain in the room, looking at one another: Francisco, Dagny, and Hank. And the looters still have a hold on the last two.

The looters count on their victim accepting their standards without him understanding those standards or being fully aware that he is sanctioning a whole different code. We see this happen with Hank. He attends Jim's wedding because he thinks he is guilty and Lillian is in the right to demand that he perform his duties as a husband. But his evaluation of his guilt and her right actually comes from her standards, not his own. And his very presence at the wedding implies that they are not looters. "In your code but not in theirs," Francisco tells him, "accepting a man's hospitality is a token of good will, a declaration that you and your host stand on terms of a civilized relationship. Don't give them that kind of sanction" (416). But Rearden can't yet understand what Lillian and the others are after and so what it is he's sanctioning.

We see the same form of error with Cherryl. She can't understand much of what Jim confesses to her, and the parts she thinks she understands, she has whitewashed by reinterpreting according to her standards. So for instance she thinks that Jim's fellow looters hate him because they envy his achievement and that when Jim flaunts that she's only a shop girl, it's "the gesture of a courageous man defying their opinion" (391). Like Rearden, she is suspicious and uneasy at times, but she gives Jim the benefit of every doubt. She can't fathom his motivation: "there are people who'll try to hurt you through the good they see in you," the sob sister tells her, "knowing that it's good, needing it and punishing you for it. Don't let it break you when you discover that" (392).

But the pull the looters have on a man of virtue is actually more precarious than the blackmails they have on each other. It will disappear if their victim identifies his own standards and those of his oppressors. And Hank is beginning to glimpse this fact: at the party he suddenly wonders why he should have to live by standards other than his own—why doesn't he just seize Dagny, as he so desperately wants to? He also momentarily applies his own standards to Lillian by thinking that a contract is not valid if "no valuable consideration had been given by one party to the other" (398). He senses that all the questions of his life would be answered if he discovered the connection between having to hide his deal with Danagger and his affair with Dagny. And he laughs at Francisco's deliberate act of destruction.

For the looters' world to collapse requires only that one of its last pillars, Hank, grasp that the answer to Francisco's question is that he, Hank, is the guiltiest man in the room. As Francisco says at the end of his speech about the meaning of money, "When money ceases to be the tool by which men deal with one another, then men become the tools of men. Blood, whips and guns—or dollars. Take your choice—there is no other—and your time is running out" (415). Time is running out—the world is descending into savagery—because Galt has been systematically removing the pillars like Hank, the pillars on which the whole (seemingly civilized) aristocracy of pull depends. The greatest symbol of Jim's power, much greater than if Mouch had attended his wedding, is Lillian's gift to him: Hank's attendance. "Your guests are quite impressed," Lillian tells Jim. "Most of them are thinking: 'If he has to seek terms with Jim Taggart, we'd better toe the line.' And a few are thinking: 'If he's afraid, we'll get away with much more.' This is as you want it, of course" (398). But Hank can end Jim's power simply by walking away.

Chapter III: White Blackmail

The few remaining pillars continue to fall—Ken Danagger quits, refusing (we learn in a later chapter) to be paid with torture for his virtues. It is this form of torture, this white blackmail, that Hank is starting to understand.

Lillian is worried, and not without reason, that Hank will do what Francisco did to d'Anconia Copper. The reason she is worried is that although Hank remains captive to alien standards in his personal life, he is beginning to see the importance of explicitly proclaiming his standards in business. This becomes evident when Ferris tries to blackmail Hank into voluntarily selling Rearden Metal to the State Science Institute for Project X. Ferris threatens to expose the business deal Hank made with Danagger, and Hank wonders why Ferris seems pleased that one of their laws has been broken. "Well," Ferris answers him, "what do you think there they're for?" Hank now sees the flaw in their racket. They don't care that their laws have been broken—they want them to be broken—but they rely on their victim caring about upholding the law and experiencing guilt when he violates it. What happens if the victim refuses to feel guilty for violating a law he rejects? You cannot blackmail a person by threatening to publicly expose that which he himself regards *and* will openly proclaim as good. This is what the looters will find out at Hank's trial.

But Hank cannot yet see that the same applies to his affair with Dagny, because he still does not fully understand the virtue involved in their affair or the vice involved in his marriage. Although he tells Dagny he thinks he was lying to himself in Wyatt's house, he still cannot accept that Dagny wants to sleep with him (or with anyone) and believes that it's right that he suffer for betraying Lillian. (In actual fact, his suffering comes from his betrayal of Dagny by remaining with Lillian.) When Lillian discovers he's having an affair, Hank thinks it's right that Lillian now dictate the terms of their relationship; he wants a divorce, but grants that the decision is hers. When she refuses him a divorce, he thinks the cause is her love for him. Yet her punishment for Hank is that he will have "to come home and face the only person who knows you for what you really are, who knows the actual value of your word, of your honor, of your integrity, of your vaunted self-esteem" (431). Hank senses that there is some flaw in her system of punishment, but cannot yet name it.

But Francisco is helping him name it. He tells Hank that the issues Hank is grappling with are much wider than business. "What I wonder about, Mr. Rearden, is why you live by one code of principles when you deal with nature and by another when you deal with men?" (451). Francisco tells him he's facing a *moral* conflict. "You who won't allow one per cent of impurity into an alloy of metal—what have you allowed into your moral code? . . . You bowed to their code and never upheld your own. . . . Their moral code is their weapon. Ask yourself how deeply and in how many terrible ways you have accepted it. . . . You have been paying blackmail, not for your vices, but for your virtues. . . . Yours was the code of life. What, then, is theirs?" (454–55). In this conflict, Francisco is indicating to Hank, the choice is either-or: either Hank applies his principles everywhere or he ends up applying them nowhere.

But if Hank is beginning to see the injustice he's been subjected to, how, Francisco wonders, can he carry such an inhuman burden? Because Hank does not see himself like Atlas—"blood running down his chest, his knees buckling, his arms trembling but still trying to hold the world aloft with the last of his strength" (455). As Hank sees himself, he is a pillar that will not break. Hank's enormous vitality, Francisco learns when Hank saves his life during the accident in the mills, masks the heavy burden Hank carries. This metaphysical issue is the looters' deepest hold on Hank, their deepest form of white blackmail. "Don't you see?" Hank tells Francisco. "We're able to act. They're not. So it's we who'll win in the long run, no matter what they do to us" (460).

Chapter IV: The Sanction of the Victim

In this chapter Hank frees himself from the guilt his family has spent its energies trying to induce in him. He sees that Lillian's attempt to punish him rested on his virtues—another form of white blackmail. Accusations of his moral depravity would affect him only if he had the virtue to take his own moral character seriously. He would worry about causing Lillian pain only if he were benevolent enough to feel concern for her. "His virtues, all the virtues she needed to achieve his punishment, came from another code and lived by another standard." But what then is the nature of *her* code? "A code—he thought—which would destroy only those who tried to observe it; a punishment, from which only the honest would suffer, while the dishonest would escape unhurt. Could one conceive of an infamy lower than to equate virtue with pain?" (465).

But does his family understand the nature of the code they espouse?

Hank senses that they do—he notes that Philip seems to enjoy that Hank is being denounced by all the newspapers and that Lillian seems to enjoy her status as the betrayed wife who has the right to seek vengeance on him. He also notes the radical difference between their reactions and that of the Wet Nurse, who has come to worship Hank and the mills. But Hank cannot believe anyone is capable of the level of evil he is sensing in his family. Yet why don't they even try to defend their code, now that he openly rejects it and asserts his own standards—as he does when he tells Philip that the next time Philip utters his depraved moral views, Hank will toss him out of the house? Hank senses that the key here too is the sanction of the victim—that he has somehow made their whole code possible—but he does not yet understand in what precise way.

But he understands how the principle pertains to his trial, and in proudly proclaiming his own standards in business and rejecting theirs, he gets off. The looters need his help to make his trial look like a tribunal of justice, and he refuses to cooperate. They scurry away, unsure of how to proceed. "But if this is what has beaten us, he thought, the guilt is ours" (483). The real sentence the trial imposes on him is to discover why men are so willing to renounce the good within them as sin.

Despite the trial's outcome, only Dagny and Willers gain inspiration from it; Hank's fellow businessmen do not join his stand; instead, they seek a middle ground. Like Francisco, Hank feels contempt for them as they struggle to evade that the issue is either-or. "Why go to extremes?"—one businessmen tells Hank. "There's always a middle ground." Hank answers: "A middle ground between you and your murderers?" (484).

But Francisco suggests to Hank that he too is caught in the middle: Hank is not consistently practicing the principle he declared at his trial. And notice that Hank in fact lost the trial and is still trying to function under the looters' unjust and non-objective laws. In the course of his conversation with Francisco, Hank learns of a whole area that he had not yet considered or understood, namely the two opposing codes' evaluation of sex; this knowledge will eventually help him understand the true scope of the sanction of the victim.

And at the end of their conversation, Hank witnesses—though he doesn't know it—a man who is *not* caught in the middle, a man who fully understands the principle of the sanction of the victim. Francisco refuses to prop up and sanction the looters' system by allowing the three ships carrying d'Anconia copper to reach New York, even though he knows it will cost him Hank's friendship.

Chapter V: Account Overdrawn

"You're the account I own!" Lillian shouts at Hank in this chapter. But the reality she senses and is trying to escape is that she no longer does. She has controlled Hank by draining his self-esteem, but she knows that his affair with Dagny, which Lillian has just discovered, has revived it. His own pleasure is now sacred to him; he would have the joy he gets from his relationship with Dagny even if it took Lillian's life. Hank still feels guilt, but not because of anything he has done to Lillian; emotionally, he is now free of concern for her. His guilt comes from what he said to Dagny in Wyatt's house and for its root within him, "the obscenity of letting impotence hold itself as virtue and damn the power of living as a sin" (530).

But though these are Hank's emotions, he is not actually free of Lillian. He still thinks she is motivated, in some twisted way, by love for him and that out of pity for her unrequited love he should take *her* standards into account. "By every standard of mine, to maintain our marriage will be a vicious fraud. But my standards are not yours. I do not understand yours, I never have, but I will accept them. If this is the manner of your love for me, if bearing the name of my wife will give you some form of contentment, I won't take it away from you. It's I who've broken my word, so I will atone for it to the extent I can" (529–30). But there is one condition: no one is to discuss Dagny or their affair. Lillian senses a last way to shackle and control Hank; her account may be overdrawn, but it is not yet closed.

More widely, across the whole nation too many pillars that the looters had been counting on are gone. The looters' seemingly bottomless account is overdrawn. Rearden Steel fails for the first time to deliver an order on schedule; Danagger is gone and coal shipments are late; Colorado's great industrialists have disappeared and the state is in its death throes; the achievement that could have fueled the Second Renaissance, the John Galt Line, is soon to be closed. Even d'Anconia Copper cannot get its shipments to the United States; they cannot get past Ragnar Danneskjöld.

So who are the looters still counting on? Dagny and Taggart Transcontinental.

But the looters evade this fact, supposedly safe in their belief that producers are a fact of nature like the sun: just as the sun will rise each day, so they believe producers will continue to produce. The looters can impose whatever schemes they dream of, and there will always be someone else to loot. The man sent from Washington, Mr. Weatherby, won't entertain the repeal of even one control; we "wouldn't even consider listening to any talk on the subject" (508). And the one person in the boardroom whom he does not need to take notice of is Dagny. No one in that boardroom wants to know what policies have brought Taggart Transcontinental to its desperate state, yet if the John Galt Line is to be closed, the Board wants it to be Dagny's decision, since she is the producer who will, somehow, makes things work out.

Francisco comes to Dagny when the decision is made to kill the John Galt Line, hoping against hope that *her* account is overdrawn and ready to be closed: that she has seen enough of the looters' world and is ready to quit. But as Francisco expected, though in pain, Dagny will keep going; for her cause, she will tear up the John Galt Line and use it to support Taggart's transcontinental system.

Although Washington can count on Dagny, it is not sure it can continue to count on Hank—not after his trial. The looters are uncertain they can control him. Jim sees his opportunity: his Washington account is overdrawn—Mouch is no longer in his pocket and Jim is losing the looters' magic title of "the public"—but he hopes to replenish his account by delivering Hank to them (via Lillian's knowledge of Dagny and Hank's affair).

Chapter VI: Miracle Metal

The looters' whole policy consists of counting on the mind while evading its nature and existence. If the looters faced what the mind was and what its requirements were, they would see the futility of their own policy and would have to face the motivation that actually drives them: hatred of values and of existence. This is the meaning of the directive issued in this chapter, Directive 10-289.

The directive attempts to freeze the economy: it attaches employees to their jobs and business owners to their businesses, "voluntarily" turns over patents and copyrights to the government, and declares that everyone must continue to produce, spend, and earn whatever they have been producing, spending, and earning. It is a moratorium on brains. It is an attempt to have a functioning industrial economy without the need for any thought or judgment on behalf of the economy's participants. It is an attempt to escape the either-or, absolute nature of reality: to enjoy the looted products of intelligence, while denying the need for intelligence to function, denying even the existence of intelligence.

But even the looters have trouble maintaining this gross of an evasion. They are frightened by so openly attacking intelligence, sensing that they are still counting on it. "It was to avoid moments such as this that all the complex twisting of their minds had been devised. They wished the directive to go into effect. They wished it could be put into effect without words, so that they would not have to know that what they were doing was what it was" (536). The more intellectual of the looters supplies the cover to cloak that which they're evading. "Naming the unnamed in all their minds," Ferris declares:

There is no such thing as the intellect. A man's brain is a social product. . . . A genius is an intellectual scavenger and a greedy hoarder of the ideas which rightfully belong to society, from which he stole them. All thought is theft. If we do away with private fortunes, we'll have a fairer distribution of wealth. If we do away with the genius, we'll have a fairer distribution of ideas. (540)

But they cannot escape the consequences of Directive 10-289, which is to drive out whatever remnants of intelligence still existed in their system. Hank's employees start to quit, industrialists vanish, Dagny resigns.

If the looters scheme is to have a chance of even momentarily succeeding, they need Hank to sign the Gift Certificate for Rearden Metal. Ferris threatens to expose Hank's affair with Dagny. In that moment and through a character-istically ruthless act of mind, Hank grasps the view of existence that underlies their code and the genesis of his own pain.

"It was proper," he thinks to himself, "that they should now call it 'Miracle Metal'—a miracle was the only name *they* could give to those ten years and to the faculty from which Rearden Metal was born—a miracle was all that the Metal could be in their eyes, the product of an unknown, unknowable cause, an object in nature, not to be explained, but to be seized, like a stone or a weed" (560). They count on his mind, yet torment him for exercising it.

> You need the products of a man's ability—yet you proclaim that productive abil-ity is a selfish evil and you turn the degree of a man's productiveness into the measure of his loss. We lived by that which we held to be good and punished that which we held to be evil. You live by that which you denounce as evil and punish that which you know to be good. . . . Such was the code that the world had accepted and such was the key to the code: that it hooked man's love of existence to a circuit of torture. (561)

His guilt was to put aside his mind and accept this view, not in the material but in the spiritual realm: he damned his love of existence by damning his desire to physically possess the spirit that was Dagny's. "My crime was com-mitted when I said to her [Lillian], 'By every standard of mine, to maintain our marriage will be a vicious fraud. But my standards are not yours. I do not understand yours, I never have, but I will accept them'" (565).

But precisely as a man of the mind, not a looter or a mystic, Hank does not accept the miraculous. He knows that there "is no escape from justice, nothing can be unearned or unpaid for in the universe, neither in matter or in spirit— and if the guilty do not pay, then the innocent have to pay it" (565). Through Hank's own reproaches and shame at their affair, Dagny has been paying for his crime. This injustice must end. He is a man who pays his way. He signs the Gift Certificate, having now fulfilled the real sentence imposed on him at his trial: he has understood the tenet—the soul-body dichotomy—through which "the victims come to sanction a code that pronounced them guilty of the fact of existing" (561).

Chapter VII: The Moratorium on Brains

In this chapter, the full effects of the moratorium on brains are being felt. Taggart Transcontinental, like most businesses, is losing its best men, replaced by human driftwood and scum. The deserters, as the men who quit are called, roam the countryside directionless. The nation is disintegrating, and in response Washington dispenses men like Chick Morrison to boost morale.

Dagny has been replaced by Clifton Locey. No one at Taggart Transcontinental now dares exercise his intelligence to make a decision, because he is the one who will be blamed. No one wants to run the railroad, only hold his job. Each tries to shift the burden of judgment to someone else's shoulders. Locey pretends to be in charge but has no thoughts of his own and tries to mimic Dagny's actions on "anything that matters" (569). To Locey and the other looters, the world is not either-or but neither-nor. The choice is not between a world of intelligence or a world devoid of intelligence. Somehow, it's possible to have neither a world of intelligence nor a world devoid of intelligence; "like everything they do today," Willers observes, "it is and it ain't, at the same time" (568).

But in fact the world is either-or—and life and production in it demand intelligence. Outlaw intelligence and catastrophes like the tunnel disaster must ensue. In a world which teaches people that the only absolute is the cries and wishes of men in power—that the way to get people to act is through fear—and that men do not live by reason—in such a world, what else is to be expected? In such a world, both the Dagny Taggarts and the Bill Brents are replaced by men who will send a coal engine into the Taggart Tunnel.

But the victims are not blameless. The passengers support and echo all the ideas that led to Directive 10-289: "there was not a man aboard the train who did not share one or more of" these ideas (607). The conductor who allows the train into the tunnel just before deserting, thinks to himself:

> there had been a time when he had placed the safety of the passengers above his own . . . . Now, he felt a contemptuous indifference and no desire to save them. They had asked for and accepted Directive 10-289 . . . they went on living and daily turning away in evasion from the kind of verdicts that the Unification Board was passing on defenseless victims—why shouldn't he now turn away from them? (604)

In the world of Directive 10-289, what mode of existence is left to men? Either "to be a looter who robs disarmed victims," Danneskjöld tells Hank, or "to be a victim who works for the benefit of his own despoilers" (575).

But Danneskjöld chooses another path: to use his mind to take up arms in defense of human ability. Hank can neither condemn Danneskjöld's chosen path—nor the path of those who've simply stepped out, like Wyatt and Danagger—nor can he follow it. Hank is still caught in the middle. He cannot renounce his mills and would rather go down with the last of his world, because he can see no possibility of a different kind of world. Yet when Danneskjöld tells Hank that despite the Gift Certificate no one will manufacture Rearden Metal, Hank wants to laugh—but he stops himself, sensing that he would never see his mills again. He senses that Danneskjöld is right and another mode of existence *is* possible; as Danneskjöld will later describe it to Galt, Hank is hanging by a thin thread.

Chapter VIII: By Our Love

Whatever the looters are fundamentally moved by, their victims—and those actually fighting the looters—are moved by their love of values. This is what we see in this chapter.

Dagny has given up Taggart Transcontinental and is in pain at the loss of an irreplaceable loved one. She wants to create, but there is nowhere to build a railroad to and no one to build it for. She is losing her right to Hank's love: "He could help her to live; he could not help her to decide for what purpose she wished to go on living" (612). Even worse than giving up Taggart Transcontinental is giving up her quest to find the secret of the motor and the world of unlimited achievement that it represents: "it was her last link to the future. To kill seemed like an act, not of murder, but of suicide" (612).

Dagny cannot understand how she has lost if evil is in fact irrational and impotent; yet nothing can shake her conviction that this *is* the nature of evil, that only the good is potent and real. She can find no solution. The clarity of her either-or world has been replaced by the nightmare of a neither-nor realm. "It seems monstrously wrong to surrender the world to the looters," she says, "and monstrously wrong to live under their rule. I can neither give up nor go back. I can neither exist without work nor work as a serf" (618).

What she now feels about the world is what she has felt all along about Francisco. In her world, one is either a great industrialist or a playboy—but Francisco seemed to be neither the great man she had known him to be nor the worthless scoundrel the newspapers had said he had become. In the ten years since he left her, she could neither lose her feeling for him nor retain it. Yet in her misery at losing her greatest love, Taggart Transcontinental, it is Francisco who comes to her. She discovers his secret.

She learns that he is still moved by the same love as she. Out of his love for d'Anconia Copper and for her, he was one of the first men to quit. He is now systematically destroying d'Anconia Copper. Francisco refuses to divorce spirit and matter, as the looters' code demands: d'Anconia Copper is just so much meaningless material when its spirit is gone, he tells her, when its purpose has gone from serving life to serving the enemies of life. "We can never lose the things we live for," he tells Dagny. "We may have to change their form at times, if we've made an error, but the purpose remains the same and the forms are ours to make" (615). The key to Dagny's dilemma, he tells her, is that she has made her enemies possible. "By accepting punishment, not for any sins, but for our virtues, we betrayed our code and made theirs possible. . . . They count on you to feel that no effort is too great in the service of your love. . . . Your unrequited rectitude is the only hold they have upon you. . . . The day when you'll discover it is the only thing they dread.

You must learn to understand them. You won't be free of them, until you do" (619).

But at this point Dagny still cannot understand the looters, nor does she see how she has made their code possible. When she hears of the tunnel disaster, she runs back in the name of her love to save Taggart Transcontinental. By returning, however, she once again saves Jim, who was about to resign. What she cannot yet grasp is that what she has saved is a being consumed with hatred of her, of life, of existence—"hatred as his claim against the universe, as a justification, as a right, as an absolute"—and that she is granting him this right (624).

Both Dagny and Hank now realize, however, that they're being held hostage by their love of life, but "price is no object any longer" (632). They will go down with their rails and mills, with the last remnants of what they love. Neither Dagny nor Hank can conceive of an alternative existence, of a world of unlimited achievement that does not contain looters. Why? Because Dagny and Hank cannot yet see that they've made the looters' whole view of existence—and so the looters themselves—possible.

Chapter IX: The Face Without Pain or Fear or Guilt

This is a chapter filled with fear, with pain, and with guilt. We witness Dagny's fear that Francisco will break and kill Hank, the man who slapped him; her pain in thinking that she lives in a world where her vision of man's limitless potential is to remain unrealized; her guilt in now thinking that it may have been she who deserted Francisco, not the other way around. We see Hank's pain from discovering that his hated rival, Francisco, is the first man who slept with Dagny. And we see Hank's guilt after denouncing a man he loves and who set him free from guilt—and who, it seems, also loved him. While Hank was driven to inflict pain on Francisco, Francisco refused to inflict the pain he knew he could have on Hank.

The source of all this suffering is divided loyalties in the pursuit of the same love—when the actual choice is either-or. Dagny thinks she is serving the man with an "intransigent mind and an unlimited ambition" who is "in love with his own life" (635). But this man, Francisco tells her, "permits no divided allegiance, no war between your mind and your body, no gulf between your values and your actions, no tributes to Caesar. He permits no Caesars" (636). Atlantis is blocked to Dagny because she is supporting its destroyers; she thinks if she works hard enough she can outlast the looters: "They need me. They know it. It's *my* terms that I'll make them accept" (636). She doesn't understand that their terms are non-negotiable: they want her dead.

Hank too is divided. He is driven to lash out at Francisco because he cannot accept that within him which responds to Francisco, even though he senses the liberation it involves; Francisco's world is one of betrayal and of renunciation, but Hank knows one must never renounce that which one loves.

And it is only the divided allegiance of Dagny and Hank that has the power to cause pain in Francisco—and in Galt. Francisco is out of reach of the looters; they can no longer inflict their tortures on him. But his pain is real: at losing Dagny, at being prohibited from defending his love for her, of being unable to answer Hank's insults and face him openly. When he stops himself from killing Hank, Dagny knows "that she was witnessing Francisco d'Anconia's greatest achievement" (641). Francisco is able to stop himself by reminding himself of his loyalty to that which he loves—undivided loyalty to the cause and to the man Dagny thinks she is serving. Francisco "was looking at Rearden, but it was not Rearden that he was seeing. He looked as if he were facing another presence in the room and as if his glance were saying: If this is what you demand of me, then even this is yours, yours to accept and mine to endure, there is no more than this in me to offer you, but let me be proud to know that I can offer so much" (641).

It is Dagny and Hank's tribute to Caesar that has produced "some vast, impersonal suffering that had made them all its victims" (641).

By contrast, the nameless Taggart Transcontinental worker possesses a face that looks as if it has "never known pain or fear or guilt" (652). Yet two events from Dagny's world even have the power to disturb his face's guiltless serenity. He's disturbed to learn that Quentin Daniels has been working to discover the secret of the motor—yet his shock turns to laughter when he hears Daniels's reasons for quitting. And he actually rushes out of the cafeteria when he learns that Dagny is sleeping with Hank. The cause of his pain comes from the divided allegiance of the woman he loves.

Chapter X: The Sign of the Dollar

The country is now rapidly decaying. As Dagny rides east to reach Daniels, she thinks of what a difference a month under the moratorium on brains has made. When she reaches the prairies, she sees "the remnants of towns" and "the skeletons of factories," now only "monuments to how much had been achieved on the edge of nature's void by men who had once been free to achieve" (655). It had once been a nation ruled by the dollar.

In Jeff Allen's recounting of the fate of the Twentieth Century Motor Company, we see the cause of the world's destruction in inception and in microcosm: what ideal, brought into full reality, replaced the rule of the dollar.

"The plan," Allen tells Dagny,

> was that everybody in the factory would work according to his ability, but would be paid according to his need. . . . None of us knew just how the plan would work, but every one of us thought that the next fellow knew it. And if anybody had doubts, he felt guilty and kept his mouth shut. . . . Hadn't we heard it all our lives—from our parents and our schoolteachers and our ministers, and in every newspaper we ever read and every movie and every public speech? Hadn't we always been told that this was righteous and just? (660–61)

The result was anything but righteous and just—as employees tried to hide their ability and exhibit their need—as competition turned from one of achievements to one of sores—and as the best men took the role of suckers and the worst, the role of bloodsuckers.

The originators and profiteers of the plan were the Starnes heirs. "But profit," says Allen, "depends on what it is you're after. And what the Starnes heirs were after, no money on earth could buy" (666). Eric Starnes was after causeless love; Gerald Starnes wanted causeless prestige and envious stares; Ivy Starnes wanted to hold the lives of her betters in her hands, degrading these men to the status of her bootlickers. But those who merely voted for the plan were not innocent: they secretly felt that their need would entitle them to the products of the ability of others.

The ideal the Starnes heirs implemented in the factory is the ideal now engulfing the nation. Gone is what the United States once was, a nation ruled by the dollar sign, the sign which stands "for achievement, for success, for ability, for man's creative power" (683).

And it is this ideal that Dagny is inadvertently sanctioning. The passengers on her frozen train need transportation; they contemptuously demand that Dagny provide it, since hers is the ability, theirs is the need. And in providing it, Dagny warrants no acknowledgment or consideration, not even the consideration of being protected from the marauding gangs of raiders. A woman onboard screams at Dagny: "I'll report you to the Unification Board!" and Kellogg underscores for Dagny the meaning of her reply: "if I give you the train to get you within sight or hearing of your Board" (677).

It is precisely this sanction that Galt withdraws when he walks out of the Twentieth Century Motor Company. He will teach the world that it is either-or: either the monstrous ideal of the Starnes heirs or the ideal of the dollar sign.

But although Dagny is unknowingly supporting the wrong ideal, consciously she is still fighting for hers. She is shocked to find how little of her world is left: her only request of Kellogg, should she die, is to tell Willers to give Allen a job and to tell Hank what happened to her. But she continues to fight for her world's remnants, unwilling to "abandon an incalculable wealth such as the brain of Quentin Daniels," ready to give her life if only she could take the destroyer's first, ready to go down with her plane in pursuit of her love (696).

But as she is crashing, she doesn't think she'll die. Another type of existence must be possible—it must be reachable—it must be real.

PART III: A IS A

In part III, all the contradictions and mysteries, small and large, are resolved. A world of identity is restored.

Dagny finds the valley in which the cigarettes with a dollar sign are manufactured and learns why Danneskjöld became a pirate. She discovers what has happened to all the men who vanished—and learns why Akston was working as a cook in a diner, Kellogg wouldn't take the promotion she offered him, and the brakeman seemed to be whistling Halley's Fifth Concerto. She discovers who the inventor of the motor is—and who the destroyer is. She learns that an existence free from the looters is possible: her world of unobstructed achievement is real, lying before her in the valley.

Part III is dominated by the figure of John Galt. He is the man who unrelentingly faces the facts for what they are. No illusions, no evasions, no misrepresentations can deflect him from identifying the nature of what is.

It is Galt who gives identity to the principles and standards that have governed the lives of those he has convinced to strike, but which they were unable to name. His new moral code is the foundation for the future of unlimited achievement that the valley represents.

It is Galt who gives identity to the nature of the enemy they all face. He defines the full meaning of the code the world accepts, the meaning that is always evaded, and he identifies the source of this code in the view of existence shared by the mystics of spirit and the mystics of muscle.

It is Galt who identifies the danger to the men of the mind of divorcing spirit from matter. He shows them the nature of their battle and how to fight the enemy: they must withdraw their sanction of the mystics' moral code and the mystics' view of existence. He thereby makes the mystics—and the world—face the true nature of their creed and of their own souls.

It is Galt who shows Dagny why she is mistaken about the looters, why she can't win her battle, and why she never had to take the looters' world seriously. It is Galt who teaches her—and the world—the full meaning of A is A.

Chapter I: Atlantis

Dagny crash lands in Atlantis. Another type of existence *is* possible. In the valley, men are free to think, to work, to trade, and to profit, each to the extent of his ability. It is a realm governed by values—the tokens of which are the gold coins Mulligan mints—in which justice and reason rule. It is a world in which spirit and matter are united. It is a world in which men reverently dedicate themselves to their own lives. "What is it that you're all doing here?" she asks Galt. "Living," he answers. "She had never heard that word sound so real" (713).

Dagny learns what it took for these men to reach and build Atlantis. She learns that Galt has called on strike the one kind of men who had never struck before, the men of the mind. They are on strike against a code that worships human incompetence and are through making terms with their enemies. Galt has withdrawn the moral sanction they had given to the mystics and granted it instead to those who had earned it but had never received it before: the strikers. Dagny hears the specific reasons why the men in Mulligan's living room quit and the price each was willing to pay. They had to be willing to give up their achievements in the world, realizing that there is no meaning to the matter they left behind absent the mind—the spirit—that animated it. They had to be willing to give up the world for a time being, knowing that this is the attitude hardest to attain: "what we now feel for their world is that emotion which they preach as an ideal: indifference—the blank—the zero—the mark of death" (741). Galt and the others went on strike without the expectation that the looters' world would collapse in their lifetimes: "We knew only that this was the only way we cared to live" (748).

Sitting before the men in Mulligan's room, she sees the *identity* of all she has sought. "*This* was the Taggart Terminal," she thinks to herself, the destination of its rails, the goal it was meant to achieve (748). "It was for the sake of this that she had dedicated herself to the rail of Taggart Transcontinental, as to the body of a spirit yet to be found. She had found it, everything she had ever wanted, it was here in this room, reached and hers" (748–49). The man at the end of the rails, whom she was serving and whom she loves, is standing before her, real.

But the price of reaching Atlantis, she thinks, is the very rail that has brought her to her destination. Although Dagny and Galt are in love, they are still pitted against one another. Galt knows the choice is either-or and is serenely confident that his judgment and choice are correct. He's strikingly open with Dagny; when she seeks to spare him the need to name the fact that he stole Daniels away from her, he names the fact proudly; he tells her he took Francisco and Danagger from her world, fully aware of the consequences to her; he deliberately shows her all the men he's taken away and openly tells her he's making it as difficult as possible for her to choose to leave the valley. More intimately, he tells her that when he saw her plane as he was flying away with Daniels, it "was the one and only time when I didn't think of you" (712). Galt has the simplicity and severity of a man who stands before the inexorable fact "that the truth is the truth" (725).

Dagny, by contrast, is conflicted: she doesn't know what is true. Galt is the destroyer she has sworn to shoot on sight, but he is also the inventor of the motor whom she wants to sleep with. She thinks that the valley *is* the Taggart Terminal, but also that she would be betraying Taggart Transcontinental by remaining here. She thinks Hank's presence in the valley would be natural, but simultaneously impossible. She thinks it would be absurd for Galt to submit to the looters by returning to the world, but not absurd for her. She is torn by a contradiction—which Galt tells her was responsible for destroying the John Galt Line and which she must resolve in order to enter Atlantis.

Chapter II: The Utopia of Greed

What is the nature of Atlantis? It is a realm where the inhabitants proudly and *greedily* dedicate themselves to the pursuit of their highest values. It is a realm where sacrifice is banished and love of life rules. This is what we witness in this chapter.

Dagny is desperately in love with Galt but she doesn't have the right to sleep with him. When she hears of Hank grimly bearing the news of her death and of the Comet crawling toward San Francisco, she feels she is betraying both by remaining in the valley—but when she thinks of leaving Galt and the existence he has created, she feels she would be betraying him. She feels homeless, "as if she were suspended in space between this valley and the rest of the earth, with no right to either" (763). She feels caught in a reality that one must never accept, "the view that man was ever to be drawn by some vision of the unattainable shining ahead, doomed ever to aspire, but not to achieve. *Her* life and *her* values could not bring her to that" (772).

Dagny wants to get word to Hank that she is alive, but she will not ask Galt for a special exception from the rules of the valley; she will not sacrifice the meaning of her love for Galt by pretending that her love for Hank is the greater. Yet it is in the name of all that she loves—of that which gives her love for Galt meaning—that Dagny chooses to leave Galt and return to the world of Rearden Steel and Taggart Transcontinental. If there is even one chance to win back the earth from the looters, to win that which is rightfully Galt's—she must take it.

Francisco too is moved by love. His love for Dagny was Galt's best argument against Francisco: he went on strike to win the kind of world she deserved (as she is now trying to win for Galt). He misses breakfast with Danneskjöld and Galt for the first time in twelve years because he is searching for the wreckage of her plane. Nor will Francisco sacrifice his love for Dagny by pretending that he no longer desires her. "Will I want to sleep with you? Desperately," he tells Dagny. "Will I envy the man who does? Sure" (768). But he will also not commit the unspeakable act of asking her or Hank or Galt to sacrifice their values and desires for his sake. He knows that they all are, rightfully, moved by the same source: "by our love for a single value, for the highest potentiality of our own existence" (768). This is what no one must be asked to betray.

Hank too is desperately in love with Dagny, and continues to search for her crash site when almost everyone else has given up. Like Dagny, if he sees even one chance for success, he will continue to fight for his values. It is only a failure of knowledge, not a failure of love, that keeps the valley hidden from him.

It is this selfishness of soul that Galt exudes and which, as the leader of the strike, he has taught the strikers to refuse to do penance for. Galt is passionately in love with his life, with his capacity to live, with the earth, and with Dagny—so passionately that he will accept no substitute, no halfway existence, no aspiration to be sought but never to be reached. Consequently, he will never divorce his end from the means necessary to achieve it; for Galt, "cost is an absolute which cannot be escaped" (780). He doesn't try to win the place he could have in the world, because he knows the price: torture at the hands of an evil whose existence he would have made possible. He didn't go to Dagny in her lonely office when she was completing the John Galt Line, despite his desire for her and hers for him, because he knew that at that point she was his enemy and would have had to try to stop him. He holds Dagny in the valley for a month because he wants her there. He wants to sleep with her, but tells her, "It's your acceptance of this place that I want. What good would it do me, to have your physical presence without any meaning? That's the kind of faked reality by which most people cheat themselves of their lives. I'm not capable of it. And neither are you" (780). And he knows that Francisco and Hank are both in love with Dagny, but Galt will not sacrifice his love for the sake of either one of them; he tells Francisco "I would have given anything to let it be otherwise, except that which is beyond giving" (810).

Stadler is thus Galt's worst enemy. Stadler's is a radically selfless soul: he has consciously betrayed that which he loved, hoping that he could evade the fact that "cost is an absolute which cannot be escaped."

In the name of an end divorced from means—of the desire to do theoretical research without the bother of having to earn the material means necessary—Stadler was willing to place his mind in service of the looters. In the process, he had to destroy that which he professed to love: the mind. He somehow expected Galt to work under the orders of Floyd Ferris; Francisco, under the orders of Wesley Mouch; and Danneskjöld, under the orders of Simon Pritchett. And then, as rationalization of his betrayal of all that he loved, Stadler wails that nothing else is possible in the material world. "What I want you to understand," Akston tells Dagny, "is the full evil of those who claim to have become convinced that this earth, by its nature, is a realm of malevolence where the good has no chance to win. . . . Let them check—before they grant themselves the unspeakable license of evil-as-necessity—whether they know what *is* the good and what are the conditions it requires" (790).

And it is out of love for the good that Galt chooses to return to the world: he will not give up that which he loves to the looters. He is certain Dagny is wrong and that her quest will fail, but knows that she must grasp the reason herself. She must not, however, commit Stadler's sin and accept the contradiction that the ideal is the unreachable. "If you fail," Galt tells her, "as men have failed in their quest for a vision that should have been possible, yet has remained forever beyond their reach—if, like them, you come to think that one's highest values are not to be attained and one's greatest vision is not to be made real—don't damn this earth, as they did, don't damn existence. You have seen the Atlantis they were seeking, it is here, it exists—but one must enter it naked and alone, with no rags from the falsehoods of centuries, with the purest clarity of mind" (812–13).

Chapter III: Anti-Greed

Dagny leaves the utopia of greed with one premise left to check: that the men of the world love their lives. And with the world near full collapse, and the looters desperate, their motivation surfaces. In this chapter, Dagny begins to see it.

Lillian tries to blackmail Dagny to appear on Scudder's radio program. Lillian boasts that for once Dagny will act as Lillian must act, by obeying a will other than her own. There is nothing Dagny can offer to prevent the blackmail, Lillian tells her, because "I'm devoid of greed. . . . I am doing it without gain. Without gain. Do you understand me?" (849). With an almost pleading tone in her voice, Lillian tells Dagny that it was she who took Rearden Metal from Hank. Dagny is beginning to see what moves them, although it "was not within the power of Dagny's consciousness ever to understand that plea or to know what response Lillian had hoped to find" (849). Lillian is seeking Dagny's acknowledgement and respect, as if Lillian's act of destroying a supreme value elevated her act into the realm of the important, as if the greatness of the value Lillian destroyed somehow made her act the greater one.

Jim too, Dagny thinks, is "going to pieces . . . the jerky impatience, the shrillness, the aura of panic were new" (839). Not even Jim's incompetent mind could believe that the new Railroad Unification Plan—a plan which purports to save the railroads by pooling all resources and revenues and then distributing the income based on need—could save Taggart Transcontinental. Jim frantically pretends the plan is practical, but his panic is palpable. "*This*," Dagny thinks to herself, "did not have even the rationality of a looter" (842). Dagny is beginning to realize that Jim's fundamental motivation is not wealth, even if looted wealth. "I see," she says quietly to Jim, and he seems to shake "with terror at that which the quiet 'I see' had acknowledged seeing" (842). She senses that the sanction Jim and his gang needs *has* to come from her, the victim—that in order for them to pretend that they belong in her shining realm, not their sewer of an existence, it is she who must concede this fact. She wonders what level of "inner degradation" these men must reach in order to require this level of self-deception (846).

This same form of inner degradation and self-deception is certainly present in Stadler. He is a man devoid of greed—of the selfishness of soul necessary to make the ideal, real. He does not want to have to bother with the effort and struggle to bring material form to his spiritual vision, to his noble pursuit of "pure" truth. Yet he still requires a laboratory and funding—how is he to get them? By seizing them. But how can he justify this? By rationalizing his action. The creation of material goods requires no thought and no intellect, he constantly tells himself; they are the products of irrational, money-chasing brutes; these products exist to be seized and this seizure is not an act directed against the mind. Nor is it even Stadler's responsibility to ensure that the work of his mind is put to the use of good and not evil, since ideals are unachievable in this world of irrational men. Over and over he tells himself, "like a voodoo formula which one recites when it is needed and beyond which one must not look: *What can you do when you have to deal with people?*" (818).

Stadler comes to *need* a world of irrational men ruled by force—because an opposite world would topple his rationalizations. This is the meaning of his sanctioning of Project X, an instrument of brute force intended to rule a mindless population. Stadler cannot face the fact that there are men who are *not* irrational, that another form of existence among men is possible, that men like Hank, Dagny, Francisco, and the inventor of the motor *are* exponents of the mind—because then he could not justify looting them. He must declare such men impractical—then evade their existence—then seek their elimination. He begins by labeling Galt an impractical idealist; he will end by demanding that Galt be killed.

Stadler's drawn-out suicide begins as he walks to the speaker's scaffold to deliver the speech extolling Project X that Ferris has prepared for him: "the crowd was about to witness an act of destruction more terrible than the destruction of the farm" (830). A young reporter cries to Stadler to tell the country the truth about Project X. The reporter's face is the only one in the crowd that exhibits a spark of ability, but Stadler denounces the man as a disloyal punk with treasonable motives; the reporter's was a young face, possessing hazel eyes with "a tinge of green" (831).

Who is Stadler's heir? Cuffy Meigs, whom Dagny discovers is the Director of Unification. He is a man the world considers the exemplar of greed: a thug who seizes whatever he can get his hands on, without concern for causes or consequences. "In the long run," he tells Dagny—stating what Jim and Jim's teachers have been saying forever, but stating it as almost self-evident fact, in light of which Meigs will simply act accordingly—"we'll all be dead" (843). He is a man devoid of thought and so of greed: he has no values, no capacity to value, no desire to give material form to any spiritual vision, no inkling of where the loot he seizes comes from.

But in this chapter, in contrast to the inner degradation and self-deception of the looters, we also see the souls of Dagny and Hank. On Scudder's radio program Dagny openly and proudly tells the world that she and Hank "are those who do not disconnect the values of their minds from the actions of their bodies," those who are driven by greed for spiritual values given material form, "those who make steel, railroads and happiness" (853). Afterward, Hank tells her he has discovered the source of his life's pain: his acceptance of "the one tenet by which they destroy a man before he's started, the killer-tenet: the breach between his mind and body" (857–58). To win back that which was rightfully his and redeem their relationship, here at its end, Hank declares his love for her and the source of that love. Despite what he has lost—both Rearden Metal and Dagny—he knows he is *richer* than he was because his capacity to value, his mind, is now whole.

Chapter IV: Anti-Life

To be anti-greed, we learn in this chapter, is to be anti-life. What Dagny must come to understand about Jim and his gang is what Cherryl discovers here—the sight of which drives her to suicide.

Jim has just helped plan d'Anconia Copper's nationalization and wants to celebrate his existence. But what is that existence? This is what he has spent his life evading—and the question is now haunting him. Tonight he wants the pleasure to be himself. "To be himself—he thought, in the drugged, precarious state of floating past the deadliest of his blind alleys, the one that led to the question of what was himself" (873).

Jim realizes he's indifferent to the money he'll seize by the nationalization; "in full truth," he realizes with a shudder of dread, "he had never cared for money" (867). "What do you want?" his enemy pursuer keeps asking (867). He boasts to Cherryl that men like Hank spend their lives "grubbing for their fortunes penny by penny" whereas he can acquire his at the snap of his fingers (869). But when she, who gives concrete form to his enemy pursuer, asks him why he hates Hank, he screams "I don't hate him!" (878). He then boasts to her that whatever such men do, "'I can undo it. Let them build a track—I can come and break it, just like that!' He snapped his fingers. 'Just like breaking a spine!'" You want to break spines?—she asks. "I haven't said that!" Jim screams at Cherryl (879).

But Jim *does* want to break their spines. It is the only way he can hope to demonstrate his superiority—the superiority of his non-ability to their ability, of his nonthought to their reasoning, of his noneffort to their work, of his impotency to their power to create. He is, as Cherryl identifies, a looter of the spirit. The only way he can demonstrate the superiority of his spirit is by killing those who choose to be and to live. The celebration Jim was seeking, he senses before he sleeps with Lillian, is the admiration she exhibits for his power to destroy. But he dare not name this fact. "I can't bring men down to their knees in admiration," Lillian tells him, "but I can bring them to their knees" (899). "Shut up!" Jim screams in terror. But this is precisely what he experiences, when he sleeps with her in order to try to wound Hank. "It was not an act in celebration of life that he had wanted to perform—but an act in celebration of the triumph of impotence" (900).

It is this, Jim's fundamental motivation, that Cherryl struggles to see and succeeds in seeing, knowing that the sight will destroy her.

Her marriage has been an orchestrated torture. Jim wants to be admired and loved, but without possessing any attribute worthy of admiration or love. In the end, the admiration and love *must* come from his victims, because only they can confirm the superiority of his impotence to their living power. He wants Cherryl to remain a hero-worshipping shop girl and "an incongruous freak" who is unable to make her way in the world (868). This would make her as abjectly dependent on him as he is on her—"two beggars chained to each other" as Cherryl describes it (903). It is she, the truly noble and spiritual person, who must give him his sense of spiritual superiority, while he acts to destroy all that she values and all that she is.

And it is Jim's soul that rules the world. Cherryl can see no way to fight it or live with it. She does not have Dagny's greater knowledge and certainty, and it is too late for her to learn from Dagny the absolutes she must hold fast to: to stand on her own judgment and, against Jim's whole world, acknowledge that what is, is. Had Cherryl grown up around Dagny—as Eddie Willers did—Cherryl could have learned the things that Willers did: the possibility and principles of another kind of existence. But Cherryl makes the tragic mistake of thinking Jim is Dagny, and his anti-life soul destroys hers. It is another demonstration of the life-giving power of the men of the mind—and the consequence of their absence.

Chapter V: Their Brothers' Keepers

In this chapter the results of the morality geared to those who are anti-life—the morality that teaches men to sacrifice because they are their brothers' keepers—are being felt across the nation.

The people of Nebraska, to take one of many examples, are sacrificed to those of Illinois, who consume the former's stock seed. The same process is occurring at Taggart Transcontinental. Meigs is looting the last of Taggart Transcontinental's supplies, with Dagny bearing the burden of trying to prevent a full collapse. As Taggart Transcontinental disintegrates, she must shift the burden of carrying it to the shoulders of the stronger, more vital parts that remain. A copper wire breaks in California and Dagny orders that Montana's spare copper be sent there; a copper wire breaks in Montana and Dagny orders that Minnesota's spare copper be sent there; a copper wire breaks in Minnesota and Dagny orders that the Taggart Terminal's spare copper be sent there. Yet she only delays the inevitable: California descends into civil war, Montana's copper mines are nationalized, and Minnesota's harvest cannot be shipped—there is no transportation because the pull-peddlers have diverted the trains. When a copper wire breaks in the Taggart Terminal, there is nothing left for Dagny to do but to try to return to the time of manual switches—to move backward—to move closer to the grave.

"There was no way to tell which devastation had been accomplished by the humanitarians and which by undisguised gangsters," Dagny thinks to herself.

> There was no way to tell which acts of plunder had been prompted by the charity-lust of the Lawsons and which by the gluttony of Cuffy Meigs. . . . Did it matter? . . . Both held the immolation of men as proper and both were achieving it. There wasn't even any way to tell who were the cannibals and who the victims—the communities that accepted as their rightful due the confiscated clothing or fuel of a town to the east of them, found, next week, their granaries confiscated to feed a town to the west. . . . Men had been pushed into a pit where, shouting that man is his brother's keeper, each was devouring his neighbor and was being devoured by his neighbor's brother. (914)

When Philip pleads with Hank for a job because he's Hank's brother—in sharp contrast to how the Wet Nurse at once eagerly and humbly asks Hank for a real job—Hank learns something more about the looters' creed of brotherly love. The enemy are men who *worship* pain. "I'm twisted by suffering, I'm made of undiluted suffering, that's my purity, that's my virtue," they declare—and "you the untwisted one," Hank thinks, "you the uncomplaining, yours is to relieve me of my pain" (931). Are such men human?

Dagny too learns from her encounter with her brother. More than ever, she senses that Jim both needs her and hates her, "as if, while clinging to her for support and protection against some nameless terror, his arms were sliding to embrace her and to plunge a knife into her back" (912). He pleads with her that he's her brother, that it's her duty to make him happy and that it is her sin if he suffers. She sees the kind of world he wants, a world where wishes rule, but she still cannot understand what could bring men to such a state of depravity. She attends the dinner Jim and his gang have invited her to, hoping that it is "the first step of their surrender. . . . But as she sat in the candlelight of the dining room, she felt certain that she had no chance; she felt restlessly unable to accept that certainty, since she could not grasp its reason, yet lethargically reluctant to pursue any inquiry" (944).

It is not that Dagny and Hank have no feelings for their true brothers—it is the vision of some brothers in spirit still remaining in the world that keeps them at work. It is for any men of the mind still left that Dagny is keeping the trains running—but when the terminal goes dark she realizes that there is not a single mind left on Taggart Transcontinental. The same is true for Hank. He is bored to death, forced by the looters' system to run his business as any criminal would. The only thing that still holds his attention are the farmers in Minnesota, "tenacious producers" who've somehow managed to survive and to produce a plentiful crop, and who need transportation. As he describes their plight to Dagny, there "was a look of intensity on his face, as if he were contemplating a rare, forgotten sight: a vision of *men*—and she knew what motive was still holding him to his job" (923). But the producers of Minnesota are soon sacrificed. Hank is almost through with the world. He laughs when he reads Francisco's message to the world. He was my friend, Hank thinks to himself, my comrade in arms, but having betrayed their brotherhood, Hank believes he has no right to seek out Francisco.

It is the world's code of brotherly love that Francisco blasts when he blows up his businesses on the day of d'Anconia Copper's nationalization. "Brother, you asked for it!" (925).

In full contrast to the world's code, there exists a man who lives by another code. In tunnels of the Taggart Terminal, Galt and Dagny sleep together. The moment is theirs. Galt will not give his mind to his brothers or their world, but he will take from them what he wants, what is his. Dagny too will not relinquish the question "what's in it for you?" or the quest for her own happiness (949). They want this moment and their joy—and they seize it. But as always, Galt will pay the cost to reach that which he desires, and in this case he knows the cost may be his life.

Chapter VI: The Concerto of Deliverance

In this chapter, Hank's family and the looters in Washington make a last, frantic attempt to—in Hank's words—"eat my mills and have them, too" (984). The attempt fails. Hank finally grasps their full natures and what they have been counting on, and when he does, he recaptures the vision of a world he had seen in his youth: a world of joy and unlimited action. He goes on strike.

When, at the request of his mother, Hank returns to his family's home for the last time, he finds that they are afraid he will quit—they recognize that out of self-preservation he should. But they don't know what to do if Hank is no longer there to exploit, and they fear the wrath of Washington if Hank deserts. But his sense of justice, which had once been their weapon against him, is now their implacable enemy. He would give them the benefit of every doubt when he could not understand their actions, their words, their feelings or their standards—thinking that, somehow, they must be like him and wish him well, as he once wished them well. "But he was through with granting respect to any terms other than his own" (971). He "would forgive miles of innocent errors of knowledge" but "would not forgive a single step taken in conscious evil" (972).

And theirs *is* conscious evil, driven by a monstrous motive, which he finally is able to identify: a hatred for values, for himself, for life. They don't want to live, they want to see him suffer and die. This, he finally understands, is why Lillian had married him, to destroy him by undercutting his moral integrity and his self-esteem. "For the same purpose and motive, for the same satisfaction, as others weave complex systems of philosophy to destroy generations, or establish dictatorships to destroy a country, so she, possessing no weapons except femininity, had made it her goal to destroy one man" (975). Hank's indifference toward her pleas forces Lillian to confront the motive that has governed her life, and the sight destroys her. Hank sees the irrationality of the looters' entire desperate scheme—the idea that Lillian could sully his moral purity by sleeping with Jim, as though "the moral stature of one is at the mercy of the action of another," and the idea that Washington could chain him to his job by threatening to hold Lillian and the rest of his family hostage (976).

But what makes these people think they can get away with this level of irrationality? This is the question that Hank faces as he sits across from the looters and hears them proposing the Steel Unification Plan. The plan will so obviously fail, yet the look in their faces says they believe they can get away with it. Why? Why do they think this? "You'll always produce," Ferris tells him, as if Hank, like all producers, is an absolute of nature, without conditions, requirements, standards, or needs, who will continue to produce no matter what (984). The first tumbler unlocking the answer falls into place. If Hank protests that under their plan he cannot continue to run his mills, they think it is *he*, not they, who is evading *reality*. "Well, after all," Lawson tells him, "you businessmen have kept predicting disasters for years, you've cried catastrophe at every progressive measure and told us that we'll perish—but we haven't" (985). The second tumbler falls into place. But how can even they think this plan will work, in which Rearden Steel must produce according to its ability but the rewards are to be distributed according to others' need? "Oh, you'll do something," Jim cries (986). The final tumbler falls into place. Hank has given the looters more than a moral sanction: he has given them a *metaphysical* sanction.

He has sanctioned their entire view of existence. "Were they illogical in believing that they existed in an irrational universe? He had made it for them, he had provided it. . . . They, the impotent mystics, struggling to escape the responsibility of reason, had known that he, the rationalist, had undertaken to serve their whims. They had known that he had given them a blank check on reality—his was not to ask *why?*—theirs was not to ask *how?*" (986). (It is this sanction, above all, that Galt has refused to grant: Hank has protected the looters from their own irrationality; Galt ensures that they experience its full effects.) Without Hank Rearden, the view of existence on which the looters' code of death rests would not be possible.

Hank realizes that he now loves his mills more than ever, seeing for the first time their full meaning as products of his own spirit and vision of existence. But that meaning is gone in the irrational existence that is the looters' world, and the mills must be abandoned, "not as an act of treason, but as an act of loyalty to their actual meaning" (988). Rearden is ready to meet the avenger working for his deliverance—and Francisco comes to claim Hank as one of the strikers' own.

The courageous struggle that Hank undertakes to win his freedom is the same struggle, in a different form, that the Wet Nurse has to undertake. But the Wet Nurse, less knowledgeable and able than Hank, more crippled by the world's teachings, pays for his deliverance with his life. The boy tells Hank that he now knows that "it's crap, all those things they taught us"—that there are in reality absolutes that must never be faked—and that by sticking his neck out for the mills he's "just discovered . . . tonight, what it means, really to be alive" (991–92). These are the very things that Rearden has also had to discover. The way the boy looks at Hank's face—"the image of that which he had not known to be his values"—is the way Rearden now looks at his mills, finally seeing their full value and meaning (994). When the boy dies, Hank experiences the desire to kill the boy's teachers, who had destroyed the boy's hold on reason and convinced the boy that he lives in an irrational world. Unknowingly, the view of existence that had destroyed the boy is the view Hank had sanctioned. In the name of everything Hank loves, he is now through with aiding evil.

Chapter VII: "This Is John Galt Speaking"

The country learns that Hank Rearden has quit. It descends into greater chaos, violence erupting in many states. Newspapers try to negate the nature of what is happening by refusing to name it, all the while echoing the same moral slogans as always, declaring to the people that greed is the cause of their problems and love, self-denial, and self-sacrifice are the solution. Mr. Thompson, however, is to broadcast a "full report" identifying the nature of the world crisis and the path to renewal (1004). But he discovers that something is interfering with the radio broadcast signal; he orders his subordinates to solve the problem, but they can't. "Isn't there anybody around to obey an order?" he cries. "Isn't there a brain left in this country?" (1009). There isn't. Mr. Thompson's time is up. In this chapter, we find out why.

John Galt tells the world that he has withdrawn the men of the mind. The identity of the man behind all the mysterious events taking place in the world in the past twelve years is revealed. And Galt gives full identity to that which everyone has been struggling *not* to see.

This is a moral crisis, he tells the people of the world, but not in the way they are pretending. The destruction they see around them is not a product of man's depraved nature or his willingness to sin; it is a product of them practicing their virtues and morality fully, with no one left to shield them from the consequences. There is no one left, because the men of the mind are on strike.

> Your ideal had an implacable enemy, which your code of morality was designed to destroy. I have withdrawn that enemy. . . . I have removed the source of all those evils you were sacrificing one by one. . . . Men do not live by the mind, you say? I have withdrawn those who do. The mind is impotent, you say? I have withdrawn those whose mind isn't. There are values higher than the mind, you say? I have withdrawn those for whom there aren't. . . . We are on strike against self-immolation. We are on strike against the creed of unearned rewards and unrewarded duties. We are on strike against the dogma that the pursuit of one's happiness is evil. We are on strike against the doctrine that life is guilt. (1010)

Galt states the standards and terms of the strikers—which he identified for them for the first time—and why they will accept no substitute. Galt states their view of existence—of a universe ruled by the law of identity and graspable only by the mind, a realm of absolutes whose price of admission is reason, a world in which all man's values are achievable if only he is moved by the spirit of logic. And Galt explains what this view of existence demands: a new moral code, the morality of life.

But this is not the world's moral code. Its code endures because people dare not face its true meaning. Galt names it. He shows why the code of sacrifice is the morality of death. And he explains the motive, the warped view of existence, of the preachers of that code, who turned the gift of existence and the virtues of thought, of ability, of intelligence, of reason, of competence, of production—into sins to be atoned for.

There can be no compromise or halfway between life and death, Galt tells the world, or between the morality of life and the morality of death. It is either-or—and the individuals remaining in the world must make a choice.

To those of you who still retain a remnant of the dignity and will to love one's life, I am offering the chance to make a choice. Choose whether you wish to perish for a morality you have never believed or practiced. Pause on the brink of self-destruction and examine your values and your life. You had known how to take an inventory of your wealth. Now take an inventory of your mind. (1052)

To make the proper choice, they must identify how the morality of death has distorted their conception of morality—how it has turned their nascent self-esteem against themselves and how it has led them to conclude that morality is a necessary evil, that compromise is always desirable, and that the men of the mind are their exploiters and enemies.

And when they identify these facts and choose to ally themselves with the morality of reason and life, they must stop supporting evil: they should go on strike and be ready to join Galt and the rest of the men of the mind when Galt decides it is time to return to the world.

Chapter VIII: The Egoist

As the looters' world crumbles, the better men remaining in that world heed Galt's call to strike: some refuse promotions, others stop showing up for work altogether, and still others retreat into their own minds. They've been armed with the necessary knowledge and courage by the man whose likes the world had never before seen: a true egoist. "Do you realize what sort of egoist you are?" Jim cries at Galt. "'Do *you*?' asked Galt, looking straight at him" (1113). *This* is the meaning of the chapter.

Galt said in his speech that he does not accept the unearned in guilt or in values. Here, in action, we see the meaning of that statement and the kind of egoist Galt is. He loves Dagny and wants to be with her, but he readily acknowledges the price: she is not yet ready to quit. When she comes to his apartment, his is "a smile of radiant greeting" (1089). He expected her to break and to need to see him, he welcomes her, he is at ease, even though he knows that what he predicted has come to pass. If his enemies were to find him, it was Dagny who would have to lead them to him.

Mr. Thompson and the other looters are paralyzed after Galt's speech, unable to determine what to do. It is Dagny who tells them: give up. "Let those who can, take over. *He* knows what to do. You don't. *He* is able to create the means of human survival. You aren't" (1073). Mr. Thompson thanks her— she doesn't understand why. "She might have something there," he says to Mouch. "*He knows what to do*" (1074). This is the origin of their plan to force Galt to support them, to harness his mind to live for them, to make him the nation's Economic Dictator. But first they must find him. They don't have the capacity to recognize him: Mouch passes over Galt's name, the name of an "unskilled railroad laborer," when they are looking for Galt (1082). But Stadler—who still has enough of a mind left to remember the homeland he has betrayed—tells them that "she's one of *his* kind," she has the capacity to recognize Galt, and so Mr. Thompson orders her followed (1075).

Galt foresaw all this and accepts it. "Gather your strength," he tells Dagny. "It will happen. Don't regret it. I won't. You haven't seen the nature of our enemies. You'll see it now. If I have to be the pawn in the demonstration that will convince you, I'm willing to be—and to win you from them, once and for all. You didn't want to wait any longer? Oh, Dagny, Dagny, neither did I!" (1091–92).

The looters capture Galt, but he proves to be the "toughest bastard" they've ever faced (1107). He is what they feared most: a man who loves his life so much that he is not open to dealing with them. He knows that they have nothing to offer him. "What I've got to offer you is your life," Mr. Thompson tells him.

> "It's not yours to offer, Mr. Thompson," said Galt softly. . . . "do you see what I meant when I said [on the radio] that a zero can't hold a mortgage over life. It's I who'd have to grant you that kind of mortgage—and I don't. The removal of a threat is not a payment, the negation of a negative is not a reward, the withdrawal of your armed hoodlums is not an incentive, the offer not to murder me is not a value." (1102)

Mr. Thompson, the man who can't be bothered with ideas, *orders* Galt to think. "How will your guns make me do that, Mr. Thompson?" (1103).

In identifying and exposing the unadulterated meaning of the morality of death, Galt, the true egoist, forces them to confront their deepest motivation. The result is inner terror. "I'll tell you more," Galt says to Mr. Thompson, "I know that I want to live much more intensely than you do. I know that that's what you're counting on. I know that you, in fact, do not want to live at all. I want it. And because I want it so much, I will accept no substitute." "That's not true!" Mr. Thompson cries, leaping to his feet (1104).

"*You* are the man who has to be destroyed!" Stadler concludes as he tries to justify his life to Galt (1119). In that moment Stadler realizes that he is the antiegoist, the man who dedicated his life to the destruction of that which he valued most.

And through Galt being the pawn in the demonstration, Dagny too finally sees the nature of the looters. She first witnesses Stadler's savage hatred for Galt; her glance at Stadler, which "began as a shock of astonishment," ends "as an obituary" (1073). But at that point she still thinks the others will give in, and that there won't be a "looters' government within ten days" (1078). Yet that government drags on, its calls to negotiate with John Galt pour out, and the nation's misery continues. The looters capture Galt, and the contrast between him and them—and all the people who accept the world's code—forces Dagny to confront the question: do they want to live? (1109, 1111).

And she must now determine *her* highest value: Galt or the world of Taggart Transcontinental? Galt has told her no middle is possible, and now she sees it. Mr. Thompson asks her if she thinks Galt will ever surrender: "The needle within her wavered for a moment, burning its oscillating way between two courses: should she say that he would not, and see them kill him?—should she say he would, and see them hold onto their power till they destroyed the world? 'He will,' she said firmly" (1110). Willers later tells her that Taggart's transcontinental rail traffic has stopped because trains are being held for ransom in San Francisco; but Dagny will not leave New York.

When the looters decide to parade Galt before the television cameras, and she sees how the faces in the crowd watch Galt with hatred, she understands:"They hate him for being himself—she thought, feeling a touch of cold horror, as the nature of their souls became real to her—they hate him for his capacity to live. Do *they* want to live—she thought in self-mockery. Through the stunned numbness of her mind, she remembered the sound of his sentence: 'The desire not to be anything, is the desire not to be'" (1124).

Chapter IX: The Generator

John Galt is the generator of life. As the foremost man of the mind, he is the source of all the values, spiritual and material, that lead to life. In this, the climactic chapter of the story, in which Galt serves as the pawn in the demonstration for Dagny, he makes this fact clear for all to see.

The looters had always known, somewhere in the recesses of their minds, hidden by the mental fog they themselves induced, that they depend for their lives on men like Francisco, Wyatt, Dagny, and Hank. But as reward, they always visited tortures upon these men. In the cellar below the State Science Institute, the distilled essence of their policy is revealed. They all know what Mouch screams: "If he dies, we die!" (1142). They hear Galt's heartbeat, knowing that it is their own as well. Yet they torture Galt nevertheless.

Even in committing this act, however, they must face their utter dependence on the mind. Just as the looters needed Hank to create Rearden Metal so that they could torture him with its confiscation—just as they needed Dagny to create the John Galt Line so that they could torture her with its destruction—just as they needed Francisco to build d'Anconia Copper so they could torture him with its nationalization—just as they needed Hank's own sense of justice to torture him with his family's accusations of injustice—just as they needed Dagny's own dedication to life to torture her with all the death-dealing obstacles placed in front of her living rails—so they need Galt's mind in order to torture *him*. Without Galt, the looters cannot create or even fix the generator. When Galt explains to the mechanic how to repair it, even this mindless drone "was able to recognize the nature of the sparkle in the dark green eyes: it was a sparkle of contemptuous mockery" (1144).

The looters had always felt safe evading their policies and their own identities, because some man of the mind would always be there to deflect the consequences and shoulder them himself. Galt, by refusing to bear this burden, makes them see themselves for what they are. Facing the fact that they need Galt even to torture him, and wanting to continue even if it means their deaths, Jim glimpses his own impotence and the motive of his entire life: "he was seeing his face as the face of a killer whom all men should rightfully loathe, who destroyed values for being values, who killed in order not to discover his own irredeemable evil" (1145). Jim collapses, and Ferris and Mouch know that they must never look for the cause, "under peril of sharing the same fate. . . . For the moment, their only certainty was that they had to escape from that cellar—the cellar where the living generator was left tied by the side of the dead one" (1146).

Galt has made Stadler confront this same fact about his own soul. Stadler felt safe in his evasion that people are irrational. Galt, by revealing another form of existence among men, has exploded Stadler's evasions. "I'll show *him* that there is no other way to live on earth!" is the wordless thought driving Stadler to the site of Project X. But by destroying the rational—looting men like Francisco and Hank—and sanctioning the irrational—the State Science Institute and Floyd Ferris—what other world did Stadler expect to generate but one ruled by irrationality? This is the terror that Stadler faces, when he discovers that Cuffy Meigs is in charge of Project X, the terror "that he was looking at his final product, that *this* was his spiritual son" (1132). As the two fight over the privilege to rule the mindless, they destroy each other.

But most of all, what Galt makes possible is for Dagny to see the earth as it could and ought to be, as it has always been in her vision of Atlantis. Seeing the looters for what they are, she is free of them and their worship of death, which never had to be taken seriously. She is now ready to strike. "With the greatest effort ever demanded of her"—the Taggart bridge has been cut in half by the explosion at Project X—she gives up Taggart Transcontinental and takes John Galt's oath (1138).

Chapter X: In the Name of the Best Within Us

Dagny—Eddie Willers heard himself crying soundlessly, as he tried to start the Taggart Transcontinental train—

> Dagny, in the name of the best within us! . . . He was jerking at futile levers and at a throttle that had nothing to move. . . . Dagny!—he was crying to a twelve-year-old girl in a sunlit clearing of the woods—in the name of the best within us, I must now start this train! . . . Dagny, *that* is what it was . . . and you knew it, then, but I didn't . . . you knew it when you turned to look at the rails. . . . I said, 'not business or earning a living' . . . but, Dagny, business and earning a living and that in man which makes it possible—*that* is the best within us, *that* was the thing to defend. (1166)

This is what Willers cannot let go of—as he watches people all around him letting go, as he sees the passengers of the Taggart train abandon it to travel by horse and buggy—this, the best within himself, is what no man should let go.

We've come back to the theme as described in the first chapter, but this time with full understanding of that which men have let go of—and with full understanding of the spiritual and moral meaning of "business and earning a living and that in man which makes it possible."

The only reason man has ascended from cave and foot to skyscrapers and locomotives is that there have been individuals like Dagny, who knew what the best within them was and who never let it go—and now these individuals know the meaning and the glory of that which they had been dedicated to. We hear again Halley's Fifth Concerto, with new understanding.

And it is in the name of their dedication to the best within themselves—and to the man who taught them the glory of it—that Dagny, Hank, Francisco, and Danneskjöld, along with half the male population of the valley, risk their lives to save Galt. It is their last fight against men who want to exist without having to rely on their own minds. "'It had to be me,'" a just-rescued Galt tells Francisco and the three others, "'if they were to try their last, and they've tried and'—he moved his hand, sweeping the room—and the meaning of those who had made it—into the wastelands of the past—'and that's that'" (1155).

Galt and the strikers have now cleared the path to do what they love—Danneskjöld goes back to reading Aristotle, Francisco to his new smelter designs, Hank to planning another business empire—they have cleared the path to live—they have cleared the path to achieving the best within themselves.

2

Who *Was* John Galt? The Creation of Ayn Rand's Ultimate Ideal Man

Shoshana Milgram

Atlas Shrugged begins with the question: "Who is John Galt?" By the end of the novel, we have had many answers—from the legend of Prometheus, to the story of Starnesville, to the speech in which John Galt himself tells the world who he is and what he has done.

I begin this essay with a different question: "Who *was* John Galt?"—Ayn Rand's creation, her ultimate ideal man. What were her first plans for the character? On what inspirations did she draw? How did her plans change, as she wrote? What do her notes and manuscripts reveal about her work with this character? What, ultimately, did Ayn Rand achieve, in the creation of this character in this novel? The topic, in other words, is Ayn Rand as the creator of John Galt, or John Galt as the creation of Ayn Rand.

The first step toward the creation of John Galt occurred in 1914, in St. Petersburg. At the age of nine, Alisa Rozenbaum found her first hero in the face, the form, and the courage of Cyrus Paltons, a British captain serving in India. She met him in the pages of *L'Écolier illustré*, a French children's magazine, in a serialized adventure novel, entitled *La Vallée Mystérieuse* [*The Mysterious Valley*] by Maurice Champagne.[1] She later said that she had been romantically in love with Cyrus, in a "serious, metaphysical" sense. Half a century later, she was still in love with him: "that kind of feeling I have for him, it still exists. . . . There's nothing I can add in quality to any serious love later on that wasn't contained in that." She honored him, in a private allusion, when she wrote her first novel, *We the Living*, giving the heroine the name Kira, the Russian female equivalent of Cyrus. He was the visual image of all her later heroes. The image of Cyrus, she said, "was everything that I wanted." The illustrations of René Giffey conveyed the perfect depiction "of my present hero. Tall, long-legged, with . . . trousers and leggings, the way soldiers wear, but no jacket, just an open-collared shirt, torn in front, . . . opened very low, sleeves rolled at the elbows and hair falling down over one eye." Cyrus helped her, she said, "to concretize: what was it I called my kind of man. That whole expression which I carried thereafter of 'my kind of man' began with that story." At nine, she was able to identify as important his "intelligence, independence, and courage"; she later said: "I don't know that I would have the word yet in my vocabulary fully or not, but 'the heroic man.'"[2]

For a fuller picture of the character who inspired her image of her "kind of man," "the heroic man," read *La Vallée Mystérieuse* in French or, in Bill Bucko's translation, *The Mysterious Valley*. You will notice several parallels between Cyrus Paltons and Howard Roark, the *first* ideal man she created: strength, courage, competence, self-confidence, resourcefulness, invincible resolution, and a ruthless sense of justice.[3] The same qualities, of course, are found in John Galt, her *ultimate* ideal man.

An additional parallel pertains to the timing of the introduction of the hero. We hear about Cyrus in the first chapter, but we do not meet him until close to the midpoint of the novel. He is described as the bravest of the brave, yet he is assumed, at the beginning of the story, to be dead and gone—actually, gone and dead, that is carried off by a tiger, and killed. We eventually learn, however, that the leader who disappeared did not die; he is discovered alive and very much kicking, along with his vanished companions, in a mysterious valley. Maurice Champagne, in other words, built the novel on a mystery—and on a surprise, a surprise that was a denial of metaphysical disaster. The hero's very existence was a kind of triumph, and a nine-year-old girl appreciated it.

When young Alisa read about the disappearance of Cyrus, in the first installment (May 14, 1914), she did not believe he was dead. She observed that he had been "planted as the hero," strong and invincible, and she wondered if he might have been kidnapped by trained tigers, and therefore, perhaps, still alive. Her governess told her that tigers cannot be trained, and Cyrus must be dead. (In other words: Grow up.) The news of Cyrus's survival appeared in the issue of September 3. (History does not record what, if anything, the governess had to say about that.) Little Alisa was an insightful reader, immediately in tune with the author's purpose in planting his hero. The rest of the novel did not disappoint her. From reading *The Mysterious Valley*, she experienced an intense admiration for a hero who was brave, intelligent, defiant, and never less than triumphant in body and spirit. It was a very good start.

The summer she discovered Cyrus was also the summer she decided to become a writer of fiction. From that time until the completion of *Atlas Shrugged*, she thought of herself as a fiction writer. The hero-worship that began with Cyrus Paltons and with her self-dedication to a career as a writer of fiction was not to be fulfilled in her work until she had created John Galt and told his whole story.

Part of that story, ultimately, involved not only the hero, but also other elements. In a different French children's magazine, at about the same time, she read another story she liked, about two adolescents participating in a submarine expedition in search of a lost city.⁴ It was a serialized novel by Georges Gustave-Toudouze, *Le Petit Roi d'Ys* [*The Little King of Ys*]. She liked the novel, she said, because the young girl was "very much, in childish terms, what Dagny would be. She acted as an absolute equal with all the adults in the story, and she was concerned with an adult purpose. And *that* I liked. . . I would say that I liked her only because she took her place, in effect, by the side of the right kind of man."⁵ In *The Little King of Ys*, the girl and boy (along with the adults) explore a sunken city, an underwater kingdom. The girl worships the boy as a hero: she crowns him king of this underground realm. What, then, did it mean for a girl who was "what Dagny would be" to take her place "by the side of the right kind of man"? It meant acting with purpose and courage, along with the man and in her own right, and seeing that man acknowledged as what he is, as the head of the city beneath the sea. Remembering this novel, nearly half a century later, Ayn Rand herself mentioned, as elements she valued, both the character and the setting: the precursor of Dagny and the location of Atlantis.

Fast forward to 1923, again in St. Petersburg. Alisa Rozenbaum was eighteen. She projected, in considerable detail, a novel she referred to as "the grandfather of *Atlas Shrugged*," or "a sense of life projection of *Atlas*."⁶ No written outline has survived, but she later retold the story, as well as she could remember it. She mentioned the following plot elements, which I will summarize:

1. One by one, the men of ability are disappearing—each after a single glance at the face of the heroine, a woman of great spiritual beauty.
2. One man has himself chained to his desk to resist temptation; he vanishes nonetheless.
3. The heroine organizes the men of ability into a kind of army.
4. This army represents the United States, with Europe as the enemy. There is no Russia at all.
5. The "real hero arises only somewhere in the middle of Part 2."
6. The final man of ability on the heroine's list is a brilliant inventor.

The parallels with *Atlas Shrugged* are obvious, although there are also several important differences. The early novel lacked the premise of the strike of the men of the mind; the men of ability, in this story, vanish from public view because the heroine's spiritual beauty has drawn them away. The inventor, moreover, does not have the narrative function of John Galt in *Atlas Shrugged*: although he is a heroic figure, he is not the prime mover. The heroine initiates the action, and the male inventor is the last prize, the last to join. The prime mover in this projected novel was the heroine, who played the role of John Galt (as the organizer and implementer of the plot).

And who was she, that early John Galt? Ayn Rand did not remember the heroine's name. She did, however, remember the name of a secondary character, the heroine's assistant, who ran her business when she was away: he acted in her place, and had always loved her in a "hopeless, non-presumptuous way." His name—was Edwin Willers. When she began *Atlas Shrugged*, she said, she "couldn't resist" using the character and the relationship from her earlier idea for a novel. She changed, of course, much else.

Twenty years later. Nineteen forty-three. New York City. Ayn Rand was thirty-eight. The strike premise—as the basis of a novel, and as a capsule summary—came to her in the year after she completed *The Fountainhead*, in August or September, some time after the publication of the novel but before she signed the movie deal with Warner Brothers. A friend had insisted, in a conversation, that she, Ayn Rand, had an obligation to write nonfiction, to explain her ideas. Ayn Rand asked: What if I went on strike? What if all the men of the mind went on strike?[7] A version of this very question, in fact, had appeared in *The Fountainhead*: "What would happen to the world without those who do, think, work, produce?"[8] In *The Fountainhead*, this is a rhetorical question. In her new novel, it became the principle underlying the plot. She said that the plot-theme came to her first. This idea—the mind on strike—was the beginning of the novel.

Not long after that, she knew who her two main characters had to be. Galt was first. "I can't remember when the character of Galt occurred to me. It *feels* as if it was always there. When I can't remember the origin of anything in my novel, it's usually the case that it's so intrinsic a part of the story that I can't separate the assignment from this particular idea, that the idea had to be *there* before the story started to gel at all. So that Galt was almost simultaneous with the conception of the story of the strike. And Dagny [was] the next one." She also decided, very early, that the climax was to be the torture of Galt.[9]

Regarding the characterization of Galt, she named, as inspiration, her husband, Frank O'Connor. She often said that he was the inspiration for all her heroes. The original dedication page of *The Fountainhead*, which was originally to be called "Second Hand Lives," read: "To Frank O'Connor [,] who is less guilty of second-handedness than anyone I have ever met."[10] A portrait of Frank O'Connor, moreover, appeared in advertisements for *Atlas Shrugged*, along with the question "Who is John Galt?"

She did not remember when she thought of the idea of "Who is John Galt?"—and she wished she could remember. "It's that fantastic, imagined or gimmick element. It kind of captures the spirit of it for me. And I think because it does it so precisely is why it feels as if I always had the idea, I don't remember when it first occurred."[11]

Within the context of the novel, too, no one remembers with certainty when the catch phrase first occurred. Jeff Allen tells the story of Starnesville and of the engineer who walked out of the meeting of the Twentieth Century Motor Company, saying he would put a stop to all this. Although Jeff Allen knows who John Galt was, he is not certain about the specific origin of the phrase. "Who is John Galt?" means: something is wrong, and no one knows why or how to fix it. "Who is John Galt?" means: distress and disappointment, without a clear source. The men who had seen the engineer walk out of the factory meeting came to believe that John Galt may have cursed them, and that he may have been responsible for everything that had gone wrong since. Perhaps, says Jeff Allen, others heard them attributing the decline to John Galt, and asked a question about the identity of this person—yet never really expected to find an answer, because the question came to mean that any search for any answer is doomed, because no effect has a known cause. What is most offensive about the catchphrase is that it is a kind of statement, rather than a question. As a statement, it means: I don't know why the world has gone wrong, and I don't care to know, and I just don't care, about anything. It is similar to one of the meanings of the Russian expression *chto delat'* (literally, "what to do"). These two words can signify "What must be done" (a statement, a program) or "What should be done?" (a question, a request for guidance) or, as in the expression "Who is John Galt," "There is nothing to be done about that" or "It is useless to ask what anyone could do."

Ayn Rand did not offer any explanation of the exact formulation of the phrase. She herself appears not to have come up with it through deliberate selection or through the rejection of alternatives. There is no page in her notes with alternative versions of the question, for example What is John Galt? Where is John Galt? And so forth. I will offer here a guess about a possible connection between the catchphrase and an insight that Ayn Rand identified (in one of her very early preparatory notes) as the most important point in the novel.

She wrote this note in Chatsworth, California, on January 1, 1945, when she was almost forty years old. It was a tradition for Ayn Rand to write on New Year's Day, in order to begin the year as one wished it to continue. From her note:

> The course of each great cultural step forward runs like this: a genius makes a great discovery; he is fought, opposed, persecuted, ridiculed, denounced in every way possible; he is made a martyr—he has to pay for his discovery and for his greatness, pay in suffering, poverty, obscurity, insults, sometimes in actual arrest, jail, and death. Then the common herd slowly begins to understand and appreciate his discovery—usually when he is too old, worn, embittered and tired to appreciate that which they could offer him in exchange, money, fame, recognition, gratitude, and, above all, freedom to do more; or long after he is dead; then the herd appropriates the discovery—physically, in that they get all the practical benefits from it, *and spiritually*, in that they appropriate even the glory. *This is the most important point of the book.* . . . The achievements of the great men are embezzled by the collective—by becoming "national" or "social" achievements. This is the subtlest trick of "collectivization." The very country that opposed and martyred a genius becomes the proud author of the genius' [sic] achievement. It starts by using his name as the proof and basis of its glory—and ends up by claiming credit for the achievement. It was not Goethe, Tchaikovsky, or the Wright brothers who were great and achieved things of genius—it was Germany, Russia, and the United States. It was "the spirit of the people," "the rhythm of the country," or whatever. The great man was only the robot—he "expressed the aspiration of the people,"

he was "the voice of the country," he was "the symbol of his time," etc. The intent in all this is single and obvious: the expropriation of the great man's credit. After taking his life, his freedom, his happiness, his peace, and his achievement, the collective must also take his glory. The collective wants not only the gift, but the privilege of not having to say "thank you.". . . *This* is how the genius is made the victim of the collective's crime and the whitewash for that crime.

Such is the relationship between the prime mover and the collective. It has been such all through history—and it is sanctioned, demanded, expected, held to be virtuous by mankind's moral codes and philosophies. *It is against this that the prime movers go on strike in my story.* . . . This is *the basis* of the whole story.[12]

Listen to her emphasis: the prime movers are on strike against not only the *physical exploitation* of the genius by the collective, but also the *spiritual appropriation of the credit.* The great man as an individual genius is obliterated, subsumed, forgotten. Who cares who *he* is, after all? Who is that John Galt, anyway? The question, in other words, is a statement, and a bad one. It is not a question at all. Asking the question "Who is John Galt?" as a guideline to assigning credit, would be a good thing. But asking the question as something other than a question, transforming the question into an admission that there is no answer, is to say that it does not matter who John Galt is, or who any of those of his ilk are, because any John Galt is "really" the voice of the collective. To ask "Who is John Galt?" as if there were no answer, or as if the answer does not matter, is to deny the facts about the role in human life of the prime mover. And it is those facts—about exactly *who* John Galt is—that the strike attempts to bring to the attention of the world.[13]

As John Galt says, in what Ayn Rand called "Galt's Speech Junior" (the one he delivers at Midas Mulligan's dinner party in the valley):

We've heard so much about strikes, and about the dependence of the uncommon man upon the common. We've heard it shouted that the industrialist is a parasite, that his workers support him, create his wealth, make his luxury possible—and what would happen to him if they walked out? Very well. I propose to show to the world who depends on whom, who supports whom, who is the source of wealth, who makes whose livelihood possible and what happens to whom when who walks out. (741)

When he says this, incidentally, he is quoting almost exactly a paragraph that Ayn Rand wrote in her notes as she planned her novel.[14] She herself was the one who proposed to show the world what happens to whom when who walks out. And she did.

Her notes on *Atlas Shrugged* shed light not only on her early thought about the novel's purpose, but also about her early plans for the characterization of John Galt. There are indications in her earliest notes that she intended the novel to have a longer time span. As she said:

When I was first considering how to implement the theme, how to construct the novel, I thought of having the strike start at least three generations earlier, and have a prologue about the originator of the strike, so that Galt would be the hero of the story, but he would be the last generation of the strike. He's the one who finally brings it to victory. And the reason why I thought that was naturalistic, in effect, or realistic. I didn't think the effect of such a strike could be felt in one generation. But very soon after I began to consider the story in more detail, I realized that a certain amount of foreshortening can be possible, that the theme could stand it. You see, if I had done it the other way, it would have had to be a much more realistic novel.

This was not a story to handle realistically, in this sense, because it's irrelevant to the theme whether certain developments take a very long time or a few months. What's essential is what *does* happen.[15]

She did not want to weaken the story, or the hero.

Even before she had decided against the multiyear span, she had chosen the novel's bookends. By New Year's Day of 1945, she had decided to open the story with the bum's asking "Who is John Galt?" and to end the novel with Galt's saying "The road is cleared. We're going back."[16]

On April 6, 1946, more than a year later, she began five months of sustained preparations, and a large body of notes. The earliest of these include the creation of John Galt legends, the existence of Galt's brilliant invention, the meeting of Galt and Dagny in the valley, the line "Most of you will never know who is John Galt," and the line "This is John Galt speaking."[17]

Her notes contain her preparations and early thoughts for several important elements of Galt's characterization, specifically: his basic nature and his relationships with other characters, his connection with the catchphrase, his romance with Dagny, his temptations, and the torture sequence. A full study of the notes is beyond my scope. I will report, selectively, on what her notes show about the characterization of John Galt: what she retained, what she omitted, what she changed. Although many elements of Galt were present from the beginning, Ayn Rand made some new, purposeful choices while she was writing.

She described Galt's basic nature as follows, in early April 1946:

John Galt—energy. Activity, competence, initiative, ingenuity, and above all *intelligence.* Independent rational judgment. The man who conquers nature, the man who imposes his purpose on nature. Therefore, Galt is an inventor, a practical scientist, a man who faces the material world of science as an adventurer faces an unexplored continent, or as a pioneer faced the wilderness—something to use, to conquer, to turn to his own purposes. In relation to the creators—*he is the avenger.* (He is *"the motor of the world."*)[18]

What she wrote here remained relevant to the final form of the characterization: energy, initiative, intelligence, independence, the avenger of the creators. Two months later, she described him further:

No progression here (as Roark had none). He is what he is from the beginning— integrated (indivisible) and perfect. No change in him, because *he has no intellectual contradiction and, therefore, no inner conflict.*

His important qualities (to bring out):

Joy in living—the peculiar, deeply natural, serene, all-pervading joy in living which he alone possesses so completely in the story. . . . It is present *even when* he suffers (particularly in the torture scene)—*that* is when the nature and quality of his joy in living is startling and obvious, it is not resignation or acceptance of suffering, but a denial of it, a triumph over it. . . . (He laughs, as answer to the crucial question of the torture scene.)

(The worship of joy as against the worship of suffering.)

Self-confidence, self-assurance, the clear-cut, direct, positive action, no doubts or hesitations.

The magnificent innocence—the untroubled purity—a pride which is serene, not aggressive—"the first man of ability who refused to feel guilty."[19]

All of these qualities, too, are relevant to the final form of the characterization. John Galt exemplifies joy in living, self-confidence, innocence, integration, and denial of the importance of suffering.[20]

She made a note, in July, about his *distinctiveness* and his perfection:

Make clear that Galt is that rare phenomenon (perhaps the *rarest*)—a philosopher and inventor at once, both a thinker and a man of action. That is why he is the *perfect* man, the perfectly integrated being. One indication of this—the fact that Galt was the star pupil, and favorite pupil, in college of both the Philosopher and the Professor. In fact, Galt was the only student who took such a peculiar (to the college authorities at the time) combination of courses.[21]

Comparing this note to the finished text, we notice that Ayn Rand ultimately decided not to make Galt "the only star pupil of both the philosopher and the professor." Instead, she gave him two friends who also excelled in both physics and philosophy. In the early stage of planning, evidently, she had not planned the integration of Francisco d'Anconia and Ragnar Danneskjöld into the narrative.

The note also indicates what she sees as perfect integration. Galt is not merely a thinker, but a thinker and a man of action at once. Her inspiration for Galt's perfect integration, as she describes it here, was her own life and work: she herself was one of the leads for the characterization of John Galt. We see this from her introspective comments.

On May 4, 1946 (two months earlier), she had written in her notes:

In my own case, I seem to be both a theoretical philosopher and a fiction writer. . . . Philosophical knowledge is necessary in order to define human perfection, but I do not care to stop at the definition; I want to *use* it, to apply it in my work (in my personal life, too—but the core, center and purpose of my personal life, of my *whole* life, is my work). . . . *This last* is my final purpose, my end; the philosophical knowledge or discovery is only the means to it. . . .

I wonder to what extent I represent a peculiar phenomenon in this respect; I think I represent the proper integration of a complete human being. Anyway, *this* should be my lead for the character of John Galt; *he*, too, is a combination of an abstract philosopher and a practical inventor; the thinker and the man of action, together.[22]

In addition to her preparations for conveying an aspect of Galt's basic nature, she made notes about his *relationships* with the other characters. On April 13, 1946, she wrote that he "must be that which is lacking in the lives of all the strikers. It is he who specifically (in events essential to and proceeding from his nature) solves their personal stories, fills the lack, gives them the answer."[23]

Two months later, she elaborated as follows:

> Here is what Galt represents to them (in specific story terms):
>
> *For Dagny*—the ideal. The answer to her two quests: the man of genius and the man she loves. The first quest is expressed in her search for the inventor of the engine. The second—her growing conviction that she will never be in love (and her relations with Rearden).
>
> *For Rearden*—the friend. The kind of understanding and appreciation he has always wanted and did not know he wanted (or he thought he had it—he tried to find it in those around him, to get it from his wife, his mother, brother, and sister).
>
> *For Francisco d'Anconia*—the aristocrat. The only man who represents a challenge and a stimulant—almost the "proper kind" of audience, worthy of stunning for the sheer joy and color of life.
>
> *For Danneskjöld*—the anchor. The only man who represents land and roots to a reckless wanderer, like the goal of a struggle, the port at the end of a fierce sea voyage—the only man he can respect.
>
> *For the composer* [Richard Halley]—the inspiration and the perfect audience.
>
> *For the philosopher* [Hugh Akston]—the embodiment of his abstractions.
>
> *For Father Amadeus* [a priest, who was ultimately dropped from the plan]— the source of his conflict. The uneasy realization that Galt is the end of his endeavors, the man of virtue, the perfect man—and that his means do not fit this end, that he is destroying his ideal for the sake of those who are evil.
>
> *To James Taggart*—the eternal threat. The secret dread. The reproach. His guilt. He has no specific tie-in with Galt—but he has that constant, causeless, unnamed, hysterical fear. And he recognizes it when he hears Galt's broadcast and when he sees Galt in person for the first time.
>
> *To the professor* [Dr. Robert Stadler]—his conscience. The reproach and reminder. The ghost that haunts him through everything he does, without a moment's peace. The thing who says "*No*" to his whole life.[24]

She followed through on some of these notes, but not all. She followed through with these plans with regard to Dagny, James Taggart, and the professor, who became Robert Stadler. In the case of Rearden, however, the role of Rearden's friend was played by Francisco, not Galt. In the novel as Ayn Rand eventually wrote it, moreover, she did not provide specific story terms and development to explain what Galt offered to Danneskjöld, to the composer, to the philosopher, or to Francisco. She had, at an early stage, envisioned doing so, by portraying Galt as an active recruiter. On April 7 and 10, 1946, for example, she wrote a speech for Galt to deliver to "one of those who is unconsciously on strike from bitterness and disillusionment." Galt's main point: your generosity to the parasites is harming you. Stop supporting your destroyers. Withdraw your sanction.[25] In her "notes on notes" of August 28, 1946, she assessed this speech as "extremely important & good—for general theme, for Rearden & for Dagny."[26] She thought of Galt as having a sequence or scene with Rearden.[27] Hence, in her earlier plans for the novel, we were to hear more of the explanation of the strike along the way, and in Galt's voice, and we would also have seen more of him in interaction with the strikers he was recruiting.

Why did she change her plan? I surmise that there were at least two reasons. One is that Francisco, who was initially simply one of the colorful strikers, became more important in the novel until he was, as she said, the "second lead." He became Dagny's childhood friend and first lover. He became the one to articulate why Atlas should shrug. And as Ayn Rand thought more and wrote more about Francisco, it made sense to her for him to take over the role of Rearden's friend and as the preview of Galt's recruiting points. Another possible purpose for the change in plans is to increase the tension and suspense as we await the appearance of Galt: to meet him *prior to* the plane crash in the valley would diminish the drama of that scene. In the novel as we have it, we first hear him explain the strike as part of his attempt to recruit the person who will be the last holdout. It is more dramatic than it would be if we had witnessed the earlier recruiting scenes.

Regarding John Galt's connection with the catchphrase, Ayn Rand planned, early, to use his name as a kind of play with language. The catchphrase means despair; when Dagny refers to the name, however, she means the *opposite* of despair. Dagny's Colorado railroad, for this reason, is called the John Galt Line. It represents her repudiation of the catchphrase and her spiritual affiliation with John Galt. And in the early planning stages, on August 24, 1946, several years before Ayn Rand wrote the scene in context, she wrote the lines that describe Dagny's plane crash in Atlantis, lines that explain the conventional meaning of the catchphrase, and Dagny's rejection of that meaning:

> And in answer to the earth that flew to meet her, she heard in her mind, as her mockery at fate, as her cry of defiance, the words of the sentence she hated—the words of defeat, of despair and of a plea for help:
> "Oh hell! Who is John Galt?" (697)[28]

The notes contained additional passages in this vein, implying that Dagny, who is in love with her railroad and the achievement it represents, is also in love with "John Galt"; her love for him is represented by the bracelet of Rearden Metal. For example: In an undated note regarding Dagny's refusal to return the bracelet to Lillian, Ayn Rand wrote: "(it represents the John Galt

Line to her.)" "In whose honor are you wearing it?" "Let's say, in honor of the man I love." "Who is he?" "John Galt." "Who is John Galt?" "I intend to find out some day."[29] I would guess that these lines were dropped in order not to undermine the romance with Rearden and not to signal too clearly the eventual union of Dagny with a real-life John Galt. The relationship between Dagny and Galt, and its complications, had an important role to play in the novel—but not immediately.

By the end of her first week of sustained work, Ayn Rand had asked herself a question: "What does Galt do, once he enters the story? Is there no conflict for him?" She answered: "This should be Dagny."[30] By July, she had identified the essence of the conflict, and decided that it was to be long-standing. She wrote:

> Galt's reason for being an obscure TT [Taggart Transcontinental] employee: he chose TT for the same reason I did, as the crucial blood system that gives him access to the whole economy of the country; by stopping TT and the key industries connected with it, he can stop the world. But while working on TT, he has fallen in love with Dagny Taggart, long ago (long before she meets him) (he knows all about her activities and her character, and he has seen her in person many times). *That* is his conflict. (He knows that he is her worst enemy, in her terms, her secret destroyer—but he knows that he must go on.) (This is reflected in his attitude toward her in the valley.)[31]

Regarding what Ayn Rand called the "enemy romance" with Dagny, the essence here was that the two of them would be in love, yet at odds. The Dagny-Galt romance is a variation on the enemy romance of Dominique and Roark, in which she acts against him while he waits for her to learn a relevant truth. In *The Fountainhead*, Dominique needs to understand that Roark will triumph in the world, and that it is not necessary to withdraw from the world to preserve one's soul. In *Atlas Shrugged*, which is set in a very different world, Dagny needs to understand that she will never triumph in *that* world, she will only get herself and Galt killed, and that they all need to withdraw from the world ruled by the death premise if they wish to preserve their souls and lives. The enemy romance was a long-standing element of the novel. Here are the key features: Dagny is in love with Galt before she even knows who he is, he is in love with her before they ever meet, their first meeting does not persuade Dagny to join the strike, and her return to the world places Galt at significant risk. These features were always part of the plan.

In her notes, from early in April 1946, Ayn Rand had planned for Dagny to awaken to sunlight, green leaves, a man's face, and the recognition of the world as she had expected to see it, when she was sixteen, "We never had to take any of it seriously, did we?"[32] And, although most of the plans for the sequence in the valley were not written until closer to the time of actual composition, Ayn Rand also planned, early and in different ways, the sequences of the contacts between Dagny and Galt, later on, in New York.

In her notes, Ayn Rand planned various scenes of betrayal by Dagny, with different degrees of intent. The April 6 outline had: "Dagny goes on strike & comes to live with Galt. ~~Dagny~~ James Taggart betrays Galt to the government."[33] How did Dagny come to go on strike before the end of the book? She finds John Galt in the subway (he is a subway guard), and goes to live with him in a garret. Then: "James Taggart finds her there. She breaks down once—by coming back to give advice in an emergency, to run the railroad, almost in spite of herself. James Taggart gets Iles Galt through Dagny (using Galt's love for her in some way—through threat or appeal)."[34]

In July 1946, a few months later:

> After the desperate search for him—Dagny comes to Galt's garret. She begs him to help them, to save TT—the temptation through love. He refuses. She asks him to escape—or she will betray him. He hands her the phone.[35]

"The temptation through love," evidently, means the temptation to abandon his strike for Dagny. This scene, viewed from the perspective of the completed novel, seems to be in violation not only of Dagny's understanding of what the strike means to Galt, but of Dagny's manifest love for Galt. Ayn Rand initially considered writing such a scene because she wanted to stress the conflict in the enemy romance and to make it dramatic. She found it possible to do so without making Dagny deliberately take action against Galt; Dagny, to be sure, is ultimately responsible for Galt's being caught, but only because she was followed, and not because she threatened and betrayed him.

In her notes, Ayn Rand lists a number of additional temptation scenes for Galt: "Further temptations: through pity—(Eddie Willers?); through fear—Dr. Stadler; through 'ambition'—Mr. Thompson; through vanity—the banquet."[36]

In the final text of the novel, there is no temptation through pity of Eddie, and the scenes with Dr. Stadler, Mr. Thompson, and the banquet are ludicrously *un*tempting in that nothing in those contexts has any possible value to offer Galt. I might almost be certain that the "temptations" were supposed to be transparently worthless—except for the fact that she also envisioned a final temptation that was *not* transparently worthless. From her notes of April 23, 1946, at the time of the torture: "word of the approaching catastrophe—his one moment of temptation when he almost speaks out of pity and natural ability, to save them—but looks at the blood running out of the wound on his shoulder and keeps silent."[37] And again in the outline of August 24, 1946: "Man rushes in—Taggart Bridge has collapsed. Galt's single moment of temptation—but he keeps silent."[38]

This final temptation of Galt, however, eventually drops out of the outlines. In the novel, Francisco experiences a similar moment of temptation when Rearden tells him that he has purchased a shipment of d'Anconia copper: "His hand was reaching for the telephone, but jerked back" (495). Dagny, too, has a final, wrenching temptation when she hears that the Taggart Bridge is gone:

"She leaped to her desk and seized the telephone receiver. Her hand stopped in mid-air" (1138). Galt, however, was always in full control of himself, after all (and, for that matter, *before* all), and never lost focus. Why did Ayn Rand ever plan such a temptation for him? Perhaps to emphasize that if he could be tempted, it would have to be by the desire to exercise his ability, not by fear or vanity or power. No other temptation could tempt him. The issue of the torture sequence does not even rise to the level of a temptation.

Ayn Rand had written: "If Dagny is the leading figure and carries the story, then the climax must be the destruction of TT (and almost the destruction of John Galt) by her attempts to deal with the parasites."[39] The torture scene itself is identified as the climax. Ayn Rand initially planned for Galt to give an important speech at this point. On April 28, 1946, during the first month of her sustained work on the novel, she wrote part of that projected speech:

He tells the men in the room that torture is the only weapon they have— and its power is limited by his own will to live. "You can get away with it only so long as I have some desire of my own to remain alive, for the sake of which I will accept your terms. What if I haven't? What if I tell you that I wish to live in my own kind of world, on my own terms—or not at all? This is how you have exploited and tortured us for centuries. Not through *your* power—but through *ours*. Through our own magnificent will to live, which you lack; the will that was great enough to carry on, even in chains and tortures. Now we refuse you that tool—that power of life, and of loving life, within us. The day we understand this—you're finished. Where are your weapons now? Go ahead. Turn on the electric current."[40] On August 28, 1946, in her notes on notes, she assessed this speech as "extra important" (underlined twice).[41]

In the novel as she wrote it, Galt makes no such speech in the torture chamber. It is not necessary. He has made these points, in words, before. Instead, his serenity and contempt in this scene, without any further exposition, illustrate his invulnerability; his enemies are revealed as powerless, and he is no longer in danger when the rescuers arrive.

The sheer amount and detail of the notes for *Atlas Shrugged* make these notes an important record of the creative decisions Ayn Rand made about the characterization of Galt, especially the changes.[42] From these notes, she wrote her drafts, generally writing straight through the chapters as we know them. I will look, very selectively, at the editing of the first draft of the manuscript, in sections pertaining to Galt, in order to see additional examples of creative revisions.

Here, for example, is a descriptive passage in which she labored to convey Dagny's first sight of Ken Danagger in the valley, and her memory of the day she sat outside Danagger's office while Galt was persuading him to quit. The goal here is to convey Dagny's awareness that Galt had been behind the door, unreachable, and that now she knows who he is and what he is, that they love each other, and that he is still unreachable.

The first draft has many versions of this passage.[43] Here is one:

> The torture of that hopeless waiting had come back to her, strangely more real than before, not as a memory of pain, but as an immediate sensation of the present. She wondered why the pain had grown more intense.

Here is another version of this moment:

> It was the sudden despair of knowing that the width of a single door which she could not open, had separated her from the door of that office, how much had depended on it, how much she had missed. She was thinking of Ken Dannager's fate and of the purpose that had brought her to his office. But somewhere within the stillness, unacknowledged and unnamed, was the thought that she had been separated by the width of a single, closed door from the sight of a face that looked like soft metal poured into harsh planes, with dark, unflinching, green eyes.

And here is the final version, in the published text:

> she stood reliving their last encounter: the tortured hour of waiting, then the gently distant face at the desk and the tinkling of a glass-paneled door closing upon a stranger.
>   It was so brief a moment that two of the men before her could take it only as a greeting [those two men are Andrew Stockton and Ken Danagger]—but it was at Galt that she looked when she raised her head, and she saw him looking at her as if he knew what she felt—she saw him seeing in her face the realization that it was he who had walked out of Danagger's office that day. His face gave her nothing in answer: it had that look of respectful severity with which a man stands before the fact that the truth is the truth. (725)

We can see Ayn Rand's intention in all of the versions. The final version, however, shortens the description of Dagny's thoughts and emphasizes Galt's understanding of what she is thinking, and his response. The final version captures the essentials of Dagny's pain and longing, and conveys also Galt's knowledge of her and his acknowledgment of that knowledge, and of all its consequences and implications.

Here is an example of the editing of a passage of dialogue, which was ultimately removed from the manuscript. In the final text, as in the manuscript, Ellis Wyatt tells her about his new process regarding shale oil, and the reasons he is happier in the valley than he was in the outside world. Afterwards, in the manuscript, she speaks with Galt as follows:

> "Funny that I feel as if I'm less afraid to speak to him [Wyatt] than to anyone else here."
>   "It's not like you to be afraid to speak to anyone."
>   "You know that?"
>   "Yes. So it's not those you speak to that you're afraid of."
>   She said openly: "That's one thing I'd rather you didn't know."

"But I do."

She remained silent, then said: "You're not making it any easier for me—in the way of a lesson about this place."

"I'm making it as hard as possible."[44]

Galt is showing Dagny what he knows about her (although he has not yet told her how long he has observed her). Part of what he knows here, is that she is not asking Galt the sort of questions she asked Wyatt, and that her selective reticence is revealing. She acknowledges that he is making it hard for her to learn about the place, and he says that he is trying to make it hard. From this sequence, the final lines are the ones that remain, and the context is changed so that the conversation in question takes place after Galt shows her the gold coins (728). The intention of the revision, I believe, was to remove the discussion of Dagny's fear (which is not quite the right way to identify her emotion regarding Galt), while retaining Galt's implacability: I am making it as hard as possible.

Similarly purposeful revisions can be seen in the editing of Galt's Speech, which Ayn Rand expected to complete in, at most, three months, and that instead took her two years. Her notes show that, in addition to all the thinking she did that was not on paper, she made notes for Galt's Speech in 1947 and 1948, then outlined the key points in 1949; wrote more in 1951, outlined again in 1953, and wrote for two years (1953–1955), including more notes while writing, in 1954.[45] The first page of the chapter "This Is John Galt Speaking" is dated July 4, 1953; the final page of the speech is dated October 13, 1955.[46]

The major changes in Galt's Speech, the large-scale editing, took place on the pages Ayn Rand did not preserve. She said that she struggled with the structure; there is, however, nothing in the notes or manuscripts that would be the equivalent of a speech organized by some other principle, for example, beginning with metaphysics or epistemology. She also said that it was important, and challenging, to tie the substance and style of this speech to the fictional context. The surviving pages of the manuscript do not provide indications of passages of starkly different substance or style. What we see in her first-draft manuscript, generally speaking, are two sorts of changes: some new development and clarification, added to what she initially wrote, and some omissions of material that is excellent, philosophically and literarily, but that she appears to have cut because the speech was clear and complete without this material.[47] I will provide selected examples of the additions, and then of the subtractions.[48]

The most philosophically significant revisions were in the wording of Ayn Rand's theory of value. In this area, there are several additions and clarifications.

In Galt's explanation for the need for a code of values, he says, in the draft: "A being of volitional consciousness has no automatic course of behavior. He needs a code of values to guide his actions. 'Value' presupposes a standard, a purpose and the necessity of making a choice" (96). "Value," was initially undefined. In between the lines, however, Ayn Rand adds: "'Value' is that which one seeks to gain; 'virtue' is the action by which one gains it." In the final text, John Galt ultimately tells us that value is "that which one acts to gain and keep" (1012).

In the first-draft manuscript: "No alternatives and no questions of value enter the existence of inanimate matter" (96). In the text, longer and stronger: "There is only one fundamental alternative in the universe: existence or non-existence—and it pertains to a single class of entities: to living organisms. The existence of inanimate matter is unconditional, the existence of life is not; it depends on a specific course of action" (1012).

Similarly, the manuscript shows a refining of the description of life. Galt adds, between the lines, the description of life as "a process of self-sustaining action" (97), later revised to "a process of self-sustaining and self-generated action" (1013).

Several paragraphs later, the draft contains the following two sentences: "Man has no automatic code of survival. He has no automatic knowledge of what is good for him or evil" (98). What sentence, in the final text, was added in *between* these two sentences? After "Man has no automatic code of survival," the final text adds: "His particular distinction from all other living species is the necessity to act in the face of alternatives by means of *volitional choice*" (1013).

This paragraph is followed, in the final text, by a paragraph that does not appear in the draft. The new paragraph reads: "A living entity that regarded its means of survival as evil, would not survive. A plant that struggled to mangle its roots, a bird that sought to break its wings, would not remain for long in the existence they affronted. But the history of man has been a struggle to deny and to destroy the mind" (1013).

The first sentence states the point; the second provides two examples (the plant that aims to mangle its own roots, the bird that intentionally breaks its wings). The third sentence relates the point to the context of the speech. The examples implicitly relate the point to living entities, within the novel, that did not survive, that is, to Cherryl Taggart and the Wet Nurse. Cherryl is "a plant with a broken stem," who asks Dagny how she managed to remain "un-mangled," and who sees the earth as "littered with mangled cripples" (892, 891, 906). Tony, the Wet Nurse, with the disadvantage of a college education, "perished in his first attempt to soar on his mangled wings" (995).

Another significant philosophical revision relates to life as the standard of value and one's own life as the purpose. The final text includes a new paragraph: "Man's life is the *standard* of morality, but your own life is its *purpose*. If existence on earth is your goal, you must choose your actions and values by the standard of that which is proper to man—for the purpose of preserving, fulfilling and enjoying the irreplaceable value which is your life" (1014, versus 104A in the draft).

Another important passage in this area, *new* in the *text*, appears in the discussion of the axioms of existence and consciousness.

Whatever the degree of your knowledge, these two—existence and consciousness—are axioms you cannot escape, these two are the irreducible primaries implied in any action you undertake, in any part of your knowledge and in its sum, from the first ray of light you perceive at the start of your life to the widest erudition you might acquire at its end. Whether you know the shape of a pebble or the structure of the solar system, the axioms remain the same: that *it* exists and that you *know* it. (1015–16)[49]

Considering the importance of the axioms, one can see why Galt thought that "existence exists" merited an additional paragraph of clear explanation, with some relevant concretes.

The manuscript shows the addition of another important paragraph:

That which you call your soul or spirit is your consciousness, and that which you call "free will" is your freedom to think or not, the only will you have, your only freedom, the choice that controls all the choices you make and determines your life and your character. (1017)

From the perspective of stylistic flow, the paragraph is an interpolation.[50] The previous paragraph ends as follows: "there is no greater, nobler, more heroic form of devotion than the act of a man who assumes the responsibility of thinking." The following paragraph begins with a natural transition: "Thinking is man's only basic virtue, from which all others proceed." In the manuscript, the new paragraph appears, by itself, on 120A. From the perspective of philosophical coherence, however, Galt is right to introduce, here, the term "free will" to describe the choice to think.

Other additions, though not always as fundamental, add integration. In the final text, Ayn Rand added a new sentence to the paragraph describing "the guilty secret that you have no desire to be moral" (378–79 in the draft): "Existence among you is a giant pretense, an act you all perform for one another, each feeling that he is the only guilty freak, each placing his moral authority in the unknowable known only to others, each faking the reality he feels they expect him to fake, none having the courage to break the vicious circle" (1052–53). This sentence describes well the interactions of the villains, and encourages one to consider the damning diagnosis in the light of past experience.

Another textual revision contributes a new paragraph on another important matter: the initiation of force. Both draft and text have Galt say: "no man may *initiate*—do you hear me? no man may *start*—the use of physical force against others" (158 in the draft, 1023 in the text). The text continues: "To interpose the threat of physical destruction between a man and his perception of reality, is to negate and paralyze his means of survival; to force him to act against his own judgment, is like forcing him to act against his own sight. Whoever, to whatever purpose or extent, initiates the use of force, is a killer acting on the premise of death in a manner wider than murder: the premise of destroying man's capacity to live."

Yet another textual revision shows Galt exposing the dangerous underpinnings of Kant's attack on reason. After the paragraph, in both draft and text, stating "The restriction they seek to escape is the law of identity" (245 in the draft, 1036 in the text), the final text adds:

Those who tell you that man is unable to perceive a reality undistorted by his senses, mean that they are unwilling to perceive a reality undistorted by their feelings. "Things as they are" are things as perceived by your mind; divorce them from reason and they become "things as perceived by your wishes."

Now a few examples of outtakes.

Here, for example, is a sentence that initially followed the phrase "the horror of a perpetual unknown" (1037 in the text):

They have created, within the vacuum of their arrested mind, the miraculous universe they wanted, where nothing is certain or solid, where entities melt at their touch, where they tremble, unable to know when the wine they drink will turn into a rock inside their throat, unable to predict what terror is advancing upon them from behind the corner they forbade their mind to see. (250 in the draft)

Here is an omitted paragraph about altruism (initially following "non-you" on 1031 in the text): "If you live to serve your neighbors, if you surrender the shirt off your back, your wife's honor and your children's food to a drunkard on the north of you and a pimp on the south—it is not their characters that motivate your action and make your behavior moral, it is not to specific entities that you owe the blood of your sacrifice, it is not to Smith or Jones, but to that shifting zero which is 'non-I'" (209–10 in the draft).

Omitted from the paragraph about those who are making an effort not to understand (1066 in the text): "It was my goal—and I have succeeded—to establish a state of existence where no one would pay for evasions of reality except the evaders themselves" (474 in the draft).

Omitted from the paragraph that begins: "You, who are half-rational, half-coward, have been playing a con game with reality, but the victim you have conned is yourself" (1054–55 in the text) is the following passage on the psychological consequences of evasion:

Every time you cheated, the lens of your mind had contracted to permit you not to see, every time you obtained the unpaid for, it was paid for by the shrinking of your brain, the extent to which you dared not face your own consciousness, was the extent of your progressive blindness to existence, whenever you tried to play it short range, the range of your vision grew shorter—and you turned from a youth of shining ambition with the range of a lifetime ahead, into a noisy evader who uses his talents to get rich in the range of five years—into a frightened chiseller who splutters with anger when someone asks him to consider next month—into a wretch with an animal's range of the moment, who dares not look within nor without, who scrambles by reflex for immediate prey and has forgotten why, what for and if it matters. (397–99)

The surviving pages of the manuscript, along with comparisons of the initial and final versions, show Ayn Rand laboring to give the definitive voice to her ultimate ideal man, the hero who has, for most of the narrative, been out of sight and out of hearing. The additions and clarifications are improvements, contributions to the presentation. The omissions, however, do not seem to indicate any errors that she decided to correct; rather, they are simply alternative—and often very eloquent—ways of making a point.

For example, very near the beginning of the speech, immediately after "You have sacrificed happiness to duty" (i.e., the end of the third paragraph of both draft and text), the draft has a paragraph that was later cut:

> Justice was evil, you said? You called it cruel? No man in your world can now claim any value of spirit or matter as his right, he can only receive it as alms. Independence was evil, you said? You called it selfish? No man in your world can now act on his own, he can only submit to the wishes of others. Reason was evil, you said? You called it arrogant? No man in your world can now judge for himself, he can only have a faith in a higher authority. Wealth was evil, you said? You called it greed? No man in your world is now above the rank of pauper, holding no shred of property he can call his own. Self-esteem was evil, you said? You called it pride? No man in your world now has cause to feel any emotion but shame. Happiness, you cried, was the most selfish of evils? There is no taint of it left to mar your world, not in any moment of man's life nor in any corner of his soul. (74–75)

This paragraph is powerful. It is replaced by a single sentence of epigrammatic conciseness: "It is your moral ideal brought into reality in its full and final perfection" (1010).

Finally, here is a passage that was removed from the opening section, but that Ayn Rand saved in a file of discards that she liked:

> You have heard it said that this is a time of moral crisis. You have mouthed the words yourself. You have wailed against evil [,] and at each of its triumphs you have cried for more victims as your token of virtue. Listen, you, the symbol of whose morality is a sacrificial oven, you *who feel bored by what you profess to be good, and tempted by what you profess to be evil, you who claim that virtue is its own reward and spend your life running from such rewarding, you who resent and despise those you hold to be saints, and envy those you hold to be sinners, you who proclaim that one must live for virtue, but dread having to live for it*—listen—*I* am the first man who has ever loved virtue with the whole of my mind and being, the man who never sought another love, knowing that no other love is possible, and thus the man who rose to put an end to your obscenity of sacrificing good to evil.[51]

That was indeed John Galt speaking.

In what ways, finally, is John Galt Ayn Rand's ultimate ideal man? He is, of course, the hero of her final novel. Her protagonists, over time, have been getting older. Kira dies at twenty-one, the age of Prometheus/Equality at the beginning of *Anthem*. At the beginning of *The Fountainhead*, Roark is twenty-two (approximately the age of Prometheus at the end of his novella); he is thirty-eight at his trial, which is approximately John Galt's age during the main events of the novel. Each one, in a sense, takes over from the last.

Galt is the ultimate ideal man, more fundamentally, for the reasons she discussed when she thought of herself as a lead for this character: he is the fully integrated human being. He is the creator of a new moral code, and he is the best representative, as Ayn Rand later said, of the Objectivist ethics. He is not only a philosopher, but a man of action, and the mind and body are integrated. He is a man the scope of whose actions is world-scale, and also one who is a hero in every aspect of his life. He is seen against the background of all history and the entire world, and he is seen from the intimate perspective of a woman in love.

One of these intimate scenes is particularly revealing. Months after Galt's Speech, Mr. Thompson asks Dagny, for the third time, where Galt is. She has nothing to say. He adds: "I hope he's still alive. I hope they haven't done anything rash" (1085). Ten days later, she goes to Galt's apartment. Galt opens the door:

> She knew that his eyes were grasping this moment, then sweeping over its past and its future, that a lightning process of calculation was bringing it into his conscious control—and by the time a fold of his shirt moved with the motion of his breath, he knew the sum—and the sum was a smile of radiant greeting. (1089)

What is happening here? Galt, obviously, is thinking. About what? He considers the past. The last time they saw each other, in the tunnel of Taggart Transcontinental, he told her: "Don't seek me here. Don't come to my home. Don't ever let them see us together. And when you reach the end, when you're ready to quit, don't tell them, just chalk a dollar sign on the pedestal of Nat Taggart's statue—where it belongs—then go home and wait. I'll come for you in twenty-four hours" (961–62).

Dagny has arrived uninvited, against his express command. Moreover, she is not ready to strike, and he knows it. This is important knowledge about the past. Everything she has seen in the outside world, has not convinced her. Everything she saw in the valley, has not convinced her. Their night in the tunnel, the power of their passion—has not convinced her. The Speech, with its special message to her—"Do you hear me, my love?"—has not convinced her. All of these episodes are in the past, and there remains a powerful question: what is it going to take to get through to Dagny? Galt refuses, wholemindedly, to rescue her against her will. It is her acceptance of the valley, and of him, that he wants. He is there to be ready for the day she chooses to join him. That day (or night) has not yet arrived. She loves him without reservations—but love is not enough. Galt has a significant problem from the perspective of the past.

He also considers the present. Dagny was manipulated by Mr. Thompson into fearing for Galt's life. Galt believes—and is correct to believe—that she has been followed. Dr. Stadler, to be sure, has some responsibility here; he was the one who told Mr. Thompson "Watch that Taggart woman. Set your men to watch every move she makes. She'll lead you to him, sooner or later" (1075). Mr. Thompson agreed, and complied. The goons are due any minute. This threat is another problem, in the immediate present.

And Galt considers the future. One way or another, he expects the outcome to make clear to Dagny what she does not yet grasp plainly enough to be ready to quit. As he tells her: "You haven't seen the nature of our enemies. You'll see it now. If I have to be the pawn in the demonstration that will convince you, I'm willing to be—and to win you from them, once and for all" (1091–92). This demonstration will be the solution to the worst problem: getting through to Dagny.

In other words: all things considered, the arrival of Dagny at this moment is good news. Even with the imminent arrival of the goons. *Because of* the imminent arrival of the goons.

Ayn Rand's characterization of Galt places him in a situation that shows how his mind takes everything relevant into account, gets to the sum, and evaluates that sum as good news.

And that's not the only reason he is smiling, and radiantly. He tells her he did not want to wait any longer to see her, and he would have been disappointed if she hadn't come. Here, too, he is calculating the past (the memory of what they have already shared together), the future (how happy they will be together for the rest of their lives), and also the present: that they are together in this moment, and that this moment is to be relished. He holds her, he kisses her, and he tells her that "It's our time and our life, not theirs" (1092).

At the end of the scene, when the doorbell rings: "Her first reaction was to draw back, his—to hold her closer and longer" (1094).[52] She draws back because she is thinking of the danger. He draws her closer not only in tenderness, to support her for the ordeal to come, but to seize one more chance to embrace her while he still can. It is still their time and their life, and he refuses to miss a minute of it. Then he helps her put on her coat, before he opens the door to the sort of men who will make possible the demonstration that will ultimately convince her. He shows no emotion when his laboratory is destroyed. That loss, too, was included in his calculation. "'Well,' said Galt, reaching for his overcoat and turning to the leader, 'let's go.'"

Who, then, is John Galt? The man we have just seen, in thought and action. Who else but John Galt could have done what he did, the way he did it? Who else but Ayn Rand could and would have written him?

Ayn Rand said:

Atlas was really the climax and the completion of the goal I had set for myself from the age of seven or nine. It expressed and stated everything that I wanted of fiction writing. Above everything else, it presented my idea of the ideal man fully. I can never equal Galt. And there's no point in equaling, and creating another character like it. I certainly can never surpass him.[53]

She went on, after this novel, to write speeches in her own voice, applying her ideas to the world in which she lived. *She* was John Galt, then.

In writing Galt's Speech, she had expressed, for the first time, the essentials of her philosophy—in the voice of a man of action, at a time when the world had to heed him or die. Either-or. In the pages of *Atlas Shrugged*, and beyond them, "this is John Galt speaking." Consider, in conclusion, one eloquent passage from Galt's Speech:

> Whoever you are—you who are alone with my words in this moment, with nothing but your honesty to help you understand—the choice is still open to be a human being, but the price is to start from scratch, to stand naked in the face of reality and, reversing a costly historical error, to declare: "I am, therefore I'll think." (1058)

I cherish the phrase "alone with my words in this moment, with nothing but your honesty to help you understand." Every reader, every thinker, every human being is alone with the words, with nothing but his honesty to help him understand. Galt is emphasizing the splendid, sacred independence of the act of thought, which is possible to human beings in this or any moment.

Ayn Rand's direct answer to the question "Who is John Galt?" appears in a letter dated September 1, 1950, while she was writing the ninth chapter of what is now part II: "John Galt is the heroic in man."[54] The heroic in man, she said later, had always meant, to her, a "sovereign consciousness and total self-esteem," a world-scale consciousness.[55] In Galt's Speech, he refers to the heroic in the following exhortation: "Do not let the hero in your soul perish, in lonely frustration for the life you deserved, but have never been able to reach" (1069). The expression "the hero in your soul" was part of a quotation from Nietzsche that Ayn Rand had underlined in her copy of an English translation of *Zarathustra*, the Modern Library volume she bought when she came to the United States, to replace the Russian translation of Nietzsche she had left behind her in Russia. The passage comes from part I of *Zarathustra* ("The Tree on the Hill"). At one point, she had intended to use it as an epigraph for Part III of *The Fountainhead* (Gail Wynand). It reads: "But by my love and hope I conjure thee: cast not away the hero in thy soul! Maintain holy thy highest hope!"[56] Her view of the heroic in man was ultimately different from Nietzsche's, because in her view, as Galt puts it, the "sovereign rational mind" is "the essence of that which is man," and also the core of the heroic in man (1069).

Another version of "the heroic in man" is expressed within the novel by Eddie Willers at the age of ten, quoting the minister: "The minister said last Sunday that we must always reach for the best within us. What," he asked the young Dagny, "do you suppose is the best within us?" (6). More than twenty years later, he again addresses himself to Dagny (although she is present only in his mind). As he tries to start a stalled train, he *answers* the question: "Dagny—in the name of the best within us, I must now start this train! . . .

Dagny, *that* is what it was . . . and you knew it, then, but I didn't . . . you knew it when you turned to look at the rails . . . I said 'not business or earning a living' . . . but Dagny, business and earning a living and that in man which makes it possible—*that* is the best within us, *that* was the thing to defend . . . in the name of saving it, Dagny, I must now start this train!" (1166). "The best within us"—is the mind; *that* is "the heroic in man." Galt himself, of course, had used the same expression in his speech: "In the name of the best within you, do not sacrifice this world to those who are its worst" (1069).

Ayn Rand's direct answer—John Galt is "the heroic in man"—is essentially equivalent to "the hero in your soul," which had been a cherished formulation ever since her teenage years in Russia. It is also the equivalent of "the best within us," or the mind, which is what makes possible business or earning a living. The mind is the heroic, the best within us, and, as Eddie Willers says, that was, and is, and will be, the thing to defend.

Who is John Galt: Cyrus Paltons and the king of the city lost beneath the sea; the glorious man of action and the serene man of thought; the man who integrates thought and action; the man who identified the nature of those who support the world, and who insisted that the world acknowledge *who* those Atlases are; the man who reversed a costly historical error and declared "I am, therefore I'll think"; the man who smiled in greeting when Dagny, trailing the goons, arrived at his doorstep, and the man who held her closer when the doorbell rang; the heroic in man, the ultimate ideal.

Who is John Galt, and who *was* John Galt?

What does it take to be that man, and what did it take to write him?

NOTES

1. The French firm Delagrave published Maurice Champagne's *La Vallée Mystérieuse*, with illustrations by René Giffey, in *St. Nicolas: journal illustré pour garçons et filles*, beginning April 16, 1914, and in its budget magazine *L'Écolier illustré* beginning May 14, 1914. From Ayn Rand's description of the publication as a magazine for boys, it appears that she read the novel in *L'Écolier Illustré*, where it appeared May 14–December 3, 1914. Bill Bucko, whose translation of the novel was published in 1994 by Atlantean Press, identified the Delagrave magazines as the publications in which the novel first appeared. For more information about the serialized novels Ayn Rand read, see Bill Bucko, *Ayn Rand's French Children's Magazines* (Ayn Rand Institute Press, forthcoming).

2. The biographical interviews (Ayn Rand Archives) are the source for Ayn Rand's comments in this paragraph.

3. Shoshana Milgram, "Three Inspirations for the Ideal Man: Cyrus Paltons, Enjolras, and Cyrano de Bergerac," in Robert Mayhew, ed., *Essays on Ayn Rand's* The Fountainhead (Lanham, Md.: Lexington Books, 2007), 177–99.

4. On the basis of Ayn Rand's description in the biographical interviews, Bill Bucko has identified the novel as *Le Petit Roi d'Ys*, by Georges Gustave-Toudouze; he has also identified the magazine in which it was serialized. The publisher Hachette serialized *Le Petit Roi d'Ys* in *Mon Journal*, January 25–July 5, 1913. Ayn Rand says, in the interviews, that she read the submarine story at about the same time as *La Vallée Mystérieuse*. She did not, however, read *Mon Journal* when the issues arrived. She was bored by the first novel she read in the magazine, a story about

an orphan—B. A. Jeanroy's *La Marraine de Carlino* (serialized October 5, 1912–January 18, 1913)—and did not become interested in reading the serialized fiction until she read Raphaël Lightone's *Herbelin contre Plock* (serialized April 26–September 6, 1913). She then went back and read the issues that had been piling up unread. Hence she may well have read *Le Petit Roi d'Ys* (1913) at about the same time as *La Vallée Mystérieuse* (1914).

5. Biographical interviews (Ayn Rand Archives).

6. Biographical interviews (Ayn Rand Archives). These interviews are the source for all information about her early novel.

7. The friend in question was almost certainly Isabel Paterson. Although Ayn Rand did not publicly identify her interlocutor, she refers to *The Strike* in a letter (October 10, 1943) to "Pat" (Michael S. Berliner ed., *Letters of Ayn Rand* [New York: Dutton, 1995], 174).

8. Ayn Rand, *The Fountainhead* (New York: Bobbs-Merrill, 1943; Signet fiftieth anniversary paperback edition, 1993), 606.

9. Biographical interviews (Ayn Rand Archives).

10. *The Fountainhead* manuscript, dedication page, dated June 10, 1940. The drafts of *The Fountainhead* are housed in the Library of Congress.

11. Biographical interviews (Ayn Rand Archives).

12. *Atlas Shrugged* Notes, January 1,1945. Published in part in David Harriman, ed., *Journals of Ayn Rand* (New York: Dutton, 1997), 393–94. The *Atlas Shrugged* Notes are in the Ayn Rand Archives. All future references to these notes, unless otherwise indicated, are drawn from the original texts in the Ayn Rand Archives; I will also indicate the pages in the *Journals of Ayn Rand* in which the notes are published in part.

13. The origin of the name "John Galt" is not entirely clear. In her biographical interviews, she specifically disavowed any connection with her friend, John Gall, an attorney involved in the defense of business and businessmen. (Several of Ayn Rand's letters to John Gall are included in Berliner, *Letters of Ayn Rand*.) Given that the character's name was not always John, it is highly unlikely that she intended any connection with the novelist John Galt (1779–1839) or any other historical or fictional characters by the name of John Galt. She owned a copy of Katharine Newlin Burt's serialized novel *No Surrender* (1940), in which there is a strong character named Jed Galt and a weak one named John Peter Galt. The last name of Ayn Rand's hero was always Galt— perhaps as a sound-similarity with Cyrus Paltons, perhaps to suggest Gold, definitely because she liked the sound. His first name, in the notes of April 1946, was "Iles," although she crossed out "Iles" and wrote "John." Why did she change the first name? The name "Iles" is unusual, exotic; perhaps she wanted a name that would *not* stand out, as his character was not to stand out during the years he worked for Taggart Transcontinental. But why was it ever "Iles"? I do not know. She may have liked the sound, possibly because, like the name she had chosen for herself, it began with the sound of the sacred word, the anthem, the I.

14. In "Who Is Ayn Rand? A Biographical Essay" by Barbara Branden, published as part IV of Nathaniel Branden, *Who Is Ayn Rand? An Analysis of Ayn Rand's Works*, with a Biographical Study by Barbara Branden (New York: Random House, 1962), 216, the passage is quoted as follows:

> The collectivists and the champions of the "common man" have screamed for so long about strikes, about the dependence of the industrialist upon his workers, about the workers supporting him, creating his wealth, making his livelihood possible, and what would happen to him if they walked out. Very well. I will now show who depends upon whom, who supports whom, who creates what, who makes whose livelihood possible, and what happens to whom when who walks out.

I have not been able to find this note among Ayn Rand's papers. I believe it was written in April, 1946, some time before April 24. "Who Is Ayn Rand?" identifies this note as having been written in April 1946, earlier in the month than a second note, beginning "Reverse the pattern of expansion" (a note that can be found in the Archives, and that is dated April 24, 1946).

15. Biographical interviews (Ayn Rand Archives).

16. *Atlas Shrugged* notes, January 1, 1945; *Journals of Ayn Rand*, 396.

17. *Atlas Shrugged* notes, April 6, 1946. In her notes of August 24, 1946, she mentioned two specific legends of John Galt: Atlantis and the Fountain of Youth. *Journals of Ayn Rand*, 533. The legend of Prometheus, which is Francisco's version, dates from April 28, 1949, if not earlier.

18. *Atlas Shrugged* notes, April 10, 1946; *Journals of Ayn Rand*, 405.

19. *Atlas Shrugged* notes, June 29, 1946; *Journals of Ayn Rand*, 512.

20. As Ayn Rand herself said later—the leitmotif of "joy in living" is ultimately particularly characteristic of Francisco (who, at this point, was not yet intended to be Dagny's former lover and the "second lead" striker).

21. *Atlas Shrugged* notes, July 18, 1946; *Journals of Ayn Rand*, 531.

22. *Atlas Shrugged* notes, May 4, 1946; *Journals of Ayn Rand*, 479–80.

23. *Atlas Shrugged* notes, April 13, 1946; *Journals of Ayn Rand*, 416.

24. *Atlas Shrugged* notes, June 27, 1946; *Journals of Ayn Rand*, 505–6.

25. *Atlas Shrugged* notes, April 7 and 10, 1946; *Journals of Ayn Rand*, 399–404.

26. *Atlas Shrugged* notes, August 28, 1946.

27. *Atlas Shrugged* notes, June 28, 1946. "Final Outline."

28. Cf. *Atlas Shrugged* notes, August 24, 1946; *Journals of Ayn Rand*, 537.

29. *Atlas Shrugged* notes, "For Dagny-Lillian," n.d.

30. *Atlas Shrugged* notes, April 13, 1946; *Journals of Ayn Rand*, 417.

31. *Atlas Shrugged* notes, July 7, 1946, *Journals of Ayn Rand*, 523.

32. *Atlas Shrugged* notes, April 11, 1946; *Journals of Ayn Rand*, 409–10.

33. *Atlas Shrugged* notes, April 6, 1946. Dagny's name is crossed out in the notes.

34. *Atlas Shrugged* notes, April 20, 1946; *Journals of Ayn Rand*, 428.

35. *Atlas Shrugged* notes, July 9, 1946; *Journals of Ayn Rand*, 524–25.

36. *Atlas Shrugged* notes, January 11, 1949; *Journals of Ayn Rand*, 587.

37. *Atlas Shrugged* notes, April 23, 1946; *Journals of Ayn Rand*, 432.

38. *Atlas Shrugged* notes, August 24, 1946; *Journals of Ayn Rand*, 540.

39. *Atlas Shrugged* notes, April 18, 1946; *Journals of Ayn Rand*, 419.

40. *Atlas Shrugged* notes, April 28, 1946; *Journals of Ayn Rand*, 471.

41. *Atlas Shrugged* notes, August 28, 1946.

42. The *Atlas Shrugged* notes chronicle a variety of creative decisions. A full account is beyond the scope of this essay. A few examples: (1) The first reference in the notes to Galt's motor—other than a reference to a new invention on January 1, 1945—is May 3, 1946; by June 25, 1946, she had decided that it was to be a major new invention, something that the professor (Dr. Robert Stadler) had stolen from him. (2) The first expression in her notes of the strikers' oath was on May 31, 1947. (3) In the course of planning, Ayn Rand changed her mind about how Galt was to be rescued. In April 1946, he was to be rescued by Dagny and Ragnar. In July 1946, he was to be saved by Dagny alone. In August 1946, he was to be rescued by Dagny, Ragnar, and Francisco. In the final text, Galt is rescued by the entire A team: Rearden, Ragnar, Francisco, and Dagny.

43. These versions are among several that appear on 163 and 164, isolated pages from the manuscript of *Atlas Shrugged*, part 3, chapter 1, in Box 165 of the Ayn Rand Papers (Ayn Rand Archives).

44. 138, an isolated page from the manuscript of *Atlas Shrugged* (Ayn Rand Archives). part 3, chapter 1.

45. She made a note on February 8, 1948, instructing herself to adhere to her note of July 1, 1947 for Galt's Speech; she wrote down, on December 13 and 14, 1949, the key points of Galt's cause; she wrote more for the speech on March 20, 1951; she outlined Galt's Speech on July 29 and 30, 1953; on January 9, 1954, she made notes for the Morality of Death.

46. *Atlas Shrugged* first-draft manuscript, part 3, chapter 7; 1 and 493. With the exception of isolated pages of the manuscript (which, as noted, are housed in the Ayn Rand Archives), the manuscripts (first, second, and third drafts) of *Atlas Shrugged* are housed in the Library of Congress, where I examined them. Subsequent references to the first draft of the manuscript of this chapter (paginated 1–493) will appear parenthetically in the text.

47. I acknowledge the assistance of Rachel Knapp, who helped me compare the draft of Galt's Speech with the final text. I read aloud the first draft of Galt's Speech, and she simultaneously read the final text, "correcting" me when necessary. When we found ourselves to be Dueling John Galts, I made notes about the differences.

48. For additional examples of revisions in *Atlas Shrugged* (in Galt's Speech and in other parts of the novel), see Shoshana Milgram, "Ayn Rand's Drafts: The Labors of a Literary Genius," New Milford, Conn.: Second Renaissance Books, 1998 (taped lecture).

49. In the first draft, this paragraph is entirely absent. The previous paragraph appears on 100 of the draft, and the next paragraph appears on 111 of the draft.

50. Rachel Knapp brought to my attention this interpolation.

51. 86, an isolated page ("to keep from Galt's Speech") from the manuscript of *Atlas Shrugged* (Ayn Rand Archives), *Journals of Ayn Rand*, 656–57.

52. Jeff Britting brought to my attention the succinct poignancy of Galt's gesture.

53. Biographical interviews (Ayn Rand Archives).

54. Berliner, *Letters of Ayn Rand*, 477.

55. Biographical interviews (Ayn Rand Archives).

56. Friedrich Nietzsche, *Thus Spake Zarathustra*, translated by Thomas Common (New York: Modern Library, 1917), 60.

3

The Spirit of Francisco d'Anconia

The Development of His Characterization

Shoshana Milgram

Atlas Shrugged, according to Ayn Rand, is "a mystery story about the murder—and rebirth—of man's spirit." It begins, accordingly, with a question: "Who is John Galt?" But this question is not the only question in the minds of first-time readers. The character of Francisco d'Anconia poses a mystery that becomes more urgent the more we learn about him. We read the flashback in "The Climax of the d'Anconias" and wonder: How are we to reconcile Dagny's private memories with Francisco's public scandals? How can a brilliant, ambitious producer waste his abilities and squander his wealth? How can the man who believed that the most depraved type of human being is the man without a purpose dedicate himself to becoming exactly that? And how can a man who appears to be a walking contradiction gravely insist that no contradictions exist? For the sort of reader who is not willing to accept an unexplained character transformation as "just one of those things," Francisco is a challenge and a puzzle. *Who is* Francisco d'Anconia?

And for the reader who is revisiting the novel after completing it, Francisco d'Anconia is absorbing for different reasons. He is the crucial link between Atlantis and the heroes who remain in the looters' world: he is, in fact, rarely seen except in the presence of Dagny Taggart, the woman he loves, or Hank Rearden, the man he seeks to conquer, rescue, and redeem. And once we know the full story, once all our questions about him are answered, reading the passages in which he appears is even more enjoyable. Francisco, after all, is irresistibly attractive with his productive energy, exuberant imaginativeness, mocking wit, and elegant grace. Francisco d'Anconia compels attention, and it's not surprising that many readers consider him their favorite character.

How did Ayn Rand first arrive at the character of Francisco?

"Strangely enough," she said in an interview, "I don't remember. Almost inspirationally. . . . Francisco, more than anyone else, seems to have been

Minerva in my mind . . . he came in ready-made."[1] Within *Atlas Shrugged*, Hugh Akston uses the same analogy to describe the genesis of John Galt himself: "I've always thought of him [Galt] as if he had come into the world like Minerva, the goddess of wisdom, who sprang forth from Jupiter's head, fully grown and fully armed" (786).[2] Dr. Akston's point is that Galt apparently had no period of development or gestation. A character, however, is not the same as the characterization. Although the novel does not indicate any process of growth in Galt, Ayn Rand's notes and drafts show that the characterization of Galt did not come in ready-made.

The *Atlas Shrugged* notes show Ayn Rand's preparatory work on the novel, much of it from April to September of 1946, as she outlined the plot. Many of her notes were substantial essays. She made notes on the important characters, explaining the motivation, qualities, and line of development for each. She made notes on the progress of events, the pattern of disintegration, the emotional main line. She made notes based on her reading about railroads, steel, and so forth, about the facts of industry and geography. She made notes on philosophy, with essays on such subjects as a possible explanation of the original reason for secondhandedness, the theory of talent, the creative process, the variations of the parasite. In successive outlines, she integrated the plot, characters, philosophy, and factual information. She made notes on notes, tying together her notes on philosophy and indicating where they supported her notes on characters, for example, her "notes on the creative process" (in her philosophical file) were intended for the characterization of Galt, and her "notes on proper cooperation" were intended for the characterization of Dagny.

Her plans for the characterizations of the positive figures in *Atlas Shrugged* emphasized Dagny Taggart and John Galt, about whom she wrote extensively during her preparations; her notes about Francisco, by contrast, are brief, few, and late. Francisco d'Anconia, designed to be one of the strikers, was initially described primarily as an aristocrat and an industrialist, who had become a playboy; the romance between Dagny and Francisco was a late addition. Francisco is, thus, far less prominent in Ayn Rand's working notes than he is in the hand-edited manuscripts or the text of the novel.[3]

Comparing the notes to the novel, we see that, in writing Francisco, Ayn Rand ultimately gave him important features that she had originally assigned to John Galt.

While preparing to write the novel, Ayn Rand had indicated, as first in the list of Galt's "important qualities (to bring out)":

Joy in living—the peculiar, deeply natural, serene, all-pervading joy in living which he alone possesses so completely in the story (the other strikers have it in lesser degree, almost as reflections of that which, in him, is the source); all-pervading in the sense that it underlies all his actions and emotions, it is an intrinsic, inseparable part of his nature (like the color of his hair or eyes), it is present *even when* he suffers (particularly in the torture scene)—*that* is when the nature and quality of his joy in living is startling and obvious, it is not resignation or acceptance of suffering—but a denial of it, a triumph over it. . . . (He laughs, as answer to the crucial question of the torture scene.)[4]

And joy, to be sure, is one of Galt's qualities. In the torture scene, as planned, Galt laughs—the "sparkle of contemptuous mockery" (1144)—when he gives instructions for repairing the generator. Moreover, "the first thing [Dagny] grasped about him was the intense perceptiveness of his eyes—he looked as if his faculty of sight were his best-loved tool and its exercise were a limitless, joyous adventure" (701). The description of Galt, however, stresses perceptiveness (a noun) more than joy (in the form of "joyous," an adjective).

Joy is more prominent and central in the characterization of Francisco. By 1947, the year after Ayn Rand wrote the notes about Galt's joy in living, Francisco appears to have taken over as the spirit of joy. Francisco, Ayn Rand writes in her notes for rewriting the chapter "The Climax of the d'Anconias," represents in Dagny's life "the entity of pure joy—the joy of ability."[5] And this plan is fulfilled throughout the characterization. In *Atlas Shrugged*, joy is Francisco's leitmotif more than it is Galt's. The contrast between the notes of 1946 and those of 1947 shows that, once Ayn Rand began writing, she assigned to Francisco a quality she had intended to make uniquely Galt's.

Similarly, the notes indicate that, while writing, she transferred to Francisco the role of Rearden's friend. Ayn Rand originally planned for Galt to provide the "kind of understanding and appreciation he [Rearden] has always wanted and did not know he wanted."[6] In the novel, Rearden is in fact referred to (once, in Dagny's mind) as Galt's "greatest conquest" (1003), after Rearden has joined the strike. But isn't Rearden really conquered by Francisco? At the Taggart wedding, Francisco said he had come there for what he believed would be his "best and greatest" conquest (416); when Rearden and Francisco seal their friendship, Rearden inquires about that remark, and Francisco says that, yes, he was referring to Rearden (998–99). It is the friendship with Francisco that is dramatized. It is Francisco who approaches Rearden, reading his thoughts, thanking him, giving him sanction, understanding, and deliverance. It is Francisco who appears when Rearden, saddened by the unexplained disappearance of Ken Danagger, wishes that someone would come for him. It is Francisco who is the man who means most to Rearden. (I will later examine the editing of these scenes, i.e., revisions of the dialogue and descriptions. My present point is that, in the initial plan, these scenes would not have been scenes about Francisco.)

Francisco swears to Rearden that he is indeed his friend, and he is. And, in the drafts, we see additional descriptions of Rearden's feelings for Francisco, passages that Ayn Rand cut—but that are not inconsistent with the text. Thinking of the sign "Rearden Metal" (and the sign "Rearden Life"), he asks himself: "For whom had you lighted it? He heard his own answer: for a man like Francisco d'Anconia . . . the only man who had ever aroused in him an emotion which he could not conquer" (Box 7, folder 8, 155-56, contrasted with 449 in the text).

Why did Francisco, rather than Galt, take on the function of Rearden's friend and conqueror? Given the eventual structure of the novel, for one thing, when would there have been time in Part III for scenes between Galt and Rearden? The more important reason is that, once Ayn Rand began to write about Francisco, she recognized his possible function in the division of labor. She knew what to do with him. Galt, to be sure, deserves considerable credit for the conquest of Rearden. Francisco is conquering Rearden by means of Galt's ideas, which are now also his ideas. Much of what Rearden gains from the friendship with Francisco, is the introduction, through Francisco, to Galt's world. And yet, although Galt has clearly prepared the intellectual ground, Francisco is the man on the scene.

When Rearden is ready to embrace his freedom, his "final certainty" is expressed in terms that recall the face of John Galt: "the radiant serenity of knowing that he was free of fear, of pain, of guilt" (997).[7] He is ready to join Galt's strike. "If it's true, he thought, that there are avengers who are working for the deliverance of men like me, let them see me now, let them tell me their secret, let them claim me, let them—'Come in!' he said aloud, in answer to the knock on his door" (997–98). But the man who enters to claim him is not John Galt, but Francisco d'Anconia. As Ayn Rand composed her novel, Francisco, and not Galt, emerged as the spirit of joy and the conqueror of Rearden.

I turn now to the first draft of the manuscript. Although the revisions reveal Ayn Rand's mind at work, the changes, with few exceptions, are both moderate and subtle. For several other Ayn Rand characters—such as Dagny and Roark—there are passages in the drafts that are not fully representative of the thoughts and actions of the characters as they appear in the final text. In the case of Francisco, such passages are rare. Although Ayn Rand did not prepare extensive notes for the characterization of Francisco, and although she did not plan for him a major role, she apparently knew—from the time she began writing about Francisco, if not sooner—who he was, how he sounded, what he might think or do. He is essentially just what Ayn Rand said, Minerva in her mind. Ayn Rand's editing of Francisco, as seen in the drafts, consists largely of stylistic enhancement (sharper wit, more elegant grace) and of altered contexts. His surroundings or interlocutors may change, but he is always what he is.

The visual image of Francisco is introduced, in the published text, through a newspaper story Dagny reads while she lies half-stretched on the couch in her apartment, listening to Richard Halley's Fourth Concerto. She does not intend to read the newspaper, but the paper falls open to a face she recognizes, and to a story she tells herself not to read—not to that music. But she does (69).

The context in the draft is significantly different. Sitting on a train, Dagny thinks about an abandoned piece of machinery she recently saw in the plant of the United Locomotive Works in New Jersey. In both the draft and the text, the sight made her angry; she felt "a scream of protest against injustice . . . an answer [changed, in the text, to: a response] to something much beyond an old piece of machinery" (Box 5, folder 6, 337 in the draft; 64 in the text). In the draft, she picks up a newspaper, as a distraction from her internal scream of protest, because the newspaper, "at least, would be safely senseless" (Box 5, folder 6, 337). In that newspaper she reads a story about a divorce scandal involving Francisco as corespondent.

In the draft, Ayn Rand juxtaposes the introduction of Francisco with the waste of a precision machine tool that has been "rotted by neglect, eaten by rust"—that is, a value unvalued, therefore neglected and destroyed. And, at the conclusion of the sequence, "Dagny let the paper slip to the floor. That story and the smile in the picture accompanying it, made her feel—not in violence, but in infinite weariness—what she had felt at the sight of the wreck that had been a matchless instrument" (Box 5, folder 6, 341). The piece of machinery is evidence of the general corruption, as well as a strongly implied analogy with Francisco. And, at that point, that was all Ayn Rand wrote about Dagny's emotions regarding Francisco.

In the published text, by contrast, Ayn Rand juxtaposes the introduction of Francisco with Richard Halley's music (which is emotionally powerful, the only source of pleasure Dagny has found outside her work, in a world grown grim) and Richard Halley's background story (which is thematically significant—he too is an unvalued value, therefore withdrawn from the world). Halley's music is important: it bookends the novel. We first encounter Halley's music when we first encounter Dagny (13). Halley's musical theme expresses the philosophical theme of deliverance. When we hear the theme at the novel's end (described, 1167, in a paragraph that repeats the first description), it is associated with Francisco's laughter: "They could not hear the music of Halley's Fifth Concerto now flowing somewhere high above the roof, but Francisco's laughter matched its sounds" (1168). In the final text, Ayn Rand introduces Francisco not simply as another example of an abandoned value, but as someone associated with the highest values of Dagny and of the novel. And, in the text only, not in the draft, Dagny, after reading the newspaper story, "sat, bent over, her head on her arms. She did not move, but the strands of hair, hanging down to her knees, trembled in sudden jolts once in a while" (69).

Looking at the draft in the light of the text, I surmise that Ayn Rand originally included no hint of any personal, romantic involvement on Dagny's part, whereas, in the text, there is at least the hint. The romantic past of Francisco and Dagny appeared late in Ayn Rand's preparatory writings. It is possible that this portion of the draft reflects a plan in which this past did not exist.[8]

However, any change or development in Ayn Rand's thinking about Francisco's relationship with Dagny is not necessarily based on a change or development in her thinking about Francisco himself. The photograph of Francisco's smile and the account of the newspaper story are virtually verbatim, in the draft and the text. Whatever Ayn Rand's changing plans for Dagny's romantic prehistory (and the notes include references to two early romantic disappointments), Ayn Rand was able, from the beginning, to envision the full and final Francisco.

The chapter "The Climax of the d'Anconias" contains an extended flashback to the childhood summers of Dagny and Francisco, to their secret romantic relationship, and to their last night together. The drafted version of the flashback contains some material Ayn Rand omitted in the final version, but nothing that clashes with the final Francisco. For example: the Francisco of the draft arrives "in the company of a diffident Argentinian tutor who barely saw him for the rest of the month. Francisco was courteously polite to the tutor, as if to make it easier for him to keep up the pretense on who was in authority between the two of them, about which neither had any doubts" (Box 5, folder 7, 455). The text reports only that Francisco had a "stern South American tutor" (90). Francisco's polite charade with the tutor, his making of his own rules, is consistent with Francisco's character; the passage was omitted not because it is wrong for Francisco, but because it is not needed.

Ayn Rand improves the presentation of Francisco without having to add elements to his character. In the draft, for example, he is described as saying, on an unspecified occasion: "The reason my family has lasted for so many centuries is that none of us has ever been permitted to think he is born a d'Anconia. We are expected to become one" (Box 5, folder 7, 456). These sentences, with a minor change ("such a long time" instead of "so many centuries"), appear in the text as well, but the set up is improved. In the text, the occasion for the remark is specified: "Eddie asked him once, 'Francisco, you're some kind of very high nobility, aren't you?' He answered, 'Not yet'" (90). In the final text, we are told how Francisco came to say that each d'Anconia is expected to become one.

Some other changes in the portrayal of Francisco arise from Ayn Rand's editing of James Taggart. The draft makes more explicit the mutual attitudes of James and Francisco:

> Francisco insisted on calling him "James," never "Jim." Francisco was unfailingly polite to him, in the same manner which he reserved for any of the young local hoodlums. It was obvious that Jim hated Francisco and that his feeling was a matter of no concern whatever to its object. The hatred had the overtones of an obsession. Dagny found herself thinking that the stories she had read were wrong: unrequited love was probably not the worst thing to bear; there was something worse: unnoticed hatred. (Box 5, folder 7, 472–73)

The passage is lucid, eloquent, consistent with everything we know of James and Francisco, and nonetheless a candidate for omission, because Ayn Rand chose to emphasize the colorful hero and to de-emphasize the sleazy villain.

The editing-down of James Taggart occurs again in the episode of "Frankie," Francisco's stint as call boy for Taggart Transcontinental. In the draft: "Jim chuckled coldly when he heard the story, and said; 'Really, Francisco, with all that talk about your ancestors, your title, your honor, with all that swashbuckling, plume-waving, medieval pose of yours—how could you take the job of a gutter-snipe? How could you be a combination alarm clock and errand boy for a lot of greasy laborers, and take orders from an illiterate master mechanic?'" (Box 5, folder 7, 478). (Although the content of James's comments is characteristically repulsive, he is uncharacteristically articulate.) "Francisco replied courteously: 'Your question answers itself. It shows why you could not do it, but I could.'"

In the corresponding scene in the novel, by contrast, James says nothing about Francisco's job on the railroad. But when Francisco tells Mrs. Taggart about his recent experience as a cabin boy, James asks a question:

> "So that's how you spend your winters?" said Jim Taggart. Jim's smile had a touch of triumph, the triumph of finding cause to feel contempt.
> "That was last winter," Francisco answered pleasantly, with no change in the innocent, casual tone of his voice. "The winter before last I spent in Madrid, at the home of the Duke of Alba." (92)

The dialogue in the final text is better because Francisco is able to devastate James simply by answering his question as if it were a straight inquiry rather than an implicit offense. The scene in the draft, by contrast, is a more direct attack on James, who is not worth attacking. The improvement is primarily in the set up. In both scenes, Francisco is truthfully and literally responsive to James's explicit remark, and he is also proudly dismissive of James's implicit disdain. In both scenes, moreover, he has the same effect on James Taggart, who—if he has not managed to evade reality entirely—must surely regret ever having opened his mouth.

Here is another example of a change in the set up. In the draft, James Taggart comments derisively on Dagny's willingness to comply with any and all of Francisco's requests. "I didn't know," he says, "that the famous South American code of honor permitted [you to] use women for running errands" (Box 5, folder 7, 472). And Francisco responds, in the draft: "It is not advisable, James, to venture unsolicited opinions. You should spare yourself the embarrassing discovery of their exact value to your listener." The same sentences appear in the text as Francisco's rejoinder to James's advice about the need to devote thought to ideals and social responsibilities (99).

A final comment on Francisco and James. The text shortens the summary of Francisco's attitude to James Taggart. In the draft: "He tolerated Jim's existence, but seldom volunteered to notice it" (Box 5, folder 7, 467); in the text, simply "He seldom volunteered to notice Jim's existence" (90). The reference to toleration is omitted; the point—that Francisco doesn't think of James—is retained.

The depiction of the love affair is essentially the same in draft and in text, but there are some stylistic improvements. Francisco's letters to Dagny, for example, are described somewhat abstractly, in the draft. "She loved them; they were eloquent through the things which he did not say; they showed that the nature of the bond between them was just what it had always been" (Box 5, folder 7, 552). In the text, more specifically, "He wrote about d'Anconia

Copper, about the world market, about issues affecting the interests of Taggart Transcontinental" (111). Ayn Rand's writing replaces Dagny's evaluation of the letters with a description of the topics of those letters.

There are a number of narrative passages dealing with their relationship that are found in the draft only, not in the text. When Francisco goes to college, for example, they "entered a road where nothing mattered except one's own journey, and that they could hold only a second place in each other's lives. But this very knowledge was the new and the greatest bond between them" (Box 5, folder 7, 505). In the draft, just before Francisco named what the act of love meant to them (108 in the text), we read "They were not in love" (Box 5, folder 7, 540). On the following page: "They never spoke of love. But nobody had ever existed for them except each other. In a world where they were strangers, it was with each other that they had to share the discovery of the greatest relationship possible. They were like two people on a desert island. It was their first test of their capacity for happiness" (Box 5, folder 7, 541).

The draft, not the text, reports that Eddie notices nothing. "Nobody ever learned the nature of her relationship with Francisco. Nobody suspected it, not even Eddie, who had remained their friend. Years earlier, Eddie had gradually granted them the privacy of their friendship which excluded him at times; but he thought of their friendship as it had been in childhood and never saw the change" (Box 5, folder 7, 546). Eddie's perspective tells us something about Eddie, but not about Francisco. The narrative about the relationship—some phrases of which, for example the desert island, are found among the few notes in the journals—do not describe any difference in Francisco. Why did Ayn Rand write, and then omit "They were not in love"? The denial of love between Francisco and Dagny supports the presentation of Galt as Dagny's final romantic choice, that is, in Rearden's words: "if love means one's final, irreplaceable choice, the only one [she has] ever loved" (860). Ayn Rand, I surmise, decided that it would be confusing to readers to be told, on the same page, that Dagny and Francisco were not in love with each other, but that no one exists for each but the other, and that they have together discovered the greatest relationship possible. At this point, we do not have sufficient context to resolve the apparent contradiction.

Another change, from draft to text, has to do with Francisco's visits to Dagny. In the draft: "That winter, Francisco came to meet her in New York, secretly, not often. He could not resist it, but it was like a break in the discipline they had established by an unspoken understanding: that they would never claim first place in each other's life. They surrendered to a break once in a while, fiercely, almost reluctantly" (Box 5, folder 7, 546–47). In the text, by contrast, we have a description of a specific scene that takes place sometimes twice a week, sometimes at intervals of months: He flies down from Cleveland, without warning, knocks at her door, takes her to an apartment in the city. When she realizes that she is his "mistress," she feels, the text tells us, "the pride a woman is supposed to experience at being granted the title of wife" (109).

The flashback shows a pattern: contrasting the draft with the text reveals no substantial change in Francisco, who was Minerva in Ayn Rand's mind. The changes are either minor stylistic improvements or differences in the set ups of his lines and the thoughts and conduct of other people. The same holds true for the series of meetings through which Francisco tries to help Hank Rearden check the premises of his moral code.

These conversations, Ayn Rand said, were exceptionally difficult for her to write. Ayn Rand had to edit out material from Francisco's philosophical speeches, not for reasons of characterization, but rather because she had to decide how much Francisco could tell Rearden (or Dagny) without "giving away" the strike too early. She did not want Francisco "to present ideas so openly that any reader would guess everything, and consequently that Rearden or Dagny would have to join the strike immediately if they hear this much." In the conversations with Rearden: "my assignment was to show by what steps he is testing and at the same time informing a future recruit. I almost felt a novice myself in his shoes, in effect, as if I didn't quite know what I should allow him."[9]

Francisco and Rearden first meet in the setting of Rearden's anniversary party. This draft scene has a number of passages unfamiliar to readers of the novel. We are told, for example, that Rearden, with surprise, observes Lillian's dislike of Francisco: "He could not hear their words, but he noted—by the pointless gestures of her hands, by the uncertain, unbecoming tilt of her head—that Lillian was not at ease in d'Anconia's presence. He knew enough about his wife to know that losing her poise had but one meaning: she disliked the man. Strange, Rearden thought indifferently, he would have expected the opposite" (Box 5, folder 9, 752). Rearden then has another thought: "'Bread and circuses,' he thought suddenly: the bread was his and that man was the circus" (Box 5, folder 9, 753). The line is clever. This sort of wit, however, is more characteristic of Francisco than of Rearden.

Francisco, who has come to the party to recruit Rearden, is aware of the risk he confronts. If Rearden learns too much about the strike before he accepts its premises, he will be even more dangerous as an opponent. The conquest (i.e. Francisco's philosophical persuasion of Rearden), thus needs to take place in several installments.

In the original plan, Francisco's first approach (as in the final text) was to offer Rearden understanding and gratitude: "of all those whom you are saving from the storm tonight, I am the only one who will offer it" (Box 6, folder 1, 802; 147). Rearden is intrigued but puzzled at such a message from such a messenger. He asks: "What is it that you're driving at?" (Box 6, folder 1, 802), revised as "What is it that you think you're doing?" and eventually "What are you trying to do?"

In the manuscript, Francisco's next sentence is revised several times, for example "I am calling your attention to the nature of those who have made you their protector and victim" (Box 6, folder 1, 802)—a formulation that comes close to identifying directly the sanction of the victim, a point that Rearden ultimately works out on his own. The final form, in the text, is "the nature of those for whom you are working" (147)—a formulation that does not give the point away.

Rearden replies: "You're a damn fool." Francisco, in the draft, responds: "Do you know the legend of Atlas, Mr. Rearden? He was a giant who supported the world on his shoulders. I wonder whether he ever looked at what he was supporting, and what he'd do if he had—crossed out—whether he would have felt pride if he did" (Box 6, folder 1, 803).

Rearden's response, which in the draft is tied to the phrase "who have made you their protector and their victim," is that he isn't a victim, because "keeping the whole lifeless bunch of them alive" means little to him.

The draft uses the image of Atlas to suggest the worthlessness of those being supported, that they do not deserve to be carried; the full point, though, includes the impact of the burden on Atlas himself. This point will be much clearer to Rearden after Rearden Metal has made his own life harder.

The next installment of Francisco's recruiting of Rearden is Francisco's speech on the nature of money. Although the speech is delivered publicly, to all the guests at the Taggart wedding, Rearden hears it, remembers it, and eventually quotes it at his own trial.

The editing of this sequence includes both additions and subtractions. To begin with, the final text introduces the speech with a description, from Rearden's point of view, of the listeners and of Francisco. In both, Rearden "found himself walking across the ballroom, toward the group that surrounded Francisco d'Anconia" (Box 7, folder 4, 2040 in the draft; 409 in the text). Rearden observes their empty, cowardly, guilty, angry appearance. In the text only: "Francisco stood cornered against the side edge of a marble stairway, half-leaning, half-sitting on the steps; the informality of his posture, combined with the strict formality of his clothes, gave him an air of superlative elegance. His was the only face that had the carefree look and the brilliant smile proper to the enjoyment of a party; but his eyes seemed intentionally expressionless, holding no trace of gaiety, showing—like a warning signal—nothing but the activity of a heightened perceptiveness" (409–10). This is an improvement: a description of the speaker, and not only of the listeners.

The content of the speech itself is the same, in both draft and text, but the organization and, hence, the order are sometimes different. The draft, for example, begins at a higher level of abstraction: the role of the mind is discussed first—that is, that the mind is the root of wealth. In the final text, Francisco develops this point at greater length, and at a later point in the speech. The text is shorter, on the whole and in regard to several points, and easier to follow because the opening sentence of each paragraph is usually the topic sentence.

The final version is, in several places, more succinct and elegant than the draft version.

Here are some typical revisions. In the draft, referring to money: "Those pieces of paper are a token of honor" (Box 7, folder 4, 2043). In the final text: "Those pieces of paper, which should have been gold, are a token of honor" (410). In the draft: "Your wallet is your statement of hope that somewhere in the world around you there are men whom you can trust" (Box 7, folder 4, 2043). In the final text: "Your wallet is your statement of hope that somewhere in the world around you there are men who will not default on that moral principle which is the root of money" (410).

In the draft:

> Money is the tool of your values—and it will achieve for you, with the most ruthless precision, just exactly what your code of values chooses to demand. Money is a tool which will carry you as far as your mind can go—but not one step farther.
>
> For money will not become a tool of evil. If one attempts to use it against its nature, it is money that destroys those who make the attempt. Money is the great scourge of the men who seek to evade the law of cause and effect—those who think they can replace the mind by seizing its products. (Box 7, folder 4, 2047–48)

In the text, much more succinctly:

> But money is only a tool. It will take you wherever you wish, but it will not replace you as the driver. It will give you the means for the satisfaction of your desires, but it will not provide you with desires. Money is the scourge of the men who attempt to reverse the law of causality—the men who seek to replace the mind by seizing the products of the mind. (411)

In the draft:

> Do not expect [men] to produce, when production is penalized and looting rewarded. Are you sick of human corruption? Do not scream that man is evil. You've set up conditions where only the evil can triumph. Do you long for a rebirth of human virtue? Then look for the root you've destroyed—and learn that money is the root of all good. (Box 7, folder 4, 2063)

In the text, more succinctly: "Do not expect [men] to produce, when production is penalized and looting rewarded. Do not ask, 'Who is destroying the world?' You are" (413–14). The revised version is more succinct, and entirely clear. The point is stated in the first sentence. The best phrase from the draft is the statement that "money is the root of all good"—and Ayn Rand (through Francisco) saves it for the final paragraph of the text of the speech (415).

In addition to the editorial revisions, there are also omissions. Here is one outtake: "The only way a man can hope to profit is to hope for a quick death before the consequences of his actions have caught him. Do not think it's hypocrisy when the looters tell you that their aim is to enshrine self-sacrifice in place of the profit motive: the society of looters is ruled by, moved by and aimed at death" (Box 7, folder 4, 2059). This paragraph, which is not needed for clarity at this point, introduces the opposition of the Morality of Death and the Morality of Life. The full explanation of this point needs to be held in reserve, because it is John Galt's assignment.

One omitted passage celebrates the industrialist as the bridge between scientific discoveries and daily life:

> Or do I hear you say that if money is the product of the mind, why does the industrialist make more money than the scientist? Because, you miserable fools, it's the industrialist who spends his life bringing the products of science into your homes! Do you think the scientist cares to bother manufacturing an electric toaster for every one of you, running the factory that makes it [this phrase crossed out], sending it across a continent to your door, pasting billboards to tell you about it and risking to lose his shirt if a rival produces a toaster that pleases you better? The scientist has no time to care whether you exist. That is not his job. Nor is it the job of a struggling housewife to spend her hard-earned dollars on the support of an abstract scientist who gives her no value in return, except the hope that his work will profit her grandchildren—if her children don't starve in the meantime. But the man who sells her the toaster is the man who lightens her work—and he makes his profit by means of a few pennies from a great number of housewives. No, wealth is not the only measure of a man's brain. In a free society, a man may make as much money as he wishes, or as little—according to his talent and purpose. But has anyone ever told you what wealth is a measure of, in a free society? You lovers of mankind, you town-criers of benevolence, you preachers of service to others—wealth is the measure of a man's brain and of the number of people who paid him for a benefit which they sought of their own free choice! (Box 7, folder 4, 2067–70)

The final sequence, in the draft, begins: "Unless and until it [the United States] breaks its chains and lifts money as its highest, noblest symbol—it is doomed to the destruction for which it asks" (Box 7, folder 4, 2074). In the text: "Until and unless you discover that money is the root of all good, you ask for your own destruction" (415). This passage is fully compatible with Francisco's characterization and does not take anything away that had to be saved for Galt. I believe that it was cut, as a derivation of the points already made about capitalism, for reasons of space.

The revisions of the Money Speech show Ayn Rand in the act of editing the prose for maximum clarity and power (tightening the syntax, improving the diction). The speech was difficult for her to write; she said she wrote at least six different versions.[10] Although the outtakes of the speech would be the gems of anyone else's writing, she removes as much as she believes she can.

That night, Rearden tries to get to the heart of Francisco's secret, by asking him why he does not practice what he preaches; when Rearden hears that Francisco is engaged in deliberate destruction, Rearden first laughs with a kind of relief, then retreats from the implications of the laugh. In a crossed-out section of the draft, Rearden begins what sounds like a condemnation of Francisco:

> "To let your mind, your life, your wealth be motivated by those people, by your hatred for them—" Francisco interrupts: "No, Mr. Rearden, that is not true. Not by those people and not by hatred."
> "By what, then?"
> "By love."
> "For whom?" (Box 7, folder 6, 64)

The omission of this passage—which is crossed out right on the page (and which, if retained in the text, would have appeared on 417 of the text)—is appropriate not because it is uncharacteristic of Francisco, who has already dropped hints he does not intend to explain (e.g., "whether there's ever been anything—or anyone—that meant a damn to me, and . . . and how much he did mean," 418), but because the question about the motivation by hatred is one that, at this point, would be hard for Rearden to ask.

Francisco's attempted philosophical conquest of Rearden, in both the draft and the final text, builds on what Rearden already understands. They meet again when Francisco appears uninvited at Rearden's office, after Ken Danagger has joined the strike.

Rearden is ready. Thinking of Ken Danagger's disappearance, he asks: "Why didn't they come for me, too, whoever they are, and give me that irresistible reason which would make me go?" At the same time, he also believes "he would murder the man who'd attempt to approach him, he would murder before he could hear the words of the secret that would take him away from his mills" (448). Rearden opens his office door, and there in the anteroom is Francisco d'Anconia. This context, in the novel, is the preparation for the conversation about Atlas, which Ayn Rand had initially planned to include as part of their first meeting.

Francisco encourages Rearden to check his premises about what is moral. Rearden chuckles when Francisco tells him he's one of the last moral men left to the world. Francisco attempts to explain that the mills are the material form of an abstract principle. Originally: "You had to choose right and you had to choose the best within your knowledge, that which works [,] and then move on and extend the knowledge and do better" (Box 7, folder 8, 167). Ayn Rand crosses out "that which works" (a formulation that appears to endorse pragmatism) and substitutes a more exact formulation and one that fits better the context of the person to whom he is speaking. Francisco tells Rearden that he had to choose "the best for [his] purpose, which was to make steel."

A little further on, the purposeful line-edits continue. Originally: "You had to weigh, to judge, to stand upon your own judgment." This formulation is crossed out, and revised to "You had to act of your own free [then "free" is crossed out] will and on your own judgment" (Box 7, folder 8, 167–68). The original version repeated "to judge" in "judgment"; the revision (although it is not retained) supplies the word "will," which sets up the eventual basis for the moral code.

A little later, Francisco, in the draft, asks Rearden: "Why don't you hold—as clearly and rigidly as you hold to the purpose of your mills—to the purpose of that much more precious entity which is your life?" (Box 7, folder 8, 169). Since the point of the question is consistent purposefulness, rather than the relative values of life and mills, the final version of the question reads: "Why don't you hold to the purpose of your life as clearly and rigidly as you hold to the purpose of your mills?" (451).

Francisco asks Rearden to contrast the payment he should properly have received for Rearden Metal, and the torture he has endured instead. Rearden immediately grasps the point. Then, Francisco asks Rearden to consider the beneficiaries of the rail of the John Galt Line. What sort of men did you think of? And who has in fact benefited? The draft has the same three types of men that appear in the final text (453), but we see Ayn Rand adding, in between the lines of the manuscript pages, specific examples for the first two: "giants of productive energy" (added: "such as Ellis Wyatt," Box 7, folder 8, 174) and "men who could not equal the power of your mind, but who would equal your moral integrity" (added: "such as Eddie Willers," Box 7, folder 8, 175). No specific names are provided for the third group, the "whining rotters." Then, after explaining that Rearden has been supporting his destroyers, Francisco asks Rearden the question about what one should tell Atlas to do, and gives him the answer. Rearden is suffering under his burden, and he has had overwhelming evidence of the unworthiness of those he supports. The context for the image of the struggling Atlas is more powerful now than it would have been at their first meeting.

Rearden wants to know what comes next. "You haven't finished, have you?" (456). They are interrupted by the furnace accident. Francisco, in spite of the strike and the full context, joins Rearden in saving the furnace. After helping a scab, Francisco no longer sees this as a good time to discuss the premises of the strike.

Ayn Rand, who was dealing with the problem of saving points for Galt's Speech, gives Francisco, within the novel, a problem that is similar in some ways to her own: Francisco needs to hold back. (After all, Rearden wanted to hear the secret that took away Ken Danagger, and he also thinks of murdering "the man who'd attempt to approach him.") At this point, Rearden wants to hear more, but the furnace accident, after which Francisco helps Rearden save the furnace, shows Francisco that this is not a good time for either of them to discuss the abandonment of a beloved career.

Francisco continues his conquest of Rearden with a conversation about the philosophy of sex. Like the Money Speech, Francisco's speech to Rearden about the philosophy of sex has at least two functions: Francisco educates Rearden, and the novel educates us. The reader, moreover, knows Francisco and Rearden are discussing a topic that has significant—but hidden—specific relevance. The reader knows—although the speakers do not—that both men are in love with the same woman, and that when Francisco says that a person's sexual choices reveal the essentials of character, he is unwittingly asserting a profound similarity between himself and Rearden.

This is not a disembodied speech. It is a dramatic scene, part of the characterization. But except for subtle line-editing, Ayn Rand, in the manuscript, did not have a large number of changes to make. Without changing Francisco's characterization, Ayn Rand improves his rhythm and syntax. In both draft and text: "They think that your body creates a desire and makes a choice for you— just about in some such way as if iron ore transformed itself into railroad rails of its own volition" (Box 7, folder 10, 163; 489). (Observe that Francisco crafts his analogy for his audience.) Then, in the text, a sentence that does not appear in the draft: "Love is blind, they say; sex is impervious to reason and mocks the power of philosophers. But, in fact, a man's sexual choice is the result and sum of his fundamental convictions" (489). This is succinct, clear, and pertinent, and it immediately precedes the parallel pair of sentences: "Tell me what a man finds sexually attractive" and "Show me the woman he sleeps with." The draft has a sentence in between these two, an earlier formulation of the point; this sentence is less clear, and it interrupts the rhythm. The draft version read: "Sex is the one aspect of existence which defeats all his frauds and betrays his essence, no matter how hard he tries to cheat himself about everything else, never mind what vicious mess of contradictions he professes to believe" (Box 7, folder 10, 164).

Other revisions enhance the philosophical clarity. Added in the text, after "He does not seek to gain his value, he seeks to express it" (Box 7, folder 10, 165; 490), is the sentence: "There is no conflict between the standards of his mind and the desires of his body." In both draft and text, Francisco says that "the man who is convinced of his own worthlessness will be drawn to a woman he despises." In the draft, he adds to the description of the despised woman, that is "the woman devoid of all those virtues which he lacks and envies" (Box 7, folder 10, 166); in the text, by contrast, Francisco gives a reason: "because she will reflect his own secret self, she will release him from that objective reality in which he is a fraud" (490), that is a perfect description of James Taggart's "attraction" to Lillian Rearden. In the draft, says Francisco: "when he [a man] believes that flaws are values, he has damned existence as evil and only the evil will attract him—because sexual hunger is the hunger to affirm one's enjoyment of being alive" (Box 7, folder 10,167). In the final text, clearer and tighter: "if he believes that flaws are values, he has damned existence as evil and only the evil will attract him. He has damned himself and he will feel that depravity is all he is worthy of enjoying. He has equated virtue with pain and he will feel that vice is the only realm of pleasure" (490). In the final text, Ayn Rand sharpens the relevant contrasts.

The editing of Francisco's philosophical conversations with Dagny follows a similar pattern. While strengthening and refining Francisco's characterization,

Ayn Rand restricts, to a necessary and appropriate extent, his divulging of the secrets, that is the philosophical premises and existential facts of Atlantis. The draft version of the country-home scene, in part 2, chapter 8, follows the usual pattern—although Ayn Rand's notes for this scene include some paragraphs that had to be saved for Galt. Ayn Rand edited out some descriptions of Francisco, when he first sees and speaks to Dagny: "the helplessness of a released convict at his first sight of space" and "He stood looking at her incredulously, as if this were his homecoming from some long journey, as if he had not seen her for years" (Box 8, folder 7, 53 and 54). "I'll tell you what those years did to me" (Box 8, folder 7, 59) becomes "I'll tell you about the years when I . . ." (615), and "not to let her see the full reflection of what his pain had been like" (Box 8, folder 7, 75) becomes "not to let her see the reflection of what his years had been like" (618). All of these changes reduce the explicit invocation of Francisco's pain (which is past) without changing the fact that he felt pain and won a victory over it.

Francisco, in the draft, utters one sentence that had to be omitted because it was inexact. "It is in the nature of the virtuous man that he is unable to understand the real nature of evil" (Box 8, folder 7, 84). Given that the following sentence is "You must learn to understand them," the two sentences together would be an apparent contradiction. But contradictions do not exist. Francisco explains part of the truth, that is, that the looters are holding her by her virtue and strength. He withholds, however, the explanation of the death premise, that is, that the looters do not want to live, they only want the good to die. Dagny does not join the strike until she finally understands this premise, when she realizes that the villains intend to kill Galt.

> She knew. She knew what they intended doing and what it was within them that made it possible. They did not think that this would succeed. They did not think that Galt would give in; they did not want him to give in. They did not think that anything could save them now; they did not want to be saved. . . . They did not want to live; they wanted *him* to die. . . . she grasped that the objects she had thought to be human were not (1135).

While composing the chapter "By Our Love" in 1950, Ayn Rand wrote a new note, dated August 27, 1950, depicting Francisco's impassioned philosophical attack on the "cannibal morality," which ties virtue to pain, and which presents moral perfection as impossible.[11] This note is approximately contemporaneous with the composition of the chapter, which Ayn Rand began writing on July 29, 1950; she began the following chapter three months later, on October 24, 1950. The pages dealing with the episode, however, are paginated continuously, with no space for this passage. I surmise that Ayn Rand wrote the note after composing much of the chapter, but decided not to include it because the philosophical content reveals too much too early.

The next meeting of Dagny and Francisco takes place in her apartment, after she returns to work in response to the tunnel disaster. The draft includes a description that the text omits. In both, Dagny says: "If Taggart Transcontinental is to perish with the looters, then so am I" (Box 8, folder 9, 178; 635). In the draft: "It seemed to her that the words hit his eyes, it was the only change she saw in his face, but by the time his glance was steady and normal again, she felt certain that he had given up the things he had come here to say" (Box 8, folder 9, 178–79). In the text: "He did not take his eyes off her face and he did not answer" (635). If Ayn Rand had retained the sentence, I believe she would have changed the word "normal." (Is Francisco's glance ever "normal"?) The effect of the sentence, however, is to emphasize Francisco's response to a conclusion of Dagny's: he realizes that she is not ready to learn the full truth. Yet even though Francisco does not reveal the secret of Atlantis, he continues to attempt to persuade Dagny to check her premises.

There is an attractive stylistic improvement in one of Francisco's remarks. In both versions, Francisco says "Dagny, we were taught that some things belong to God and others to Caesar" (Box 8, folder 9, 189; 636). In the draft, he continues: "Perhaps God would permit that, though I doubt it," which becomes, in the text, "Perhaps their God would permit it." The revised version is shorter, and free of the implication that there could be such a God.

The apartment scene in the draft is very close to the scene in the novel, including the dramatic conclusion, after Rearden walks in. In the draft, when Rearden warns Francisco to keep away from Dagny, he says: "I want you to learn that she is not to be thought of by you, not to be looked at, not to be approached" (Box 8, folder 9, 215). The final text, by contrast, reads as follows: "I want you to learn that you are not to think of her, not to look at her, not to approach her" (640). The active voice in the final version is more appropriate, because Rearden is concerned here more with Francisco's action than with Dagny as object of the action—as we see in the next sentence ("Of all men, it's you who're not to appear in her presence") and in Rearden's emotion toward Francisco ("driven by a desperate anger at his own feeling for this man").

Francisco's remaining scenes with Dagny and Rearden take place after the revelation of the secret of Atlantis. Francisco, who has believed Dagny dead in a plane crash, finds her alive in the valley. In the description of Francisco's embrace of Dagny in the text (764), the following passage from the draft is omitted: "His hands grasped on her waistline, holding on to her as to a last branch over an abyss" (Box 9, folder 8, 85). The description is complete, and sufficiently intense, without it.

In the draft, Francisco says that the industrial system in the outside world is "run, not by bankers, but [in the draft] by any unshaved professor in any basement beer joint" (Ayn Rand omits "humanitarian" and substitutes "professor") (Box 9, folder 8, 96). For the text, however, she restores "humanitarian" (766). Humanitarians and professors are both bad, on the whole, but humanitarians are worse. When Francisco welcomes Dagny to his home, and says that the rebirth of d'Anconia Copper (and of the world) must start in the United States, he identifies the relevant principle, in both draft and text, as "the supremacy of reason" (Box 9, folder 8, 127; 771). In the draft only, Francisco also says that this is the "basic premise . . . of life, not death." The point about the Morality of Death had to be saved for Galt, and was omitted.

The sequence also includes a thought of Dagny's that was omitted in the analogous section of the novel (772). As Dagny looks at Francisco's designs for a smelter, "she felt as if some part of her mind leaned back for an instant to observe them both and to note that their road had brought them to reverse the parts they had played on their last night together: it was she who had then spoken of her railroad and her future with an eagerly confident fire, to a man silent under the weight of a tragic conflict; now, he had reached full certainty, while she listened, guiltily torn between her enjoyment of this moment and the unsolved question mark of her own future" (Box 9, folder 8,132). The parallel between the two scenes is not as strong as Dagny thinks it is. All things considered, in both scenes Francisco was right, and Dagny was wrong. In any event, the characterization of Francisco is the same regardless.

Back in the grim world outside Atlantis, the reunion scene of Francisco and Rearden, after Francisco saves Rearden's life, contains some dialogue that was omitted in the text. In both, Francisco tells Rearden that he's been working as Rearden's furnace foreman. "I didn't think you'd mind that. You offered me the job yourself" (Box 11, folder 2, 231; 998). In the draft, Rearden responds:

> "God, how I wish you'd accepted it then!"
> Francisco shook his head. "You'd have made me superintendent within a month or demanded to know the reason why."
> "Didn't you . . . didn't you break that reason tonight, by saving the mills?"
> "It wasn't the mills that I was saving. It was lives—our kind of lives. Those thugs had orders to spare the machinery and go after blood. They'd marked the best of your men for slaughter to eliminate future recalcitrants. Incidentally, they know that you're more valuable to them than all the machinery put together, and they didn't intend to harm you, at present—but this is what happens when they release a bunch of killers and expect to be able to control them." (233)

Francisco's view of the looters here is relatively benevolent, that is, that they want to keep Rearden alive because he is valuable. Francisco does not present the final argument—the morality of death, which is coming up in the next chapter—and Rearden does not need it, as indeed the novel does not need these paragraphs. This sequence, if included, would have answered a question a reader might have asked: isn't Francisco breaking his oath? Ayn Rand evidently did not consider this objection important enough to deal with it, at this point.

The Francisco of the draft is fundamentally the same as the Francisco of the final text. But one type of revision, visible through the drafts, shows an interesting pattern of changes: the actions and remarks pertaining to Francisco's masquerade. When Ayn Rand first developed Francisco's characterization, she made him appear to be more of a liar and a cynic. His masquerade, as she origi-nally depicted it, included more overtly, explicitly negative elements. But that would not do. Ayn Rand, in editing the drafts, eliminated some untruths.

Francisco would not typically wish to utter a direct lie. In both draft and text, Dagny asks Francisco to explain why he bought the San Sebastián mines, knowing they were worthless, knowing they would be seized. She accused him of trying to harm his American stockholders, and he agreed that he was, and that this was part of the truth. "What's the rest?" asks Dagny.

"It was not all I was after." "What else?" In the draft, Francisco replies:

"I was after Senorita Conception Gomez who had the most beautiful legs I've ever—oh, I beg your pardon! it was not Senorita Conception Gomez at all, it was the Senora Dolores Garcia—you see, that was six years ago, so it's a little hard to remember—but it was the Senora Dolores Garcia—her legs were not the most beautiful ones I've ever seen—yours are—but she had beautiful shoulders [eyes crossed out]. Her husband owned those acres of vacant mountains that nobody wanted, and he was pressed for cash—so that's how I became interested in the San Sebastiáno project. Much the more plausible explanation, isn't it, Dagny?"

She had been unable to notice at what point the expression of his face had changed, but the look of mockery was obvious now, yet he had never moved his eyes from her; and the mockery was the more blatant because it was impossible to tell whether he was taunting her with the preposterous story or laughing at her because the story was true. (Box 5, folder 7, 600–1)

In the text, by contrast, when Dagny asks Francisco what else he was after, he replies: "That's for you to figure out" (119).

Moments later, commenting on James Taggart and his friends, Francisco, in the draft, says "their theory was valid" (Box 5, folder 7, 607). This is not true. In the final text, he says, instead: "their theory was not new" (120). He adds in the draft, "nothing is foolproof"—which is untrue. In the text, instead, he says: "it wasn't foolproof."

When Dagny asks Francisco: "Why did you start that project?" he replies, in the draft:

Oh, just to do something. One has to go through the motions of being a great industrialist, once in a while. I was bored with the whole goddamn business. I didn't care what I started, whom I hired or what they did, so long as I didn't have to be bothered. I left it up to my employees and went on a trip around the world. It's much more exciting to spend money than to make it. (Box 5, folder 7, 611–16)[12]

Not for him, it isn't—not in reality.

In the text, instead of asserting his worthlessness, Francisco poses rhetori-cal questions: "But haven't I the right to be what is now accepted as human? Should I pay for everybody's mistakes and never be permitted one of my own?" (120).

In the draft: "If you think I did it on purpose, you still give me credit for having a purpose. But I haven't any." This is false. In the text: "Did you intend me to notice that if you think I did it on purpose, then you still give me credit for having a purpose?" The revised version is a question, rather than a lie.

The examples abound. In the draft: "My motive, Dagny? It's the simplest one of all: the spur of the moment" (Box 5, folder 7, 617). This is another false statement. In the text: "You don't think that it's the simplest one of all—spur of the moment?" (121).

When he points out that Mrs. Vail has claimed they spent a romantic evening together in the Andes at a time when he was presiding at the opening of the San Sebastián Line in El Paso, Dagny asks him, in both draft and text, how he can explain the discrepancy. In the draft, he says: "Oh, just that charming women do not have accurate memories for dates. Mrs. Gilbert Vail is a very charming woman" (Box 5, folder 7, 625). His statement is false twice: some charming women have accurate memories, and Mrs. Vail is not a very charming woman. In the text, by contrast, he tells Dagny: "Draw your own conclusions" (122).

He continues, in the draft: "You'd appreciate Mrs. Vail if you had a sense of humor. But then, if you had a sense of humor, you'd appreciate so many things!" (Box 5, folder 7, 625). Francisco does not sound like himself here. Have we been visited by the ghost of Ellsworth Toohey, who said that nothing was sacred except a sense of humor?[13] In the novel itself, of course, Francisco says nothing of the kind.

And as for the San Sebastián disaster, he comments, in the draft: "I didn't stage it intentionally. I only wish I had. I would have broken the record of the Emperor Nero" (Box 5, folder 7, 627). But he did stage it intentionally; his denial is a lie. In the text, by contrast: "If I had staged it intentionally " (122).

He continues to misstate the truth. When Dagny asks Francisco if he knows Ellis Wyatt, he says that he does, in both draft and text, but in the text he leaves it at that. "Sure" (125). In the draft, he adds a comment: "Ellis Wyatt is a brilliant young fool" (Box 5, folder 7, 638). Brilliant, yes, but a fool? False.

This section has the highest concentration of literally false utterances converted to truths, but there are others elsewhere. For example, when Dagny asks Francisco for money to finance the John Galt Line, Francisco cries out, "My love, I can't," and then, to cover up, adds, in the draft, "Please excuse the mixture in styles of expression. I've said that to so many women, but in regard to somewhat different occasions" (Box 5, folder 7, 1099). In the text, he avoids a direct lie: he says, instead, "I've been supposed to say that to so many women, but on somewhat different occasions" (200).

These examples of purposeful editing-out of Francisco's lies are a salient pattern in the drafts regarding Francisco. Perhaps the masquerade itself was hard to present. Most masquerades are designed to conceal vices; Francisco's masquerade conceals his virtues.[14] This sort of masquerade is not natural for Francisco, or for Ayn Rand. But she solved her problem. The ultimate portrait of Francisco shows his ability to create a misleading impression without lying—while also, especially with Dagny, encouraging the observer to penetrate the disguise.

Francisco, as Ayn Rand said, came in ready-made. She improved him, enhanced him, but never had to develop him in the way she developed Dagny or Rearden or Roark. And once he arrived on the page, Francisco assumed tasks Ayn Rand had not originally assigned to him. He presented two challenges unique to his characterization. As the chief recruiter, he needed to explain, in some way, the idea of the strike, yet she had to edit his philosophical conversations in order not to give away too much too soon. As a man in disguise, moreover, he is creating a false impression about himself, but she edited his remarks in order to minimize bold-faced lies. As we have seen, Ayn Rand's revisions are purposeful. The purpose is evident—with one partial exception: The editing of the manuscript led to the omission of an entire scene in the extended flashback.

One summer night, when Dagny was thirteen, and Francisco two years older:

> It was on the evening before his departure that they sat alone together in a hidden corner by the edge of the water. A rocky hill rose in a bend of the river ahead. There were long, thin strips of fire in the sky, beyond the black rock, and red sparks floating lazily on the water. Francisco pointed ahead and asked: "Dagny, if you walked around the turn of that rock, what would you expect to find there?" "Something exciting and wonderful." He chuckled, nodding, and said: "So do I. So does everybody else. That is what people always expect to find around every corner they turn. And they're always disappointed. But you and I won't be. We know something they've never discovered. When we turn a corner, there will always be something exciting and wonderful there: we will be there."
>
> She laughed, lying stretched on the soft pine needles of the shore; she had no desire to turn any corner right now. He said:
>
> "We'll never go seeking anything. We'll make it. Just remember that that's the difference between us and everybody else."
>
> He sat half-stretched, propped up on his elbows. She put her head in the crook of his arm and lay looking peacefully up at the sky. She felt what she had never felt before: contented and lazy. She felt that only here, only with him, and under his protection, was it proper for her to let herself feel such a strange thing as rest. (Box 5, folder 7, 48–90)

Neither part of this passage—not Francisco's remark about the wonder and excitement that the two of them represent, not Dagny's thought about allowing herself to feel rest—appears in the corresponding section of the text (96). There are parallels, elsewhere in the novel, to Dagny's thought. When we first meet Dagny, she is listening to a whistled musical theme: she releases the controls, and permits herself just to feel (13). Later, when she meets John Galt, she recalls this feeling without at first recognizing what it is (703).

The spirit of Francisco's remark pervades Ayn Rand's fiction. "When we turn a corner, there will always be something exciting and wonderful there: we will be there." Ayn Rand refers elsewhere to the excitement to be expected around the corner. For example, Cherryl Brooks has "a look that expected the world to contain an exciting secret behind every corner" (258). "More than any other writer," Ayn Rand said, "O. Henry represents the spirit of youth—specifically, the cardinal element of youth: the expectation of finding something wonderfully unexpected around all of life's corners."[15] The other references, however, do not include Francisco's explanation of the specific reason that there will always be, for him and for Dagny, something wonderful around any corner.

What is Francisco saying here? In miniature, it is the essence of *The Fountainhead*, the self-sufficient ego, invulnerable and uncrushable, the reverence of the noble soul for itself. *We* will be there. We will be what we have made of ourselves.

For the evil characters, their hell is what they have done to themselves, what they have made of themselves. For example: "The burning pressure on his temples and the faint, dizzying nausea of unreality came from the fact that he could not recapture the sense of being Dr. Robert Stadler" (1117). In view of the evil he has sanctioned and committed, Dr. Stadler is no longer there. Around every corner he will seek in vain the self he abandoned. Instead of something exciting and wonderful, instead of "the fearless mind" and "the inviolable truth" (185), he will find instead something awful, the spectacle of the mind he has betrayed.

Similarly, James Taggart, who shaped his evil self long ago and has been running from the awareness of it ever since, is destroyed by the vision, so to speak of himself. "The sight he was confronting was within him" (1145). For Taggart, beyond every corner, at the end of every blind alley—once the fog is cleared away—there is and will always be something horrible: he will be there.

The tragedy within *The Fountainhead* is Wynand's realization that he has committed the unforgivable sin, treason against his own greatness.[16] The fulfillment of one's own promise, by contrast, is Rearden's triumph. On the night of Dagny's broadcast, when Rearden tells Dagny everything he has learned and accepted (including her use of the past tense in talking about their relationship), Dagny sees his spiritual achievement:

> Looking up at his face, she realized that for the first time he was what she had always thought him intended to be: a man with an immense capacity for the enjoyment of existence. The taut look of endurance, of fiercely unadmitted pain, was gone; now, in the midst of the wreckage and of his hardest hour, his face had the serenity of pure strength; it had the look she had seen in the faces of the men in the valley. (861)

He is finally what she has thought him intended to be. Hank Rearden is there, at last.

For Ayn Rand's heroes, from Kira with her enduring smile and her salute to the possibilities of life, to Prometheus in the act of discovering the self as the greatest treasure, to Howard Roark and the great-souled heroes of *Atlas Shrugged*, spiritual splendor is the reward that, at every moment and forever, will always be there. It's what can't be lost. Whatever the turns of the plot, whatever the setbacks and difficulties, the heroes, in the plenitude of their grandeur, will be there.

So why did Ayn Rand remove this passage? Perhaps because Francisco's self-praise is too abstract to be a proper expression of pride. Or perhaps because his emotional intensity, and Dagny's response to a man's protection, could not be vouchsafed to anyone but Galt. After that speech, how could any other man be Dagny's final romantic choice and the novel's greatest hero?

Whatever the reason for the omission, the serene self-confidence Francisco expresses is thoroughly justified, and dramatized throughout a colorful characterization that, as we have seen, was developed not by calculation but by inspiration, as if Ayn Rand had, always before her sight and within her mind, the spirit of Francisco, the epitome of relentless ambition, ruthless justice, elegant self-confidence, and radiant joy. Whatever the turn of the plot of *Atlas Shrugged*, whatever else Ayn Rand labored to accomplish in her masterpiece, there was always something exciting and wonderful there: because Francisco d'Anconia was there. Thanks to Ayn Rand, he always will be.

CONCLUSION

I conclude with a thought that addresses a question I've frequently encountered. People sometimes say that we need a sequel to *Atlas Shrugged*, in which Francisco would find a woman worthy of him. Well, I also used to feel sorry for Francisco, but not any more. What I'm sharing with you is fantasy, not literary scholarship, but I'm no longer worried about Francisco's happiness. The solution exists. If one wished to find a woman who would love and cherish Francisco, one would not have far to look.

This woman is already in Atlantis. She has high standards and excellent judgment where men are concerned. Although we do not learn her name, we know who she is because she looks remarkably like someone we know. She is "stretched on the sun-flooded planks" of a pier, "watching a battery of fishing rods," with her "dark, disheveled hair and large eyes" (719).[17] In addition to being the valley's "best fishwife," she is "the kind of writer who wouldn't be published outside. She believes that when one deals with words, one deals with the mind" (720). She is, of course, in love with Galt, and Francisco is in love with Dagny; the dramatic development of the novel would be violated by a sudden, new relationship between Francisco and this woman. Nonetheless, the possibility exists, in the future beyond the novel, for a romantic union of Francisco and the character based on Ayn Rand.

Ayn Rand is really all of her heroic characters, She is both Dagny and Galt, Dominique and Roark. But the fishwife-novelist is uniquely similar in appearance to Ayn Rand. She said, moreover, that this character was "strictly me, . . . in a Hitchcock way . . . what I call a private joke."[18] Francisco's names, moreover, are suggestive. Three of his many names are Francisco, Carlos, and d'Anconia, which correspond to the three parts of the name of her husband, Charles Francis O'Connor, who was known as "Frank."[19] In the fullness of postfictional time, Francisco will be joyous, as always, and not alone. Ayn Rand named him after Frank, and she saved him for herself.

NOTES

1. Biographical interviews (Ayn Rand Archives).
2. Ayn Rand described John Galt in a note, on June 29, 1946: "No progression here (as Roark had none). He is what he is from the beginning—integrated (indivisible) and perfect. No change in him, because he has no intellectual contradiction and, therefore, no inner conflict." For information about the characterization of John Galt, see "Who *Was* John Galt? The Creation of Ayn Rand's Ultimate Ideal Man" in the current volume.
3. The *Atlas Shrugged* manuscripts (three drafts, one set of galleys, and one set of proofs) are housed in the Library of Congress, where I examined them. In the first draft, which will be my major focus, each chapter is paginated separately. Because the chapter divisions in the drafts are not always the same as those in the novel, I will identify quotations from the first draft by the numbers of the box, folder, and page. The *Atlas Shrugged* notes, along with some isolated pages from the manuscript, are housed in the Ayn Rand Archives. All references to these notes are drawn from the original texts in the Ayn Rand Archives; I will also indicate the pages in David Harriman, ed., *Journals of Ayn Rand* (New York: Dutton, 1995) in which the notes are published in part.
4. *Atlas Shrugged* notes, June 29, 1946; *Journals of Ayn Rand*, 512.
5. *Atlas Shrugged* undated notes, "Main Problems" [From rewrite of chapter VI], concerning the Dagny-Francisco romance, partially reprinted in *Journals of Ayn Rand*, 561.
6. *Atlas Shrugged* notes, June 27, 1946; *Journals of Ayn Rand*, 505.
7. Eddie Willers says: "Do you know what's strange about your face? You look as if you've never known pain or fear or guilt" (652). Dagny awakens in Atlantis to see "a face that bore no mark of pain or fear or guilt" (701).
8. It is difficult to date with certainty Ayn Rand's decision to describe a romantic relationship between Dagny and Francisco. Her notes of 1945 and 1946, which make no mention of such a relationship, list Francisco as one of the strikers, not as the "second lead." In the first-draft manuscript (Box 5, folder 5, 271–74, in a chapter begun on March 1, 1947) and in the final text of that chapter, "The Top and the Bottom" (53), we initially learn that Dagny knows him as an industrialist who appears to have wasted his ability. The absence, at that point, of any reference to a romance obviously does not mean that there was no such relationship; we know that, in the completed novel, there was. But the subsequent first-draft references to Francisco appear to exclude (or, at rate, to conceal) a romance. In the first draft of the same chapter (Box 5, folder 5, 297–98, corresponding to 57), James Taggart refers to Dagny's "hero worship" of Francisco (a judgment and an emotion he does not and did not share), but does not hint at any suspicions of what Francisco and Dagny "did" together. And, as I have noted in the text of this article, the first description of Dagny's reading of the newspaper story about Francisco (in a chapter begun on March 31, 1947) shows no indication of a romantic past; Francisco is simply another wasted value, like the rusted piece of machinery (Box 5, folder 6, 337–41). In the first draft of this passage, moreover, Ayn Rand wrote that Dagny had not seen Francisco for "three or four years"—as

if Dagny might not remember exactly when she saw him for the last time. I assume, therefore, that Ayn Rand, in March and April of 1947, had not yet intended to give Francisco and Dagny a romantic past. The chapter in which she ultimately did so (Box 5, folder 7, 447–645) is undated; it is paginated relatively continuously with the preceding chapter and the following chapter, which she began writing on July 4, 1947. I assume that it was written in between the end of April and July 4. After writing this chapter, she wrote notes (also undated) for an extensive rewrite, developing in greater detail the episodes dealing with the childhood and adolescent summers of Dagny and Francisco.

9. Biographical interviews (Ayn Rand Archives).

10. Biographical interviews (Ayn Rand Archives). The manuscripts housed in the Library of Congress have two drafts of the chapter containing the Money Speech.

11. *Atlas Shrugged* notes, August 27, 1950; *Journals of Ayn Rand*, 626–27.

12. This section has, in the draft, indications of missing pages. Page 611 is only half a page, and page 616 begins: 611–15 cut. Ayn Rand wrote more passages in this vein, and removed them from the draft, as later she removed the literal lie from these as well.

13. Ayn Rand, *The Fountainhead* (New York: Signet, 1993), 232.

14. Another example of an editorial change in Francisco's masquerade is the omission, in the final version of the chapter "The Climax of the d'Anconias" of an episode, reported in the newspapers, that appears only in the draft. Dagny "read the story of the great ball in Paris and of the Countess who attempted to commit suicide; he was to escort the Countess to the ball, and he arrived at her residence as promised, but it was her maid that he took with him to the party; the maid was much the prettier of the two" (Box 5, folder 7, 578; cf. 115 in the text). Francisco, courteous under all circumstances, would not have committed this sort of rude act, even for the sake of outrageousness. The masquerade can go only so far.

15. Ayn Rand, *The Romantic Manifesto: A Philosophy of Literature* (New York: Signet, 1975), 110.

16. *The Fountainhead*, 663.

17. In the notes, Galt tells Dagny that the fishwife (the writer) is in love with him, and that the outside world regards unrequited love with scorn:

> men hold love to be a supreme virtue, yet a woman who loves a man without answer is supposed to be ridiculous, she is supposed to hide her feeling as some sort of disgrace or shame, in order to protect her "pride"; or else she makes a claim and a burden upon the man out of her unrequited feeling and pursues him, half as a beggar, half as a sheriff. But *here*, love is what it actually is by its nature: a recognition of values and the greatest tribute one human being can give another, gratefully to be accepted, whether one returns it or not. (*Atlas Shrugged* notes, January 4, 1952; *Journals of Ayn Rand*, 636.)

18. Biographical interviews (Ayn Rand Archives).

19. Ayn Rand commented that she did not know the source of the name (Biographical interviews, Ayn Rand Archives). She also noted that she owed to Frank O'Connor several of Francisco's lines, including "Brother, you asked for it!" Ayn Rand therefore asked him to write the line (with the full name: Francisco Domingo Carlos Andres Sebastian d'Anconia) in the manuscript (Box 10, folder 9, 142).

4

A Note on Francisco's Ancestry

Tore Boeckmann

One evening in her late teens, in a Petrograd theater, sitting in a balcony seat that afforded a view of only half the stage, Ayn Rand saw her first play by Friedrich Schiller. The play was *Fiesco; or, the Genoese Conspiracy*, and she thought it was magnificent. She went to see it again the next evening.[1]

Fiesco deals with a sixteenth-century republican revolt against Andrea Doria, the Duke of Genoa, and his nephew Gianettino. The hero is Fiesco, a Genoese count. He is described by his wife Leonora as "he who from the chisel of the exhaustless artist, Nature, sprang forth all-perfect, combining every greatness of his sex in the most perfect union."[2] When she stood beside him at the altar, Leonora thought to herself: "thy Fiesco . . . will free Genoa from its tyrants!"[3]

But Leonora's hopes for her husband's political heroism are disappointed when Fiesco starts throwing decadent parties. He declares: "Let the floors swim with Cyprian nectar, soft strains of music rouse midnight from her leaden slumber, and a thousand burning lamps eclipse the morning sun. Pleasure shall reign supreme, and the Bacchanal dance so wildly beat the ground, that the dark kingdom of the shades below shall tremble at the uproar!"[4] The play opens at one of these parties, where Fiesco, before his wife's eyes, courts another woman.

When a courtier tells Fiesco that he has "become a mere votary of pleasure" and that "[t]he great world has lost much in you," Fiesco answers: "But [I have] lost nothing in giving up the world. To live is to dream, and to dream pleasantly is to be wise. Can this be done more certainly amid the thunders of a throne . . . than on the heaving bosom of an enamored woman? Let Gianettino rule over Genoa; Fiesco shall devote himself to love."[5]

Fiesco's hedonism bitterly disappoints his wife. "Go now, and see this demigod of the Genoese amid the shameless circles of debauchery and lust! Hear

the vile jests and wanton ribaldry with which he entertains his base companions! *That is Fiesco!* Ah, damsels, not only has Genoa lost its hero, but I have
lost my husband!"[6]

Now consider the character of Francisco d'Anconia in *Atlas Shrugged.*

Like Fiesco, Francisco is an aristocrat stylized to perfection by nature. "It
was as if the centuries had sifted the family's qualities through a fine mesh
. . . and had let nothing through except pure talent; as if chance, for once, had
achieved an entity devoid of the accidental" (93).

Like Fiesco, Francisco promises much for the future. When he inherits the
family business, leaders of industry think that d'Anconia Copper "would
sweep the world now, under what his management promised to become"
(111).

Like Fiesco, Francisco disappoints all expectations when he starts throwing
decadent parties. At an Algerian resort, "he built a pavilion of thin sheets of ice
and presented every woman guest with an ermine wrap, as a gift to be worn for
the occasion, on condition that they remove their wraps, then their evening
gowns, then all the rest, in tempo with the melting of the walls" (115).

Like Fiesco, Francisco gives a hedonistic reason for his transformation.
"Why should I wish to make money? I have enough to permit three generations of descendants to have as good a time as I am having" (116).

Like Fiesco, Francisco causes great pain to the woman who loves him—
Dagny Taggart. "The boy she had known could not have become a useless
coward. An incomparable mind could not turn its ingenuity to the invention
of melting ballrooms. Yet he had and did, and there was no explanation to
make it conceivable and to let her forget him in peace" (116).

Francisco's and Fiesco's transformations have an air of mystery and in-
trigue—for two reasons. First, as Schiller said in a different context, "the nobler
a thing is, the more repulsive it is when it decays."[7] Yet neither Francisco nor
Fiesco elicits repugnance. Dagny tells Francisco: "The way you live is depraved.
But the way you act is not. Even the way you speak of it, is not" (199). How
does he speak of it? With a self-confident, nondefensive wit that is inconsistent with the assumption that he is a man of high purpose turned hedonist.
The same is true of Fiesco.

Second, both men drop hints that suggest a hidden purpose. Fiesco tells a
young man: "It is not for the eye of the youthful artist to comprehend at once
the master's vast design. Retire . . . and take time to weigh the motives of Fiesco's conduct."[8] By "the master's vast design," Fiesco means God's purpose. His
point is that the universe, as created by God, holds no contradictions—and
one would see the logic of everything if only one knew the totality. Apart from
the religious aspect, Francisco makes the same point to a bewildered Dagny
when he tells her: "Whenever you think that you are facing a contradiction,
check your premises. You will find that one of them is wrong" (199).

The character of Francisco d'Anconia, I believe, is directly inspired by Schiller's Fiesco.

In a broad sense, Francisco is the culmination of a long line of literary heroes, like the Scarlet Pimpernel and Zorro, who affect what we may loosely call a playboy persona in order to mask some more serious purpose. But Fiesco is (to my knowledge) the first of this line, and the one most similar to Francisco in the details. We know that Ayn Rand admired Schiller's play. And it is worth noting that she originally thought of Francisco as more typically Italian than Spanish (or Latin American) and wanted to name him "Francesco."[9] For these reasons, it is plausible to conclude that she created Francisco with Fiesco as her model.

Yet Francisco is not simply a copy of Fiesco. To see the difference between the two characters, and its significance, consider first the *theme* of *Fiesco*.

Schiller writes in his preface to the play that "it becomes necessary to lay aside the feelings of a man in order to become a political hero."[10] He expresses the same general idea in his *Letters on Don Carlos*, where he writes that "the capacity for sacrifice is the essence of all republican virtue."[11] Leonard Peikoff formulated the theme of *Don Carlos* as "the primacy of freedom over selfishness."[12] Each of these formulations expresses a slightly different angle on the idea (dear to Schiller) that in order to fight for and institute political freedom (a republic), men must sacrifice their selfish emotions and passions.

This is the meaning openly embodied in the character and actions of Fiesco. As the republicans in the play bemoan, a Fiesco who pursues his every sensualistic whim cannot lead the fight for Genoa's freedom. Or as the tyrannical Andrea Doria says complacently: "Fiesco, wearied with his rioting, sleeps and has no time to think of Doria."[13]

The meaning embodied in the character of Francisco is different. The theme of *Atlas Shrugged* is "the role of the mind in man's existence."[14] This theme is dramatized by showing what happens to society when the mind is absent—when the men of the mind go on strike. And what happens when the mind is absent—what happens to a man who stops thinking, and to the industrial company he runs—is precisely what is illustrated by Francisco's turning into a playboy. It does not matter, from this perspective, whether he is *really* a playboy, or is one of the strikers. As he tells Dagny after he wastes part of his fortune: "Whether I did it on purpose, or through neglect, or through stupidity, don't you understand that that doesn't make any difference? The same element was missing" (124). He means the element of the mind.

Both Schiller and Ayn Rand present a man of exceptional nobility of mind who turns (seemingly) into a decadent playboy. Yet if Fiesco and Francisco are meant to concretize different abstract meanings, one would expect them to differ concretely as well. And so they do. First and foremost, they differ in what their new, playboy personas are a change *from*.

Francisco embodies the essence of "the mind's role in man's existence" because he is *a man of the mind*—an expected genius of reason-guided production—who becomes a playboy. Fiesco embodies the essence of "the opposition of selfishness and freedom" because he is an expected *hero of liberty*, of republican revolt, who becomes a playboy.

It is telling that both Schiller and Ayn Rand stress the nature of their hero's youthful ambition, political or productive. Schiller has Leonora recall her husband in youth: "Such was his noble and majestic deportment, as if the illustrious state of Genoa rested alone upon his youthful shoulders."[15] Ayn Rand includes the flashback to Dagny and Francisco's childhood, which illustrates that "[t]he d'Anconia heirs had been men of unusual ability, but none of them could match what Francisco d'Anconia promised to become" (93).

It is not their playboy personas as such that differentiate Francisco and Fiesco, but the respective natures of the youthful destinies that those personas betray.

Or, rather, seemingly betray. Of course, the two men have not really become playboys.

Francisco is on strike. Like the other strikers, he wants to remove from the altruist-collectivist society the benefits of the rational mind—in his particular case, the benefits both of his *own* mind and of the minds of his ancestors, who built his copper company. To prevent the company from being taken over by the looters, he must destroy it. His playboy persona, he says, "was a part that I had to play in order not to let the looters suspect me while I was destroying d'Anconia Copper in plain sight of the whole world" (765).

Fiesco, too, has a secret purpose: he wants to overthrow the Dorias. To do so, he must amass armaments and troops. His playboy persona is a cover for such activities. As he tells a group of republicans, who are to be his fellow conspirators: "All Genoa was indignant at the effeminate Fiesco; all Genoa cursed the profligate Fiesco. Genoese! my amours have blinded the cunning despot. . . . Concealed beneath the cloak of luxury, the infant plot grew up."[16]

The "real" motives of Fiesco and Francisco seem superficially similar: both men seek the destruction of political tyranny. But a closer look reveals crucial differences.

Observe first that the conspirators in *Fiesco* want to topple the Dorias by force, seize control of the government of Genoa, and institute a republic. They want to bring freedom to their state by means of a personnel change at the top. This poses a problem. As Fiesco's wife, Leonora, says when she learns about the conspiracy: "Seldom do angels ascend the throne—still seldomer do they descend it such."[17] In other words, given the opportunity to wield arbitrary power, even the most idealistic and freedom-loving man is in danger of giving way to his selfish passions. Thomas Jefferson would later express the same general idea in his first inaugural address: "Sometimes it is said that man cannot be trusted with the government of himself. Can he, then, be trusted with the government of others? Or have we found angels in the forms of kings to govern him?"

Fiesco proves no angel. When he has cast aside his playboy act and taken lead of the republican conspiracy, he finds it in his reach to become the tyrant of Genoa. "To obey! or to command! To be, or not to be! . . . To tame the stubborn passions of the people, and curb them with a playful rein, as the skilful horseman guides the fiery steed! With a breath—one single breath—to quell the rising pride of vassals, whilst the prince, with the motion of his sceptre, can embody even his wildest dreams of fancy! . . . I am resolved."[18]

Like Fiesco the sensualist playboy, Fiesco the power-luster embodies the theme of "selfishness versus freedom." Nothing has changed except the particular selfish passion that sidetracks him from the pursuit of liberty.

Observe next that Francisco and the other strikers in *Atlas Shrugged* do not want to replace the altruist-collectivist rulers and hand freedom to the people as an altruistic gift from above. Relevant here is John Galt's answer to Mr. Thompson, "the Head of the State," when Mr. Thompson offers him the job of Economic Dictator of the nation. "If you want a free economy," Mr. Thompson says, "order people to be free!" (1100). Galt replies: "I don't want to be an Economic Dictator, not even long enough to issue that order for people to be free—which any rational human being would throw back in my face, because he'd know that his rights are not to be held, given or received by your permission or mine" (1101).

John Galt knows that man survives by the use of his mind—and that the mind does not function by *permission*, only by *right*. This is why it is useless for Galt to order men to be free, or to think. They won't—not so long as they know that Galt, or Mr. Thompson, has it in his power to order the opposite tomorrow.

Just as Galt refuses power for the altruistic end of setting people free, so he refuses power for "selfish" ends—to Mr. Thompson's befuddlement. As Mr. Thompson sees it, he is offering Galt everything that the most rapacious egoist could possibly desire. "If it's money that you want—you couldn't make in three lifetimes what I can hand over to you in a minute, this minute, cash on the barrel. . . . [I]f it's power that you're after, I'll guarantee you that every man, woman and child in this country will obey your orders and do whatever you wish" (1101–2). Yet Galt turns him down, and Mr. Thompson can't understand it. He says: "I thought you were an egoist" (1101).

Galt *is* an egoist—but he is a special kind of egoist. Historically, it has been taken for granted that it *would* be in a man's self-interest to "quell the rising pride of vassals" or have every man, woman, and child obey his orders. But Galt knows that enslaved men, women, and children have nothing of value to offer *him*, the man of the mind.

What *is* in a man's self-interest, in a social system based on the rule of brute force (provided no foundation has been laid for a mass rebellion)? To pursue such values as he can, out of sight of the rulers—and to hasten their collapse by withdrawing the service of his mind. Or, in other words, *to go on strike.*

This is what John Galt does—and what Francisco does. Francisco destroys his entire copper company, except the small mine he operates in "the valley," out of the looters' grasp. As he tells Dagny,

> It may be that at the end of my life, I shall have established nothing but this single mine—d'Anconia Copper No. 1, Galt's Gulch, Colorado, U.S.A. But, Dagny, do

you remember that my ambition was to double my father's production of copper? Dagny, if at the end of my life, I produce but one pound of copper a year, I will be richer than my father, richer than all my ancestors with all their thousands of tons—because that one pound will be *mine by right* and will be used to maintain a world that knows it! (771)

Francisco d'Anconia's real purpose—the purpose he disguises by affecting the playboy persona—is to go on strike against the altruist-collectivist society, for his own selfish benefit. He neither tries to be a benevolent, altruistic dictator, nor a selfish, tyrannical one. In this, he differs from Schiller's Fiesco, who plans and plots to grant mankind the gift of liberty—and then changes his mind out of selfishness.

Just as the "real" Fiesco, the man behind the playboy façade, embodies the theme of *Fiesco*, so the "real" Francisco embodies the *full* theme of *Atlas Shrugged*: "the role of the mind in man's existence—and, as corollary, the demonstration of a new moral philosophy: the morality of rational self-interest."[19]

In a 1946 journal entry, "Philosophical Notes on the Creative Process," Ayn Rand wrote:

> [I]f creative fiction writing is a process of translating an abstraction into the concrete, there are three possible grades of such writing: translating an old abstraction (known theme) through the medium of old fiction means, i.e., through characters, events, or situations used before for that same purpose (this is most of the popular trash); translating an old abstraction through new, original fiction means (this is most of the good literature); or creating a new, original abstraction and translating it through new, original means. This last, as far as I know, is only *me*—my kind of fiction writing. May God forgive me (metaphor!) if this is mistaken conceit. As near as I can now see it, it isn't. (A fourth possibility—translating a new abstraction through old means—is impossible; if the abstraction is new, there can be no means used by anyone else before to translate it.)[20]

Schiller falls in the second category: he translates an old abstraction through new, original fiction means. The idea that liberty requires the self-sacrifice of the best and noblest is not new with Schiller. For instance, it is a constant theme in the writings of the Ancient Romans.[21] (It is also popular among modern conservatives.) By contrast, Schiller's *means*—the portrayal of a hero who fakes a playboy persona to mask a strike against tyranny—is new with him.

Ayn Rand is a different case. The abstraction she translates into the concrete—man's radical dependence on his mind, and the morality of rational self-interest—is new with her. Being so, the abstraction cannot be translated through old fiction means. But such means can be *adapted* to fit her purpose. Ayn Rand can take old fiction means and change, not merely some surface details, but that which makes the concrete in question speak to the essence of an abstract idea; and so doing, she can turn old means into new.

She can take Schiller's character of Fiesco as her model and create a Francisco who embodies a new, original abstraction through new, original means.

And this is why Ayn Rand does not need God's forgiveness for any mistaken conceit.[22]

NOTES

1. Biographical interviews (Ayn Rand Archives).
2. Friedrich Schiller, *Fiesco; or, the Genoese Conspiracy: A Tragedy*, trans. by Henry G. Bohn, in *The Works of Frederick Schiller*, vol. IV (London: Bell & Daldy, 1871), 135.
3. Schiller, *Fiesco*, 135.
4. Schiller, *Fiesco*, 140.
5. Schiller, *Fiesco*, 142
6. Schiller, *Fiesco*, 136.
7. Friedrich Schiller, *On the Aesthetic Education of Man*, trans. by Elizabeth M. Wilkinson and L. A. Willoughby (Oxford: Clarendon Press, 1967), 27.
8. Schiller, *Fiesco*, 145.
9. See David Harriman, ed., *Journals of Ayn Rand* (New York: Dutton, 1997), 390.
10. Schiller, *Fiesco*, 132.
11. Friedrich Schiller, *Letters on Don Carlos*, trans. by Jeanne R. Willson, in Friedrich Schiller, *Plays*, Walter Hinderer, ed. (New York, Continuum, 1983), 311.
12. Leonard Peikoff, "Eight Great Plays as Literature and as Philosophy," (Ayn Rand Bookstore, 1993), lecture 4, "Don Carlos."
13. Schiller, *Fiesco*, 216.
14. Ayn Rand, "Basic Principles of Literature," *The Romantic Manifesto: A Philosophy of Literature*, revised edition (New York: Signet, 1975), 85.
15. Schiller, *Fiesco*, 135.
16. Schiller, *Fiesco*, 180.
17. Schiller, *Fiesco*, 214.
18. Schiller, *Fiesco*, 184.
19. Ayn Rand, *For the New Intellectual* (New York: Signet, 1963), 103.
20. Harriman, *Journals of Ayn Rand*, 481–82.
21. The historian Sallust, writing about Catiline's conspiracy to destroy the freedom of the Romans and establish dictatorship, says: "The whole truth—to put it in a word—is that although all disturbers of the peace in this period put forward specious pretexts, claiming either to be protecting the rights of the people or to be strengthening the authority of the Senate, this was mere pretence: in reality, every one of them was fighting for his personal aggrandizement." Sallust, *The Jugurthine War/ The Conspiracy of Catiline*, trans. by S. A. Handford (London: Penguin, 1963), 204–5. I owe this example to John Lewis.
22. I am grateful to Robert Mayhew for helpful comments on earlier drafts. This chapter is excerpted from my lecture "The Originality of *Atlas Shrugged*," given to the OCON Objectivist Summer Conference 2007, Telluride, Colorado, July 6–15. My lecture discusses at much greater length Ayn Rand's originality, and explores a further parallel between a Schiller play (*Mary Stuart*) and *Atlas Shrugged*. It is available from The Ayn Rand Bookstore (www.aynrandbookstore.com).

5

Working for Ayn Rand

Selections from *Facets of Ayn Rand*

Mary Ann Sures

Editor's note: *What follows is a set of excerpts from* Facets of Ayn Rand: Memoirs by Mary Ann Sures and Charles Sures *(Ayn Rand Institute Press, 2001), a book based on interviews conducted by Scott McConnell for the Oral History Program of the Ayn Rand Institute. The excerpts selected for inclusion here focus on Ayn Rand's work on* Atlas Shrugged. *Mary Ann Sures was a personal friend of Ayn Rand for twenty-eight years, beginning in 1954, and was her secretary during the last stages of work on* Atlas Shrugged, *from the fall of 1956 to the spring of 1957.*

Key: ARI: Ayn Rand Institute; MAS: Mary Ann Sures

WORKING FOR AYN RAND

ARI: Mary Ann, you were one of Ayn Rand's typists of *Atlas Shrugged*. Let's talk about that experience. How did it come about?

MAS: In the fall of 1956, Ayn was nearing the end of the writing, and needed a typist and proofreader. I had just finished a teaching assignment at NYU and was looking for employment that would leave me some free time to do graduate work. By that time, she knew me well enough to know that she could trust me not to divulge the content of the novel to anyone.

ARI: How long did the job last? And what did you do?

MAS: It lasted until the spring of 1957, when she turned the completed manuscript in to Random House. In the beginning, it wasn't full-time work. Some days there wasn't much to type, but as the weeks progressed, the workload increased. On some days, I was there from morning to evening.

When I started, the work consisted of typing and proofreading the newly written pages of the novel. That was a memorable experience. I had the pleasure, and the privilege, of reading the last part of the novel in her handwriting—hot off the press, so to speak.

In the fall of 1956, she was writing the closing chapters of part III. She was also editing the entire novel from page one, all of which had been typed by previous secretaries. I retyped the extensively edited pages that were difficult to read. On the pages that had very little editing, I made the changes in pencil on the carbon copies. In the beginning, we always discussed which pages needed retyping, and which pages could get by with pencil changes. After a while, she left it up to me. She wanted to present a manuscript that could be read easily. One of the sections she especially wanted to submit in clean pages was Galt's speech. I did considerable retyping of it.

ARI: Let's talk about those months.

MAS: Having had Ayn Rand as a mentor and friend for twenty-eight years was itself a matchless experience. But that period, the fall of 1956 and spring of 1957, has a unique place in my thoughts and memories, because it was during this period that I really got to know Ayn and Frank [O'Connor, her husband], and they got to know me, on a personal basis. We developed a closer relationship. Until then, I had seen them mainly in the company of others, or if I was alone with her, the discussion was usually about an aspect of philosophy. Now, I was alone with them almost on a daily basis, and the context was different. There were just the four of us in the apartment—Ayn, Frank, Frisco the cat, and me. . . .

ARI: Where were they living at the time?

MAS: In the fall of 1956, Ayn and Frank lived at 36 East 36th Street, Apt. 5-A. Across the street from the apartment house was the splendid Morgan Library. Around the corner was B. Altman, a department store which has since closed; Frank enjoyed shopping there. Across from B. Altman was a hamburger shop, Tailor Made, from which the O'Connors ordered.

ARI: Could you describe their apartment?

MAS: Their apartment was a one bedroom with den; it was not very spacious. You entered into a short hallway which opened into a larger entrance foyer. A black-lacquered dining room table was kept in the foyer, pushed up against a mirrored wall. I worked at the dining room table. Beyond the foyer was the living room, long and rectangular, with windows at one end. To the left of the foyer, there was a short hallway leading to the bathroom, linen closet, and the kitchen. Around the corner, there was another short hallway leading to her study and to their bedroom. It was very compact. The foyer, where I worked, was very close to her study—not more than ten or twelve steps. She kept the door to her study open, and, when necessary, we could talk back and forth.

ARI: She didn't close the door for privacy?

MAS: Only when she had a personal phone call. Otherwise it was always open.

ARI: What was her study like?

MAS: It was very small, and very simple. Actually, it was quite bare. There was only one window, and her desk was placed right in front of it. She didn't have an inspiring view, just windows of an apartment house across the way. To the left of her desk, along an adjoining wall, there were book shelves. On one of the bottom shelves, she kept the typed manuscript of *Atlas Shrugged* in boxes that had contained typewriter paper. The handwritten pages she was working on were kept in manila folders on the desk; she did her writing on a blue-green blotter. Opposite the desk were filing cabinets, on which there was a telephone and a pencil sharpener.

ARI: No decoration, no personal touches in the room?

MAS: Two personal touches. On the wall to the right of the desk, there were three photographs of Frank which were publicity stills from the Hollywood days, taken when he was a young man. He was strikingly handsome. Hanging next to these photographs was a print of an industrial site. So she had Frank and modern industry nearby, both what she would call "top values." And, the desk was a gift from Frank; he had had it made for her. So that's a personal touch, too.

The floor was parquet, not carpeted. She sat in a straight-backed, wooden chair that had a thin cushion covered in blue-green material. When she got up, she scraped the chair against the wooden floor, and I could easily hear it. The floor in the hallway was tiled, and I could hear her brisk footsteps. And Frank's, too, which were longer and more leisurely. And she could hear my typing—which didn't seem to disturb her.

ARI: Let's talk about a typical workday. How did it start?

MAS: Starting time was 9:00 a.m., unless we had agreed to a different schedule. Frank usually answered the door. He always told me what Ayn was doing—"Ayn is at her desk," or "Ayn is having coffee in the bedroom," or, very seldom, "Ayn is still sleeping." If Ayn was not working yet, he would tell me to help myself to the freshly made coffee, and join them in the bedroom for a morning visit.

ARI: What did you talk about?

MAS: Movies or television shows we had seen, or current events, sometimes art. They were not lengthy discussions.

One morning, early on, I rang the doorbell and I heard her quick steps approaching the door, and then her deep voice: "Hallo?" she said. "It's Mary

Ann," I answered. Then she opened the door a crack and asked me to excuse her because she wasn't dressed. That's how I learned that Ayn Rand often worked in a nightgown. The one she wore was made of a soft material, like brushed jersey. It was pale aqua, and it fell to the floor in long, regular folds, like a Greek column. The sleeves were long and full, and the neckline was a wide V decorated with rhinestones. It was quite glamorous. She had slippers in aqua leather, to match. She once jokingly assured me that she had other nightgowns, but this one was her favorite, and it was warm and heavy enough to wear without a robe.

When she was dressed, which was most of the time, she usually wore a navy wool skirt and a simple, short-sleeved silk blouse—in navy or dark green. And her favorite pair of high-heeled red leather sandals.

The first time I saw her in the nightgown, she explained why she wasn't dressed: if, when she woke up, she felt refreshed and eager to start writing, she didn't want to lose the momentum. So, she would quickly splash water on her face, brush her teeth, run a comb through her hair, get a cup of coffee, and get right to work.

ARI: What was she like when she was writing?

MAS: She was very disciplined. She seldom left her desk. If she had a problem with the writing—if she had what she called the "squirms"—she solved the problem at her desk; she didn't get up and pace around the apartment, or wait for inspiration, or turn on the radio or television. She wasn't writing every minute. Once I heard a flapping sound coming from the study—she was playing solitaire. She might read the newspaper. At times, I entered the study to find her sitting with her elbows on the desk and resting her chin on her hands, looking out the window, smoking, thinking.

One morning when I arrived, she was still in bed. I started my work, and soon I heard her call out: "Oh, Frank. I'm falling asleep. Oh no, I can't!" A few minutes later I heard her slippers slapping on the tiles. She washed her face, took a cup of coffee, and went to work. Later that morning, she explained that she had been up very late the night before, and had had little sleep. She had a deadline to meet with Random House, and she was determined to meet it—exhausted or not.

ARI: Did she ever play music while she worked?

MAS: Only once, in my experience. When she was writing the last chapter of the novel. One afternoon she put a record on the stereo, which was in the living room, and asked me to replay it when it stopped. It was the last movement of Rachmaninoff's *Second Piano Concerto*.

ARI: Do you know what scene or dialogue she was writing then?

MAS: No, I don't, and I was curious, too. But I didn't think it was my business to ask. And, had I asked, she would have answered—or explained why the question was too personal.

ARI: This brings me to the question: what kind of a boss was Ayn Rand?

MAS: She was, in a word, a lovely boss, very easy to work for. She never issued terse orders, or showed impatience, or stood over my shoulder. She was not your stereotypical temperamental genius. There was a graciousness in her manner—there was always "please" and "thank you" when she had a request. But she wasn't chatty; there was seldom any small talk before I started to work, if she was already at her desk. We agreed on the day's work and I got right to it. This raises what I call the spiritual atmosphere of the household. In a few words, it was sheer, unadulterated, never-ending good will—an atmosphere created by both Ayn and Frank. Here were two unpretentious and considerate people. In that home, there were no meta-messages or hidden agendas or speaking between the lines—there was always complete candor. And no tension hanging in the air. It was, truly, a benevolent universe.

When there wasn't a full day's work for me, she apologized. I didn't mind; I used to float to work, eager to get there. Once, I told her that I liked coming over because it was a sane and friendly place, and she said, "Oh?" in her characteristic way, and nodded and said, "Well, yes it is, you're right." And she added that I was free to come over and bring work of my own on days when I wasn't scheduled to work for her.

ARI: And did you?

MAS: Only a few times, because I thought it was an intrusion. But, she was sincere about it; they treated me like one of the family. I should have taken her at her word, because she meant everything she said.

She was a woman without moods. Or, if she were in a mood, she knew it. She would say so and offer a reason.

ARI: Such as?

MAS: If her work had been interrupted for some reason—like attending to some business matters or going to the dentist. That always got her down, and she knew it.

In the morning when I entered the study to get my work, I tapped lightly on the open door so I wouldn't startle her. There were only a few times when she didn't acknowledge me with a smile and a hello.

She was patient. It took me a while to get used to her handwriting. So, in the beginning, on the days I typed up the newly written pages, I read them over first. And if I had any questions, she wanted me to interrupt her. I tried to keep interruptions to a minimum. In all the months I worked for her, she only got angry with me once.

ARI: About what?

MAS: She didn't like typewritten pages with just a few lines. She thought they interrupted the flow of the story for the reader at Random House. Short pages resulted from deletions or additions to the typed manuscript, and were often

unavoidable. However, when we were nearing the end of the editing and retyping, one of her changes resulted in adding some lines to the manuscript; I
ended up with a page that had only three or four lines. To make it a complete
page would have required retyping all the pages up to the end of that section,
and there just wasn't time. Well, when she saw it she got angry. She reminded
me, in very stern tones, of our agreement to avoid short pages. She explained
again her reasons for not wanting to trouble the reader. I thought her point
was valid. But, I have to add here that I wasn't feeling very sympathetic toward
that reader, who had the pleasure of reading the novel in large sections, in one
sitting—while I had had to wait for Saturday nights to read single chapters and
then spend the week wondering what was going to happen next! So, when
she finished, I just said, "Ayn, it's *Atlas Shrugged* we're talking about." She just
looked at me, and her expression changed; she said, simply, "You're right." I
think we were both a little on edge, working against a deadline.

ARI: What were the working conditions, physically?

MAS: I worked on an old manual typewriter, with a cotton ribbon that wound
around spools, and the ribbon and the keys stuck occasionally. I heard once
that she had brought a typewriter with her from Soviet Russia. I don't know if
this was that typewriter, but it could have been. It was like an old tank, and just
as noisy! I typed an original and several carbon copies, and I made corrections
with a typewriter eraser. This was long before the days of word processing!

In the beginning, I was quite slow and didn't think I was earning my day's
wages, so I suggested that she pay me by the page. It would have been to her
financial advantage, but she insisted on paying me by the hour at the going
rate. She said she knew I would pick up speed after I got used to the typewriter.
And she insisted that I keep records of minutes, and if I stayed 10 minutes over
an hour, she insisted on paying me for a quarter of an hour.

She didn't expect me to do personal errands for her. I did shop at a nearby
stationer's for typing supplies, and that was part of the job. The one time I
volunteered to do a personal errand, there was a long discussion.

ARI: What was that?

MAS: A few times a week, in the early afternoon, she would interrupt her
work to call in the grocery order. The O'Connors bought their groceries from
Verde's, a small, specialty grocer on Third Avenue, near 36th Street, which was
a few blocks from their apartment. She had to get the order in by a certain time
so that it could be delivered late in the afternoon. One day, she missed the
deadline. Verde's delivery boy was gone for the day, and Frank wasn't home,
so I volunteered to pick up the groceries.

ARI: What happened?

MAS: First she said it was out of the question, that she couldn't ask me to do
that, that doing personal errands was not part of my job, and so on. She re-

ferred to types she had known in Hollywood and of which she disapproved—executives who always expected personal favors and errands. And I explained that the situation was an exception, that it was necessary, and that I didn't mind the walk. I don't remember the entire exchange, but I managed to convince her. But she insisted on paying me for the time and having me stay for dinner. She definitely didn't exploit her employee. I was always treated with respect; she always held my context. They both did.

ARI: Were there any house rules?

MAS: I remember three. First, to make sure that all cigarettes one smoked were put out in the ashtrays, especially in the ashtray on her desk. She was very strict about that. I often saw her carefully stubbing out a cigarette in the desk ashtray. If she thought there might be something still burning, she carried the ashtray into the kitchen. Another rule was the way I destroyed manuscript pages of *Atlas.*

ARI: Are you saying that you actually destroyed pages of that novel?

MAS: Yes. If a typewritten page had extensive editing and had to be retyped, the original page was destroyed. Her rule was that the page would first be torn into small pieces, and then the pieces mixed up and thrown down the incinerator in the hallway. She showed me how she wanted it done. She never, ever, discarded anything she had written without tearing it up completely—she didn't take whole pages, squash them up, and throw them as a ball into the wastebasket.

ARI: What about handwritten pages? Don't tell me you destroyed any of those?

MAS: Oh, yes. If her changes on a handwritten page were so extensive that the page was difficult to read, she rewrote that page and gave me the original page to destroy. To tear up and incinerate.

ARI: How could you bring yourself to destroy them?

MAS: Because that's what she wanted. She didn't want those pages lying around. They weren't of any use to her. She wasn't like some artists who save every scrap of paper they touch. She was concerned with the finished product, not with the process.

ARI: But this is an historic document we are talking about! Didn't you want to keep the pages as souvenirs? How many of those pages were there?

MAS: I don't remember the exact number, but there were not a great many. It never occurred to me to ask for them. I think that would have been the height of presumption. And, had I asked, I think she would have been annoyed and refused. And rightly so. . . .

ARI: You said there were three house rules.

MAS: The third one was never to open a window, even if Frisco was not in the room. They were concerned that he might jump out. This was a strict rule, and not just for Frisco. Later, there were other cats in the household, and the same rule applied. . . .

ARI: Earlier, you mentioned having dinner with the O'Connors. Didn't they dine out?

MAS: During that period, when she was completing *Atlas*, dinner was almost always at home. Sometimes she cooked it, sometimes Frank did. Being invited to dinner was the exception, not the rule. But as the work progressed, I sometimes stayed into the evening to finish up, and I was asked to stay for dinner. Especially when there was a casserole already made. Frank nicknamed it the "Atlas Shrugged casserole." I don't think we ever told her about that. It was a recipe they discovered on a Mueller's macaroni box. It was delicious, quick, and easy. Frank and I prepared it a few times—macaroni, onions, hamburger, and cheese. And one casserole was dinner for three nights!

They ate simply. They did something interesting with canned peas—they were served at room temperature, mixed with mayonnaise. Once in a while, we had hamburgers from Tailor Made. She would consult Frank and me, make up the order, call it in, and then Frank and I would walk over to pick it up.

ARI: Didn't you think it a bit odd—for the author of *Atlas Shrugged* to be calling in grocery orders and hamburger orders?

MAS: At first, yes, I did think so. But she never behaved as if she were the great genius who was above doing mundane things. She was the brilliant philosopher and writer. But if groceries and hamburgers had to be ordered, then she did that, too. She looked upon getting dinner ready as, primarily, the wife's responsibility.

ARI: Where did you eat, on the dining table that was your desk?

MAS: No. Never there, because of the typewriter and supplies on it. Frank and I set up TV tables in the living room, and we ate there. If there was something interesting on TV, we watched it; otherwise, it was just friendly chat. A relaxed atmosphere. . . .

FINISHING *ATLAS SHRUGGED*

ARI: Were you there when Miss Rand finished writing *Atlas Shrugged*?

MAS: Yes, that is one of my most vivid memories.

ARI: What happened?

MAS: *Atlas Shrugged* was finished on the afternoon of Wednesday, March 20, 1957. That, incidentally, is the date she wrote on the last page of the manuscript. The only people there, besides Ayn, were Frank, Joan, Leonard,[1] and me.

At the time, Ayn was working against a deadline, a date when she was scheduled to turn in the final typed manuscript of the novel to Random House. My job was to get the typing and proofreading finished by that deadline. I had agreed with Ayn not to let the work pile up; I was to keep up with her. On March 20, there were typewritten pages to be proofread. I had typed them earlier in the week, and I asked Joan to proofread with me. Ayn knew we were coming over.

We arrived at the apartment after lunch, about 1:00 p.m. We knew Ayn was writing the last chapter but we didn't know how close to the end she was. Frank answered the door, and said something like "I think this is going to be it, kids. . . ."

As I said earlier, whenever I went over to do some work and she was writing, I would tap on the study door, enter, take my work, and leave. But, after hearing Frank, I decided that we should not disturb her. We sat in the living room, whispering. More than an hour passed. Finally, I thought that one of us should quietly enter the study and quickly take the manuscript pages we needed—I knew exactly where they were on the bottom shelf of the bookcase. But, which one of us?

ARI: Which one was it?

MAS: Joan. How we decided that Joan should be the one is amusing. We concluded that since she was petite, she would be less noticeable! I told her to tap lightly and enter. She walked back to the study, and here is what I heard: a few taps on the study door, followed by Ayn's voice speaking in a stern manner: "If you come in here, I'll kill you." That's an exact quote.

Joan returned, and we retreated to the farthest corner of the living room and sat whispering and wondering. I decided to call Leonard and tell him what was happening. I had to go down to the lobby to use the pay phone, because the only telephone in the apartment was in Ayn's study. Leonard lived a few blocks away, and he came right over. He joined us in the corner of the living room, and we three whispered and waited. I'm not sure how much time passed; it seemed like hours, but it wasn't. And then we heard the loveliest sound in the world—Ayn's chair scraping against the wooden floor. We heard her footsteps walking out of the study, we heard Frank say, "Congratulations, darling." Then we heard her walking into the living room. She entered, dressed in a skirt and short-sleeved blouse, her hair was somewhat disheveled, her face was a little shiny. She was walking toward us, holding up a manuscript page with her thumb and index finger. We approached her and read the words "The End" at the bottom of the page. She looked young, she was smiling broadly, her eyes were bright. Frank followed her in, and he was beaming.

ARI: Was she angry about the interruption?

MAS: She didn't even mention it. After hugs and congratulations, we apologized for disturbing her. She dismissed it with a wave of her hand. She said it was all right, that we had no way of knowing what page she was on. She was so happy in those moments, I don't think anything could have undercut her joy at having finished *Atlas*. She wanted to have the Collective[2] over that night to celebrate. Then we left. It was still daylight.

ARI: How did you celebrate?

MAS: We had champagne. The "If you come in here, I'll kill you" story was told, to everyone's amusement. Ayn said that she didn't know who was tapping on the study door. We had coffee and pastries. I remember picking up some at the bakery on Third Avenue that the O'Connors used, Versailles Patisserie.

ARI: Were there any pictures taken, just after she finished writing the last page?

MAS: Right after she finished? No. No one had a camera. If we'd had a camera, we would have snapped her as she walked into the living room holding up the last page!

ARI: Do you remember typing the last page?

MAS: I typed only part of it. As I was typing the last chapter, Ayn said I could type everything but the last lines. She wanted to type those herself. When that time came, she sat down at the typewriter and said that even though she was a fast typist, she made a lot of mistakes. She added that she better not make any this time. So she typed, very slowly, from "He raised his hand . . ." to "The End." After she finished, she said, "Now it *really* does say 'The End.'"

NOTES

1. Joan Mitchell Blumenthal, an artist, who was then a friend of Ayn Rand's, and Leonard Peikoff, Ayn Rand's legal and intellectual heir and her close friend for thirty years.
2. "The Collective" was Ayn Rand's tongue-in-cheek name for a small group that met on Saturday nights to discuss her works and philosophy.

6

Publishing *Atlas Shrugged*

Richard E. Ralston

SELECTING A PUBLISHER

Ayn Rand had to struggle for years to *find* a publisher for each of her first three novels. That was not necessary for *Atlas Shrugged*, for which she merely needed to *select* a publisher. The success of *The Fountainhead*, its ongoing sales, and the well-known motion picture based on that novel for which she wrote the screenplay, meant that her next novel was eagerly anticipated by the publishing industry. The publication of her first three novels in America required a tenacious strategy to find a single publisher for each that was capable and willing to reach those she knew to be her potential readers. In contrast, the publication of *Atlas Shrugged* was the result of making the most discerning and appropriate choice among many willing publishers.

Ayn Rand also had to struggle with the literary agents who had represented her first three novels. Although she exercised more plain sense about book publishing than many publishers ever displayed, and had a very clear understanding of the unique characteristics of each novel and the precise readership it would attract, she eagerly sought out any agent with specialized knowledge and established contacts in the industry who might help find the right publisher. Yet after years of frustration with the representation of *The Fountainhead* she removed it from her agent and represented it herself until it was published by Bobbs-Merrill. For the rest of her life, that novel was not represented by any U.S. agent.

After the publication of *The Fountainhead* Rand began a relationship with Alan Collins at Curtis Brown Ltd. to represent the rights for a film adaptation. (The sub-agent in Hollywood was Berg-Allenberg—which was acquired after the production of the film by William Morris in December, 1949.) Although Rand was not impressed by the performance of Berg-Allenberg during production, she became increasingly confident with the relationship with Alan Collins. By 1950 she had moved her earlier works still handled by the Ann Watkins Agency to Curtis Brown, and at that time made the decision that her next novel would also be represented by Collins.[1] From 1943 the relationship with Collins, and after his death with Perry Knowlton at Curtis Brown, continued until Rand's death nearly forty years later. This provided Rand with the trusted assistance of a well-established agent in selecting a publisher for *Atlas Shrugged*. She was effectively able to benefit from or overrule his judgment as appropriate.

As early as 1946 before Rand had even started writing the book Collins received an offer of a combined advance and advertising guarantee of $125,000 from Appleton. In 1950 they were approaching Collins again with an offer for half that amount. At that time Archie Ogden, Rand's former editor at Bobbs-Merrill—who had famously put his job on the line to publish *The Fountainhead*—was working for them, and Rand thought they assumed she would like to work with Ogden again (she would have). But she was not yet ready to talk to publishers.[2]

Rand began the search for a publisher in late 1955 after completion of the radio broadcast speech by John Galt. (She did not include the speech in manuscripts provided to publishers, but held it back until she made the final selection.) The contract for *The Fountainhead* with Bobbs-Merrill gave them the first look at a new novel. Other than her contacts with her editor Archie Ogden—who had long since left Bobbs-Merrill—she had been very dissatisfied with their production, advertising, and promotion of the book. The only one at Bobbs-Merrill that she had enjoyed working with after Ogden was their editor Hiram Haydn, and he had recently departed for a position at Random House.

After reviewing the manuscript Ross Baker at Bobbs-Merrill invited Rand to dinner to discuss his list of proposed changes and cuts, and another long list of changes prepared by their editors. She did not consider that an appropriate subject for dinner conversation and declined the offer. After appealing without success to Alan Collins to be given a hearing for his cuts, Baker asserted that the book as written was unsalable and unpublishable. Although he was not shown the long speech by John Galt, Baker particularly objected to the other speeches which he thought were inappropriate in the context of the novel—especially mentioning his dislike of the "Money Speech" in that regard. From the publisher of *The Fountainhead*, with its own important speeches, that was a remarkable comment. Rand concluded of Bobbs-Merrill: "they remembered nothing and learned nothing."[3] (Although Rand was clearly in the driver's seat for the first time in selecting a publisher for her fourth novel, that did not mean that most publishers had any better idea of what they were dealing with than they ever had.)

Word about Bobbs-Merrill circulated quickly and many publishers began to contact Curtis Brown about the book. McGraw-Hill had already been aggressively making inquiries of Alan Collins. As a strong business publisher they were evidently looking for more best-selling fiction, and offered a strong promotional campaign. Rand was initially suspicious of the religious views of the Catholic owners. Collins had a high regard for the ability of Knopf to sell the book, but they were having a bit of a management crisis as the owners had difficulty in turning control of the firm over to their son and kept going into and out of retirement. Archie Ogden had an arrangement with Viking for bringing it titles for which he would freelance as an outside editor. Neither Collins nor Rand were comfortable with such arrangements.[4]

Hiram Haydn then proposed a luncheon meeting with Random House President Bennett Cerf and his partner Donald Klopfer. They had acquired what became Random House in 1925 and turned it into a major publisher.[5] Rand liked the intellectual atmosphere but not their left-wing reputation in the 1930s and 1940s. However Haydn told her that a single editor of many years was largely responsible for the political bias which had improved since he left the company.

Collins strongly opposed a first meeting over lunch with publishers at that level and thought Random House had too large a list to give the title adequate attention. Haydn was persistent; and then Cerf, who was publishing a lot of Curtis Brown's authors, called Collins and asked him what he had against Random House regarding this title. That was a bit awkward for Collins and he scheduled a lunch. Rand was very impressed by that as she felt she would have done the same thing as Cerf.

Rand later called the lunch "the most exciting publishing meeting I have ever had in my career." She felt they listened, faced ideas openly, were enthusiastic, and gave straight answers to her questions. She was most impressed by a suggestion of Cerf and a question by Klopfer. Cerf proposed the unusual step of submitting the book simultaneously to several publishers and requesting proposals on how they would respond to its ideological content and how they would handle the book. Their respective responses to the controversial nature of the book would give a good indication of what could be expected from them if they were to publish it. Rand was delighted, but Collins was horrified as that sort of thing was just not done. He did say he would consider it and let them know. Rand told them nothing about the book except its theme as an uncompromising defense of capitalism, and that any publisher would encounter opposition from both the political Right and Left. Klopfer then asked, "But if this is an uncompromising defense of capitalism, wouldn't you have to clash with the Judeo-Christian tradition of ethics?" She had never heard anyone else observe that and responded that that was her main point—that capitalism needed a moral defense because it does clash with Judeo-Christian tradition—which increased his interest.[6] Later due to the response of Cerf and Klopfer, Collins conceded that the lunch was not such a bad idea. Rand appreciated the fact that her agent was open to reason and changing his mind on such issues.

Collins and Rand also met with Pat Knopf from whom there were some indications of competence if not maturity, but he could not agree to the idea of a competition with other publishers because his supposedly retired father (Alfred A. Knopf) would never approve of such an exercise.[7] (It was just as well that Rand did not become associated with this corporate version of a family dispute. By 1960 Alfred Knopf had sold his firm to Random House after Pat Knopf had left in 1959 to found Atheneum Publications—with Hiram Haydn who had left Random House. A not unusual turn of events in American book publishing.)

Rand prepared a list of "Qualifications of Ideal Publisher" as follows:

1. Understanding of the nature of the book.
2. Understanding of the nature of the book's appeal.
3. Ability to sell the book aggressively and properly.
4. Independence of judgment, which would withstand influence when under fire.
5. Enthusiasm: a. for job of publishing. b. for me specifically.
6. Rationality in method of approach to issues and to communication with me.[8]

About a dozen major publishers had expressed interest to Collins. Of these three were chosen to consider the manuscript and their responses were evaluated and charted based on these criteria. Random House received two question marks and five pluses; Viking Press received seven minuses; McGraw-Hill four question marks and three minuses. Rand also wrote a narrative summary of her judgment on each of the points for each publisher. The following are brief extracts from these evaluations.

1. Remarks about Random House included: "They appeared to want *me* specifically, and not just an author who sold." "They seemed to be on the policy of figuring things out, *not* of acting on precedent and routine." "If they go after readers as they went after me, I could not ask for anything better." "The direct, open and purposeful method of conversation; I had the feeling of being heard and being answered, the conversation was fully in focus."
2. Remarks about Viking Press: "[The publisher] had not read *The Fountainhead* and did not ask a single question about me or my new book" and "he displayed enormous reluctance to enter into an issue of *intellectual values* and to take a stand on his own ideas."
3. Remarks about McGraw-Hill: There were one or two signs of hope as when the publisher remarked that "*The Fountainhead* sold because it made people think." But he "never asked a single question about the nature of the new book." "*Most dangerous sign for me*: his statement that, as an editor, he '*might*' say that some paragraph is wrong because he so feels, without being able to state his reasons."[9]

Rand had some concern if Random House would be able to "fight for a controversial book," and in the event she was disappointed at Cerf's "helplessness and fear" in the face of frightful reviews. (Random House did have a record from early days of supporting controversial authors, famously winning a court case to publish James Joyce in the United States.[10]) But Random House was the clear winner of the competition which Cerf had proposed, and Collins and Rand paid him a visit to tell him Random House would receive the first submission of the manuscript. They received the manuscript complete up to Galt's speech in Part III. After Cerf, Klopfer, and Haydn read the script, Collins and Rand were invited to Cerf's office where he announced: "It's a great book; name your terms." Rand told them about the length of the speech and the three final chapters. Then terms were agreed to on the advance, royalty, initial press run, and advertising guarantee in five minutes. A press release on September 7, 1956, conveys the tone of the relationship at that time:

> Author of THE FOUNTAINHEAD joins Random House. Ayn Rand's First Novel under Random House imprint to be called ATLAS SHRUGGED.
>
> Random House is gratified to announce one of the most noteworthy author-publisher associations in the firm's history, in the signing of Ayn Rand. Author of THE FOUNTAINHEAD, which sold over 700,000 copies in the original trade edition and was one of the most widely discussed books in recent decades, Miss Rand's first novel under the Random House imprint is a major work. Approximately 1,000 pages in length, the new book is titled ATLAS SHRUGGED. The publisher expects to bring it out sometime in 1957.[11]

The top management of Random House seemed genuinely enthusiastic about the book. Haydn reported that after reading the end of Part I on the completion of the John Galt Line railroad project, Cerf came running out of his office waiving the manuscript and calling it a great book. What impressed Rand was that both Cerf and Klopfer, while not claiming to agree with most of her ideas, took them seriously and thought they were very important. When Donald Klopfer told her that *Atlas Shrugged* had changed his mind about many issues, Rand invited him to lunch to find out what they were. He told her that he had not previously realized the extent to which success in industry and business depended on intelligence and ability. He had himself felt guilty when reproached for his success but could not understand why. He told Ayn Rand that she had solved that problem for him. While Cerf was friendly toward her ideas, he was intellectually and emotionally ill-equipped to survive the vicious reviews of the book with equanimity. That had not surprised Rand (nor had the reviews which would not have been easy for any publisher to take).

Although Rand had remained friendly for many years with her editor at Bobbs-Merrill, Archie Ogden, long after he left that publisher, she had never had a friendly personal relationship with the chief executives of any publisher. She had succeeded in establishing a substantive relationship with perhaps the two most prominent leaders in American publishing in the twentieth century. For a book that would challenge the entire intellectual establishment and culture, that was extremely fortuitous.

That relationship lasted for several years through their licensing of a paperback edition, and their publication of *We the Living* and *For the New Intellectual*. Eventually it would crumble under the pressure of Cerf's inability to stand up to the conformity of his editors—to what today would be described as "political correctness"—when during the perceived Camelot of the Kennedy Administration they could not live with a projected book project on "the Fascist New Frontier." But by that time the course for *Atlas Shrugged* had been set on its way toward reaching millions of readers.

Ayn Rand did come to regret that when finalizing the business arrangement, things were going so well that she forgot to require her approval for any advertising by Random House for *Atlas Shrugged*.[12]

MARKETING AND PROMOTION

The advertising for the book was not significantly less inept than that for her previous novels. Suggested advertising copy given to Cerf was well received by him, but did not survive in his advertising department. (One challenge in working with any large publisher is that advertising and artistic staffs do not have time to read—much less understand—most of the new books they are promoting. They did not have a clue about what they were trying to sell.) Random House did attend at least adequately to the basics of publicity and getting out review copies.[13]

One exception was an ad done as a personal favor. It reproduced a painting of Ayn Rand's husband, Frank O'Connor, over the headline "This is John Galt." More typical were small ads whose only message other than the title of the novel was "Ayn Rand's First Novel Since *The Fountainhead*." Eloquent in its simplicity, but needless to say more could have been said.[14]

As disappointed as Ayn Rand was with the advertising she was generally forgiving of Random House. She felt they did the best job they were capable of doing, and a better job than any other publisher would have done. Her judgment at that time was: "Random House is wonderful and the best of what there is today."[15]

Rand herself took up the primary role of promoting the book. She had projected her highest vision of man's potential as a heroic being in *Atlas Shrugged*. If that was to serve what she later described as "the motive and purpose of my writing" it would need to reach those worthy of and in need of that vision.[16]

Ayn Rand did not enjoy public speaking yet she had welcomed opportunities to speak for many years in order to call attention to her novels *We the Living* and later *The Fountainhead*. After the publication of *Atlas Shrugged* she began to respond to invitations from colleges to lecture. She also made herself available and gave frequent interviews to print and broadcast media. Over the years, talks such as "The Objectivist Ethics" (at the University of Wisconsin) or "Philosophy: Who Needs It" (to the U.S. Military Academy) became the leading articles in published anthologies of her nonfiction. In one sense, all of her writing and public speaking over the next twenty-five years can be understood as a means of elaborating on and explaining concepts introduced in *Atlas Shrugged*, but just as importantly of promoting that book to new readers. More than twenty extensive interviews were conducted at Columbia University from 1962–1966 and broadcast on radio. A remarkable series of seventeen substantive lectures were delivered for the Ford Hall Forum in Boston between 1961 and 1981. Many television interviews were broadcast including those with Johnny Carson, Tom Snyder, Phil Donahue, Edwin Newman, Louis Rukeyser, and Mike Wallace. Substantial printed interviews were given to such diverse publications as *Playboy* and *The Christian Science Monitor.*[17]

Rand also tried to answer as much fan mail as she could, as she had for earlier novels. She especially liked to respond to any spark of understanding revealed in a fan letter. To give one example, in 1960 she responded to a letter expressing concern about the indeterminate fate of the character Eddie Willers at the end of *Atlas Shrugged*: "Eddie Willers is not necessarily destined to die; in a free society, he will live happily and productively; in a collectivist society he will be the first to perish. He does not have the ability to create a new society of his own, but he is much too able and too honest ever to adjust himself to collectivism."[18]

One specific objective of Rand's in the publication of *For the New Intellectual* was to promote sales of the paperback edition of *Atlas Shrugged*. (It probably did that, as *For the New Intellectual* itself has sold more than one million copies.) This was the first of seven books of philosophy prepared in her lifetime ranging from ethics and epistemology to political economy and literature. They all referred to and were rooted in the philosophical principles incorporated in *Atlas Shrugged*.

An editor at one of Ayn Rand's publishers, when asked many years later how they had sold Rand's books, answered "they sell themselves."[19] While that may be insightful, it is not entirely true as a publisher is definitely needed to both produce and effectively distribute any book so that those who are looking for a book can easily find and acquire it. Rand would have said that "word of mouth" was the most effective means of promotion.

Realizing this, it is obvious that Ayn Rand nonetheless vigorously and continuously supported this phenomenon with her own speaking and writing. Since her death in 1982 this confrontation of the culture with the vision of man presented in *Atlas Shrugged* has been sustained by the Executor of the Estate of Ayn Rand, Dr. Leonard Peikoff, in his own writing and lecturing, and in his close oversight of the publication and sale of *Atlas Shrugged* and Rand's other books. His establishment of The Ayn Rand Institute also created an enduring institutional structure that continues to promote Ayn Rand's works, including *Atlas Shrugged*, to young people and their teachers, scholars, business professionals, and other new readers.

PUBLISHING HISTORY AND SALES

The initial press run by Random House was 100,000 copies. Three days after the publication date of October 10, 1957, the book appeared on the *New York Times* best-seller list as #6. It remained on the list for twenty-one weeks, peaking at #4 for a six week period beginning December 8, 1957.[20] Net sales of the book were nearly 70,000 copies in the first twelve months, which in those days put the book firmly in the "best-seller" category.[21] *Atlas Shrugged* was Ayn Rand's first novel to achieve that status immediately upon publication. Total sales of the Random House hardcover editions reached 250,000 copies by the time Dutton, a division of Penguin Group (USA) became the publisher in 1992.[22]

By the time *Atlas Shrugged* was published, it had become clear to Ayn Rand that a paperback edition, if preceded by a successful hardcover edition, would reach far more readers and have the most impact on the culture. This reflected a major change in book publishing following the publication of *The Fountainhead*, which did not go into a paperback edition until nine years after it was first published. The paperback publisher was New American Library (NAL). Ayn Rand had a good working relationship with Victor Weybright, one of the founders with Ken Enoch of NAL. In many ways they held a similar stature as major figures in American paperback publishing to that of Cerf and Klopfer at Random House for hardcover books. They had been hired in 1945 to head an American branch of Penguin Books. They went on to found their own firm in 1948, the New American Library of World Literature. (In 1987 NAL was acquired by Penguin Group (USA), closing the circle, as it were.)[23] The fact that *Atlas Shrugged* benefited from a literary agent, a publisher, and a paperback publisher at this level in whom Ayn Rand had confidence was entirely unprecedented in her experience.

The first paperback edition was published by NAL in July of 1959 with an initial press run of 150,000 copies. It also had a net sale of nearly 70,000 copies in the first 12 months.[24] *Atlas Shrugged* appeared on the paperback best-seller list of the *New York Times* on at least a couple of occasions including #8 on January 15, 1961, and #8 on April 7, 1963.[25]

Many translations have been published in the last fifty years. Those currently in print include Chinese, German, Italian, Japanese, Korean, Marathi, Russian, Spanish, Swedish, and Turkish.

Most remarkable about a novel in print for fifty years is the increasingly strong trend in sales over recent years. Paperback sales by New American Library to the book trade averaged 77,600 copies a year in the 1980s, 95,200 copies a year in the 1990s, and 134,600 copies a year so far in the first decade of the twenty-first century. In its fiftieth anniversary year (2007), annual sales reached an all-time high of more than 180,000 copies. A new British edition was published in 2007 by Penguin Modern Classics in London, and a new Penguin edition in Australia in 2008. Penguin Group (USA) currently publishes four editions: hardcover, two trade paperback editions, and one mass market edition. At this writing total sales exceed 6,250,000 copies[26]—a remarkable total for a lengthy, serious, intellectual novel that enshrined businessmen and industrialists as the unacknowledged heroic leaders of human progress, and directly challenged the traditional moral and philosophical pretensions of modern society.

While marketing and sales activities of the publisher have expanded and become more effective in recent years, and have taken optimal advantage of opportunities such as the centennial of Ayn Rand's birth and the fiftieth anniversary of the publication of *Atlas Shrugged*, that alone cannot explain the steady increase in sales far beyond those achieved during the author's lifetime. Ayn Rand always respected the important role that word-of-mouth promotion played in the gradual increase in sales of all of her books. She was always confident that if she reached enough of "my kind of readers" they in turn would reach even more. No one promotes *Atlas Shrugged* to new readers more effectively than readers of *Atlas Shrugged*. That is the most enduring of all sales trends. It is the direct result of the immutable and eternal artistic achievement of *Atlas Shrugged* dedicated "to the glory of Man."[27]

NOTES

1. Michael S. Berliner, ed., *Letters of Ayn Rand* (New York: Dutton, 1995), 488.
2. Berliner, *Letters of Ayn Rand*, 469.
3. Biographical interviews (Ayn Rand Archives).
4. Biographical interviews (Ayn Rand Archives).
5. "A History of Random House" (Random House website).
6. Biographical interviews (Ayn Rand Archives).
7. Biographical interviews (Ayn Rand Archives).
8. Unpublished notes (Ayn Rand Archives).
9. Unpublished notes (Ayn Rand Archives).
10. "A History of Random House."
11. Random House Press Release (Ayn Rand Archives).
12. Biographical interviews (Ayn Rand Archives).
13. Biographical interviews (Ayn Rand Archives).
14. Press Clippings (Ayn Rand Archives).
15. Biographical interviews (Ayn Rand Archives).
16. Ayn Rand, "The Goal of My Writing," *The Romantic Manifesto* (New York: Signet, 1975), 162.
17. Published and broadcast interviews preserved in Ayn Rand Archives.
18. Berliner, *Letters of Ayn Rand*, 564.
19. Interviews, Ayn Rand Archives.
20. Press Clippings and Publishers' Reports in Ayn Rand Archives.
21. Royalty Ledgers, Curtis Brown Ltd., New York City.

22. Publishers' Reports (Estate of Ayn Rand).
23. "About Us" New American Library, Penguin Group (USA) website.
24. Royalty Ledgers, Curtis Brown Ltd., New York City.
25. Press Clippings in Ayn Rand Archives.
26. Publishers' Reports (Estate of Ayn Rand).
27. Rand, "The Goal of My Writing," 172.

7

The *Atlas Shrugged* Reviews

Michael S. Berliner

With the publication of *Atlas Shrugged*, Ayn Rand's world changed. The novel established her as the foremost philosophic defender of capitalism. But she was no longer met with the polite and often positive reaction that greeted publication of *We the Living, Anthem,* and *The Fountainhead.*[1] The response to *Atlas Shrugged* was principally negative and often vicious—making her infamous in some circles and a controversial figure for the rest of her life.

The reason for this change is not difficult to discern. *We the Living* (1936) was a political novel involving a love triangle. *Anthem* (1937, revised in 1946) was a short, poetic novella that projected a future society without the word "I." And *The Fountainhead* (1943) dramatized the virtue of independence, as it followed the story of an architect battling the Establishment. But with *Atlas Shrugged*, the themes were no longer so limited nor was the philosophy even slightly implicit. By 1957, Ayn Rand had become an uncompromising advocate of reason, egoism, and laissez-faire capitalism, and an uncompromising opponent of altruism, collectivism, and mysticism (including religion). With her three previous works, there may have been some doubts about where she stood philosophically; with *Atlas Shrugged*, there could be no doubts. It had become much more difficult for critics (and readers) to ignore or evade her ideas.

The changed attitude towards Ayn Rand was reflected in the reviews of her novels. *We the Living* received mixed but generally positive reviews, somewhat surprising given its anti-Soviet message and that it was published during the Red Decade. *Anthem*'s paean against collectivism was welcomed even in socialist England. *The Fountainhead* evoked some nascent philosophic opposition, but most critics ignored the theme of "individualism vs. collectivism, not in politics but in a man's soul" and treated the novel as a love story, a book about architecture, or—at most—an attack on conformity.

The *Atlas Shrugged* reviews constitute a microcosm of American intellectual life: the Left was appalled by its blatant pro-capitalism; the religious Right rebelled against its rejection of religion. Most reviewers were dismayed by its immoderation, that is, its absolutism, and horrified by its opposition to altruism. Thus were revealed the principal intellectual trends against which Ayn Rand would fight the rest of her life.

A SURVEY OF THE REVIEWS

Let us now look in some detail at the *Atlas Shrugged* reviews. Of the hundred reviews in Ayn Rand's personal files, about half were in folders she marked as "Junk," "Mixed," or "Medium."[2] The other half were in general files and contained mostly negative reviews. Only fourteen (found mainly in "Mixed" and "Medium") were basically positive, and that number drops when only major publications are included. However, *Atlas Shrugged* did get some positive reaction from the majors. Paul Jordan Smith, writing in the *Los Angeles Times*, correctly identified the philosophy, about which he was completely approving, calling the book "challenging" and "fascinating," and he was sure that left-wingers would hate it. The *Wall Street Journal* published a review by M. E. Davis (October 10, 1957) that was positive though weak, especially given that Ayn Rand was championing the businessman. Davis wrote that the novel favors selfishness and individualism, is a tense and gripping story, and—though he makes little mention of the ideas—he concluded by pointing out that Ayn Rand provides a bright future at the end by having a character add "freedom of trade and production" to the rights guaranteed by the Constitution. There were positive reviews in the *Boston Herald* (October 13) by Alice Dixon Bond, who called it "monumental," and the *Seattle Post-Intelligencer* by Berne Jacobson, who deemed it a book "for those who feel that man is a thinking animal and has a right to the products of his mind." Other positive reviews appeared in San Francisco (Alma Oberst, October 19 in the *News*), Fort Worth (Thelma Cash, October 27 in the *Star-Telegram*) and some smaller cities. The most positive review in a national magazine came from *Playboy*, which described the theme rather imprecisely as: those who believe in reality believe in themselves and live for themselves. *Newsweek* began its review by quoting Ayn Rand on her "philosophy in essence"[3] and proceeded through a non-sneering description of the plot and the philosophy. "Despite laborious monologues, the reader will stay with this strange world, borne along by its story and eloquent flow of ideas." In sum, said *Newsweek*: "Powerful argument." (And *Newsweek* followed with a respectful interview with Ayn Rand.)

For more significant reviews, let us turn to those from what might be termed the "liberal establishment."

Earle P. Browne in the *Washington Post and Times-Herald* (October 13) alleged that "her industrialists are so ruthless they make Hollywood's worst producers seem like Bernard Baruch," and the book's major weakness, he wrote, was its neglect of the ordinary individual. Miss Rand, wrote Browne, seems to believe that to be a "heroic being" and fight oppression, you have to be the inventor of a new metal, the girl vice-president of a railroad, or the creator of a motor which harnesses energy from the sun. The *Washington Star,* in a review by Mary McGrory (October 13) labeled "junk" by Ayn Rand, called the book preposterous and endless, with no charm, humor, or nuances of character; a paean to survival of the fittest written like a battering ram. Another "junk" review appeared in the *Christian Science Monitor* (October 13) by Ruth Chapin Blackman, who maintained that the novel does its own purpose a disservice through caricature. There was, the reviewer lamented in a paradigm of nonconceptual analysis, no relevance to the book because, she wrote, the American economy is booming; furthermore, the novel is full of extremes and absolutes, with no middle ground or compromise; in fact, Blackman claims, had Rearden et al exercised their political responsibility, they wouldn't have been taken over.

The reviews in New York City—which Ayn Rand thought to be the only important reviews for any book—were mostly negative. The *New York Times Book Review* (October 13), selected by then ex-Communist Party member Granville Hicks as its reviewer. Hicks, in fact, had been an editor at Macmillan in 1936 and, according to Ayn Rand[4] had tried unsuccessfully to prevent Macmillan from publishing *We the Living.* Hicks called *Atlas Shrugged* a harangue and not a serious novel. He made fun of having heroes and villains and attacked the novel for being a tribute to the superior individual. The book, he concluded, was written out of hate, a conclusion whose sole basis was that it was set in a dying New York City. An unlikely plot, wrote *New York Post* reviewer W. G. Rogers (October 13), who would rather have read four shorter novels of the same total length. The novel, he said, is preposterous and endless, praises cutthroat competition, and lacks charm and humor. The review in the *New Yorker,* by Donald Malcolm (October 26), was predictably snide. It called the theme unbelievable and pointless. "After all," wrote Malcolm, "to warn contemporary America against abandoning its factories, neglecting technological progress and abolishing the profit motive seems a little like admonishing water against running uphill." (He obviously didn't foresee the ecology/environmentalism movement, which Ayn Rand termed "the anti-industrial revolution."[5]) *Time* magazine (October 14) began: "Is it a novel? Is it a nightmare? Is it Superman in the comic strip or Nietzschean version? The reader can't be sure. Then the truth emerges: Ayn Rand is smashing the world in order to rebuild it according to her own philosophy. And that philosophy must be read to be believed." After making fun of the story and Ayn Rand's writing, *Time* asserted that her philosophy is merely Nietzsche's inversion of Christianity and is ludicrously naïve. In fact, opined *Time,* her version of capitalism is such a hideous caricature that it will destroy faith in capitalism. Charles Rolo, in the *Atlantic Monthly* (November) said that *Atlas Shrugged* might be mildly described as execrable claptrap. In a typical distortion, he claimed that Ayn Rand is a Nietzschean and "holds that egoism can be deduced from A is A. Makes our most reactionary journals sound like do-gooders." *Atlas Shrugged*, he wrote, is an extreme expression of the aggressiveness and power worship which have been the Black Death of this century (a none-too-subtle way of calling Ayn Rand a Nazi).

In the *Saturday Review of Literature*, H. B. Woodward (October 12) called Ayn Rand a writer of "dazzling virtuosity" and *Atlas Shrugged* the equivalent of a fifteenth-century morality play which challenges the welfare state and the whole Christian ethic. However, Woodward thought the book to be over-simplified with its good guys and bad guys, had too much philosophy, demolished straw men and was shot through with hatred: of moralists, mystics, income taxes, professors, altruists, Communism, and Christianity. Demonstrating a certain inability to identify abstract principles, Woodward concluded that Ayn Rand's solution is the same as that of nineteenth-century altruists: a small, controlled Utopia. E. Nelson Hayes, writing in the *Progressive*, the journal of the Humanist Society (November), attacked selfishness, equated heroes with superheroes and referred to Aristotelian logic as "the blind almost mystical belief in either-or and in absolutes and the unreality of contradictions." In fact, he maintained, man has survived because of his power to love and has produced because of his ability to cooperate.

The Book-of-the-Month Club selected as its reviewer Clifton Fadiman. Fadiman was a prominent liberal and one of the models Ayn Rand used for Ellsworth Toohey, villain of *The Fountainhead*,[6] but his review wasn't worse than mixed. He found *Atlas Shrugged* to be "slightly mad," with an improbable thesis and a belief in the profit motive to the point of anti-Christianity. However, he praised Ayn Rand's narrative power and cunning plot and concluded with the opinion that she "possessed the story-telling ability of a Dumas or a Margaret Mitchell, as rare in our day as is her frenzied power-philosophy."[7]

Ayn Rand's uncompromising support of capitalism and its foundations had elicited predictable opposition from the liberal establishment. But what might seem surprising was the level and depth of opposition from Ayn Rand's supposed allies on the political right. So let us look at those reviews and then assess their significance.

The review on the front page of the *New York Herald-Tribune Book Review* (October 6) was written by well-known conservative John Chamberlain. Chamberlain praised the novel as monumental and inspired, a book that could satisfy readers on many levels: "First-rate pedagogy combined with first-rate entertainment." But the philosophic lesson to be learned, he thought, was merely that government interference with private property will destroy the economy. Demonstrating his lack of understanding of the novel, Chamberlain found one fault: the rejection of Christian morality. "To the Christian, everyone is redeemable. But Ayn Rand's ethical hardness may repel those who most need her message that charity should be voluntary. . . . She should not have tried to rewrite the Sermon on the Mount." Chamberlain repeated this theme in his review in *The Freeman* (December 1957), where he suggested she should have made "voluntarism" (i.e. subjectivism) rather than selfishness her philosophical touchstone. In a similar vein, E. Merrill Root, a conservative professor at Earlham College, praised the book and maintained that Rand's atheism was a mere superficial aberration and that her metaphysical roots tended toward religion despite her denial.[8]

Catholic publications, such as *The Sign* and *The Tablet*, were scandalized by her abandonment of God and belief that we have a right to exist for ourselves. Patricia Donegan in *Commonweal* (November 8) complained about the opposition to Original Sin and the lack of compassion, charity, and humility. Another Catholic reviewer, Francis E. O'Gorman, in the *Catholic Telegraph Register* (November 22), branded it "the most immoral and destructive book he'd ever read," but was mollified that its 500,000 words would not endure.[9] And Riley Hughes, in *Catholic World* (January 1958), opined that Rand subscribed not to reason but to rationalism, or why else would she sneer at anything mystical. But these reviews were mild, compared to the harshest attack on *Atlas Shrugged*.

WHITTAKER CHAMBERS'S REVIEW
IN THE *NATIONAL REVIEW*

The most significant review from the political right appeared in *The National Review* (December 28, 1957) and signaled the "official" conservative position.[10] The 2,700-word review was written by another ex-Communist, Whittaker Chambers, and was republished in 2005 and yet again on the *National Review* website in 2007 on the occasion of the fiftieth anniversary of the publication of the novel. Chambers spent a good part of his review sneering at the novel, which he characterized as "remarkably silly," "bumptious," and "preposterous"—a book that no sensible adult could take seriously. All of the characters were mere caricatures, which he thought spared Miss Rand the necessity of explaining "how they came to exist at all"—this despite the fact that Ayn Rand's novels are unusual, if not unique, in identifying and explaining the philosophic roots of her characters. His review came across as so non-objective to Rand's colleague Leonard Peikoff that he stated in his letter to the *National Review* (which they did not publish): "Mr. Chambers is an ex-Communist. He has attacked *Atlas Shrugged* in the best tradition of the Communists—by lies, smears, and cowardly misrepresentations. Mr. Chambers may have changed a few of his political views; he has not changed the method of intellectual analysis and evaluation of the Party to which he belonged."[11]

It is significant that the *National Review* wanted (and wants) to go on record as seeing no redeeming value in what has become a classic and a favorite novel of so many Americans, from businessmen to Hollywood stars.[12] But even more significant is Chambers' attack on Ayn Rand's ideas. His criticisms show how intent the *National Review* was (and is) to distance itself from Ayn Rand's philosophy.

Chambers advanced the claim—popular mainly with the Left—that Ayn Rand is a Nietzschean, with political views leading to Nazism. "Miss Rand acknowledges a grudging (sic) debt to one, and only one, earlier philosopher: Aristotle. I submit that she is indebted, and much more heavily, to Nietzsche. Just as her operatic businessmen are, in fact, Nietzschean supermen, so her ulcerous leftists are Nietzsche's 'last men.'" These supermen heroes are, according to Chambers, a "technocratic elite," who will "head us into dictatorship, however benign, living and acting beyond good and evil, a law unto itself (as Miss Rand believes it should be)." "From almost any page of *Atlas Shrugged*," he charges, "a voice can be heard, from painful necessity, commanding 'To a gas chamber—go!'" What are we to make of these charges? For one thing, it is impossible to take Chambers as an honest critic: he charges her with ideas (e.g., that some people are "beyond good and evil") that she went to great lengths to denounce (both dramatically and in Galt's Speech), so it seems as though Chambers' hatred of the book is beyond fact. But let us look briefly at some specifics. Is Ayn Rand's philosophy Nietzschean? It is beyond the scope of this chapter to explain why the answer is "no." Suffice to say that—although, as a teenager in Soviet Russia, she was temporarily attracted to Nietzsche's poetic paean to the individual— she soon realized that his philosophy was antithetical to hers, particularly his opposition to reason and his advocacy of determinism and of power over other people. "You are wrong," she would write later to a fan, "when you see any parallel between my philosophy and Nietzsche's."[13] As to her views on dictatorship (and its philosophical antecedents), those views were too well-established even in 1957 to necessitate any refutation of Chambers' claim. Her novella *Anthem*, published in 1937, established her credentials as anticollectivist, and in 1942, Mussolini's fascist government banned the Italian film of *We the Living* when the government realized that Rand was attacking collectivism per se, not merely Soviet Communism. By 1957, Ayn Rand was even more established as a champion of reason and individual rights, placing her in the tradition of the Founding Fathers and the Declaration of Independence. One might think that such ideas would endear her to the political Right—until one realizes that those ideas are precisely what the *National Review* conservatives oppose, as is evidenced by Chambers' other criticisms of *Atlas Shrugged*.

Rand's approach to ethics is not to Chambers' liking, because "everybody [in *Atlas Shrugged*] is either all good or all bad." Of course, perhaps employing some dialectical logic from his past, he also claimed that her heroes were presented as being "*beyond* [my italics] good and evil." Nevertheless, he is obviously opposed to Rand's moral absolutism. He is also unsympathetic to her individualism, because it leaves "no other nexus between man and man other than naked self-interest," a view he claims allies her with Marxism, although his criticism is almost identical to that leveled by Marx against individualism: "The concern of the French Constitution of 1793," wrote Marx, "is with the freedom of man as an isolated monad withdrawing into itself. . . . The human right of freedom is not based on the connection of man with man but rather on the separation of man from man. It is this right of separation, the right of the *limited* individual, limited unto himself."[14] Beyond his sneers at "naked self-interest" and his attempt to turn her ethics upside down by character-izing it as promoting a technocratic elite, Chambers makes no mention of her opposition to altruism or her insight that altruism is the ethical basis of dictatorship.

With respect to Ayn Rand's views on knowledge, Chambers' review is none too clear. His rejection of her absolutism regarding morality would likely ap-ply to knowledge in general, but he doesn't say so. However, he does charge her with advocating dogmatism and being "the bringer of a higher revela-tion." Apparently Chambers believed that any advocacy of certainty must be taken as Revealed Truth and thus dogma. But what is Chambers' alternative? We can't be sure from the review. It is not the alternative offered by the liber-als: skepticism. It is not reason, for nowhere does he laud the use of reason or chastise Ayn Rand for being anti-reason. In fact, his alternative to what he sees as Rand's dogmatism is his own religious dogmatism, which he described five years earlier in the first chapter of *Witness*, the story of his rejection of Communism and of his testimony against Alger Hiss: "I am an involuntary witness to God's grace and to the fortifying power of faith."[15] The Communist, he wrote, cannot admit "that there is something greater than Reason, greater than the logic of the mind."[16]

But it is with respect to Ayn Rand's metaphysics—her view of the nature of man and reality—that Chambers saves his major criticism. The story of *Atlas Shrugged*, he writes, "serves Miss Rand to get the customers inside the tent, and as a soapbox for delivering her Message. The Message is the thing. It is, in sum, a forthright philosophical materialism." This is a truly astounding claim and one explained only by holding, as Chambers clearly does, that anyone who is an atheist (i.e., does not accept the existence of invisible supernatural entities) is ipso facto a materialist. For Chambers, materialism is the only alternative to supernaturalism, a long-ago exposed false dichotomy that was at the heart of his rejection of Marxist philosophy: while gazing upon his infant daugh-ter's ear, he concluded that it couldn't have been constructed by chance, and therefore there must be a Divine Plan (the possibility of a natural explanation eluding him).[17] In fact, materialism is the view that only physical matter exists; anything else, for example, ideas, is reducible to physical matter. Thus Marx maintained "It is not the consciousness of men that determines their being, but, on the contrary, their social being that determines their consciousness."[18] But, for Ayn Rand, consciousness is not reducible to matter or to anything else; it is an irreducible primary, as she made clear in Galt's speech.[19]

The actual theme of *Atlas Shrugged*, one that is obvious in virtually every page, is the role of the *mind* in human existence. Ayn Rand's message is: human existence and progress depend on the mind, that is, the independent thinking of those who choose to think. Marx's materialism, which Chambers believes Ayn Rand accepts, is in direct contradiction to the message of *Atlas Shrugged*. The materialist (or labor) theory of value, a cornerstone of Marxism, is the direct opposite of Ayn Rand's views on production: the pages of *Atlas Shrugged* are replete with the message that it is ideas and intellectual labor—not physical labor—that move the world.

Chambers' philosophic foundations are revealed by his exploration of Ayn Rand's supposed materialism: "Like any consistent materialism, this one begins by rejecting God, religion, original sin, etc. etc. . . . Thus Randian Man, like Marxian Man, is made the center of a godless world." For Chambers, that's all it takes. "The Communist vision," he wrote in *Witness*, "is the vision of Man without God," with "man's mind replacing God as the creative intelligence of the world." [20] Accepting the Marxist pretense at being pro-reason and pro-science, Chambers writes that "to the challenge of God or Man, [Communism] gives the answer: Man." [21] So, despite its demand for blind obedience (to the Party), and its elevation of historical-economic forces over individual minds as the basic cause of human action, Communism is pro-reason—or so Chambers believes. Despite its decades of slavery and mass murder, Communism is pro-man—or so Chambers believes. Such are the blinders leading Chambers to lump Ayn Rand with Marxism. For there is, he recognizes, no other way to preserve religion. [22]

The irony of Chambers' rejection of Communism in favor of Christianity is that the two are really philosophic brothers under the skin. Both advocate altruism ("from each according to his ability, to each according to his need" said Marx, echoing the Bible [23]), reject free-will, demand obedience to an unseen entity (society or God). Both are—as Ayn Rand noted—"enemies of the independent mind." [24]

From the time that Ayn Rand—at the age of nine—decided to become a fiction writer, her goal had been the creation of "the ideal man." That ideal was first manifested in Howard Roark in *The Fountainhead* and culminated in the men and women of *Atlas Shrugged*. As she wrote in her postscript, "About the Author": "My philosophy, in essence, is the concept of man as a heroic being, with his own happiness as the moral And that is the purpose of his life, with productive achievement as his noblest activity, and reason as his only absolute." This view of man, I submit, is at the heart of Chambers' antipathy to *Atlas Shrugged*. The Christian view has no place for man as heroic or for life on earth as the ultimate happiness. The best that Chambers can provide as an alternative to what he thinks is Ayn Rand's animalistic pursuit of happiness is tragedy, and he laments her view, in which man's "tragic fate becomes, without God, more tragic and much lonelier." [25] From the standpoint of the philosophy of *Atlas Shrugged*, the most damning statement in Chambers' book is his false description of Marxism: "[Marxism] is the vision of man's liberated mind, by the sole force of its rational intelligence, redirecting man's destiny and reorganizing man's life and the world."[26]

Four years after the publication of *Atlas Shrugged*, Ayn Rand presented—at Princeton University—a lecture entitled "Conservatism: an Obituary." In this, and many subsequent talks and essays, she argued that no matter how philosophically bad was the Left, the conservatives were worse, because they attempted to justify freedom and capitalism on faith and altruism, views that undermined capitalism rather than supported it. Freedom, she argued, is impossible on any philosophy that holds an individual to be moral only if he lives for others. On that ethical view, his life would belong to others, that is he would be a slave.

> Intellectually, to rest one's case on *faith* means to concede that reason is on the side of one's enemies—that one has no rational arguments to offer. The "conservatives" claim that their case rests on faith, means that there are no rational arguments to support the American system [that they're supposedly defending], no rational justification for freedom, justice, property, individual rights, that these rest on a mystic revelation and can be accepted only *on faith*—that in reason and logic the enemy is right, but men must hold faith as superior to reason.[27]

CONCLUSION

Ayn Rand did not expect much from reviews of her books. As she stated in her biographical interviews, "I had read too many book reviews of books that I had read, and I had seen the terrible contradictions, [with] no standards nor reasons given." Nor did she blame herself for bad reviews: "If anybody praises me I want to know why. And, particularly, if anybody criticizes me I want to know why. And if I see arbitrary statements, I discount them immediately, particularly if they're distorting statements." Nevertheless, the reviews of *Atlas Shrugged* had an important effect on Ayn Rand: they helped convince her of the urgent need to spread her philosophy.

> The worst part for me of the after-*Atlas* period, was the fact that I could not make up my mind am I a fiction writer or am I a philosopher. Or rather, I knew that I was both, and neither prospect alone quite appealed to me. I did not know what I wanted to undertake next. I was enormously shocked by the state of the culture and by the attacks on *Atlas*, not by the attacks themselves, but by the fact that there was nobody to oppose them. I had expected more *intelligent* smears. Actually in the thirties, reviewers and columnists and everybody else was on a higher intellectual level. I had predicted the smears to some extent. I had told Random House not to count on a single good review; if they got one it's possible, but that would be gravy. But what shocked me was the abysmal, stupid, hooliganism of the reviews, that they were self-contradictory even within their own terms. Total distortions, and that there was nobody objecting to it. That the whole state of the culture suddenly appeared much worse than I had imagined.[28]

She was not willing to concede the battle to her philosophic enemies, to let them be the only ones speaking about the philosophy of *Atlas Shrugged*. And when she was convinced by Leonard Peikoff and others that her philosophy was not only more unique than she realized but wasn't as self-evident to others as it was to herself, she resolved to explain the details of that philosophy, which she did in lectures, essays, and books for the next twenty-five years.

NOTES

1. See my other essays on the reviews of Ayn Rand's novels: "Reviews of *We the Living*," in Robert Mayhew, ed., *Essays on Ayn Rand's* We the Living (Lanham, Md.: Lexington Books, 2004); "Reviews of *Anthem*," in Robert Mayhew, ed., *Essays on Ayn Rand's* Anthem (Lanham, Md.: Lexington Books, 2005); "*The Fountainhead* Reviews," in Robert Mayhew, ed., *Essays on Ayn Rand's* The Fountainhead (Lanham, Md.: Lexington Books, 2007).

2. All reviews quoted herein are from Ayn Rand's collection in the Ayn Rand Papers, located in the Ayn Rand Archives, Irvine, Calif.

3. See the "About the Author" afterword to *Atlas Shrugged*.

4. In her Biographical Interviews (Ayn Rand Archives).

5. See "The Anti-Industrial Revolution," in Ayn Rand, *Return of the Primitive: The Anti-Industrial Revolution*, Peter Schwartz, ed. (New York: Meridian, 1999).

6. Ayn Rand noted that she "always thought of [Harold] Laski and Fadiman as the main sources [of Ellsworth Toohey]. . . . Well [Fadiman] was the arch literateur of the Left. In other words, the intellectual who had enormous influence in Leftist circles and was kind of an elegant literary type. Enormously phony. . . . And it was that intellectual superciliousness of his, combined with Leftism, that was just right for Toohey." Biographical Interviews (Ayn Rand Archives).

7. As a consequence of that review and a shorter one he wrote in *Holiday* magazine, under the heading "Current Books I've Liked," Miss Rand—as she related in the same interviews—"sort of lifted him a few rungs in hell." Biographical Interviews (Ayn Rand Archives).

8. E. Merrill Root, "What About Ayn Rand," *National Review*, June 30, 1960, quoted in George H. Nash, *The Conservative Intellectual Movement* (Wilmington, Del.: ISI Books, 2006), 240.

9. Similarly, in a classic case of wishful thinking, William F. Buckley began his obituary of Ayn Rand with: "Ayn Rand is dead. So, incidentally, is the philosophy she sought to launch dead; it was in fact stillborn" (*National Review*, April 2, 1982). Note that more than fifty years later it still sells more than 130,000 copies per year.

10. Whittaker Chambers, "Big Sister is Watching You," *National Review*, December 28, 1957.

11. Peikoff's letter is published for the first time in this volume. See chapter 7.

12. A 1991 survey by the Library of Congress found *Atlas Shrugged* to be second in influence only to the Bible.

13. Ayn Rand, letter to Libby Parker, in Michael S. Berliner, ed., *Letters of Ayn Rand* (New York: Dutton), 614.

14. Karl Marx, from "On the Jewish Question," quoted in Eugene Kamenka, *The Ethical Foundations of Marxism* (New York: Praeger, 1962), 64.

15. Whittaker Chambers, *Witness* (Washington, DC: Regnery Gateway, 1952), 6.

16. Chambers, *Witness*, 15

17. Chambers, *Witness*, 16.

18. Karl Marx, Preface to "A Contribution to the Critique of Political Economy" in Eugene Kamenka, ed., *The Portable Karl Marx* (New York: Viking Penguin, 1983), 160.

19. See *Atlas Shrugged* (933). For a discussion of Rand's position, see Leonard Peikoff, *Objectivism: the Philosophy of Ayn Rand* (New York: Dutton, 1991), 4ff.

20. Chambers, *Witness*, 9.

21. Chambers, *Witness*, 13.

22. M. Stanton Evans, in his 1967 critique of Ayn Rand in *The National Review* lamented that she tried to justify capitalism without its supposedly necessary base, that is "the Christian culture which has given birth to all our freedoms." M. Stanton Evans, "The Gospel According to Ayn Rand," *National Review*, October 3, 1967, quoted in Nash, 541.

23. Karl Marx, "Critique of the Gotha Program" in Kamenka, ed., *Portable Karl Marx*, 541. "And all that believed were together, and had all things common; And sold their possessions and goods, and parted them to all men, as every man had need " (*Acts* 2:44–45) "Neither was there any among them that lacked: for as many as were possessors of lands or houses sold them, and brought the prices of the things that were sold, and laid them down at the apostles' feet: and distribution was made unto every man according as he had need." (*Acts* 4:34–35)

24. Ayn Rand, letter to Stephen Sipos, in Berliner, *Letters of Ayn Rand*, 565. For the similarities in the two supposedly opposed views, see Leonard Peikoff, "Religion vs. America," in Ayn Rand, *The Voice of Reason* (New York: New American Library, 1989), 76–77.

25. Gary Wills, as part of *National Review's* ongoing angst over Ayn Rand and *Atlas Shrugged*, echoed this tragic view of man: "When [John] Galt asserts the immediate perfectibility of man . . . he is working from the first principle of historical Liberalism," in contrast to conservatism. Gary Wills, "But is Ayn Rand Conservative?" *National Review*, February 27, 1960, quoted in Nash, 241.

26. Chambers, "Big Sister is Watching You."

27. Ayn Rand, "Conservatism: an Obituary," in *Capitalism: the Unknown Ideal* (New York: New American Library, 1967), 197. Rand could have had Chambers in mind, for he wrote in *Witness*: "[God] is the only guarantor of freedom," and political freedom "is only a political reading of the Bible" (16).

28. Bibliographical interviews (Ayn Rand Archives).

8

Reply to Whittaker Chambers

Leonard Peikoff

Editor's note: *Leonard Peikoff wrote this letter to the editors of the* National Review *(William F. Buckley and Frank S. Meyer) in response to Whittaker Chambers'* review of Atlas Shrugged *in the December 28, 1957 issue. (Dr. Peikoff's letter was also dated December 28.) The* National Review *did not publish it. The original letter is located in the Ayn Rand Archives; it is published here for the first time. Note that although Ayn Rand's disagreements with conservatives go back to the 1930s, at the time this letter was written she and her associates (including Dr. Peikoff) still used "conservative" to refer broadly to anyone who claimed to defend capitalism and the original political philosophy of the American Founding Fathers.*

Sirs:

Whittaker Chambers' irresponsible review of Ayn Rand's *Atlas Shrugged*, in your issue of Dec. 28th, is a combination of distortion and fear-inspired invective. It is a review which a respectable magazine—to say nothing of a conservative one—would not publish.

To compare Miss Rand's heroes to Nietzschean supermen, to say of her that she "consistently mistakes raw force for strength," to identify her politically with the Hitlerian "Right," and to attribute to her the advocacy of a Big Brother-technocratic elite "living and acting beyond good and evil"—is not stupidity on Mr. Chambers' part. It is willful perversion. Were I in philosophic agreement with Mr. Chambers, I would say that his review is the proof of his doctrine that men are born with Original Sin and are inherently corrupt. But I am not in agreement with Mr. Chambers. He cannot blame Adam or God for that review. It is his responsibility.

Miss Rand's philosophy, unequivocally stated and demonstrated in *Atlas Shrugged*, is that man's life depends upon the constant and unremitting use of his mind in the task of identifying reality and gaining knowledge; it is, she

shows, the process of thinking, the adherence to logic, the exercise of rationality, that makes it possible for man to take the productive actions necessary
to achieve the values upon which his survival depends. The heroes of *Atlas
Shrugged,* as an expression of this philosophy, are the men of greatest rationality and greatest achievement. Where in this does Mr. Chambers discover any
vestige of the Dionysian frenzy and anti-reason rampant in Nietzsche's characterization of his supermen? Where in this does Mr. Chambers discover the advocacy of raw force by Miss Rand, or the equation of raw force with strength?

Miss Rand's philosophy states further that, since the use of the mind is
man's cardinal virtue, a moral social system must guarantee each and every
man the inalienable right to freedom—freedom of thought and of action,
and the freedom to keep the property his thought and action have created.
Miss Rand clearly states that there are only two choices in the construction
of political systems: a system that respects individual rights—or all those systems which violate them. She points out that contemporary political theorists
argue only over *whose* rights are to be violated, by whom, and for whom, but
that all agree that the sacrifice of some men to others is a moral ideal and a
political necessity. To dramatize her unalterable opposition to any form of
human sacrifice, to any form of the idea that a ruling elite may dispose of the
lives of other men and live and act "beyond good and evil," she has her hero,
John Galt, offered by the collectivists total dictatorial power over America. He
refuses. He is tortured by the collectivists for refusing to rule. The collectivists,
the advocates of raw force, all but kill him, but he remains adamant. In the
name of his vision of a country where there will be no masters and slaves, no
rulers and ruled, no commissars or Gestapo or ruling elite of any kind, he is
willing to risk his life. There is no honest way of interpreting this philosophy
as akin to Hitler, Big Brother, or technocracy.

Mr. Chambers declares that Miss Rand's philosophy is materialism. How
can a philosophy which worships the creative, thinking mind be called materialism? How can a philosophy be called materialism which declares that
one should go on strike against the world and abandon all its goods rather
than renounce his mind? It could only be so called by a mystic such as Mr.
Chambers, for whom there are only two alternatives: either you love life on
earth—in which case you are a vulgar materialist; or you hate life on earth and
believe in a mystical super-dimension whose existence and nature you know
by blinding revelations—in which case your anti-materialism consists in hating everything material.

Mr. Chambers is an ex-Communist. He has attacked *Atlas Shrugged* in the
best tradition of the Communists—by lies, smears, and cowardly misrepresentations. Mr. Chambers may have changed a few of his political views; he has
not changed the method of intellectual analysis and evaluation of the Party
to which he belonged. And the *National Review,* an ostensibly conservative
publication, permitted these tactics to be used on the first book which has ever
provided a philosophic, rational basis for capitalism.

I am a lecturer in philosophy at two New York universities. I have occasion frequently to discuss with students the unfortunate state of political affairs in America and to recommend conservative publications to them. I will sooner in future recommend the *Daily Worker* than the *National Review*. The *Daily Worker* at least is open and honest in stating its political position. It is a tragedy of America that it is the *National Review*, which is supposed to serve as the conservative counterweight. The desperate state of America is easily explained if it is you at the *National Review* who represent contemporary conservatism.

9

Atlas Shrugged and the Metaphysics of Values

Tore Boeckmann

In *The Fountainhead*, Dominique Francon visits the construction site of the Enright House, a building designed by her lover, Howard Roark.

> She thought, standing there in the heart of the building, that if she had nothing of him, nothing but his body, here it was, offered to her, the rest of him, to be seen and touched, open to all; the girders and the conduits and the sweeping reaches of space were his and could not have been anyone else's in the world; his, as his face, as his soul; here was the shape he had made and the thing within him which had caused him to make it, the end and the cause together, the motive power eloquent in every line of steel, a man's self, hers for this moment, hers by grace of her seeing it and understanding.[1]

As readers of *The Fountainhead*, and Ayn Rand's other novels, we can have nearly the same kind of experience that Dominique has in the Enright House. None of us is Ayn Rand's lover, as Dominique is Roark's—but here, in her novels, is the rest of her, accessible to all. "An artist reveals his naked soul in his work,"[2] wrote Ayn Rand—and so she did in hers.

She did so primarily by means of her themes and her plots.

THEME AND PLOT-THEME

An art work's theme is the core of its abstract meaning.[3] And observe that Ayn Rand's themes express her personality.

The theme of *We the Living* is "the individual against the state."[4] The theme of *Anthem* is "the meaning of man's ego."[5] The theme of *The Fountainhead* is "individualism versus collectivism, not in politics, but in man's soul."[6] The theme of *Atlas Shrugged* is "the role of the mind in man's existence."[7] These themes address, each from its own angle, Ayn Rand's main thematic concern: the sanctity of the individual, the ego, the sovereign mind—as opposed to any form of collectivism. On the basis of theme alone, a reader familiar with some of her novels would easily recognize any other as "a typical Ayn Rand novel."

Such a main thematic concern, expressing the personality of the writer, is not unique to Ayn Rand. For instance, Friedrich Schiller is concerned with the preconditions of political liberty. Edmond Rostand is concerned with man's quest for integrity in the face of the split he thinks exists between man's mind and his body. This is partly why the authorship of a Schiller or a Rostand play is easily recognizable.

"The theme," writes Ayn Rand, "sets the writer's standard of selection, directing the innumerable choices he has to make and serving as the integrator of the novel."[8] However, a theme, as an abstraction, has a major limitation: it yields only abstract integration, not the concrete unity an artist seeks. Suppose Ayn Rand tried to create *Atlas Shrugged* armed only with the abstract theme: "the role of the mind in man's existence." She might think of the first man who discovered how to make fire, the building of an American railroad, Aristotle writing the *Analytics,* and, by contrast, the backwardness of mystical India. But these concretes are separated by continents and millennia. They are a grab bag, impossible to combine into the unity of art.

To achieve concrete unity, a writer needs a concrete standard of selection. He or she needs a *plot-theme* (or its equivalent). "Plot-theme," a concept originated by Ayn Rand, means "the central conflict or 'situation' of a story."[9] This conflict isolates in the story's subject matter a particular abstract meaning—the theme—and then, by virtue of its inner logic, unfolds into a unified progression of events in which the thematic abstraction remains highlighted.[10]

Ayn Rand stated the plot-theme of *Atlas Shrugged* as "the men of the mind going on strike against an altruist-collectivist society."[11] This is the essence of the central conflict, and it isolates the thematic meaning: "the mind's role in man's existence." It does not, however, unfold in a logical progression of events; all it leads to is one person going on strike, and another, and another. On its own, Ayn Rand's essentialized formulation is too general to do the work of a plot-theme. To reach a full plot-theme, she had to expand her idea into a complex conflict between specific individuals.

Let us put ourselves in her situation. We start with the idea of "the men of the mind going on strike against an altruist-collectivist society." This indicates two obvious categories of characters: the men of the mind, and the looters against whom they go on strike. Less obviously, a third category is indicated: those men of the mind who are not *yet* strikers.

We now have looters, strikers, and scabs—but no individuals. However, if there is a strike, somebody must have called the strike. This would be the novel's hero. Let us call him John Galt. Also, if there are scabs, one particular scab must be the last holdout and the hero's most formidable antagonist. Let us call her Dagny Taggart. And if these two characters fall in love, we have an even more complex central conflict.

The conflict depends on the premises of the characters. The looters uphold altruism and collectivism, and so claim the right to enslave man's mind. The strikers uphold a new morality of rational self-interest which condemns such enslavement as evil. Dagny is against enslaving the mind, but also against the strike, since she thinks that the looters might yet be swayed by an appeal to reason and self-interest. Galt knows that this is impossible, since the looters' attack on the mind is caused, fundamentally, by their hatred of life.

Like its rudimentary precursor, this expanded conflict situation isolates the abstract meaning "the mind's role in man's existence"—but *now* the conflict is complex enough to generate a logical progression of events. For instance, if Dagny comes to suspect the existence of a "destroyer" who is draining the minds of the world, and if she can somehow predict which man of the mind the destroyer will remove next, she will logically try to reach him in order to convince him to remain. In the actual novel, this happens when Dagny flies to Afton, Utah to reach Quentin Daniels, and then follows Galt's plane to the valley.

These derivative events convey the same abstract meaning that was isolated in the plot-theme: the role of man's mind. Dagny follows Galt's plane in order to stop the destroyer from removing the world's minds—because she recognizes the importance of the mind and how much the world needs it. At the same time, Galt is taking Daniels to the valley—because he recognizes both that the mind cannot work under compulsion and that the looters, who set the terms of society, hate the mind and will never stop enslaving it until they are utterly crushed.

By means of the plot-theme, the theme of *Atlas Shrugged* is carried from the novel's inceptive idea onward to every derivative part. The theme becomes like an aspect of the DNA of a living organism. Present in the first cell, it is carried on intact through every cell division, and thus to every part of the organic unity that it helps to shape and build.

EXTRA-THEMATIC VALUES

Just as a writer may have a main thematic concern, so he may have favorite fields of human action from which he draws his concrete subject matter. Schiller's plays deal with matters of politics, statesmanship, and warfare. Rostand's plays deal with poetry, swordsmanship, and love. Ayn Rand's novels deal with productive work and love.

In *The Fountainhead*, Howard Roark battles for his building career against a collectivist public, and as a result is thrown into romantic conflict with Dominique, who thinks the collective will win. In *Anthem*, Equality 7-2521 discovers his ego primarily through his reinvention of the electric light, but partly also through his love for Liberty 5-3000. In *We the Living,* the two highest values that the totalitarian state denies Kira are her engineering career and the man she loves. In *Atlas Shrugged,* the men of the mind go on strike—that is, leave their professions—so the novel obviously deals with productive work. And as noted, it is also a love story.

Ayn Rand's focus on work and love conveys a premise: that these are the two crucially important fields of human values. This premise is not unique to Ayn Rand, but it is characteristic of her. Its projection is part of what makes an Ayn Rand novel "an Ayn Rand novel."

Yet the premise of "the primacy of work and love" is (usually) not an aspect of Ayn Rand's themes. It is an *extra-thematic* premise.

To grasp the role of extra-thematic premises, or values, observe first that *any* concretization of an abstraction will have aspects that are incidental to that abstraction. Take the character of Howard Roark. He concretizes the abstraction of "individualism," because he consistently goes against collective opinion. He also is described as having a body of long, straight lines and angles, which has nothing to do with individualism. But as a concrete human being, he must have *some* appearance; Ayn Rand's only choice is whether to leave his description partly up to chance or make it reflect values of hers other than the theme—that is, extra-thematic values. Since nothing in art should be chance, she does the latter: the long lines of Roark's body reflect Ayn Rand's image of her ideal man. (For evidence of this, see any photograph of her husband.)

The same pattern holds for the construction of a story's plot-theme. The plot-theme corresponds to the theme but is itself a concrete and as such has many thematically incidental characteristics. And a good author will make these express extra-thematic values and premises—as Ayn Rand does in featuring love and productive work as the main fields of plot action.

GOOD-VERSUS-GOOD CONFLICTS

Now take another thematically incidental characteristic of the plot-theme of *Atlas Shrugged*: the most important conflict strand puts in opposition two morally good persons, Galt and Dagny. Their conflict is not the most fundamental—it is derivative of the conflict between strikers and looters, which sets good against evil—but the Galt-Dagny conflict is the most emotionally intense, the most difficult to solve, and the most dangerous. For instance, it is only because Galt loves Dagny that he follows her from the valley and back to the world, risking capture by the looters. As he tells her: "My actual enemies are of no danger to me. *You* are" (961).[12]

The same pattern holds for the other good-versus-good conflicts in *Atlas Shrugged,* such as that between Hank Rearden and Francisco d'Anconia, and for Roark's conflict with Dominique in *The Fountainhead,* and Kira's conflict with Leo and Andrei in *We the Living*. These are good-versus-good conflicts which depend on, but supersede in importance, the clash of good and evil.

The supremacy in her novels of good-versus-good conflicts expresses definite premises of Ayn Rand's. First, the relegation of the good-versus-evil conflicts to secondary status projects the relative impotence of evil, the view that evil is a minor concern in human life. Second, on the positive side, the supremacy of good versus good projects a benevolent view of life. Since the good is the rational, the good but mistaken person can always come to see the truth, which means that the most difficult and painful of life's conflicts can potentially be resolved—and resolved not merely through the victory of one party and the defeat of the other, but through the ultimate spiritual victory of both.

The premises of the impotence of evil and the benevolence of life are extra-thematic to Ayn Rand's fiction. Yet the concrete material that projects these premises is not added on to the dramatization of the theme. Ayn Rand does not "throw in a love affair" in order to convey the importance of love, and neither does she throw in, say, the arrest of a criminal to convey the impotence of evil, or a trip to an amusement park to convey benevolence. Rather, all of these extra-thematic premises are projected through the characteristics of the central conflict which dramatizes the theme.

In this plot-theme, the extra-thematic premises join the theme to become part of a story's DNA, and thus in turn are carried forward to every limb and feature of the full-grown whole.

ROMANTIC TESTS OF STRENGTH

Ayn Rand's novels are love stories, but so are the novels of many other writers. Her fiction projects her individual personality not merely by the fact that it deals with love, but by virtue of the distinctive Ayn Rand *approach* to the issues of love and sex.

Consider the following two passages from *We the Living*, featuring the heroine, Kira.

> Victor's arm slowly encircled Kira's shoulders. She moved away. Victor bent close to her and whispered, sighing, that he had waited to see her alone, that he had known romances, yes, many romances, women had been too kind to him, but he had always been unhappy and lonely, searching for his ideal, that he could understand her, that her sensitive soul was bound by conventions, unawakened to life—and love. Kira moved farther away and tried to change the subject.[13]

Later, Kira meets Leo, the love of her life.

> He was tall; his collar was raised; a cap was pulled over his eyes. His mouth, calm, severe, contemptuous, was that of an ancient chieftain who could order men to die, and his eyes were such as could watch it. . . .

He stopped and looked at her. "Good evening," he said.

And Kira who believed in miracles, said: "Good evening."

He stepped closer and looked at her with narrowed eyes, smiling. But the corners of his mouth did not go up when he smiled; they went down, raising his upper lip into a scornful arc.[14]

It is no coincidence that Kira, an Ayn Rand heroine, responds to Leo and not to Victor. Victor is pleading, manipulative, and weak; Leo is masterful and strong. And to Ayn Rand, masculinity is strength, while femininity is hero worship—the desire to look up to man.

A woman is not an inferior human being; intellectually and morally, she ought to be the equal of the man she worships. What she desires to look up to is specifically his masculinity—his strength, physical and mental.[15] (Generally, men are physically stronger than women, but they do not have any superior mental capacity. If they have greater mental fortitude, it is, in my view, an issue of living up to a greater responsibility posed by their superior physical strength.)

Now consider this description of Dagny, the heroine of *Atlas Shrugged*:

> She stood as she always did, straight and taut, her head lifted impatiently. It was the unfeminine pose of an executive. But her naked shoulder betrayed the fragility of the body under the black dress, and the pose made her most truly a woman. The proud strength became a challenge to someone's superior strength, and the fragility a reminder that the challenge could be broken. (154)

Note Dagny's psychology here. As a woman, she expects to look up to a lover's superior strength—and therefore she expects of a potential lover that he demonstrate his strength in some appropriate way—and therefore she posits a *challenge* to such a man. A similar psychology is at work when young lovers run along a beach, the woman trying to avoid capture by the man. And it is at work in a classic erotic motif in art: nymphs fleeing from a pursuing satyr.

A writer who shares (at least in essence) Ayn Rand's view of masculinity and femininity can project that view in his story. He can project it in isolated touches of characterization, as in Kira's encounters with Victor and Leo. Or he can project it much more forcefully through the nature of his plot conflicts. He can turn a conflict of lovers into a romantic test of strength.

A famous example is *Turandot*, the play by Gozzi and adapted by Schiller on which the libretto for Puccini's opera is based. Turandot, princess of China, regards any yielding of control to a man as an intolerable breach of her independence. She therefore demands of any suitor that he solve three riddles, and the price of failure is death. When she finally falls in love with one of her suitors, her extravagant challenge becomes a romantic test of strength.

Turandot was a favorite of Ayn Rand's. And in her own fiction, she presents equally grand test-of-strength conflicts: between Roark and Dominique in *The Fountainhead*, and between Galt and Dagny in *Atlas Shrugged*.

Dagny first meets Galt when she crashes in the valley. She learns that he is the destroyer who has been draining the minds from the world, and from her railroad. She learns that he loves her; and she falls in love with him. And as soon as they are in love, their conflict over the issue of the strike turns into a romantic test of strength.

Consider the scene where Dagny refuses to claim the money in her account at the Mulligan Bank—the gold Ragnar Danneskjöld has seized on her behalf from the looters. Galt tells her: "If you don't claim it, some part of it—a very small part—will be turned over to me in your name." "Why?" "To pay for your room and board."

Galt explains that he intends to hold Dagny in the valley for a month.

> "There's no rule demanding that I hold you, but by forcing your way here, you've given me the right to any choice I make—and I'm going to hold you simply because I want you here. If, at the end of a month, you decide that you wish to go back, you will be free to do so. Not until then."
>
> She sat straight, the planes of her face relaxed, the shape of her mouth softened by the faint, purposeful suggestion of a smile; it was the dangerous smile of an adversary, but her eyes were coldly brilliant and veiled at once, like the eyes of an adversary who fully intends to fight, but hopes to lose. . . .
>
> "I shall comply with your terms," she answered; her voice had the shrewd, confident, deliberating slowness of a trader. "But I shall not permit the use of that money for my debts."
>
> "How else do you propose to comply?"
>
> "I propose to earn my room and board."
>
> "By what means?"
>
> "By working."
>
> "In what capacity?"
>
> "In the capacity of your cook and housemaid." (759–60)

In this conflict scene, Dagny is acting to preserve her integrity as a non-striker, and even an antistriker—and from this perspective, her actions project thematic meaning. But at the same time, and as an additional aspect of the same conflict, she is challenging Galt romantically—which projects Ayn Rand's extra-thematic values in the field of love and sex.

Now compare this conflict with that between Kira and Leo in *We the Living*. Kira falls in love with Leo at first sight—because of the strength she reads in his face. And she is not mistaken: there are scenes in the novel where Leo shows tremendous strength. But his strength is not evidenced in the central conflict. The Kira-Leo conflict arises because of her actions to save his life—actions she takes only because he himself has given up the struggle. So in regard to the central problem and conflict of the novel, Kira is in fact stronger than Leo.

Leo is not unworthy of Kira's love. He has given up, not from weakness, but from disgust. When Kira tells him, "One can fight," he answers: "Fight what? Sure, you can muster the most heroic in you to fight lions. But to whip your soul to a sacred white heat to fight lice!"[16]

Leo's giving up might be understandable, but it prevents the novel's hero-heroine conflict from being a romantic test of strength. And thus Ayn Rand's view of the essence of man-woman relationships, while present in many smaller touches, is absent from the central conflict. It is not part of the novel's DNA.

As a result, *We the Living* is not as characteristic of Ayn Rand as are her later novels.

THE SPIRITUAL NOBILITY OF MATERIAL PRODUCTION

It is a common view that romanticism, which evokes a quest for the ideal, may be congruous to medieval romances but not to the modern world of capitalism and industrial production. One exponent of this view was the nineteenth-century German writer Theodor Fontane, who said that "romanticism is finished on this earth; the age of the railway has dawned."[17]

Another exponent of the same view is Lillian Rearden in *Atlas Shrugged*. Her husband, Hank Rearden, gives her the first thing made from the first heat of the first order of Rearden Metal. "He did not know that he stood straight and that the gesture of his arm was that of a returning crusader offering his trophy to his love, when he dropped a small chain of metal into her lap." Her reaction? "You mean it's fully as valuable as a piece of railroad rails?" (36).

Unlike Fontane and Lillian, Ayn Rand upholds the spiritual nobility of material production, including the railroad industry. She is both a romantic novelist—and in perfect sympathy with her greatest heroine, Dagny, who feels that the concourse of the Taggart Terminal "looked like a temple" and its "vaulting held the solemn peace of a cathedral" (59).

Or take the description of John Galt as he lies strapped to the torture machine:

> His naked body looked strangely out of place in this cellar. . . . The long lines of his body, running from his ankles to the flat hips, to the angle of the waist, to the straight shoulders, looked like a statue of ancient Greece, sharing that statue's meaning, but stylized to a longer, lighter, more active form and a gaunter strength, suggesting more restless an energy—the body, not of a chariot driver, but of a builder of airplanes. And as the meaning of a statue of ancient Greece—the statue of man as a god—clashed with the spirit of this century's halls, so his body clashed with a cellar devoted to prehistorical activities. The clash was the greater, because he seemed to belong with electric wires, with stainless steel, with precision instruments, with the levers of a control board. (1141)

Like a Greek statue, Galt's body represents the idea of "man as god"—but in a form appropriate to the post-Industrial Revolution world, where man is God-like specifically in his mastery of the power of reason; in his ability, not to drive chariots, but to build airplanes.

For Ayn Rand, material invention and production belong on the most exalted level of human values. This premise is a distinctive aspect of her personality—and of her fiction, where it is reflected in the *professions* of her heroes. They are engineers, inventors, businessmen—men who translate the theoretical products of reason into the practical requirements of human life.

Kira in *We the Living* studies engineering. Equality 7-2521 in *Anthem* reinvents the electric light. Howard Roark in *The Fountainhead* is an architect. The most important strikers in *Atlas Shrugged* are an inventor (Galt) and a copper magnate (Francisco). The most important scabs are a railroad executive (Dagny) and a steel magnate (Rearden).

The material-production professions of Ayn Rand's heroes are not generally directed by the themes of her novels. The theme of *We the Living* is "the individual against the state," but the totalitarian state is opposed to *any* private career, not just an engineering career. The theme of *Anthem* is "the meaning of man's ego," which the hero discovers through engineering; but as far as the theme is concerned, he could as well have discovered it through a pursuit of art (as his friend International 4-8818 starts to do). The theme of *The Fountainhead* is "individualism versus collectivism, not in politics, but in man's soul," but the individualist in any field, not just architecture, confronts the social obstacle of psychological collectivism.

In other words, the professions of Ayn Rand's heroes project the nobility of material production as an *extra-thematic* premise.

However, the mere fact that a fiction character has a material-production profession does not convey spiritual grandeur. A naturalistic author like Sinclair Lewis could write a novel about "a typical American architect of the nineteen-twenties and thirties" and yet convey little sense of nobility. Why, then, does the fact that *Roark* is an architect convey nobility? Only because he is presented as a hero of individualism and individual integrity—which *in combination* with the fact that he is an architect logically implies that such exalted moral concepts apply just as much to a practical field like architecture as it does to, say, art or science.

The extra-thematic projection (of the nobility of material production) is a function of a theme-incidental characteristic of the plot (Roark's profession) but only within the context of the novel's dramatization of its theme (individualism).

Similarly, *We the Living* projects the view that engineering can be a sacred calling only because the *theme* of *We the Living*—the sanctity of the life and values of the individual—is dramatized by the heroine's loss of her engineering career. And *Anthem* projects the view that practical invention springs from the source of spiritual values, man's ego, only because the *theme* of *Anthem*—the importance of the ego—is dramatized by means of the hero's reinvention of the electric light. In all these cases, we see essentially the same extra-thematic premise ("the spiritual nobility of material pursuits") being projected by a thematically incidental characteristic of the story—in the context of the dramatization of the theme.

Now observe that Ayn Rand's view of material production is projected in somewhat different forms, and with varying strength, in her novels.

Ayn Rand said about *We the Living* that "it is as near to an autobiography as I will ever write." Yet she did not follow the time-honored convention of writers of making their fictional alter ego a painter. Nor did she make Kira a student of history, as she herself had been. She made her an engineering student. Why? Her explanation is found in the following statement: "My view of what a good autobiography should be is contained in the title that Louis H. Sullivan gave to the story of his life: *The Autobiography of an Idea*. It is only in this sense that *We the Living* is my autobiography and that Kira, the heroine, is me."[18] And what is the *idea* that Ayn Rand shared with Kira and that directed her choice of Kira's profession? The spiritual nobility of material production.

In the first draft of *We the Living*, Kira did study history at university. Ayn Rand later changed her subject to engineering, for the reason given above; but note that in doing so, she would have had to make no major plot changes. It does not really matter for the story what Kira studies in college. Her profession is incidental to the nature of the central conflict.

We the Living is the story of a girl who happens to study engineering. By contrast, *The Fountainhead* is the story of an architect. Roark's profession could not be changed without the whole novel changing. The extra-thematic premise of the nobility of material production is here projected by an aspect of the story—Roark's being an architect—that is crucial to the central conflict, even though incidental relative to the theme. This adds strength to the projection of the nobility of architecture.

Atlas Shrugged is a more complex case. The theme—the idea that man depends on his mind—applies to all legitimate fields, including science, philosophy, medicine, law, and art. Accordingly, the strikers in the novel include professors of philosophy, economics, history, and psychology, a doctor, a judge, a composer, several writers, a sculptor, and an actress. A novel about the mind on strike—demonstrating the importance of the mind—could be told from the perspective of any of them. And observe that Ayn Rand's statement of the plot-theme, "the men of the mind going on strike," mentions no particular professions. Even if one expands the plot-theme to include the Galt-Dagny conflict, no professions need be specified. As far as the essence of their conflict is concerned, Dagny could have been a historian and Galt a sculptor.

Yet the fact that the main heroes are industrialists, inventors, businessmen, and so on, clearly projects the nobility of material production—as a central motif of the novel.

Is this motif extra-thematic? I would say no.

The reason is that the novel's actual plot-theme consists of more than the Galt-Dagny conflict strand. There are at least two adjunct strands. The first of these is the battle for the industrial economy of America, a battle that pits

Dagny and Rearden (struggling to keep the economy afloat) against the loot-ers (looting the economy) and the strikers (withdrawing from the battle). The second adjunct conflict strand is the Rearden-Dagny-Lillian triangle. Both of these adjunct strands have their own themes, which are *aspects* of the overall theme of the novel. The overall theme is "the mind's role in human existence." The theme of the battle for America's industrial economy is "the mind's role in material production." The theme of the Rearden-Dagny-Lillian triangle is "the mind's role in love and sex."

The spiritual stature of material production is in turn an aspect of the theme "the mind's role in material production" (since that role is crucial). The importance of love is an aspect of the theme "the mind's role in love and sex" (since love is an expression of the mind's highest values). Furthermore, these aspects of the novel's adjunct themes are issues on which the characters disagree, which is crucial to their conflicts with one another. If the looters had upheld production as a noble endeavor, or if Lilllian had upheld the im-portance of romantic sexual love, the adjunct plot strands would have been impossible. This is what makes the importance of love and the nobility of production *thematic* premises in *Atlas Shrugged*.

In Ayn Rand's last and greatest novel, certain premises of hers that were extra-thematic in her earlier fiction are lifted to thematic status. But the fact that a premise is made thematic does not diminish the power of its projection in a novel. Quite the contrary: this means that the value-projection involved is firing on all engines—which is one reason why *Atlas Shrugged*, more than any of her previous novels, represents the quintessence of Ayn Rand.

THE GLORY OF AMERICA

In her introduction to Victor Hugo's *Ninety-Three*, Ayn Rand wrote that "[t]o a Romanticist, a background is a background, not a theme. His vision is always focused on man—on the fundamentals of man's nature, on those problems and those aspects of his character which apply to any age and any country."[19]

This statement of Ayn Rand's notwithstanding, a novel's setting can relate to its abstract message in different ways. At one end of the spectrum are novels where the setting is an aspect of the theme itself, in which case the theme di-rects that particular setting. For instance, the theme of *Quo Vadis* is "the rise of Christianity," which virtually directs the setting: Rome under Nero. The theme of *Gone with the Wind* is "the passing of the old South," which directs the set-ting: the old South. You could not have *Gone with the Wind* set in Maine.

At the other end of the spectrum is a novel like *Anthem*, which is set in the future, in some place unrecognizable to contemporary readers. The reader does not know whether the City is really Chicago, Paris, Moscow, or what-ever—nor does it matter.

Between these extremes, we find Ayn Rand's other novels.

We the Living, she herself said, "is *not* a novel 'about Soviet Russia.' It is a novel about Man against the State."[20] Yet the Russian postrevolutionary background is presented in great detail; and in conjunction with the dramatization of the theme, that background does project the extra-thematic premise "the misery and horror of Communist Russia."

This projection is not the fundamental purpose of the book, but it is *one* purpose. When Ayn Rand left Soviet Russia, a guest at her farewell party said to her: "If they ask you, in America—tell them that Russia is a huge cemetery and that we are all dying slowly." Ayn Rand said, "I'll tell them."[21] *We the Living* is her fulfillment of that promise.

In her first novel, Ayn Rand was obligated to tell the truth about where she happened to come from. Later, in her two greatest novels, she would tell the truth about where she chose to go. In both *The Fountainhead* and *Atlas Shrugged*, the American setting is used for the extra-thematic projection of *positive* values, making them more fully Ayn Rand novels than *We the Living*.

The theme of *The Fountainhead*, "individualism versus collectivism," is neutral in regard to setting: this clash is found in any country. But when the plot concretizes the virtue and triumph of individualism, the fact that this plot is set in America opens the way to the extra-thematic projection of the premise "America as the glorious country of individualism."

As Howard Roark says in his courtroom speech: "Now observe the results of a society built on the principle of individualism. This, our country. The noblest country in the history of men. The country of greatest achievement, greatest prosperity, greatest freedom."[22] To this country, Roark says, "I wish to give the ten years which I will spend in jail if my country exists no longer. I will spend them in memory and in gratitude for what my country has been. It will be my act of loyalty, my refusal to live or work in what has taken its place."[23]

But the America of *The Fountainhead* is still ruled by the principle of individualism, at least as far as politics and law is concerned, and Roark is acquitted at his trial.

Throughout the novel, Roark faces social opposition, but this opposition is not backed by the power of a gun. When his first building is completed, the distinguished architect Ralston Holcombe remarks: "It's a disgrace to the country that a thing like that Heller house is allowed to be erected. It's a blot on the profession. There ought to be a law."[24] But Holcombe's attitude is satire on Ayn Rand's part. None of Roark's enemies has the political power to stop him.

The theme of *Atlas Shrugged*, "the role of the mind in man's existence," is similarly neutral in regard to setting: the mind's role is the same in any country. But when the plot concretizes the role of the mind, the fact that this plot is set in America opens the way to the extra-thematic projection of the premise "America as the country of the mind." As Francisco puts it: "This country was the only country in history born, not of chance and blind tribal warfare, but as a rational product of man's mind. This country was built on the supremacy of reason—and, for one magnificent century, it redeemed the world. It will have to do so again" (771).

Part of the mind's role is to make possible the values required for man's survival. This role is dramatized in *Atlas Shrugged*, which is why the novel's American setting opens the way to the projection of yet another extra-thematic premise: "America as the country of wealth creation." In Francisco's words: "To the glory of mankind, there was, for the first and only time in history, a *country of money*. . . . For the first time, man's mind and money were set free, and there were no fortunes-by-conquest, but only fortunes-by-work, and instead of swordsmen and slaves, there appeared the real maker of wealth, the greatest worker, the highest type of human being—the self-made man—the American industrialist" (414).

The American setting of both *The Fountainhead* and *Atlas Shrugged* is accidental relative to each novel's theme—and the premises this setting helps project are extra-thematic. But is this extra-thematic projection of the strong or weak kind? In other words, is the American setting of these two novels comparable to Roark's being an architect (crucial to the plot) or to Kira's being an engineering student (incidental to the plot)?

This is a debatable issue. My own view is that the novels could have been set outside America with no change in basic plot-themes—but only with a loss of plausibility. In *The Fountainhead* and *Atlas Shrugged*, the characters—especially the morally good secondary characters like Kent Lansing and Ken Danagger—are much more American than European. They have a particularly American independence and indifference to social status, which makes it convincing that they would fight for their own judgment and give a commission to Roark, or follow Galt when he goes on strike. Conversely, a European or Asian jury would not be likely to acquit Roark.

Roark and Galt, as Ayn Rand's projections of the ideal man, could have been given any nationality. They depend only on her personal vision. But they could not realistically have found the various minor allies that would enable them to *win* in any culture. Only in America.

THE METAPHYSICS OF VALUES

The essential attribute of romanticism in literature, Ayn Rand wrote, is "the independent, creative projection of an individual writer's values."[25] Having seen a variety of ways in which Ayn Rand accomplishes this task, we can now draw certain lessons relevant to the nature of art in general and to romanticism in particular.

Let us start with art as such. Art, in Ayn Rand's definition, "is a selective re-creation of reality according to an artist's metaphysical value-judgments."[26]

A man's metaphysical value-judgments are his answers to such questions as: Is the universe intelligible to man or not? Does man have the power of choice or not? Can he achieve his goals in life or not? Is he a harmonious unity of mind and body, or is he by nature torn between spirit and matter? Can he find happiness on earth or is he doomed to frustration and despair? "These are *metaphysical* questions," writes Ayn Rand, "but the answers to them determine the kind of *ethics* men will accept and practice; the answers are the link between metaphysics and ethics."[27]

Take Ayn Rand's evaluation of America. America is great, she holds, because it is the country of the mind. But why is it *good* to be "the country of the mind"? Only because the universe is intelligible to man—which conclusion is a metaphysical value-judgment. If reason were impotent, a mystical country like Russia would more logically be considered great. Observe that someone like Dostoevsky might agree that America is the country of the mind, but since his metaphysics would reject the efficacy of reason, his evaluation of America would not be positive.

Or take Ayn Rand's admiration for the professions of science, engineering, and business. Her evaluation is based on her metaphysical premise of mind-body union, her view that "man is an indivisible, integrated entity—and his place is here, on earth." She rejects the belief in an opposition between man's spiritual aspirations and his material existence—a view which to her "represents the debasement of man and of this earth."[28] These metaphysical value-judgments direct Ayn Rand's evaluation of specific professions as especially worthy of admiration.

Or take Ayn Rand's view of love as a crucial human value. This premise, too, rests on deeper foundations. Most immediately, it rests on the premise that the unique values of individual human beings are of crucial importance.

Consider a story told by Morton Hunt in *The Natural History of Love*. An anthropologist who lived among the Bemba of Zambia in the 1930s once "related to a group of them an English folk-tale about a young prince who climbed glass mountains, crossed chasms, and fought dragons, all to obtain the hand of a maiden he loved. The Bemba were plainly bewildered, but remained silent. Finally an old chief spoke up, voicing the feelings of all present in the simplest of questions: 'Why not take another girl?'"[29]

The old chief viewed human beings as interchangeable. He did not regard the unique values of individuals as important—and therefore he did not grasp the idea of an irreplaceable spiritual bond between individuals—and therefore he did not regard love as important—and therefore he did not understand love stories.

John Galt has a different outlook. Consider the nature of his response when he first sees Dagny on a passenger platform of the Taggart Terminal. He later tells her:

> You wore an evening gown. You had a cape half-slipping off your body—I saw, at first, only your bare shoulders, your back and your profile—it looked for a moment as if the cape would slip further and you would stand there naked. Then I

saw that you wore a long gown, the color of ice, like the tunic of a Grecian goddess, but had the short hair and the imperious profile of an American woman.
You looked preposterously out of place on a railroad platform—and it was not
on a railroad platform that I was seeing you, I was seeing a setting that had never
haunted me before—but then, suddenly, I knew that you *did* belong among the
rails, the soot and the girders, that that was the proper setting for a flowing gown
and naked shoulders and a face as alive as yours—a railroad platform, not a
curtained apartment—you looked like a symbol of luxury and you belonged in
the place that was its source—you seemed to bring wealth, grace, extravagance
and the enjoyment of life back to their rightful owners, to the men who created
railroads and factories—you had a look of energy and of its reward, together, a
look of competence and luxury combined—and I was the first man who had ever
stated in what manner these two were inseparable—and I thought that if our age
gave form to its proper gods and erected a statue to the meaning of an American
railroad, yours would be that statue. (778–79)

Galt falls in love with Dagny because of his values—and hers. What are
these values?

First, he upholds mind-body union and the spiritual nobility of material
production. This is the deeper meaning of his comment that Dagny seems "to
bring wealth, grace, extravagance and the enjoyment of life back to their rightful owners, to the men who created railroads and factories."

Second, there is something god-like in Galt's image of post-Industrial
Revolution man—or in this case woman: not merely does Dagny wear a gown
"like the tunic of a Grecian goddess" but, Galt thinks, "if our age gave form to
its proper gods and erected a statue to the meaning of an American railroad,
yours would be that statue."

Third, Galt specifies "an American railroad," and earlier he notes that while
Dagny resembles a Grecian goddess, she has "the short hair and the imperi-
ous profile of an American woman." In other words, Galt values Dagny's
Americanness—and regards it as fitting her other qualities.

The values Galt sees in Dagny obviously match those of Ayn Rand herself, as
projected through her novel's central conflict. But the more immediately relevant point is the fact that these values—which are what Galt's love for Dagny
is all about—are individual in nature.

An individual value is one that is characteristic of a human being qua individual, as opposed to, say, the generic values of social conformity. Both kinds
of values can be observed in actual human beings. But what decides which
kind someone will regard as important, as representing the essence of a human being? The premises of free will or determinism.

If one sees man as a volitional being, capable of *choosing* his values, one
will naturally regard as important those values of his which bear the mark
of individual choice. By contrast, if one sees man as a determined being, one
will regard as important only those of his values which seem to represent, not
individuality, but the impersonal powers of fate.

Thus the metaphysical premise of man's power of choice directs the premise of the importance of individual values, which directs the premise of the crucial value of love, which directs the treatment of love in a novel like *Atlas Shrugged*.

And thus, in reverse, the treatment of love in a novel like *Atlas Shrugged* projects the metaphysical premise of man's power of choice.

So does the treatment of all the *other* values individual to the author. Individual values are front and center in a romantic art work—and the importance given to them projects the premise of choice. It is no coincidence that Ayn Rand defined romanticism as "a category of art based on the recognition of the principle that man possesses the faculty of volition."[30]

Except for choice, romantic art is not limited to the projection of any *given* individual values or metaphysical value judgments. Walter Scott portrayed medieval knights, Ayn Rand portrayed railroad executives. Edmond Rostand upheld the mind-body dichotomy. Joseph Conrad disliked America, the country of "the silver dollar" (or in other words the country of money, which for Conrad was not a compliment). However, in regard to *method*, as opposed to any given value-content, all of these writers are romanticists, upholding individual values and choice.

The romantic method is more specific than a general injunction to "feature individual values." For one thing, a collection of unrelated values of an artist's would not be a standard of selection for the creation of a unified whole. What the romantic artist needs is a single standard that contains within itself a spectrum of his own values, beyond those implied by the theme. And this kind of standard cannot be found ready-made in the world, but has to be *created* by the artist.[31]

Compare a romantic novel like *Atlas Shrugged* to a naturalistic one like Tom Wolfe's *The Bonfire of the Vanities*. The theme of the latter is "New York City in the 1980s." Wolfe's method is simple: he records certain characteristic patterns of valuing and acting that he observed in New York in the 80s. These patterns are his standard of selection, and although he is acutely perceptive in recognizing them, they are in effect found ready-made in reality. They are not *creative* standards of selection. But then they do not have to be, since Wolfe is concerned with presenting other people's values, not his own.

By contrast, in *Atlas Shrugged* Ayn Rand was concerned with presenting her own values—a set of values which formed a unique and unprecedented personality. Therefore, no ready-made standard of how to present them was to be found. Ayn Rand had to create her own standard.

She did so in the form of the plot-theme of *Atlas Shrugged*.

I do not mean that she constructed her plot-theme with the conscious, laborious assignment of filling in the theme-incidental cracks with extra-thematic values chosen from a list like "material production, hero-worshiping femininity, America, and romantic love." No, her immediate standard (alongside the theme) was a simpler and more general one. As she herself put it: "My basic test for any story is: Would I want to meet these characters and observe these events in real life? Is this story an experience worth living through for its own sake? Is the pleasure of contemplating these characters an end in itself?"[32]

But the answers to such questions depend on individual values, which in turn imply metaphysical value judgments. This is the reason why an artist reveals his naked soul in his work—and why, reading Ayn Rand's novels, we can experience the equivalent of Dominique's feeling in Howard Roark's Enright House.

The conflicts and the characters and the logical progressions of events are Ayn Rand's and could not have been anyone else's in the world; hers, as her face, as her soul; here is the shape she made and the thing within her which caused her to make it, the end and the cause together, the motive power eloquent in every line of dialogue, a woman's self, ours for a while, ours by grace of our seeing it and understanding.[33]

NOTES

1. Ayn Rand, *The Fountainhead* (New York: Bobbs-Merrill, 1943; Signet fiftieth anniversary paperback edition, 1993), 287.

2. Ayn Rand, "Art and Sense of Life," *The Romantic Manifesto: A Philosophy of Literature*, revised edition (New York: Signet, 1975), 44.

3. See Ayn Rand, "Basic Principles of Literature," *Romantic Manifesto*, 85.

4. Ayn Rand, *For the New Intellectual* (New York: Signet, 1963), 60.

5. Rand, *New Intellectual*, 64.

6. Rand, *New Intellectual*, 68. The word "versus" is italicized in the original.

7. Rand, "Basic Principles of Literature," 85.

8. Rand, "Basic Principles of Literature," 81.

9. Rand, "Basic Principles of Literature," 85.

10. See my "What Might Be and Ought to Be: Aristotle's *Poetics* and *The Fountainhead*," in Robert Mayhew, ed., *Essays on Ayn Rand's* The Fountainhead (Lanham, Md.: Lexington Books, 2007), 155–75.

11. Rand, "Basic Principles of Literature," 85.

12. See Ayn Rand, *The Art of Fiction: A Guide for Writers and Readers*, Tore Boeckmann, ed. (New York: Plume, 2000), 41.

13. Ayn Rand, *We the Living* (Sixtieth anniversary paperback edition, New York: Signet, 1996), 59.

14. Rand, *We the Living*, 61.

15. See Ayn Rand, "About a Woman President," *The Voice of Reason: Essays in Objectivist Thought*, Leonard Peikoff, ed. (New York: New American Library, 1989), 268.

16. Rand, *We the Living*, 65

17. Quoted in William Vaughan, *German Romantic Painting* (New Haven: Yale University Press, 1994), 239.

18. Rand, *We the Living*, xvii.

19. Ayn Rand, "Introduction to *Ninety-Three*," *Romantic Manifesto*, 156.

20. Rand, *We the Living*, xiii.

21. Quoted in Nathaniel Branden and Barbara Branden, *Who is Ayn Rand?* (New York: Random House, 1962), 171.

22. Rand, *Fountainhead*, 683.

166   *Tore Boeckmann*

23. Rand, *Fountainhead*, 685.
24. Rand, *Fountainhead*, 137.
25. Ayn Rand, "What is Romanticism?" *Romantic Manifesto*, 111.
26. Ayn Rand, "The Psycho-Epistemology of Art," *Romantic Manifesto*, 19. Italics removed.
27. Rand, "Psycho-Epistemology of Art," 19.
28. David Harriman, ed., *Journals of Ayn Rand* (New York: Dutton, 1997), 551.
29. Morton M. Hunt, *The Natural History of Love* (New York: Alfred A. Knopf, 1959), 10.
30. Rand, "What is Romanticism?" 99.
31. I explore the nature of such created standards, or what I call "core combinations," and their function in romantic art, in "*The Fountainhead* as a Romantic Novel" in Mayhew, *Essays on Ayn Rand's* The Fountainhead, 119–53, as well as in "Caspar David Friedrich and Visual Romanticism," *The Objective Standard*, 3.1, Spring 2008.
32. Ayn Rand, "The Goal of My Writing," *Romantic Manifesto*, 163.
33. I am grateful to The Ayn Rand Institute for a grant which supported the writing of this essay, and to my fellow participants in the Philosophers' Workshop on *Atlas Shrugged* held at A.R.I. January 18-19, 2008: Yaron Brook, Onkar Ghate, Robert Mayhew, Jason Rheins, Gregory Salmieri, and Tara Smith. In addition, Harald Waage tracked down for me an old Danish translation of *Turandot*, and Robert Mayhew and Kristi Boeckmann made astute comments on earlier drafts.

10

Atlas Shrugged as the Culmination of the Romantic Novel

Andrew Bernstein

In *The Romantic Manifesto*, Ayn Rand establishes that volition is the essence of the romantic approach to literature. In contrast to naturalist writers, romantic authors show human beings confronted by fundamental alternatives among which they must choose. In the novels of Victor Hugo, Fyodor Dostoyevsky, and Ayn Rand, characters face a constant alternative involving the most important issue of all: good and evil. Further, these geniuses explicate their understanding of good and evil by showing it as an integrated element of a comprehensive philosophy—a philosophy dramatized brilliantly in their greatest novels: *Les Misérables*, *The Brothers Karamazov*, and *Atlas Shrugged*.[1]

Because romantics recognize that men possess free will, the best writers of this school are passionate moralists, who believe that men can and must choose the good over the evil and put it into practice in the world. They are not like Shakespeare, who, although a magnificent literary genius, depicts man as a tragically flawed being in whose doomed existence morality is an ineffectual force. In contrast to the amorality of the naturalist school, the romantics are concerned to dramatize a vision of a world morally transfigured.

But on their own terms, Hugo and Dostoyevsky show their respective moral codes as incapable of promoting the sweeping social changes that each seeks. Only Ayn Rand shows her moral-philosophical vision as triumphantly capable of transfiguring the world.

The principle of volition, although profoundly important, is not a philosophical primary. What are the deeper principles held by Hugo and Dostoyevsky that prevent them from projecting their moral codes as capable of bettering the world? What basic premise held by Ayn Rand enables her to dramatize her system of thought as sweeping aside all obstacles and bringing vast improvements to men's lives and social systems? The answers to these questions will give us a deeper understanding of the contrasting philosophical convictions held by the

167

leading romantics. Most important, we will gain greater appreciation of the role played by philosophy in the structure and outcome of their plots.

It is possible to go through these three books one at a time and identify the underlying philosophical principles embodied in each. The answers will be inductively extracted from the details of each story, that is, the method employed will be to begin with the concretes of each plot and proceed to climb the ladder of abstractions to broader levels of intellectual understanding. In what follows, an inductive method similar to Ayn Rand's is employed to arrive at (and validate) her understanding of the plot-theme and theme of *Les Misérables* and *Atlas Shrugged*. This method is further applied to *The Brothers Karamazov*.[2]

The three principles of rational literary analysis to be employed are: (1) master the concretes of the author's universe; (2) condense the number of concretes into increasingly essentialized formulations; (3) extract all explanatory principles from, and reduce them back to, the level of perceptual concretes.

So the essay is divided into four parts: the first part analyzes Hugo's *Les Misérables*; part two examines Dostoyevsky's *The Brothers Karamazov*; part three explicates Rand's *Atlas Shrugged*; and the final part identifies the reasons permitting Rand to fulfill the romanticist program and preventing Hugo and Dostoyevsky from doing so.

PART ONE: HUGO'S *LES MISÉRABLES*

Les Misérables tells the story of Jean Valjean, a hardened ex-convict in nineteenth-century France who is converted to religious humanism by Bishop Myriel, the saintly prelate of Digne. But before his conversion is completed, he robs a young boy and is a fugitive hunted by the relentless detective, Inspector Javert. In disguise as Monsieur Madeleine, he rises from his job as a factory laborer by virtue of discovering a new manufacturing process that revolutionizes the local industry of Montreuil-sur-Mer. He brings prosperity to the locale, makes a fortune, and is appointed mayor. But when he saves an innocent man, he reveals himself as Jean Valjean and is captured by Javert. He escapes prison, rescues the young, cruelly mistreated Cosette, daughter of the dead (and equally cruelly mistreated) prostitute, Fantine, and is pursued by Javert, eventually finding refuge in a convent. Years later, Cosette falls in love with Marius Pontmercy, who, distraught at the impossibility of their relationship, intends to die on the barricades with his revolutionary friends, Enjolras and the Society of ABC. Jean Valjean rescues both Marius and Javert from the battle, then escapes the police by fleeing through the sewers. Javert, upon realizing the existence of a moral law higher than, and sometimes clashing with, the one to which his entire life is dedicated, commits suicide. Jean Valjean unites Marius and Cosette—who are wed—and then withdraws from their lives. Without his adopted daughter, he begins to waste away. Though Marius and Cosette finally realize the great man's true moral stature and rush to him, it is too late. Jean Valjean dies from a combination of starvation and a broken heart.

To understand a novel's plot, it is first necessary to answer the question: Who is the main character? That is, who is principally responsible for advancing the action? The main character, in pursuing a goal, clashes with whatever forces oppose that goal. It is his value quest that initiates, sustains, and carries to climax the story's central conflict.

The main character of *Les Misérables* is Jean Valjean. His value quest and actions drive the story. He steals a loaf of bread to feed his sister's starving children. He puts into practice the benevolent message of Monsieur Myriel, developing a revolutionary manufacturing technique that transforms his town's economy. It is Jean Valjean who rescues Fauchevelent, although he realizes it will arouse Javert's suspicion—and it is he who both promises the dying Fantine to save her daughter and who carries through on his vow. He is the one who takes the youthful Cosette to a convent for safety, and then, years later, removes her so that she can experience life. He saves Marius from the soldiers and Javert from the revolutionaries. He unites Marius and Cosette, then withdraws from their life together and passes on to them the bishop's message of love. Jean Valjean's values and actions dominate this story.

The second question is, what does he want? *Les Misérables*, at the level of action, is the story of a man seeking liberty from an oppressive system of criminal justice. Jean Valjean is, first and foremost, a fugitive. The next question is: Who or what stands in his way? Clearly, it is Javert who, as a relentless representative of the state, provides the primary opposition, the main obstacle standing in Jean Valjean's path. Javert, as the individual most ruthlessly devoted to the enforcement of the strict letter of the law, is and must be the hero's primordial antagonist.

From this understanding, it is possible to extract a statement of the essentialized conflict of *Les Misérables*: Jean Valjean seeks freedom but is relentlessly pursued by the police officer, Javert. In *The Romantic Manifesto*, Ayn Rand defines a novel's plot-theme as: "the central conflict or 'situation' of a story . . . the core of its events." The plot-theme of *Les Misérables* is: "the life-long flight of an ex-convict from the pursuit of a ruthless representative of the law."[3]

But what does it all mean? What is significant about all of this? What is the meaning of the injustices heaped upon Jean Valjean? It is now possible to search for the theme. In doing so, it is important to integrate the novel's main action with its other events, to widen the range of the units, to incorporate all of a story's events under its theme in the way that all particulars of a certain kind are united under a concept. Here, the specific questions to be asked are: Is there some connection between Jean Valjean's mistreatment and the abuses suffered by Fantine? Between his misfortune and the harsh cruelty imposed on the youthful Cosette? Is there some connection between the injustices borne by the main character and those that Enjolras and his band of revolutionaries seek to redress? What is the connection between the harsh life imposed on the innocent fugitive and the torrent of examples of human misery depicted in the novel?

What are the principles that tie together these concretes and explain their abstract meaning? There are two: (1) the terrible suffering borne by the poor; (2) the cruel indifference of society and its legal system to such suffering. The book's action, reduced to its essentials, adds up to an overwhelming picture: the terrible injustices of society toward the poor. This realization leads directly to the novel's theme: the injustice of society toward its lower classes.[4]

The next question is: What should be done about such injustice? What can be done? Should it be supported, ignored, redressed—and if the latter, by what means? The theme alone does not provide an answer. It is necessary to identify the moral stand the author takes toward his own theme. Such an identification may be termed: the novel's meaning. To identify the novel's meaning requires further analysis. The book's theme is indubitably social—showing what Hugo considers the inhuman lack of civilization permeating nineteenth-century French society—but there are more fundamental philosophical premises that are dramatized in the story. For example, even on a casual reading it is apparent that religion, in some form, is central to Hugo's worldview and to the meaning of this book.

Its ethic of social service, its emphasis on the importance of relieving poverty, does not proceed from a modernist, that is, a Marxist basis. The premises at work are not dialectical materialism, economic determinism, or philosophical atheism. There is a profound spirituality to this book, in a distinctively religious—although not necessarily Christian—sense.

For example: Bishop Myriel morally regenerates the hardened ex-convict. Following this, the bishop is perennially with him, helping him make difficult moral decisions for the rest of his life. Jean Valjean keeps the candlesticks, symbolic of the bishop's enduring influence, by his side in a case dubbed by Cosette "the inseparable."[5]

The bishop imbues him with an understanding of, and reverence for, Jesus' teachings: love the weak, cherish the downtrodden, and, above all, take action—perform good deeds, engage in heartfelt charity, succor society's victims. Dedicate one's life to an *active* service of humanity. The regenerated Jean Valjean feels the presence of God in his life in the form of a burning exhortation: love and serve mankind. Even Javert is not immune to the religiosity of Hugo's universe, for when he realizes that Jean Valjean serves a higher law than that of the state, he understands that the two often conflict and that God's law takes precedence. But this truth contradicts every aspect of his life—and he cannot change. The only recourse is: suicide.

Religion permeates this book. The bishop's life, Jean Valjean's reconstituted life, Javert's death—all are dominated by the moral presence of God. But the book's religiosity is not in strict accordance with orthodox Christianity. For one thing, there is no belief in Original Sin. On the contrary, man is depicted as clean, pure, even noble. Further, there is no adherence to organized religion:

the hero belongs to no church, receives no sacraments, seeks no blessing from priests and no absolution from confession. He clearly is not a Catholic (as was the vast majority of Hugo's French audience). Neither does he read the Bible, attend revivals or prayer meetings or cherish a personal faith relationship with Jesus Christ. He is clearly not a Protestant. Bishop Myriel himself holds beliefs that are non-Christian, even anti-Christian. Myriel expresses many of Hugo's own ideas: belief in general education, in progress, and in man's earthly happiness. In one of the novel's most powerful scenes, he kneels for a blessing from an atheistic, regicidal revolutionary of 1793.

On this same theme are Enjolras and the revolutionaries, who love man, reject Christianity, and who are "for religion against religions." These firebrands, out to overthrow the existing social order, are as representative of the author's religious views as is the bishop. Many religions and moral codes stress help to the needy—such beliefs are not distinctive to Christianity.

The moral commandment accepted by Jean Valjean to aid the poor does not come from social institutions. On the contrary, they are cruelly inhumane, and must be purified or even overthrown. The moral principle animating Jean Valjean's benevolence emanates from a non-Christian conception of God.

This point leads to the heart of *Les Misérables*. As stated by the eminent scholar of French Literature, Paul Benichou: "Against society and social strength, against the law itself, stands a spiritual premise which can alter the course of injustice. . . . This Conscience above the Law was for Victor Hugo, God himself. . . . Thus the quartet of the Policeman, the Bishop, the Convict and the Prostitute strikingly act out the fundamental idea of *Les Misérables*: the appeal to a spiritual force in order to regenerate the social order." This insight—the appeal to a spiritual force in order to regenerate the social order— is the essence of 1400 pages of text reduced to a clause. Here is the book's meaning: the importance of embracing a spiritual force as a necessary means of bringing justice to human society.[6]

Nevertheless, it is possible to analyze *Les Misérables* at a still deeper level of philosophy. With what view does the novel leave its readers? Man is great but Society is corrupt. Man the individual is noble but social institutions are not. How can it be that individuals are pure but the group is debased?

Because to attain such nobility of character one must be influenced by a love of humanity which comes exclusively from God. There are only a few rare individuals who dedicate themselves to God's teachings and who achieve this degree of spiritual grandeur. In *Les Misérables* there are three: the bishop—Myriel; the convict—Jean Valjean; and the revolutionary—Enjolras. These are the crusaders and the saints, imbued with the moral fire of a higher authority, fighting for justice in the here-and-now. In devotion to the metaphysical order, they seek sweeping reform of the social order. Despite their love of man, the saints of *Les Misérables* are alienated from men; their stature places them apart and higher; their devotion to God elevates them above their peers.

Hence the bittersweet irony that the fighters for mankind, though they live in God's graces, die as lonely outcasts from men. Enjolras, fighting for the people, dies alone on the barricades because the people fail to rise. Jean Valjean, whose life was dedicated to Cosette, dies of a broken heart because neither she nor Marius—nor anyone—recognizes him for the moral giant he is. This is the deepest level of conflict in Hugo: the great man, by virtue of his devotion to a higher order, makes himself a rebel and outcast in this one. In fighting for the world, he fights against the world. In fighting for man, he is rejected by men. The social order resists the moral crusader; it stands opposed to or does not recognize the reforms for which he fights.

But there are other foes besides human cruelty that oppose the hero: natural forces like starvation, illness, freezing winter weather, and the need of exhausting physical labor. There is a recalcitrant element to the physical world itself that resists the reforming efforts of the moral giant. There is a wealth of examples of this struggle in *Les Misérables*: Fantine's sickness and death, Cosette's helpless shivering in the cold, the harsh manual labor performed by the poor to escape starvation, and so forth.

The saint's struggle with physical nature is not the focus of Hugo's story; his conflict with society is.[7] But it underlies that struggle: the one-step-ahead-of-starvation-and-freezing lifestyle of the poor gives to that struggle a life-and-death urgency. So what is Hugo showing us? The great man dedicated to a higher law that emanates from a spiritual realm seeks to put that law into practice in this one—a world where society and nature combine to resist him.

Service to a higher spiritual world versus resistance from a lower, material world. God and Heaven versus the earth. The soul versus the body. There is a mind-body conflict in *Les Misérables*. It is not merely a cruel, greedy society that rejects the saint's message of love; deeper than that lies an incorrigible physical world that is not malleable to the demands of the spirit.

There is a Platonic dualism that lies at the base of Hugo's metaphysics—a universe divided into a spiritual and bodily realm, in which the two are separate, unequal, and opposed; in which the soul is noble and pure but the body is debased, resistant to the higher moral principles of the spirit. This is why there is an element of the heroes being "too fine for this world;" why they don't merely live in poverty and/or die alone—but, more fundamentally, perish with their moral vision unrealized.

At the end of the book, Bishop Myriel, Enjolras, and Jean Valjean are all dead. Perhaps their spirit will live on in a newly awakened love of humanity in the souls of Marius and Cosette. Beyond that, nothing has changed. The same injustices exist as before. The world has not been transfigured in accordance with the moral vision of the heroes. It could not be. On a Platonic metaphysics, an imperfect world could never absorb the perfection of a spiritual giant.

This is the bottom line and final lesson of *Les Misérables*: man can achieve spiritual grandeur, but the very requirements of his moral greatness preclude worldly success. The rejuvenation of the social order is a tortuously uphill struggle that is not possible in the universe of *Les Misérables*.

PART TWO: DOSTOYEVSKY'S *THE BROTHERS KARAMAZOV*

Dostoyevsky's universe in *The Brothers Karamazov*, although as teeming, robust, and religious, differs sharply from Hugo's in its essential thematic meaning. The novel tells the story of four brothers and their antagonistic, ultimately murderous relationship with their despicable father.

The essence of the story is: Alyosha Karamazov, a young disciple of the saintly Father Zossima, is instructed by the elder to attempt to resolve the dispute within his family between his father and his older brother, Dmitri. Alyosha is unsuccessful at reconciling the two regarding either Dmitri's inheritance or the jealous rivalry over the young coquette, Grushenka. Dmitri threatens to kill the old man rather than allow him to possess Grushenka. Karamazov's other legitimate son, Ivan, is an atheistic intellectual—and the bastard, Smerdyakov, is his philosophical protégé. When Dmitri can't find Grushenka, he rushes to his father's house—sees that she isn't there—but badly beats a servant who tries to stop him. Shortly after, Dmitri and Grushenka are united, but Dmitri is arrested for the murder of his father. Ivan discovers that Smerdyakov is the killer but, overcome by his guilt, goes mad. Smerdyakov commits suicide. Alyosha, having had no success at sharing Father Zossima's message of love with the adults, seeks to bring it to the children.

Such a summary reduces the conflict to seven key figures—the four brothers, the father, Zossima, and Grushenka—and a limited range of highly essentialized actions.

What does the story show? A murder—by Smerdyakov. It raises the question: Is he the only one morally responsible? Dostoyevsky's answer is an emphatic: no.

It is necessary to examine the central situation that Dostoyevsky presents to his readers. Dmitri and the old man are locked in a death struggle over Grushenka. Alyosha sees disaster approaching—attempts to avert it—but fails because he does not put forth a maximum effort. Ivan refuses to be his brother's keeper—or his father's—and claims that in a world without immortality all actions are morally permissible. Smerdyakov, the cynical lackey, takes Ivan's words to heart and puts them into brutal practice.

The conflict, in part, is: Dmitri versus his father over Grushenka. In part, it is also Alyosha's earnest but ultimately half-hearted and unsuccessful attempt to bring Father Zossima's message of kindness to his warring family members. But the conflict is extraordinarily complex. It also involves both Ivan inciting a senseless murder and his struggle to come to terms with his own culpability—*and* Smerdyakov bashing his father's skull for no other reason than to show that in a world devoid of God there exist no constraints on his whims.

The compound conflict intimately involves all five members of the Kara-mazov clan. Grushenka is a secondary figure, because although a flirtatious coquette, she is not fundamental to the seething familial struggle.

Dostoyevsky brings together a combustible cast of characters. The two crude sensualists—Dmitri and his father—are bent on a collision course. The intellectual, Ivan, indifferently observes that "If one wild beast devours another, it's good riddance to both of them." The whim-driven flunky, Smerdyakov, is a third beast who murders the first before the second one can do so. The ineffectual monk, Alyosha, sees the murder coming but is too weak to take the necessary actions to prevent it.[8]

In essential terms, Dostoyevsky tells a story of four brothers, each of whom is responsible, in his own way, for the murder of their reprehensible father. One brother commits the murder—Smerdyakov; a second brother desires it—Dmitri; a third provides the moral justification for it—Ivan; and a fourth is unwilling to stop it—Alyosha.

This understanding provides Dostoyevsky's plot-theme: The actions of four brothers, in varying ways, lead to the murder of their loathsome father.

Such a condensation explains the complex conflict by uniting it around a thread that runs through the story's entirety: the four brothers, distinct and separate in so many ways, are united in their responsibility for the murder. There is the sensualist, the intellectual, the nihilist, and the monk—men as varied as can be found—brought together by their mutual complicity. Their shared guilt exists at three levels: the moral-practical, the psychological-existential, and the metaphysical-theological. These can be analyzed one at a time, starting with the level of personal moral responsibility.

Dmitri, despite being neither the trigger man nor the intellectual instigator, is the prime mover of the crime. It is his out-of-control, volatile use of force that not only gives Smerdyakov a convenient fall guy but, more fundamentally, establishes a context of violence against the old man, creating a situation ripe for murder.

Ivan, with his belief that the absence of immortality makes all actions permissible, gives a moral sanction to the murderer—and more, Ivan's own secret desire to be rid of his father motivates him to leave town at the propitious moment, thereby providing the murderer with an opportunity.

Alyosha, although kindly, is far too passive in his attempt to prevent the crime. He is certain disaster is coming; but when he fails to convince Ivan to stay, he does not leave the monastery to himself reside at his father's home, thereby providing the murderer a clear shot at his intended victim. His lack of protective action at the decisive moment may indicate that he, too, like Ivan, at the subconscious level, desires to be rid of the despicable old man. He is certainly not prepared to go the distance in preventing the crime—this despite Father Zossima's insistent exhortation that he devote himself to resolving his family's quarrels.

Smerdyakov murders his own father for no better reason than an irrational whim—the desire to corroborate the nihilistic belief that all actions are morally permissible. His motive is not even a desire to curry favor with his philosophical mentor, but one that is infinitely worse: an all-out destructiveness—a desire based not on a hatred of the good but on indifference to everything. The man who holds nothing as sacred or even valuable brings about the ruin of his mentor, as well as that of himself, his older brother, Dmitri, and their father.

Dmitri, Ivan, and Smerdyakov are guilty because of the actions they take; Alyosha by virtue of the actions he does not. The responsibility of the first three is active; Alyosha's is passive. Theirs is a guilt of commission, his is of omission. Such guilt leads to a second level of analysis: the psychological-existential consequences.

Ivan lives out a deeply held Dostoyevskian conviction: the correlation of crime with sickness. He has visions of devils, suffers from a raging fever, and there is fear he is going mad. Smerdyakov commits suicide, befitting a man with no values and nothing to live for. Dmitri is arrested, imprisoned, and doomed to an escape that will exile him from the land and people he loves. He is overwhelmed with remorse at the realization that though he is not guilty of this crime, he is guilty of a violent and wantonly self-indulgent existence. Alyosha must live with the realization that his failure to take decisive action violates not only his duty to his father—but, more fundamentally, his duty to his elder. For all four, the consequences of guilt are dramatic: one dies, one goes mad, one is imprisoned, one must immediately reform his character to bring his actions into accord with his stated convictions.

But it is the third, theological level of guilt that is critical to understanding the book's action and its theme. Karamazov and Dmitri are hardly the only self-indulgent hedonists who fill this story. There are also hordes of background drinkers, gamblers, revelers, lechers, and prostitutes; a thief (Dmitri), a killer (Smerdyakov), a coquette (Grushenka), a deeply neurotic woman (Katerina), and endless acts of passion-driven violence. Over it all lies Father Zossima's sainthood, Alyosha's struggle to live by the elder's teachings, relentless protestations by the hedonists of their deep love for God, and the author's reverence for the ascetic holiness of the Russian Orthodox monks. What does it all mean? What does it add up to?

This is Christianity: the sinfulness of man; the lustful, bestial, violent desires that form the core of his nature and motives; the purity of God; the on-the-brink, life-and-death desperation of the human condition in the absence of God; the need of suffering, of a soul howling from the edge of the abyss to gain redemption.

This is a picture of man and of life, not generically religious but specifically Christian. In contrast to Hugo, this is not religious humanism, but pietistic, evil-stressing, sin-bashing, Bible-thumping Christianity (of a Russian Orthodox variety).

We are all sinners, the story proclaims—not just the murderers, but all men, even Alyosha, who fails to consistently carry out Father Zossima's code; even Zossima himself, who insists that each is responsible for the sins of all. We are all responsible; we are all sinners; we are all Karamazovs, as Alyosha discovers. Life for such a creature is endless, bloody conflict over who can scratch, snort, gorge, drink, belch, brawl, and fornicate the most. It is violent, it is cynical, it is self-indulgent, it is criminal, it is desperate; ultimately, it is murderous.

This is the loathsome life and death of Fyodor Karamazov; the lives of Smerdyakov and Dmitri; this is, as Dmitri observes, the insect-like existence of reprobate man. This is, vividly, brilliantly dramatized, the theme of the novel.[9]

To state the theme succinctly: the desperate condition of human existence in a world without God.

In this novel, Dostoyevsky thunders against nineteenth-century positivism, determinism, materialism, and atheism—against the dominant philosophical and scientific theories of his era. These theories are embodied in Ivan's philosophy. Ivan is consumed by his intellectual life—he thinks, questions, doubts, seeks logical answers, finds none, rejects God, lives alone, despairs over evil, instigates a murder, broods over his guilt, sees devils, goes mad. In the character of Ivan Karamazov, Dostoyevsky depicts and rejects Western rationalism. Ivan's fate shows the necessity of reaffirming Russian faith, Russian mysticism, Russian Christianity.

Modern Western man, Dostoyevsky in effect proclaims, has rejected God; he scorns the commandments, embraces liberal permissiveness, believes that "anything goes." All actions are morally permissible, state the "enlightened" modern thinkers, thereby liberating violent emotionalists like Dmitri and cynical nihilists like Smerdyakov from all ethical constraints. The necessary result is violence and murder. Ivan's prose poem, "The Grand Inquisitor," is an eloquent example of Dostoyevsky's theme.

In it, Jesus returns and is imprisoned by the Inquisition. You are guilty, the Grand Inquisitor says to Christ, of condemning man to freedom. You rejected the temptation of Satan and set an example for man. You expect men to emulate you. But you are divine and can make that choice. They are sinful and cannot. The temptation is too much for them and they fall. Few are capable of choosing the moral law and salvation. Most choose hedonistic indulgence and Hell. Therefore, for man's good, the Church has been forced to enslave him, to end his freedom, to provide metaphysical law and order.

The Grand Inquisitor's enslavement of man (and his imprisonment of Jesus) is justified only because man's sinful nature made it impossible for all but a select few to choose God. A few, like Father Zossima, can venture into the wilderness, face Satan and return stronger. The rest fall.[10]

Man's sick soul was such that he had to reject God. The nineteenth-century intellectuals have declared that "God is dead!" Now, says Dostoyevsky, man is left with *the* question of the modern world: How do men live in a world without God? In *The Brothers Karamazov*, the author provides a succinct answer: they don't. Herein lies the meaning of this novel: Man's unequivocal need to affirm Christian faith.

In providing a Christian view of existence, Dostoyevsky focuses on what a great novelist must: the nature of man. His primary characters dramatize a key principle of human nature. Alyosha, as one example, struggles to live by Father Zossima's teachings. He has doubts when God causes his mentor's corpse to decompose rapidly—he yields to temptation (he, too, is a Karamazov), rushes to Grushenka's house, rights himself, but still does not carry through Zossima's teachings consistently.

Ivan agonizes over the choice between fundamental alternatives: God or reason. He is ambivalent regarding the theism-atheism question but clearly rejects God's world, a realm where the innocent are unjustly condemned to suffer. He rejects the Christian belief that a man is his brother's keeper, and, by leaving town at the climactic moment, involves himself in responsibility for the murder.

Dmitri's agony involves a related issue, the choice of honor versus base living, morality versus self-indulgent hedonism, God's laws versus the temptations of Satan. He falls repeatedly; but finally, his role in the murder of his father fills him with remorse, and he is ready to choose another kind of life.

In the struggles of his main characters, Dostoyevsky shows a fundamental alternative—in varying forms—faced by all human beings. This is the choice between: faith or disbelief. A man can choose God, like Father Zossima—or he can choose Satan, like Fyodor Karamazov—or he can choose God and then struggle with his wavering faith, like Alyosha—or he can choose to love God but follow the devil, condemning himself to the agonizing attempt to live a contradiction, like Dmitri—or he can abandon God, not for pleasure but for logic, and then find himself alienated from the good, driven inexorably to evil, then to madness, like Ivan. In brief, man must choose God, Satan, or some tortured attempt to combine the two.

God or Satan are the fundamental alternatives, and men must choose between them. Volition is man's nature—he is condemned to freedom—and his salvation depends on the right choice. The inescapable necessity to choose, and awareness of the momentous consequences of his choice, explains the frenzied torment in which Dostoyevskian man exists. He knows God is good, but is unable to resist lustful passion, and then is tortured by alienation from God.

The power to choose between God and temptation is the essence of human nature as depicted in *The Brothers Karamazov*. "God and the devil join battle," Dmitri bitterly observes, "and their battlefield is the heart of man."[11]

Dmitri's assessment is literally accurate. The battle lines between good and evil in this novel are defined strictly on theological grounds, and Dostoyevsky's artistic genius weaves the theology into a literary fabric that provides a vivid, chilling depiction of a Christian view of man.

For Hugo, God is necessary to imbue the social order with kindness, with a gracious goodwill of man to fellow man. But for Dostoyevsky, God is necessary at a more fundamental personal level: to cleanse man's sick soul of sin. In Hugo's world, the problem is merely the social system's lack of benevolence; the great man, with God's aid, can fight this. But in Dostoyevsky's world, there are and could be no great men, only misshapen creatures howling from the edge of the Pit. Hugo's man in *Les Misérables* needs God to make society more humane. Dostoyevsky's man in *The Brothers Karamazov* needs God to cleanse his contaminated soul and thereby spare his eternal life. But whatever the weighty matters on which they disagree, they concur regarding a fundamental belief: man needs God.

Ayn Rand's man in *Atlas Shrugged* needs no God.

For Hugo, man without God can achieve nobility of character but is trapped in a cruel society. For Dostoyevsky, man without God is a loathsome creature doomed in every conceivable form. But for Ayn Rand, only man without God can achieve nobility and a flourishing life.

For Hugo, society is malevolent. For Dostoyevsky, human nature is malevolent. But for Ayn Rand, religion is malevolent (and its secularization in modern culture is similarly evil).

She dramatizes this point consistently in *Atlas Shrugged*.

PART THREE: AYN RAND'S *ATLAS SHRUGGED*

The book tells the story of a man who vows to stop the motor of the world—and then does. For the overwhelming preponderance of the novel, he operates behind the scenes, giving the story an air of mystery on a global scale. To those who suspect his existence, like Dagny Taggart, he is a destroyer responsible for the collapse of industrial civilization.

Dagny is the Vice-President in Charge of Operation of Taggart Transcontinental Railroad in an America of the not-so-distant future. Industrial production is falling sharply due to two causes: the statist policies of the political leaders and the disappearances of the country's best minds. To signify despair and hopeless resignation, people ask the seemingly rhetorical question: "Who is John Galt?" Dagny works to rebuild the crucial Rio Norte Line as a means of saving the railroad and stemming the decline. She suspects the existence of an active agent working for destruction, and in defiance of society's pervasive expectation of doom rechristens her line the "John Galt Line." In the teeth of virtually unanimous social opposition, she builds the line not of steel but of Rearden Metal, a new alloy developed by industrialist Hank Rearden. She and Rearden successfully construct the line, and then become lovers.

On vacation, they find the abandoned wreck of a motor that could transform the world. She searches unsuccessfully for the inventor, and then hires a scientist to attempt its reconstruction. But the government issues a decree, enslaving men to their jobs, and the scientist quits. Dagny flies to Utah, finds him leaving with the destroyer, flies after them, and crashes in the Colorado mountains.

She finds herself in a hidden valley—"Atlantis"—the home of John Galt, the man who is both the motor's inventor and the "destroyer." Here she finds the great thinkers who have disappeared. They are on strike against the creed of self-sacrifice that enslaves the mind.

Although Dagny returns to her railroad, she and Galt are in love and become lovers. The looting politicians try to take over Rearden's mills; he sees the nature of their code and joins the strike. John Galt gives a radio address to the nation, explaining both the existence and the nature of the strike, and the conditions for ending it. The looters take Galt prisoner; they torture him, seeking to force him to become economic dictator of the country. Galt's allies, now including Dagny, rescue him and return to the valley. With the great minds on strike, the looter's regime collapses. The strikers are free to return to the world.

This is the essence of one thousand pages of an extraordinarily complex story line. At this point, there is enough information to raise the question: Is there a main character, a hero, whose specific value quest drives the action? Clearly, there is: John Galt. He is the one who conceives of the strike, initiates it, and leads it to its successful resolution. What, specifically, does he want? His goal is to successfully complete the strike—to withdraw from the world the men of the mind, to precipitate the collapse of the looters' regime and the creed upon which it rests; then to return to the world and rebuild it on the basis of a philosophy recognizing the role of the mind in human life, that is, a philosophy of reason, egoism, individualism, and capitalism.

Are there antagonists who oppose him? Yes—fundamentally, Dagny Taggart and Hank Rearden. The looters are Galt's philosophical enemies, but they survive by force and parasitism, as leeches on the productive effort of the philosophers, scientists, engineers, industrialists, and others. When the rational, productive men withdraw, the looters starve; they cannot stand on their own. In the terms of *The Fountainhead*, they are utterly second-handed in the mode by which they seek survival. The parasites need productive individuals like Dagny and Rearden to support their existence.

One of the many bold and distinctive aspects of the novel is the good versus good nature of its essential conflict. Although Galt and his allies are determined to bring down the parasites' regime, the parasites themselves are helpless to offer opposition. Incapable of so much as independent survival, they are not the slightest match for the intellectual and moral giants who seek the end of their rule. Only the nonstriking producers, such as Dagny and Rearden, can defeat them, and temporarily prop up the looters' moribund regime.

Because this is a novel about a strike, it is possible to understand all of its characters in terms of strike-related categories. These reduce to four: the strikers (Galt and his allies), the scabs (primarily Rearden and Dagny), management (the statist politicians and their intellectual supporters), and share-holders (the American people, to whom Galt addresses his radio broadcast). This understanding holds the essence of Ayn Rand's story: the thinkers go on strike against the philosophical-moral code that enslaves them. This is the plot-theme of *Atlas Shrugged*: the men of the mind going on strike against an altruist-collectivist society.[12]

The story presents a stark alternative regarding human nature: fundamentally, there exist the men of reason and the men of unreason. Just as Hugo shows a fundamental division and conflict between the kindhearted and the cruel—and Dostoyevsky between the godly and the sinful—so Ayn Rand presents a similar dichotomy between the men of the mind and the men of force, that is, between the rational and the irrational. She shows vividly what the two sides stand for in action.

In the world of the thinkers, John Galt creates both a motor and a philosophy that revolutionize men's lives. Rearden's metal, Ellis Wyatt's innovative method of extracting oil, and many other advances greatly improve human life on earth. In real life, of course, it was the men of genius who created the electric lighting system, the airplane, the cures of modern medicine, and numerous other inventions and new methods that promoted men's well-being. The author's principle is clear: where the mind is free to function, there is creativity, inventiveness, productivity, abundance, prosperity, and flourishing life.

In contrast is the world of the looters, the force initiators, in which government officials such as Mr. Thompson, Wesley Mouch, Floyd Ferris, and others, pass directives that enable less productive states to suck the life blood of Colorado—that make it impossible for Hank Rearden to profit on the product of his brains—that establish Railroad and Steel Unification Plans, demanding that the producers work at a loss, and so forth. They chain men to their jobs, shackle the mind by imposition of brute force, and ultimately drive the best thinkers to join the strike. In real life, the periods and nations in which independent thought was stifled by church or state—medieval western Europe, such past and present Communist tyrannies as Soviet Russia and North Korea, and various Third World dictatorships—led to regression, backwardness, and abysmal collapse. Again, Ayn Rand's principle is clear: where the mind is shackled by force, human life is tragically undercut.

The clash of rationality versus irrationality is dramatized in the novel's *dramatis personae*, as well as by its events—for every primary character is a carefully etched variation on the theme of reason versus unreason. Ayn Rand's literary skill creates characters who are breathing, flesh-and-bone individuals embodying philosophical principles—whether rational or irrational. In her main characters, she brings philosophical theories to pulsating life. Several examples of both heroes and villains will suffice to illustrate the point.

Ragnar Danneskjöld—philosopher, pirate, and collector of Internal Revenue—is a character only Ayn Rand could create. Before the reader directly encounters him, other characters whisper about him—that he is a ruthless criminal, a renegade, a pirate, a man devoid of moral scruple or regard for justice. Then the reader, with Hank Rearden, meets him. Danneskjöld accosts Rearden on a lonely road on a dark night a short while after the looters have stripped the industrialist of the rights to Rearden Metal. He hands him a bar of gold. He states: "I know that you don't need this gold at present. What you need is the justice which it represents, and the knowledge that there are men who care for justice." Ragnar describes himself as a policeman who restores to productive men the wealth stolen from them by the looters. In returning the gold sooner than he had intended, Ragnar breaks every rule that he had set for himself—but the sight of the looters robbing Rearden of his right to his metal was too much even for him. Why? Because the terrible crime abrogated his highest love. "Which is what?" "Justice," Ragnar replies.

Danneskjöld, the international police officer, is a stylized embodiment of the virtue of justice—the virtue requiring that men be judged by as *"rational a process of identification"* as is inanimate matter, that is, the virtue holding that the character of men must be evaluated by the same inviolate objectivity employed to assess the forces of nature. His victorious struggle to reclaim stolen property from the looters and restitute it to its proper owners dramatizes the principle that force backed by mind will always triumph over brute force (572–84, 1019).

John Galt, the strike's progenitor, is obviously a man of prodigious genius. In three distinct disciplines—philosophy, physics, statesmanship—he is a revolutionary thinker. In real life, only the greatest minds of human history— Aristotle, Michelangelo, Leonardo, Newton—could be considered his equal. Galt describes himself as "the man who loves his life," which is accurate. But fundamentally and above all, he is the man who perceives reality, the individual who permits no other consideration, no matter how painful, to interfere with his cognitive apprehension of the facts. He leaves his motor moldering on a scrap pile—he gives up for years the opportunity to woo the woman he loves—he lives through the agony of knowing that she is sleeping with another man—he knows it is very possible that he might never be able to achieve any of his specific goals. But he knows the strike is right, that it represents the only chance to create the kind of world in which he could flourish, and that he must do it. Observe that Ayn Rand characterizes him by reference to his ruthlessly perceptive eyes, those eyes that see facts for what they are, no matter his feelings about them or any other consideration (701, 954, 1009).

Galt's cognitive method of operation may be termed: heroic rationality. Such a method involves an undeviating allegiance to the facts of reality, if necessary in the teeth of any and all opposition, and any and all consequences. In the short term, the consequences may be painful. But in principle such a method is the core of a man's self-interest—for his survival, prosperity, and happiness depend on it. Its antipode—irrationality, the willful denial of reality—can bring only demise, destruction, and death.

Heroic rationality is, therefore, not a duty, a renunciation or a tight-lipped stoic acceptance. It is rather a celebration. It is the recognition that the achievement of values, of joy, of life depend on it—and that any other course leads to suffering and, ultimately, to death.

This proactive eagerness to seek out truth, and the inviolable willingness to accept it—this profoundly selfish adherence to reality—is the essence of John Galt's characterization. This is the deepest reason that Galt can properly say: "I am the man who loves his life." Such a truthful emotional claim is an effect of enacting the necessary epistemological cause. Joyous life requires heroic rationality. Certainly, Galt's genius is not representative of everyman; but his cognitive method might be and ought to be.

Ayn Rand's villains, as well as her heroes, offer a colorful and enlightening cast of philosophical players. Fundamentally, *Atlas Shrugged* shows that either a man is for the mind or he is against it. Therefore, every major character in the story—and many of the minor ones—is a specific variation on this theme. Countless examples could be adduced, but a few will be sufficient.

Mr. Thompson, head of state, is a consummate statist politician, utterly contemptuous of theory, principles, and ideas, concerned solely with practical action in the immediate moment. He has regard for one thing only: preserving his rule for the next day, hour or second. When a military march is played on the radio following Galt's speech, Wesley Mouch screams for it to be cut off. "It will make the public think that we authorized that speech," he says. Mr. Thompson insists that the radio station go on playing it. "Would you rather have the public think that we didn't?" he asks. He seeks to find Galt, because the strike leader has "a pressure group: he's cornered all the men of brains." Mr. Thompson believes that Galt is open to a compromise, that the looters will "have to make a few concessions to big business," and that Galt will then work with them. When Mouch objects regarding Galt's ideas, Mr. Thompson impatiently interjects: "Who cares about ideas?" When Mouch persists, claiming that Galt will not be open to a deal, Mr. Thompson responds with the essence of his wisdom: "There's no such thing" (1071, 1075–76).

Mr. Thompson is a consistent practitioner of the philosophy of pragmatism. On such a world view, developed and made popular by William James and John Dewey, there are no absolutes and no principles valid beyond the next instant—truth is whatever satisfies human needs for the moment—ideas are solely instruments for taking immediate action—and, above all, the theoretical is eschewed in favor of the practical. Expressed simply, truth is whatever helps satisfy the desire of the moment—whether individual or social. For Mr. Thompson, an arch-power seeker, whichever policy supports his rule temporarily— even if a deal with his sworn philosophical enemy—is the true and the right. His character, therefore, by rejecting principles, theory, and long range thinking in favor of short term activism, dramatizes one variation of a virulent anti-mind philosophy. Consequently, his myopic vision of human life leads necessarily to the country's collapse and to his own ruin.

A more powerful and tragic example in *Atlas Shrugged* is provided by Dr. Robert Stadler, a brilliant abstract scientist and former teacher of Galt and his principal allies. Stadler, a true genius in his field, studies cosmic rays and is unconcerned regarding practical matters of life on earth. When Dagny shows him the remnants of Galt's motor and manuscript, Stadler immediately recognizes the extraordinary "feat of pure, abstract science" the inventor had achieved—but then wonders: "Why did he want to waste his mind on practical appliances?" (355–56).

Philosophically, Stadler is a Platonist. He draws a sharp distinction between the theoretical and the applied, studies the realm of pure, abstract science and repudiates practical applications, is fascinated by cosmic rays and uninterested in man's earthly existence. In effect, he posits a separate realm of ideas beyond the prosaic concerns of this world, a higher world superior to this one that represents the true object of study by great intellects. But, on his view, the common man is a vulgar philistine interested only in his earthly life and utterly unconcerned with a higher world of ideas. Left free, ordinary men will never support impractical research into purely theoretical questions. Therefore, they have to be forced to do so; hence, his advocacy for the coercively established State Science Institute. For their own good, the illiterate plebeians must be ruled by their intellectual and moral superiors, in effect, by a Scientist King; and Stadler is driven remorselessly by the logic of his own premises to first set himself up as the aristocratic ruler of the state established science foundation, and, subsequently, to seek mastery of Project X and proclaim himself baron of a personal fiefdom in Iowa.

His death in the ensuing disaster is a just recompense for a genius turned dictator. His gravest sin is that he divorced the mind—mankind's survival instrument—from all considerations of survival; and that, holding men incapable of reason, he turned himself into the thinkers' primordial antagonist—a man of brute force.

The timeless clash between rationality and irrationality permeates every aspect of this novel.

Because of this, the story effectively dramatizes the author's central point: the source of progress, prosperity, and, indeed, every value that enhances human life is not manual labor but the mind. In the absence of genius, no amount of muscular effort could create Galt's motor or Rearden Metal—nor learn to grow crops, build cities or skyscrapers, cure diseases, or advance in any field from literature to music to physics to a hundred others. Such understanding leads directly to the novel's theme, which is now clear: the role of the mind in man's existence. Ayn Rand expresses her theme by dramatizing both the mind's free functioning and its suppression—by showing its presence in human society and its absence—presenting her point in positive terms and in negative ones.[13]

The question can be raised: What is *Atlas Shrugged* really about? The clearest answer can be provided by contrast with *Les Misérables* and *The Brothers*

Karamazov. Hugo, of course, seeks to regenerate social institutions. Dostoyevsky looks to purify man's nature. What does Ayn Rand attempt to accomplish?

She does not hope to transform human nature, à la Dostoyevsky. This, she
recognizes, is not possible; for it is fixed by nature, by reality; it is, in her technical terms, metaphysical, not man-made, and is not subject to choice. Nor is
it necessary—for, as the story vividly dramatizes, man's rational faculty is life
giving.

Certainly, Rand, like Hugo, seeks to promote political/social change, but
even this goal is neither fundamental nor sweeping. Observe in this regard
that near the end of *Atlas Shrugged,* Judge Narragansett revises portions of
the *United States Constitution,* and adds the clause: "Congress shall make no
law abridging the freedom of production and trade" (1167–68). In so doing,
he merely applies the document's fundamental principle of individual rights
more consistently, including in the economic realm. Ayn Rand's point is clear:
the original founding principles of the United States are superb, but there have
been and remain inconsistencies of formulation and application that enabled
the statists to push the nation toward dictatorship. These inner contradictions
must be expunged and the principle of individual rights affirmed across the
board. Important though this is, however, it is not the primary goal of the
book's hero. Ayn Rand's masterpiece is not fundamentally about politics, for
she is after much bigger game.

Atlas Shrugged is an impassioned plea for man to discover and embrace his
rational nature, including and especially in regard to moral principles.

Changes in human nature are neither possible nor necessary—and social-
political changes, though significant, are secondary consequences.

Atlas Shrugged is about man's discovery of himself.

The author makes clear by means of both her story's events and its dialogue
that human history and philosophy have been largely an attempt to deny and/
or suppress man's mind. Religion rejects it for faith. Emotionalism rejects it for
feelings. Materialism rejects it for neural firings, internal chemical reactions,
and manual labor. Modern education, entrusted with the sacred responsibility
of nurturing it, has instead labored to cripple it. Dictatorships of every conceivable ilk have suppressed it in favor of blind obedience. Conquerors, plunder-
ers, and common thieves have eschewed it for brute force and/or fraud. Even
the common man has too often innocently rejected it for drudgery and an unthinking work-a-day grind. The mind, the faculty responsible for every magnificent achievement and for sustaining human life itself, is and has been ignored,
reviled, stifled. Relentlessly, the human race has sought to commit suicide.

Ayn Rand, the atheist, has written a religious hymn to the glory of man's
mind. In it, she sings of the great and notable deeds already performed by
rational men, and provides them with both heartfelt gratitude and a moral
sanction. She further sings of the potential lying still untapped within the human spirit—the discoveries, the inventions, the explorations, the innovations

that thinking man can yet attain. She exalts the abundance that man could create. In the *Aeneid*, writing about a mighty warrior, Virgil "sings of arms and of a man." In *Atlas Shrugged*, writing about a peerless genius, Ayn Rand sings of the mind and of a rational man.

Atlas Shrugged is a love poem written to man's mind.

This is the core of its meaning.

PART FOUR: THE TRIUMPH OF THE GOOD

The questions this essay seeks to answer are: Why are Hugo and Dostoyevsky unable to artistically project the triumph of the good as they conceive it? And why is Ayn Rand alone, of all the great romantics, capable of it? The information necessary to provide the answers has now been examined.

Observe first an important truth regarding human nature shared in common by these writers. In *Les Misérables*, man is confronted by a fundamental alternative: humane benevolence or callous indifference. In *The Brothers Karamazov*, man is confronted by a different basic alternative: God or the devil. In *Atlas Shrugged*, man is again confronted with a fundamental alternative: rationality or irrationality. It is not just Jean Valjean or the four Karamazov brothers or John Galt and the strikers who face these choices in their respective universes; rather, all human beings must choose between them; none can escape the necessity of fundamental choice. All men are ultimately either humane or inhumane—Godly or ungodly—rational or irrational. When the intellectual themes are inductively extracted from the specific events of these books, the truth of one of Ayn Rand's esthetic principles is confirmed: romanticism is the literary school that recognizes and upholds the principle of man's volition.

But more to the point: romantics recognize man's ability to know the good, that is, the fundamental moral truths of human life. Hugo argues that a benign humaneness in action is the good, that man can and should recognize and affirm it. Dostoyevsky claims that Godliness is the good, and that man can and should embrace it. Ayn Rand shows that an unbreached rationality is man's tool of survival, that this is the good, and that man can and must honor his rational nature. *Romantics repudiate skepticism.*

A fundamental reason that romanticism is currently out of literary vogue is that romantics reject the modernist belief that intellectual issues are hopelessly complex, that everybody has differing viewpoints, and that no one viewpoint is more truthful than any other. In the most important area of human life— ethics—romantics claim to have answers. They hold that there is a moral truth—and that men can know it. This is inherent in the principle of human volition: if men's choices are to be meaningful, then they must have the ability to choose the good and reject the evil; otherwise, volition is a trivial, inconsequential faculty. But to choose between X and non-X, one must know them. To choose the good, men must know the good.

But in Hugo's universe, and in Dostoyevsky's, the good upheld by each author loses its struggle with its antipode. In Hugo's universe, the saints are deceased and the world remains the same inhumane place it was before they lived. In Dostoyevsky's universe, it is true, Dmitri is ready to renounce sin, and Alyosha perhaps has some success bringing Christian teachings to children, but these Christian gains are severely delimited. The world remains the same roaring pesthole of iniquity that the author depicted at his tale's start. It is only in *Atlas Shrugged* that the fundamental villain—in this case, irrationality—is routed, and the fundamental hero—in this case, the mind—succeeds in transfiguring the world. Why?

Let's start with Dostoyevsky, whose ideas have the least chance of promoting positive change. As a devout Orthodox Christian, he upholds faith as the essential solution to the problems of human existence. But in fact, in reality, faith is hopeless. The eras and nations in which faith was/is culturally prevalent bear tragic witness to this claim. Western Europe during the Dark Ages, for example, was utterly dominated by Christian faith—and was abysmally backward regarding living standards, educational levels, and life expectancies. (Similarly today, the Arab-Islamic world, mired in medieval faith, depends on the secular West for whatever degree of modernization it achieves.)[14]

Employing an epistemological method telling them that burning bushes speak, men live inside whales, and virgins give birth, what could Father Zossima or Alyosha hope to accomplish? Could they learn to formulate scientific theories, increase crop production, cure diseases, build cities, and so forth, on such a method? Could they raise living standards, increase life expectancy, promote men's earthly happiness? Could they develop—or even accept—the theory of evolution or any other factual claim clashing with their faith-based beliefs? Clearly not. Their best is to give sermons, fight sin, preach love, and fervently pray as men die in their twenties of famine and bubonic plague. Faith is utterly powerless to bring about flourishing, successful, joyous life. Only reason, philosophy, science, technology, and industry are capable of this. The mind is man's instrument of survival.

But the mind is exactly what Dostoyevsky rejects. In the character of Ivan Karamazov, the Western-style intellectual, Dostoyevsky repudiates reason, science, and secular philosophy. Since, in reality, religion in an undiluted form brought (and could bring) only a Dark Age, the question must be asked: Is this Dostoyevsky's ideal? In many ways, it is. Certainly, he repudiates the secular philosophy and scientific advances that greatly improved human life on earth.

Ayn Rand once said that she did not write her planned last novel because she found it impossible to project her kind of hero, events, and universe in the world of the late twentieth century. A romantic realist projects men choosing among fundamental alternatives in the world as it is in his day. Notice in this regard that modern collectivists, in one form after another, not religionists, always constitute the villains of her novels. This is so, because the collectivists constituted the mind's worst enemy in the world of Ayn Rand's day. Romantic realist writers may project heroes changing the world of their day, but the world of their day is always the baseline from which they start.

Dostoyevsky certainly falls into this category. His story takes place in Russia as it was in his era, not in a historical past or a hypothetical fantasy realm. How realistic would it be to project the triumph of sin-bashing, medieval Christianity in the midst of nineteenth-century Europe, even Russia? It would be out of the question for two reasons. The relatively minor problem is that nineteenth-century European intellectual culture is becoming so secular that Nietzsche can accurately declare that God is dead. Even Russia's near term future at that time lay in Marxism, which although it embraces a Christian ethic, repudiates its transcendent metaphysics for materialism and atheism. To project the triumph of otherworldly, ascetic Christianity in nineteenth-century European Russia would not be realistic; it would require Dostoyevsky to lurch into fantasy to tell such a tale.

But the major problem is not that such a story is socially unrealistic—but that it is metaphysically impossible. Because an antimind, Zossima-like reliance on faith, and an utter repudiation of an Ivan-style Western rationalism, is incapable of achieving values in reality, it is consequently impossible for an artistically honest genius like Dostoyevsky to realistically project such an occurrence in fiction.

It is possible to write a fantasy about God interceding to perform various miracles; and, in fact, such a fantasy has been written. It's called the Bible. But a realistic portrayal of such events, in the kind of narrative Dostoyevsky would create, is impossible. Dostoyevsky, then, by the logic proceeding from his own fundamentals, finds it impossible to project the triumph of the good as he conceives it.

Hugo, although holding an enormously noble vision of human nature, in contrast to Dostoyevsky's sin-based viewpoint, is in essentially the same position. The central problem in the universe of *Les Misérables* is man's inhumanity to man. Hugo's solution, in effect? All you need is love. But in fact, men are able to project the power and triumph of the good only to the extent that they embrace the mind.

In Hugo's universe, the good has far greater power than in Dostoyevsky's, because Hugo, at least implicitly, recognizes that the mind plays a positive role in man's life. For example, Jean Valjean performs his greatest good by creating an innovative manufacturing process that transforms the economy of his town. In this, Hugo recognizes the virtue of the technological and industrial revolutions emanating from Great Britain and sweeping through the Western world during the nineteenth century. More broadly, there is no Ivan Karamazov-type character in this universe to serve as the author's whipping boy, and no railing against Western rationalism and science.

But for all his implicit acceptance of the mind, Hugo is explicitly primarily an emotionalist. In the end, it is love—an emotion—that is lacking in the world, and which constitutes the necessary ingredient to ameliorate the human condition. But, in reality, love is not the means by which men deal effectively with nature; it is not the means, for example, by which they grow food, build cities, cure diseases, and so forth; all of which is necessary to remediate the terrible sufferings of the starving masses that Hugo so powerfully depicts. Obviously, only reason can accomplish this.

Further, love is not even a primary in promoting men's ability to interact positively with society, never mind nature. Benevolent good will toward our fellow man is truly a valuable characteristic, but it rests upon underlying fundamentals. To effectively care about and aid another man, it is necessary to respect his rights, fundamentally his right to his own life and to his own mind, the means by which he furthers his life. To do this, it is necessary to first revere the mind and its life-giving nature.

There are exhilarating elements of a rational philosophy in Hugo's universe, but it is not consistent and far from dominant. Enjolras is a brilliant intellectual; the bishop is not; and Jean Valjean generally is not. Hugo's heroes are simply unequipped to battle their malevolent social antagonists and to reform the social order. John Galt could bring the sweeping social changes Hugo seeks. But the saints of *Les Misérables* cannot. Love is not the instrument that will transform human life on earth.

Observe that Christianity has promoted "love" as the answer for 2,000 years, but the clearest practical expression of its full philosophy was the Dark Ages. Marxists claim to love the people—and have proved it by murdering 100 million of them in ninety years. Love is not the answer—and Hugo, for all his monumental genius and profound nobility of spirit, has not found the answer to the social problems he addresses. Consequently, his heroes have no chance to transfigure the social order.

A life-promoting philosophy must be formulated and then spread throughout a culture before sweeping social change becomes possible. Enjolras had the best chance to bring profound change in the universe of *Les Misérables*. He is brilliantly intellectual and holds fundamentally the right philosophy, but made the tragic error of opting for political revolution before his ideas were widespread in French society. His only chance lay in education, not in battle. He fails to understand this point, because Hugo has not fully grasped or embraced the role of the mind in man's life.

By contrast, John Galt did not start a political revolution; he did not lead his supporters on the barricades against the oppressive forces of the statists. He understands that philosophical education is a necessary step toward sweeping political change. His strike is, in effect, an educational tool—as is his climactic radio address. Once the strike has demonstrated, in action, the utter reliance of mankind on the men of the mind—and only then—can Galt present to the American people the ideas that explain it. In terms of logic, Galt is an inductive thinker: he shows the facts first, and then he theoretically explains them. The result is a devastating demonstration of philosophical truth; the American people understand it; the regime of the looters cannot long survive; and, eventually, the strikers are free to return to the world. John Galt succeeds fully in his selfish mission to remake the world into a place where he and the other men of the mind are free to flourish.

Since, in fact, the mind is the means by which men achieve values and promote life, Ayn Rand is able to realistically portray the mind's triumph over irrationality and brute force. Although Ayn Rand does not dramatize the specific deeds by means of which the men of the mind rebuild the world from the shattered remnants of the looter's regime, she leaves no doubt that such reconstruction is imminent and that the thinkers, now free, will lift men to exalted heights of progress and prosperity. The author shows this in the book's final scene, as the strikers plan their return. Midas Mulligan, for example, chooses the companies in which he will invest; Francisco completes the drawing of his new smelter, as Rearden and Ellis Wyatt discuss business; and, of course, Judge Narragansett edits the *U.S. Constitution*, adding a clause upholding the freedom of production and trade (1167–68).

The men of the mind are coming—and with them comes philosophy, the arts, research, science, medicine, technology, industry—and spiritual/material wealth. Since, in reality, the men of the mind have already accomplished this to a significant degree—especially in America, where the full benefits of the Scientific, Technological, and Industrial Revolutions were achieved—Ayn Rand is able to realistically project such a series of events in the universe of the novel.

Regarding a romantic realist's ability to project the triumph of the good as he conceives it, his attitude toward the mind must be identified. It needs to be asked: Who, if anyone, is the main proponent of the mind in the author's universe? The specific characters in these universes are Ivan Karamazov, Enjolras, and John Galt. The authors' attitudes toward them are made clear in the stories. Though Dostoyevsky sympathizes with Ivan's honest and tormented soul-searching, he repudiates his method and values. Though Hugo admires Enjolras enormously, he subordinates his Enlightenment philosophy of reason and the rights of man to a religiously based love of mankind. Only Ayn Rand fully understands the mind's creative role in promoting human survival and prosperity; consequently, only she is capable of projecting the triumph of the good in her fictional universe.

Because the mind is required to bring success in reality, it is likewise required to bring success in realistic fictional projections. It is important to recognize, as all the romantics do, that men possess the faculty of volition, the capacity to promote both individual and social betterment. But until they recognize that the essence of the good versus evil conflict is rationality versus irrationality, they will be unable to achieve the good in either reality or in realistic fiction. Because Ayn Rand is the only one of the great romantics to identify this monumental truth, she is the only one capable of realistically dramatizing the triumph of the good. This is the answer to the question raised in this essay.

NOTES

1. Ayn Rand, *The Romantic Manifesto* (New York: Signet, 1975), 91–93.

2. Rand, *Romantic Manifesto*, 73–78. I am indebted to Ron Pisaturo for his identification of a method of replicating inductions.

3. Rand, *Romantic Manifesto*, 76–77.

4. Rand, *Romantic Manifesto*, 77.

5. Victor Hugo, *Les Misérables*, translated by Lee Fahnestock and Norman MacAfee (New York: New American Library, 1987), 880–81.

6. Paul Benichou, "Introduction" to *Les Misérables*, abridged version (New York, Washington Square Press, 1972), xiv–xv.

7. But see Hugo's *Toilers of the Sea*, which is such a story.

8. Fyodor Dostoyevsky, *The Brothers Karamazov*, translated by Andrew MacAndrew (New York: Bantam, 1981), 168.

9. Dostoyevsky, *Brothers Karamazov*, 126, 127.

10. Dostoyevsky, *Brothers Karamazov*, 297–319.

11. Dostoyevsky, *Brothers Karamazov*, 127.

12. Rand, *Romantic Manifesto*, 77.

13. Rand, *Romantic Manifesto*, 77.

14. See my "The Tragedy of Theology: How Religion Caused and Extended the Dark Ages," *The Objective Standard*, Winter 2006–2007, 11–37.

11

A Tale of Two Novels

Harry Binswanger

Editor's note: This editorial originally appeared in the Las Vegas Review-Journal, *August 27, 1998. It has been slightly revised for republication here.*

In the "culture wars," a major battle erupted recently on the literary front. At issue: What is the best English-language novel of the century? The two opposing camps picked two opposite novels. Here is a representative passage from each.

Novel A:

He kissed the plump mellow yellow smellow melons of her rump, on each plump melonous hemisphere, in their mellow yellow furrow, with obscure prolonged provocative melonsmellonous osculation.

The visible signs of postsatisfaction?

A silent contemplation: a tentative velation: a gradual abasement: a solicitous aversion: a proximate erection.

Novel B:

She sat listening to the music. It was a symphony of triumph. The notes flowed up, they spoke of rising and they were the rising itself, they were the essence and the form of upward motion, they seemed to embody every human act and thought that had ascent as its motive. It was a sunburst of sound, breaking out of hiding and spreading open. It had the freedom of release and the tension of purpose. It swept space clean, and left nothing but the joy of an unobstructed effort. Only a faint echo within the sounds spoke of that from which the music had escaped, but spoke in laughing astonishment at the discovery that there was no ugliness or pain, and there never had had to be. It was the song of an immense deliverance.

Clearly, one of these novels is a stylistic masterpiece, and the other is trash. The fighting is over which is which.

Novel A is James Joyce's *Ulysses*, named best by a panel of "experts" at the Modern Library division of Random House.

Novel B is Ayn Rand's *Atlas Shrugged*, named best by the "unenlightened masses" who voted online in an Internet poll also conducted by Modern Library.

The culture wars, correctly conceived, actually reflect the clash between the intellectual establishment and the American people.

It has been said that everyone, in terms of his own philosophy, is either a Platonist or an Aristotelian. In broadest terms, the intellectuals are Platonists but the American people are Aristotelians.

Plato held that there are two realities—a higher realm of perfect, timeless abstractions and the degraded, illusory world we think we perceive by our senses. For Platonists, "higher truths" are revealed to the intellectual elite and cannot be communicated or explained to the masses, who stubbornly cling to "common sense"—i.e., reason and logic.

Aristotle, the father of logic, held that there is only one reality, the world we perceive by our senses. For Aristotelians, all knowledge is derived from sensory observation by a process of abstraction and conceptualization. Aristotle rejected Plato's mystical, elitist tendencies and held that by adherence to logic we can and must make rational sense of everything. Joyce and his coterie of academic admirers are Platonists, Rand and her fans are Aristotelians.

Joyce's style alternates between gibbering wordplay ("mellow yellow smellow") and ponderous, woozy abstractions ("tentative velation"), the style conforming to Plato's dichotomy between perceptual concretes and ineffable abstractions. *Ulysses'* alleged meaning can be "intuited" only by a special circle of Joycean scholars. Rand's style, as in the third sentence, takes us by Aristotelian abstraction from the concrete (notes flowing up) to the more abstract ("the essence and form of upward motion"), to the still more abstract ("every human thought and effort that had ascent as its motive"), making the meaning vividly clear to any rational mind.

Platonists view man as a metaphysical misfit, caught in a conflict between the spiritual realm and this debased world. Man's earthly concerns, such as sex, drag him down to a smarmy, animalistic level, making him appear infantile and ridiculous.

Aristotelians, as the passage from Rand expresses, view man as a noble, potentially heroic being, whose highest moral purpose is to achieve his own happiness on this earth ("the joy of unobstructed effort").

A poll conducted by the Library of Congress and the Book of the Month Club asked what book has most affected reader's personal lives. *Atlas Shrugged* placed second only to the Bible. Many report that reading the novel was a profoundly emotional experience, as well as an intellectual one. Readers of *Atlas Shrugged* talk about the book changing their lives, and that change is due not only to the explicit, philosophical content of the book, but also to its exalted vision of what life, and man, can be.

It is not really fair to ask if *Ulysses* holds similar meaning for the Platonists, because the book is practically impossible to read—which is the reason for its snob appeal. *Ulysses* recalls the saying, "They muddy the waters to make them appear deep."

Until a generation of Aristotelian philosophers converts the pseudo-intellectuals to reason and reality, the deeper culture wars will rage on.

12

Adapting *Atlas Shrugged* to Film

Jeff Britting

INTRODUCTION

A motion picture version of Ayn Rand's novel *Atlas Shrugged* has been in development for over thirty-five years. Reports in the media of failed efforts to develop a filmable screenplay and to secure production funding now fill a thick clipping file. Hollywood's first reported interest in the novel as a film property appeared in 1957. Its most recent producing efforts extend to the present; yet, to date, no film has been made. As a result, *Atlas Shrugged* has developed a reputation as an unfilmable novel. The reasons cited by observers vary. These include the novel's 1,168-page length. Its story—the strike by the men and women of the mind against a collectivist world that does not recognize their fundamental value—is a mystery-thriller written in a dramatic, action-adventure style and is well suited to Hollywood. Yet the novel depicts a radical, new philosophy: a moral code of rational self-interest, which is summarized in speeches of daunting length.[1]

During Rand's lifetime, the integrity of *Atlas Shrugged* and its potential film adaptation were a real concern to her. Beginning in 1972 and ending in 1982, the year of her death, she was active in her novel's development as a film, which included her final approval of its script. However, Rand's involvement raised an issue in Hollywood. As summarized by Michael Jaffe, a film producer who spearheaded one such effort:

> The reputation [in Hollywood] is that her stories are too idea-filled to make into films; if she had stayed out of it and let them just make the movies, take the best of the plot and not be whipsawed by all the philosophy, they'd be great stories. But it was the whipsawing that always killed it. It was the sense that the stories were too full of philosophy, and the people who controlled the rights to her stories would never let you just go out and *make the movie*.[2] [Emphasis added.]

At issue is what it will take to "make the movie." Can a screen adaptation of *Atlas Shrugged* render the book's "great" story without the "whipsawing" of its philosophy and plot?

The historic failures notwithstanding, the evidence suggests that Ayn Rand's answer was: *it can be done.* In fact, Rand was writing such an adaptation at the end of her life. Although she did not live to complete her script, the work and its underlying literary method are worth studying, particularly by any writer struggling to adapt the novel today. And *plot* is the *crucial* aspect of her underlying method to study. Plot, she wrote, is a "purposeful progression of logically connected events leading to the resolution of a climax."[3] In Rand's view, creating a plot is the primary means of constructing a story. It is also the primary means of conveying a story's content, including its philosophical content. *Atlas Shrugged* is an illustration of her theory in practice. If one knows her theory, then adapting the story and retaining both its drama and philosophy is possible.[4]

As a writer, Rand had a particular view of the connection between storytelling and the concept of *value.* And she viewed plot as a literary means of underscoring the importance of one's values. Further, as a philosopher, she saw a connection between values and philosophy. In the first part of this chapter, the connection between storytelling and values will be introduced and illustrated with examples from Rand's early film experience.[5] Next we will present Rand's view of the link between values and philosophy. We will then consider how complex actions on screen can carry and express, correspondingly, complex philosophical content. Building on this base, the second part of this paper explores Rand's unfinished 1981–1982 adaptation of *Atlas Shrugged.* We will examine the script's basic plot situation and her efforts to elaborate it, addressing issues of characterization and style as well. Our study concludes with a brief parting comment, intended partly for writers, on how best to proceed practically.

Rand's unfinished adaptation of *Atlas Shrugged* presents scripted action and dialogue that fuses seamlessly with the book's philosophy. The "whipsawing" of philosophy and plot feared by Hollywood is, actually, a groundless fear. At the end of this study, we will see why. We will know a *principle* that will help us adapt an "idea-filled" novel, while keeping its philosophy intact and flowing through a page-turning, filmable script.[6]

PLOT AND PHILOSOPHY

In the context of storytelling, a plot sequence underscores the importance, the merit, the worth, the *value* of a specific theme by means of depicting the actions taken in its pursuit.[7]

Now let us illustrate this point with an actual plot example from Rand's early work, one that underscores the value of "romantic love." Fittingly, her story was originally conceived as a silent-film scenario. It is a simple situation without a title, yet, it contains all the basic elements of drama. The story concerns a young woman whose husband is captured during a war and awaits execution:

> Determined to save him, and with only hours left, the [young woman] devises an ingenious method of rescue. She has just begun to carry out her plan when she receives word that their child is gravely ill and needs her. She must choose between abandoning her child and leaving her husband to certain death. She makes her choice: she will not desert the greatest of her values—her husband. The story does not end with disaster: she is successful in freeing him, and their child recovers.[8]

This brief sequence of events brings the value of romantic love sharply into focus. The woman's love for her husband is not simply asserted: it is demonstrated in action. In the face of her husband's imminent execution, she attempts his rescue. However, her devotion to the value of her husband is challenged. Their gravely ill child, another important value, is introduced and requires immediate attention. The young woman now faces a clash of pursuits—a conflict of values—a conflict that must be resolved in one direction or the other. The climax of the story occurs when the woman chooses her husband, rather than her child, as the value most essential to her happiness. The resolution of her choice is the successful rescue of her husband and the eventual reunion with their child, who recovers.

In its brief statement, the story anticipates literary principles true of Rand's future work. Her story incorporates theme, value, choice, conflict, climax, resolution, characterization (her early focus on female protagonists) and even a certain style (film versus literature). But, what is most important, the story's attributes arise during their enactment. They are brought to life in action and organized in a logically connected sequence. This germ of a story contains action, choice, value, pursuit and, most important, conflict. In the context of the young woman's story, asserting a value judgment is meaningless without the enactment of it in reality. And the primary way to underscore the importance of a value is to place the value in danger and to demand effort to overcome the danger in order to retain the value. "Value is that which one acts to gain and or/keep," writes Rand in *Atlas Shrugged*. The value of the young woman's love for her husband is demonstrated by the magnitude of the effort expended by her to "gain and/or keep" him. Plot ("a progression of *events*—and 'events' in this context means actions in the physical world") is the crucial literary element by which a novelist or a screenwriter depicts such actions, actions which are in pursuit of values and—simultaneously—plot is the method of depicting the importance of values literarily.[9]

The scope of the possible action in the novel *Atlas Shrugged* and, therefore, the scope of possible values at stake, define the scope of a potential screen adaptation.

In *The Art of Fiction*, Rand condensed the novel's theme as "the importance of reason."[10] *Atlas Shrugged* takes a specific position on "reason." And the book's view of reason and its place in man's life is enormously abstract. It covers the entire range of man's existence, including the universe in which he exists, his means of knowledge, the standards he adopts in the pursuit of his values, including the values he can properly seek from other men and in what context. The compass of the theme "the importance of reason," raises, in its very statement, the whole sphere of philosophy. The fullest statement of the theme of *Atlas Shrugged* is: "the role of the mind in man's existence—and, as corollary, the demonstration of a new moral philosophy: the morality of rational self-interest."[11]

In the storytelling context that is our focus here, value is tied to plot action and, literarily, values are underscored by such action. In Rand's silent-film scenario, a young woman seeks to rescue the husband she values. The magnitude of her pursuit expresses her valuation. But how does this apply to more complicated actions and values—let alone the theme of "the importance of reason," which encompasses not just one or two values, but the universe of values, including the value of human life? Obviously, the role of the mind in preserving human life is a story essential. But how can such a complicated, controversial subject appear on screen? The basic issue to clarify is: What can actions carry in terms of content? How can the complex actions in a screenplay express, correspondingly, complex philosophical content? As a lead, Rand relates an experience at the start of her writing career while employed in a story department under director Cecil B. DeMille:

> I had already developed a strong plot sense; but although I could recognize a good plot story, I had not consciously identified what characteristics made it good. DeMille told me something that clarified the issue for me.
>
> He said that a good story depends on what he called "the situation," by which he meant a complicated conflict, and that the best stories are those which can be told in one sentence. In other words, if the essential situation (not the whole story, of course) can be told in one sentence, this makes for a good plot story.

Rand related how DeMille decided to purchase the story for *Manslaughter*, which was originally a novel and eventually a successful silent film. "A friend," she continues, "wired [DeMille] in Hollywood advising him to buy it for the screen. The friend included only one sentence about the story: 'A righteous young district attorney has to prosecute the woman he loves, a spoiled heiress, for killing a policeman in an automobile accident.' This is all DeMille knew about the story, and he bought it."[12]

The "situation" is a complicated conflict that lays out the framework of a story. In effect, it is adaptation in reverse, whereby one reduces a larger literary whole to its most important, transferable elements. From the "situation" a story could be repositioned, extended, and enacted in multiple ways. As a silent film directed by Cecil B. DeMille, it was presented without dialogue in the course of a one-hour-and-forty-minutes running time. As a novel, the situation unfolded over hundreds of pages—with subordinate parts, including secondary characters, shifts in time and location—all implied by the central conflict. As a contemporary, feature-length motion picture—or television miniseries— this situation could be rendered in action and dialogue in the course of 126 (or more) pages. In each case, the situation remains the same, while the forms elaborating the situation's inherent complexity differ in scope.

The pattern is evident in "Red Pawn," an early film scenario written in the 1930s.[13] Philosophically, Rand's purpose in "Red Pawn" was to expose "the evil of dictatorship and equate Communism with religion. Like *We the Living* [her first novel, set in Soviet Russia], the plot of 'Red Pawn' involves a love triangle: a woman becomes the mistress of a Soviet prison commandant in order to secure the freedom of a prisoner she loves."[14] For the first time, Rand writes explicitly on the subject of plot, philosophy, and film. She calls her method writing in "tiers or layers of depth."

In a 1934 letter to Kenneth MacGowan, a producer and director, Rand summarizes her theory:

There is only one common denominator which can be understood and enjoyed by all men, from the dullest to the most intelligent, and that is plot. . . . The novelty of what I propose to do—and I believe it is a novelty, for I have never seen it done deliberately—consists in the following: in building the plot of a story in such a manner that it possesses tiers or layers of depth, so that each type of audience can understand and enjoy only as much of it as it wants to understand and enjoy.

Rand explains how her technique would not "burden" the viewer with more meaning than he or she was prepared or willing to entertain. "[T]he same story can stand as a story without any of its deeper implications, so that those who do not care to be, will not be burdened with any intellectual or artistic angles, and yet those who do care for them will get those angles looking at *exactly the same material*." [Emphasis added.] She illustrates by reference to the plot situation. On the surface,

["Red Pawn" is] merely the story of a woman who comes, at the price of a great sacrifice, to rescue her husband from a life sentence in prison and of her worst enemy's great, unhappy love for her. There is nothing very intellectual or difficult to understand about that. . . . Those who cannot go any further will be held merely by these physical facts of the plot as it develops, merely by the most primitive suspense of the story, by the quality they would enjoy in a plain serial.

But those who can see further, will have before them the spectacle of a rather unusual emotional crisis involving the three characters of the story, and the picture of a life and conditions which they have not seen very often.

Those who want to go still further, will see the *philosophical problem* of the main figure in the story—the Commandant of the prison island—the clash of his belief in a stern duty above all with the belief in a right to the joy of living above all, as exemplified in the woman. And this clash is not merely a matter of details and dialogue. *It is an inseparable part of the very basic plot itself.*[15] [Emphasis added.]

If Rand regarded plot as *"the* crucial attribute of the novel," then she regarded the plot of *Atlas Shrugged* as its *industrial formula.* The logically connected series of actions leading to its climax are essential to the book's literary
values, its enduring popularity, and its adaptability on screen.

The industrial metaphor is apt. It surfaces in her notes regarding the choice
of film director for *Atlas Shrugged,* one on the order of a "Fritz Lang or Alfred
Hitchcock," and whom she describes as an "engineer" and not a *"comedia
dell'arte"* improviser.[16] The engineering metaphor is also present in her writings on literature, where she describes the fundamentality of plot in relation
to other literary attributes:

> The plot of a novel serves the same function as the steel skeleton of a skyscraper:
> it determines the use, placement and distribution of all the other elements. Mat-
> ters such as the number of characters, background, descriptions, conversations,
> introspective passages, etc. have to be determined by what the plot can carry, i.e.,
> have to be integrated with the events and contribute to the progression of the
> story. Just as one cannot pile extraneous weight or ornamentation on a building
> without regard for the strength of its skeleton, so one cannot burden a novel [or
> screenplay] with irrelevancies without regard for its plot. The penalty, in both
> cases, is the same: the collapse of the structure.[17]

The integrity of plot structure occasioned a long, 1945 letter to Henry
Blanke—the Warner Bros. producer responsible for her own screen adaptation of *The Fountainhead.* In this excerpt Rand expressed concerns that apply
equally to *Atlas Shrugged:*

> Do not attempt to devise a different plot or a different climax. It can't be done.
> It took me seven years to work out this one—and I know. Don't waste your time
> and money. This story—to be what it is—has to be told in these particular events.
> If you change them—you won't get "something like *The Fountainhead.*" You'll get
> *nothing like The Fountainhead.*[18]

Rand never wrote about film at length. But scattered throughout her works
and commentaries are statements that reinforce the primacy of plot.

In a 1960s radio discussion of the visual arts, Rand offers a more detailed
estimate of the medium:

> Film is a composite art, made up of an integration of other arts. . . . Film combines
> all other human arts that the medium can employ. Primarily, of course, it is a dra-
> matic medium; therefore, it involves literature. It is presented visually; therefore, it
> involves painting. It involves sculpture and architecture, in the sense of the three-
> dimensional projection of sets. It involves acting, which is an interpretive art. It
> involves music, singing, dancing—any art form can be used in film. A similar art is
> opera, which combines drama and music, along with acting and singing. But film
> is a much wider composite; it is a sum of all the other arts. Therefore, potentially,
> film is probably the greatest of the composite arts.[19]

In a 1960s essay on esthetics, Rand describes film's highest expression to
date:

As an example of film direction at its best, I shall mention Fritz Lang, particularly in his earlier work. His silent-film *Siegfried* is as close to a great work of art as films have come. . . . Lang is the only one who has fully understood the fact that *visual art is an intrinsic part of films in a much deeper sense than the mere selection of sets and camera angles—that a "motion picture" is literally that, and has to be a stylized visual composition in motion.*[20] [Emphasis added.]

In 1980 Ayn Rand was asked her goal for a proposed television miniseries of *Atlas Shrugged* and whether the "projection of an ideal man" was her purpose. "No," she replied, "That's accomplished by the book." However, she continued, a motion picture adaptation of the novel,

will make the ideas more vivid. More dramatic. Literature, a book, is a very abstract art, probably the most abstract art. And a television show would be the perfect vehicle to concretize the meaning of the book's events. Not philosophical teaching so much, as the overall, what I call, "sense of life," the basic abstraction of the book. To tell people what kind of world it would be. Not tell them. Show them."[21]

To show the basic abstraction of *Atlas Shrugged* is to show the concrete events out of which the abstraction of the book is formed. The entire arsenal of filmmaking is available to serve that end, but only if that end is guided by the basic principle guiding the selection of the building blocks that form the abstraction, that is, the plot, which makes the story possible—*and adaptable.*

ADAPTING A PHILOSOPHICAL NOVEL

Let us turn to Rand's unfinished teleplay "Atlas Shrugged" (1981–1982). In the nature of the case, the evidence is incomplete. Rand finished a little under one third of a proposed nine-hour teleplay of *Atlas Shrugged*. Nevertheless, Rand's script, as well as her notes and outlines on earlier efforts—written over the course of a decade—are pregnant with insight. These manuscript materials are indicative of her basic "plot" driven orientation. The script's 326 handwritten pages stop immediately after the successful launch of the John Galt Line and at the start of the Dagny Taggart and Hank Rearden love affair. The notes, outlines, and comments on previous efforts are part of an incomplete mosaic of writing preparation, commentary, editing, and actual writing. However, the basic literary principle of plot, which has been our focus, as well as the other basic principles—theme, characterization, style—are present in the materials we will now examine.

Plot "Situation" and Its Elaboration

As we have noted earlier, *plot* is the "purposeful progression of events . . . leading to the resolution of a climax." Among Rand's existing notes, there is no indication that the basic situation or "plot-theme," as Rand later renamed DeMille's idea, changes. The script's theme remains "the role of the mind in man's existence." The situation is "the men of the mind going on strike against an altruist-collectivist society."[22] Albert S. Ruddy, producer of *The Godfather*, who first took on the project of producing *Atlas Shrugged* in 1972, summarizes an early view of the situation:

> [I]t was going to be a thriller, a love story, with the underpinnings of a man who wanted to turn off the motor of the world and to restart it again. But it was going to be a thriller and have a lot of suspense, and be a terrific love story. And it was going to be a mystery of trying to figure out who was pulling these strings. The main line was Dagny trying to save the railroad and Rearden trying to save the alloy and how they come together.

Ruddy projected a feature film of two and a half to three hours in length. The challenge was selecting what to omit from the book's 1,168 page length. In Ruddy's words, this involved "knowing what to abstract."[23]

In an undated early note, most likely written around 1972, the process of abstraction begins. Rand elaborates the "situation" by listing a series of discrete events or "keypoints," which sketches the arc of the film's story. The events are essential to the "main line" of focus, which, as Ruddy puts it, is "Dagny trying to save the railroad and Rearden trying to save the alloy and how they come together." Rand's 1972 note is the shortest summary of the film-to-be. And being the most condensed of Rand's notes, in some respects it is one of the most valuable:

THE KEYPOINTS

PART I

The John Galt Line – The search for the Inventor of the Motor – Wyatt's Torch

PART II

The Moratorium on Brains (Directive 10-289) – The tunnel catastrophe – Dagny and "frozen train," her flight, her crash.

PART III

"Atlantis" & Galt – The progressive destruction of Chapter V (the copper wire) Dagny-Galt affair – the Siege of Rearden Steel, & Rearden quitting – Galt's speech – Galt's arrest – the torture scene – the rescue. The Finale in Atlantis.[24]

Elsewhere, Rand suggests an underlying reason for the "keynote" events. As presented in a separate discussion from the 1960s, Rand describes what she must show in order to demonstrate "the importance of reason." Her comments mention two of the keynotes listed above: "The John Galt Line" and "The tunnel catastrophe." In the novel (and screenplay) Rand must establish "what reason is, how it operates, and why it is important":

> The sequence on the construction of the John Galt Line is included for that purpose—to concretize the mind's role in human life. The rest of the novel illustrates the consequences of the mind's absence. In particular, the chapter on the tunnel catastrophe shows concretely what happens to a world where men do not dare to think or to take the responsibility of judgment. If, at the end of the novel, you are left with the impression "Yes, the mind is important and we should live by reason," these incidents are the cause. The concretes have summed up in your mind to the abstraction with which I started, and which I had to break down *into* concretes.[25]

The basic "situation" of *Atlas Shrugged* and its elaboration imply a number of possible formats, from the simple to the complex. These would determine what selection (or condensation) of characters are necessary to enact the "mind on strike." Aside from the projected nine-hour miniseries and a two and one half hour theatrical release previously mentioned, several other formats were discussed. There are reports of a four-hour two-part theatrical film as well as two shorter miniseries. The documentary evidence of this is sometimes brief but it is not cryptic. On the contrary, because of Rand's fundamental reliance on plot structure, any note on plot by dint of its inclusion becomes significant. However, the most fully worked-out example is her teleplay.[26]

Summary: "Atlas Shrugged" teleplay, 1981–1982

The first third of her 1981–1982 screenplay opens with a world at the end stage of decay and with the despairing expression: "Who is John Galt?" Rand's adaptation runs close to the novel. This includes the building of the John Galt Line both as a showcase for Rearden Metal and the incident leading to the Dagny Taggart and Hank Rearden love affair. The final sequence, which Rand wrote on January 1, 1982, begins with Dagny awakening in bed, smiling radiantly in recognition of their newly experienced intimacy. Rearden, on the opposite side of the room, is a moment away from exploding in contempt for the both of them—which the altruistic morality he has embraced requires—having succumbed to a sexual desire he views as depraved. At this point, Rand stopped writing, and the script remains unfinished.[27]

This summary appears to follow several earlier and undated outlines prepared by Rand. Of special interest is her handling of the subplot depicting the country's reaction to the building of the John Galt Line. Her adaptation includes the introduction of new characters. It also introduces a dramatic device with unfulfilled implications for the unfinished portions of the script.

In the novel, public opinion against Rearden's new metal is expressed grad-ually: first through dismissal by James Taggart, followed by the indifference of Rearden's family and culminating in a disinformation campaign initiated by the government to discredit Rearden's achievement. In the script, protests against the metal begin with picketing at the factory on the night that the metal is first poured. The culture's hostility towards Rearden escalates. Rand intro-duces a "hippie" character leading a street protest. College campus protests are also introduced. The student movement becomes television talk-show fodder featuring negative commentary from intellectuals of the day. In the novel, such views were expressed explicitly and at length during a party celebrating Rearden's wedding anniversary. In the script, the party is retained, allowing for the initial meeting between Rearden and Francisco, but is shortened. In the script, media coverage of the countrywide protest against Rearden's Metal and the John Galt Line is conveyed though the camera point-of-view, moving through the television screen into the actual party in progress.

The unfulfilled implications of television are interesting. Rand frequently planted important dramatic devices at the beginning of her stories. Although there is no evidence of this in her notes, the use of the television "eye" to con-dense and dramatize the negative intellectual state of the country would have afforded, at the end of the teleplay, a means to revise Galt's speech. Instead of a radio address, Galt's speech could have been dramatized as a documentary proper to television. A visualization of the world "as it is" against Galt's vision of "what it ought to be," while underscoring his own words, is a fertile dramatic opportunity. In the novel, a radio speech is entirely appropriate. The passage of time is not specified nor are we aware of the passage of time during our reading of the speech. This could not be so in a motion picture. Its presentation in a film version would require a dramatic equivalent, an example of which is suggested here. "By the time I come to an abstract speech," Rand commented, "I've given you all the concretes required for you to draw a conclusion—and then I draw the conclusion."[28] Michael Jaffe recalls discussing Galt's Speech, which runs over sixty pages in the novel. Rand read and timed the speech:

> It was four hours and twenty minutes or something, so she knew you weren't go-ing to take three nights on TV to read John Galt's speech. So, she said, "You have to find a dramatic equivalent for that. But I am going to edit that speech for you, so don't worry, and I will get that speech down to three to seven minutes. I'll have to do it; no one else is equipped to do that."[29]

Unfortunately, Rand did not indicate the nature of her own "dramatic equiva-lent," but the first third of the script is suggestive, nonetheless.

A Scene in Detail

With the basic summary of the extant script in mind, let us now take a closer look at the development of an actual scene, starting with the novel and moving to the script. This will further our illustration of Rand's process of adaptation.

In constructing her script, Rand appears to work from two sources: the dialogue lifted from the novel directly (which will be examined in a subsequent section) and the selection of logically connected sequences. Although the line leading from the "the key points" to any one of the several proposed and one actual (though unfinished) versions is not known, Rand appears to flesh out the plot through intermediary outlining.

To get a sense of the rendering, let us focus first on the opening chapter as it appears in the novel. Then we will turn to the outlines and their narrowing focus, and then, ultimately, to the opening sequence as it appears in the script. (This pattern of adaptation demonstrated here is true of the finished portion of the unfinished script.)

In the novel, chapter one is appropriately named "The Theme." The chapter introduces all the basic elements of the story: the time period, the location, the key individuals, but also the overall sense of apprehension of a decaying world entering its twilight. The chapter introduces its characters against the immediate problem of the imminent loss of a vital branch line. This presents both the general disintegration of the railroad and the opportunity for each character to respond in relation to the railroad, setting their course for the remainder of the story. The characters and their responses include: the intelligent resignation of the New York City bum; the diffused apprehension of Taggart Transcontinental Railroad employee Eddie Willers; the drained resentment of railroad president James Taggart; the cynical resignation of chief clerk Pop Harper; the overabundant joy and vitality of railroad Vice-President in Charge of Operation Dagny Taggart; the distant curiosity of the young brakeman; the passivity of the railroad train crew; the courteous professionalism of music publisher Mr. Ayers; the placid emptiness of railroad employee (and first striker) Owen Kellogg when he resigns from Taggart Transcontinental.

In the novel, the only character not related in some way to the railroad is the bum. He is indicative of the world as such. He opens the novel with a particular tone, and it occasions the reflection (via exposition) of railroad employee Eddie Willers. After Eddie's initial encounter with the bum, the remaining and substantial portion of the opening sequence is devoted to Eddie's diffused apprehension and his struggle to pull himself together. The novel's exposition introduces his anxiety, whose origin he cannot pinpoint. He surveys the city, which is in obvious decay, but he sees nothing unusual about it. The sight of a public calendar makes him uneasy but he is not clear why. He tries to remember but cannot recall some popular expression associated in his mind with the calendar. After glancing at the city, which includes the noting of signs of competence among its inhabitants, Eddie shifts his focus to the memory of his childhood friendship with the Taggart railroad family. A giant oak tree stood on a section of the Taggart estate. One day lightning strikes and topples the tree. However, Eddie finds the oak rotted to the center. The memory arises inexplicably. All these thoughts occur to Eddie as he returns hurriedly to the office of the railroad, where he is employed as the assistant of his childhood friend Dagny Taggart. From the street the Taggart Building looms above the city, untouched by the surrounding decay. As Eddie enters the building, he recalls the slogan of his childhood and corporate slogan of the Taggart Enterprise: Taggart Transcontinental, From Ocean to Ocean.

In adapting the script, Rand's two outlines show her work on chapter 1. The first outline is excerpted from a complete chapter by chapter outline of the novel. The second outline is an (earlier) document containing a smaller subset of sequences to include in an earlier proposed script. After analyzing these outlines, we will examine the opening sequence as it appears in the script.

Here is the complete outline from chapter 1 of the novel:

ATLAS SHRUGGED

September 18, 1977
(Chapter Outline)

PART I "NON-CONTRADICTION"

I. "The Theme"

"Who is John Galt?" – Eddie Willers & bum. The calendar. Eddie and James Taggart: exposition about Colorado and the Rio Norte Line; Orren Boyle and Associated Steel; the Phoenix-Durango railroad; Ellis Wyatt and Wyatt Oil; ending on "Damn my sister!" Pop Harper and "Your days are numbered." Dagny Taggart on train, Halley's Concerto – and the young brakeman. The stop at the red light (general deterioration). Return to New York – the brakeman watching her. Dagny – Jim: the order for Rearden Metal rails. Dagny – Music Publishers, re: Halley's Concerto. Dagny- Owen Kellogg (he quits inexplicably).

The second outline is a "tentative" selection of sequences selected for an early, proposed version of the script. (Note the inclusion of "plants"):

May 16, 1972

TENTATIVE OUTLINE (MOVIE)

Part I

Eddie Willers & bum – Eddie & city: the calendar, The Taggart Building – Eddie & James Taggart (plant: state of Rio Norte Line, Taggart's resentment of Rearden & Dagny.) Dagny of train: the Halley Concerto – Dagny & Taggart (plant: importance of Colorado, order for Rearden Metal rail) Dagny & music publisher – Dagny & Owen Kellogg[30]

Both outlines contain opening sequences described as: "Eddie Willers & bum – Eddie & city: the calendar, The Taggart Building." In the novel, these two sequences introduce a decaying world, the slogan "Who is John Galt?," Eddie Willers and his diffused apprehension, plus his struggle to pull himself together and, lastly, his appreciation for his employer as a symbol of strength. As presented in the novel, these sequences run approximately four single-spaced pages and 2,000 words, including description, dialogue, inner-monologue, and exposition. As presented in the script, the same sequences run approximately 300 words of scenic description and acting direction—and 150 words of spoken dialogue.

The following are the opening sequences from Episode One, Act One. (They have been reformatted and adapted for easier reading):

We fade in on Eddie Willers and a bum standing on a New York City street at sunset. The bum is middle-aged, ragged, with a deeply lined face and intelligent eyes.

"Who is John Galt?" says the bum.

Eddie replies tensely: "Why did you say that?"

The bum mockingly replies: "Why does it bother you?"

"It doesn't," he replies sharply. Eddie reaches into his shirt and extends a dollar-bill to the bum. "Go get your coffee."

The Bum takes the money indifferently: "Thank you, sir."

Eddie starts walking away, but glances up and sees at an opening between two skyscrapers. Long streaks of grime run down the soot-eaten walls of the skyscraper. There are cracks in the walls, and broken windows. In the center of the shot there is a page of a gigantic calendar, erected on a roof that looks suspended in the sky over the city. The page says: September 2.

Eddie's face fills the screen looking up. His face is tense. He shudders slightly, as if from the cold, and looks away, as the camera moves back to include the bum.

"Now what is bugging you?" says the bum.

Involuntarily, Eddie points upwardly: "I don't like that damn thing."

The bum glances up mockingly at the calendar: "That? Why his honor the mayor put that up for the citizen's convenience, so we'd know the day and the date, and . . ."

"That calendar seems to be saying something," Eddie says interrupting, "some sort of phrase or question, but I can't recall it. I've tried, but I can't."

"Oh, I can tell you that," said the bum, "I know what it's saying."

"What?" asks Eddie.

"Your days are numbered" replies the bum.

Eddie looks startled then nods faintly, in reluctant agreement. Then he turns sharply and walks away.

Eddie continues walking down a main thoroughfare. It is Fifth Avenue, but it is obviously decaying; every fourth store window is dark and empty, bankrupt. He turns another corner and stops. The Taggart Building rises in the distance, untouched by decay, in contrast to its neighbors. Eddie Willers smiles, looking up at the building, and touches his fingers to his forehead in a kind of military salute. Then he hurries forward.

As Eddie enters the building, the camera moves to the sign over the entrance, which reads:

TAGGART TRANSCONTINENTAL
From Ocean to Ocean

The scene dissolves to the same inscription on the top of a map, then pulls back to reveal a large map of the United States, crisscrossed by a network of red lines from New York to San Francisco. The camera moves further back and reveals the luxurious office of James Taggart, president of the railroad. [End of sequence.]

As presented in the script (and above), the exchange with the bum includes new dialogue, which explains the meaning of the calendar. "Your days are numbered." (In the novel, Eddie's recollection occurs toward the end of chapter one.) The oak tree episode and all references to the past are omitted. The general sense of decay is present. And so is a telling bit of characterization for Eddie: he attempts to conduct himself as usual, which includes a military salute offered to the "untouched" Taggart Building, whose strength and days are numbered, also.

Characterization

Characterization is "the portrayal of those essential traits that form the unique, distinctive personality" of a human being.[31] Rand viewed action and dialogue as the "means of characterization" through which we come to know a character's motives. "To know a person well," writes Rand in her lectures on fiction, "is to know 'what makes him tick'":

> There is no way to know the soul (the consciousness) of another except by means of physical manifestations: his actions and words (*not his words in the sense of philosophical declarations, but his words in the context of his actions*). [Emphasis added.] The same applies to fiction. As part of characterization, a writer can sum up in narrative passages a character's thoughts or feelings, but *merely* to do that is not characterization.[32]

In the novel, the issue of characterization through dialogue is severalfold. As Rand explains in a 1944 letter to friend and aspiring writer, Gerald Loeb, one must make "dialogue sound as if this is the way people really talk—and yet write it with a brevity, clarity and economy of words never achieved by anybody in real-life talk." The dialogue must not contain lines without a specific purpose: one "must have every line carry either exposition or characterization—and usually both." The characters must speak in a fluid, unstilted manner: "[the writer] cannot allow his characters to talk so precisely that they will sound stilted. The trick is to select out of people's normal expressions those lines that are representative, that can give you—in one flash—the whole idea of the person or subject discussed, while sounding completely natural. It is a very difficult trick."[33]

The same principles apply to extracting dialogue from *Atlas Shrugged* for use in a film script.[34]

During her lifetime, Rand was amenable to adjustments in the construction of subplots. However, she was extremely sensitive to substantive changes in dialogue that affected changes in character motivation. She approved smaller changes in dialogue, which were expected and necessary. Nevertheless, the identity of a character on film is realized primarily through his action and dialogue. Jaffe recollects: "Every author goes out and spends however many years creating a character and having them speak in a certain way. Why would a screenwriter change the way they speak? I can understand not using all of the dialogue, but I can't understand changing the dialogue. The whole point is that people read the book because the dialogue is written the way it is, why change it? So she was very upset about that."[35]

A speech delivered by Francisco d'Anconia illustrates Rand's process, including the necessity of editing dialogue lifted from the book. In the novel, James Taggart, President of Taggert Transcontinental Railroad, confronts Francisco d'Anconia, a copper industrialist, over his involvement in the San Sebastián mine affair—an inherently worthless property that has wasted millions in investor money, and which has been nationalized by the Mexican government. Beginning with its short introduction, here is the speech as presented in the novel:

> Francisco stood looking at him in polite astonishment. "Why James," he said, "I thought you would approve of it."
>
> "Approve?!"
>
> "I thought you would consider the San Sebastián mines as the practical realization of an ideal of the highest moral order. Remembering that you and I have disagreed so often in the past, I thought you would be gratified to see me acting in accordance with your principles."
>
> "What are you talking about?"
>
> Francisco shook his head regretfully. "I don't know why you should call my behavior rotten. I thought you would recognize it as an honest effort to practice what the whole world is preaching. Doesn't everyone believe that it is evil to be selfish? I was totally selfless in regard to the San Sebastián project. Isn't it evil to pursue a personal interest? I had no personal interest in it whatever. Isn't it evil to work for profit? I did not work for profit—I took a loss. Doesn't everyone agree that the purpose and justification of an industrial enterprise are not production, but the livelihood of its employees? The San Sebastián Mines were the most eminently successful venture in industrial history: they produced no copper, but they provided a livelihood for thousands of men who could not have achieved, in a lifetime, the equivalent of what they got for one day's work, which they could not do. Isn't it generally agreed that an owner is a parasite and an exploiter, that it is the employees who do all the work and make the product possible? I did not exploit anyone. I did not burden the San Sebastián Mines with my useless presence; I left them in the hands of the men who count. I did not pass judgment on the value of that property. I turned it over to a mining specialist. He was not a very

good specialist, but he needed the job very badly. Isn't it generally conceded that when you hire a man for a job, it is his need that counts, not his ability? Doesn't everyone believe that in order to get the goods, all you have to do is need them? I have carried out every moral precept of our age. I expected gratitude and a citation of honor. I do not understand why I am being damned. (143)

Here is the same passage with Rand's revisions, including cross-outs and new words enclosed with brackets:

Francisco stood looking at him in polite astonishment. "Why James," he said, "I thought you would approve of it."

"Approve?!"

"I thought you would consider the San Sebastián mines as the practical realization of an ideal of the highest moral order. Remembering that you and I have disagreed so often in the past, I thought you would be gratified to see me acting in accordance with your principles."

"What are you talking about?"

Francisco shook his head regretfully. "I don't know why you should call my behavior rotten. I thought you would recognize it as an honest effort to practice what the whole world is preaching. Doesn't everyone believe that it is evil to be selfish? I was totally selfless in regard to the San Sebastián project. Isn't it evil to pursue a personal interest? I had no personal interest in it whatever. Isn't it evil to work for profit? I did not work for profit—I took a loss. Doesn't everyone agree that the purpose and justification of an industrial enterprise are [is] not production, but the livelihood of its employees? The San Sebastián Mines were the most eminently successful venture in industrial history: they produced no copper, but they provided a livelihood for thousands of men who could not have achieved, in a lifetime, the equivalent of what they got for one day's work, which they could not do [were unemployable]. Isn't it generally agreed that an owner is a parasite and an exploiter, that it is the employees who do all the work and make the product possible? I did not exploit anyone. I did not burden the San Sebastián Mines with my useless presence; I left them in the hands of the men who count. I did not pass judgment on the value of that property. I turned it over to a mining specialist. He was not a very good specialist, but he needed the job very badly. Isn't it generally conceded that when you hire a man for a job, it is his need that counts, not his ability? Doesn't everyone believe that in order to get the goods, all you have to do is need them? I have carried out every moral precept of our age. I expected gratitude and a citation of honor. I do not understand why I am being damned.

Here is the same encounter presented in screenplay format:[36]

FRANCISCO

(Stands looking at him in polite astonishment)

TAGGART

Approve?!

FRANCISCO

I thought you would recognize it as an effort to practice what the whole world is preaching. Doesn't everyone believe it is evil to be selfish? I was totally self-less in regard to the whole Sebastián project. Is it evil to work for a profit? I did not work for a profit – I took a loss. Doesn't everyone agree that the purpose of an individual enterprise is not production, but the livelihood of its employees? The San Sebastián mines produced no copper, but they provided a livelihood for thousands of men who were unemployable. I have carried out every moral precept of our age. I expect gratitude and a citation of honor. I do not understand why I am being damned.[37]

Style

Style, Ayn Rand writes,

has two fundamental elements . . . : the "choice of content" and the "choice of words." By "choice of content" I mean those aspects of a given passage (whether description, narrative or dialogue) which a writer *chooses* to communicate (and which involve the consideration of what to include or to omit). By "choice of words" I mean the particular words and sentence structures a writer uses to communicate them.[38]

Novels and screenplays are different dramatic mediums with different stylistic possibilities. The run of the John Galt Line is one of the most tightly integrated literary sequences presented in the novel. It conveys both action and explicit philosophical content. Rand's adaptation of this passage for the screen demonstrates her sensitivity to word and content choices across two mediums. The importance of such word and content choices can by seen by comparing the original, more novelistic version of the John Galt Line sequence and its final, more filmic revision.

The successful run of the John Galt Line is a climax of both the first third of the book and the first third of the screenplay. As presented in the book, the run of the train is a physical demonstration of the power of reason. The run brings into focus—both in dialogue and in action—the methodical application of man's rational faculty to the problems of his survival. In so doing, the sequence involves a concern with facts (the problem of a faltering branch line), evaluation (the preservation of a valuable line essential to the continued expansion of industrialism) and action (the successful building of the line in the face of obstacles). It is also the sequence in the novel explicitly dramatizing Rand's view of the unity of mind and body: the integration of thought and action in "solving the problem of one's survival," that is, in successfully pursuing his own life and happiness on earth.

In the novel the sequence is presented from a moving train, crossing the earth over plains and through mountains at a speed of one hundred miles per hour. The train is a machine, a material product of human intelligence. And

Dagny Taggart, the person responsible for the train's successful operation, rides in the cab of its engine. During the ride she experiences the physical consequences of her success—the smooth operation of the train, the integrity of the track bed, the positive, celebratory reactions of those who have come to witness the run—but, as she descends into the heart of the engine's motor, she also reflects upon the event's "spiritual" or mental aspects. During a substantial inner monologue, Dagny moves among the moving parts of the train motor and reflects on the unity of mind and body—and the role such a unity plays in the successful run of the train. Dagny's inner monologue is substantial. The entire mechanism of the engine's motor was designed with a specific purpose and that purpose originates in a thinking mind. The engine roaring around her is a constant, perceptual reminder of this integration.

There are two drafts of this sequence among Rand's teleplay manuscripts. (This material is the longest example of editing on paper within the screenplay itself.)

First, Rand prepared this sequence in outline form. (The transcription here omits page numbers.) On one side of the page are the specific actions depicting the sequence. Among these are: "Show speed of train – signal light 2 miles apart," "attitude of Logan [the engineer]," "Rearden looking down at Dagny," "Crowd of people under the 'Stop. Look. Listen.' signs," "good description of the start of mountains." On the other side is the column called "Her thoughts." Under this column are "Ownership," "the meaning of this day for them," "Wish & Fulfillment," "Mind & body, physical pleasure," "Who made the engine" and so forth. A total of thirteen physical descriptions are listed as are twelve key "thoughts."

In the first draft of this sequence, the physical description and the inner monologue are combined in a montage. Rand coordinates specific monologue with specific actions. However, in the final version, which stands in the script, this entire section is cut.[39] Apparently, the translation required to capture the scene in the novel and render it effectively in the script meant abandoning her first approach entirely. In the second version, she omits the inner monologue and its reflection on "mind and body" integration. In notes from the script (reproduced below), she explains her revision:

> **Note:** The visual aspects of the following sequence (the train ride) are, properly, the job of the director, and I shall leave them to him. I shall present here only the shot necessary to the progression of the story. I shall not attempt to break down into individual shots the enormous visual complexity of projecting a train traveling through the mountains at a hundred miles an hour. (I have done that job verbally in the novel.)
>
> I suggest that the director read carefully pp. 239 – 247 of *Atlas Shrugged* (Random House edition), because he has to convey visually the equivalent of what I have conveyed in narrative. He should avoid any suggestion of the notion of "how small is man in the face of nature"—since the meaning of this sequence is: How great are man and his achievement in the conquest of nature.

THE WRITER'S PERSPECTIVE

Any writer facing the task of adapting Rand's universe onto the screen will no doubt have heard—and may possibly share—the concerns listed by journalists at the opening of this study: The novel is too long, too idea-filled or too propagandistic in its advocacy of capitalism. In one form or another during her lifetime, Rand faced these same criticisms. She was asked repeatedly whether she was "primarily a novelist or a philosopher" and whether her stories were "propaganda vehicles for ideas, whether politics or the advocacy of capitalism" was her "chief purpose." Rand replied that "all such questions are so enormously irrelevant, so far beside the point, so much not my way of coming at things." Her explanation, reproduced below, also serves as a summary of the issues introduced and discussed in this paper:

> My way is much simpler and, simultaneously, much more complex than that, speaking from two different aspects. The simple truth is that I approach literature as a child does: I write—and read—for the sake of the story. The complexity lies in the task of translating that attitude into adult terms.
>
> The specific concretes, the *forms* of one's values, change with one's growth and development. The abstraction *"values"* does not. An adult's values involve the entire sphere of human activity, including philosophy—most particularly philosophy. But the basic principle—the function and meaning of values in man's life and in literature—remains the same.
>
> My basic test for any story is: Would I want to meet these characters and observe these events in real life? Is this story an experience worth living through for its own sake? Is the pleasure of contemplating these characters an end in itself?
>
> It's as simple as that. But that simplicity involves the total of man's existence.[40]

If the simplicity of a story "involves the total of man's existence," then we have answered our opening question: Can a screen adaptation of *Atlas Shrugged* render the book's story without the "whipsawing" of philosophy and plot alleged by Hollywood? The answer is: Yes, as long as you incorporate its philosophy into a script by simply *showing* men *living* it—a simple answer that "involves the total of man's existence."

Abstractions like the "the importance of reason" or "rational self-interest" or "the conquest of nature" are ultimately reducible to concrete, specific entities and their actions. The whole goal of a novel (and of art in general) is to express such abstractions by embodying them in a perceptual form. In terms of film, this means the action and dialogue of a script and everything that this implies on a film set.

In *Atlas Shrugged*, every event or fact implies a *value*. Every value pursued (or dismissed) by a character, implies an estimation of that value in action. Philosophy (value) and plot (the facts) do not whipsaw. They are different perspectives on the same real, concrete, perceptible, and, therefore, *filmable* human actions. Each event in *Atlas Shrugged* the novel—whether enacted by an individual or a government, by a hero or a villain—expresses some estimate of the mind and its relation to human survival. The estimate is embedded in the actions of the characters. In other words, to paraphrase a well-known expression: philosophical actions speak louder than empty words. In the literary arts, what empties words of their meaning and turns them into meaningless assertions is any disconnection between a word and the observable, concrete things (and their actions) that give those words meaning. Disconnecting *Atlas Shrugged* from the "logically connected events leading to the resolution of a climax" would empty the book (or screenplay) of drama.

A collectivistic society disregards individual effort. (See the attacks on Rearden's Metal.) Such a society disregards the connection between independent judgment and its root in the mind, which makes judgment possible. (See the attacks on Dagny as she attempts to build her railroad.) A collectivistic society seeks to undermine the institutionalized protection of such judgment by undermining individual rights. (See Washington, DC and the pressure group warfare described in the novel.) A collectivist society is antagonistic to the achievement of wealth and the trading of values in a market place that is capitalism. (See Directive 10-289.) What happens in a world where men do not think or assume the responsibility of judgment? (See the tunnel catastrophe.) And what is the proper response to such a world? (See the strike by the men and women of the mind.) And, lastly, to the extent that a man struggles to live, to this extent he needs the guidance of philosophy if he wishes to remain alive and achieve his happiness. (See Galt's Speech.)

In a plot-story, the extent to which a man seeks a value and struggles to "gain and/or keep it" is the extent to which he is in both the domain of fiction *and* philosophy. Men and women do not float above or beyond the earth (and reality). They are living beings in *this* reality, who reap directly the benefits (or detriments) of their basic choices: to live or not, to think or not. These are philosophical choices. In Rand's view, such choices are inescapable to real men and women and to their equivalent in fiction. To live and to think or to refrain from thinking, therefore, to die—are actions expressing the two clashing philosophies presented in the novel: the Morality of Life and the Morality of Death. They differentiate the heroes and villains of *Atlas Shrugged*, whose stands on the "role of the mind in man's existence" are enacted over the course of 1,168 pages by what they do. In the words of producer Albert S. Ruddy: "It's knowing what to abstract."

If plot shows us *what* to abstract from the novel, Rand describes *how* to abstract (or adapt) by indicating the state of mind one needs to achieve before doing so:

> When you master the relationship of abstractions to concretes, you will know how to translate an abstract theme into action, and how to attach an abstract meaning to an action idea. . . . Only when your mind is geared to dancing back and forth—and I mean *dance*, with that kind of ease—between abstractions and

concretes will you be able to give the philosophical meaning to an action idea or the action story to a philosophical idea.[41]

CONCLUSION

Dramatizing *Atlas Shrugged* (and its ideas) on-screen is not only possible, it is *necessary*—if the result is to remain *Atlas Shrugged*. Rather than creating obstacles, a thorough understanding of the novel's plot would clarify the job. But this requires an understanding of the underlying theory of story telling, without which the book is nothing, and any adaptation is less than nothing. The plot of *Atlas Shrugged* is the book's industrial formula, the key to solving the billion-dollar question weighing, no doubt, heavily on producers, distributors, exhibitors, the viewing public—and, perhaps most of all, writers. How does one adapt *Atlas Shrugged*?—is a question we have attempted to answer here. The plot of *Atlas Shrugged* is like the algebraic formula: 2a = a + a. And to paraphrase Rand from another context, any number of specific events may be substituted for "a" without altering the truth of the plot. The situation of the novel is true of a three-hour film and a nine-hour miniseries. Delivered intact, the plot of *Atlas Shrugged* will attract the book's enormous public and "fill seats." Without its plot, the public will exit theatres shrugging, and screenings will empty because the screen will be empty.[42]

Rand is feared (groundlessly) in Hollywood for her philosophizing speeches. On the same erroneous grounds, she goes unrecognized for her philosophizing action. For any writer facing the practical job of writing an adaptation today, simply reading the novel will flood him with Rand's philosophy and its *dramatic* equivalents. But that is not enough. He must put down the book and look out at the world, totally on his own—while taking stock of his own experience—in order to begin dancing, as observes Rand, "literally" between the novel's abstract philosophy and its concretes.

Ironically, it is not a motion picture with dialogue but a *silent film* that merits Rand's esteem as the greatest motion picture yet produced. Perhaps Rand's view of film greatness reveals the truest test of all: not until the writer of record is ready and willing to dramatize *Atlas Shrugged* in *total silence*, will he be able to adapt the novel—with sound, picture, and the "technological radiance" of the medium Rand loved, confident of her drama *and* his own ingenuity in matching it.[43]

NOTES

1. This study is confined primarily to works and commentary generated during Ayn Rand's lifetime. This includes items found among her personal papers, interviews or written statements by Rand, or oral histories conducted with people associated with historic efforts to produce a film

version of her novel. Since the focus here is Rand's approach to dramatizing ideas, a great deal of interesting material pertaining to the film's development process is omitted, including the evolution of the long format dramatic television or "miniseries," which was anticipated by Rand. Also omitted is a review of innovative legal contracts crafted to insure Rand's control over the script. A longer study would have permitted the use of the interesting literature on adaptation and film esthetics in general. However, since Rand is a philosopher in her own right, and her views on film are comparatively little known, she deserves the special focus presented here.

For a short, informative history of *Atlas Shrugged* producing efforts and the general concerns raised in Hollywood, see Kimberly Brown, "Ayn Rand No Longer Has Script Approval," *New York Times*, 12 January 2007, 9,14 (AR).

2. Scott McConnell, "Interview with Michael Jaffe," *One Hundred Voices: An Oral History of Ayn Rand* (Irvine, Calif.: Ayn Rand Institute Press, forthcoming).

3. Ayn Rand, *The Romantic Manifesto: A Philosophy of Literature*, revised edition (New York: Signet, 1975), 82.

4. Plot is not the only literary element necessary. Rand held that other attributes of storytelling—theme, characterization, style—are essential, too. However, she regarded events as primary. She writes: "Since art is a selective re-creation [of reality] and since events are the building blocks of a novel, a writer who fails to exercise selectivity in regard to events defaults on the most important aspect of his art . . . . The means of exercising that selectivity and of integrating the events of a story is the plot." Rand, *Romantic Manifesto*, 82. For a further discussion of philosophy and art, see note 11.

5. "The purpose of all art is the objectification of values. The fundamental motive of a writer—by implication of the activity, whether he knows it or not—is to objectify his values, his view of what is important in life. . . . In this sense, every writer is a moral philosopher." Ayn Rand, *The Art of Fiction: A Guide for Writers and Readers*, Tore Boeckmann, ed. (New York: Plume 2000), 13–14.

6. The theory of plot (and its associated principles) presented in this paper is Ayn Rand's and flows out of her literary philosophy. Her theory of plot, actually, is the starting point of an examination of film adaptation, including derivative issues (and further principles) that are outside the scope of this paper. However, within this paper's scope is an examination of the connection between plot and *philosophy*. For a complete examination, see Rand, *Romantic Manifesto*.

7. In a narrative film, our primary goal is to depict or show human beings in action, thereby depicting a subject of human interest. Some motivation is involved, something besides the sheer existence of a subject matter. A subject must *matter*. Something about one set of activities (or concerns) sets it apart from another set, something makes this set interesting and worth pursuing to the viewer. This human perspective on any given fact or facts is our *entrée* into the whole realm of values. Rand defined a value as "that which one acts to gain and/or keep." The fact of human valuing leads, in turn, to morality, which Rand defined as an entire branch of philosophy. For a summary of Rand's argument, see Leonard Peikoff, *Objectivism: The Philosophy of Ayn Rand* (New York: Dutton, 1991).

8. Ayn Rand, quoted in Nathaniel and Barbara Branden, *Who is Ayn Rand?* (New York: Random House, 1962), 152.

9. Peikoff, *Objectivism*, 429–30.

10. Rand, *Art of Fiction*, 13.

11. Rand defined *philosophy* as a "comprehensive, integrated view of man and man's relationship to existence." Man needs this perspective out of practical necessity. As Rand puts it: "In order to live, man must act; in order to act, he must make choices; in order to make choices, he must define a code of values; he must know what he is and where he is—i.e., he must know his own nature (including his means of knowledge) and the nature of the universe in which he acts—i.e., he needs metaphysics, epistemology, ethics, which means: philosophy." Rand considered esthetics the fifth branch of philosophy. She defined art as "a selective re-creation of reality according to an artist's metaphysical value-judgments." See Rand, *Romantic Manifesto*, 45, and Peikoff, *Objectivism*, 417.

12. Rand, *Art of Fiction*, 57.

13. Leonard Peikoff, ed., *The Early Ayn Rand: A Selection from Her Unpublished Fiction*, revised version (New York: Signet, 2005), 149.

14. Jeff Britting, *Ayn Rand* (New York: Overlook Press, 2005), 40.

15. Michael S. Berliner, ed., *Letters of Ayn Rand* (New York: Dutton, 1995), 6–9. Although "Red Pawn" was never produced as a film, her work on it, which includes an early screenplay, shows Rand incorporating her theory into the story.

16. *Ayn Rand Papers*: 58-12-19, Ayn Rand Archives, A Special Collection of the Ayn Rand Institute, Irvine, Calif.

17. Rand, *Romantic Manifesto*, 84.

18. She also states: "You know that people receive a sense of exaltation from this book. And you know that from the sublime to the ridiculous is just one step." Berliner, *Letters of Ayn Rand*, 245.

19. "Interview with Ayn Rand," Ayn Rand On Campus: "The Visual Arts", undated, *Special Collections*, Ayn Rand Archives.

20. Rand, *Romantic Manifesto*, 71–72.

21. Jerry Schwartz, "Interview with Ayn Rand, Part II," *The Objectivist Forum* 1, no. 4 (August 1980): 1.

22. For a discussion of "plot-theme," see Rand, *Romantic Manifesto*, 85.

23. McConnell, "100 Voices," "Interview with Albert S. Ruddy."

24. *Ayn Rand Papers*: 58-12-19, Ayn Rand Archives.

25. Rand, *Art of Fiction*, 13.

26. Ayn Rand, "Atlas Shrugged, a Teleplay," *Ayn Rand Papers*, Ayn Rand Archives.

27. Rand, "Atlas Shrugged, a Teleplay," pp. 1–324, 1–2, *Ayn Rand Papers*.

28. Robert Mayhew, ed., *Ayn Rand Answers* (New York: New American Library, 2005), 193.

29. McConnell, "Interview with Michael Jaffe."

30. *Ayn Rand Papers*: 58-12-19, Ayn Rand Archives.

31. Rand, *Romantic Manifesto*, 87.

32. Rand, *Art of Fiction*, 59–60.

33. Berliner, *Letters of Ayn Rand*, 133–34.

34. "She got out her copy of *Atlas Shrugged*, underlined the dialog she wanted to keep, scene by scene. Then she sat down and in longhand on her blue paper, in screenplay form, with the proper formatting, wrote everything down. She got all the way through the first third, and I typed it up for her." McConnell, "100 Voices," "Interview with Cynthia Peikoff."

35. McConnell, "100 Voices," "Interview with Michael Jaffe."

36. For full effect, reading the speech aloud is recommended.

37. Rand, "Atlas Shrugged, a Teleplay," 150–52.

38. Rand, *Romantic Manifesto*, 94.

39. In the novel this sequence of activity and the monologue omits the measure of a specific passage of time. In reading the novel, one can put down the passage and then resume reading. One can, in effect, reenter the sequence and pick up where one stopped. This is because a novel presents physical space at a high level of abstraction. (The same is true of movement.) The amount of information in a novel sufficient to give an impression of movement, sound, and the passage is far less than what is required in motion pictures. The latter must keep moving, literally.

40. See Rand, *Romantic Manifesto*, 162–63. On why she wrote *Atlas Shrugged*, see Mayhew, *Ayn Rand Answers*, 230.

41. See also Rand, *The Art of Fiction*, 55.

42. Ayn Rand, *Introduction to Objectivist Epistemology*, Expanded Second Edition, Harry Binswanger and Leonard Peikoff, eds. (New York: New American Library, 1990), 18.

43. I would like to thank Donna Montrezza and Michael S. Berliner for proofreading assistance and comments; Sharyn Blumenthal for her illuminating thoughts on film theory; Robert Mayhew for his wise and patient editing.

13

Atlas Shrugged on the Role of the Mind in Man's Existence

Gregory Salmieri

Ayn Rand described the theme of *Atlas Shrugged* as "the role of the mind in man's existence," and my aim in this essay is to call attention to what the novel has to say about this role.[1] The novel operates on a grand, social-political scale dramatizing not only the mind's role in an individual human life, but also in society as a whole.[2] As the story of "the mind on strike" (738),[3] it conveys this role by depicting what happens to a society when "the men of the mind" withdraw.[4] What the novel shows about society at large, however, follows from what it shows about individual men; and, in the present essay, I will focus on the role of the mind in an individual life.[5]

Since *Atlas*'s plot centers around the "men of the mind," it is necessary to comment briefly at the outset about what distinguishes these men from others. The phrase itself implies that the mind plays a central role in the lives of some people that it does not play in the lives of others, and this might be taken to suggest that the mind is somehow the exclusive province of a select few—a view that has loomed large in the history of thought. I will say more about what the mind (or reason or intellect) is on Rand's view shortly, but we can begin by identifying it as the faculty responsible for thinking and epitomized in such uniquely human achievements as science, mathematics, philosophy, and (Rand would insist) industry. Plato and a train of subsequent thinkers, noticing that most people do not devote their lives to science or philosophy, and thinking that they lack the native intelligence required to do so, concluded that reason could figure in the lives of most people only (or primarily) through their relations to their intellectual superiors—usually relations of obedience or subjugation. The Platonic view is a *metaphysical elitism*, on which innate differences between men divide them into castes of rulers and ruled; it is incompatible with the political freedom that *Atlas Shrugged* vigorously defends and is precisely what the American Founders denied when they declared that "All men are created equal." Despite attempts of some hostile reviewers to attribute this sort of elitism to *Atlas Shrugged*, the novel could not be clearer in rejecting it.[6]

While many of the heroes are unusually intelligent, others, though exceptional in many respects, are not portrayed as being endowed with any special native intelligence. Think of the young mother in the valley (784) or the truck driver who doesn't want to remain one (721), or of Owen Kellogg, the young engineer who goes on strike in the first chapter (25)—he is portrayed as unusually competent but not in any way that implies a special innate intelligence. Even Dagny does not have the sort of genius characteristic of Rearden and Francisco, and they themselves lack the sort of brilliance personified by Galt, who Rearden describes as "the sort of mind that's born once in a century" (290). Moreover, such characters as Eddie and Cherryl, who represent the best among average men, are shown as having deep similarities with the strikers that make them too qualify as "men of the mind." Cherryl for example is likened to a scientist when Jim complains that her "constant asking of a why for everything" amounts to treating him "as if [he] were a scientific object in a laboratory" (882). Think also of the many characters, often unnamed, whose competence or effort gives them a bond with the heroes: the cigarette vender with whom Dagny sometimes chats in the terminal (61, 353, 382); the people responsible for the "clean white curtain," fresh vegetables, and expert steering of a bus that lift Eddie's spirits when he sees them en route to the Taggart Building early in the first chapter (4); and so forth. Since, as we'll see, Rand sees all forms of competence as of a piece and attributes them to the minds of individuals, it is clear that these characters all have minds in the sense that matters to Rand's theme.

What the positive characters share is not a certain degree of intelligence, but the commitment to using such intelligence as they do possess.[7] Similarly, the villains are not portrayed as lacking intelligence—indeed Stadler is a genius; rather their evil consists in a choice to subvert their minds.[8] The consistent position of the novel is that, though there are differences in degrees of intelligence, we all possess the faculty of reason, and it can and should play the same role in each of our lives. What unites the men of the mind, is not genius, but "an *unbreached rationality*"—"not the degree of your intelligence, but the full and relentless use of your mind, not the extent of your knowledge, but the acceptance of reason as an absolute" (1059).

The novel's primary message with regard to the differences in the degrees of men's intelligence is: first, that each man, in proportion to the degree of his intelligence and his consistency in employing it, benefits himself and all the people with whom he interacts; and, second, that the dominant moral code (which is rooted in a failure or refusal to recognize the role of the mind in man's existence) damns each of us in this same proportion. The strike depicted in the novel is the refusal by the men of the mind to submit to this injustice any longer. Every man who is committed to the fullest use of his mind is a "man of the mind," but the title applies most dramatically to those men of rare intelligence who are mankind's greatest benefactors and have been its greatest victims, and these are the men who Galt makes it his special mission to remove from society, though he recruits others to his cause along the way.[9]

Because *Atlas'* heroes have powerful intellects and exercise them consistently, they epitomize the function of a mind. But the mind of any individual can and should play the same role in his life, regardless of the degree of his intelligence.

THE HUMAN FORM OF CONSCIOUSNESS

Before we can say anything substantive about the mind's role, we must first get clearer on what the mind or reason is. We have said already that it is the faculty that is responsible for thinking and that distinguishes us from other animals. Like people, animals—at least many of them—are conscious. In particular, they have the faculty of sense-perception, by means of which they are aware of the objects in their immediate environment. Some animals have memory, which enables them to learn about these objects, making use of information from past encounters with an object to better deal with it in the present. By associating perceptibly similar objects, these animals can also apply material learned about one object or situation to others that are perceptibly like it, and so they are able to master such basic skills as hunting. But such skills represent the upper limit of consciousness for the (nonhuman) animals, whereas human knowledge extends far further.[10] Man is able to acquire vast sums of knowledge about categories of objects which are not perceptibly similar, and which may not be perceptible at all. For example, he can grasp laws of motion that apply alike to apples, planets, and molecules. From the human perspective, the world is not, as it is for an animal, a succession of objects and situations that are more or less reminiscent of one another. Instead, we are aware of the world *conceptually.* A concept is a unit of thought, of the sort normally represented in speech by a single word, that applies to a whole category of objects that have a common nature and act accordingly. Concepts enable man to grasp causal connections that are inaccessible to animals and so to achieve an *understanding* of the world. Reason, since the birth of philosophy in ancient Greece, has been identified as the faculty that enables this distinctly human perspective.

Rand, following in the philosophical tradition of Aristotle and Thomas Aquinas, held that reason functions by processing the information we acquire about the world in sense-perception into a new and more powerful form of consciousness, which remains grounded in perception.[11] Thus Galt defines reason as "the faculty that perceives, identifies, and integrates the material provided by man's senses."[12] He elaborates:

> All thinking is a process of identification and integration. Man perceives a blob of color; by integrating the evidence of his sight and his touch, he learns to identify it as a solid object; he learns to identify the object as a table; he learns that the table is made of wood; he learns that the wood consists of cells, that the cells consist of molecules, that the molecules consist of atoms. All through this process, the work of his mind consists of answers to a single question: *What* is it? (1016–17)

We identify, for example, a particular man, by subsuming him and his characteristics under concepts such as "man," "animal," "rational," "virtue," "inventor," "genius," and so forth. And in forming a concept we integrate our knowledge about many objects into a single, unitary awareness of them.[13] This makes it possible to think, for example, about animals in general—or, more widely, about entities or actions as such, or even about existence as a whole.

Increasingly abstract concepts enable a grasp of increasingly complex causal connections, ranging over greater expanses of time. Thus, an animal, without any concepts, might be able to learn that eating a berry will satiate its hunger, but only a man can learn that planting bushes will result in a crop of berries months into the future, or that by irrigating a field, he can make it possible for berries to grow on what would otherwise be barren land. Moreover, he can go on to learn that his ability to produce berries in this manner and to benefit from the harvest depends on political freedom, which cannot be defended except on the basis of a whole philosophy.

Whereas the functioning of our sense organs is automatic, the formation and use of concepts are (to a large extent at least) under our conscious control, and this imposes a responsibility on us. Galt makes this point when describing the development of a human consciousness:

> the day when [a child] grasps that he is not a passive recipient of the sensations of any given moment, that his senses do not provide him with automatic knowledge in separate snatches independent of context, but only with the material of knowledge, which his mind must learn to integrate—the day when he grasps that his senses cannot deceive him, that physical objects cannot act without causes, that his organs of perception are physical and have no volition, no power to invent or to distort, that the evidence they give him is an absolute, but his mind must learn to understand it, his mind must discover the nature, the causes, the full context of his sensory material, his mind must identify the things that he perceives—*that* is the day of his birth as a thinker and scientist. (1041)

Unlike the senses, then, reason is a faculty that man must self-consciously exercise and learn how to exercise. Man must discover the laws of logic, and then adhere to them *by choice*. It is only by doing this that he manages to attain his distinctive form of awareness—a point Galt captures by describing man as a "being of volitional consciousness." As Rand makes the point in her nonfiction, man must choose to engage in the process of *thinking*, which is "not a passive state of registering random impressions" but

> an actively sustained process of identifying one's impressions in conceptual terms, of integrating every event and every observation into a conceptual context, of grasping relationships, differences, similarities in one's perceptual material and of abstracting them into new concepts, of drawing inferences, of making deductions, of reaching conclusions, of asking new questions and discovering new answers and expanding one's knowledge into an ever-growing sum.[14]

The heroes of *Atlas Shrugged* are constantly engaged in this process. We can observe it in detail in the cases of Dagny and Rearden, the only major heroes whose thoughts are often narrated, and sometimes in the cases of Cherryl Taggart and Eddie Willers.[15] The novel also depicts a variety of people who do not engage in this activity. The simplest examples are minor characters like the residents of Starnesville. Consider the woman who "looked on without reaction" as a local child threw a rock at Rearden's windshield:

> She had stood there silently, watching, without interest or purpose, like a chemical compound on a photographic plate, absorbing visual shapes because they were there to be absorbed, but unable ever to form any estimate of the objects of her vision. (286)[16]

The woman can be taken as a symbol of mental passivity. Her senses function, but her mind does not; and so she forms no estimate of what she sees. She is likened to a photographic plate rather than to an animal (which also sees without thinking) because for animals this form of consciousness is complete and sufficient: they have automatic desires which lead them to act on what they perceive in the ways necessary to secure their survival. As we will see in greater detail later, this is not true in the case of man, and so the woman's mental passivity renders her passive existentially as well, and reduces her to a subanimal state.

Significantly, the woman is described not merely as failing to form any estimate of what she sees, but as being unable to do so. This may be true in the sense that, after a lifetime of mental passivity, she lacks the context necessary to make meaningful evaluations of what she sees, but she is not (on Rand's view) literally unable to think. In his speech, Galt says that "in every hour and every issue" one has a "basic moral choice" between "thinking and non-thinking," and Rand elaborates on this choice in her nonfiction:

> In any hour and issue of his life, man is free to think or to evade that effort. Thinking requires a state of full, focused awareness. The act of focusing one's consciousness is volitional. Man can focus his mind to a full, active, purposefully directed awareness of reality—or he can unfocus it and let himself drift in a semiconscious daze, merely reacting to any chance stimulus of the immediate moment, at the mercy of his undirected sensory-perceptual mechanism and of any random, associational connections it might happen to make.[17]

There is, then, a fundamental alternative between the states Rand calls "focus" and "drift." The heroes are people who characteristically focus their minds and have developed a clarity-seeking psychology to which focus comes easily and drift is unnatural. The woman in Starnesville represents a different sort of psychology, habituated to drift, to which focus would be unnatural. There is a third alternative in addition to focus and drift. Galt describes it as:

> that nameless act which all of you practice, but struggle never to admit: the act of blanking out, the willful suspension of one's consciousness, the refusal to think— not blindness, but the refusal to see; not ignorance, but the refusal to know. It is the act of unfocusing your mind and inducing an inner fog to escape the responsibility of judgment—on the unstated premise that a thing will not exist if only you refuse to identify it, that A will not be A so long as you do not pronounce the verdict "*It is.*" (1017)

Following Rand in her nonfiction, we can call this act "evasion."[18] *Atlas Shrugged*'s most dramatic portrayals of it involve Jim Taggart, who "jerks his head to stop" his thoughts when he feels as if they are "slipping down a dangerous blind alley, the end of which he must never permit himself to see" (866). Indeed, his first words in the novel are "Don't bother me, don't bother me, don't bother me" (7). They are addressed in irritation to Eddie Willers, who has come to discuss an important issue on the railroad, but they may as well be addressed to reality as such.

Some evasion is required to maintain a state of drift over an extended period of time—and certainly over a lifetime: one cannot avoid periodically noticing signs that greater attention is called for, so one must evade these signs in order to remain in drift.[19] The residents of Starnesville for example have ample evidence that a better life existed there in the past and exists elsewhere in the present, and they must push this out of their minds in order to continue in their thoughtless, stagnant routine. Nevertheless, there is a difference between these characters who are perpetually adrift (evading as necessary to maintain it), and characters, like Taggart, whose perpetual mental state is one of evasion. The following descriptions would not apply to the residents of Starnesville:

> This was the way he had lived all his life—keeping his eyes stubbornly, safely on the immediate pavement before him, craftily avoiding the sight of his road, of corners, of distances, of pinnacles. (867)

> . . . danger to him was a signal to shut off his sight, suspend his judgment and pursue an unaltered course on the unstated premise that the danger would remain unreal by the sovereign power of his wish not to see it—like a fog horn within him, blowing not to sound a warning, but to summon the fog. (868)[20]

Here we see a mind habituated to evasion, and it is such people who are the villains in *Atlas Shrugged*. They are people who do not merely fail to use their minds, but who live their lives on the principle of subverting them.

Evasion is, in Galt's words, "an act of annihilation, a wish to negate existence, an attempt to wipe out reality" (1018), and it is a thesis of *Atlas Shrugged*'s that the psychology of an evader is centered around a fundamental antipathy for existence as such, and for all the values that make human existence possible. The psychology of evil will not be my focus in the present essay, but it is necessary to mention it here, because it is not only minor negative characters like the passive residents of Starnesville, but also villains like Jim Taggart who serve as contrasts by which the role played by the mind in the lives of the heroes is brought out. While the passive characters represent the mere absence of mental functioning, the villains represent its antithesis.[21]

As a final topic connected with drift and evasion, it will be instructive to say a few words about an epistemological doctrine that is an expression and rationalization of the psychology of passive men and evaders. The doctrine is "mysticism," which Rand defines as follows:

> Mysticism is the acceptance of allegations without evidence or proof, either apart from or *against* the evidence of one's senses and of reason. Mysticism is the claim to some non-sensory, non-rational, non-definable, non-identifiable means of knowledge, such as "instinct," "intuition," "revelation," of any form of "just knowing."[22]

Mysticism is the source of the "Morality of Death" against which Galt calls the strike, and he discusses it at some length in his speech (1027).[23] I mention it here because this doctrine is diametrically opposed to *Atlas Shrugged*'s position on the role of the mind, and we will have occasion to note the contrast in connection with the aspects of the mind's role that we will focus on in the remaining sections of this essay.

For the present, we can use the contrast to help sum up what we have already seen about Rand's conception of the mind. Man's means of knowledge is reason, and there can be no such thing as "just knowing," because reason does not function automatically; rather, knowledge is something that must be achieved by integrating our sensory material to form progressively wider concepts, by identifying what we observe in conceptual terms, and integrating these observations into an ever-growing conceptual awareness of reality. This is what it means for a man to be conscious, and reason is man's means of consciousness.

What, then, is its role in man's existence? We can begin our answer with an observation Rand makes in her nonfiction: "Consciousness—for those living organisms which possess it—is the basic means of survival. For man, the basic means of survival is *reason*."[24]

THE PRODUCTIVE FACULTY

Have you ever looked for the root of production? Take a look at an electric generator and dare tell yourself that it was created by the muscular effort of unthinking brutes. Try to grow a seed of wheat without the knowledge left to you by men who had to discover it for the first time. Try to obtain your food by means of nothing but physical motions—and you'll learn that man's mind is the root of all the goods produced and of all the wealth that has ever existed on earth. (410)

The words are Francisco's. In her nonfiction, Rand describes production as "the application of reason to the problem of survival," explaining that "The action required to sustain human life is primarily intellectual: everything man needs has to be discovered by his mind and produced by his effort."[25] This point is a central theme in *Atlas Shrugged*: its philosophical speeches underscore, and the progression of its plot dramatizes, the many ways in which our lives depend on technologies and how these technologies are produced and sustained by thought.

At their first meeting, looking out on a stormy night from a formal party with "summer flowers and half-naked women," Francisco says to Rearden: "It's a terrible night for any animal caught unprotected on that plain. . . . This is when one should appreciate the meaning of being a man." He describes Rearden as "saving" his guests "from the storm." The truth and significance of Francisco's remark becomes increasingly clear as the men of the mind withdraw from society. Dr. Stadler finds it too cold to work in the laboratories of the State Science Institute, which lack oil for heat during the winter following Wyatt's disappearance (339). The next winter, when the rest of the Colorado industrialists have gone, people do "not care to remember that there had been a time when snowstorms did not sweep, unresisted, down unlighted roads and upon the roofs of unheated houses, did not stop the movement of trains, did not leave a wake of corpses counted by the hundreds" (496). "The last of the trucks made by Lawrence Hammond" and "the best of the airplanes once made by Dwight Sanders" are lost in vain attempts to fight the storm. Earlier in the novel, Dagny describes such machines as "alive,"

> because they are the physical shape of the action of a living power—of the mind that had been able to grasp the whole of this complexity, to set its purpose, to give it form. . . . They *are* alive, she thought, but their soul operates them by remote control. Their soul is in every man who has the capacity to equal this achievement. Should the soul vanish from the earth, the motors would stop, because *that* is the power which keeps them going. (246)

With Saunders and Hammond gone, the motors stop—the machines die; and so do the people whose lives depend on them.

When nature is more hospitable, as it is the following year in Minnesota, when they have "a bumper crop," it is only through reason that men are able to take advantage of it (923). Agriculture itself and all the tools it requires are products of reason, and this particular crop only exists because the ingenuity of the farmers found a way to plant their wheat despite such obstacles as the deteriorating state of their equipment. The crop could not have been harvested if not for the foresight of Rearden, who recognizing the situation, turned his full attention to providing metal on credit to the manufactures of farm equipment, who then sold it to the farmers on the same terms. Before the harvest can feed the nation (or profit the farmers and their suppliers), it needs to be transported to market, and this too requires technology and the intelligence to use it. In this case, despite a heroic effort by Dagny and Eddie, the harvest rots due to the irrationality of the bureaucrats who control the nation's railroads.

Unlike animals who survive by repeating patterns of behavior that are innate or learned passively in childhood, in order to survive man must initiate and sustain a process of thought. And the result of this process is a sort of survival that is not possible for animals. Each new discovery enables us to live longer and better—a point made eloquently by Wyatt:

> "I add an extra span of time to [my customers'] lives with every gallon of my oil that they burn. And since they're men like me, they keep inventing faster ways to make the things they make—so every one of them grants me an added minute, hour or day with the bread I buy from them, with the clothes, the lumber, the metal"—he glanced at Galt—"an added year with every month of electricity I purchase." (722)

Earlier in the novel Rearden speaks in similar terms of "what [Galt's] motor would have meant if built":

> about ten years added to the life of every person in this country—If you consider how many things it would have made easier and cheaper to produce, how many hours of human labor it would have released for other work, and how much more anyone's work would have brought him. (290)

Even the poorest among modern Americans now take for granted a standard of living and a longevity that was not possible to anyone prior to the Industrial Revolution. Throughout most of its history most of mankind was engaged in the sort of back- and spirit-breaking labor illustrated in the novel by the people of Starnesville. The passive woman there, discussed earlier, has "stooped shoulders" and "shuffling movements" that give her the "the mark of senility" at the age of thirty-seven. Dagny and Rearden wonder how she could have "come to such a state." The answer is implied by the following paragraphs:

> The last thing they saw, as they left the town, was a billboard. A design was still visible on its peeling strips, imprinted in the dead gray that had once been color. It advertised a washing machine.
> In a distant field, beyond the town, they saw the figure of a man moving slowly, contorted by the ugliness of a physical effort beyond the proper use of a human body: he was pushing a plow by hand. (286)

Our conception of what it is like to be thirty-seven—or any other age—is colored by the availability of labor-saving technologies that are products of the mind. They vanish when it does, leaving man to labor "from sunrise to sunset at the shafts of a hand-plow for a bowl of rice" (1052) and woman to sit "with her shriveled face and pendulous breasts . . . grinding meal in a bowl, hour after hour, century by century" (1049).

In addition to being needed to create and sustain technology, intelligence is required for its use, if it is to be beneficial rather than harmful. This point is illustrated by the explosion in the Winston Tunnel (584-608), and by Project X, which, in the hands of a drunken Cuffy Meigs destroys everything within a hundred mile radius, including the Taggart Bridge (1132).[26] Mulligan, who predicts the destruction of the bridge, elaborates on this theme:

> Consider the physical risks of complex machinery in the hands of blind fools and fear-crazed cowards. Just think of their railroads—you'd be taking a chance on some such horror as that Winston tunnel incident every time you stepped aboard a train—and there will be more incidents of that kind, coming faster and faster. They'll reach the stage where no day will pass without a major wreck. . . . And the same will be happening in every other industry, wherever machines are used—the machines which they thought could replace our minds. Plane crashes, oil tank explosions, blast-furnace break-outs, high-tension wire electrocutions, subway cave-ins and trestle collapses—they'll see them all. The very machines that had made their life so safe, will now make it a continuous peril. (805–6)

Just as technology is a product of the mind that depends on it for its sustenance and use, so too is wealth. To maintain a fortune over time, one must invest it wisely, as the stories of the Starnes heirs, Lee Hunsacker, and others illustrate (313–24). And the fortune itself only has value in a world populated by productive men with products for sale. Francisco explains:

> When you accept money in payment for your effort, you do so only on the conviction that you will exchange it for the product of the effort of others. It is not the moochers or the looters who give value to money. Not an ocean of tears nor all the guns in the world can transform those pieces of paper in your wallet into the bread you will need to survive tomorrow. Those pieces of paper, which should have been gold, are a token of honor—your claim upon the energy of the men who produce. Your wallet is your statement of hope that somewhere in the world around you there are men who will not default on that moral principle which is the root of money. (410)

The point is illustrated in the action of the novel. Mr. Thompson summarizes the result of Galt's withdrawal of the mind when he observes that "people are starving and giving up, the economy is falling to pieces, nobody is producing any longer" (1089). When, in an effort to entice Galt to solve the problem, he offers Galt a "a billion dollars—a cool, neat billion dollars," Galt points out that the money will not buy him anything in a world lacking producers—in a world without the mind.

Just as technology and wealth are products of the mind, which can neither be sustained nor be of any benefit in its absence, so too, though in a less obvious way, are natural resources. These are not man-made in the normal sense of that term, but their *value* is produced, and is a product of reason. Oil, for example, is not created by man, and would continue to exist if men were to vanish entirely or if they stopped using their minds. But intelligence is needed to find oil, to extract it from the earth, and to refine it. In the novel we see that Wyatt is able to do this—and to do it in new and innovative ways—whereas the drudges at the State Science Institute are not (248–49, 343, 519, 720–23). More importantly, though, intelligence is needed to discover oil's uses and to implement them. It is of no use to an animal, and is only of use to men like Jim Taggart because there are other men who know how to put it to use powering and lubricating machines that he does not understand. Without the minds of such men, Dagny observes, the oil would "become primeval ooze again" (246). The same point applies to the static electricity in the air, which due to Galt's genius, replaces oil as a source of power for the residents of the valley. The point applies even to the wild berries picked by a primitive hunter-gatherer, as Rand points out:

> Man could not survive even as an herbivorous creature by picking fruit and berries at random. He has no instinct to tell him which plants are beneficial to him and which are a deadly poison. He can learn it only by conscious experimentation or by the observation of other living creatures who do not touch poisonous plants— a procedure which, in either case, is a process of thought.[27]

Galt makes this same point more succinctly in *Atlas Shrugged*, when he says that man "cannot obtain his food without a knowledge of food and of the way to obtain it" (1012).

We can appreciate, now, why Francisco describes the mind as the "root of all the goods produced and of all the wealth that has ever existed on earth" (410). All goods, from gold, to land, to food, to oil, to technology, are created by applying reason to the problem of survival, in the way that is most obvious in the case of sophisticated technologies, and they cease to be useful and, in most cases, even to exist unless reason is constantly employed to maintain and utilize them.

The recognition that we need reason to produce, maintain, and utilize the goods necessary for survival dates back at least to ancient Greece, but the form in which this view is presented in *Atlas Shrugged* is both strikingly modern and distinctive to Rand. To see how, it is instructive to begin by considering briefly some of what the Greeks had to say on this issue.[28] Plato recounts the myth that Prometheus bestowed mankind with "vocational wisdom," after his brother Epimetheus neglected to provide us with a means of survival.[29] And Aristotle, in the first book of his *Politics*, details the role in human survival of such vocations as hunting, agriculture, animal husbandry, and household management. The word I'm translating "vocation" here is *technê* (the root of our word technology); it amounts to knowledge of how to produce something.[30]

The Greeks saw a significant divide between the sort of reasoning involved in the vocations and the "theoretical" reasoning involved in the sciences (including, especially, philosophy and mathematics).[31] The sciences were more intellectually demanding but their discoveries seemed not to make any significant contribution to production. Instead, they were experienced as containing their own reward in the form of a sense of exercising one's mind to the utmost, which the philosophers regarded as an end in itself—something that has value intrinsically, quite apart from its relation to the rest of life.

By contrast, little intellectual satisfaction was to be found in the vocations, which, though they did require some thinking, were more labor intensive than any job in the modern world. It is significant in this connection that the Greeks did not see the vocations as involving the discovery of *new* methods of production. What Prometheus handed down to man were complete (or nearly complete) bodies of knowledge, which needed only to be applied, and this application consisted largely in tedious (and often excruciating) manual labor. Thus, while theoretical reasoning was engaged in for its own sake, the vocations were practiced only for the material rewards they yielded (and indeed, they were most often practiced by slaves, who had no choice in the matter).

We have here a dichotomy between theoretical reasoning, which is seen as useless but intrinsically valuable, and productive reasoning, which is valued only for its effects. Theoretical reason, which is reason in the fullest sense, aims at truth, whereas productive reason, which is barely reason at all, aims at profit or sustenance. Thus the alleged impracticality of theoretical reasoning came to be seen as ennobling it, and the utility of productive reason as debasing it.

This attitude, which persists to this day, is represented in *Atlas Shrugged* by a number of characters. Among these is the bum who Dagny encounters in a slum diner:

> Man's only talent is an ignoble cunning for satisfying the needs of his body. No intelligence is required for that. Don't believe the stories about man's mind, his spirit, his ideals, his sense of unlimited ambition. . . . Spirit? There's no spirit involved in manufacturing or in sex. Yet these are man's only concerns. Matter— that's all men know or care about. As witness our great industries—the only accomplishment of our alleged civilization—built by vulgar materialists with the aims, the interests and the moral sense of hogs. It doesn't take any morality to turn out a ten-ton truck on an assembly line. (177)

Morality, he thinks, is "judgment to distinguish right and wrong, vision to see the truth, courage to act upon it, dedication to that which is good, integrity to stand by the good at any price" all traits associated with scientists and philosophers, but not with practitioners of vocations.

The novel's most significant exponent of the distinction between theoretical and productive reasoning is Robert Stadler.[32] We can see this in his responses to the two most significant technological achievements in the novel, Rearden Metal and Galt's motor. He calls the first "an excellent piece of smelting" which he regards as of negligible value when compared to the State Science Institute, "the last center of science left on earth, and the whole future of human knowledge" (190). Notice that Rearden Metal is a significant scientific achievement, which gives the lie to Stadler's claim that the State Science Institute is the *last* center of science. Stadler does not count Rearden's laboratories as centers of science precisely because they have a productive purpose. And in describing the metal as a "piece of smelting" he treats it as though it were a mere application of the ancient vocation of blacksmithing.[33] The new discovery involved in Galt's motor is too profound for Stadler to ignore or minimize, but consider what he says in response to it:

> He arrived at some new concept of energy. He discarded all our standard assumptions, according to which his motor would have been impossible. He formulated a new premise of his own and he solved the secret of converting static energy into kinetic power. Do you know what *that* means? Do you realize what a feat of pure, abstract science he had to perform before he could make his motor? . . . Did you say you found this in the research laboratory of a plain, commercial motor factory? . . . A man with the genius of a great scientist, who chose to be a commercial inventor? I find it outrageous. He wanted a motor, and he quietly performed a major revolution in the science of energy, just as a means to an end, and he didn't bother to publish his findings, but went right on making his motor. (355–56)

Stadler, enraptured by Galt's "pure, abstract science," is *offended* that Galt saw it as a means to a productive end. "Why," Stadler asks, "did he want to waste his mind on practical appliances?"

This question and Dagny's involuntary reply, "Perhaps because he liked living on this earth," go to the heart of Stadler's thematic role in the novel. Through the character, Rand draws out an implication of the dichotomy between theoretical and productive reasoning. If reason, in its highest functions, is useless and its value is entirely disconnected from the rest of life, then the mind—and the man of the mind—is not at home in the world. This implication was explicitly embraced by Plato, who portrayed philosophers as longing to be separated from their bodies in death.[34] His thesis was in part motivated by the significant mystical elements in his conception of reason; but even Aristotle, who had no patience for mysticism and was this-worldly in orientation, found it difficult to account for the place of reason in the world.[35] Stadler, the pure theoretical scientist who looks down on productive reasoning, is portrayed, like Plato's philosophers, as a man who does not belong on Earth. But the reason that he does not belong is, on Rand's view, not because he is a scientist as such, but because he represents a mistaken view of the role of science, and of the mind generally, in man's existence.

Atlas Shrugged portrays and celebrates reason as a single, unitary faculty. The differences between so-called "productive" and "theoretical" reasoning are differences in degree rather than in kind. Knowledge as such has survival-promoting applications, and because of this, even the most abstract science or mathematics qualifies as productive, even when the scientist himself does not yet know of a specific application for it. Thus theoretical reasoning differs from the deliberations of a blacksmith only in the *immediacy* of its use in the production of material values. Though the productive consequences of scientific discoveries may be less immediate, they are ultimately greater. This point is not unique to Rand: it has found other defenders in the modern world, most famously Francis Bacon, who is reputed to have said "knowledge is power."[36] There is, however, another aspect to Rand's integrative view of reason which is uniquely hers: she ascribes to production the features long recognized as noble in abstract science, and in so doing she reconceives the nature of this nobility.

Recall the traits that the bum in the diner thought could not be found in the modern world: "vision to see the truth, courage to act upon it, dedication to that which is good, integrity to stand by the good at any price." Notice what reason Rearden gives in the very next scene for his refusal to sell the rights to his Metal *at any price* or to be intimidated by any threat into taking it off the market: "You see, it's because Rearden Metal is *good*" (182).[37] He and Dagny have the vision to see the truth about the metal, and the courage to act upon this truth, when the whole world is against them. In showing us how this vision and courage is necessary to produce the John Galt Line, *Atlas Shrugged* shows us that it is necessary for production as such.

In contrast to Stadler, Rearden is portrayed as the man who does belong on Earth—the man, Dagny thinks, "to whom the Earth belongs"—and, in his creation of Rearden Metal, we see at once the scientist dedicated to truth, and the industrialist out to make a profit by putting this truth to life-sustaining work.

Two hundred tons of metal which was to be harder than steel, running liquid at a temperature of four thousand degrees, had the power to annihilate every wall of the structure and every one of the men who worked by the stream. But every inch of its course, every pound of its pressure and the content of every molecule within it, were controlled and made by a conscious intention that had worked upon it for ten years. . . .

—the nights spent in the workshop of his home, over sheets of paper which he filled with formulas, then tore up in angry failure— . . .

—the meals, interrupted and abandoned at the sudden flash of a new thought, a thought to be pursued at once, to be tried, to be tested, to be worked on for months, and to be discarded as another failure—

—the moments snatched from conferences, from contracts, from the duties of running the best steel mills in the country, snatched almost guiltily, as for a secret love—

—the one thought held immovably across a span of ten years, under everything he did and everything he saw, the thought held in his mind when he looked at the buildings of a city, at the track of a railroad, at the light in the windows of a distant farmhouse, at the knife in the hands of a beautiful woman cutting a piece of fruit at a banquet, the thought of a metal alloy that would do more than steel had ever done, a metal that would be to steel what steel had been to iron—

—the acts of self-racking when he discarded a hope or a sample, not permitting himself to know that he was tired, not giving himself time to feel, driving himself through the wringing torture of: "not good enough . . . still not good enough . . ." and going on with no motor save the conviction that it could be done. (29–30)

Here we see the nobility of a reason that is at home in the world—a power-ful, intense reason that isn't the luxury of aristocrat philosophers fed by slave labor (or of a State Science Institute funded with money taxed from the pro-ductive), but a reason which is itself productive, and on a grand scale.

The scale is important: Rearden is as different as can be from the "household managers" Aristotle describes—functionaries who oversee muscular drudges in the performance of a stagnant routine. He is an innovator, who, through the work of his mind, opens up new worlds of life-sustaining possibility:

To take the pounding violence of sixteen motors, she thought, the thrust of seven thousand tons of steel and freight, to withstand it, grip it and swing it around a curve, was the impossible feat performed by two strips of metal no wider than her arm. What made it possible? What power had given to an unseen arrangement of molecules the power on which their lives depended and the lives of all the men who waited for the eighty boxcars? She saw a man's face and hands in the glow of a laboratory oven, over the white liquid of a sample of metal. (245)

As an inventor, and so a scientist, Rearden exemplifies the productive charac-ter of the very functions of the mind that the Greeks thought were inherently impractical; and Galt does this on an even greater scale. It is in such dramatic cases of technological innovation that the error of the Greek view is most read-ily apparent (which is why it was not apparent to the Greeks who did not yet have any such examples to draw on).

Atlas Shrugged also shows us how the same intransigent devotion to truth epitomized by science is present in all productive work, from running a rail-road or a steel mill to mining coal or investing in the stock market. We see its presence even in such mundane tasks as toasting bread or cooking a ham-burger when they are performed *well* (176–77, 328). It is true, of course, that all of these productive endeavors require some manual labor (though nothing like the backbreaking labor with which most of mankind was occupied prior to the Industrial Revolution); but an important theme of *Atlas* is that this labor is not what is primarily responsible for the product, because it is the mind that creates the context in which the physical labor can be of value. Galt explains:

When you work in a modern factory, you are paid, not only for your labor, but for all the productive genius which has made that factory possible: for the work of the industrialist who built it, for the work of the investor who saved the money to risk on the untried and the new, for the work of the engineer who designed the machines of which you are pushing the levers, for the work of the inventor who created the product which you spend your time on making, for the work of the scientist who discovered the laws that went into the making of that product, for the work of the philosopher who taught men how to think and whom you spend your time denouncing.

The machine, the frozen form of a living intelligence, is the power that expands the potential of your life by raising the productivity of your time. If you worked as a blacksmith in the mystics' Middle Ages, the whole of your earning capacity would consist of an iron bar produced by your hands in days and days of effort. How many tons of rail do you produce per day if you work for Hank Rearden? Would you dare to claim that the size of your pay check was created solely by your physical labor and that those rails were the product of your muscles? The standard of living of that blacksmith is all that your muscles are worth; the rest is a gift from Hank Rearden.

Physical labor as such can extend no further than the range of the moment. The man who does no more than physical labor, consumes the material value-equivalent of his own contribution to the process of production, and leaves no further value, neither for himself nor others. But the man who produces an idea in any field of rational endeavor—the man who discovers new knowledge—is the permanent benefactor of humanity. Material products can't be shared, they belong to some ultimate consumer; it is only the value of an idea that can be shared with unlimited numbers of men, making all sharers richer at no one's sacrifice or loss, raising the productive capacity of whatever labor they perform. It is the value of his own time that the strong of the intellect transfers to the weak, letting them work on the jobs he discovered, while devoting his time to further discoveries. (1064)

Galt's position here (and Francisco's in the passage quoted at the beginning of this section) is presented in explicit opposition to the view that wealth is essentially the product of physical labor, with its corollary that industrialists grow rich by "exploiting" their workers. This position, which was most prominently defended by Marx, is simply a twist on the Greek marginalization of productive reasoning applied (preposterously) to an industrial society. The twist is that, where the Greeks had exalted theoretical reasoning and disdained manual labor, Marx exalted toil and dismissed as empty the theorizing that the Greeks saw as an end in itself. He regarded men's thoughts as effects of their economic circumstances and activity, describing them as "the efflux of their material behavior" and "ideological reflexes" that are "echoes of life-processes."[38] Galt aptly dubs this position "mysticism of muscle," because it views knowledge not as something that must be achieved through a process of self-directed reasoning, but as something that arises in us passively as a by-product of manual labor, which we somehow *just know* how to perform. Lee Hunsacker speaks for this view when he says:

Any enlightened person knows that man is made by the material factors of his background, and that a man's mind is shaped by his tools of production. But people wouldn't wait for the laws of economic determinism to operate upon us. We never had a motor factory before. We had to let the tools condition our minds, didn't we? (320)[39]

It is because tools cannot condition a mind that the factory closes; and in the absence of a mind competent to understand its nature and value, Galt's motor, the greatest of all tools, rusts while the mindless residents of Starnesville sink into a life of true toil. This is only one of the many episodes in the novel that dramatize the falsehood of the mysticism of muscle. One further example will suffice, both to convey this point and to underscore the mind's role as the productive faculty. Consider how Rand describes the relay room in the Taggart Terminal, and Dagny's thoughts concerning it, after the interlocker system has failed:

Through the open door of the relay room, she saw the tower men standing grimly idle—the men whose jobs had never permitted a moment's relaxation—standing by the long rows that looked like vertical copper pleats, like shelves of books and as much of a monument to human intelligence. The pull of one of the small levers, which protruded like bookmarks from the shelves, threw thousands of electric circuits into motion, made thousands of contacts and broke as many others, set dozens of switches to clear a chosen course and dozens of signals to light it, with no error left possible, no chance, no contradiction—an enormous complexity of thought condensed into one movement of a human hand to set and insure the course of a train, that hundreds of trains might safely rush by, that thousands of tons of metal and lives might pass in speeding streaks a breath away from one another, protected by nothing but a thought, the thought of the man who devised the levers. But they—she looked at the face of her signal engineer—they believed that that muscular contraction of a hand was the only thing required to move the traffic—and now the tower men stood idle—and on the great panels in front of the tower director, the red and green lights, which had flashed announcing the progress of trains at a distance of miles, were now so many glass beads—like the glass beads for which another breed of savages had once sold the Island of Manhattan. (951–52)

Without the interlocker, the trains must be directed manually, by an army of men with lanterns, following written orders, a process that "will take hours to do what used to take minutes" (953). In response to the signal master's surprise, Dagny says:

"Yes, brother! Now why should *you* be shocked? Man is only muscles, isn't he? We're going back—back to where there were no interlocking systems, no semaphores, no electricity—back to the time when train signals were not steel and wire, but men holding lanterns. Physical men, serving as lampposts. You've advocated it long enough—you got what you wanted. Oh you thought that your tools would determine your ideas? But it happens to be the other way around—and now you're going to see the kind of tools your ideas have determined!"

But even to go back took an act of intelligence—she thought, feeling the paradox of her own position, as she looked at the lethargy of the faces around her. (952)

THE VALUING FACULTY

In discussing reason's role in production, we focused on what philosophers call "instrumental reasoning"—that is, calculating the means necessary to achieve an end. To return to our last example, Dagny sought to move trains through the Taggart Terminal, and figured out *how* to do it. The broken interlocking system, a product of reason, was likewise devised as a *means* to this end. Again, consider the ten-year long process by which Rearden designed his Metal. There was something he sought—a metal with certain properties—and he thought about the means of creating it. However, Rand maintained that reason is responsible for determining our ends as well as our means.[40]

Before taking up *Atlas Shrugged*'s treatment of this point, it will be instructive to briefly consider it independently of the novel. We can begin by imagining the content of an animal's consciousness. Take the case of a tiger on the hunt: he is seeking his prey, and in some manner—perhaps in the form of an image—he must be aware of this goal. In this way, the tiger can consciously pursue the prey or a mate, but he cannot consciously pursue good nutrition or parenthood as such; much less can he consciously pursue life or any particular sort of life. The tiger's consciousness is limited to the perceptual level, and he cannot project goals that cannot be perceived. Because his life as a whole is outside the range of his consciousness, he cannot consciously pursue or direct it. Its direction is provided by genetically programmed desires or learned habits that nonconsciously cause him to be motivated to pursue various perceptible goals and to take various concrete actions, which, unbeknownst to him, cohere into a self-sustaining way of life. Thus, as Rand explains,

> an animal's life consists of a series of separate cycles, repeated over and over again, such as the cycle of breeding its young, or of storing food for the winter; an animal's consciousness cannot integrate its entire lifespan; it can carry just so far, then the animal has to begin the cycle all over again, with no connection to the past. *Man's* life is a continuous whole: for good or evil, every day, year and decade of his life holds the sum of all the days behind him.[41]

A man can—and, indeed, must—project goals that are outside of the range of his perceptual awareness. He must *conceive purposes*, holding them in mind over a span of time, directing himself toward them. Think, for example of how Rearden held "the one thought" of his metal "immovably across a span of ten years, under everything he did and everything he saw" (30). Further, man can integrate his purposes into wider and wider values, to be pursued over longer and longer expanses of time, culminating in a conception of his life as a whole, as a value to be achieved and maintained. Thus Rearden, seeing the neon sign above his mills as he walks home after pouring the first heat of his Metal, thinks of the other neon signs in different parts of the country reading "Rearden Ore—Rearden Coal—Rearden Limestone" and wishes "it were possible to light a neon sign above them, saying: Rearden Life" (32): each sign represents a value achieved, and he conceives of his life as an ever-growing sum of such achievements.

A purpose conceived and pursued over time is a *value* in the sense in which that term is properly applicable to man. Galt, in his speech, defines a value as "that which one acts to gain and keep" (1012), and there is a sense in which a man chasing after something in the short-range manner of an animal might be said to be pursuing a value; but human beings cannot survive in this manner, nor can they even find such values desirable, except in a context where they see them contributing to further values. Whereas an animal is motivated to pursue certain perceptible things by innate desires, all of man's desires derive from the purposes he has chosen.

This difference between men and animals is highlighted in Dagny's thoughts, during her stay in Woodstock. Having quit the railroad, which has been her central purpose in life since she was a child, she retreats to the country to regroup; with nothing else to do, she finds herself rebuilding the path from her cabin.

The work gave her the calm needed; she had not noticed how she began it or why; she had started without conscious intention, but she saw it growing under her hands, pulling her forward, giving her a healing sense of peace. Then she understood that what she needed was the motion to a purpose, no matter how small or in what form, the sense of an activity going step by step to some chosen end across a span of time. The work of cooking a meal was like a closed circle, completed and gone, leading nowhere. But the work of building a path was a living sum, so that no day was left to die behind her, but each day contained all those that preceded it, each day acquired its immortality on every succeeding tomorrow. A circle, she thought, is the movement proper to physical nature, they say that there's nothing but circular motion in the inanimate universe around us, but the straight line is the badge of man, the straight line of a geometrical abstraction that makes roads, rails and bridges, the straight line that cuts the curving aimlessness of nature by a purposeful motion from a start to an end. The cooking of meals, she thought, is like the feeding of coal to an engine for the sake of a great run, but what would be the imbecile torture of coaling an engine that had no run to make? It is not proper for man's life to be a circle, she thought, or a string of circles dropping off like zeros behind him—man's life must be a straight line of motion from goal to farther goal, each leading to the next and to a single growing sum, like a journey down the track of a railroad, from station to station. (609)

A tiger would not experience the process of acquiring food when he had no further purpose as an "imbecile torture," because his awareness does not reach beyond the meal. The direction of his life and the place of the meal in it is set for him by nonconscious mechanisms. For Dagny, whose consciousness does reach further, the meal can only be a value as a means to or part of something more. And she must conceive and choose this something herself. At this point in the novel she has abandoned what had been her central purpose in life and, because of certain philosophical confusions, is unable to choose another one.[42] It is for this reason that she can find no joy in such short-range goals as preparing a meal. (Notice how she delights in this very same task, later in the novel, when cooking for Galt in the valley [774–75].)

Dagny's mind is fiercely active, and she experiences her lack of a purpose during her time in Woodstock as an unbearable departure from her normal way of functioning. Other characters, who lack a purpose because they are mentally passive or evasive, do not experience the lack as Dagny does, but it is nonetheless present. Such people, like the "old woman" of Starnesville, come as near as a human being can to an animal's mode of action; but they do not have the vitality that we associate with animals. Instead they drift through life without feeling the passions that even animals experience for such things as food and sex. Consider in this connection how James Taggart and Betty Pope's relationship is described:

> There was no passion in it, no desire, no actual pleasure, not even a sense of shame. To them, the act of sex was neither joy nor sin. It meant nothing. They had heard that men and women were supposed to sleep together, so they did. (71)

The negative characters are similarly indifferent to money. In part III, for example, Jim absentmindedly hands a bum a hundred dollar bill, which is "the first wad of paper" he finds in his pocket. He notices that the bum accepts the money in the same "automatic and meaningless" manner in which he gave it—"as if he would have been indifferent had he received a hundred dollars or a dime or, failing to find any help whatever, had seen himself dying of starvation within this night" (864). Over the course of the evening, Jim has "thrown dollars about by the hundreds" for "unfinished drinks," "uneaten delicacies," "unprovoked tips," and such "unexpected whims" as a "long distance phone call to Argentina" to check "the exact version of a smutty story." Reflecting on this, he realizes that "he had never cared for money" and feels a "shudder of dread" at the recognition that "he would be equally indifferent were he reduced to the state of the beggar" (867).

This indifference comes from the abdication of the mind, as Francisco explains in his speech at Taggart's wedding on "the meaning of money":

> [Money] will take you wherever you wish, but it will not replace you as the driver. It will give you the means for the satisfaction of your desires, but it will not pro-

vide you with desires. . . . Money will not purchase happiness for the man who has no concept of what he wants: money will not give him a code of values, if he's evaded the knowledge of what to value, and it will not provide him with a purpose, if he's evaded the choice of what to seek. (411)

There are two crucially connected points here. The first is that valuing as such is a *conceptual* process, which requires using one's mind to project new possibilities, and to direct oneself toward them over time. This is the case regardless of what one values. To be purposive at all, a man must be a thinker—he must have a "concept of what one wants" (though there is a certain, degenerate respect in which nonthinkers may be said to have purposes). The second point is that some purposes are rational and right and others irrational (or, at least, mistaken) and wrong: man must use his mind to discover "the knowledge of what to value." Crucial to Rearden's valuing of Rearden Metal, for example, is his identification of it *as good*. Ultimately validating this judgment requires an explicit code of values, and later I will comment briefly on the need for such a code and reason's role in defining one. But it is possible to have values even in the absence of an explicit code, as is the case with Rearden who (initially at least) evaluates the metal as good based on his recognition of the way in which it promotes a constellation of other values that he recognizes as promoting human survival.

At present, our focus is on the role of reason in having purposes at all, and especially on the implications of this for motivation. It is by *choosing what to seek*, by projecting and committing to goals, that reason gives rise to desires and emotions, including both those drives that are thought to be innate, such as sexual passion and the desire to live, and those profound values that give shape and meaning to one's life and generate one's deepest emotional responses. In its capacity as the valuing faculty—and specifically the faculty that gives rise to values of this second sort—the mind is the *spirit* or *soul*. Just as there is a dichotomy, rejected by *Atlas Shrugged*, between theoretical and productive reason, so there is a dichotomy between spiritual values and bodily desires. The former, which are more often attributed to some mystical faculty than to reason, include moral and aesthetic values and love; the latter, desires for sex, food, and creature comforts. The spiritual values are supposed to be sublime and bodily desires debased—an attitude we witnessed earlier in the person of the bum who attributes technology to man's "ignoble cunning for satisfying the needs of his body":

There isn't any human spirit. Man is just a low-grade animal, without intellect, without soul, without virtues or moral values. An animal with only two capacities: to eat and to reproduce. . . . You go through life looking for beauty, for greatness, for some sublime achievement, and what do you find? A lot of trick machinery for making upholstered cars or inner-spring mattresses. (177)

It does not occur to the bum that there may be anything sublime or spiritual in creating an innerspring mattress (or in maintaining a transcontinental railroad) because such accomplishments are related to bodily needs, and he conceives of spiritual values as independent of, and higher than, bodily concerns.

In opposition to the spirit-body dichotomy, *Atlas Shrugged* maintains that bodily desires and pleasures are expressions of spiritual values, and that spiritual values must be given expression in material form. The novel's most extended treatment of the unity between spirit and body, especially as regards the spiritual character of bodily pleasures and desires, occurs in connection with Rearden, whose initial acceptance of the spirit-body dichotomy leads him to damn himself for his sexual desire for Dagny (254). Through his affair with her and friendship with Francisco he comes first to appreciate the spiritual nature of material production, and then to grasp that "my mind and my body [are] a unit," that sex is "an experience of superlative joy to unite my flesh and my spirit," and that his desire for her "did not come from the sight of her body, but from the knowledge that the lovely form I saw, did express the spirit I was seeing" (564). In the course of this development he learns how to enjoy his wealth, and realizes that there is a "vicious and important" "perversion" in the idea that it is mindless playboys who are the real enjoyers of material pleasures (371).[43]

Dagny understands these points from the beginning, but some of the novel's most dramatic expressions of them occur in the narrations of her thoughts. We can see clearly the novel's position on the relation of sexual desire to spiritual values as she struggles against an overpowering desire for Galt:

> as she lay in bed in the darkness of her room, unable to think or to sleep—and the moaning violence that filled her mind seemed only a sensation of her muscles, but its tone and its twisting shades were like a pleading cry, which she knew, not as words, but as pain: Let him come here, let him break—let it be damned, all of it, my railroad and his strike and everything we've lived by!—let it be damned, everything we've been and are!—he would, if tomorrow I were to die—then let me die, but tomorrow—let him come here, be it any price he names, I have nothing left that's not for sale to him any longer—is this what it means to be an animal?—it does and I am. . . . She lay on her back, her palms pressed to the sheet at her sides, to stop herself from rising and walking into his room, knowing that she was capable even of that. . . . It's not I, it's a body I can neither endure nor control. . . . But somewhere within her, not as words, but as a radiant point of stillness, there was the presence of the judge who seemed to observe her, not in stern condemnation any longer, but in approval and amusement, as if saying: Your body?—if he were not what you know him to be, would your body, bring you to this?—why is it *his* body that you want, and no other?—do you think that you are damning them, the things you both have lived by?—are you damning that which you are honoring in this very moment, by your very desire? . . . She did not have to hear the words, she knew them, she had always known them. . . . After a while, she lost the glow of that knowledge, and there was nothing left but pain and the palms that were pressed to the sheet—and the almost indifferent wonder whether he, too, was awake and fighting the same torture. (780–81)

Dagny's desire for Galt is intense and intensely physical, but it stems from her deepest spiritual values and her recognition of his—from the *things they have lived for*. Throughout the novel we see how sexual passion is a result of such values, and how the characters, like James Taggart and Betty Pope, who lack such values do not experience intense sexual desires or find any joy in sex.

The mere physical sensation of an orgasm, taken in isolation, may be pleasant, but such tactile pleasures alone do not account for the superlative joy we take in sex or the painful intensity with which we sometimes desire it. Rather the tactile pleasures are a form in which we experience spiritual values:

> It was not the pressure of a hand that made her tremble; but the instantaneous sum of its meaning, the knowledge that it was *his* hand, that it moved as if her flesh were his possession, that its movement was his signature of acceptance under the whole of that achievement which was herself—it was only a sensation of physical pleasure, but it contained her worship of him, of everything that was his person and his life [...] it contained her pride in herself and that it should be she whom he had chosen as his mirror, that it should be her body which was now giving him the sum of his existence, as his body was giving her the sum of hers. These were the things it contained—but what she knew was only the sensation of the movement of his hand on her breasts. (956–57)

The same point applies to luxuries. The flowers and lights at Dagny's first ball do not make the occasion gay for people who have nothing to celebrate (103); and looking at the "dim sculptured beauty" of a fancy restaurant and at its patrons, Rearden notices their "look of rancorous anxiety" and "manner of self-conscious display, as if the enormous cost of their clothes and the enormous care of their grooming should have fused into splendor, but didn't." "They sit there, waiting for this place to give them meaning, not the other way around. . . . They are the playboys, while we're just tradesmen, you and I. Do you realize that we're much more capable of enjoying this place than they can ever hope to be?" (371–72). Unlike other patrons, Dagny and Rearden can enjoy the luxurious restaurant because they have values to give it meaning.

It is primarily for these values, rather than for the pleasure they take in sex or luxury items, that the spirit-body dichotomy denigrates mere "tradesmen" like Rearden and Dagny. When, earlier in the novel, under the influence of the dichotomy, he described the two of them as "a couple of blackguards" who "haven't any spiritual goals or qualities" and care only for "material things" (87), the material things he had in mind are not sexual pleasures or creature comforts. He and Dagny were standing at the window of his office watching "silently" and "intently" the motion of a crane as it loaded the first shipment of Rearden Metal rails into a string of gondolas. Dagny pronounced the name of the metal "as if greeting a new phenomenon of nature," and the two agreed that it is "great" and "the most important thing happening in the world today" because of "what that metal can do, what it will make possible":

They spoke of the metal and of the possibilities which they could not exhaust. It was as if they were standing on a mountain top, seeing a limitless plain below and roads open in all directions. But they merely spoke of mathematical figures, of weights, pressures, resistances, costs.

This was reality, she thought, this sense of clear outlines, of purpose, or lightness, of hope. This was the way she had expected to live—she had wanted to spend no hour and take no action that would mean less than this.

She looked at him in the exact moment when he turned to look at her. They stood very close to each other. She saw, in his eyes, that he felt as she did. If joy is the aim and the core of existence, she thought, and if that which has the power to give one joy is always guarded as one's deepest secret, then they had seen each other naked in that moment. (87)

The spirit-body dichotomy vilifies the heroes because they value nothing above the production of material goods. What Rearden Metal makes possible is such things as heavy-freight air traffic, new types of motors, durable and inexpensive chicken wire and kitchenware, and so forth. These goods are of value because they contribute to the fulfillment of "needs of the body" for such things as food and shelter, and a life around such needs is supposed to be that of a "low-grade animal" without any spiritual qualities.

We saw in the last section how reason is the root of production, and the greatest productive achievements, such as Rearden Metal, involve the fullest use of the mind. And, earlier in this section we saw that, though these achievements are our means of satisfying the bodily needs that we share with animals, the motivation involved is quite different. A tiger in pursuit of his prey is acting to sate an automatic urge that has come over him, but there is no such automatic desire to create a new metal. That goal itself is a value that Rearden conceived and chose; and, like the pleasure he takes in the taste of expensive wine (372), the sight of Hawaiian Torch Ginger on a winter's day (368), or the feeling of Dagny's "slender, sensitive body" trembling under his fingers (309), his enjoyment of the metal is an expression of his spirit.

Dagny first formulates this point to herself, in the moment of her greatest achievement, as she rides in the cab on the first run of the John Galt Line. The narration of her thoughts, from which I quote at length, gives what I think is the novel's most eloquent expression of the relation between spirit and body:

The glass sheets of the cab's windows made the spread of the fields seem vaster: the earth looked as open to movement as it was to sight. Yet nothing was distant and nothing was out of reach. She had barely grasped the sparkle of a lake ahead—and in the next instant she was beside it, then past.

It was a strange foreshortening between sight and touch, she thought, between wish and fulfillment, between—the words clicked sharply in her mind after a startled stop—between spirit and body. First, the vision—then the physical shape to express it. First, the thought—then the purposeful motion down the straight line of a single track to a chosen goal. Could one have any meaning without the other? Wasn't it evil to wish without moving—or to move without aim? Whose malevolence was it that crept through the world, struggling to break the two apart and set them against each other?

She shook her head. She did not want to think or to wonder why the world behind her was as it was. She did not care. She was flying away from it, at the rate of a hundred miles an hour. She leaned to the open window by her side, and felt the wind of the speed blowing her hair off her forehead. She lay back, conscious of nothing but the pleasure it gave her.

Yet her mind kept racing. Broken bits of thought flew past her attention, like the telegraph poles by the track. Physical pleasure?—she thought. This is a train made of steel . . . running on rails of Rearden Metal . . . moved by the energy of burning oil and electric generators . . . it's a physical sensation of physical movement through space . . . but is that the cause and the meaning of what I now feel? . . . Do they call it a low, animal joy—this feeling that I would not care if the rail did break to bits under us now—it won't—but I wouldn't care, because I have experienced this? A low, physical, material, degrading pleasure of the body? . . .

She did not want to think, but the sound of thought went on, like the drone of the motors under the sounds of the engine. She looked at the cab around her. The fine steel mesh of the ceiling, she thought, and the row of rivets in the corner, holding sheets of steel sealed together—who made them? The brute force of men's muscles? Who made it possible for four dials and three levers in front of Pat Logan to hold the incredible power of the sixteen motors behind them and deliver it to the effortless control of one man's hand?

These things and the capacity from which they came—was this the pursuit men regarded as evil? Was this what they called an ignoble concern with the physical world? Was this the state of being enslaved by matter? Was this the surrender of man's spirit to his body?

She shook her head, as if she wished she could toss the subject out of the window and let it get shattered somewhere along the track. She looked at the sun on the summer fields. She did not have to think, because these questions were only details of a truth she knew and had always known. Let them go past like the telegraph poles. The thing she knew was like the wires flying above in an unbroken line. The words for it, and for this journey, and for her feeling, and for the whole of man's earth, were: It's so simple and so right! (240–42)

She recognizes that the pleasure she takes in the feeling of the wind through her hair, is due not to the feeling itself but to what it means to her; it is the physical sensation of the achievement of a great value. She has worked tirelessly for months against great odds to bring the John Galt Line into existence. She thinks the Line will save Colorado and, with it, the country and the railroad to which she has devoted her life; so the Line's success represents the triumph of her view of life against the sense of futility and despair that have become the leitmotif of the culture.

Her view of life is summed up in the "single absolute" with which she later tells Galt she has held since childhood: "that the world was mine to shape in the image of my highest values and never to be given up to a lesser standard, no matter how long or hard the struggle" (812).[44] And the swift motion of the train symbolizes the process of shaping the world in the image of one's values: one sees a goal ahead, moves purposefully toward it, and then reaches it. A value is "that which one acts to gain and keep" (1012), and so requires action toward it. But our actions are bodily, and to gain a value is to bring it into physical reality—to reshape the world in its image. Any alleged value that cannot be given "physical shape" or expression cannot be acted for and is a contradiction in terms. And, as Galt explains in his speech, anyone who doesn't act to give his values "expression in material form" is "a cheap little hypocrite" whose "existence is unrelated to his convictions" (1029). Productive work is the epitome of valuing. Galt defines it, echoing Dagny's words, as: "the process by which man's consciousness controls his existence, a constant process of acquiring knowledge and shaping matter to fit one's purpose, of translating an idea into physical form, of remaking the earth in the image of one's values" (1020). Far from "being enslaved by matter" or "surrendering his spirit to his body," the person who devotes his life to production takes mastery over matter and makes the world his own.

The values alleged to be nonbodily and superior to the productive purposes to which Dagny and Rearden devote their lives fall into two categories. Some are legitimate values that have been thought incorrectly to be unrelated to physical survival. In this category fall art, romantic love, and the intellectual values prized by the Greeks.[45] The second category of values alleged to be superior to productive achievement are not values at all but the undefined ideals espoused by "mystics of spirit."

The novel's two most prominent mystics of spirit are James Taggart and Lillian Rearden.[46] Lillian consistently demeans Rearden's values as "crude," "materialistic," "commercial," "sensual," and so forth, and professes devotion to the "non-commercial" or "non-material," offering no positive identification of her ideal. When asked by Rearden what "enlightened people do with their lives," she suggests that their enlightenment consists in their not attempting to do anything—"they certainly don't spend [their time] on manufacturing plumbing pipes" (302). Jim speaks of "a hunger for something much beyond" achievements such as the John Galt Line—for things that "can't be tagged or measured" or "named in materialistic words"—for "the higher realms of spirit, which man can never reach" (265). Again, he defines the phenomena of the spirit for which he longs only by stating what they are not. Galt explains:

> They claim that they perceive a mode of being superior to your existence on this earth. The mystics of spirit call it "another dimension," which consists of denying dimensions. The mystics of muscle call it "the future," which consists of denying the present. To exist is to possess identity. What identity are they able to give to their superior realm? They keep telling you what it is *not*, but never tell you what it *is*. All their identifications consist of negating: God is that which no human mind can know, they say—and proceed to demand that you consider it knowledge—

God is non-man, heaven is non-earth, soul is non-body, virtue is non-profit, A is non-A, perception is non-sensory, knowledge is non-reason. Their definitions are not acts of defining, but of wiping out. (1035)

A value that is not rational, cannot be given material expression, and cannot be achieved, is a contradiction in terms, and the claim that there are such self-contradictory values is simply an attempt to *evade* the necessity of conceiving and pursuing rational values and the existence of those who do so.

Jim Taggart and Lillian are among the true villains of *Atlas Shrugged*, the conscious mystics and inveterate evaders. I mentioned earlier that such characters develop a special, perverse form of motivation centered around an antipathy toward existence and values as such. For them mystical pseudo-values are an instrument of destruction, a means to tear down genuine values.[47] But the acceptance of mystical values is not always motivated by such vicious motives. Consider, for example, how the disillusioned bum Dagny meets in the slum diner is described:

His gaunt face, with staring eyes and shrunken features that had been delicate, still retained a trace of distinction. He looked like the hulk of an evangelist or a professor of esthetics who had spent years in contemplation in obscure museums. She wondered what had destroyed him, what error on the way could bring a man to this. (177)

The error that destroyed the man is the acceptance of mystical pseudo-values, and the tone of description suggests that the error was venial and that his destruction is tragic, whereas Jim Taggart's is not. Dagny sums up the effect the acceptance of such pseudo-values would have on a man nicely when she contrasts her love of electric lights with "what others claimed to feel at the sight of the stars." The lights represent an achievable goal—"the aspiration drawing her upon her upward course," with the earth as "the height that she wanted to reach." By contrast, because the stars are "safely distant by millions of years," they impose no "obligation to act," but serve "as the tinsel of futility" (691). This sense of futility and resigned hopelessness, represented by the question "Who is John Galt?" is pervasive in the world of *Atlas Shrugged* and sadly prevalent in the world in which we live. So too are feelings of guilt experienced by productive men, such as Rearden, who, because they give credence to a mystical standard, mistakenly impugn the values to which they devote their lives.

What mysticism mandates is the sacrifice of one's values—the goals that one has rationally projected and is pursuing in action—to undefined pseudo-ends that cannot be achieved or even pursued. In denying that reason is the source of values and that values are achievable on Earth, mysticism erects an imposter code of values. The possibility of such an aberration and the havoc it can wreak even on the lives of honest men, underscores the need for a rationally defined code of values—a *morality of reason*, which, unlike mystical codes, is based on and consistent with the facts that give rise to the phenomenon of valuing. Though the content of this morality is too large a topic to take up in the short space remaining, it is necessary to say a little bit about its function in life, in order to complete our sketch of *Atlas Shrugged*'s theme.[48]

In her nonfiction Rand defines a "morality" as "a code of values to guide . . . the choices and actions that determine the purpose and course of [man's] life," and "ethics" as the "science" charged with "discovering and defining such a code."[49] What morality specifies is not such concrete values as who to love or what career to pursue, but rather the broad principles by which one can assess such concrete values. It performs the function that, in animals, is served by the innate desires that direct them toward certain things and away from others and so make their actions cohere into a life—"a process of self-sustaining and self-generated action" (1013). Like animals, man needs such direction, but possesses no innate code to provide it—a point made heartbreakingly by Cherryl Taggart:

> We've always been told that human beings have such a great power of knowledge, so much greater than animals, but I—I feel blinder than any animal right now, blinder and more helpless. An animal knows who are its friends and who are its enemies, and when to defend itself. It doesn't expect a friend to step on it or to cut its throat. (890)

Cherryl has begun to realize that prevailing morality condemns as evil all the things that make life possible and elevates as virtues the traits most inimical to life, thus turning morality against man. When she realizes the full extent of this problem, believing herself to be helpless in the face of it, she takes her own life. The train of thought that leads her to this highlights the crucial role of intelligence in the formation of a morality. Observing the traffic light change from red to green,

> she stood trembling, unable to move. That's how it works for the travel of one's body, she thought, but what have they done to the traffic of the soul? They have set the signals in reverse—and the road is safe when the lights are the red of evil—but when the lights are the green of virtue, promising that yours is the right-of-way, you venture forth and are ground by the wheels. All over the world, she thought—those inverted lights go reaching into every land, they go on, encircling the earth. And the earth is littered with mangled cripples, who don't know what has hit them or why, who crawl as best they can on their crushed limbs through their lightless days, with no answer save that pain is the core of existence—and the traffic cops of morality chortle and tell them that man, by his nature, is unable to walk. . . .

> She could not deal with people any longer, she could not take the paths they took—but what could she say to them, she who had no words to name the thing she knew and no voice that people would hear? What could she tell them? How could she reach them all? Where were the men who could have spoken? (906–7)

The men who could have spoken are the men of the mind, who are on strike, and the strike itself is their means of "reaching them all." In less than four months after Cherryl's suicide, Galt speaks in a voice that everyone does hear. It takes Galt, "the sort of mind born once in a century," to find the words to name the thing Cherryl knew—to identify that the world is perishing because of a Morality of Death and to define a Morality of Life. Galt's moral code—The Objectivist Ethics—is based on a recognition of the nature of the mind and its role in man's existence, and it enables the mind to play that role fully, self-confidently, and without contradiction for the first time.

But this is a topic for another occasion. I'd like to close this essay by returning once again to Dagny's thoughts during the first run of the John Galt Line, when she first articulates the key aspects of the mind's role that we have been discussing.

> Why had she always felt that joyous sense of confidence when looking at machines?—she thought. In these giant shapes, two aspects pertaining to the inhuman were radiantly absent: the causeless and the purposeless. Every part of the motors was an embodied answer to "Why?" and "What for?"—like the steps of a life-course chosen by the sort of mind she worshipped. The motors were a moral code cast in steel.
>
> They *are* alive, she thought, because they are the physical shape of the action of a living power—of the mind that had been able to grasp the whole of this complexity, to set its purpose, to give it form. For an instant, it seemed to her that the motors were transparent and she was seeing the net of their nervous system. It was a net of connections, more intricate, more crucial than all of their wires and circuits: the rational connections made by that human mind which had fashioned any one part of them for the first time.
>
> They *are* alive, she thought, but their soul operates them by remote control. Their soul is in every man who has the capacity to equal this achievement. Should the soul vanish from the earth, the motors would stop, because *that* is the power which keeps them going—not the oil under the floor under her feet, the oil that would then become primeval ooze again—not the steel cylinders that would become stains of rust on the walls of the caves of shivering savages—the power of a living mind—the power of thought and choice and purpose. (246)

Here we can see all the elements we have discussed of *Atlas Shrugged's* distinctive vision of the mind and its role in human existence. We see the mind as the source of the technology that keeps us alive, and as the setter of purposes. We see the mind as the soul or living power. It brings life to wires, metal, and primeval ooze by shaping them into the physical form of a life-sustaining value it has conceived. In like manner, man brings himself to life by exercising his power of thought and choice and purpose to set the values—the moral code—that give self-sustaining direction to his actions. This is what it means to live *as a man*. *Atlas Shrugged* shows us both grand-scale examples of such living and "that state of living death" which is man's only alternative to it (1015).[50]

NOTES

1. Ayn Rand, *Capitalism: The Unknown Ideal* (New York: Signet, 1967), 1, and "Basic Principles of Literature," in *The Romantic Manifesto: A Philosophy of Literature* (New York: Signet, 1975), 81. In some contexts, she gave a fuller statement of the theme: "the role of the mind in man's existence and, as a corollary, the presentation of a new code of ethics—the morality of rational self-interest" ("Is Atlas Shrugging," in *Capitalism*, 15, and *For the New Intellectual* [New York: Signet, 1963], 88). I discuss how the novel demonstrates a new moral philosophy in my essay "Discovering Atlantis" in this volume.

2. As Allan Gotthelf has pointed out to me, this broader focus is reflected in Rand's statement of the theme as the role of the mind "in man's *existence*" rather than "in man's *life*."

3. Rand identifies this as the "plot-theme" of the novel in her lectures on fiction (reprinted, in an edited form, in *The Art of Fiction: A Guide for Writers and Readers*, Tore Boeckmann ed. [New York: Plume, 2000], 18). The concept of "plot-theme," a term coined by Rand, is explained in "Basic Principles of Literature" (*Romantic Manifesto*, 84) and *Art of Fiction*, 17. For an illuminating analysis, see also Tore Boeckmann, "*The Fountainhead* as a Romantic Novel," in Robert Mayhew, ed., *Essays on Ayn Rand's* The Fountainhead (Lanham, Md.: Lexington Books, 2007), especially 123ff.

4. In this respect *Atlas Shrugged* is anticipated by *Anthem*, which dramatizes the "meaning of the concept 'I'" by showing a world in which it has been eradicated and the steps by which a lone genius recaptures it. In Rand's view, the "I" or "ego" and the "mind" are the same thing (see especially *Atlas Shrugged*, 1057). For discussion of *Anthem* from this point of view, see my "Prometheus' Discovery: *Anthem* on Individualism and the Meaning of the Concept 'I'," in Robert Mayhew, ed., *Essays on Ayn Rand's* Anthem (Lanham, Md.: Lexington Books, 2005).

5. As Rand wrote in another connection: "A great deal may be learned about society by studying man; but this process cannot be reversed: nothing can be learned about man by studying society—by studying the inter-relationships of entities one has never identified or defined." ("What is Capitalism," in *Capitalism*, 15.)

6. See Michael S. Berliner, "The *Atlas Shrugged* Reviews," and Leonard Peikoff, "Reply to Whittaker Chambers," in the present volume.

7. In a letter to John Hospers, Rand expresses uncertainty as to whether there even are innate degrees of raw intelligence. See Michael S. Berliner, ed., *Letters of Ayn Rand* (New York: Dutton, 1995), 539.

8. It is, however, a thesis of *Atlas* that one can permanently destroy one's mind through long and consistent misuse. This is the state of people like James Taggart who Galt refers to as "teachers of the Morality of Death" and who he says "will never know who is John Galt."

9. Galt describes this mission as follows:

> I went out to become a flame-spotter. I made it my job to watch for those bright flares in the growing night of savagery, which were the men of ability, the men of the mind—to watch their course, their struggle and their agony—and to pull them out, when I knew that they had seen enough. (746)

The men Galt has in mind here are those like Rearden, Wyatt, and Dagny, and we get several indications in the novel that Galt, Francisco, and Ragnar have lists of such "future strikers" (795, 804, cf. 579, 758). But not all strikers were targeted in this manner. There are indications that when Rearden strikes, he takes with him much of his staff (most notably his secretary, Gwen Ives), though none of these people had been specifically sought out by Galt or Francisco (1000). These people and presumably many others were invited to join the strike, whereas some equally virtuous people were not, because the strikers happened to know of them. A third, intermediate, category of striker comprises those, like Owen Kellogg and Dick McNamara, who Galt targets in order to undermine Taggart Transcontinental. These men, though likely not of sufficient stature to be on Galt's initial list of potential strikers, acquire special significance because of Dagny's reliance on them.

10. Henceforth, I will use "animal" to refer only to animals other than man.

11. This tradition should be distinguished from both the rationalist tradition (exemplified by Plato and Descartes), which holds that we have some knowledge entirely independent of the senses, and the empiricist tradition (exemplified by Locke and Hume), which held that all knowledge derives from the senses and retains an essentially sensory character, as well as from the Kantian tradition which is a synthesis of these two and maintains that the objects we know are constructed by the mind out of sensory material in accordance with innate structuring principles.

12. Rand repeated this definition, speaking in her own voice, in her 1960 talk "Faith and Force" (reprinted in *Philosophy: Who Needs It* [New York: Bobbs-Merrill, 1982; Signet paperback edition, 1984].). In later writings, she dropped the word "perceives," defining reason as "the faculty that identifies and integrates the material provided by man's senses." (See especially "The Objectivist Ethics," in *The Virtue of Selfishness: A New Concept of Egoism* [New York: New American Library, 1964].). Most likely the change was made because it came to Rand's attention that the initial formulation could be taken to mean that there is reasoning involved in the process of sense-perception itself, a view that she rejected. For further discussion of this issue see my chapter "The Objectivist Epistemology" in Allan Gotthelf and Gregory Salmieri, eds., *Ayn Rand: A Companion to Her Works and Thought* (Oxford: Blackwell, forthcoming).

13. Rand presents her theory of concepts in *Introduction to Objectivist Epistemology*. Further exposition and elaboration can be found in Leonard Peikoff, *Objectivism: The Philosophy of Ayn Rand* (New York: Dutton, 1991), chapters 3–5, my "Objectivist Epistemology," and Allan Gotthelf's unpublished paper "Ayn Rand on Concepts: Another Approach to Abstraction and Essence."

14. "Objectivist Ethics," 22.

15. I discuss Rearden and Dagny's developing thinking in some detail in my other contribution to this volume, "Discovering Atlantis." Cherryl's thought is narrated across part III, chapter IV; see especially pp. 873–83 and 900–8. We see Eddie's thoughts in the novel's opening scene (3–7) and he expresses them throughout the novel in his conversations with Galt and with Dagny.

16. Similar characters include the store keeper in Woodstock, with whom Dagny deals during her stay there (610), and the members of Cherryl Taggart's family (on which, see 261). None of these characters seek to improve their lots in life, because doing so would require conceiving of an alternative to the status quo, and that would require a sort of mental exertion that, after a lifetime of passivity, would be unnatural to them (and perhaps impossible).

17. "Objectivist Ethics," 22.

18. See, for example, "Objectivist Ethics," 20,"The 'Conflicts' of Men's Interests" (in *Virtue of Selfishness*), 59, "Philosophy and Sense of Life" (in *Romantic Manifesto*), 26, and "Our Cultural Value Deprivation" (in *The Voice of Reason: Essays in Objectivist Thought*, Leonard Peikoff ed. [New York: New American Library, 1989; paperback edition, Meridian, 1990]), 102. For further discussion, see Peikoff, *Objectivism*, 61.

19. There is helpful discussion of this point in Harry Binswanger's lectures on *Free Will* from the 1999 Second Renaissance Conference in Lake Tahoe (recording of which are available from the Ayn Rand Bookstore).

20. Such fog imagery occurs also in connection with Lillian Rearden, in whose eyes Hank sees "not the look of understanding, but of a furious refusal to understand—as if she wanted to turn the violence of her emotion into a fog screen, as if she hoped not that it would blind her to reality, but that her blindness would make reality cease to exist" (538).

21. On the psychology of evil, see Onkar Ghate's discussion of the chapter "Anti-Life" in his essay "The Part and Chapter Headings of *Atlas Shrugged*," also in the present volume (40–41, 49–50) and Tara Smith's discussion of "The Death Premise" in her essay "No Tribute to Caesar: Good or Evil in *Atlas Shrugged*" in the present volume (280–87).

22. "Faith and Force," in *Philosophy: Who Needs It*, 85.

23. See especially 1027 and 1034–46. For discussion, see Allan Gotthelf's "Galt's Speech in Five Sentences (and Forty Questions)" in the present volume (381).

24. "Objectivist Ethics," 22–23.

25. *Capitalism*, 17.

26. It is worth noticing that an area over nine times the size would have been destroyed if Rearden had not heroically withheld Rearden Metal from the State Science Institute, when it requested it for Project X (360, 432–38). As built, the device is able to "produce rays to cover . . . the entire countryside within a radius of one hundred miles." Floyd Ferris and his goons had "the technical knowledge to build generators with a range of two and three hundred miles—but due to the fact that we were unable to obtain in time a sufficient quantity of a highly heat-resistant metal, such as Rearden Metal, we had to be satisfied with our present equipment and radius of control" (822–23). When initially asked to sell the Metal for use in the secret project, Rearden gives as one of this reasons for refusing: that "I created that Metal" and "It is my moral responsibility to know for what purpose I permit it to be used" (365). This is just the sort of responsibility defaulted on by Stadler, who does not object to his discoveries being used to create Project X. Rand discusses the responsibility of scientists in this connection in her essay "To Young Scientists," in *Voice of Reason*.

27. David Harriman, ed. *Journals of Ayn Rand* (New York: Dutton, 1997), 252. The passage is from a nonfiction treatise *The Moral Basis of Individualism*, which Rand worked on in the period between *The Fountainhead* and *Atlas Shrugged*, but never completed.

28. My treatment of the Greeks here owes a great deal to Leonard Peikoff's explanation (in an unpublished lecture on the importance of historical knowledge to philosophy) of Rand's comment that she could not have formulated her philosophy prior to the Industrial Revolution. See his briefer discussion of this issue in *Objectivism*, 195–96.

29. *Protagoras* 321d. Significantly, allusions to Prometheus figure prominently in Rand's work. Francisco describes Galt as "Prometheus who changed his mind" (517) and Equality 7-2521, the hero of *Anthem*, renames himself Prometheus at the end of the novella (Fiftieth anniversary paperback edition [New York: Signet, 1995], 115). The mythological Prometheus represents reason and is supposed to have stolen fire for man from the gods and to have been punished for this by being bound to a mountain where he was pecked at by birds of prey. Similarly, Galt and the hero of *Anthem* are paragons of reason who make a new form of energy available to mankind and suffer for having done so. But in Rand's version, unlike the myth, the suffering is caused by mankind itself; and, instead of submitting to it, the heroes (to paraphrase Francisco) withdraw their fire until the day when men withdraw their vultures (517). This point was called to my attention by Jason Rheins, who observed that Steve Ingalls, the hero of Rand's 1939 play "Think Twice" (posthumously published in Leonard Peikoff ed., *The Early Ayn Rand: A Selection from Her Unpublished Fiction*, revised version [New York: Signet, 2005]), also creates and withdraws a new form of energy and so can be seen as a third instance of Rand's reconceiving the Prometheus myth. Rheins elaborates: "All the central protagonist-heroes in works that Rand conceived of and finished after starting *The Fountainhead* fit the Prometheus model. Rand sees in the Prometheus myth and many others an implicit recognition of society's hostility against (the men of) the mind—an identification made by Roark [*Fountainhead*, 678], whose destruction of the Cortland housing project is a similar revolt against self-sacrifice. Rand's 'New Prometheus' archetype not only emphasizes the life-giving power of reason, as some other versions of the myth had done, but also epitomizes the moral revolution of rational egoism that liberates the mind from the code of self-sacrifice."

30. In *Nicomachean Ethics* VI 4, Aristotle defines a *technê* as a "productive state involving true reason."

31. For completeness, it is worth mentioning a third category of reasoning, which both Aristotle and Plato discuss: the *practical reasoning* by which we make decisions about how to conduct our lives. Plato, especially, stresses the role of this sort of reasoning in making material possessions of value to us (*Euthydemus* 278e-282a, *Meno* 87e-88b, cf. *Apology* 30b), and thinks that it is closely related to (or perhaps identical with) theoretical reasoning, which he regards as quite distinct from the sort involved in producing food. Aristotle treats theoretical, practical, and productive reasoning as fully distinct categories (see especially *Nicomachean Ethics* VI).

32. See Galt's reference to Stadler in his speech, 1066.

33. Similarly Lillian refers to it as "a new kind of tin" (37).

34. See especially the *Phaedo*.

35. This difficulty gives rise to a number of often-remarked-on tensions in his corpus. He is frequently tentative when discussing issues bearing on the relation of mind to life and nature; and his identification, in *Nicomachean Ethics* Book X, of the life centered around theoretical contemplation as the highest good, has seemed to many commentators to be out of tune with the loving attention paid in the rest of the treatise to a constellation of virtues and values that are associated with civic life and would seem to be relegated to a merely instrumental role in the life Aristotle ultimately advocates as best.

36. Rand often quoted approvingly Bacon's other famous dictum, that "Nature, to be commanded, must be obeyed" (*Novum Organum* Book 1, aphorism 3 [Spedding trans.]), and once gave it as a one-sentence summation of her metaphysics (see "Introducing Objectivism," in *Voice of Reason*, 3, "Who is the Final Authority in Ethics?" in *Voice of Reason*, 18, *For the New Intellectual*, 15, "The Metaphysical vs. the Man-Made," in *Philosophy: Who Needs It*, 25; cf. *Introduction to Objectivist Epistemology*, 2nd. ed. [New York: Meridian, 1990], 82, and "The Stimulus and the Response," in *Philosophy: Who Needs It*, 202.)

37. Francisco, in Rearden's office, makes a similar point, describing the dedication to the good that is inherent in the way Rearden runs his business and makes his Mills constitute a "material" expression of the "abstract principle" of "moral action" (451).

38. For an especially clear statement of Marx's position on this issue (from which I draw my quotes) see "Premises of the Materialist Method," in *The Materialist Conception of History* (in David McLellan, ed. *Karl Marx: Selected Writings*, 2nd ed. [Oxford: Oxford University Press, 2000], see especially 180–81).

39. Rand regarded Marxism as a form of mysticism in its methodology as well. See *For the New Intellectual*, 33–34, "The Left: Old and New" (in *Return of the Primitive* [New York: Meridian, 1999]), 169, and "To Dream the Non-Commercial Dream" (in *Voice of Reason*), 246. Marxism is based on so-called "dialectical logic," which is different from and allegedly superior to traditional Aristotelian logic in two respects: first it views thought as inherently social, whereas Aristotelian logic views it as individualistic; second, it views contradictions between premises as a necessary stage in reasoning from which we progress to new conclusions by "transcending" the contradiction. Aristotle and Rand, by contrast, maintained that contradictions arise only from missteps in one's reasoning that must be corrected by "checking your premises," so as to discover and reject the false ones. Rand interpreted appeals to dialectical reasoning as attempts to lull people into abandoning their minds and submitting to authority, and illustrated this with the characters of Simon Pritchett and Floyd Ferris (132–33, 542).

40. For an especially emphatic statement of this position, see Robert Mayhew, ed., *Ayn Rand Answers: The Best of Her Q&A* (New York: New American Library, 2005), 107. See also Darryl Wright's 2005 lecture "Ayn Rand and the History of Ethics" (available from the Ayn Rand Bookstore). Taking this statement as his point of departure, Wright gives a masterly exposition of Rand's meta-ethics and its relation to the views of several landmark thinkers.

41. "Objectivist Ethics," 26.

42. For further discussion see my "Discovering Atlantis," 226 ff.

43. See "Discovering Atlantis," 406, 416–20.

44. Galt echoes her wording in his speech, when he defines "productive work" as "the process by which man's consciousness controls his existence, a constant process of acquiring knowledge and shaping matter to fit one's purpose, of translating an idea into physical form, of remaking the earth in the image of one's values" (1020).

45. For *Atlas Shrugged*'s view of the role of art in life, see 65–66 and 781–84. Rand discusses the value of art at length in *The Romantic Manifesto*.

46. Taggart and Lillian, of course, are not the source of the doctrine. They are taught by intellectuals such as Simon Pritchett, who themselves stand at the end of "a long line of men stretched through the centuries from Plato onward" (559).

47. Because they do not focus their minds, these characters have no values and so no desires in the normal, healthy sense of that term. But, even in their out-of-focus state, they cannot help but be aware in some form of their own impotence to deal with reality and of their dependence

on rational men. As a result, they come to resent the world for its inhospitality to them and to hate rational men for their ability to succeed in it. Ultimately they become motivated to destroy or demean the great. This is why the only moment of enthusiasm from either Taggart or Pope during their time together comes when he tells her of his plans to "put the skids" under his sister (71), and the closest he or Lillian ever comes to sexual passion is when they sleep with one another in a pathetic, futile attempt to defile Rearden (898–900). That act satisfies a desire Jim has had all evening to "celebrate." It is the only time in the novel when he wants to celebrate, and what he wants to celebrate is specifically the deal that will lead to the nationalization—that is, the destruction—of d'Anconia Copper (866).

48. See Darryl Wright's "Ayn Rand's Ethics: From *The Fountainhead* to *Atlas Shrugged*" and my "Discovering Atlantis," both in the present volume, for a discussion of the essential ethical content of the novel and its validation.

49. "Objectivist Ethics," 13.

50. The Anthem Fellowship for the Study of Objectivism at the University of Texas at Austin and The Ayn Rand Institute cosponsored a workshop on *Atlas Shrugged* in January of 2008 at which there was much valuable discussion of my plans for my two contributions to this volume, and of *Atlas Shrugged* more generally. Both essays are better for it, and I would like to thank Tara Smith and Debi Ghate, who both organized and participated in the event, and the other participants: Robert Mayhew, Tore Boeckmann, Yaron Brook, Onkar Ghate, and Jason Rheins. Thank you also to Allison and Jason Roth for valuable comments on a draft of the essay, to Allan Gotthelf and Harry Binswanger for discussion and comments, and to Charlotte Jarrett for some unexpected, last-minute line editing. Finally, I'd like to acknowledge the Chicago Objectivist Club, where I delivered a version of this paper in April 2008 and received valuable feedback—in particular, I'd like to thank Keith and Pari Schacht for organizing the talk; Keith also, along with Ben Bayer, had insightful comments and questions about the structure of the material.

14

Ayn Rand's Ethics

From *The Fountainhead* to *Atlas Shrugged*

Darryl Wright

Ayn Rand first envisioned *Atlas Shrugged*—originally entitled *The Strike*—as something of a postscript to *The Fountainhead*. The novel would dramatize the world's need for and injustice toward its prime movers—its Howard Roarks. But its philosophic frame of reference would be the philosophy of egoism and individualism set forth by its predecessor. In time, however, *The Fountainhead* became—as Rand later put it—the overture to *Atlas Shrugged*.[1]

The postscript view—the view of *Atlas* as the subordinate work—is evident in Rand's very first notes for the novel, dated January 1, 1945. "The theme," she says, "requires showing who are the prime movers and why, how they function; who their enemies are and why, what are the motives behind the hatred for and the enslavement of the prime movers; the nature of the obstacles placed in their way, and the reasons for it."[2] That sounds familiar enough; it sounds like *Atlas*. But she immediately adds: "This last paragraph is contained entirely in *The Fountainhead*. Roark and Toohey are the complete statement of it. Therefore, it is not the direct theme of *The Strike*—but it is part of the theme and must be kept in mind, briefly re-stated in order to have the theme clear and complete."[3] The point is evident: *Atlas* will inherit its main philosophic content from *The Fountainhead*. By the late '40s, however, Rand realizes that *Atlas* will be "bigger in scope and scale than *The Fountainhead*," as she puts it in a 1949 letter to Archibald Ogden (her former editor at Bobbs-Merrill).[4]

In part, *Atlas* is bigger in "scope and scale" because it has a metaphysical theme (the role of the mind in human survival), not just an ethical one (egoism and individualism). But *Atlas* also presents a more detailed, more complex, more systematic, more fully validated—and, in some ways, different—view of ethics from *The Fountainhead*. And this is my focus here: how Ayn Rand's ethical thought develops and why.

I start by exploring Rand's changing conception of the relationship between
The Fountainhead and *Atlas*. This will point up three issues on which the moral
philosophy of *Atlas* diverges from or moves beyond that of *The Fountainhead*,
and I then explore each of these issues more fully. Although these issues do
not exhaust the important differences between *Atlas* and *The Fountainhead*
(even in ethics), they are among the most important of those differences. The
three issues are: (1) rationality rather than independence as the primary moral
virtue; (2) altruism as a means of exploitation; and (3) the proper validation
of a moral standard and the role of choice in morality. Finally, I draw some
general conclusions concerning the progression of Rand's ethical thought in
the period between her two major novels. I refer frequently to Rand's notes
and draft material for *The Moral Basis of Individualism*, a book she never completed but that was to have been a nonfiction presentation of the moral philosophy of *The Fountainhead*. She worked on this project from 1943 to 1945.

ATLAS SHRUGGED IN RELATION TO *THE FOUNTAINHEAD*

Let us return to Ayn Rand's early notes for *Atlas*, specifically, to her further
analysis of the thematic relationship of *Atlas* to *The Fountainhead*. *The Fountainhead*, she writes, "showed that Roark moves the world—that the Keatings feed
upon him and hate him for it, while the Tooheys are consciously out to destroy him. But the theme was Roark—not Roark's relation to the world. Now
[in *Atlas*] it will be the relation."[5] *The Fountainhead* "was Roark's story."[6] But
Atlas "must be the world's story—in relation to its prime movers. . . . I do not
show directly what the prime movers do—that's shown only by implication.
I show what happens when they don't do it."[7] This last statement is striking. The
completed novel does, of course, "show directly what the prime movers do";
it shows a great deal of how they approach life and how they use their minds,
which is just what makes it inspiring. Similarly astonishing is the statement in
Rand's early notes that the novel "do[es] not set out to glorify the prime mover
(that was *The Fountainhead*)."[8]

Six months into her work, Rand is having doubts about her original conception of the novel:

> I must consider very carefully the statements I made . . . to the effect that *the world*
> is featured in the story, and *the relation* of society to its prime movers. . . . [T]he
> second-handers *must not* be allowed to steal the show . . . . Even though I do not
> here treat of the *nature* of prime movers but of *their relation* to society—it is still
> *the prime movers* who are to be the stars: it is still *their story*.[9]

Although she still does not expect *Atlas* to add to *The Fountainhead*'s depiction
of "the nature of [the] prime movers," she perceives that the novel's social emphasis threatens to give the second-handers[10] center stage. The danger is that
"[t]he predominant emotion left by the book would be contempt, hatred, ridi-

cule, gloating over the second-handers and their plight—but no uplift to the spirit of the strikers. The strikers would become only a kind of plot means to expose the parasites."[11] Thus, in rethinking her initial conception of the novel, Rand makes a decisive change. Whereas originally *Atlas* was to have been the world's story, not the strikers' story, now, referring to the strikers, Rand writes: "it is still *their* story."

But this change presents an awkward problem. How can *Atlas* be the prime movers' story without "treat[ing] of the *nature* of [the] prime movers"? Focusing on the strikers seems repetitive and unnecessary in light of *The Fountainhead*, but without such a focus the novel will lack an uplifting meaning. The solution, Rand concludes, is for the events of the novel to dramatize "[t]he nature of the *prime movers' martyrdom*," which is the "spirit" and "justification" of the strike and "*the very thing that made me want to write this novel.*"[12] Now the strike, once complete, *ends* their martyrdom. Thus, to *dramatize* their martyrdom requires showing the prime movers when they are *not* on strike. Rand discusses the advantages of this approach in subsequent notes: "There is the danger of having mere action, without emotional content, if I start with the strikers already on strike. Their decision [to strike] is then undramatized, behind the scenes—and the story can become passive, like their action of just doing nothing."[13] She adds, "*The actual plot must contain emotional conflict.*"[14] What is needed, then, is to show the strikers being victimized by society, and going on strike as a result, in a way that centers the emotional content of the story on their decision to do so. Rand then indicates the nature of the emotional conflict they face: "*Here*—show that it is not easy for them to break the ties."[15] It is not easy for any of the strikers. The emotional content of *Atlas*, however, centers on Dagny and Rearden—on their resistance to the strike and eventual realization that it is they themselves, as well as the other prime movers, who have empowered the evil destroying them and the world. In the remainder of this section, I take an overview of the steps involved in that realization, highlighting the importance of the three issues mentioned in the introduction. As we will see, the novel presents Dagny's and Rearden's decisions to join the strike as the direct result of a growth of moral understanding centered on these issues.

Why do Dagny and Rearden oppose the strike? In effect, they make the opposite error from Dominique Francon in *The Fountainhead*. Dominique believes that evil—second-handedness—is powerful, and that the good can succeed in the world only by making terms with evil, thereby destroying itself as good. By contrast, Dagny and Rearden consider evil impotent, not powerful; they regard the policies of the second-handers (the "looters" in the vernacular of *Atlas*) as a self-defeating aberration. Galt sees the full truth that the novel seeks to convey: that evil *is* impotent in itself but gains its destructive power through the forbearance of the good. In this respect, *Atlas* places the theme of *The Fountainhead* into a wider and richer context, in which that theme is both confirmed and refined. If *The Fountainhead* said that evil cannot touch the good, then *Atlas* adds: unless the good empowers it.

Rearden (rather than Dagny) is first to see this and go on strike. A long development lies behind his decision to do so. But the last straw is the looters' total imperviousness to reason, as displayed in the expectation that the prime movers will always save them from the consequences of their actions, will always find a way to make reality suit the looters' wishes *somehow*. Rearden had long recognized that the looters were cowardly, dishonest, and completely dependent on the judgment and actions of better men; that they were what Roark would have called "second-handers." He assumed, though, that even they would eventually have to alter their disastrous course. It is the Steel Unification plan that finally convinces him otherwise. Objecting to the plan, which would force profitable steel manufacturers to subsidize unprofitable ones, he tells James Taggart, Floyd Ferris, and the others, "There is no way to make the irrational work"—to which Taggart replies, "Oh, you'll do something!" (986). The assumption that the looters would eventually concede their errors and relent presupposed some basic rationality on their part—some basic respect for reality. Taggart's reply crystallizes for Rearden that this basic rationality is what the looters have rejected; he sees that they are not just second-handers but irrationalists. If second-handedness, for Rand, represents a contemptible and self-defeating way of dealing with the world, then the looters' irrationalism represents a profound evil—a rejection of the precondition of any form of successful, life-sustaining action. By working under the looters' directives, Rearden realizes, he has helped them to prolong their hold on the country and sustain the illusion that the irrational *can* be made to work. He has thus unwittingly collaborated in his own exploitation (and that of the other prime movers). At the beginning of the next chapter, he goes on strike.

But nothing Rearden learned about the looters could have had its full effect before he had grasped an important truth about himself, namely, that the sense of moral guilt he carries for much of the novel is undeserved. He condemns himself for his affair with Dagny, which he considers both a salacious betrayal of his respect for her and an unpardonable violation of his marriage vows. This verdict on his actions has two disastrous results: first, it damages his estimation of himself and, so, his capacity to enjoy his life and achievements; second, it opens him up to "white blackmail" by the looters when he is asked to sign the Gift Certificate making Rearden Metal public property. The blackmail is white because, in Rand's view, Rearden has no actual guilt. In the circumstances, the affair is morally justifiable (his wife neither loves nor respects him, and she actively works to deprive him of happiness); indeed, it is admirable (what draws him to Dagny are her moral virtues and way of facing life). Dagny, who speaks for Rand on this issue, recognizes this and subsequently chooses to reveal the affair herself. But Rearden—not questioning the necessity of unconditional marital fidelity or the assumption that sexual passion is a morally anomalous animal response—signs the Gift Certificate in order to prevent the affair's being exposed. He allows guilt over the affair and pity for Lillian's unhappiness to tie him to her, treating his marriage vows as though they gave her unlimited license to maltreat him. In these respects, his actions are shaped by the ethics of altruism, of self-sacrifice, that the novel as a whole condemns.[16] Although his acceptance of altruism is merely passive and implicit, and contradicted by all he does that is motivated purely by love of his work, it damages him as well as signalizes a deeper problem. As conscientious as he is in other respects, Rearden has given little explicit attention to the importance of moral values and ideals in human life. The irrationality of the looters could not have driven him to strike had he not first come to grips with this issue and revised the moral standards by which he judged his own actions.

Dagny has a richer explicit understanding of morality and is more morally consistent than Rearden. But she, too, crucially misunderstands the looters' motivating aims. She can see that their policies have the *effect* of preventing the prime movers from functioning, and that those policies will be harmful not only to the prime movers but ultimately even to the looters themselves, since they will inevitably bring down the entire national economy. But she does not see that the destruction of the prime movers is the unadmitted intent of those policies. She does not see that the looters have a psychological stake in the destruction of the prime movers, and in branding them as evil, for if the prime movers represent virtue and success, then the looters can only represent evil and impotence. The looters sense something that Galt expands on in his speech:

> By a feeling he has not learned to identify, but has derived from his first awareness of existence, from his discovery that he has to make choices, man knows that his desperate need of self-esteem is a matter of life or death. As a being of volitional consciousness, he knows that he must know his own value in order to maintain his own life. He knows that he has to be *right*; to be wrong in action means danger to his life; to be wrong in person, to be evil, means to be unfit for existence. (1056–57)

Precariously, the looters have staked their self-esteem on being the moral opposites of prime movers. What is inconceivable to Dagny is that they will not right themselves come what may but will persist in seeking vindication from an uncooperative reality. They struggle not to make themselves fit for existence but—impossibly—to make existence fit for them (and unfit for the prime movers). This is what explains their insistence on political and economic policies that are a disaster by any sane standard.

Dagny's own love of life runs so deep, and her commitment to the fulfillment of her life's potential is so fundamental, that it simply eludes her that others do not share it or that there is even an issue on which a choice must be made, a stand taken. When she discovers late in the novel that the looters would rather kill Galt than change course and save themselves, the truth becomes clear to her: she sees that the looters have no real desire to live and that what motivates them ultimately is a nihilistic hatred for all human success and ability. That is when it becomes clear to her that she must quit. Until then, she assumed that the looters would eventually have to recognize the futility of their own policies and give up. On that assumption, her struggle to keep Taggart Transcontinental alive was a struggle *against* the looters—a struggle to hold out until they were forced to concede and relent. But if their motive is destruction, then there is no bringing them around, and holding out merely amounts to accepting victimization for herself and others.

The realizations that Rearden and Dagny come to, and that are decisive in their decision to strike, become central themes in the moral philosophy presented in Galt's Speech. In regard to each of them, the moral philosophy of *Atlas* takes important steps beyond the moral philosophy of *The Fountainhead*. Rearden's discovery of the looters' rejection of reason emerges as the view that rationality rather than independence is the basic moral virtue; in *The Fountainhead* the basic virtue was said to be independence. His awakening to the costs of his own moral passivity emerges as the issue of the "sanction of the victim" and the exploitative character of altruism. Dagny's recognition of the looters' nihilistic motives emerges as the view that the choice to live or not is the basic choice a human being must confront, and the requirements of living, the proper standard of morality. I turn now to the development of Rand's views in each of these areas.

FROM INDEPENDENCE TO RATIONALITY AS THE PRIMARY MORAL REQUIREMENT

The unreason of the looters' society is all over *Atlas Shrugged*. It is best embodied in the character of James Taggart. We repeatedly see Taggart refusing to think, evading what he knows, and placing feelings over facts. By contrast, Dagny, Rearden, and the other prime movers use their minds fully, straining every nerve to understand, to know the truth, even in periods of anxiety, discouragement, and exhaustion. Reflecting this basic contrast, in *Atlas* Ayn Rand casts rationality as the basic requirement of morality—an important shift from *The Fountainhead*.

The case for independence as the basic moral requirement is made in Roark's courtroom speech. Here are two key passages:

> Man cannot survive except through his mind. He comes on earth unarmed. His brain is his only weapon. Animals obtain food by force. Man has no claws, no fangs, no horns, no great strength of muscle. He must plant his food or hunt it. To plant, he needs a process of thought. To hunt, he needs weapons, and to make weapons—a process of thought. From this simplest necessity to the highest religious abstraction, from the wheel to the skyscraper, everything we are and everything we have comes from a single attribute of man—the function of his reasoning mind. . . . But the mind is an attribute of the individual. There is no such thing as a collective brain.[17]

The choice is not self-sacrifice or domination. The choice is independence or dependence. The code of the creator or the code of the second-hander. This is the basic issue. It rests upon the alternative of life or death. The code of the creator is built on the needs of the reasoning mind which allows man to survive. The code of the second-hander is built on the needs of a mind incapable of survival. All that which proceeds from man's independent ego is good. All that which proceeds from man's dependence upon men is evil.[18]

Roark's argument is as follows: (1) we face the alternative of life or death; (2) the requirements of life are the proper standard for moral evaluation; (3) the mind is our means of survival; (4) but the mind is an attribute of the individual and independence is its basic requirement; (5) therefore, independence—forming one's own judgments and living by the work of our own mind—is one's primary moral obligation. The conclusion is really only implied, but it is explicit in Rand's early notes for *The Moral Basis of Individualism*, where she makes essentially the same argument and concludes: "To preserve the independence of his mind is man's first and highest moral duty. It stands above any other precept."[19]

Notice how much that is familiar from *Atlas* (and from *The Virtue of Selfishness*) is already clear to Rand by 1943: (a) the connection between morality and the alternative of life or death; (b) the requirements of man's life as the proper standard of moral value; (c) the mind as man's basic means of survival; and, therefore, (d) its needs as the source of moral requirements. Still, she identifies independence, not rationality, as the basic requirement to be derived from the moral standard of "man's life" and from man's nature as a rational being. Why is this? Her views at this time about the nature of human volition are the decisive factor. She says in *The Moral Basis of Individualism* that the choice of independence or dependence "is the crucial choice; primary in its nature, based on the manner of his survival, on the issue of life or death, this choice will determine all his subsequent behavior, his actions, his motives, his character, the style of his soul."[20] If independence or dependence is our basic choice, and one leads to life and the other to death, and life is the standard of morality, it makes sense to take independence as the basic moral requirement.

Why does Rand think the choice of independence or dependence is psychologically basic? She writes:

There is nothing in nature to hinder the function of man's rational faculty. That function follows a simple pattern: to observe through his own senses, to make the proper deductions through his own reasoning power. Nothing must stand between the material and man's mind. No intermediary is possible. What can assume the role of such an intermediary? Only other men. The conclusions, the thoughts, the opinions, the wishes or the orders of other men. . . . The only threat to man's rational faculty lies in the person of others.[21]

This seems to imply that if no one else were around, a person would use his mind fully. Interestingly, in the same set of notes she recognizes that "[l]eft alone, man has a single alternative: think or perish."[22] Further, in some earlier notes, she recognizes that thinking involves choice: "It is not only that man survives through the rational faculty which functions through constant choice. It is that he also has the choice of exercising his rational faculty or not. He can make an error in judgment. He can act against his own judgment. He can suspend all judgment."[23] But she does not appear to consider the choice to suspend one's judgment a psychologically realistic one in desert-island cases. In society, she thinks, suspending one's judgment is a realistic possibility, since one has the apparent (but actually only temporary) alternative of "think or be supported by the thinking of others."[24] The presence of others, she seems to assume, supplies a potential motive for nonthinking that would be absent on a desert island. Why is this? She seems to be making two assumptions about those who choose to be dependent on the thinking of others: first, that they have nothing against thinking *per se*; second, that they do want to live. In that case, if such a person found himself on a desert island, he might wish that there were someone else to do his thinking for him, but he would choose to think rather than allow himself to perish. But, as we will see, these are two assumptions about dependent people that Rand will modify later.

On Rand's early view, the choice to suspend one's judgment just *is* the choice to be a second-hander. If independence or second-handedness is the primary choice, then morality has a primarily social function, a function essentially concerned with guiding our relations to others. And this seems to be how Rand first views morality in working on *The Moral Basis of Individualism*. If moral principles are to be delineated by reference to the requirements of human survival, she says, then "the first moral principle deduced from [this standard], the first commandment to guide man in his relations with other men, is the principle of independence. Independence of man from men is the Life Principle. Dependence of man upon men is the Death Principle."[25]

In *The Moral Basis of Individualism*, Rand does not call independence a *virtue* but rather a *moral duty*, by which she means not a duty in the technical, Kantian sense of a categorical imperative, but rather a moral obligation teleologically grounded in the goal of sustaining one's life. She uses the term "virtue" more narrowly than she later does in *Atlas*: "Man's virtues are the qualities required for the preservation of his independence."[26] The virtues, in this presentation, have roughly the same relation to independence as the virtues of independence, honesty, justice, and integrity have to rationality in Rand's later thought (indeed honesty, justice, and integrity are among the virtues Rand discusses as subordinate to independence, along with courage, confidence, honor, wisdom, strength [of mind], and self-respect). Presumably she later concluded that it was not necessary to have a separate category for the master moral requirement of which these virtues are applications; the master requirement (e.g., rationality in Galt's Speech) could also be considered a virtue (and no doubt she later would have wanted to avoid the Kantian overtones of the term "duty"[27]). Terminology aside, her attempts to depict the subsidiary virtues as aspects of *independence* are rather strained. For instance, she writes, "The incentive to dishonesty comes when one deals with other men," which turns it into an issue of independence or dependence (in the sense that the dishonest person is dependent on those he exploits).[28] But that seems incorrect: isn't there such a thing as self-deception—and isn't it precisely the point of Rand's characterization of men like James Taggart that they deceive and manipulate others in order to fake, to themselves, a self-esteem they do not have? Similarly, can't one be unjust in one's assessment of *oneself*, as Francisco argues that Rearden has been when they speak at Rearden's mills? (455).

A great deal of the characterization in *Atlas Shrugged*, both of the prime movers and of the looters, involves aspects of rationality or irrationality that are not primarily matters of independence or dependence. To take one more (negative) example, what drives the looters' material exploitation of the prime movers—their expropriations, regulations, and so forth—is not primarily a desire for wealth but a desire to take over the stature held by the prime movers as beneficent, efficacious men crucial to the well-being of the nation. But it is part of the theme of *Atlas* that wealth has its source in the moral stature of the individuals who produce it, and that it is impossible apart from moral virtue. The novel thus presents the looters' attempt to gain moral stature through material expropriation as a futile and irrational attempt to reverse the actual direction of causal influence.

Shortly before stopping work on *The Moral Basis of Individualism*, Rand makes some notes assessing what she has written. A two-year gap separates these notes from the earlier ones:

> Before you come to any "principle as a guide in his relations to other men," cover the point of how the morality of reason applies to man alone—even to a man on a desert island. The first commandment is to exercise his reason. *Morality is not social* (and don't forget the evils that come from thinking that it is). Only after you have established this, can you come to morality in relation to other men.[29]

In his editorial comments in the *Journals of Ayn Rand*, David Harriman notes that this passage marks the beginning of Rand's transition from taking independence as the primary moral requirement to taking rationality as the primary requirement.[30] Independence is a virtue that can only be exercised in a social context;[31] if morality is not primarily social, then independence cannot be its primary requirement. What accounts for this transition? The notes in which Rand revises her thinking on this point, deciding that morality must be defined nonsocially, come at the end of June 1945, six months after she has started working on *Atlas Shrugged*. It may be that the thinking she had now done concerning the respective psychologies (as she projected them) of the prime movers and the looters had convinced her that there is a genuine, nonsocial choice that a person faces between using his mind fully and failing to do so (e.g., sometimes evading facts or giving in to the promptings of unconsidered emotions). From this, she may have concluded that there is a need for nonsocial moral guidance identifying and characterizing this choice, and evaluating the full and consistent use of one's mind as morally good. This, in essence, is what Rand's concept of "rationality" (as a moral virtue) serves to do.[32] Her views concerning the fundamentally nonsocial nature of ethics and the primacy of the virtue of rationality, in other words, may have grown out of her having reached a clearer view of the nature of human volition, as a result of her having started to work out the psychologies of the positive and negative characters of *Atlas Shrugged*. And *Atlas* not only presents rationality as the basic virtue but presents the choice to think (or not) as the basic choice (1017).

ALTRUISM AS A MEANS OF EXPLOITATION

In her first notes for *Atlas Shrugged*, Ayn Rand writes that the novel must show "exactly *how* the second-handers live on the creators, both in *spiritual* matters *and* (most particularly) in concrete physical events."[33] Some fifteen months later, she reverses this emphasis: "John Galt is the Roark in the story, but the others are not, and it is against the exploitation by the world, particularly . . . spiritual exploitation, that Galt teaches them to strike."[34] Here, as elsewhere in Rand's writings, "spiritual" has a purely naturalistic sense and means "pertaining to consciousness"—to man's moral-intellectual and emotional life.[35] Broadly speaking, spiritual exploitation is Rand's term for the looters' attempt to deprive the prime movers of recognition, admiration, and self-esteem.

Why does Rand decide that the prime movers' spiritual exploitation should have primacy? This reversal of emphasis corresponds to changes in her thinking about the nature and causes of the spiritual exploitation that the prime movers are subjected to. Early on, she envisions the looters exploiting the prime movers by taking credit for their achievements.[36] This form of exploitation is similar to what occurs in *The Fountainhead* (e.g., when Keating accepts credit for architectural plans actually drawn by Roark). Although this kind of exploitation also occurs in *Atlas* (e.g., when James Taggart claims credit for Dagny's decision to build the John Galt Line out of Rearden Metal or when Rearden Metal is made public property and renamed Miracle Metal), it is not of primary importance *per se*. Rather, it is an indication and consequence of a much larger issue, an issue not seen in *The Fountainhead* that Rand seems not to have formulated previously.

The looters in *Atlas* have a sense of the psychological power of morality that the prime movers largely lack (the leaders of the strike, and to some extent Dagny, are the exceptions). According to Rand, man needs morality not only to be able to sustain himself physically but because "to live requires a sense of self-value, but man, who has no automatic values, has no automatic sense of self-esteem and must earn it by shaping his soul in the image of his moral ideal" (1020–21). Thus, "he must acquire the values of character that make his life worth sustaining" (1020). To sustain himself psychologically, Rand holds, a person must acquire the self-esteem that proceeds from a dedication to moral rectitude, which Rand calls the virtue of pride.[37] The prime movers all have the virtue of pride; what they lack (the strike leaders again being exceptions) is a full and explicit grasp of the moral standards—the moral ideal—that should inform this virtue, and a grasp of their own heroic stature when judged by those standards. Their lack of complete and well-articulated moral standards enables the looters to use the prime movers' moral conscientiousness against them. Attuned to the psychological necessity of morality, the looters have attached themselves to a moral code that allows them seemingly to reverse their own sense of moral inferiority to the prime movers while continuing to reject the virtues required by a code geared toward human survival.

The moral code embraced by the looters is *altruism*, not in the confused popular sense of an indiscriminate combination of self-sacrifice and mere generosity, but in the precise philosophic sense deriving from Auguste Comte's use of the term to mean a morality of self-denying service to others.[38] In the novel, altruism enables the looters to cast their antipathy toward the prime movers as a moral crusade against selfishness and for the general good. Altruism thus serves as a vehicle for the exploitation of the prime movers. But *Atlas Shrugged* is not Rand's first attack on altruism; her first explicit attack is in *The Fountainhead*. Nor is *Atlas* the first time she shows the prime movers (as opposed to others) being victimized by altruism. Roark is certainly harmed by the pervasive demand that he sacrifice his own architectural standards in order to serve the standards of the public; it makes his struggle harder. He is harmed by the unauthorized alteration of his design for Cordlandt Homes, which is justified by reference to the public interest. *The Fountainhead* presents "second-handedness" as the unavoidable psychological result of altruism, in the sense that altruism drives people to set aside their own values and seek self-esteem in catering to the wishes of others.[39] And the second-handedness of others devastates Henry Cameron and nearly destroys Steven Mallory, neither of whom is able to sustain the same degree of inward self-sufficiency as Roark. Indeed, Roark points out in his statement at his trial that "the second-hander [uses] altruism as a weapon of exploitation," suggesting that not only does altruism foster second-handedness but that second-handedness, once it takes root, depends on altruism for its moral justification.[40] But *The Fountainhead* does not show Roark and the other prime movers being victimized by *their own* acceptance of altruism. In *Atlas*, however, the focus is on the damage done to the prime movers by their own acquiescence (to varying degrees) in the altruistic code of the looters' society. This was never an issue in *The Fountainhead*. In *Atlas Shrugged*, it is an issue and it has a name: "the sanction of the victim," the prime movers' own toleration of and deference to a moral code on which their rationality, their productiveness, their dedication to their own happiness, and all their other virtues are denigrated as forms of immoral self-indulgence, inimical to the good of society.

Dagny is one case in point here. Misled by an overly charitable reading of the looters' motives, she struggles to run Taggart Transcontinental in conditions demanding a growing effort to stem crises, while offering shrinking room for the pursuit of positive goals. Not surprisingly, her energy wanes and her ability to find joy in life shrivels. But Dagny's acquiescence is not inward acceptance, not even in a latent or implicit form, and this saves her from the worse consequences endured by Rearden, on whom I will focus for the remainder of this section. Rearden's suffering in the novel runs deeper than Dagny's, because Dagny has an explicit awareness of morality that he lacks. In his conscious convictions, Rearden is largely oblivious to morality, and that, the novel shows, makes him specially vulnerable, for morality has a power rooted in our need for moral guidance and justification, a power it exerts on us whether we realize it or not. Francisco warns him of this in the moments before the furnace breakout at Rearden's mills: "You who won't allow one percent of impurity into an alloy of metal—what have you allowed into your moral code? . . . You knew that man needs the strictest code of values to deal with nature, but you thought that you needed no such code to deal with men." (454)

The distinction that Francisco makes in this passage parallels the distinction that led Rand to view rationality rather than independence as the basic virtue. Whereas Rand had, in effect, neglected the purely individual, "desert island" aspect of morality in making the basic virtue independence, Rearden, according to Francisco, makes the reverse error: he neglects interpersonal moral issues. But that is really only the tip of the iceberg. For Rearden's knowledge of the code of values needed for dealing with nature is at best implicit; he does not explicitly see himself as operating by a moral code in his work. His lack of moral self-awareness comes out most clearly in the scene between him and Dagny after her radio appearance: "I took pride in my ability to think, to act, to work for the satisfaction of my desires. But I did not know that this was virtue, I never identified it as a moral value, as the highest of moral values" (858). Rearden does not just neglect interpersonal morality; he neglects morality as such as an explicit intellectual concern:

> While I was busy conquering matter, I had surrendered to them the realm of the mind, of thought, of principle, of law, of values, of morality. I had accepted, unwittingly and by default, the tenet that ideas were of no consequence to one's existence, to one's work, to reality, to this earth. (858)

In short, he "had accepted the one tenet by which they destroy a man before he's started . . . : the breach between his mind and body" (857–58). And he had accepted it "like most of their victims . . . not knowing even that the issue existed" (858).

As long as Rearden has not identified the sources of his pride as *moral values*, he cannot regard his pride as morally justified, and therefore he cannot regard his self-esteem as morally deserved. Rearden *has* earned the self-esteem that he feels. But it is not enough that his fundamental emotional estimate of himself is positive, for his lack of insight into the moral basis of this emotional estimate leaves him tragically vulnerable. We see his vulnerability in the inner conflict he faces in regard to his affair with Dagny. He regards his sexual desire for Dagny as an animal lust degrading to both of them; meanwhile, he is wracked by guilt over his violation of his marriage vows, even though Lillian offers him neither love nor respect. He cannot feel guilty for wanting Dagny, and he cannot hate himself in any fundamental sense. Yet having absorbed societal moral standards he barely knows exist, he condemns himself. The condemnation does not shake his core self-esteem; what it shakes is his conviction that he has any moral *right* to that self-esteem, or, consequently, to any happiness his life has to offer him.

The prime movers' spiritual exploitation is the cause of their material exploitation. And that is surely one reason why Rand reverses the novel's emphasis, giving primacy to the issue of spiritual exploitation. But it is not the most important reason. As Rearden says to Dagny, "wealth is a means to an end" (858). The deepest damage Rearden suffers is not the loss of his wealth. As he comes to recognize,

> I . . . created the means [the wealth] and let them [the society's intellectual trend-setters] prescribe the ends. I, who took pride in my ability to achieve the satisfaction of my desires, let them prescribe the code of values by which I judged my desires. I, who shaped matter to serve my purpose, was left with a pile of steel and gold, but with my every purpose defeated, my every desire betrayed, my every attempt at happiness frustrated. (858)

Besides its connection to their material exploitation, the spiritual exploitation of the prime movers is important in its own right, for the same reason that happiness is important in its own right. Happiness, in Rand's view, is a moral person's deepest purpose in living. But happiness, she holds, proceeds from success in attaining one's values, including, above all, the moral values one aspires to embody in one's character. Thus, happiness, for Rand, depends on moral virtue and thus on pride, understood as "moral ambitiousness," dedication to upholding high moral standards.[41] Pride, in this sense, requires not just living up to one's standards but taking *explicit* charge of the moral standards by which one judges oneself. For all his rightful pride in his abilities, it is pride in this moral sense that Rearden lacks and that makes his exploitation by the looters (both spiritual and material) possible.

THE CHOICE TO LIVE AND
THE VALIDATION OF A MORAL STANDARD

Rearden lacks an understanding of his own virtue and of the importance of morality in human life. He comes to see that his lack of explicit moral values has harmed him. But why is this? Paraphrasing Francisco, what *is* it that a code of moral values does to a man's life, and why *can't* he exist without one? Further, what standard should govern the formulation of such a code, and why, and what would qualify as moral virtue by that standard? The world learns the strikers' (and Rand's) answers to these questions in Galt's Speech, and the individual strikers hear them privately at the time of their recruitment. Clearly, answers to these questions are necessary; the recognition that one has suffered by allowing others to set one's moral values is at best a first step toward solving this problem.

It is not surprising, then, that the validation of a standard of morality is a matter of intense concern for Ayn Rand in the period between *The Fountainhead* and *Atlas*. I will trace some of the evolution of her thinking on this issue. We will also see her reach a conclusion that is vital not for Rearden's self-liberation but for Dagny's: the idea that one's need for, and thus one's potential receptiveness to, morality depends on a basic choice to live. Dagny, recall, shares none of Rearden's moral errors; she does, however, assume that she and the looters share some common moral ground as fellow human beings with the same fundamental aims. What Rand's exploration of the foundations of morality brings out is not just the need for morality in human existence but that there is a choice involved in valuing one's life, a choice that is the precondition of one's being reachable by moral appeals.

Recall Roark's statement that the morality of independence was based on "the needs of the reasoning mind" and, beneath that, the requirements of man's life in the face of the alternative of life or death. This approach to justifying moral requirements takes life as the end to which morality will be the means, and thus makes the requirements of man's life—of man's long-range survival—the standard of what is moral or immoral. So, for example, if we learn that human survival requires rationality, rationality will qualify as a moral virtue. Without a clearly formulated moral standard, any claim one makes about what is moral or immoral is arbitrary. In *The Fountainhead*, Rand sets forth her moral standard but does not present its validation. She first tackles the question of how to validate the standard in *The Moral Basis of Individualism*. This is a crucial issue, since not only do particular moral principles need to be validated by reference to a moral standard, but the standard itself has to be validated in some way; it cannot just be arbitrarily picked out of the air or else the principles based on it will themselves be arbitrary and unjustified.

In *The Moral Basis of Individualism*, Rand says that the basis of morality is a *moral axiom*, which she formulates as "Man exists and must survive as man."[42] Given this axiom, she holds, man's life is the proper moral standard, the proper criterion for determining what is right and wrong. By the time she writes Galt's Speech, however, she has rejected the view that morality is based on a moral axiom. Let us explore why she held her earlier view, what problems there were with it, and how her later view deals with those problems.

Consider again the proposed moral axiom, "Man exists and must survive as man." As she uses the term, an axiom is a self-evident, primary truth lying at the base of a discipline, a truth that must be accepted in any attempt to deny it.[43] Before judging whether the statement just mentioned qualifies as an axiom, we must get clear on what the statement means. The first part—that man exists—is easy enough. But what about the second part, *Man must survive as man*? What does "must" mean, in this context? We are talking about human beings with the faculty of volition, so the "must" cannot refer to deterministic causal necessity—it cannot mean that man necessarily acts in a certain way, just as a pen necessarily falls to the floor when you drop it. This is supposed to be a *moral* axiom, and so the "must" has to be the kind of "must" we encounter in morality—that is, a "should" or an "ought." Rand says that if you wanted to deny this part of the axiom, you "would have to claim either that [man] exists, but his survival is not desirable, or . . . [that] he can survive as a sub-human creature."[44] This part of the axiom thus makes two claims: that man's survival is desirable—that is, that man *should* seek to survive; and that man cannot survive by subhuman means—that is, that *if* man seeks to survive, he *should* act in accordance with his nature.[45] Thus we have three points built into the axiom: (1) Man exists; (2) man should seek to survive; (3) if man seeks to survive, he should act in accordance with his nature. Now it is easy to see why Rand might have thought that (1) has the status of an axiom within ethics. Since ethics prescribes guidance for human conduct, and so presupposes that there are such things as human beings, ethics must take the existence of human beings as a given.[46] It is also easy to see why she might have considered (3) to be axiomatic for ethics: it can be seen as an inference from, or application of, the law of identity, which for Rand is a metaphysical axiom. The law of identity, as she formulates it, says that everything that exists has some definite nature; (3) says that human nature is a given that must be yielded to if one is to be able to survive.[47] But what about (2), the claim that man's survival is desirable or that he should seek to survive? There are two problems with taking this claim to be axiomatic. First, why accept that we should seek to survive? Where does this "should" come from? Second, why accept that survival should be the ultimate end toward which all moral requirements are calibrated? Some moral systems claim that a person should subordinate his life to a higher end. What proves that these systems are wrong?

As she works on *The Moral Basis of Individualism*, Rand seems to recognize that this middle component of her axiom is contestable. She takes two important steps, which, in effect, respond to the objections just mentioned and suggest that her views are evolving—or at least that she is articulating them more fully and precisely. First, she raises the issue of what to say to someone who challenges the claim that man's survival is desirable: "If anyone now asks: But why do I have to hold my survival as desirable?—The answer is: You don't have to. It is an axiom, to be accepted as self-evident. If it is not self-evident to you, you have an alternative: admit that your survival is not desirable and get out of the way."[48] This is a pretty relaxed attitude to have about an axiom (or any true proposition), and it suggests that she is *not* really thinking of "survival is desirable" as a self-evident *truth* that we apprehend, which is how she thinks of metaphysical axioms like the law of identity. For she does not suggest that the person envisioned here would be mistaken or deluded; she is willing to grant him the premise that his own survival is not desirable. One could imagine Rand telling a person who denied metaphysical axioms, "Suit yourself." But it seems unlikely that she would tell him he should admit that a thing can be nothing in particular, or admit that things can act in conflict with their natures.[49]

It seems, then, that the middle part of the axiom—"man's survival is desirable"—is something other than an axiomatic truth that one can grasp and would be mistaken to deny. Confirming this impression, in the same stretch of her notes Rand explains this part of the axiom as follows: "Man needs a rational decision, an axiom understood and consciously accepted: I wish to survive—my survival is desirable. In accepting this, he has accepted the standard and the first axiom of morality."[50] Here, the "axiom" sounds less like an axiomatic *truth*—a truth whose identification lies at the base of a field of study—and more like what we might call an "axiomatic decision"—a decision lying at the base of one's concern to discover correct moral guidance. On this approach, the answer to the question about the source of the "should" in "man should seek to survive" is that there really *is* no "should"; rather there is a decision to embrace one's survival as a goal and, in this sense, take it as "desirable." Although Rand's view seems to be developing in this direction, it still remains somewhat ambiguous.

What about the second objection I mentioned—the issue of why we should take survival (even if it is desirable) as our ultimate end and as the standard for morality? Here the key beginning step comes as Rand is rewriting some earlier draft material for *The Moral Basis of Individualism*. She has the idea that instead of starting her argument by setting forth her axiom she should "begin by asking whether a moral code is necessary? Prove that it is—for a rational being."[51] Later, in *The Virtue of Selfishness*, she begins the presentation of her ethics with just this question, emphasizing that it is the question from which any ethical theory must properly begin. Starting with the question of why moral values are needed provides a way of validating a moral standard without recourse to a moral axiom. If we can explain why—for what purpose—man by his very nature needs a code of moral values, then that purpose will have a clear claim to be the standard of moral value.[52]

Interestingly, it is not until quite some time after Rand thinks of this procedure that she believes she has a satisfactory answer to the question of why man needs moral values. She mentions this question a couple of times more in her notes for *The Moral Basis of Individualism* and in her working notes for *Atlas*, but she mentions it as a question still to be answered, rather than as one to which she already has the answer. This may seem puzzling since she has already stated explicitly that all living things need values in order to live and that man needs morality because he has no preprogrammed values. One might think that she could just put these two points together and obtain the answer she's looking for. But that's not what happens.

What holds her back? What does she think is missing? There is something present in the *Atlas Shrugged* and *Virtue of Selfishness* arguments for the standard of moral value that is only hinted at previously: her analysis of our grounds for forming the concept of "value." Why is such an analysis necessary? The claim that man needs values to live (and more broadly that all living things need values to live) reflects a certain view of the concept of value, a view of what the concept refers to. Since the classifications we make here will impact our conclusions about why we need values, any answer to this question is liable to be accused of changing the subject by someone who sees those classifications differently. Either there is some way of escaping that kind of impasse, or an objective resolution of fundamental ethical disputes is impossible. In her epistemological writings, Rand argues that, along with epistemic standards for justifying beliefs, there are epistemic standards for justifying conceptual classifications.[53] As far as these standards are concerned, Rand contends that our ordinary evaluative vocabulary is a mixed bag. There are parts of it that have no rational grounds and should be jettisoned, such as the concept of "duty" in its Kantian sense (and the artifacts of that sense found in ordinary moral discourse) and the concept of the "common good" as opposed to the good of an individual human being (or other individual living thing).[54] Other parts are in better shape, though, and Rand's analysis of the basis of the concept "value" is an attempt to recover those aspects of this familiar concept that are epistemically legitimate. If she has done this correctly, then she cannot be accused of changing the subject.

To answer the question of why we need values, then, we have to first know what values are—what, if anything, we are talking about when we talk about "values." Knowing this, on Rand's account of the way our concepts work, involves knowing what facts of reality enable and require us to form the concept "value."[55] By the time of *The Moral Basis of Individualism*, Rand has already concluded that values are integral to the functioning of all living things. But this conclusion depends on extending the concept "value" very broadly, to cover not only things pursued by humans but by animals and plants. Is this classification of the objects of animal and plant action as "values" warranted? Rand has some grounds for it in observable similarities between humans and other species.[56] But before Galt's Speech, she does not have a full, systematic account of the basis of the concept "value."

She does have some leads. She writes at one point, "The concept of 'value' presupposes an entity to whom an object or action is valuable."[57] She also has the idea that what is of value to an entity is of value to it for the sake of some goal or end. What does not appear until *Atlas* are these two crucial points from Galt's speech:

(1) "'Value' presupposes a standard, a purpose and the necessity of action in the face of an alternative. Where there are no alternatives, no values are possible" (1012).

(2) "There is only one fundamental alternative in the universe: existence or non-existence—and it pertains to a single class of entities: to living organisms. The existence of inanimate matter is unconditional, the existence of life is not; it depends on a specific course of action. Matter is indestructible, it changes its forms, but it cannot cease to exist. It is only a living organism that faces a constant alternative: the issue of life or death" (1012).

The concept of "value," Galt says here, can only be formed with reference to an entity facing "the necessity of action in the face of an alternative"; omit the issue of such an alternative and it would be impossible to form the concept.[58] But if living organisms and only living organisms confront an action-necessitating alternative, then a "value" is properly defined as an object of a living thing's goal-directed action. And in that case, according to Rand, it is possible to give an objective, nonarbitrary answer to the question of why living organisms need values and, more specifically, why man needs a code of *moral* values. The answer is that we and they need values in order to live—and that means that life *is* the proper standard by which to delineate a code of morality.

Once Rand has this analysis of the roots of the concept "value" in place, she is also able to reframe her account of the basis of morality, to eliminate the problems and ambiguities we noted earlier. In particular, she drops the idea that morality is based on the axiom that man's survival is desirable. To say that survival is desirable or that one should survive, she now holds, is to use the evaluative concepts "desirable" and "should" outside of the only context in which they acquire meaning—the context of a living organism acting to sustain its life.[59] We can evaluate things as desirable, and actions as ones that we should take, in relation to the goal of sustaining our lives; but strictly speaking that goal itself qualifies neither as desirable nor undesirable, in Rand's view (though, of course, it can be desired or undesired). Nor is there any "should" attaching to it, for it is precisely this goal that gives the concepts of "should" and "desirable" meaning. Thus Galt says, "My morality, the morality of reason, is contained in a single axiom: existence exists—and in a single choice: to live. The rest proceeds from these" (1018). This formulation replaces the problematic axiom that "survival is desirable" with the basic choice to live. What about the "existence exists" part? "Existence exists" is a metaphysical not a moral axiom, for Rand, the axiom that there is a reality (1016).[60] But it has moral implications. It implies that if one chooses to live, one must take specific steps to implement that choice—the steps required by the nature of the reality in which one acts, by the "nature of things," including one's own human nature. In effect, Rand is retaining point (3) of her original axiom here, but making its deepest metaphysical foundation explicit.

CONCLUSION

What can we say overall about the development of Ayn Rand the moral philosopher in the period spanning the publication of her two greatest novels? The theme that runs through each of the topics we have considered is our profound *need* for morality. It is her conclusion that we would need morality even on a desert island that prompts her shift from taking independence to taking rationality as the primary virtue. It is her recognition of the indispensability of moral ideals that motivates her concern with spiritual exploitation and her critique of altruism. And it is her quest for the deepest philosophical justification of the thesis that we need morality to live that drives her to one of her most important insights—that the very idea of "value" is inconceivable apart from the concept and phenomenon of life.

These are striking philosophical contributions. But it is worth remarking that they are also more than that. They are part of the abstract background that makes all the concrete magnificence of *Atlas Shrugged* possible. For all of this extraordinary philosophical thinking was born of the aim not of writing a philosophical treatise but of creating something geared toward yet another crucial human need: the need for moral inspiration through art.

NOTES

1. See "About the Author," which follows the text of *Atlas Shrugged*.
2. David Harriman, ed., *Journals of Ayn Rand* (New York: Dutton, 1997), 390.
3. Harriman, *Journals of Ayn Rand*, 390.
4. Michael S. Berliner, ed., *Letters of Ayn Rand* (New York: Dutton, 1995), 437. The letter is dated April 23, 1949.
5. Harriman, *Journals of Ayn Rand*, 390–92.
6. Harriman, *Journals of Ayn Rand*, 392.
7. Harriman, *Journals of Ayn Rand*, 392–93, emphasis in original.
8. Harriman, *Journals of Ayn Rand*, 392.
9. Harriman, *Journals of Ayn Rand*, 397, emphasis in original.
10. "Second-handers" is Rand's term for those who live lives of intellectual, psychological, and existential dependency, drawing their ideas, values, goals, self-esteem, and (in some cases) material support from the "creators" or "prime movers" who think and produce for themselves. See Ayn Rand, *The Fountainhead* (New York: Signet, 1993), 679–85.
11. Harriman, *Journals of Ayn Rand*, 397.
12. Harriman, *Journals of Ayn Rand*, 396 and 397, emphasis in original.
13. Harriman, *Journals of Ayn Rand*, 399.
14. Harriman, *Journals of Ayn Rand*, 399, emphasis in original.
15. Harriman, *Journals of Ayn Rand*, 399.
16. For discussion of the meaning Rand attaches to the term "altruism," see section 3, below.
17. Rand, *Fountainhead*, 680.
18. Rand, *Fountainhead*, 682.
19. Harriman, *Journals of Ayn Rand*, 258.
20. Harriman, *Journals of Ayn Rand*, 259.

21. Harriman, *Journals of Ayn Rand*, 257.

22. Harriman, *Journals of Ayn Rand*, 258.

23. Harriman, *Journals of Ayn Rand*, 253.

24. Harriman, *Journals of Ayn Rand*, 253–54.

25. Harriman, *Journals of Ayn Rand*, 258. Brackets are Harriman's.

26. Harriman, *Journals of Ayn Rand*, 260.

27. See Ayn Rand, "Causality Versus Duty," in *Philosophy: Who Needs It* (New York: Signet, 1984), 95–101.

28. Harriman, *Journals of Ayn Rand*, 261.

29. Harriman, *Journals of Ayn Rand*, 275.

30. Harriman, *Journals of Ayn Rand*, 275.

31. This is not to say, however, that independence can only be exercised *in the company of others*. A person on a desert island (or alone in his house) lacks independence if, say, he adjusts his thinking or action out of fear of "what others might think" if he said or did such-and-such. Conceivably, a person might have become so habituated to this sort of dependence on others that he might persist in it even under circumstances in which the actual likelihood of encountering other people's disapproval was nil—for example, if he had become stranded someplace where there was no hope of being rescued. The point, however, is that dependence on others can only originate where there are others to be concerned with. (If there were no others to be concerned with, a person would face the alternative of being rational or irrational, but the alternative of independence or dependence would not apply; he could have neither the virtue of independence nor the vice of dependence.)

32. For her fullest summary statement of what this virtue involves, see Ayn Rand, *The Virtue of Selfishness* (New York: Signet, 1964), 28. Her most comprehensive elaboration of what rationality entails comes in the form of the characterizations of the prime movers in *Atlas* and thus must be gleaned from the novel as a whole. For Rand's account of the function of literature, in this regard, see *The Romantic Manifesto*, revised edition (New York: Signet, 1975), chapter 1, esp. 21–22.

33. Harriman, *Journals of Ayn Rand*, 393, emphasis in original.

34. Harriman, *Journals of Ayn Rand*, 404.

35. See Ayn Rand, *Introduction to Objectivist Epistemology*, Expanded Second Edition, Harry Binswanger and Leonard Peikoff, eds. (New York: Meridian, 1990), 33–34.

36. Harriman, *Journals of Ayn Rand*, 394.

37. Rand, *Virtue of Selfishness*, 29. For Rand's use of the phrase "psychological survival," see Rand, *Romantic Manifesto*, 169; see also 16–17.

38. See *Oxford English Dictionary*, Second Edition (1989), s.v. "Altruism" (dictionary.oed.com/cgi/entry/50006618?single=1&query_type=word&queryword=altruism&first=1&max_to_show=10) (accessed October 17, 2008). Also see Auguste Comte, *System of Positive Polity, or Treatise on Sociology*, Volume IV, translated by Richard Congreve (Paris: Carilian-Goeury and Vor Dalmont,1854), *passim.* and esp. 43–45, 145–47, 247–48, and 228.

39. Rand, *Fountainhead*, 607.

40. See Rand, *Fountainhead*, 681.

41. Rand, *Virtue of Selfishness*, 29–30.

42. Harriman, *Journals of Ayn Rand*, 255.

43. See Rand, *Introduction to Objectivist Epistemology*, 55; see also Leonard Peikoff, *Objectivism: The Philosophy of Ayn Rand* (New York: Dutton, 1991), chapter 1.

44. Harriman, *Journals of Ayn Rand*, 255.

45. It is clear, in context, that "man" refers to any and every individual human being and not to mankind as a whole, and that what Rand's axiom prescribes is that each human being make his own survival his end (and seek that end in a manner consistent with his human nature).

46. This would actually be a more contentious claim in some quarters than I have made it out to be. A Kantian in ethics might argue, as Kant did, that ethics prescribes guidance for the conduct of *rational* beings and thus does not presuppose that there are *human* beings. That is clearly not how Rand views the subject matter of ethics, but the existence of the Kantian view points

up that what one could consider axiomatic within a given field will depend on some potentially controversial prior conception of that field's subject matter. The reasons why Rand would reject the Kantian view are complex and largely beyond the scope of this essay. In essence, however, Rand's view is that a *rational* being is a certain kind of *living* being, and that our need for ethical guidance derives *both* from our rational nature (in virtue of which we must act by choice and by the guidance of principles) and from our nature as living things (in virtue of which we confront a basic alternative of life or death and the consequent necessity of taking action to sustain our lives). Some aspects of this perspective are discussed further in the text, in the remainder of the present section. (For Rand's elaboration of this perspective, see *Virtue of Selfishness*, chapter 1.)

Finally, even Kantians are normally interested in ethics for the sake of settling questions about *human* conduct, and see their discussions of ethics as being addressed to their fellow human beings. The existence of human beings, then, though it may not be a theoretical presupposition of Kantian ethics, certainly appears to be a practical presupposition of the enterprise of Kantian ethical theorizing.

47. Rand takes the law of identity to be a substantive truth of metaphysics, but one that is arrived at by conceptualizing a self-evident fact known in sense perception, and not through any sort of a priori insight. See *Atlas Shrugged*, 1016. See also Peikoff, *Objectivism*, chapter 1. The connection between a later variant of (3) and the law of identity is made in *Atlas Shrugged*; see 1016.

48. Harriman, *Journals of Ayn Rand*, 303.

49. She might tell him to go ahead and try to act successfully on the basis of these premises. But that would be toward the end of exhibiting the premises as false. She could not use a parallel strategy to exhibit as false someone's denial that his survival was desirable.

50. Harriman, *Journals of Ayn Rand*, 303.

51. Harriman, *Journals of Ayn Rand*, 272.

52. See Rand, *Virtue of Selfishness*, chapter 1; and Peikoff, *Objectivism*, chapter 7. There is obviously more to be said in order to make this argument fully, but my intention here is only to indicate the direction in which Rand's thinking develops. I discuss Rand's argument from the need for ethics to the standard of morality further in my "Evaluative Concepts and Objective Values: Rand on Moral Objectivity," *Social Philosophy and Policy* 25.1 (2008): 149–81.

53. See, for elaboration, Rand, *Introduction to Objectivist Epistemology*, esp. chapter 7.

54. For her criticisms of these two concepts, see, respectively, Rand, "Causality Versus Duty," and Ayn Rand, "What is Capitalism?" *Capitalism: The Unknown Ideal* (New York: Signet, 1967), 11–34, esp. 20–25.

55. See Rand, *Introduction to Objectivist Epistemology*, 51.

56. See, for example, Harriman, *Journals of Ayn Rand*, 298–99.

57. Harriman, *Journals of Ayn Rand*, 299.

58. In *Virtue of Selfishness*, Rand uses the example of an "immortal, indestructible robot," which, she claims, could not form any value-concepts, to clarify and support the claim that the presence of (and one's awareness of) an alternative is necessary for the formation of these concepts. See Rand, *Virtue of Selfishness*, 16.

59. See Rand, "Causality Versus Duty," and Rand, *Virtue of Selfishness*, 97.

60. See, for discussion, Peikoff, *Objectivism*, chapter 1.

15

No Tributes to Caesar

Good or Evil in *Atlas Shrugged*

Tara Smith

Atlas Shrugged helps us to understand the life-and-death consequences of rationality and irrationality. Correlatively, it illustrates the inescapability of value choices. By demonstrating how the law of excluded middle plays out in the realm of human action, Ayn Rand vividly dramatizes how every choice that a person makes is good or evil insofar as it carries repercussions on his existence. Only with a firm grasp of this fact can we fully understand the action of the novel. This fundamental "either-or" also explains the absolutist character of Rand's moral philosophy.

To help us digest the significance of Rand's insight, this paper will examine the choice between good and evil. In particular, it will focus on the mutually exclusive and jointly exhaustive nature of these alternatives to make plain their life-or-death consequences. It will proceed in four stages. First, to indicate morality's roots in the issue of life or death, I will outline Rand's view of the basic nature of value. Second, we will trace pivotal elements in the protagonists' steadily increasing understanding of the character of their alternatives over the course of the story. Next, we will observe how this increased knowledge alters their course of action. Finally and more briefly, we will indicate how the "either-or," mutually exclusive character of this alternative dictates the absolutist character of Rand's moral code. All of this, I believe, will help the reader to understand the theme of *Atlas Shrugged*—the role of the mind in human existence—more richly.[1]

THE NATURE AND FOUNDATIONS OF VALUE

To understand the life-or-death stakes of morality's authority and the inescapability of value choices, we must first understand Rand's view of what morality is. While this is a large subject that warrants extensive explanation in its own right, a basic sketch must suffice here.[2]

In *Atlas*, Rand illustrates how morality and rationality go hand in hand. "Man's reason *is* his moral faculty," Galt observes, and "thinking is man's only basic virtue" (1017, emphasis in original). The rational is the moral. Rand was led to this conclusion by investigating the roots of morality.[3]

"Morality is a code of values to guide man's choices and actions—the choices and actions that determine the purpose and the course of his life."[4] But, Rand asks, why should a person be moral? On what grounds does it make sense to consider certain things good or valuable? What she finds, in answer, is that it is only in relation to living organisms that anything can be good or bad. For inanimate objects, no values exist. Nothing can be good or bad for a bench or a clock or a stone insofar as these entities have nothing to gain or to lose as a result of anything's effects on them. "Gains" and "losses" are possible only in relation to some end. Indeed, this is precisely how we measure gains and losses: by things' impact on the achievement (or maintenance) of a goal. As Rand explains,

> "Value" is that which one acts to gain and/or keep. The concept "value" is not a primary; it presupposes an answer to the question: of value to *whom* and for *what*? It presupposes an entity capable of acting to achieve a goal in the face of an alternative. Where no alternative exists, no goals and no values are possible.[5]

Values arise, in other words, only in relation to entities that pursue an end whose achievement stands to be positively or negatively affected by those entities' actions.

Since life literally is a process of self-generating and self-sustaining action, living beings do have such an end: their continued existence.[6] To be a living entity is to be engaged in the process of self-*sustaining* action. (To the extent that an entity is not engaged in such action, it is not functioning as a living organism.) In relation to that end (its existence), various things can be beneficial or harmful. This is not to imply that all human beings necessarily embrace that end or adopt their existence as a conscious objective. Man is free to reject his life and to suffer the consequences. The point, rather, is that ends make possible benefits. Apart from their relation to an end, the concept of "benefits" would be meaningless.

Living organisms are not simply helpless, passive recipients of external events' impact, however. Their actions affect their survival. Thus it is important to appreciate that this, more specifically, is what gives rise to the phenomenon of values. It enables us to identify certain objects of organisms' actions as objectively good for them.

All living organisms need to act in ways that sustain their existence. Accordingly, that which is conducive to the existence of an organism is good for it; that which is detrimental is bad. For a plant, absorbing sunlight or water might be a value; for a given animal, the acquisition of nuts or berries or a safe environment to hibernate. For a human being, food or money or knowledge or friendship would typically be values. Obviously, particulars vary with the species.[7] The shared basis for all values, however, is the fact that organisms' existence depends on their acting in ways that sustain their existence.

For all of human beings' similarity with other organisms, the distinctive way in which human beings confront the alternative of existence or nonexistence creates our unique need for morality. Because human beings volitionally select our actions, we must rationally evaluate our options, identifying things' probable impact on our lives in order to pursue those things that offer a positive contribution and to avoid those that threaten harm. Only the former are objective values. A person *should* seek to gain and to keep certain things, in other words—and he requires guidance from a moral code that identifies objective values—only if and because he seeks his existence. What underwrites morality's authority is causality: if a man seeks a certain end, he must respect its necessary conditions and enact the requisite means by achieving appropriate values. A rational moral code is designed to guide him in doing this. Without the desire to live, the mandate for morality dissolves; no moral "shoulds" are warranted.[8] (This explains Galt's statement that a moral "commandment" is a contradiction in terms [1018].)

What Rand identifies, then, is the fact that for human beings, "the standard of value . . .—the standard by which one judges what is good or evil—is *man's life*, or: that which is required for man's survival *qua* man."[9] And a man's own life is his proper purpose. Rand stresses that "life" refers not only to physical subsistence, but to the overall fit and healthy condition of an organism such that it is poised to prosper in the future. Insofar as human beings are mental as well as material beings and insofar as a man's psychological and physical conditions affect one another, the standard of life subsumes the condition of a man's psyche (his beliefs, values, emotional dispositions, cognitive methods, and the like).[10] What is important for our purposes is that this standard provides the basis for the identification of objective values. That is, the basis for distinguishing between those things that truly are in a person's interest and those things that are treated as such by particular individuals, but which are not, in fact. While their dimension can vary considerably, all objective values offer some positive net contribution to a person's well-being.[11] (Henceforth, my references to "values" will be restricted to values for human beings, unless the context clearly indicates otherwise.)

Because morality's authority is contingent on a person's embrace of his life—his desire for his continued existence—it is important to have a sound understanding of what this is. The "choice to live" does not consist of a purely intellectual preference for a clinical medical status, exerted on an isolated occasion. Rather, it is a wholehearted commitment manifested in countless actions that a person takes every day. A man chooses to live by conducting his days in a life-advancing manner, by seeking to make his life go as well as possible, by actively and continuously going after goals that enhance it. The man who truly embraces his life treats his flourishing as the overriding reason for all that he does.[12] This stance is palpable in *Atlas'* heroes. And it is noticeably absent among the villains.

Notice that certain of the villains' ends which would normally function as values in a person's life do not, for them. Jim's money, for instance, is sterile. It does nothing life-nourishing for him. His wealth does not result from his own life-supporting action and is not used by him to achieve his objective well-being. This does not mean that he might not enjoy having money; by pretending that it proves something about his relative merit vis-à-vis others, Jim occasionally takes a fleeting reassurance from it. But his wealth does not represent his achievement of objective values and does not actually further his life.

Similarly, Lillian's marriage is not a genuine value for her. The desire to exert a perverse sense of moral superiority over Hank and her anticipation of pleasure in catching her husband with his mistress reveal her ends as anything but healthy (525–26). Her marriage to Hank does not reflect a celebration of his objective value to her, nor of the fact that she is a value to him; rather, it reflects Lillian's futile desire to gain value through the destruction of another man's virtue. She belittles the bracelet made of Rearden Metal (which *is* a value to Dagny and to Hank) and sleeps with Jim only as a testament to their common wish to deface values (900).

A different kind of case to consider is Taggart Transcontinental. Dagny treats the railroad as a value through most of the book, until she finally joins the strike. Yet her viewing it as a life-serving enterprise does not make it so. Attitude does not determine the positive or negative effects that things carry for human existence. While the railroad was a great value to many, in its earlier history, its value is not intrinsic. Its ability to serve anyone's life cannot withstand the abuses imposed by the looters. As distorted by altruist demands and coercive restrictions, the sad fact that Dagny finally confronts is that her beloved railroad, and her work in directing it, are no longer a constructive contributor to her life.[13]

These are just a few examples of how characters in *Atlas* do or do not embrace their lives. When it comes to spelling out a code of morality to guide the man who does wish to live, Rand identifies the central principle as rationality. For this is the fundamental requirement of our existence. Human beings must deliberately utilize our powers of conceptual thought in order to create the values that satisfy our needs. "Man's mind is his basic tool of survival," Galt observes.

> To remain alive, he must act, and before he can act he must know the nature and purpose of his action. He cannot obtain his food without a knowledge of food and of the way to obtain it. He cannot dig a ditch—or build a cyclotron—without a knowledge of his aim and of the means to achieve it. To remain alive, he must think. (1012)

As Rand elaborates elsewhere,

> For an animal, the question of survival is primarily physical; for man, primarily epistemological.
>
> Man's unique reward, however, is that while animals survive by adjusting themselves to their background, man survives by adjusting his background to himself. If a drought strikes them, animals perish—man builds irrigation canals; if a flood strikes them, animals perish—man builds dams; if a carnivorous pack attacks them animals perish—man writes the Constitution of the United States. But one does not obtain food, safety or freedom—by instinct.[14]

All of this should help us to understand the bond between reason and morality expressed in Galt's declaration that a man's basic moral choice "in every hour and every issue" is "thinking or non-thinking, existence or non-existence" (1018). Given that values are grounded in the alternative between existence and nonexistence, every decision that stands to further or detract from a man's existence is an issue of morality. Correspondingly, the choice between good and evil that a man confronts in any of his actions is, at root, the choice between life and death. The questions "Should I be moral or immoral?" or "Should I follow rational principle or cheat?" amount to: "Should I act to live, or to die?"

UNDERSTANDING THE ALTERNATIVES

Having sketched Rand's basic understanding of good and evil, we can now consider the way in which the central figures in *Atlas* come to appreciate this.

At the book's opening, the men on strike understand what "choosing life," as a human being, requires. Hank and Dagny do not. Suspended in a kind of limbo, Hank and Dagny do not consciously embrace the looters' code, yet their actions defer to substantial portions of it. The reason is a lack of knowledge on their parts and as the story unfolds, we witness the steady growth of their understanding. When Dagny retreats to the cabin in the woods, for instance, she misframes her conflict as whether to give up on life by quitting, as so many others have, or to labor on, on the looters' terms (611).[15] Gradually, she and Hank come to appreciate that the strikers have not given up. They, uniquely, have "chosen" their lives, on a full understanding of what the terms of human life are.

Essentially, what Hank and Dagny eventually realize is that the world is animated by two basic premises—life and death—and that the alternative between them is mutually exclusive. Their opponents do not seek life, they learn, and consequently, no values can be gained from these people. Concessions to the demands of death cannot advance life. It is these realizations that convince Hank and Dagny to withdraw their sanction of irrational standards as the only way to champion their own happiness. It is by recognizing the self-defeating character of their concessions to the looters that they finally renounce those burdens and join the strike.

The Death Premise

The evil that *Atlas'* heroes battle is not a freestanding force in the universe; it is not an anonymous, inevitable presence. While the concept of evil has acquired all sorts of murky and largely mystical connotations over the years, in fact, "evil" refers to those actions, ideas, objects, policies, and persons whose nature is essentially antagonistic to the conditions of human flourishing. Just as the good is that which advances human life, evil is that which works against it.[16] The single most decisive discovery that Hank and Dagny make is that their adversaries do not value their lives. They are dedicated, instead, to what Galt calls the morality of death (1025, also see 1046–47). Whether or not they recognize this in such explicit terms, death is the goal and the standard of their course.

Through much of the plot, Hank and Dagny grant the benefit of the doubt to their adversaries, even as they impose ever more onerous demands, penalize the producers' success, and seek to inflict guilt and suffering. "Surely they're after what we're after," Hank and Dagny assume; "surely they want to live." "I can carry Jim (the railroad, the family);" "I can endure these vacuous social appearances with Lillian;" "I can put up with their irrationalities." Particularly as the looters' political policies backfire and the resulting economic contraction intensifies, surely, Hank and Dagny expect, the others will recognize the error of their ways. In fact, however, what the heroes come to realize is that there *is* no error in the looters' course. Having accepted the premise of death, the destruction that their philosophy inflicts is what they're after.[17]

Notice that Hank and Dagny's charitable assumption that all people are "on the same side" is exactly what is challenged in several of their encounters with strikers. When Francisco pays a call on Rearden at his mills, Francisco tells him that he has been placing his "virtue in the service of evil" (453). Needless to say, that is hardly how Rearden views his course. Francisco explains:

> You're guilty of a great sin, Mr. Rearden, much guiltier than they tell you, but not in the way they preach. The worst guilt is to accept an undeserved guilt—and that is what you have been doing all your life. You have been paying blackmail, not for your vices, but for your virtues. You have been willing to carry the load of an unearned punishment—and to let it grow the heavier the greater the virtues you practiced. But your virtues were those which keep men alive. Your own moral code—the one you lived by, but never stated, acknowledged or defended—was the code that preserves man's existence. If you were punished for it, what was the nature of those who punished you? Yours was the code of life. What, then, is theirs?" (455)

In the valley, after Dagny explains her reason for returning to the "real" world, Akston's response names the fact that she has not yet identified. She begins the exchange:

> "If you want to know the one reason that's taking me back, I'll tell you: I cannot bring myself to abandon to destruction all the greatness of the world, all that which was mine and yours, which was made by us and is still ours by right—because I cannot believe that men can refuse to see, that they can remain blind and deaf to us forever, when the truth is ours and their lives depend on accepting it. They still love their lives—and *that* is the uncorrupted remnant of their minds. So long as men desire to live, I cannot lose my battle."
>
> "Do they?" said Hugh Akston softly. "Do they desire it? No, don't answer me now. I know that the answer was the hardest thing for any of us to grasp and to accept. Just take that question back with you, as the last premise left for you to check." (807)

Consider an earlier exchange, also, in which Dagny explains her perseverance to Francisco:

> She glanced at the city. "The life of a man of ability who might have perished in that catastrophe, but will escape the next one, which I'll prevent—a man who has an intransigent mind and an unlimited ambition, and is in love with his own life . . . the kind of man who is what we were when we started, you and I. You gave him up. I can't."
>
> He closed his eyes for an instant, and the tightening movement of his mouth was a smile, a smile substituting for a moan of understanding, amusement and pain. He asked, his voice gravely gentle, "Do you think that you can still serve him—that kind of man—by running the railroad?"
>
> "Yes."
>
> "All right, Dagny. I won't try to stop you. So long as you still think that, nothing can stop you, or should. You will stop on the day when you'll discover that your work has been placed in the service, not of that man's life, but of his destruction." (635)

A little later, she continues,

> "If I can keep Taggart Transcontinental in existence, it's the only benefit I want. What do I care if they make me pay ransoms? Let them have what they want. I'll have the railroad."
>
> He smiled. "Do you think so? Do you think that their need of you is your protection? Do you think that you can give them what they want? No, you won't quit until you see, of your own sight and judgment, what it is that they really want. You know, Dagny, we were taught that some things belong to God and others to Caesar. Perhaps their God would permit it. But the man you say we're serving—he does not permit it. He permits no divided allegiance, no war between your mind and your body, no gulf between your values and your actions, no tributes to Caesar. He permits no Caesars." (636)

At one level, Francisco is denying any inherent conflict between the demands of a man's mind and of his body. These are not warring rulers between which man is doomed to unceasing strife. (Hank, in particular, is tormented by a struggle between serving rational standards in the material realm and the irrational standards of others in regard to spiritual values. This is most painfully evidenced in his attitude toward his relationship with Dagny.[18] Obviously, he eventually learns the proper relationship.) More fundamentally, however, Francisco is observing that a man is beholden to no sovereigns other than reality. If a man wishes to exist—if he seeks to achieve his own happiness—then he must respect the demands imposed by the nature of reality. He must respect the fact that A is A—in his beliefs, in his desires, in his actions. That is the price that his life demands. Because reality is not a part-time master, however, and because its sovereignty is shared with no competing masters, the causal conditions necessary for a man's own happiness are his only God. Reality allows no deference to rivals. To the extent that a man pays tributes to any alternative sovereign, he defies the requirements of his own happiness.

The claim that *Atlas'* evil characters function on the premise of death may initially seem overly dark, I think, because it *is* a difficult fact to accept, as Akston remarks to Dagny (807, cited above). To appreciate the truth of this and its significance for the plot, we need to understand more precisely what the death premise is and how it is manifested in various characters.

Essentially, acceptance of the death premise means that a person does not value his life. The alternative between A and not-A, when the A in question is life, is the alternative between life and death. To the extent that a person's actions are not animated by the ambition of advancing his life, therefore, they, and he, are anti-life.

Just as embracing one's life is not simply an attitude experienced on a single occasion, accepting the death premise is not necessarily a conscious declaration made in a single moment. People on the death premise need not explicitly resolve: "I hate life. I pledge to hinder life wherever I can." Their governing premise is manifested, rather, in the way they spend their days. More specifically, it consists of their spurning (and often actively opposing) the pursuit of objective values.

Individuals on the premise of life are fundamentally thinkers and valuers. They acknowledge that human survival depends on the exercise of reason. And they accept the correlative responsibility of using their rationality as their means of acquiring knowledge, embracing ends, and achieving values. We observe this throughout *Atlas* in the heroes' basic orientation. All of the admirable characters, from Dagny and Galt through Eddie Willers and Gwen Ives, repeatedly respond to problems with logical thought and practical follow-through. They take command—of their minds and of their actions.

Those on the premise of death, by contrast, are, at their least destructive, passive. They do not exercise their rational faculties. Rather than focus and think in order to achieve any ends, they characteristically "summon the fog" (as Rand puts it in a description of Jim Taggart, 868). They evade, they shirk, they count on others to fulfill their needs and satisfy their desires. Jim, for instance, expects Dagny to make the railroad run and Cherryl—or *someone*—to shower unearned love on him (and, he hopes, in defiance of causality, to gain worth thereby). The tunnel catastrophe is the logical combustion of numerous individuals' cumulative evasions.[19]

James Taggart

Late in the story, when a beggar is blasé about receiving Jim's hundred-dollar offering, Jim is disturbed by dimly recognizing that the beggar's indifference to values mirrors his own (864). Whatever Jim's social position or job title or money might be, that breathing driftwood embodies Jim's basic character. We also come to know far more vicious depths of Jim's devotion to the death premise, however. He belligerently evinces positive hatred of objective values as such and of those who achieve them.[20] From childhood, Jim is jealous, resentful, and disparaging of Francisco and Dagny. He rides on their coattails while ridiculing their accomplishments as not truly impressive or as only so much good luck. His attitude toward men of ability is naked in the animus he spews toward Hank, in a conversation with Lillian: "'I'd like to see him beaten,' he said. 'I'd like to hear him scream with pain, just once'" (899).

After perfunctory sex with Betty Pope (emblematic of the utter void of values in both their lives), their gloomy next morning of lethargic, irritable sniping and indignation at life in general brightens when he turns his attention to "putting the skids" under his sister at a board meeting later that day (71).[21] Jim and Betty bond over their resentment of Dagny's success and Jim's plans to "put her in her place" (71). Only the prospect of a producer's downfall rekindles some semblance of desire in this pair. "Maybe I *will* take you out tonight," Jim chirps to Betty, after contemplating his trap for Dagny (72).[22]

In a telling conversation with Cherryl, Jim confesses his attitude toward all achievers: "Whatever they do, I can undo it. Let them build a track—I can come and break it, just like that!" He snapped his fingers. "Just like breaking a spine!" (879). When Cherryl suggests the significance of this statement, Jim retreats, in the manner typical of the evader:

"You want to break spines?" she whispered, trembling.

"I haven't said that!" he screamed. "What's the matter with you? I haven't said it!" (879)

Jim's response presumes that if he refuses to acknowledge his nature, it won't be what it is.

Lillian Rearden

Lillian reflects another variation of the death premise. She does not seem as directly committed as Jim does to destruction as such, but is more intent on deriving a certain sense of superiority over Hank, in particular. She acts, Hank gradually understands, as if she believes that puncturing his strength will somehow bestow value on her (974–75). She seeks to destroy him precisely for his virtues, "as the symbol of man's living power" (974).

Notice, for example, that after discovering that Hank is having an affair, Lillian does not acknowledge what that means about her place in his life. She does not mourn the erosion of their marriage as one would, if it were a genuine value. Rather, she is gleeful at what she regards as the "collapse" of his "vaunted sense of honor" and she relishes the prospect of his being condemned to the life of a "hypocrite." By remaining his wife, Lillian hopes to stand as a relentless reminder of his "depravity" (429–31).[23]

In response to Jim's saying that he would like to see Hank broken (noted above), Lillian muses: "I can't build his mills—but I can destroy them. I can't produce his Metal—but I can take it away from him. I can't bring men down to their knees in admiration—but I can bring them down to their knees" (899). When Lillian and Jim proceed to have sex (another pair of well-matched bedfellows), their mutual motive is hatred of the good (900). Their intention is to degrade Hank's character (deluding themselves that they hold the power to do that). Similarly, when Lillian tells Dagny that it was she who had revealed Hank's affair to the bureaucrats who then used it to extort his signature on the "Gift Certificate," Dagny detects a hint of pleasure in Lillian's admission. It was *she* who took Rearden Metal away from him, Lillian boasts (849). Perversely, if not pathetically, she implies that this is something to be proud of. Lillian continues, in the conversation with Dagny:

> You can't fight me. You can't buy your way out of it, with those dollars which you're able to make and I'm not. There's no profit you can offer me—I'm devoid of greed. I'm not paid by the bureaucrats for doing this—I am doing it without gain. Without gain. Do you understand me? (849)

The evil of her attitude—her attitude toward *all* values—is exactly what Dagny, Hank, and the reader do come to understand about Lillian. What Lillian chooses not to understand is what this boast reveals about herself. For to not seek values is to not seek life.

Robert Stadler

Rand recognizes that most people are not self-conscious haters of the good.[24] Other forms of evil can be just as virulent, however. Stadler, for instance, represents a still different facet of evil than Jim and Lillian do. Stadler is a paradigm of pragmatism. As such, he is an appeaser of evil who thereby eases the way for the more deliberately destructive to be effective.[25]

On the surface, Stadler seems to champion a noble end: the progress of science. He tells himself that he must make concessions to opponents of reason (government bureaucrats, society's demands) in order to advance that end. Sacrifices are unavoidable (188–92, 1117–19). Yet over the course of the story, we see that his pragmatic compromises are not motivated by innocently misguided tactical judgments. Underneath, Stadler is a whim worshipper. As he pleads to Galt,

> What I saw ahead, what I wanted, what I *felt*, was not to be measured in their miserable dollars! I wanted a laboratory! I needed it! What do I care where it came from or how? I could do so much! I could reach such heights! Don't you have any pity? I *wanted* it! (1118)

Stadler's attitude is: he wants what he wants; getting it is all that matters. To do so, he tunes out the longer-term repercussions of the means he adopts and the preconditions for the results to be objectively valuable. He offers numerous rationalizations for his compromises, groping to persuade himself that one *must* use deceit and force, that "men are not open to truth or reason" (191), that he "had no choice" and "there is no way to live except on their terms" (1118). Stadler is, in principle, no different from any whim worshipper who elevates his desires above the facts of reality. His crime is in certain respects worse than Jim's, however, because Stadler had the mind to know better. Through the pragmatic course he adopts, his prodigious intellect is directed not to the creation of valuable knowledge, but to the State Science Institute's thwarting Rearden Metal and to Project X, an exercise of annihilation for its own sake (816 ff.). By the end, Stadler can no longer evade the life-destroying essence of his pragmatism when, in his extended confession *cum* apologia to Galt, he finds himself declaring: "You are the man who has to be destroyed" (1119). The either-or alternative between the path of reason and life and the path of irrationality and death is inescapable.

While aspects of both Lillian and Stadler certainly reflect hatred of the good as such, Jim is most fully and brazenly committed to this. Lillian, in however warped a way, believes that she gains some value out of standing in a certain relationship to a man such as Hank. Stadler kids himself that the noble end of science justifies his corrosive means. Jim, however, seeks destruction as such. His campaign against values is much more total and unreserved than the others'. This is evident in his relationship with Cherryl, whom he repeatedly sets up to suffer failure and humiliation. Jim relishes his scheme to exterminate her ambition and to crush her earnest efforts to become the best person she can be (874). When she finally enjoys a successful social evening, he scolds her for embarrassing him (875).

In Jim, Cherryl confronts "evil for evil's sake" and the chilling realization that he is "a killer . . . for the sake of killing" (901, 904). His bloodthirsty character is even more plain when, during the torture of Galt, he is not satisfied with anything short of Galt's death. Consider his exchange with Ferris:

> "Jim, hasn't he had enough? Don't forget, we have to be careful."
> "No! He hasn't had enough! He hasn't even screamed yet!"
> "Jim!" cried Mouch suddenly, terrified by something in Taggart's face. "We can't afford to kill him! You know it!"
> "I don't care! I want to break him! I want to hear him scream! I want—"
> And then it was Taggart who screamed. It was a long, sudden, piercing scream, as if at some sudden sight, though his eyes were staring at space and seemed blankly sightless. The sight he was confronting was within him. The protective walls of emotion, of evasion, of pretense, of semi-thinking and pseudo-words, built up by him through all of his years, had crashed in the span of one moment—the moment when he knew that he wanted Galt to die, knowing fully that his own death would follow. (1144–45)

The horrific truth that Jim faces is that he had sought destruction for its own sake. His motive was "the lust to destroy whatever was living, for the sake of whatever was not" (1145).[26]

This is the death premise.

Given what the good is and does, hatred of the good is hatred of life. The paths of *Atlas'* villains help us to understand Galt's analysis of those on the premise of death:

> They do not want to own your fortune, they want you to lose it; they do not want to succeed, they want you to fail; they do not want to live, they want you to die; they desire nothing, they hate existence, and they keep running, each trying not to learn that the object of his hatred is himself. (1046)[27]

The worship of death is by far the most difficult thing that Hank and Dagny need to understand about their enemy before they can free themselves of evil's clutches. After a steady accumulation of hints and insights, however, both of them finally recognize the ugly truth. In a final conversation with his family when they are panicked by Hank's cutting off their allowance checks and they attempt fresh psychological tactics to win his renewed support, he realizes that his mother's desperate plea, "we want to live," is not true.

> "Why, no—" he started in quiet astonishment and ended in quiet horror, as the thought struck him fully, "I don't think you do. If you did, you would have known how to value me." (973)

To have heaped only mocking ridicule and "hammering derision" (975) on that which keeps them alive—Hank's work and achievements—reveals a damning picture of their regard for their lives. They do not know how to treat a value because they do not know what a *value* is. Why did they never bother to find out? Because they do not value their lives.

Dagny has a similar solemn epiphany when, in explaining to Jim and Cuffy Meigs the inevitably disastrous results that would come of their proposed course for the railroad, it dawns on her that both of them already know everything she could tell them about its futility. It simply does not matter to them (842). She realizes, more broadly, that "inanimate indifference was the permanent state of the people around her" (1111). Other encounters with the looters, under increasingly dire conditions, prompt the recurrent wonder about this seemingly alien species, "*did* they want to live?" (1109, 1111).

The Impotence of Evil

While recognition of their enemies' embrace of the death premise is critical to Hank's and Dagny's ultimate refusal to cooperate any longer, a second and closely related fact they must grasp is the impotence of evil and, correlatively, its utter dependence on the good. Given the essential nature of evil—"the irrational, the blind, the anti-real"—it contributes nothing to the furtherance of human life (1048). Those who seek to live have nothing to gain from evasion, irrationality, or any of its progeny. As Galt observes, a man has "no benefits to seek from human vices" (1023).

The demands that evil imposes on the good are not merely neutral or benign, however. They are poison. A man stands only to lose by any cooperation with evil. The "ransoms" that the heroes pay to buy off their adversaries do *no* good because they are paid in exchange for no positive value. Even the Wet Nurse eventually realizes this, evidenced in his explanation of his defending Rearden's mill from the assault to seize control of it. When Rearden observes, in semi-astonished admiration, that the Wet Nurse had stuck his neck out, he responds:

> But I had to! . . . I couldn't help them wreck the mills, could I? . . . How long was I to keep from sticking my neck out? Till they broke yours? . . . And what would I do with my neck, if that's how I had to keep it? (990)

The Wet Nurse has come to understand, in other words, that if living requires taking a great risk for the sake of his values, that is the price he will pay. For, after a long period of confused ambivalence, he has decided that *that* is what he wants: to live. And he gains nothing by taking any actions based on the antithetical code of death. (The contrast with Stadler is striking.)

Because evil is itself incapable of sustaining life, its endurance is entirely due to the support it receives from the good. The power of the irrational results from the power that the rational grant it. Early on, from his meeting with the official described as a "traffic cop," Hank detects that his adversaries need something from him, although he is not yet sure what it is (364–67).

Later, at Thanksgiving dinner, Hank realizes that the guilt that Lillian seeks to induce depends on his accepting her standards (464–65), and he has a similar realization in discussing with Dr. Ferris the blackmail based on his affair with Dagny (559–62, 564–65). Much later, when Jim cries his assurance to Hank that "you'll do something" to maintain production even under suffocating restrictions (986–87), Hank more fully recognizes that he had made the looters' exploitation possible. They wholly depend on us, he realizes; we have been feeding our own predators. (Notice that when Hank begins to pay less deference to his family's wishes, refusing many of the demands that he had met in the past, even they have trouble any longer evading their abject dependence on him.) In another scene with Philip, Hank recognizes that Philip is asserting his weakness and lack of values as the source of his claim on him (927–32, especially 929–32; this is an instance of what Galt calls zero worship).

Francisco actually explains this dependence to Dagny, although she does not yet understand it. Francisco begins this exchange:

> "It was our own guilt. We produced the wealth of the world—but we let our enemies write its moral code."
>
> "But we never accepted their code. We lived by our own standards."
>
> "Yes—and paid ransoms for it! Ransoms in matter and in spirit—in money, which our enemies received, but did not deserve, and in honor, which we deserved, but did not receive. *That* was our guilt—that we were willing to pay. We kept mankind alive, yet we allowed men to despise us and to worship our destroyers. We allowed them to worship incompetence and brutality, the recipients and the dispensers of the unearned. By accepting punishment, not for any sins, but for our virtues, we betrayed our code and made theirs possible." (619)

Eventually, Dagny comes to see the validity of Francisco's charge that *she* acts as a destroyer, by sustaining the looters. She and Hank have both been unwittingly complicit in their own strangulation and in the assault on all that is good. What they finally appreciate is that, as Galt puts it, "evil [is] impotent . . . and . . . the only weapon of its triumph [is] the willingness of the good to serve it" (1048).

The Need to Withdraw

Crucial to Hank's and Dagny's acceptance of the need to abandon the looters' society is their eventual recognition that there is no refuge from the alternative between life and death; no "in between" can be sustained. *Every*thing is ruled by the law of excluded middle, including their own actions. They themselves, therefore, are either fundamentally for their happiness or against it; they support their lives or they support their deaths. "There's no such thing as a temporary suicide," as Hank observes (984). Dagny believes for a long time that concessions to her enemies will not damage her own values (evident in her readiness to pay ransoms as long as she can keep the railroad (636). Yet because of the inextinguishable, polar antagonism between life and death, any concession to evil is toxic to oneself.

Stadler is a chilling illustration of this. As a pragmatist, Stadler tries to skirt the fundamental alternative by circumscribing and compartmentalizing. He denounces Dagny and Galt as "impractical idealists" (790), implying that the ideal and the practical inhabit independent realms. People are the problem, he insists, implying that people supersede reality (818). Stadler pretends that he can somehow escape the either-or character of human existence—that he can survive without respecting the law of excluded middle, which means: without respecting the basic nature of reality, the fact that A is A. (The irony of his being the most respected mind in science is rich.) As a result of these evasions, we watch Stadler descend into ever greater depths of destruction, culminating in his call for the death of Galt. Yet in that scene, we also witness Stadler's *self*-destruction. He begins the meeting with Galt by pleading his innocence (against his internal knowledge of his guilt) and ends in agony, moaning "No . . . No . . ." against "the full meaning of his own words" that call for Galt's death (1117, 1119).

The sanction given by the good protects evil and obscures its utter dependence on the good. The cushion afforded by these "death buffers" makes it more difficult to grasp that the alternative *is* one or the other.[28] But it is recognition of the mutually exclusive and jointly exhaustive alternative between the standard of life and the standard of death that enables the heroes to eventually see who their allies and enemies are and the actual path necessary for their happiness. When Francisco first tells Dagny that she is the enemy whom he must defeat, rather than Jim or Mouch, she is disbelieving (636). Much later, in the gulch, Galt similarly observes that her course is that of his enemy (961). It is only when she and Hank understand the truth of this—that they have been aiding Galt's enemies and that to have been fighting against the "quitters" is to have been fighting against themselves—that they accept the imperative to strike.

As we noted earlier, while Hank and Dagny try to coexist with the looters, they do so on a mistaken premise. For as long as they believe that ransoms are their only means of achieving their values, it is their integrity in devotion to those values that leads them to continue that course. Eventual recognition of their opponents' death premise and of the complete dependence of evil on *their* support shows them the propriety of withdrawing that support. Contrary to Dagny's initial assumption, abandoning the looters' world is not "giving up." It is, rather, testament to her love of her life—as is captured in the requisite oath for entry into Galt's gulch: "I swear by my life and my love of it that I will never live for the sake of another man nor ask another man to live for mine" (731). And it reflects knowledge and acceptance of the necessary conditions of life. A man cannot live on the premise of death. It is when Hank and Dagny recognize *this*, in the end, alongside their adversaries' allegiance to death and the utter impotence of evil, that they join those who have seen it before them.[29]

KNOWLEDGE OF THE "EITHER-OR" IN ACTION

Hank's and Dagny's growing understanding of the nature of their enemies clearly informs their actions. Indeed, a reader can only fully understand the novel if we grasp, as they do, the do-or-die opposition between good and evil. Without that, certain features of the story may seem unjustified. Let us examine next, then, how a proper understanding of the nature of good and evil illuminates what might otherwise be troubling aspects of the novel.

Consider, first, some of the book's terminology. "Destroyers" may initially seem too harsh a term to characterize either those who are recruiting producers to quit or those of Jim's ilk. To call them "destroyers" seems disproportionate to the actual disagreements between the opposing camps. Yet in fact, this term is exactly right, for it names the essence of what evil or irrationality does: it thwarts life. Destruction is destruction, regardless of the degree to which it is deliberate.

"Looters," similarly, may seem an ill-fitting epithet for the good guys' adversaries. These people are not breaking into stores and running away with merchandise, after all. Yet it is entirely apt, in truth, because this *is* their essential character. Given that those who are irrational create no values and thus have nothing to trade in their interactions with others, they rely completely on what others produce. Notice that in Mr. Thompson's most urgent, final attempt to persuade Galt to cooperate, for instance, all he can offer is the threat to use force (1102). In the qualities and values that human life depends upon, however, Thompson is penniless, as Galt points out to him (1102).[30]

We may have a little more difficulty accepting Galt's calling Dagny his "enemy" (961), responsible for the dangerous condition of the world for him. What this unsparing characterization reflects, however, is the fact that evil, on its own, *is* impotent. Whatever efficacy it enjoys is a result of the power that the good provide it by cooperating with its standards. Dagny's well-meaning intentions are not enough. Causality dictates proper action, not wishes, however innocent. And a person who is truly on the strikers' side will not make things any easier for those who would thwart them. Individuals who sanction evil in any form or degree are the enablers of evil, and thereby make themselves the enemies of the good.

When we turn from language to characters' actions, the principal choice that reflects the heroes' recognition of the either-or nature of their alternative is the decision to go on strike. There is no minimizing how profound an action that is. Galt, in launching the strike, is abandoning his motor and the joy of bringing its transformative potential to full fruition. *All* the strikers are leaving life as they have known it. They are giving up the specific values that they have been passionately devoted to (most significantly, their work). For Francisco, striking entails hurting the woman he cherishes. He must allow Dagny to think him a worthless playboy and must make her life harder by recruiting other producers, steadily draining material and spiritual nourishment away from her. Needless to say, it also pains him to abandon their relationship and to watch her struggle as she does.

By refusing to any longer cooperate with those who would destroy them, the strikers are leaving behind many decent people, such as Eddie Willers and Gwen Ives.[31] They are not indifferent to this. The heroes' regard for other rational men is palpable in several episodes. Hank's compassionate treatment of the Wet Nurse, well before he shows anything near to Eddie's or Gwen's moral stature, is indicative of Hank's genuine concern for anyone who does value life. Hank had detected certain promising traits in the Wet Nurse, an assessment later vindicated by his heroic performance fighting the assault on the mills. Similarly, Dagny's generosity toward Cherryl and the tramp testify to her respect for those on the premise of life. This sincere benevolence notwithstanding, the strikers recognize that they are not responsible for the welfare of others. The idea that they should risk their lives for others' need reflects the code of irrationality that they are rejecting. The strikers are compelled to desert the looters' world, knowing that some good people will suffer heavier burdens as a result, because no compromise between life and death is sustainable. If a man chooses to live, he must accept that his options are one or the other. "Life—and a little death" is not a viable prescription.

Once one understands why the strike makes sense, it is easier to dissolve any nagging misgivings about some of the other actions of the heroes. Hank's peremptory divorce of Lillian against her will, for instance, with "no alimony and no property settlement" (571), reflects his final recognition that after her treatment of him over their years together, he owes her nothing. Any obligation he incurred from marrying her has been long since discharged. She has offered no genuine value to him and she offers none now; indeed, she actively seeks to destroy him. Therefore, he has no reason to continue to support her in any way. Or consider Galt's refusal of Francisco's request to have Dagny spend her last week in the valley at his place (796). Acquiescing would have betrayed how Galt feels about Dagny. The truth is, *he* wants her. To have made such a sacrifice for Francisco would have faked the value that she is to him. Sacrifices fake the value that different things are, for a person, and they fake the nature of value itself. Any sacrifice of a man's values hurts *him*.[32]

Two of the heroes' other choices might seem more disturbing. When Dagny is 'captive' in the gulch, missing and feared killed by those outside, Galt does not allow her to notify Rearden that she is all right.[33] This might seem cruel, since the reader knows that Hank and Dagny are actually good guys. Once one understands the strict opposition between good and evil, however, the reasoning for this policy is not difficult to see. Anyone who is not a committed resident of the valley is an enemy, whether by design or by accident. This includes scabs and prospective members, such as Dagny and Hank. To the extent that they are still cooperating with the destroyers, they are making life harder for the strikers. Consequently, the strikers must give them no quarter. To lighten *their* load in any way would add to the strikers' own and endanger their safety.

Bear in mind that there is nothing that the looters won't do in order to obtain Galt's cooperation. This is plain as we see them, increasingly desperate, resort to guns and torture.[34] Since the good guys who are still on the outside are unwittingly assisting their destroyers (and the destroyers of all who embrace the premise of life), any knowledge that these people possess of the gulch makes them dangerous, insofar as they might divulge its existence (inadvertently or under coercion) and thereby jeopardize its residents' security. In short, any cooperation with the world of the looters is a threat to all the strikers. And for that reason, the strikers cannot permit it. Hank's "need" for information about Dagny's welfare does not obligate the strikers to provide that information, particularly given that his course of action continues to oppose them.[35]

Finally, consider Dagny's shooting the guard during the rescue of Galt (1147-48). Does she really have to *kill* him?

The fundamental incompatibility between the code of life and the code of death makes the answer clear. The guard sees his choice as between obeying Ferris' orders or Dagny's. When he whines that he doesn't know what to do—how can *he* decide?—she matter-of-factly responds: "It's your life." This, Rand has shown, is what is at stake for each of us, in every decision. The guard tries to escape the fundamental alternative and his need to choose between the two, seeking to wiggle out to some enclave in between. But a man cannot escape that choice. The only alternative to life is destruction, as the guard's death makes graphic.

By defending Galt's imprisonment, the guard is defending the collectivist, altruist, irrational principles that have been eating Dagny alive. Dagny aims at his heart because *she* chooses life. Having done so—and with knowledge, now, of life's nonnegotiable conditions and of the nature of the enemy—she will take no chances by prolonging any threat to it. It's his life or hers, she realizes (and, of course, his life or Galt's). On behalf of their love of their lives, the heroes must kill that which is killing them.

The concern that any of the actions I have just analyzed is cruel or unduly harsh, we should recognize, reveals the lingering belief that a person *can* straddle incompatible standards, serving the mutually contradictory ends of one's life and one's death without cost. Galt observes as much about Dagny's decision of whether to leave the gulch: "If it seems hard, it's because you still think it does not have to be one or the other. You will learn that it does" (749). This is precisely what all those who eventually join the strike do learn.

Man cannot fudge the law of identity and the law of excluded middle. Life or death is either-or. The pursuit of one's life must be, correspondingly, uncompromising. Remember that the heroes come to realize that their opponents stand on the premise of death. Jim, Lillian, and Stadler are not misguided allies of theirs who are after the same thing. If they were, the heroes might reasonably think, "oh, they'll come around, eventually; they will appreciate that ours is the better way." The ugly fact is that the looters do not seek what the producers do. Accordingly, all that the looters are doing and can be expected to do in the future is obstruct the producers' lives. The only thing for those who love their lives to do, consequently, is to withdraw the sustenance they have provided to their destroyers and renounce the burdens they have borne on their enemies' behalf. The heroes' deliverance depends on their total rejection of all irrational standards. Their full commitment to their own happiness depends on their recognition that anything less than that is suicide.

MORAL ABSOLUTISM

Ayn Rand's moral philosophy is absolutist. The authority of moral principles is unequivocal. When a moral principle properly applies, it may not be violated. "There are two sides to every issue," Galt observes, "one side is right and the other is wrong, but the middle is always evil" (1054). Absolutism does not mean that all moral answers are easy to reach, but that there is a definite fact of the matter as to something's ultimate value and the proper course of action. The complexity of certain cases is not a license to pretend otherwise. A man's adherence to rational moral principles, correspondingly, must be uncompromising. "In the realm of morality nothing less than perfection will do" (1059).[36]

"Absolutism" is sometimes used slightly differently, to refer to the wide breadth of a moral code that governs all (or nearly all) of the kinds of choices that a man encounters. Such a code is absolute in being all-encompassing, allowing no "time-outs" from morality's demands. While the scope of morality's authority is strictly distinct from the relative rigor or laxness of any of its individual principles (that is, the question of whether or not it is ever permissible to violate a particular moral principle is independent of the number of issues that are governed by moral principles), these two senses of absolutism both stem from the same source, as we shall see. In what follows, I will use "absolutism" in the first sense, to refer to the fact that moral principles permit no violations. It will be apparent, however, that both senses of absolutism are often involved.

Interestingly, the absolutism of Rand's moral philosophy is the source of much hostility toward it. It is not only the substance of her moral theory—its unorthodox advocacy of egoism—that many people find objectionable, but the "extreme," unqualified character of that code. Skepticism toward absolutism is understandable, since its assertion is usually arbitrary (as with religious dogma). Moreover, given that the reigning moral doctrine of altruism requires violations (since no one could survive if he consistently obeyed a code of self-sacrifice), most people subconsciously conclude that any demand for perfect adherence is utterly impractical. This breeds a lack of seriousness about moral standards, as such.[37] While moral absolutism is too large a subject to explore in any detail here, it is useful to see that its foundation lies in the mutually exclusive alternative between good and evil that we have been examining. Before concluding, then, let me briefly indicate this basis for it.

Rand shows that the evil is anti-life. Whatever its particular manifestation or degree, whatever its motivation or an agent's awareness of its impact on a given occasion, that which is evil works to impede human life. Because the good is that which advances human life and because every choice that a man makes stands to either nourish or poison his life, the either-or between good and evil is both inescapable and of profound consequence. This either-or character of a man's choices thus dictates absolutism in regard to both morality's comprehensive scope and its "100%-ism," its refusal to permit compromise. A man cannot serve his life by pretending that morality's domain is more circumscribed than it is, just as a man cannot serve his life by pretending that violations of rational principles will be beneficial to him. Galt indicates the basic reason for this:

> In any compromise between food and poison, it is only death that can win. In any compromise between good and evil, it is only evil that can profit. In that transfusion of blood which drains the good to feed the evil, the compromiser is the transmitting rubber tube. (1054)[38]

The advancement of life, as we have seen throughout, has nothing to gain from that which damages life.

Notice that as long as the destructive nature of evil is murky to a person, he may understandably be lax about avoiding it. If morality is a game, then goodness is a game and the propriety of individual choices seems of no real consequence. A person must clearly grasp the stakes of moral principles in order to see the price of deviating from them. By making these stakes and the fundamental incompatibility of good and evil plain, Rand demonstrates that to compromise on a valid moral principle is to damage oneself. Such an action's premise is, in effect: "I'm not really committed to my happiness," or "I want to live—sort of, kinda, but not fully." Because all of a man's choices do carry consequences for his existence, however, the man who seeks to live cannot afford to drift between life-advancing and life-diminishing actions. Rather, he must identify each specific option that he contemplates as essentially a "death action" or a "life action," vigilantly restricting himself to the latter. It is the mutually exclusive and jointly exhaustive nature of the alternative between life and death and, correspondingly, between good and evil, in other words, that dictates the absolutism of morality.

Just as *Atlas* shows that a man should lend no support to the evil of others, the point of moral absolutism is that he should tolerate no evil in himself. Such concessions to the irrational are equally self-destructive. Given that a man's fundamental alternative is between life and death, he can do himself no *good* by cheating on rational, life-fostering principles. Existence permits no tributes to competing Caesars.

In the end, moral "shoulds" are unyielding because reality is unyielding. Everything is governed by the law of excluded middle, including the effects of a man's actions. A moral code that is intended to serve human life must respect the conditions of life. And so must any person who seeks his life.

CONCLUSION

In the opening chapter of *Atlas Shrugged*, Eddie recalls a childhood conversation in which he and Dagny affirmed a devotion to "the best within us," even while he was uncertain of exactly what that was. It was not "business or earning a living," he thought at the time, but it consisted in "things like winning battles, or saving people out of fires, or climbing mountains." It seemed a matter of doing "whatever is right" (6).

In the book's final chapter, Eddie identifies this quality more accurately. What is right *is* "business and earning a living and that in man which makes it possible—*that* is the best within us, *that* was the thing to defend" (1166).

The best within us is that which wants to live—wholeheartedly, unequivocally, and with full understanding of what human life demands. *Atlas* illustrates that this love of one's life incorporates knowledge as well as desire. Love of life is not simply an ardent wish for one's happiness, the grip of an emotion or a mood. It is a deliberate, informed commitment. The quality within us that makes all values possible depends on knowledge of the causal requirements of one's happiness as well as the commitment to achieving one's happiness, in light of that knowledge. To love one's life—to withdraw all sanction of evil, to refuse tributes to false gods, to swear the oath—requires the complete repudiation of anything and everything that impedes life. As symbolized in Dagny's shooting of the guard, it requires the denial of all quarter to poisonous premises and practices.

The alternative between good and evil, Rand demonstrates in *Atlas*, is, fundamentally, the alternative between one's life and one's death. Coming to appreciate that no neutral territory is available, that one can take no action that does not support one or the other and that concessions to irrational standards achieve no value but bring only some form and degree of self-destruction, is what enables the heroes ultimately to recognize the imperative to strike. It is their understanding of the inescapable and mutually exclusive nature of the choice between life and death—and of how the choice between the rational and the irrational and between good and evil reflects this—that allows them to fully love their lives *in action*. It liberates them to pursue, without apology, the joy of their existence. And it allows them to experience that joy.[39]

NOTES

1. Rand remarks on the theme in *The Art of Fiction*, Tore Boeckmann, ed. (New York: Plume, 2000), 17–18.

2. Extensive explanation can be found in Ayn Rand, *The Virtue of Selfishness* (New York: Signet, 1964); Leonard Peikoff, *Objectivism: The Philosophy of Ayn Rand* (New York: Dutton, 1991), chapter 7; and Tara Smith, *Viable Values: A Study of Life as the Root and Reward of Morality* (Lanham, Md.: Rowman & Littlefield, 2000), chapters 4 and 5.

3. By "reason," Rand means "the faculty that perceives, identifies and integrates the material provided by [man's] senses," *Atlas*, 1016. For more on the nature of reason, see Peikoff, *Objectivism*, 152–53, 159–63, 220, and on reason as man's primary virtue, 220–29. On the latter, also see Tara Smith, *Ayn Rand's Normative Ethics—The Virtuous Egoist* (New York: Cambridge University Press, 2006), 48–74.

4. Rand, "The Objectivist Ethics," *The Virtue of Selfishness*, 13, emphasis in original.

5. Rand, "The Objectivist Ethics," 16.

6. "Life" is defined in the *Oxford English Dictionary* as "the series of actions and occurrences constituting the history of an individual (especially a human being) from birth to death." 1971 edition. Also see definitions in the online edition, which include: "The property which constitutes the essential difference between a living animal or plant, or a living portion of organic tissue, and dead or non-living matter; the assemblage of the functional activities by which the presence of this property is manifested. . . ; Continuance or prolongation of animate existence; opposed to *death*." Online edition. Also see Natalie Angier, *The Canon—A Whirligig Tour of the Beautiful Basics of Science* (New York: Houghton Mifflin, 2007), 172–73, and Harry Binswanger, *The Biological Basis of Teleological Concepts* (Marina del Rey, Calif.: Ayn Rand Institute Press, 1990), 6–7, 63–64.

7. Particulars can also vary within a species, within boundaries that are set by the nature of that species. For discussion of this, see Smith, *Viable Values*, 99–101, 127–28, 183 and *Ayn Rand's Normative Ethics*, 27, 30.

8. For thorough explanation of this, see Rand, "Causality vs. Duty," *Philosophy: Who Needs It* (New York: Bobbs-Merrill, 1982), 118-119; Rand, "Objectivist Ethics," 17–18; Peikoff, *Objectivism*, 241–48; Smith, *Viable Values*, 84–90, 93–95, 101–3; *Ayn Rand's Normative Ethics*, 21–23.

9. Rand, "*Objectivist Ethics*," 25. Also see 25–27 and *Atlas*, 1014.

10. For much more on the intimate relationship between existence and flourishing, see Rand, "Objectivist Ethics," 25–27, and Smith, *Viable Values*, 125–51.

11. Notice that this is the familiar yardstick by which we assess well-being and distinguish health from disease or deficiency in all organisms. Moreover, in the realm of ethics, many philosophers have sought to explain that which is good for human beings as rooted in the needs of a man's nature (pithily expressed in Peter Geach's claim that "men need virtues as bees need stings"). See Peter Geach, *The Virtues* (Cambridge: Cambridge University Press, 1977), 17; Philippa Foot, *Natural Goodness* (Oxford: Clarendon Press, 2001); Rosalind Hursthouse, *On Virtue Ethics* (New York: Oxford University Press, 1999); Berys Gaut, "The Structure of Practical Reason," in Garrett Cullity and Berys Gaut, eds., *Ethics and Practical Reason* (Oxford: Clarendon Press, 1997); James D. Wallace, *Virtues and Vices* (Ithaca, N.Y.: Cornell University Press), 1978; Aristotle, *Nicomachean Ethics*.

For more on the difference between objective, subjective, and intrinsic value, see Smith, "The Importance of the Subject in Objective Morality: Distinguishing Objective from Intrinsic Value," *Social Philosophy and Policy* 25, no. 1 (Winter 2008): 126–48; Smith, "'Social' Objectivity and the Objectivity of Value," in *Science, Values, and Objectivity*, Peter Machamer and Gereon Walters, eds., *Science, Values, and Objectivity* (Pittsburgh: University of Pittsburgh Press, 2004), 143–71; Darryl Wright, "Evaluative Concepts and Objective Values: Rand on Moral Objectivity," *Social Philosophy and Policy* 25, no. 1 (Winter 2008): 149-81; and Wright, "Evaluative Concepts and Objective Value," paper delivered at Conference on Concepts and Objectivity, University of Pittsburgh, Sept. 22–24, 2006.

12. This formulation is borrowed from Wright.

13. Thanks to Greg Salmieri for conversation that led me to appreciate this point more keenly.

14. Rand, "For the New Intellectual," *For the New Intellectual* (New York: Random House, 1961), 10.

15. Similarly, in an earlier scene, she tells Danagger that she is not ready to surrender the world to the looters, 445.

16. See Rand, "Objectivist Ethics," 25. Insofar as evil is a moral concept, it refers to that which *deliberately* works to oppose human life. It is intentional human action and its products that can be evil, not accident or natural processes beyond man's control.

17. For discussion of the death premise, see Rand, "The Age of Envy," *Return of the Primitive: The Anti-Industrial Revolution*, Peter Schwartz, ed. (New York: Meridian, 1999), 130–58.

18. See his self-denunciation after their first night together, 254–55.

19. For excellent discussion of the death premise and the life premise, see Onkar Ghate, "The Death Premise in *We The Living* and *Atlas Shrugged*," in Robert Mayhew, ed., *Essays on Ayn Rand's We The Living* (Lanham, Md.: Lexington Books, 2004), 335–56.

20. He exemplifies hatred of the good for being the good, which Rand identifies as the lowest rung of evil in "The Age of Envy."

21. Before that, Jim "did not feel like moving to find his watch . . . it was too much trouble to look for his slippers," and Betty had resentfully declared: "I hate morning. Here's another day and nothing to do" (70).

22. Ghate offers this vivid example, "Death Premise," 344.

23. The punishment she seeks to impose is a graphic indictment of *her* character (see 431).

24. Rand, "The Age of Envy," 149. Also note her remark that "deliberately evil men are a very small minority," "Altruism as Appeasement," *The Objectivist* 5, January 1966, 6.

25. See his exchange with Dagny, 188–89.

26. I recommend reading the fuller account of what Jim realizes about himself, on 1145.

27. Eric Starnes' suicide on the wedding day of the girl he pines for (an act carried out in her bedroom, so as to be discovered by the newlyweds that night) is another grotesque illustration of this, 321. Thanks to Jason Rheins for reminding me of this example. Also see Rand, "The Age of Envy," 133–34.

28. Galt refers to such "buffers" on 1047.

29. Peikoff provides an illuminating explanation of how the virtue of integrity, in Rand's view, demands *seeing* one's alternatives accurately, more than strength of doing in the familiar idea of willpower, *Objectivism*, 261–62. This is clearly on display in *Atlas*, as we witness Hank's and Dagny's coming to see the true nature of their enemy and their unwitting role in their own destruction. (See Gregory Salmieri, "Discovering Atlantis: *Atlas Shrugged*'s Demonstration of a New Moral Philosophy," in the present volume.)

30. Hank offers a similar rejoinder to Ferris' suggestion that Hank would have been better off had he taken the chance to join Ferris' side early on: "But if I had joined you . . . what would I have found worth looting from Orren Boyle?" (560).

Separately, while people who do not create material values certainly sometimes receive goods voluntarily from others, this is not what is dominantly on display in *Atlas*. The heroes' adversaries are looters insofar as they claim that which they neither deserve nor have rights to.

31. The fate of Gwen Ives is actually left unstated, in the novel, but since we have no report that she reaches the gulch, it seems fair to refer to her alongside Eddie, here.

32. A sacrifice is the surrender of a greater value for a lesser value. It is not to be confused with an investment, in which a person forgoes a smaller value for the sake of gaining a greater value later. See Rand, "The Ethics of Emergencies," *Virtue of Selfishness*, 50–53; Peikoff, *Objectivism*, 232–36; Smith, *Ayn Rand's Normative Ethics*, 38–40.

33. After explaining that residents in the Gulch are permitted no communication with those in the outside world, Galt does ask whether Dagny wishes to request a special exception. It is not entirely clear that he would grant it, however, if she were to make such a request, 763–64.

34. Reliance on force is the natural culmination of a code of irrationality. Once one abandons reason, force is the only fundamental alternative. See Rand, "Faith and Force," *Philosophy: Who Needs It*, 70–92.

35. Also bear in mind the logic of this decision from the perspective of the plot. At this stage in the story, Dagny has found a love greater than her love for Hank. Given this, placing Hank's well-being above Galt's would risk a greater value, Galt, for a lesser (albeit a tremendous) value, Hank. And we know by now that Dagny does not knowingly make sacrifices. (The choice of whether to

contact Hank is not ultimately hers, of course, but this helps to explain why she doesn't resist the policy and seek an exception.)

Later, by contrast, when Hank meets Galt and sends Dagny a note from the valley—"I have met him. I don't blame you" (1002)—the very different context justifies this breach of the barrier against communication between the two realms. Dagny is already aware of the gulch and of the strike. Hank is thus not disclosing any new, potentially threatening information. When Dagny had been in the valley, however, Hank had no clue of its existence.

36. Bear in mind that Rand firmly distinguishes an innocent error from a moral failing, writing that "errors of knowledge are not breaches of morality," and that "no proper moral code can demand infallibility or omniscience," "The Cult of Moral Grayness," *Virtue of Selfishness*, 88. It is also important to appreciate that the proper application of moral principles is contextual. See Peikoff, *Objectivism*, 274–276, and Smith, *Ayn Rand's Normative Ethics*, 36, 94–105. On moral perfection, see Smith "Morality Without the Wink: A Defense of Moral Perfection," *Journal of Philosophical Research* 29 (2004): 315–31, and the discussion of pride in Smith, *Ayn Rand's Normative Ethics*, chapter 9.

37. Consider Galt's observation: "A moral code impossible to practice, a code that demands imperfection or death, has taught you to dissolve all ideas in fog, to permit no firm definitions, to regard any concept as approximate and any rule of conduct as elastic, to hedge on any principle, to compromise on any value, to take the middle of any road. By extorting your acceptance of supernatural absolutes, it has forced you to reject the absolute of nature" (1054).

38. For related discussion of the way in which the power of the good depends on its consistency, see Peikoff, *Objectivism*, 264–67.

39. Thanks for many valuable comments to participants in a workshop cosponsored by the Anthem Fellowship for the Study of Objectivism at the University of Texas at Austin and the Ayn Rand Institute, held in Irvine, Calif. in January 2008: Tore Boeckmann, Yaron Brook, Onkar Ghate, Robert Mayhew, Jason Rheins, and Greg Salmieri, and to Debi Ghate, for co-organizing this workshop with me. Greg Salmieri's lecture course "*Atlas Shrugged* as a Work of Philosophy," given at OCON, Telluride, July 2007, was also very helpful for my thinking about these issues. Robert Mayhew's editorial comments have improved the paper.

16

The Businessmen's Crucial Role

Material Men of the Mind

Debi Ghate

INTRODUCTION

In describing *Atlas Shrugged*, Ayn Rand wrote, "its theme is: the role of the mind in man's existence."[1] This is a very broad theme, one that Rand could have illustrated via countless different story lines. Among the many possibilities, she chose a specific plot-theme. As she explained:

> The link between the theme and the events of the novel is an element which I call the plot-theme. . . . A "plot-theme" is the central conflict or "situation" of a story—a conflict in terms of action, corresponding to the theme and complex enough to create a purposeful progression of events. . . . The plot-theme of *Atlas Shrugged* is "The men of the mind going on strike against an altruist-collectivist society."[2]

In other words, to show the role of the mind in man's existence, she chose as the central action a most unusual kind of strike: what would happen if a certain group of men—the men of intellect—were to withdraw from the world?

Among Rand's heroes in *Atlas Shrugged*, we find several businessmen: Hank Rearden, Dagny Taggart, Francisco d'Anconia, and others. This is intriguing; it is rare to find businessmen portrayed as the protagonists in modern literature and movies, and even rarer if the story involves men of the intellect. Businessmen are generally treated with suspicion—they are considered greedy, soulless money-grubbers, out to take advantage of anyone in the name of making a profit. Even when we have no solid reason to doubt their motives, the strong message delivered to the businessman who rises above the crowd is: Don't stand out or we'll relevel the playing field; don't earn too much through your chosen profession, or we'll find a way to redistribute your wealth. We expect caped crusaders to save the day, not suited businessmen.

Yet Ayn Rand cast businessmen as *heroes* in the novel. Was this an optional selection on her part? Could she have written her novel with scientists, philosophers, engineers, lawyers, or doctors as her central heroes? John Galt, the leader of the strike, says that the strikers will return to the world only when the lights of New York City are extinguished. What will it take to extinguish those lights? Who keeps those lights on?

I argue that *Atlas Shrugged*, because of its chosen plot-theme, had to have businessmen such as Hank Rearden and Dagny Taggart as its heroes *by necessity*.

THE POPULAR CONCEPTION OF
THE BUSINESSMAN AS MATERIALIST

While I was writing this essay, the United States was facing tremendous economic uncertainty caused by a "credit crisis." During the frenzy, the typical cries against businessmen were once again heard. Presidential candidate John McCain vowed that his administration, if elected, would "put an end to the reckless conduct, corruption and unbridled greed that have caused the crisis on Wall Street."[3] Profit-seeking businessmen are society's downfall: they are the source of our economic woes, and the public suffers for their vice of pursuing wealth. They are certainly not described as "men of the mind," the type of man that *Atlas Shrugged*'s strike removes from society. Instead they are considered men of corruption and sin.

In the novel's setting, what is the response to the businessman? As in today's media accounts, the wealthy businessman in *Atlas Shrugged* is deemed evil and blamed for the current economic crisis facing the country:

> The newspapers had snarled that the cause of the country's troubles . . . was the selfish greed of the rich industrialists; that it was men like Hank Rearden who were to blame for the shrinking diet, the falling temperature and the cracking roofs in the homes of the nation . . . that a man like Hank Rearden was prompted by nothing but the profit motive . . . as if the words "profit motive" were the self-evident brand of ultimate evil. (476)

Far from being considered a candidate for a strike by men of the mind, a businessman like Hank Rearden is denounced as a "predatory savage" who is nothing but an "ex-ore-digger" (404). Business is dismissed as a trivial activity that any greedy brute can undertake to make a quick buck. When Dagny speaks with Dr. Stadler, a brilliant but corrupt scientist, about an abandoned motor that she believes could revolutionize industry, he spurns the businessman's role, stating: "You'd think any greedy fool of an industrialist would have grabbed it in order to make a fortune. No intelligence was needed to see its commercial value" (356). When a member of the "intellectual class" attempts to flatter Jim Taggart, the businessman with a "social conscience," he says "the best compliment I can pay you is that you're *not* a real businessman." In response, Jim preaches the mantra of the looters: "We are breaking up the vicious tyranny of economic power. We will set men free of the rule of the dollar. We will release our spiritual aims from dependence on the owners of material means. We will liberate our culture from the stranglehold of the profit-chasers" (404).

The contempt for the businessman and the corresponding attitude that he is a force of destruction and chaos, rests on the view that he is an emotion-driven thug who mows down the intellectual as he lustily pursues profit, nurturing greed in others. What is behind this view?

"*We will release our spiritual aims from dependence on the owners of material means,*" says Jim Taggart (404). A well-known author who frequented many parties concurs: "Our culture has sunk into a bog of materialism. Men have lost all spiritual values in their pursuit of material production and technological trickery. . . . They will return to a nobler life if we teach them to bear privations. So we ought to place a limit on their material greed" (133). "Intellectual pursuits are not learned in the marketplace," said the hostess (144). The dominant view is that business is corrupt *because* it is material, and therefore by necessity is nonspiritual.

What is praised as spiritual by those who find the material distasteful? It is the abstract, indefinable, intangible, and impractical realm, the subject matter of highbrow discussion amongst the popular intellectuals in the novel. "No," says an author at a gathering of socialites, "you cannot expect people to understand the higher reaches of philosophy. Culture should be taken out of the hands of the dollar-chasers. We need a national subsidy for literature. It is disgraceful that artists are treated like peddlers and that art works have to be sold like soap" (141). The art works and books that no one wants to buy are spiritual. The ideas that are beyond the grasp of the rational individual are spiritual. "You must learn to see beyond the static definitions of old-fashioned thinking. Nothing is static in the universe. Everything is fluid," said the professor of philosophy at the same party (132). The common view is that it is the *unknowable* and *otherworldly* that constitutes the spiritual.

Because what the businessman does is definable, tangible, concrete, and of-this-world, his work is disdained as material, and therefore not of the intellect or spirit.

BUSINESS AS AN INTELLECTUAL AND SPIRITUAL PURSUIT

Ayn Rand completely rejected the conventional view of the businessman, the view that he is nothing more than a "used car salesman" with a bigger dealership. Rather, Ayn Rand celebrated the businessman and his pursuit of material wealth as *virtuous*. As Francisco d'Anconia states:

> To the glory of mankind, there was, for the first and only time in history, a *country of money*—and I have no higher, more reverent tribute to pay to America, for this

means: a country of reason, justice, freedom, production, achievement. For the first time, man's mind and money were set free, and there were no fortunes-by-conquest, but only fortunes-by-work, and instead of swordsmen and slaves, there appeared the real maker of wealth, the greatest worker, the highest type of human being—the self-made man—the American industrialist. (414)

Why did Rand hold the businessman as the "highest type of human being"? To judge whether business requires intellect or not, one must examine what it consists of. What does a businessman do on a daily basis and over the span of his career?

Much of the novel concentrates on the lives of two businessmen whom the strikers consider their greatest enemies, and their greatest potential conquests: Hank Rearden and Dagny Taggart. Through them, we are exposed to the role of the mind in business and the full range of activities it involves—when it is pursued actively and purposefully as a productive venture. Does business require men of intellect?

Hank Rearden

Hank Rearden is an industrialist whose chosen purpose was to invent a new Metal that would outlast, outperform, and outsell any other material known to man. He had worked since the age of fourteen in mines, foundries, and mills, learning the industry from the mine shafts up. By thirty, he owned the mine. He eventually owned Rearden Ore, Rearden Coal, and Rearden Limestone before opening Rearden Steel. Every stage of his career was an advancement over the last; every advancement brought him closer to his goal: Rearden Metal. As Rearden says to Francisco d'Anconia, "To me there's only one form of human depravity—the man without a purpose" (148).

On the night that he finally pours the first heat of Rearden Metal, he reflects on what it took to reach this day. It took him ten years to develop the metal and "every inch of its course, every pound of its pressure and every molecule within it, were controlled and made by a conscious intention that had worked upon it" (28). Rearden envisioned a world built and shaped by his Metal. He foresaw what multitudes of applications would result if he succeeded in his quest—from kitchen knives to communication wire to airplanes. With his purpose firmly in mind, Rearden spent years in research laboratories in front of scorching ovens, poring over formulas on paper, testing material, learning from each failed attempt—reformulating, recalculating, reinventing, and always reasoning, reasoning, reasoning—until the solution was found, until the day he could hold the cool metal in his hands. Consider what this required: an integrated understanding of chemistry, physics, mathematics, engineering, metallurgy, among other fields. It required the ability to conceptualize beyond previously identified and readily accessible metals, and to reconfigure existing materials into combinations not previously thought of. It required an ability to persist in the face of failure. On the day his metal is poured for the first time, Rearden finds that his mind is still sharply focused on what had been his ten-year goal: "The sight of the running metal was still burned into his mind, filling his consciousness, leaving no room for anything else" (34).

Yet, during that ten-year period, as the owner of the most efficient and productive steel mills in the country, Rearden undertakes this inventive effort while expertly overseeing all other aspects of his business. In order to garner the greatest profit and reward from his mills, Rearden must continually identify or create new or larger markets for his metal. He must envision new, industry-advancing solutions for his customers' manufacturing and engineering needs. For instance, when Taggart Transcontinental wants to build a new bridge using his Metal, Rearden sketches a design that leads to a new method of construction, at a fraction of the previously estimated cost—construction that takes into account the superior quality of Rearden Metal. He has just created a new market segment of unlimited potential, with colossal profits as his just reward. And his customers are now able to pursue new industrial endeavors more efficiently, leading them to increase their own production and wealth—leading them to place larger and more frequent orders for his Metal. Rearden's attitude is summed up in his reply to Dagny, when she tells him a story she once heard in school about the sun losing energy and growing colder and colder each year: "I never believed that story. I thought by the time the sun was exhausted, men would find a substitute" (171).

As an industrialist, Rearden must oversee the design, construction, and any expansion of the physical mills. What methods and efficiencies can he introduce to maximize production and continuously increase the output of his mills? Has he hired the right employees to carry out the work? What directions should he give his superintendent in the face of a crisis? The more the mills produce, the more he produces; the more he produces, the more he sells; the more he sells, the more he earns. How can he produce 600 tons of metal a day on fewer furnaces compared to Orren Boyle's 100 tons using many more furnaces? Rearden is ruthlessly focused on squeezing the most production out of Rearden Steel, leading to larger and larger profits.

But he does not take a short-term, pragmatic view in generating those profits. He recognizes that he must earn the loyalty of the kind of customers he wants to deal with—those who will pay for his Metal and put it to the uses he had envisioned. He must determine at what price to sell his Metal so that his customers can afford it and will return. He must hire and fire employees with varying skills, from researchers to floor sweepers—the right decisions advance his long-term goal to maximize his profits. He must put out a fire at his mills and shovel coal if necessary in an emergency rather than watch and direct the action from afar. And, unfortunately, he must also deal with the Floyd Ferrises, the Wesley Mouches, the Paul Larkins, and their collaborators, who not only distract him from his purpose but actively try to undermine it. Rearden, the industrialist, must personally and simultaneously respond to multiple demands and pressures calmly, with focus, all the while engaged in the creative process of making Rearden Metal. Hank Rearden *is* Rearden Steel.

It was not easy; he experienced fatigue, frustration, and anger. He experienced occasional failure. But Rearden succeeded nevertheless. He was committed to a well-defined purpose, a purpose that he knew *had to be possible to achieve* given his hard-acquired knowledge. He knew that the goal he set—a new, revolutionary metal—would require a high level of sustained effort to attain. He recognized that his mind and spirit were the only sparks he needed to keep himself going (30).

In offering us Hank Rearden, Ayn Rand presents us with a business hero who proudly relies on his mind in the relentless pursuit of his business—for the express purpose of making as much money as possible. She presents us with a man who, through his confident dedication to his purpose, offers the world a product, Rearden Metal, that has the potential to revolutionize industry, providing a wide range of new products at a cheaper price. Through Hank Rearden, we see what intellectual and physical effort must be invested to achieve this, and the overwhelming range of intermediary decisions that rest on his judgment. When combined together in a man like Rearden, a business giant is born, the kind of man who changes the world product by product. Jim Taggart protests: "Rearden. He didn't invent smelting and chemistry and air compression. He couldn't have invented his Metal but for thousands and thousands of other people. *His* Metal! Why does he think it's his? Why does he think it's his invention?" His future wife, Cherryl, asks, puzzled, "But the iron ore and all those other things were there all the time. Why didn't anybody else make that Metal, but Mr. Rearden did?" (262). Without him, there is no revolution in manufacturing. He knows it, as does John Galt and his fellow strikers, as do the looters who try to deny that a man like Rearden is a man of the mind.

Dagny Taggart

Dagny Taggart decided as a child that she would one day run Taggart Transcontinental—"From Ocean to Ocean, forever"—better and faster than anyone, including her legendary grandfather, Nat Taggart. She knows all other industries depend on motive power to gather manufacturing components and transport their finished goods to market. The work she does moves the country—the better and faster she does that, the more her company earns, and the more she earns as a stockholder and employee. And that profit is earned from other businesses that are also actively creating wealth from products they make. The more those businesses manufacture, the more her railroad earns by providing them with transportation.

Dagny started as a night station operator and worked her way up to Vice-President in Charge of Operation. In her, we find a competent, energetic professional who is always ready to act on her judgment in a swift and decisive way. Consider this exchange between Dagny and her mealy-mouthed brother and boss, Jim, when she announces her decision to replace the Rio Norte Line using track made of Rearden Metal, something no one has dared to attempt before:

> "The consensus of the best metallurgical authorities," he said, "seems to be highly skeptical about Rearden Metal, contending—"
> "Drop it, Jim."
> "Well, whose opinion did you take?"
> "I don't ask for opinions."
> "What do you go by?"
> "[My] Judgment." . . .
> "Then what on earth do you know about Rearden Metal?"
> "That it's the greatest thing ever put on the market . . . because it's tougher than steel, cheaper than steel and will outlast any hunk of metal in existence."
> "But who says so?"
> "Jim, I studied engineering in college. When I see things, I see them."
> "What did you see?"
> "Rearden's formula and the tests he showed me."
> "Well, if it were any good, somebody would have used it, and nobody has." He saw the flash of anger, and went on nervously: "How can you *know* it's good? How can you be sure? How can you decide?"
> "Somebody decides such things, Jim. Who?" (21)

Dagny Taggart, Taggart Transcontinental's Vice-President in Charge of Operation, decides these things.

Dagny always seems to know what to do and why. She has a seemingly pure clarity in her thinking. This clarity comes from knowing with certainty that she can make the right decision. This certainty is not without basis, it does not come from arrogance but from an earned confidence. What is the source of that confidence? Dagny knows every aspect of the company's business from the lonely station post to the powerful board room. She has invested in learning every key aspect of Taggart Transcontinental's business. She can read every map, operate any signal, construct a complex train schedule, hire expert contractors, and build a new railroad line. Before making her business decisions, Dagny personally examines the evidence, gains a firsthand understanding of the data in front of her, and evaluates all of the known facts. Because she has done so, she has no hesitation in issuing the necessary directions. On whose judgment? Her own. On whose authority? Her own. At whose risk? Her own. Dagny repeatedly and consistently tells employees, government officials, Jim, and the Taggart board of directors, that she personally assumes responsibility for her decisions when no one else dares to act. Her confidence is such that she decides to personally assume the risk of building the John Galt Line, entering into an agreement with Taggart Transcontinental that has it garnering all of the benefit if she succeeds.

What does building the John Galt Line require of Dagny? Her constant goal is: the best, fastest, safest railroad the world has ever seen. Her constant motivation is: to make as much money as possible for herself and the railroad, boosting the other industries that depend on rail transport along the way so that her own company has long-term customers. Dagny knows that the fate of Colorado's industries, such as Wyatt Oil, Nielsen Motors, Hammond Cars, Stockton Foundry, depends on whether the Line is built or not. She knows that if Colorado's industries vanish, so does the entire country's economy.

Dagny has relied on her own judgment to identify that Rearden Metal is the best material to use for her endeavor even if it has never been used to build a railroad track. Because she is ultimately responsible for making the Line as profitable as possible, she must ensure that it is built to last and to transport as much traffic as possible while doing no harm to Taggart Transcontinental's passengers, or to the cargo entrusted it. To construct a railroad made of a new, untried material, she must resolve numerous engineering, manufacturing, and personnel issues. The consequences of an error are potentially costly to her given her agreement to bear all the risk—passengers could be killed if the rail is unsafe, the shareholders' investment may not pay off, Taggart Transcontinental's profits could crumble, or the commerce of Colorado could wither away, leaving the country's economy in jeopardy. What Dagny's business activities provide is a lifeline—a mechanism for people to move their goods and themselves—a way for them to carry out their own businesses, and therefore earn their livelihoods.

Because she has fully evaluated every component of the Line (human, mechanical, or otherwise), because she has planned for its construction, taking into account all known facts, because she has carefully calculated, designed, tested, and verified her vision, she succeeds—with nothing but her judgment to stand on. As she proudly rides in the engine car on the day the line opens,

> She wondered why she felt safer than she had ever felt in a car behind the engine, safer here, where it seemed as if, should an obstacle rise, her breast and the glass shield would be the first to smash against it. She smiled, grasping the answer: it was the security of being first, with full sight and full knowledge of one's course—not the blind sense of being pulled into the unknown by some unknown power ahead. It was the greatest sensation of existence: not to trust, but to know. (240)

Because of her dedication to fully understand every aspect of the railroad business, Dagny is able to quickly identify obstacles and, at a rapid-fire pace, direct the necessary actions to remove them. She uses the results of her mind's effort to *act*. When the John Galt Line is built, and she has claimed victory over the naysayers, she decides to lay a track made of Rearden Metal across the country—"From Ocean to Ocean, forever." She is in a position to immediately conclude that this is the best course of action for the success of the railroad.

However, Dagny is not able to pursue that goal. Instead, she must respond to calamity after calamity in an attempt to save Taggart Transcontinental. When the tunnel disaster occurs in Colorado, Dagny's focus immediately turns to solving the problem of how to provide ongoing transportation with the least amount of disruption. She pulls maps from the railroad's early days and issues work orders to begin rerouting tracks in order to resume cross-country operations as soon as possible. When the Comet stalls on the tracks and is abandoned, she personally walks down the track to contact help. Her guiding principle is that "so long as she was still in existence she would know that action is man's foremost obligation, regardless of anything he feels" (334). Her mind is in constant drive and she acts on its output to continuously reach for her goal: a faster and better railroad than has ever been offered to the country before.

But, like Rearden, she must excel at overseeing the details of the business while pursuing her long-term, visionary goal. She must have the kind of intellect and dedication to purpose it takes to revolutionize the transportation industry of an entire nation. It is Dagny that recognizes the value of Rearden Metal in spite of the doubts cast upon it by the country's leading metallurgists. *She* conceives of the Rearden Metal bridge and track, recognizing the durability and speed it would provide. And she recognizes the value of the abandoned motor at the Twentieth Century Motor Company's ghost town factory. It is she who pursues the answer to the motor's riddle, knowing what it would mean for her railroad and for the entire economy.

What is it about the motor that convinces Dagny she must do everything in her power to resurrect it? Dagny understands the potential wealth that the motor could bring, not only to its inventor but to anyone who has the ability to harness its power. The motor is *self-generating*, requiring no outside source to continually replenish it. This means that any motorized process could be significantly accelerated, making more time and materials available for other use. As Rearden responds to her query as to whether he recognizes the value of the motor, if built: "I'd say: about ten years added to the life of every person in this country. . . . That motor could have set the whole country in motion and on fire" (290). And it is Dagny who extracts that invisible potential from an unidentifiable junk heap in the corner of an abandoned factory.

Taggart Transcontinental could not continue to exist but for Dagny's purpose, knowledge, and capacity for action. John Galt and his fellow strikers know this. Dagny senses it. And so do Jim, his board of directors, and the other looters who want to use her mind's products while cursing her existence.

Other Businessmen

There are other businessmen in the novel through whom we learn more about the intellectual power required to properly engage in business. Midas Mulligan, the financier, only makes loans to customers who he judges will pay them back with sufficient interest; he does not run a bank built on hopes, dreams, and pity, but on reality. What does that require? Mulligan must understand enough about the intended activities of his loan applicants to evaluate whether to incur the risk of supporting them (whether they be in mining, car manufacturing, or any other productive venture). In order to decide whether an investment is worth his gold, Mulligan must be in a position to *judge* whether his injection of capital will make that business grow. Ellis Wyatt, the man with no time to waste, works on drawing oil out of shale—previously considered an impossible task. What does that require? Wyatt must first conceive of the possibility, and then sufficiently understand the science and technology involved to lead the effort and hire the right specialists to convert the possibility into fact. He must then work on methods that will allow him to refine more of the oil he draws out of that shale, at a faster rate, in order to fulfil increasing demand from his customers. Ken Danagger, who owns a coal mine, judges that Rearden is a man worth dealing with under any circumstances, including the threat of legal sanction. What does that require? Danagger must be able to exercise independence in the face of popular opinion and evaluate Rearden as a business associate upon whom to stake the future of his coal mines. Danagger must be able to judge the material—and spiritual—benefits of such a business decision. Through these characters, Rand continues to show that business requires a thoroughly engaged and active mind, a mind capable of simultaneously asking a broad range of industry-redefining questions while yielding innovative answers that generate significant wealth for its owner and those he trades with.

What Business Is

Business, when pursued as Rearden, Dagny, and other businessmen in *Atlas Shrugged* pursue it, is indisputably a material endeavor that is equally intellectual and spiritual. Ayn Rand describes the businessman as follows:

> The businessman carries scientific discoveries from the laboratory of the inventor to industrial plants, and transforms them into material products that fill men's physical needs and expand the comfort of men's existence. By creating a mass market, he makes these products available to every income level in society. By using machines, he increases the productivity of human labor, thus raising labor's economic rewards. By organizing human effort into productive enterprises, he creates employment for men of countless professions.[4]

In other words, the industrialist channels the inventions and discoveries of highly specialized professions through carefully designed processes that result in goods and services, elevating our standard of living and making our lives more enjoyable, efficient, and effortless. The businessman converts the raw output of the researcher into a viable product that he can sell as widely and as profitably as possible. Along the way, he hires and therefore sustains many others of varying skill and ability, at all levels of society. That is, at the broadest level, what a businessman does.

This type of businessman is not a work of fiction created by Ayn Rand. Consider one of the earliest industrialists, James Watt (1736 to 1819). Watt is credited with commercializing a key piece of technology that brought about the Industrial Revolution, and thus our modern civilization: the steam engine. While he did not invent the steam engine, it was Watt who recognized its potential value. He began working on existing steam engines in 1764 to increase their output over longer periods of time. In 1765, Watt finally gained the critical insight of separating an engine's condenser from its piston, allowing it to maintain the requisite temperature. He then created a test engine and raised capital to mass produce the improved engine. By 1775, he had gone into business with fellow industrialist Matthew Boulton, and what followed was rapid progress in creating a commercial version of the test engine. Over the next few years, he worked to overcome other major design challenges involving the piston and beam. The result was the birth of the first steam engine of commercial value. Watt continued to work to improve the engine and adapt it for use in more specialized markets. By developing a rotary-motion steam engine in 1781 (replacing the earlier up-and-down pumping model) and introducing other mechanical improvements, Watt made available a steam engine for use in paper, flour, cotton, and iron mills, as well as distilleries, canals, and waterworks. He continued to improve and sell engines, generating significant profits. By the time he retired in 1800, he had patented the steam locomotive and was very wealthy, having reaped the rewards for his intellectual efforts. Watt's commercialization of the steam engine is credited as supplying the foremost source of energy, which made possible the Industrial Revolution.[5]

An industrialist's mind must therefore be such that he can take the scientist's creation, recognize its potential value, adapt it for commercialization and sell it to larger and larger markets. He expects to reap significant financial rewards for his efforts. But as Francisco points out to Rearden, there are easier ways to make money (452). Ultimately, what is it that motivates the businessman to engage in the demanding intellectual work required to successfully achieve his purpose?

It is precisely because the material pursuit of business is *spiritual* that the industrialist is dedicated to it. The businessman's ultimate goal is to create *values*. When Francisco asks Rearden why he spent ten years making his Metal and what he had hoped to achieve by giving his life to this activity, Rearden responds that he is proud of his achievement. He is proud of the John Galt Line because it is the best rail ever made and he wishes to make money by exchanging his best efforts for the best efforts of others. Rearden wants to see his Metal used by the best among men—those whom it will help reach greater and greater achievements—those who understand and appreciate the greatness of his own achievement (452).

Business is an activity that offers the mind challenges of a tremendous scale (on the order of how to create a new metal, how to revolutionize the transportation industry, or how to bring oil out of shale), the successful completion of which leads to the attainment of values. The night that Rearden pours the first heat of his Metal, he thinks: "Whatever it was . . . whatever the strain and the agony, they were worth it, because they had made him reach this day" (31). As Dagny rides in the engine car on the first run of the John Galt Line, she goes to look at the generators, exhilarated:

> She stood in a swaying, sealed chamber of metal, looking at the giant generators. She had wanted to see them, because the sense of triumph within her was bound to them, to her love for them, to the reason for the life-work she had chosen . . . "The John Galt Line!" she shouted, for the amusement of feeling her voice swept away from her lips . . . They *are* alive, she thought, but their soul operates them by remote control. Their soul is in every man who has the capacity to equal this achievement. (245–46)

The pride and immense satisfaction of having created an industry—having accomplished what no one else could with the iron ore, the railroad system, or the shale—and the pleasure and happiness one derives from seeing one's product put to the uses one envisioned, is the spiritual reward the business-man receives for his intellectual effort.

The financial reward that the businessman expects to earn as a result of creating these values is the objective measure of his success. But it also adds to his spiritual reward. It is his means of pursuing and maintaining other values: the friends, ideas, art, projects, and hobbies that he has chosen because they bring him fulfillment and happiness. As Francisco puts it:

> Money . . . will take you wherever you wish to go but it will not replace you as the driver. It will give you the means for the satisfaction of your desires, but it will not provide you with desires. . . . Money will not pursue happiness for the man who has no concept of what he wants: money will not give him a code of values. (411)

The pursuit of business so that it generates as much profit as possible therefore supplements the spiritual rewards that the work itself provides: it supplies the means for the businessman to enjoy a full life.

Finally, business is spiritual precisely because it involves material products—the definable, tangible, concrete products created by it. Francisco explains this relationship between material goods and man's spirit:

> Dagny, we who've been called "materialists" by the killers of the human spirit, we're the only ones who know how little value or meaning there is in material objects as such, because we're the ones who create their value and meaning . . . *You* do not have to depend on any material possessions, they depend on you, you create them, you own the one and only tool of production. Wherever you are, you will always be able to produce. (620)

The one and only tool of her production is her mind. Absent her mind, there is no tangible product for her to sell, and there is no resulting wealth for her to pursue her values with or no spiritual satisfaction to derive out of the creative process.

Without the material objects generated by business, the industrialist is unable to derive the spiritual wealth he gets from creating values out of his work. Without the spiritual investment of the industrialist's soul into his business, there is no material wealth possible to him. The two are indivisible. Business is a material *and* spiritual pursuit, demanding the best of one's mind.

As the composer Richard Halley comments in the valley:

> Miss Taggart, do you see why I'd give three dozen modern artists for one real businessman? . . . Whether it's a symphony or a coal mine, all work is an act of creating and comes from the same source: from an inviolate capacity to see through one's own eyes. . . . That shining vision which they talk about as belonging to authors of symphonies and novels—what do they think is the driving faculty of men who discover how to use oil, how to run a mine, how to build an electric motor? That sacred fire which is said to burn within musicians and poets—what do they suppose moves an industrialist to defy the whole world for the sake of his new metal . . . ? . . . [I]f there is more tragic a fool than the businessman who doesn't know that he's an exponent of man's highest creative spirit—it's the artist who thinks that the businessman is his enemy." (782–84)

What Business Isn't

Not all of the characters who claim the title of businessman in *Atlas Shrugged* illustrate the proper role of the mind in man's existence. Jim Taggart, Orren Boyle, Paul Larkin, Horace Bussby Mowen claim to be "businessmen." And why not? After all, they work *at* businesses, claim lofty titles such as president or owner, have big offices and staff scurrying about them, and take high-level meetings with the "who's-who" of Washington and Hollywood. These men are engaged in the full-time activity of trying to steal the income of hard-working people, using as minimal a level of effort as possible. They are corrupt, greedy thieves. *These* are the "predatory savages" that populate the prevailing notion of businessmen and what they do.

Recall Rand's description of the businessman and his role. Do the pseudo-businessmen transform inventions into new products, creating mass markets for them? No, they think of ways to steal the products of others and beg loans from Washington. Do they organize people into effective teams creating productive output? No, they look for ways to have the most number of people do as little productive work as possible. These characters spend their time currying favors, evading facts, avoiding decision-making, trading pull with other pull-peddlers, attending parties to see and be seen, and speaking in half-truths and code. They do everything in their power to remain in a hazy fog and avoid the necessity of action, preferring instead to rely on the Reardens and the Dagnys to do their thinking for them. A day's work for a man like Jim Taggart is to wake up cursing the dawn, to think of who he needs to avoid that day in order not to have a favor called in, and more importantly, who he needs to entertain and play the sycophant to in order to gain a favor. A man like Orren Boyle spends his days lobbying for increased regulations to throttle his competitors so that he can avoid the difficult task of figuring out how to produce steel. These are not businessmen, they are thugs. Rather than produce, they contrive new mechanisms by which to force others to do their thinking for them. They serve as a stark contrast to Rearden, Dagny, and the other heroic businessmen in the novel. They illustrate the role of the *mindless*.

The Spiritual Field that Sustains Other Fields

But men of the mind exist in every field requiring specialized knowledge and skill. Obviously one must think rationally, have a purpose, and act on one's judgment if one is a physicist designing a self-generating motor, a composer who writes uplifting music, or a philosophy professor who teaches future generations of thinkers. What makes the businessman unique? Why would the strike have lacked success if all the other men of the mind shrugged, but the businessman did not?

On a practical and visceral level, other professions rely on the businessman for their livelihood. The physicist needs the businessman to recognize the potential value and create commercial markets for his invention. The composer needs the businessman to record and sell his music. The philosophy professor needs the businessman to build and operate the university where he teaches. Even if the professional is engaged in certain business-like activities himself (for example, a self-employed doctor who markets his practice, provides services of value, issues invoices, and collects payment, pays the bills), he relies on others to put up the financing and carry out the construction of buildings that house his practice; to supply and sell the specialized equipment he needs to carry out his profession; to make commercially available new medicines and therapeutic products that will allow his own profession to grow. Who provides all of these elements? The businessman.

In the context of the novel, note that John Galt was temporarily employed by a motor company, Richard Halley performed in concert halls and recorded his music at studios, and Hugh Akston taught at Patrick Henry University. Each of them looked to the businessman for employment or for providing a means of earning an income. The products of their minds had limited exposure and were therefore of limited benefit, until the businessman recognized their value.

But the businessman supplies other professions with much more than employment, capital, and industrial products. He is the provider of *material and therefore spiritual wealth*, which makes possible the pursuit of other professions.

Rand, in her discussion of the businessman's role, expanded on what he makes possible: "*He* is the great liberator who, in the short span of a century and a half, has released men from bondage to their physical needs, has released them from the terrible drudgery of an eighteen-hour workday of manual labor for their barest subsistence, has released them from famines, from pestilences, from the stagnant hopelessness and terror in which most of mankind had lived in all the pre-capitalist centuries—and in which most of it still lives, in non-capitalist countries."[6]

Because J. D. Rockefeller refined oil into petroleum and other key materials, new products, including cars, tractors, and bulldozers emerged, freeing men from physical labor and allowing more than a small elite under the protection of patrons to engage in professions such as teaching, painting, or lawyering. Because Thomas Edison manufactured the electric light bulb, men were free to continue their activities after dark, allowing them to produce more in a day, making them wealthier. In their new-found leisure time, they could afford to buy books, listen to recorded performances, and watch movies, resulting in income for authors, musicians, and film directors. Because J.P. Morgan financed corporations, including manufacturing and drug companies, scientists and engineers were able to secure private employment rather than work for the state or under the protection of an aristocratic patron who was entertained by the abstract intellectual work done by the creator.

As *Atlas Shrugged*'s Ellis Wyatt identified:

> What's wealth but the means of expanding one's life? There's two ways one can do that: either by producing more or by producing it faster. And that's what I'm doing, I'm manufacturing time . . . I'm working to improve my methods, and every hour I save is an hour added to my life . . . Wealth, Dagny? What greater wealth is there than to own your life and spend it growing? Every living thing must grow. It can't stand still. It must grow or perish. (721–22)

Every hour that a man like Ellis Wyatt adds to his life means that more efficient industrial processes and products now exist. With the advent of those comes the growth of many other professions—and the wealth to support them.

THE DEVASTATING EFFECTS OF THE STRIKE

As the businessmen join the strike, taking their minds and wealth-generating abilities with them, what effect is there?

In the areas of the country where industries have vanished, a regression from modern life to preindustrial conditions takes place. As Rearden and Dagny drive through Michigan's countryside, they visit an abandoned ore mine—and see the "remnants of a crane like a skeleton bending against the sky," a discarded lunchbox at their feet. As they drive through nearby towns, they observe run-down houses, sagging structures—and horse-drawn carriages where cars once traveled. When they reach the area where Dagny finds the abandoned motor, the village of Starnesville, they are met with people dressed in rags with no shoes, drawing water from wells, living by candlelight in highly unsanitary conditions—who blankly stare at their car as if they have appeared from another dimension of space and time. They see the remains of gasoline stations, and isolated telegraph poles. They see chickens loose in the meager vegetable garden, and pigs waddling in refuse. The people appear bedraggled and hopeless. They look much older than their age and as if they are incapable of feeling anything but exhaustion (280–83).

What image does this account invoke?

> English peasants in 1086 had little more than enough food to keep them alive, and sometimes not even that. Houses were crude temporary structures. A peasant owned one set of clothes, best described as rags, and little else. As late as the fifteenth century expenditures of the masses on non-food items such as clothing, heat, light, and rent were probably only 13 percent of all expenditures.[7]

When Michigan's industries shut down, its people find themselves living in conditions similar to what eleventh-century peasants endured. They have lost centuries' worth of progress. They are reduced to a state of bare subsistence, and one can no longer afford the luxury of employment as a scientist, composer, or philosophy professor. They are on the path to returning to what the West was like prior to Watt, his steam engine, and all of the other advances of the Industrial Revolution: "The hovels of the poor in London and elsewhere were health hazards of the highest order. . . . Sanitation was primitive and sewage much the same. In many parts of London, people simply threw their garbage into the street. . . . There were outhouses and cesspools instead of sewers."[8] The tangible effects of the wealth generated through industrialization are plainly visible when looking at how life expectancy has improved as society has become more industrialized.

> The pre-industrial period could generate only minor fluctuations in life expectancy, averaging in the mid-to-high 30s, but the Industrial Revolution created a sustained upward movement. "People lived longer because they were better nourished and sheltered, and cleaner, and thus were less vulnerable to infectious . . . diseases . . . that were peculiarly susceptible to improved living standards." The industrial era initiated a gradual but steady march upward regarding English life expectancy, which is currently 74.7 years on average for men and 80.2 for women. "It took thousands of years to increase life expectancy at birth just over 20 years to the high 20s. Then in just the past two centuries, the length of life . . . in the advanced [i.e., industrialized] countries jumped from less than 30 years to perhaps 75 years."[9]

Starnesville—the town of filthy shacks amongst ruins—provides a stark reminder of what history has already shown us. It illustrates what happens when the source of material and spiritual wealth, the industrialist, has withdrawn. Remove the businessman, remove our ability to sustain civilization. Without the mind, and the businessmen's use of it to create wealth, it is not possible for others to pursue values beyond those utmost crucial values for physical survival: food and shelter.

In the absence of industrialists, society returns to a pre-nineteenth century level of existence. Human life shortens in span—death comes more quickly for all. *This* is the result of the mind on strike.

In the days that followed Rearden's strike, what effect was there on the spirit of the people? A steel shortage causes a number of businesses to fail and close, shop owners give up their stock to looters, small businessmen commit suicide and panic ensues. In the hours following Dagny's strike, the lights of New York City go out. All that is left is Wyatt's torch, burning incessantly. There is no mind left to bring the much-needed oil out of the ground. As Francisco tells Dagny:

> The rebirth of d'Anconia Copper—and of the world—has to start here, in the United States. This country was the only country in history born, not of chance and blind tribal warfare, but as a rational product of man's mind. This country was built on the supremacy of reason—and for one magnificent century it redeemed the world. It will have to do so again. (771)

WHY THE STRIKE REQUIRED BUSINESSMEN

Given Rand's choice to write a novel about the men of the mind going on strike in the midst of a collectivist society, her selection of businessmen as the lynchpins holding the looters' society together was essential. Rand views the businessman as the "field agent of the army whose lieutenant commander-in-chief is the scientist."[10] She describes her character, Francisco d'Anconia, the industrialist, as being the perfect blend of his two intellectual fathers, a philosopher and a physicist. In her view the businessman and the professional intellectual are partners.

Why was the businessman crucial to the strike given its purpose? Because of all the professions, his mind was the most disdained for being dedicated to pursuing what is considered the lowest of realms: the material world. Yet his mind was the one that all others most depended on for the requirements of human flourishing. Industrial civilization and all that it depends on—our release from physical labor, leisure time, art, culture—demands that the businessman be given a special place of honor amongst its "men of the mind." The industrialist not only provides the material means for other professions to exist, his success makes possible our pursuit of spiritual values. Only the businessman is in a position to simultaneously withdraw the material and spiritual wealth that the looters have looted. Only he can sever both sources at once, and with such devastation, simply by uttering one word: "Enough." Only his act of shrugging can figuratively, and literally, turn off the lights of New York City.[11]

NOTES

1. Ayn Rand, *For the New Intellectual* (New York: Signet, 1963), 88.

2. Ayn Rand, *The Romantic Manifesto: A Philosophy of Literature,* revised edition (New York: Signet, 1975), 85.

3. B. Reinhard, "McCain blames Wall Street's 'unbridled greed' for economic woes," the *Miami Herald* (Sept. 16, 2008), retrieved from www.miamiherald.com.

4. Rand, *For the New Intellectual*, 27.

5. *The New Encyclopedia Britannica Micropaedia Ready Reference* 15th edition, Vol. 12 (Chicago: Encyclopedia Britannica, 2002), 528–29.

6. Rand, *For the New Intellectual*, 27.

7. J. Simon, *The State of Humanity* (Cambridge, MA: Blackwell, 1995), 137.

8. Andrew Bernstein, *The Capitalist Manifesto* (Lanham, Md.: University Press of America, 2005), 64.

9. Bernstein, *The Capitalist Manifesto*, 120 (see n. 31 for sources cited).

10. Rand, *For the New Intellectual*, 27.

11. I wish to thank the Ayn Rand Institute's Yaron Brook, Executive Director, and Onkar Ghate, Senior Fellow, for their insightful editorial advice and their moral support, and its Academic Coordinator, Christopher Elsee, whose valuable assistance made it possible for me to have the time to write this essay. For an excellent discussion of the issues addressed in this essay, see the title essay by Leonard Reikoff in *Why Businessmen Need Philosophy* (Ayn Rand Institute Press, 1999).

17

The Traits of Business Heroes in *Atlas Shrugged*

Edwin A. Locke

There are many aspects of *Atlas Shrugged* that the reader can enjoy. It is a mystery with a totally original and suspenseful plot. It presents a revolutionary new philosophy that is demonstrated in action. It is a study of good against evil and an examination of the mind-body relationship from perspectives never before identified by a novelist or philosopher. It is a study of business heroes and their struggle to succeed against overwhelming odds. In the novel, of course, all these aspects are brilliantly interconnected and fully integrated.

In this chapter I will focus on the business heroes and the traits that made them great—and contrast, in limited fashion, these traits with those that characterized the business villains. The business heroes of the novel, such as Dagny Taggart, Hank Rearden, Ellis Wyatt, and Ken Danagger, were all brilliantly competent and, to the extent allowed, initially, by the altruistic society they were living in, successful. In what follows, I focus on their success and what made it possible, not on what happened later in the novel.

What traits did the heroes possess that would make successful production possible?

FOCUS ON REALITY

To the business heroes, reality is an absolute. To the villains, it is something to be evaded at all costs. Early in the book we are shown the contrast between Dagny Taggart, the Vice-President in Charge of Operation, and her brother James, the President of Taggart Transcontinental. Dagny predicts, based on her own evidence, that the Mexican government is going to nationalize Taggart's San Sebastián Line, but James refuses to consider it. His first concern is to

altruistically help an underprivileged country. Facts are secondary in his mind
to that wish. Further, because Associated Steel, led by a looter, Orren Boyle,
has not fulfilled its previous rail order, Dagny has ordered new rails for the
Rio Norte Line made from Rearden Metal, an entirely new product that no one
else had dared to order. James does not want to face reality. James's look is
described at one point as "gliding off and past things in eternal resentment of
their existence" (7). He does not want to think in order to form his own opinion of Rearden Metal. But Dagny is adamant, because she studied engineering
and knows the metal's value. She demands that James either approve the order
or refuse it. James whines: "That's the trouble with you. You always make it
'Yes' or 'No.' Things are never absolute like that. Nothing is absolute." Dagny
replies: "Metal rails are. Whether we get them or not, is" (23).

No matter what setback or disaster she is faced with—the loss of key employees, contractors, and suppliers, the shortages of rail and engines, the Winston Tunnel explosion, the shortage of money needed to build the John Galt
Line, the passage of productivity-destroying legislation by the government—
she never once considers faking reality in any way. Every fact, no matter how
unpleasant, is faced and evaluated fully and honestly.

Furthermore, every evaluation of the facts leads to action when action is
necessary and possible (an issue I will expand on later). For example, when
James refuses to support her plan to build the John Galt Line, which she regards as critical to the survival of Taggart Transcontinental—and to the whole
country—she "officially" leaves the company and takes charge of building the
line herself.

Hank Rearden is equally focused on reality. When visited by Dr. Potter
from the State Science Institute, who wants him to stop producing Rearden
Metal, Rearden has only one question for him: "Is Rearden Metal good or
not?"(179). As with Dagny, when he is faced with setbacks such as the loss of
his iron ore or copper or coal supplies, he fully accepts the facts as given and
works to find new sources.

In contrast to the villains, in whose minds wishes always take precedence
over facts, for the heroes reality is always primary in their thinking. At Lillian
Rearden's party, a corrupt philosopher Dr. Pritchett tells a guest that "nothing
is anything" (141)—which means that reality is whatever you want it to be.
Soon after, Francisco explains what Dr. Pritchett's predecessor at the Patrick
Henry University, Dr. Akston, taught: "that everything is something" (142).
The law of identity (A is A) is ingrained into the minds of the business heroes
like it was part of their DNA—only it's there by choice.

Even when they are wrong, both Dagny and Rearden act on the facts as they
understand them. Dagny, knowing her own, incredible, productive capacity,
believes she can save the world with her own brilliance and energy, but fails,
until late in the book, to see that she cannot succeed and is simply aiding
in her own destruction. When she understands this fully, she quits—as does
Rearden.

Unlike the villains, the business heroes *want to know*. Dagny wants Eddie Willers to tell her everything that has happened when she returns from being on her vacation with Rearden and after her stay in Galt's Gulch. She gets news about the railroad from him regularly when she is building the John Galt Line. In contrast, the first words we hear in the novel from James Taggart, when Eddie asks to consult with him, are: "Don't bother me, don't bother me, don't bother me." (7) James only wants to "know"—so long as he does not have to know his own motives—when he has gotten away with something dishonest such as a swindle or the crushing of a rival, such as Dan Conway or anyone who was productive, through his machinations. Otherwise he wants only to blank out existence.

Another example of the contrast between Dagny and Jim occurs later in the novel when a government thug, Cuffy Meigs, is appointed to replace Dagny after her plane crashes in Galt's Gulch. Meigs proceeds to loot the company, which Dagny discovers and reveals to Jim upon her return. Jim does not want to talk about it or deal with it. She thought: "*there* was the method of his consciousness: he wanted her to protect him from Cuffy Meigs without acknowledging Meigs' existence, to fight it without admitting its reality" (915). Dagny refuses to evade anything, including her brother's evil.

Nor does Dagny confuse the metaphysical with the man-made. She sees through Jim's unstated premise that "there is no difference between a law of nature and a bureaucrat's directive" (917). She grasps that nature must be accepted and obeyed whereas bureaucrats' directives must be evaluated by a process of thought.

Rearden wants to know the results of every experiment when he works to develop Rearden Metal, even though for many years the experiments were total failures. Ayn Rand writes: "He had never spared himself in any issue. When a problem came up at the mills, his first concern was to discover what error he had made" (128). Rearden also wants to know everything Francisco has to teach him about philosophy, including his own wrong premises concerning the mind-body relationship and his own sanctioning of the victim—the victim being himself. He grasps that such knowledge is critical to the future of his business and to his own happiness.

ABILITY AND CONFIDENCE

The business heroes in *Atlas Shrugged* are brilliantly competent. They are also aware of their own natural abilities, but not boastful about them. Ability is not a self-esteem issue for them but simply a fact of reality. (By natural ability, I mean inborn capacity, not acquired knowledge.) Dagny thinks:

> Studying mathematics, she felt quite simply and at once: "How great that men have done this" and "How wonderful that I am so good at it." It was the joy of

admiration and of one's own ability, growing together. Her feeling for the railroad was the same: worship of the skill that had gone to make it, of the ingenuity of someone's clean, reasoning mind, worship with a secret smile that said she would know how to make it better someday. (51)

In school Dagny got A's in all her classes with almost no effort (100). Ability breeds confidence. She tells Eddie Willers, when she is twelve years old, that someday she will run the railroad, although she decides this for herself when she is nine (51).

She starts at a low position at the railroad but her rise is "swift and uncontested. She took positions of responsibility because there was no one else to take them" (51). She never doubts her ability to be the Vice-President in Charge of Operation of Taggart Transcontinental and make the hundreds and thousands of decisions the job requires. When she presents the plan for the Rio Norte (John Galt) Line to James, she asserts without any expression of doubt: "I will act as my own contractor. I will get my own financing. I will take full charge and sole responsibility. I will complete the line on time" (193). And she does.

Hank Rearden is equally able. One day he thinks back on the struggles he had endured to make Rearden Steel a success. "All he remembered of those jobs was that the men around him had never seemed to know what to do, while he had always known" (30).

Rearden's confidence goes beyond this, however. He says to Dagny, "You and I will always be there to save the country from the consequences of their actions" (84). Later he says, "it's we who move the world and it's we who'll pull it though" (88). Dagny agrees. They were wrong, but they came as close to achieving the impossible as anyone could have because of their extraordinary competence.

It is Francisco d'Anconia, however, who is the symbol of "pure talent" (93) in the novel:

> Francisco could do anything he undertook, he could do it better than anyone else, and he did it without effort. There was no boasting in his manner and consciousness, no thought of comparison. His attitude was not: "I can do it better than you," but simply: "I can do it." What he meant by doing was doing superlatively.
>
> No matter what discipline was required of him by his father's exacting plan for his education, no matter what subject he was ordered to study, Francisco mastered it with effortless amusement. (94)

During his summer visits to the Taggart estate, he masters baseball and driving a speedboat in no time. He also designs a system of pulleys to make an elevator to the top of a rock using a primitive form of a differential equation. He does this when he is twelve years old (93). Later, he secretly becomes the best furnace foreman Rearden ever had. And it required a brilliant mind to destroy d'Anconia Copper over many years without the public detecting it. The destruction, of course, was in the name of his freedom to produce in the future. We know that Francisco has the ability to rebuild his copper empire once he is free to do so.

John Galt is a genius inventor whose motor will someday revolutionize the production of electricity.

The self-confidence of the heroes in the novel, however, goes deeper than their scholastic or business ability. They have the confidence that comes with genuine self-esteem caused by their unceasing reliance on their power to think.[1] In a passage that would astonish modern psychologists who believe that self-esteem comes from social approval, Dagny and Rearden have the following exchange:

> "[Most women are] never sure that they ought to be wanted. I am."
> "I do admire self-confidence."
> "Self-confidence was only one part of what I said, Hank."
> "What's the whole?"
> "Confidence of my value—and yours. . . ."
> "Are you saying . . . that I rose in your estimation when you found that I wanted you?"
> "Of course."
> "That's not the reaction of most people to being wanted. . . . Most people feel that they rise in their own eyes if others want them."
> "I feel that others live up to me, if they want me." (375)

Contrast Dagny with her brother. James has little or no ability and does not want to try to be great, only to be thought great by others. (Note the similarity, in this respect, to Peter Keating in *The Fountainhead*.) Thus James' deception of Cherryl who believes, until she learns the truth, that he is the guiding genius behind Taggart Transcontinental. His "self-esteem" is only self-delusion.

In addition to being able and confident themselves, the heroes in *Atlas Shrugged* value—virtually worship—ability in others. Others' ability is not viewed as a threat to their self-esteem, as with the villains, but as a pre-condition of their own business success. John Galt knows this too, which is why he takes away every person of ability that Dagny and Hank—and the country—need.

Before Dagny lost Owen Kellogg, she had planned to promote him. "[S]he had always looked for sparks of competence, like a diamond prospector in an unpromising wasteland" (17). Later: "It was only in the first few years that she [Dagny] felt herself screaming silently, at times, for a glimpse of human ability" (52). Later, as society collapses, she does not have time to feel, only to act.

In Galt's Gulch one of the strikers, Andrew Stockton, says to Dagny: "Any man who's afraid of hiring the best ability he can find, is a cheat who's in a business where he doesn't belong. To me—the foulest man on earth, more contemptible than a criminal, is the employer who rejects men for being too good" (725). But the character in *Atlas Shrugged* who risks his life specifically for ability, is a pirate, Ragnar Danneskjöld. He explains to Rearden: "my only love, the only value I care to live for, is that which has never been loved by the world, has never won recognition of friends or defenders: human ability. That is the love I am serving—and if I should lose my life, to what better purpose could I give it?" (580).[2]

It must be stressed that the business heroes in *Atlas Shrugged*, like Ayn Rand in real life, despite being exceptionally talented, put enormous effort into their work. For Ayn Rand and her fictional characters, natural ability was critical, but only the starting point for adult success, not its effortless guarantee. (I will come back to the issue of effortful action in a later section.) Effort aside, however, it is obvious that some people are just more able than others, including with respect to wealth creation.[3]

Why do the heroes in the novel, and Ayn Rand, worship ability?

The answer is metaphysical. In reality, our lives depend on the capacity of men to formulate and attain productive goals. It takes ability to create wealth or to make any great discovery. In contrast, the novel's villains fear and resent ability in others. They fear it because it makes them look inadequate—which they are. But, more fundamentally, they resent it because it means that some people achieve more success and rewards than others, which threatens their ideal of altruism.

INDEPENDENCE

Ability, in addition to rational thinking and practical success, breeds confidence. Confidence encourages independence. Independent thinking reciprocally builds confidence. The business heroes do not decide what to believe or how to act on the basis of feelings, the opinions of authority figures, or on majority opinion. They look at the facts firsthand, evaluate them firsthand, and decide what is right. Consider Dagny's response when James challenges her choice of Rearden Metal for the new rails.

> ". . . whose opinion did you take?"
> "I don't ask for opinions."
> "What do you go by?"
> "Judgment."
> "Well, whose judgment did you take?"
> "Mine." (20–21)

Later in the book Ayn Rand writes of Dagny: "She was fifteen when it occurred to her for the first time that women did not run railroads and that people might object, To hell with that, she thought—and never worried about it again" (51). Observe here that Dagny is defying the whole of society, and yet does not give it second thought. Seeking the approval of others is totally alien to her way of drawing conclusions and making decisions.

One of the best lines in *Atlas Shrugged* comes just before the first run of the John Galt Line. Dagny is asked by a reporter: "Tell me, Miss Taggart, what's going to support a seven-thousand ton train on a three-thousand ton bridge?" Dagny answers: "My judgment" (238).

Rearden recognizes her independence (and ability) when he recognizes what the initial success of the John Galt Line means: "All the roads to wealth that they're scrambling for now, it's your strength that broke them open. The strength to stand against everyone. The strength to recognize no will but your own" (268).

Independence is a trait that Rearden shares with Dagny. Early in the novel Paul Larkin is lamenting Rearden's bad press.

> "The newspapers are against you. . . ."
> "What do they write about me? . . ."
> "That your only goal is to make steel and to make money."
> "But that *is* my only goal."
> ". . . .They think that your attitude is anti-social."
> "I don't give a damn what they think." (39)

Dagny is fully conscious of his independence:

> [During the first run of the John Galt Line] She glanced at Rearden. He stood against the wall, unaware of the crowds, indifferent to admiration. He was watching the performance of track and train with an expert's intensity of professional interest; his bearing suggested that he would kick aside, as irrelevant, any thought such as "They like it," when the thought ringing in his mind was: "It works!" (243)

Rearden's independence is also revealed at his trial. He defies the conventional moral slogan—the public good—that dominates the country and the entire world in the name of his right to trade freely with other men in his own self-interest. His defiant statement: "The public good be damned" (481) is based on a statement made by William Vanderbilt, the son of a famous real-world wealth creator, Cornelius Vanderbilt,[4] and expresses Rearden's refusal to accept the morality of altruism. Even his fellow businessmen condemn him for his ideas, but he does not back down.

The business heroes are also independent because they are self-reliant. Unlike James Taggart and Orren Boyle, they seek no favors or handouts from the government and would be horrified at the thought of getting them. They want only to be left alone to do their work and take their own risks.

VISION AND PURPOSE

The term "vision" is widely used in the business world today, though the definitions of the term vary. In the context of business, I will use the term to mean seeing the future or potential value of a product, technology, or service.[5]

As we will see, however, some of the heroes in the novel are visionary in an even wider sense.

Purpose refers to the conscious intent to achieve a certain end. Francisco tells Dagny when she is fifteen years old that the most depraved type of human being is: "The man without a purpose" (99). Later, Rearden says the same thing to Francisco, not realizing at this point how much Francisco, who poses as a worthless playboy, actually knows (148). But why is purpose important? Because it motivates goal-directed action, including the actualization of a vision, and goal-directed action is the essence of life itself.[6] The man without a purpose is negating his own existence. In the most fundamental sense, he is not human even though he may physically survive owing to the purposeful actions of others. The converse of purpose is: stagnation—the state of living death.

Now consider Rearden's thoughts about his new metal:

> the one thought held immovable across a span of ten years, under everything he did and everything he saw, the thought held in his mind when he looked at the buildings of a city, at the track of a railroad, at the light in the windows of a distant farmhouse, at the knife in the hands of a beautiful woman cutting a piece of fruit at a banquet, the thought of a metal alloy that would do more than steel had ever done, a metal that would be to steel what steel had been to iron. (30)

Observe the purposeful, visionary thinking process involved here. He is considering the potential of a product that does not yet exist but which he plans to bring into existence. He is thinking of the numerous uses to which such a metal could be put.

Note also the time span involved: ten years. Dagny is equally purposeful in building the John Galt Line. Although the time span was shorter, she understands the Line's potential value. Compare Rearden and Dagny to the villains who subject the businessmen to a never-ending series of regulations without any thought (or rather the deliberate evasion) of the long-range consequences. There is no vision, only self-induced blindness. Labor leader Fred Kinnan is the most "honest" of the looters in that he does not engage in any self-deception regarding the consequences of the looters' stream of business-destroying directives. He says to them: "I'm playing the game as you've set it up and I'm going to play for as long as it lasts—which isn't going to be long for any of us!" (542). Because the government directives are based on emotion and altruism, and not reason, there is no thought about the inevitable consequences. Nor is there a desire for any thought, because that would force the villains to acknowledge the real goal of their actions: destruction for the sake of destruction.

Francisco d'Anconia knows the potential of d'Anconia Copper as well as his own ability. His initial life purpose reveals enormous ambition. In his childhood he is quizzed in a hostile manner by James Taggart, who asks "What are you after?" Francisco replies, "Money." When James asks, "Don't you have enough?" Francisco answers, "In his life time, every one of my ancestors raised the production of d'Anconia Copper by about ten percent. I intend to raise it by one hundred"[7] (96).

Banker Midas Mulligan is also visionary—about men. He can see from talking to a man and looking at his record, which meant judging his character and ability, whether he is a good risk or not. He finances Rearden's business enterprises, early in Rearden's career, because he sees Rearden's potential for earning wealth. He goes on strike when a court orders him to lend money to an incompetent moocher, Lee Hunsacker. Mulligan envisions the disastrous consequences of financing men like Hunsacker instead of men like Rearden (742).

Dagny expresses her own vision to John Galt during her stay in Galt's Gulch: "I want you to know this. I started my life with a single absolute: that the world was mine to shape in the image of my highest values" (812). Her more specific purpose is to save Taggart Transcontinental from bankruptcy and then to make it grow and prosper. She has the ability and drive to succeed but has to fail ultimately in the face of the altruist code that makes success impossible. She is overconfident, because she does not see until the end of the novel that ability and effort cannot overcome a moral code that leads a person to help his enemies survive at the expense of his own life and values.

John Galt has the vision to see the potential of his motor which is based on an entirely new concept of energy and would revolutionize the production of electricity. But he is visionary on an even more fundamental scale—on a scale that, in the real world, only an Ayn Rand or her equal could grasp or formulate. Galt's broadest vision is: a complete philosophical revolution. His vision is the precondition of saving the world from destruction by establishing the foundation for all future production. He grasps that irrationalism, including altruism, is destroying the world. He identifies that altruism is the morality of death, and that the world's moral code has to be changed so that wealth creators and all men of mind, including himself, have a chance—not to mention the people of lesser ability whose survival depends on them.

Galt is also visionary in another way. He sees how his philosophy could be made to come to fruition: by convincing men of ability to refuse to work under the code of altruism and thus let altruism destroy itself.

Galt's long-range purpose then becomes, first, to drain the brains of the world so that there will be no one left to help altruism succeed and the world would collapse—a process that requires twelve years. Second, he would slash away centuries of error and present a totally new, pro-life philosophy based on reason and egoism and make possible a world in which businessmen, and all men, were free to function. Third, he would then be free to further develop and sell his motor—and make an enormous profit.

PASSIONATE LOVE OF WEALTH CREATION

The business heroes in *Atlas Shrugged* are passionate valuers—they value their work because they value the process of thinking and creating, and, at the deepest level, the process of living itself—they love purposeful action. In her youth, Dagny "felt the excitement of solving problems . . . of taking up a challenge and then disposing of it . . . the eagerness to meet another, harder test" (51). Much later in the book, when she decides to leave the valley, she explains her reason: "I cannot bring myself to abandon to destruction all the greatness of the world, all that which was mine and yours, which was made by us and is still ours by right" (807). She loves her work too much, as well as being too confident about her ability to save the world.

Francisco then acknowledges her love for her railroad but expresses the conviction that she will eventually join the strikers: "The only man never to be redeemed is the man without passion" (808).

Rearden is not one of the irredeemable. His mooching brother Phil accuses Rearden of having a neurosis, because he loves his work so much (34). In reality, neurotic obsession with one's work does exist, but it stems from fear and self-doubt. The motivation is negative. The goal of such work is to relieve the doubt, but it does not work, because the self-doubt does not stem from lack of work achievement but from deeper feelings of inadequacy. Rearden's "obsession" with his work is healthy; it stems not from self-doubt but from positive motivation, from love for what he is doing.

It may be asked, what do the business heroes love more: the process of production or the money they make from it? The answer is: they love both. In reality the two are ultimately inseparable in the realm of business. It is through production, and only through production (direct or indirect) that wealth is created. Money, that is, currency, is only a claim on actual wealth.[8] Furthermore, the money earned through past production provides the fuel for future production.

The man who is willing to spend his career trying to produce without material rewards (e.g., for "spiritual rewards") is a martyr. In reality, a true altruist (e.g., a Mother Teresa) would not be motivated to *produce* anything. And a man like Orren Boyle, who wants to get money without earning it through production, is a looter who can only survive as a parasite. Both types are anathema to the business heroes in *Atlas Shrugged*.

There is one other possible category to consider: a man, like Mr. Mowen, who wants money but does not really enjoy the process by which he makes it, that is, does not love his work. A common cause of such a condition is mistakenly basing self-esteem on the amount of money one makes (and can show off) rather than its real cause, reliance on one's power to think.[9] Such a man is dooming himself to a lifetime of misery. His work would be drudgery, devoid of all pleasure. Nor will such a man be a creator. As Howard Roark says to Peter Keating in *The Fountainhead*, "to get things done you must love the doing."[10]

There is no dichotomy between love of production and love of money in the business heroes. They hold the same view as Francisco that, "To love money is to know and love the fact that money is the creation of the best power within you" (412). In this sense, making money, rather than being shameful, is, to the business heroes—and in reality— virtuous. Observe also Ayn Rand's total rejection of the widely held (Marxist) view that making money is a purely materialistic endeavor which has nothing to do with man's consciousness. Wealth creation, as *Atlas Shrugged* demonstrates, is the product of man's mind.[11]

The villains in the novel, of course, have a very different motivation. They have no ability to create and do not love—or more precisely, they resent— both production and money. James agrees with the Bible that (love of) money is the root of all evil. He does not have any actual (positive) values at all. He does not actually *want* money any more than he wants to have adulterous sex with Lillian Rearden. He and the other villains, however, do seek to *get*, rather than earn, money—through scheming, manipulation, and government favors. They want power for the "pleasure" of destroying the real producers. (The deepest motive of the looters and power lusters, the Morality of Death, is explained in Galt's Speech.)

COMMITMENT TO TENACIOUS ACTION

The business heroes are not content to formulate visions and feel passionate. They want to act to make the visions real, the passion to lead to something concrete. Dagny's commitment to action is shown in the first chapter of the book when she takes charge of a train stalled due to a malfunctioning signal. She felt "the hard, exhilarating pleasure of action" (17).

Later, James sarcastically says to the Board of Directors: "My dear sister does not happen to be a human being, but just an internal combustion engine" (229). His observation has an element of truth: Dagny is an internal combustion engine, one driven to persistent action by thought and values. Contrary to James's assertion, however, she is not only human but represents the essence of what it means to be human.

During the first run of the John Galt Line she thinks:

First, the vision—then the physical shape to express it. First, the thought—then the purposeful motion down the straight line of a single track to a chosen goal. Could one have any meaning without the other? Wasn't it evil to wish without moving—or to move without aim? (240–41)

Commitment to action persists even when the heroes are faced with seemingly insurmountable obstacles or setbacks. When Dagny learns of the new government regulations that will ultimately destroy Colorado, she is horrified. She knows that Ellis Wyatt will go on strike and that she has to try and stop him. Her unbreached determination is revealed in her thoughts at this moment:

> And because, were she lying crushed under the ruins of a building, were she torn by the bomb of an air raid, so long as she was still in existence she would know that action is man's foremost obligation regardless of anything he feels—she was able to run down the platform [to a telephone booth and try to call Wyatt]. (334)

Rearden is equally tenacious. He recalls how difficult it was to create Rearden Metal:

> —the nights spent in the workshop of his home, over sheets of paper which he filled with formulas, then torn up in angry failure . . . [his staff fighting] a hopeless battle . . . [and thinking] ". . . it can't be done."
> —the meals, interrupted and abandoned at the sudden flash of a new thought . . . to be tried . . . to be worked on for months, and to be discarded as another failure. (29)

It required ten years of unrelenting work before he succeeded. Even when he was totally exhausted, he did not quit:

> He saw an evening when he sat slumped across his desk. . . . He was tired. . . . He had burned everything there was to burn within him; he had scattered so many sparks to start so many things—and he wondered whether someone could give him now the spark he needed, now when he felt unable ever to rise again. He asked himself who had started him and kept him going. Then he raised his head. Slowly, with the greatest effort of his life, he made his body rise until he was able to sit upright with only one hand pressed against the desk and a trembling arm to support him. He never asked that question again. (30–31)

During the furnace breakout when Francisco and he work together to stop it, Rearden is described as having "the exultant feeling of action, of his own capacity, of his body's precision, of its response to his will" (457). Earlier in the novel he is described as having "joyous, boundless power" (40). No matter what burdens and setbacks Rearden faces—the loss of ore supplies, of coal, of copper, of competent workmen, or strangling government directives—he never stops taking action until the day goons try to take over his business by force, and Francisco explains to him the philosophical issues involved in this attack, his own past struggles, and the collapsing economy. One is reminded here of Aristotle's concept (discussed by him in a cosmological context) of the unmoved or prime mover (which was his conception of god): "If everything in motion is moved by something, and the [prime] mover is moved but not by anything else, it must be moved by itself."[12] Rearden, Dagny, and the other business heroes were self-movers in the deepest sense. They thought and acted by volitional choice.

Only when the copper suppliers on whom Rearden depended are virtually destroyed by a new set of government edicts does he temporarily lose the desire to do anything. He recalls that he had never before "reached the ultimate ugliness of abandoning the will to act" (374) even during times of struggle and suffering. But faced with the use of physical force by the government, he sees that purposeful action is, right then, impossible. By crushing the possibility of action, by paralyzing the mind, the government is crushing his spirit— his love of existence, even his desire for Dagny. But even here, he soon regains his love of the world, his desire to act and his romantic passion. His spirit is not to be destroyed by a setback.

Dagny too was temporarily bereft of any desire to act after McNamara, the only good contractor left, quit. "She felt suddenly empty of energy, of purpose, of desire, as if a motor had crackled and stopped" (65). But, like Rearden, she recovered.

Contrast Rearden and Dagny to Ben Nealy, Dagny's main contractor for the John Galt Line. Nealy does not want to destroy the producers but resents the effort that doing a good job requires, especially the effort of thinking. His belief is: "muscles—that's all it takes to build anything in the world" (162). Ayn Rand is here alluding to Karl Marx's erroneous view that only physical labor creates value. Nealy is not a villain in the novel, but his commitment to action is much weaker than that of the heroes. He is sullen and passive in the face of obstacles and resents being held to his assigned objectives. He is not a self-mover but needs constant instruction from Dagny.

The passionate commitment to action, including the integration of thought and action, in the heroes of *Atlas Shrugged* reveals Ayn Rand's rejection of any version of the mind-body dichotomy as well as her conviction that integrity is a cardinal virtue.[13]

JUSTICE

The business heroes are uncompromisingly pro-justice. Dagny is infuriated at the destruction of a competitor, the Phoenix Durango Railroad, by the National Railroad Alliance, a collectivistic, private organization.

Dagny and Rearden always seek the best talent available and pay everyone what they are worth. They deal with their customers through mutual self-interest. They function by what Ayn Rand calls "the trader principle," exchanging value for value through voluntary consent.

Dagny, Rearden, and the novel's other heroes do not hire or reward people who do not deserve it. For example, consider the attempt of Rearden's mother to convince him to give his worthless brother, Philip, a job. She whines:

"He [Philip] wants to be independent of you."
"By means of getting from me a salary he can't earn for work he can't do?"
"You'd never miss it. You've got enough people here who're making money for you."

"Are you asking me to help him stage a fraud of that kind?"
". . . You have no mercy for anybody."
"Do you think a fraud of this kind would be just? . . . Don't ever speak to me
again about a job for Philip." (208)

Francisco's pro-justice actions are focused on punishment rather than on reward or on the refusal to hire incompetents. The punishment, of course, is indirect. He lets the looters count on his judgment and productivity while actually withholding them. Francisco "discovers" the San Sebastián mines and the looters take it on faith that the mines must be valuable, because they know that Francisco is involved. But they never look for any facts about the mines, nor do they investigate the political risks of investing within a socialist state. They buy up the stock only to see the mines nationalized; furthermore, the mines turn out to be worthless. The looters think they can get money through theft, without thinking. The justice here is that the looters, including the Mexican government, get exactly what they deserve: nothing.

The same thing happens later in the novel on a larger scale when d'Anconia Copper is nationalized by the People's State of Chile. The government finds that there is no d'Anconia Copper left to nationalize. Francisco has gradually and secretly destroyed it. The Chilean government gets nothing and the various looters who invested in the company lose everything. Again, the enraged looters get just what they deserve.

In a different way, Ragnar Danneskjöld also promotes justice—by correcting injustice. He turns looted wealth into gold and deposits it into accounts that he creates for the business heroes in proportion to the income taxes they have paid.

More broadly, the whole of Atlas Shrugged is a hymn to justice. The altruists loot and undermine every man of ability that they can get their hands on, until there are no more victims to be found. John Galt has taken them away. The victims have withdrawn their sanction. The looters then suffer the logical and just consequences of their corrupt philosophy: the total collapse of society. In organizing the strike, John Galt is the prime orchestrator of justice on a world scale. At a deeper level, however, the avenger in the novel is reality itself. The looters are trying to practice a contradiction. They want to enforce altruism, an irrational and antilife moral doctrine, through coercion and to get wealth (at least temporarily), while at the same time destroying freedom and thus making production of wealth—and life—impossible.

On the positive side, Galt's speech gives the producers the justice they deserve: the recognition of their morality.

MOTIVE POWER AND THE PROFIT MOTIVE

The term "motive power" is used throughout the novel. When first introduced, it refers to the need for engines to power Taggart Transcontinental trains. James

Taggart, trying to explain why the railroad is running just one, coal-burning engine a day on the San Sebastián Line, explains: "we had a little trouble with our motive power" (49). Dagny thinks, "Motive power . . . rested on the engines that rolled across a continent" (64). Eddie Willers, still referring to engines, makes a more profound statement than he realizes: "Motive power—you can't imagine how important that is. That's the heart of everything" (63).

The term, even when used in the context of engines, is really a metaphor. Its deeper meaning (which James, Eddie, and even Dagny are unaware of) pertains to the motivation of men. Dagny talks about being "the motive power of her own happiness" (65), but does not identify the root issue. Francisco identifies it for Rearden: "Man's motive power is his moral code" (455). The moral code of the business heroes is: rational egoism, the code that makes it possible to produce engines—and everything else on which man's life depends. Given their motive power in the realm of morality, the business heroes are prime movers of the economy. They are to the country what the engines are to the train.

The business heroes possess motive power in abundance. Rearden feels no guilt about the fact that he is working for himself. He tells Francisco at Lillian's party: "the man who works, works for himself. . . . I don't want any part of that tripe about working for others. I'm not" (147).

In his conversation with Dr. Potter of the government's State Science Institute, who wants to buy the rights to (stop making) his Metal, Potter asks, "why do you want to struggle for years, squeezing out your gains in the form of pennies per ton. . . Why?" Rearden answers, "Because it's *mine*" (181). At his trial, Rearden, to the astonishment of the judges and the courtroom audience, asserts, "I work for nothing but my own profit" (480).

There is one point at which Rearden tells Dagny: "We're a couple of blackguards, aren't we?" (87). Later he says to Francisco "you're thinking . . . that I'm selfish, conceited, heartless, cruel. I am" (147). What he means is that Dagny and he are evil according to conventional morality (altruism). However, Rearden does not really believe, deep down, that he is a blackguard. He does not experience any genuine guilt about his business—in contrast to what he feels about his relationship with his wife.

Rearden's unjust burden is symbolized early in the novel after he gives Lillian a bracelet made from the first batch of Rearden Metal: "'A chain,' she said. 'Appropriate, isn't it? It's the chain by which he holds us all in bondage'" (43). The irony of this statement is only revealed later. It is Rearden who is in bondage to his family, whose contemptuous treatment of him he sanctioned for years, because he did not understand the evil of their moral code nor the virtue of his own. Even in business, though free of fundamental guilt, he cannot experience full moral pride, because he does not understand how virtuous he is.

Rearden's implicit philosophy is correct, but like the other business heroes, he cannot validate it. They do not know how to identify or defend their virtues philosophically. As Francisco explains to Rearden: "You have been willing to carry the load of an unearned punishment—and to let it grow the heavier the greater the virtues you practiced. . . . Your own moral code—the one you lived by but never stated, acknowledged or defended—was the code that preserves man's existence" (455). Galt's speech provides the full validation of rational egoism.

Dan Conway presents an intermediate case of motive power. He is a good businessman who selfishly loves his work, but he does not have enough motive power to protest being sacrificed by the National Railroad Alliance. He accepts, at some level, the legitimacy of collectivism (what he calls "majority rule") even while hating it. As a result he is unable to act when confronted by a monstrous injustice.

The villains in the novel possess no motive power at all. They possess only one weapon: knowing how to cash in on the morality of altruism, and thereby to get the men of mind to serve them by sanctioning a wrong moral code. The villains exploit their philosophically helpless victim—until John Galt and his allies identify and validate the moral code held subconsciously by the producers.

Galt convinces them to withdraw their sanction and thereby stops the motor of the world. The ultimate motor was not an engine but an idea: genuine moral virtue—rational egoism.

CONCLUSION

In today's intellectual climate, just as "business ethics" is considered an oxymoron, so is it considered ludicrous to pair "making money" and "virtue." Moneymaking is widely considered to be a product of irrational, mindless greed and dishonesty. The selfish pursuit of profit is considered axiomatically to be evil and altruism to be good. No moral credit is given for making money, only for giving it away. This is called "giving back," as though you took something that you had no right to.

Atlas Shrugged smashes these distortions and misconceptions at root.

Making money, which means creating wealth, is shown to be caused by virtue. But the virtues involved are not the conventional ones such as altruism, piety, mercy, and faith. The core virtue is rationality, which includes taking reality seriously, which requires honesty. Other corollaries of reason include independence (reliance on one's own judgment), integrity (taking actions consistent with one's judgment), and justice. Productiveness is a consequence of reasoned action. Pride is the sum of all virtues. (Of course, these virtues are not only for making money. They apply to every sphere of human functioning.)

Ability too is required to earn money. Wealth is not created by mindless manual labor but by creative intelligence, which includes the ability to envision products or services that customers value. Wealth creators must value ability in others because any business exceeding a one-man shop requires the work of other (even hundreds or thousands of) individuals. Ability alone, of course, is not enough. Long term effort and tenacious action are required to make ability pay off.

Finally, the wealth creator must have a profoundly selfish interest in his work. He must put forth enormous effort, passionately love what he does, and value the rewards productivity brings, including money.

These traits are not mere fictions applicable only in the universe of *Atlas Shrugged*. The traits that made the business heroes in *Atlas Shrugged* successful are the same traits that make real-life businessmen successful.[14] But this earthshaking novel provides something which, prior to its publication, no real businessman ever had: an explicit validation of the morality of wealth creation, which means: of capitalism.

John Galt's great gift to the businessman was this:

> I have called out on strike the kind of martyrs who had never deserted you before. I have given them the weapon they had lacked: the knowledge of their own moral value. I have taught them that the world is ours, whenever we choose to claim it, by virtue and grace of the fact that ours is the Morality of Life. They, the great victims who had produced all the wonders of humanity's brief summer, they, the industrialists, the conquerors of matter, had not discovered the nature of their right. They had known that theirs was the power. I taught them that theirs was the glory. (1051)

NOTES

1. See Edwin A. Locke, "The Educational, Psychological, and Philosophical Assault on Self-Esteem," *The Objective Standard*, Vol. 1, No. 4, 2006–2007, 65–82.

2. One might ask why Ayn Rand put such stress on natural ability—as opposed to acquired ability or skill. The explanation could be partly autobiographical. She taught herself to read. She was a brilliant student from a very young age. She found school boring and secretly wrote novels in class. Like Dagny, she excelled in mathematics. At the age of twelve she identified conceptually the process of thinking in principles and the use of reason. She also rejected the ethics of altruism. And at the age of thirteen she chose atheism over religion, based on her previous discovery of reason. In college, which she entered at sixteen, she was intelligent enough to see the value of Aristotle's philosophy and its superiority to other philosophies. (See Jeff Britting, *Ayn Rand* [New York: Overlook Duckworth, 2004] for a short biography of Ayn Rand.) She rejected Plato's ideas and indicated to her professor that she had her own ideas about philosophy. She was already confident that her ideas would become part of the history of philosophy. There is no doubt that Ayn Rand was a prodigy who had supreme confidence in herself. She had to know that not just anyone could achieve what she achieved.

However, it is also clear from the events of her own life that natural ability, by itself, did not imply an easy road to practical or career success. In her life in America she endured a terribly difficult struggle, not only to earn a living but to become a successful writer—a writer whose philosophy defied the entire Judeo-Christian ethic. She worked endless hours for decades on her writing—and had to master a new language to do it. It took her seven years to write *The Fountainhead* and thirteen years to write *Atlas Shrugged*.

3. See Edwin A. Locke, *The Prime Movers: Traits of the Great Wealth Creators*, second edition (Irvine, Calif.: Ayn Rand Institute Press, forthcoming).

4. Locke, *Prime Movers*.

5. Locke, *Prime Movers*.

6. Ayn Rand, *The Virtue of Selfishness: A New Concept of Egoism* (New York: Signet, 1964).

7. A technical clarification is needed here. Assuming production increases are roughly proportional to profit increases, increasing production/profits by ten percent in a lifetime would be extremely poor performance. Consider a forty-year career as CEO—that would be an increase in profits of only 0.25 percent per year, which would be virtual stagnation. An increase of 100 percent over forty years would only be 2.5 percent per year—which would also be considered relatively poor performance. In business an increase in profits of 10 percent per year is considered good performance. I believe that Ayn Rand could have meant the percentage increases to be annual. A 100 percent per year increase, though not sustainable indefinitely, could be sustained for many years by a brilliant businessman starting from a low enough base. Technical issues aside, however, the best way to interpret the above quote is that Francisco is markedly more able, confident, and ambitious than his family predecessors.

8. See Ayn Rand "Egalitarianism and Inflation," *The Ayn Rand Letter*, Vol. III, Nos. 18–20, and the "Money Speech" in *Atlas Shrugged* (410–15).

9. See Locke, "Educational, Psychological, and Philosophical Assault on Self-Esteem."

10. Ayn Rand, *The Fountainhead* (New York: Bobbs-Merrill, 1943; Signet fiftieth anniversary paperback edition, 1993), 578.

11. See Locke, *Prime Movers*.

12. Aristotle, *Physics* VIII 5, in J. Barnes, ed., *The Complete Works of Aristotle*, Vol. 1 (Princeton, NJ: Princeton University Press, 1984), 428.

13. For a discussion of the virtue of integrity see Leonard Peikoff, *Objectivism: The Philosophy of Ayn Rand* (New York: Dutton, 1991), 259–67.

14. See Locke, *Prime Movers*.

18

"Humanity's Darkest Evil"

The Lethal Destructiveness of Non-Objective Law

Tara Smith

INTRODUCTION

The law is an ominous presence throughout *Atlas Shrugged*, as we witness its society's government impose increasingly restrictive laws that send people tumbling back to primitive conditions. Yet law's role is secondary; the novel is not *about* political issues. What the prime movers gradually realize is not simply that theirs is a corrupt legal system, but that the entire philosophy on which it is premised—and which is the source of all the forms of victimization they are subjected to, in their personal lives as well as those imposed through law—is invalid. While *Atlas* clearly carries lessons for the legal realm, at its most fundamental, the book concerns the role of the mind in human life and the code of values that that necessitates.

Against that knowledge, it is striking to read Judge Narragansett observe that non-objective law is "humanity's darkest evil, the most destructive horror machine among all the devices of men" (737). Given the depth of the other vices that Ayn Rand exposes in the book (which include hatred of the good for being the good and the rejection of life itself), surely, one might suppose, this sweeping condemnation is literary hyperbole.[1] If politics is derivative from ethics, how can a certain character of law be humanity's darkest evil?

Ayn Rand typically chooses her words carefully. Whatever cautions are appropriate against reading fiction as an exact statement of an author's philosophical convictions, the unqualified character of Narragansett's statement on such a significant topic merits serious consideration. How destructive *is* non-objective law? The answer is important not only for better understanding the novel, but for understanding our own political situation.[2]

This paper will investigate the meaning of Narragansett's assessment. To understand his claim, we must understand the stakes. Thus I will begin by explaining the essential nature and the profound value of objective law. I will then focus on the distinctive character of non-objective law, to appreciate its destructive effects. Because the proper nature of law depends on the proper nature of government, which itself depends on the nature of physical force and on human beings' need for freedom, much of the discussion will be rather abstract, as we must unpeel several layers of foundational premises. Only by explaining these, however, will we be able to appreciate the truly devastating destruction wrought by non-objective law, both in *Atlas* and in the world around us.

WHAT OBJECTIVE LAW IS

Skepticism toward Narragansett's assessment arises, in large part, from widespread haziness about exactly what objective law is. Most people do have a dim sense of objective law from their familiarity with the ideal of the rule of law. That ideal is typically understood to consist of a number of conditions. Among them: that a government's powers and the rules by which it exercises those powers be stated in plain, readily intelligible terms, promulgated in advance of their application. Retroactive laws are not permitted. Laws must be stable in that they do not frequently or abruptly change and they remain binding until formally altered through pre-established procedures. No contradictory rules may be enacted; laws must be mutually consistent so that each of them can actually be obeyed. Consistency in application is important, as well: laws must be applied equally to like cases. The law is authoritative; its resolutions of disputes are respected as final.

While different scholars would delineate the precise features of the rule of law in slightly differing terms, all accept at least these core ingredients.[3] In deliberate contrast with the rule of men, the requirements of the rule of law are designed to protect individuals from the passions, prejudices, mistakes, and sheer arbitrariness to which human beings are susceptible.[4] When law is what governs a society, a government's rules are spelled out in objectively verifiable terms, for all to know. People are able to plan and coordinate their activities with knowledge of what steps would incur legal penalties. They know what to expect and are able to comply. Moreover—crucially—the rulers themselves are constrained by the law.[5] While it is obviously men who enact any government's laws, the distinction with the rule of men highlights the fact that under the rule of law, the authority of rulers must itself be law-governed. Any actions that rulers take and any rules they impose must be created within the scope of their legitimate authority and must then be applied to them as well as to everyone else in that society. Rulers are bound by laws as much as ordinary citizens.

While all of this goes some way toward clarifying the nature of objective law, it does not go far enough. Notice that these most commonly cited elements of the rule of law address the form of law, rather than its substance. Yet there would be no point in maintaining the niceties of objective form if the substance that those formally correct laws served were unwarranted. Invalid content would sabotage the value of objective form in law, just as invalid form would sabotage the value of objective content. Laws that restricted aspects of individuals' actions that the government had no basis for restricting would not be made any more valid by the precision or lead time with which they were announced, for instance. By the same token, the validity of a law that violated formal requirements of clarity or mutual consistency could not be rescued by the fact that that law sought to achieve a perfectly valid substantive end (such as protection of private property). Both valid form and valid content are crucial to truly objective law. Indeed, knowledge of the proper content of law helps to establish what law's proper form is, since form follows function.[6]

What is the proper content of law? And what determines objectivity in regard to both the law's content and form?

In order to grasp the fundamental character of objective law, first consider the nature of objectivity itself. In any realm, objectivity is a matter of reaching conclusions on the basis of logical inference from relevant facts. Broadly, a conclusion (or policy, procedure, decision, etc.) is objective insofar as it is governed by the way things are—the relevant things—rather than by any person(s)'s subjective beliefs about or attitudes toward the way things are.[7] In a legal system, which facts are relevant depends on the purpose of law, which, in turn, depends on the purpose of government. Since law is the means through which a government carries out its charge, it is the purpose of government that sets the standard for objectivity in law.

Accordingly, "objective law" designates a legal system that strictly serves the proper purpose of government. All of its specific laws are necessitated by that purpose and advance it by means that carry no countervailing damage.[8] What determines what a particular law should be is that which authorizes the existence of law, in the first place. The mission of law as a whole establishes the proper parameters around the content and form of any particular law. In order to be objective, a law may neither do something *else*, attempting to advance some additional goal that is beyond the authorized role of government, nor do anything that directly undercuts the government's ability to serve its proper function as effectively as possible. A legal system that deviates from objectivity in regard to either law's form or law's content amounts to an abuse of power. For through such departures, it licenses the government to exercise its power in ways that are not justified by the specific function for which it was given that power. (I will expand on this below.)

Given that the objectivity of law is established by the purpose of government, we need, next, to look more closely at what that purpose is.

The Purpose of Government

"A country's political system is based on its code of morality," Rand writes in Galt's Speech. A proper political system is built on "the premise that man is an end in himself, not the means to the ends of others, that man's life, his freedom, his happiness are *his* by inalienable right" (1061). The purpose of government is to protect man's rights.

Rights are the moral principle that defines and sanctions a man's freedom of action in a social context. More specifically, rights define an individual's entitlement to be free from "physical compulsion, coercion or interference" imposed by others. Rights protect a man's "freedom to take all the actions required by the nature of a rational being for the support, the furtherance, the fulfillment and the enjoyment of his own life."[9] Since the government is that institution within any society that holds the exclusive authority to force people to act in certain ways, the only reason for having such a coercive institution is the protection of individual rights.[10] To appreciate the crucial value of objective law in confining government to its proper purview, we must first understand the necessity of respecting individual rights.

Man survives by the use of his reason. Unlike other organisms, we are not genetically coded or instinctually "programmed" to act automatically in ways that will preserve our existence. Reason is our only means of acquiring knowledge and thereby enabling ourselves to obtain and create the goods required for our survival. We must identify "what's what" and draw logical inferences about it—we must grasp the nature of the existents around us and of the causal relations among them—in order to generate values, those things that sustain and advance our lives. Because the use of reason is volitional, however, a human being "cannot function successfully under coercion."[11] Where a man is not free to direct his own actions, he is denied his capacity to reason. This is as lethal an assault as a bullet to his heart. For whether one kills a man by a single, fatal blow or through a prolonged ordeal that bleeds him to death, one kills. Since reason is man's means of survival and since the exercise of reason requires freedom, deprivations of a man's freedom kill. Let's examine the issue still more closely.[12]

An individual's freedom is violated when another person initiates the use of force against him against his will. The direct application of physical pressure is the clearest instance, such as by beating, stabbing, poisoning, shackling, shooting, or imprisoning. Further, however, "you are forced to do something if the alternative is physical damage: you'll be seized, imprisoned, deprived of property, or killed."[13] This fact stands on the obvious difference between being persuaded to do something and being forced to do something. If I want something from you, and I attempt to persuade you to give it to me, it remains your choice whether or not to surrender it. This is so regardless of whether I employ rational arguments or nonrational tactics such as flattery or assurances of fame. Your mind, by attending to the case offered, is able to freely reach a conclusion about the advisability of agreeing to my request. If I claim the sought object by means of force, in contrast, such as by picking your pocket or threatening to beat you or to damage other of your property unless you surrender it, I render your beliefs about the wisdom of giving it to me irrelevant.

My use of force declares: "I'm getting that object and the only choice left for you is whether you will submit quietly or kick up a fuss, thereby bringing even worse upon yourself. By the power of my guns (clubs, knives, etc.), however, I am getting it; that much has been decided unilaterally, by me."[14]

The person who is subjected to force is prevented from acting as he chooses at the cost of something else that is his. He is made to choose between his money and his life, for example, or between his freedom to run his business as he likes and his ability to avoid legal penalties. He is thus thrust into a "must lose" situation. The problem is not simply that he cannot any longer retain two things that he wants and is entitled to, however (serious a problem as that is). More fundamentally, the very mechanism by which any human being can maintain his life—his capacity for rational thought—is denied him. As Galt puts it, "To interpose the threat of physical destruction between a man and his perception of reality, is to negate and paralyze his means of survival" (1023). Because this is what the initiation of force does, it is a uniquely intolerable evil.

Here again, in order to fully digest this, we should probe more deeply the destructiveness of force.[15]

When a person does something because he is forced to, he is not acting on the basis of evidence and logic. Those considerations are replaced by the need to appease the aggressor. Under such conditions, the victim is unable to proceed by reason. Force "negates" the mind, as Galt declares, not merely by depriving a man of the natural effects of his thinking, but by bringing to a halt the very *process* of thinking. As Leonard Peikoff has observed, "to the extent that someone's gun becomes a man's epistemological court of final appeal, . . . he cannot perform the processes essential to human cognition; he *cannot* think."[16]

What is at issue is not brain injury or malfunction; the paralysis is epistemological. A mind is not a physical entity like a billiard ball or a sponge or a pincushion that can be manipulated by physical objects. The mind is rooted in the brain, of course, but that is not what a mind *is*. No combination of physical pressures can generate *thought* or result in a man's believing anything. A man could feign belief by mouthing certain words, but physical sounds are not convictions. As Rand acutely demonstrates through the torture of Galt, even the infliction of excruciating pain cannot initiate a process of thinking in a man's mind. Force cannot make a mind *go*.[17] Just as intellectual activity alone cannot move physical objects, so physical manipulation alone cannot achieve intellectual effects.[18] Whether a mind thinks and what a mind thinks are the result of a series of cognitive (rather than physical) activities—of mentally focusing, identifying, attending, weighing evidence, pursuing logical implications, and so on. All of these activities are volitional, however; physical force has no power to bring them about. The upshot is well-expressed by Galt: Any threat of the form "your money or your life"—whatever the particular values being attacked—amounts to the ultimatum: "'Your mind or your life'—and neither is possible to man without the other" (1023). When a man is unable to use his mind—to reason—he is unable to act as his life requires.[19]

Since physical force has the unique capacity to thwart man's ability to reason, then, if human beings are to live together, the initiation of force must be
banished. To accomplish this, "men need an institution charged with the task
of protecting their rights under an *objective* code of rules. *This* is the task of a
government . . . [which is] *the means of placing the retaliatory use of physical force
under objective control—i.e.,* under objectively defined laws."[20] Government is
strictly "an agent of man's self-defense, and, as such, may resort to force *only*
against those who *start* the use of force" (1062).[21]

Implications for Objective Law

This function of government, again, provides the standard for objectivity
in the law, since law is the instrument through which a government fulfills
its function. While Rand is not the first to have recognized the protection of
rights as the proper task of government, as long as the object of rights has
been murky, so have the proper activities of government. When notions of
what individuals possess rights *to* are confused or invalid, different people will
demand conflicting "rights" and the government will seek to balance these
competing claims. How that balance is achieved—exactly what constitutes a
proper "balance," and of what particular factors—has historically been fluid,
left largely to a reading of the mood of the populace at a given moment. Given
this, it is crucial to an objective determination of what a government may and
may not do to pin down the exact object that rights protect.

This is what Rand's identification of rights as guardians of individual
freedom of action provides. Her identification of the fact that rights can be
violated only by the use of physical force enables us to objectively implement
the proper theory of government.[22] For the initiation of physical force against
a person is a definite, knowable activity. Rand's insight into the pivotal role
of force means that the violator of rights "is not to be detected by 'intuition,'
feeling, or vote; his action is a tangible fact, available in principle to sense perception."[23] This is not to say that the proper application of this standard will
always be transparent or that the layers of abstract reasoning beyond immediate perception that are sometimes required will never be demanding. We cannot expect the proper resolution of every new question about the parameters
of rights in cyberspace or in genetic materials, for instance, to be a snap. It is
to say, though, that the standard to be upheld to meet such challenges is firm
and clear and rationally justified.

THE VALUE OF OBJECTIVE LAW

All of this places us in better position to appreciate not only the nature but
also the critical importance of objectivity in the law. The value of objective law
lies in its crucial service to human life. More exactly, it might be summarized

in a single word: freedom. Only through a system of law that is fully objective can the government subordinate might to right. By banishing the unjustified use of force, objective law allows man the freedom that his survival demands. Indeed, because human life is sustained by rational action and because the ability to take rational action relies on a man's being free, the value of objective law is difficult to overstate. By protecting a man's freedom, objective law enables him to engage in the kind of action without which he cannot live.[24]

In order to protect individual freedom, the law must be objective in regard to both what it does and how it does it. The substance of its rules as well as their implementation (encompassing enactment and enforcement) must be justified by their service to the government's singular mission. The standard for measuring law's objectivity, again, follows straightaway from the reason for having a government in the first place. As Rand writes:

> The nature of the laws proper to a free society and the source of its government's authority are both to be derived from the nature and purpose of a proper government. . . . Since the protection of individual rights is the only proper purpose of a government, it is the only proper subject of legislation: all laws must be based on individual rights and aimed at their protection. All laws must be *objective* (and objectively justifiable): men must know clearly, and in advance of taking an action, what the law forbids them to do (and why), what constitutes a crime and what penalty they will incur if they commit it.[25]

It is not difficult to appreciate the threat posed by laws that lack legitimate content. When law restricts activities that fall within an individual's rightful domain, the individual is victimized by the very institution whose role is to protect him. His freedom is unjustifiably infringed. Less apparent but no less critical to the security of individual rights, however, is the form of law. Laws which are not implemented objectively (due to vague and ambiguous wording, for instance, or due to lax standards of proof for criminal conviction) bring the same unjust effects as laws whose content is invalid. When an ambiguous law is applied to a particular individual, for instance, that person has been denied fair notice of the rules to which he is held legally accountable and thereby denied the full, rightful exercise of his freedom. In order to stay within the confines of a law that could reasonably be interpreted to mean different things, he must refrain from certain activities that he is actually entitled to engage in. To keep the government from penalizing him, that is, he is compelled not simply to obey valid laws and to respect others' rights (which are perfectly proper demands for the law to make of him), but to constrict his activities to a still narrower course.

Because of the power of government, objectivity is vital throughout every aspect of a legal system. A government cannot be limited if its rules of operation are, thanks to non-objective form, unlimited. Insistence on objectivity is a means of ensuring that the power of government not be misapplied. No fail safe guarantees are available, of course, but the objectivity of law disciplines the government to serve only its proper purpose. Every legal restriction of a citizen poses a threat to use force against him, if he fails to obey that restriction. Only such threats that are required for the respect of individual rights can be justified. In an objective system, therefore, law's substance is limited exclusively to measures that are necessary to achieve the government's purpose and the law's form introduces no features that sabotage that purpose. While both objective content and objective form of law are extremely valuable, it is also important to recognize that we cannot truly enjoy the fruits of objectivity in regard to either without objectivity in the other. Any failure to maintain strict and complete objectivity permits an unjustified use of force by the government and thus violates individual rights. As such, it contradicts the government's reason for being.

The fact that Galt's Gulch lacks a formal government should not be taken to imply that Rand considers the true ideal to be the absence of government. While Galt tells Dagny that "we have no laws in this valley, no rules, no formal organization" (714), the gulch is not meant to be a model for large scale societal living; it is not an example of Rand's political philosophy, in practice. Mulligan remarks that the gulch is "not a state . . . not a society of any kind," but simply "a voluntary association of men" (747).[26] Bear in mind that its population consists of an extremely small number of carefully chosen residents. While Rand defends a government of strictly limited powers, she is emphatically not an anarchist. Nor does she regard government as a necessary evil. On the contrary, all of the argument thus far should make plain that government is a necessary good. For an objective legal system is a *liberator* to human beings and as such, a monumental value. Since this aspect of Rand's political philosophy is sometimes misunderstood (often, by people professing agreement with her political ideas), further clarification is useful.

Anarchy is not a prescription for liberty, Rand recognizes, but for the rule of the strongest. For its practice amounts to the complete unleashing of force. Since government is the institution designed for the objective protection of individual rights, the rejection of government as such amounts to the rejection of those rights. Contrary to its frequent lip service to rights, anarchism's "anything goes" policy implies that individuals do not possess rights that warrant respect or objective protection. And if individuals do not hold moral claims against others' forceful interference, the only thing left to stop the imposition of force is opposing force.

Anarchism is usually defended as necessary to honor *complete* freedom, in order for people to be *fully* free. Its driving contention is that no shackles whatsoever, private or public, should be tolerated. The problem, however, is that this conception of "shackles"—of what would constitute an infringement of individual freedom—reveals a subjectivist conception of rights that confuses freedom with license. In truth, the freedom to which individuals are entitled by right has a distinct identity and definite boundaries. My rights protect my freedom of action from others' initiation of physical force—period. Rights do not protect me from having unfulfilled desires. Not *anything* that a person might like to do constitutes a rightful exercise of his freedom. Correspondingly, not any restriction of my actions constitutes a violation of my freedom (or an unwarranted shackle). My desire to help myself to your wallet, for instance, would not make my seizing it an innocent exercise of my rights. If that were the case, the concept of rights would be meaningless, since any apparent violation of one man's rights would simply be the exercise of another man's rights and as such, immune to legitimate restriction. Your right to your wallet would collapse as soon as another person tried to grab it. On this view, nothing could qualify as a violation of rights. But rights that could not possibly be violated are rights that could not shield anything; *nothing* is required to respect them.[27]

The implication for the propriety of government is direct. If one views rights as license to do whatever one pleases such that anything goes in the exercise of rights, one will have no basis for recognizing a government's authority to enforce laws declaring that certain actions may not "go." Without recognition of the objective nature of rights, a government can have no valid principle of operation, no valid means of distinguishing what individuals should and should not be free to do. The subjectivist about rights, in other words, is committed to subjectivism about government (evidenced in the anarchists' frequent embrace of "competing," "private" governments). The person who recognizes the objective nature of rights, on the other hand, will recognize the propriety of a government dedicated to the objective enforcement of those rights. The need for government is a direct outgrowth of the objective nature of rights.[28]

NON-OBJECTIVE LAW . . .

Fortified with this understanding of the exact nature and value of objective law, we can now investigate more directly the malignant character of non-objective law.

Essentially, non-objective law is law that does not serve the legitimate purpose of government. It exercises coercive power to accomplish ends other than the protection of citizens' rights. Whether intentionally or unwittingly, non-objective law transgresses the boundaries that the function of government imposes on the government's activities. This might be done through the adoption of substantively invalid laws, laws whose content forbids or requires some action that it is not a government's legitimate authority to restrict. The advancement of a moral crusade to encourage people to volunteer more time to charity, for instance, or paternalistic restrictions on the foods that people consume would both reflect this sort of non-objectivity.[29] Law could also be non-objective in virtue of being poorly crafted. Ambiguous language or retroactive law or the imposition of requirements by one law that conflict with those imposed by other laws would make it impossible for individuals to know exactly what is required of them. In these cases, although the offending laws might intend to achieve the government's legitimate ends, their non-objective formulation invalidates them. For, as we have already indicated, such laws can only be enforced at the expense of the rights that the government is charged to protect. A person who is uncertain of the range of his legal rights in business because of a vague regulatory edict, for example, will naturally play it safe and curtail his activities in order to avoid possible government penalties. In this way, however, his freedom is wrongly constricted.[30]

Further, laws that are perfectly objective in both content and written form could be applied improperly. Mayor Bascom is an all-too-familiar practitioner of this sort of abuse, treating the law as "rubber," readily stretchable for friends (295).[31] When the standards that people are actually compelled to obey are subjectively determined by the transient preferences of particular bureaucrats, people are as vulnerable as they are under retroactive law. A hallmark of the rule of law—knowing what to expect—is obliterated.[32]

Atlas Shrugged is littered with non-objective laws. The Economic Emergency Law forbids any discrimination "for any reason whatever against any person in any matter involving his livelihood" (317). Hiring job applicants on the basis of their training, experience, or ability, for instance, is forbidden. Wesley Mouch, the government's Top Coordinator of Economic Planning and National Resources, issues a blizzard of directives that impose restrictions on business operations, taxes on the most productive, and assure "fair shares" to all. The steel mills of the country are "ordered to limit the maximum production of any metal alloy to an amount equal to the production of other metal alloys by other mills placed in the same classification of plant capacity—and to supply a fair share of any metal alloy to all consumers who might desire to obtain it" (333). Similar restrictions are imposed on the railroad and steel industries (333-335, 836ff., 840, 980). Project Soybean is designed to "recondition" people's dietary habits (937ff). And "[a]ll the manufacturing establishments of the country, of any size and nature, were forbidden to move from their present locations, except when granted a special permission to do so by the Bureau of Economic Planning and National Resources" (333).

Like a virus, the non-objectivity of such a legal regime gradually infects people's private interactions. Consider the Anti-dog-eat-dog-Rule,

> a measure of "voluntary self-regulation" intended "the better to enforce" the laws long since passed by the country's Legislature. The Rule provided that the members of the National Alliance of Railroads were forbidden to engage in practices defined as "destructive competition"; that in regions declared to be restricted, no more than one railroad would be permitted to operate; that in such regions, seniority belonged to the oldest railroad now operating there, and that the newcomers, who had encroached unfairly upon its territory, would suspend operations within nine months after being so ordered; that the Executive Board of the National Alliance of Railroads was empowered to decide, at its sole discretion, which regions were to be restricted (75).

Under non-objective law, such "voluntary self-regulation" is increasingly adopted as a means of preemptive self-defense. Industries "agree" to restrict their own rights in an attempt to forestall even more restrictive regulations that a government threatens to impose. ("Jawboning" is the contemporary euphemism for this sort of extortion, most commonly inflicted on the oil, tobacco, and media industries in the United States.)[33] Businesses are sent the message: do this, or else we will impose worse.[34]

Notice, further, that none of the Anti-dog-eat-dog-Rule's pivotal terms is objectively defined. The rule prohibits competition that is "destructive" to whom? By what standard? What constitutes "unfair encroachment"? And by what right is a given segment of the market *another's* territory? How much power—and of exactly what type—does the Executive Board's "sole discretion" encompass?[35]

The only type of "destruction" that government is properly concerned with is the violation of its citizens' rights. When extraneous aims are introduced (such as avoidance of "unfair encroachments" and provision of "fair shares"), the government exceeds its authority. For any ends other than the protection of individual rights can only be advanced by means that violate rights. Given that the government properly is an institution authorized solely to protect individual rights and which does not itself produce anything (other than the services necessary to fulfill that mission), the only way for a government to serve any alternative agendas is through forcibly compelling some people to supply the things that the government promises to give to others. In doing so, however, the government becomes an agent of injustice, wronging those whose property it seizes. It restricts the very freedom that it is designed to protect.[36]

Among the novel's myriad non-objective laws, the prize winner in perversity is Directive 10-289, which prohibits individuals from changing jobs, businesses from closing, changing their amounts of production or income or spending, and everyone from creating new goods or inventions. It authorizes the government to seize all patents and copyrights (538–39). Aptly dubbed the "moratorium on brains" by Francisco (551), this law essentially seeks to freeze the economy in place—by exterminating the liberty that fuels human production of goods and services and thereby allows there to be an economy.[37]

When Mr. Weatherby derides Dagny's "old-fashioned idea about law," her response indicates the basic reason that a legal system must be objective:

> "Why speak of rigid, unbreakable laws? [Weatherby asks] Our modern laws are elastic and open to interpretation according to . . . circumstances."
> "Then start being elastic right now, because I'm not and neither are railroad catastrophes." (631)

Dagny's point is that the laws of identity and causality must be respected in running a government as much as in running a railroad or any other enterprise.

Non-objective laws cannot succeed. The exercise of government power for any end beyond its proper purpose undermines its ability to achieve that purpose.[38] Once a legal system abandons the objective standard of individual rights as its means of determining its activities, what fills the void is the arbitrary. Non-objective law is utterly unfathomable; it *cannot* be applied objectively. Rearden, for instance, has no objective means of discovering what the Fair Share Law actually requires of him since no one could know how to "determine what constituted a fair share of what amount. . . . There was no way to form an argument; the figure could have been one pound or one million tons, with the same validity" (361).[39]

Essentially, what the kaleidoscope of non-objective law in *Atlas* makes clear is that without objectivity, laws no longer govern. No legal question is ultimately answered by reference to written, duly enacted rules. Rather, those men who wield the most brute power have their way. A given citizen's legal status is hostage to whatever those particular men believe or want, today (which may differ from what they believe or want, two weeks from today).

It is important to appreciate that this is the case not only in regard to government officials who would deliberately abuse their authority to serve ulterior agendas. When the law itself is non-objective, it cannot be objectively understood and applied even by those who earnestly attempt to. Just as you cannot fit a square peg into a round hole, you cannot apply laws that are not rationally justified in accordance with strictly rational methods. When the content or formulation of law is non-objective, laws *must* be treated as "rubber," since human beings cannot survive by strict adherence to irrational rules. It is only the violation of such rules that allows people to satisfy the needs of their existence.[40] Non-objective laws require that even the most upright government officials resort to irrelevancies in order to determine precisely how a non-objective law will be applied in a particular case.[41]

Consider laws that erect "the public good" as their basis. Exactly who *is* the "public"? And who, among a nation's citizens, is not? How secure is anyone's membership in this fortunate class? On what basis is a government to champion the interests of certain segments of the population and not others? Further, for any particular group, which of its interests is the government to serve (other than the rights that all citizens possess equally)? The impossibility of valid answers to these questions (answers that are rationally grounded in the function of government) means that non-objective law *requires* subjectivism from even the most conscientious government worker. In practice, "the public" is invariably identified with a continually revolving cast of subgroups, such that "the public" allegedly served by today's legislation (the country's teachers or single parents, for instance) is different from "the public" served by tomorrow's (farmers or coal miners or overweight middle schoolers). Certain groups are repeat beneficiaries, while other groups never receive such favor. Non-objective law thus divides the populace into rival constituencies who can merely hope that their day will come and deliver as many goodies as those paid out to others—and that they are not displaced by a fresher flavor-of-the-month before having won a big enough payday to last them a while.

The larger point, again, is that in the absence of objective law, no legal question is ultimately answered by reference to what is written. Every question remains indefinitely open, capable of infinitely many answers, depending on the views of the particular enforcers on a particular day. Pull with "the right people" is a person's only path to the satisfactory resolution of a dispute with the government; rights are no longer relevant. As Dr. Potter observes, what a person needs in such circumstances is "friends" (182). Dave Mitchum recognizes the same basic truth. Although he "knew nothing about the philosophy of law," Mitchum realizes "that when a court is not bound by any rules, it is not bound by any facts, and then a hearing is not an issue of justice, but an issue of men, and your fate depends not on what you have or have not done, but on whom you do or do not know" (596).

. . . AND ITS FALLOUT

The material destruction caused by non-objective law confronts the people of *Atlas* at every turn. Strangled by laws that dictate precisely how businesses will be run, companies are increasingly unable to produce, to ship, to deliver on contracts. Shortages, delays, equipment and facility failures mushroom and progressively envelop the entire economy. Remedies adopted to solve the problems created by earlier non-objective laws, because they themselves are non-objective, inevitably aggravate problems and extend the paralysis. Eventually, every aspect of people's standard of living is sent careening backward as rationing is imposed, leisure venues are closed to conserve fuel, and basic infrastructure fails (e.g., bridges, railroads) (350, 499, 496ff). By the end of the novel, people resort to horses for transportation in a society where the lights are out.[42]

It is a commonplace that the rule of law, with its requirements of written, stable, objectively knowable rules, is essential to a person's ability to plan his life. The arbitrariness of the legal system in *Atlas* makes such planning impossible. Instead of proceeding in a legal environment where fixed rules govern cooperation and trade, producers such as Rearden must invest their resources "upon the sole evidence of a man's face, manner and tone of voice, . . . pouring money into unknown hands in exchange for unsupported promises, . . . into unenforceable contracts—both parties knowing that in case of fraud, the defrauded was to be punished, not the defrauder" (302). Under non-objective law, *all* of a person's plans acquire this perpetually precarious character. A man literally does not know what is his from one day to the next. Consequently, even the normally most capable people are rendered helpless. For the absence of a clear, well-defined challenge prevents their adoption of a logical course. A person cannot effectively build something or battle something if he is left continually guessing about the nature of his tools and of his obstacles. (Which bureaucrat do I have to please? By what means? Will the pitch that works today continue to appease the relevant personalities tomorrow? Which of the constantly morphing "rules" will apply then?) Without the protection of objective law, a person has no means of rationally pursuing his values.[43]

Admittedly, in *Atlas*, the economic regulations' stifling effects are exacerbated by the strikers' withdrawal. Yet this merely hastens the inevitable. Even without the strike, people would eventually confront the same consequences; this is only illustrated more graphically by removing the "men of the mind." For non-objective law equally removes the men of the mind—along with all the products of rational thought—by removing individual freedom. Non-objective law extinguishes the condition that is necessary for men to use their minds and to create the benefits that rational thought uniquely makes possible.

Directive 10-289, as we have already noted, is the most egregious of the book's array of government restrictions. By using an example of such drastic dimensions, Rand starkly exposes the life-choking principle that is shared by all non-objective law. This extreme instance simply makes its consequences more plain. Yet less sweeping regulations are of the same essential nature and carry the same destructive effects. The label "moratorium on brains" highlights the fact that the mind drives all genuinely productive activity.[44] Laws such as 10-289 cripple independent thought, however, by making the use of one's mind to devise a different way of producing anything a punishable offense. (No "better mousetraps" will be permitted.) The message that unites all economic regulations is: *Don't think. We'll make all the decisions; we (the government) know best.* The people are simply to follow orders. The tunnel episode illustrates the disastrous culmination of this ethos, in practice. While it is not the direct result of a specific law, the disaster clearly reflects the philosophy that informs such non-objective regulations. The greater the number of dictates handed down from Washington, the less freedom an individual has to exercise his independent judgment and the less we can expect individuals' decisions to be ruled by independent judgment. The reign of non-objective law teaches that the way to stay out of trouble is through mindless obedience. *Don't raise questions or suggest alternatives. Don't attend to the relevant facts confronting you. Simply do as others command.* The result of widespread adherence to such a policy is catastrophe.[45]

The destruction wrought by non-objective law is not confined to the material realm. Its spiritual destruction is equally vast.

Notice that phoniness permeates human interactions in such a regime. When a government sets itself against individual freedom and sets individuals against one another through non-objective law, winks, charades, and double-dealing become the essential tools of survival. Mexico's promise to respect a contract with Taggart Transcontinental, for instance, is pretended to provide assurance, despite the common knowledge that Mexico does not respect property rights (53). (Indeed, it promptly violates that promise by nationalizing the San Sebastián Railroad and Mines [72].) Abiding by the Equalization of Opportunity Bill, Eddie explains to Galt, requires elaborate charades about who owns what (217). Producers and looters alike must break laws in order to get by, as we see in Rearden's and Danagger's private agreement to circumvent legal restrictions, Dagny's bribing officials to get resources needed to keep the railroad running, and Hank's buying his divorce (224, 163). In the rescue of Galt, Dagny shoots a man (1148).

The heroes are reduced to the methods of criminals—Rearden meeting "furtively" with Danagger, searching like a "scavenger," "hiding, sneaking, lying" to obtain the materials he needs in order to produce (383, 922; also see 474). Dagny wonders at the debasement of this:

> There was a time, she thought, when [Rearden's] mind, his energy, his inexhaustible resourcefulness had been given to the task of a producer devising better ways to deal with nature; *now*, they were switched to the task of a criminal outwitting men. She wondered how long a man could endure a change of that kind. (922)

Under non-objective law, as one of Jim's cronies candidly acknowledges, it is not a government of "principles anymore . . . it's only a question of who robs whom" (541). Far from protecting individual rights against aggression, a government of non-objective law creates conflicts between people who are made to fight over a finite pot of loot. Human relations *become* "dog eat dog," as such law converts the great value of other people into a threat.[46] Individuals get by being at once slave and slave master (654), compelled by the government to satisfy others' demands and to meet their own needs by the only means available: coercion. The freedom to reason and to produce for themselves has been extinguished.[47]

The moral inversion of non-objective law is crystallized in the fact that a pirate is one of the good guys. Ragnar, who never takes rightful property but only things stolen from the innocent (576, 577), is the agent of justice in this upside-down universe, avenging the exploitation of the producers. "It is a policeman's duty to retrieve stolen property and return it to its owners," he explains. "But when robbery becomes the purpose of the law, and the policeman's duty becomes, not the protection, but the plunder of property—then it is an outlaw who has to become a policeman" (577–78). When Rearden, on a dark road, tells the police that Ragnar is his new bodyguard, he does not realize how apt a description that is (583).[48]

Shocked as we may initially be by the presentation of a pirate as a hero, defiance of the law is what the rulers of a non-objective system themselves expect—and count on. In a confrontation with Rearden, Ferris explains:

> Did you really think that we want those laws to be observed? . . . We *want* them broken. . . . We're after power and we mean it. . . . There's no way to rule innocent men. The only power any government has is the power to crack down on criminals.

Well, when there aren't enough criminals, one *makes* them. One declares so many things to be a crime that it becomes impossible for men to live without breaking laws. Who wants a nation of law-abiding citizens? What's there in that for anyone? But just pass the kind of laws that can neither be observed nor enforced nor objectively interpreted—and you create a nation of law-breakers—and then you cash in on guilt. (436)

Non-objective law invites disrespect, disobedience, and eventually, contempt. While eager for the first, Ferris is oblivious to the second (in the fashion typical of a short-range mentality). When people realize that their legal system does not respect any valid moral ideals and must be routinely violated, they will view it as a sham; the guilt that Ferris is counting on will wear thin. This is evident with the deserters, who are not deterred by the illegality of their actions.[49] When men no longer respect the legitimacy of their legal system, it loses its power to induce guilt. And the pretense of a society that is ruled by law, rather than by muscle, is fully exposed. Ragnar and the strikers simply catch on more quickly.[50]

By casting men into conditions that render survival by rational methods impossible, non-objective law is inimical to the practice of morality. (By "rational methods" here, I mean those based on the fundamental nature of man and his long-term survival needs.) Non-objective law directly assaults reason, as we have already explained. Because all moral virtues are applications of reason, however, non-objective law is an assault on objective morality across the board. Economic regulations clearly penalize the virtue of productiveness by imposing special burdens on those who exercise it (taxes, fees, restrictions on production and contract terms, etc.). Yet non-objective law equally impedes independence, integrity, justice, honesty, and pride.[51]

Independent thought and action are not possible when a person is not free to act by his rational judgment. His thoughts are useless if he is not permitted to act on them and his actions are useless if they are not grounded on *his* convictions.[52] Integrity—fidelity to one's values—is not possible when a person is penalized for pursuing any values that the government disapproves of (disapproval enforced through laws that restrict a man's rightful activities). Justice is not possible when a person must deal with others on the basis of government decrees (about hiring, termination, pay, etc.) rather than his own objective judgment. Honesty is not possible when a person must feign compliance with laws that he cannot actually obey and must pretend respect for a justice system that is a fraud. Pride is not possible to a man whose range of ambition is trimmed to satisfy mandated caps and "fair shares" and who is not permitted to live by means of reason, productiveness, independence, integrity, justice, and honesty.[53]

By its basic rejection of rationality, non-objective law pits a man's morality against him. By requiring conformity to irrational standards, it renders the exercise of objective virtues self-destructive.[54]

The spiritual destruction of non-objective law is also evident in its emotional toll. At times, Dagny's, Rearden's, and Francisco's pain at the conditions they face is searing. After the passage of the Equalization of Opportunity Bill, Rearden's sense of futility is palpable:

> He stood at the window, trying not to think. But he kept hearing words in his mind: Rearden Ore . . . Rearden Coal . . . Rearden Steel . . . Rearden Metal . . . What was the use? Why had he done it? Why should he ever want to do anything again? (215)

Non-objective law's systematic evisceration of the conditions of human life drains natural motivation. Dismayed and discouraged as they are at times, though, *Atlas'* heroes are never broken. For the strikers are not the quitters. It is the looters who quit on living as a human being *must*, if he wants to live. One of *Atlas'* major themes is that those who quit reason (through non-objective law or any other means) quit life.

Some will no doubt object that the laws on display in *Atlas* are too far-fetched to teach us much; their provisions are too extreme to be actually imposed, thus they are not a realistic basis for lessons about the nature of law. Unfortunately for this wishful thinking, however, the US today suffers from a plethora of non-objective laws that are no less devastating in their effects.[55] Regulations of trade are ubiquitous. Consider, to cite just a handful: minimum wage laws and calls for caps on corporate executives' pay; the Family Leave Act (requiring employers to extend leave time to employees) and the Fair Pay Act, which would mandate equal pay for "comparable" work.[56] Oil companies are routinely threatened with laws against price gouging (earning "excessive" profits) while an endless carousel of "price supports" are given to farmers of corn or cotton or wheat or whatever on the basis of which voting bloc can exert the greatest political pull in a given session of Congress. The Farm Bill is a notorious piñata bursting with prizes designed to satisfy an array of special interests.[57] Regulations of particular industries—health care, coal mining, banking, transportation, food, clothing manufacture, entertainment, telecommunications, and on and on (try to find an industry devoid of regulation)—are so plentiful that most people take them for granted without a second thought.

Antitrust law alone imposes a dizzying array of unjustified restrictions on voluntary transactions. Since enactment of the Sherman Antitrust Act in 1890, one scholar has observed, "The courts in the United States have been engaged . . . in deciding case by case exactly what the law proscribes. No broad definition can really unlock the meaning of the statute."[58] This is the epitome of non-objective law. In the century-plus since Sherman, a cascade of additional restrictions has only further obscured antitrust laws' meaning and tightened the noose on businesses' freedom. The Federal Trade Commission was established in 1914 to prosecute "unfair methods of competition" and "anti-competitive practices."⁵⁹ The standards for determining what is "unfair" or "anti-competitive" are opaque. Indeed, antitrust law has grown

> into a haphazard accumulation of non-objective laws so vague, complex, contradictory, and inconsistent that any business practice can now be construed as illegal, and by complying with one law a businessman opens himself to prosecution under several others. No two jurists can agree on the meaning and application of these laws. No one can give an exact definition of what constitutes "restraint of trade" or "intent to monopolize" or any of the other, similar "crimes." No one can tell what the law forbids or permits one to do.⁶⁰

Danagger faces this very predicament: "One gang in Washington is yelling that I am expanding too much and something should be done to stop me, because I am becoming a monopoly. Another gang in Washington is yelling that I am not expanding enough and something should be done to let the government seize my mines, because I am greedy for profits and unwilling to satisfy the public's need of fuel" (383).

Again, this is far from fanciful fiction: In the 1950s, General Electric and Westinghouse, among others, were convicted for fixing prices.⁶¹ Yet by the law, companies were liable for charging prices deemed *either* too low or too high: for being "predatory" by charging so little as to run competitors out of business or for charging too much and thereby "gouging" the consumer. Nonobjective regulations leave companies damned if they do and damned if they don't, with no way to avoid the penalties of the law.⁶²

Antitrust law is but one example. It enjoys no monopoly on the employment of arbitrary and thus unknowable standards. Whether a person is striving to comply with affirmative action laws that require respect for the "compelling state interest" served by "diversity"⁶³ or with sexual harassment law that prohibits creating a "hostile or offensive" work environment⁶⁴ or with the Fairness Doctrine's mandate that broadcasters guarantee "ample play" for the "fair competition" of opposing views on the airwaves,⁶⁵ the individual is placed in the untenable position of not truly knowing what he legally may and may not do. The guessing game that is so conspicuous in antitrust and that we see so vividly on the dramatic canvas of *Atlas* is essentially the same in numerous non-objective laws.

Moreover, all regulatory law is non-objective insofar as it preemptively substitutes the government's judgment about the wisdom of a particular action for an individual's own. By declaring that a given food or drink or drug is too dangerous to be consumed (the Food and Drug Administration) or that a given radio or television program is too "indecent" to be heard (the Federal Communications Commission) or that a certain activity is too important to practice without a license or too risky to be engaged in without satisfying government restrictions (activities that include, in some states, interior decorating and fortune telling), regulatory law unjustifiably prevents a person from exercising his freedom to rule his own life. Advance restrictions of a person's activities, when those activities would not infringe on others' rights, violate *his* rights by removing from that person decisions and options that are properly his. The good intentions that may sometimes be involved do not alter the fact that this tramples his rightful freedom.[66]

While details of actual and fictional laws naturally vary, then, many current laws in force are the same, in principle, as those in *Atlas*. And they carry the same malignant consequences.

Non-objective law is, we have seen, forever unsettled and unknowable. Indeed, released from the discipline of objective validity, *the* law becomes a fiction. Those remnants that resemble law (such as the terms for creating a binding legal contract) offer no protection to those who conform to them. This is vividly illustrated when Rearden signs the papers transferring owner-ship of his ore mines to Paul Larkin:

> Paul Larkin reached for the papers hesitantly; he looked ingratiatingly helpless. "It's only a legal technicality, Hank," he said. "You know that I'll always consider these ore mines as yours."
>
> Rearden shook his head slowly; it was just a movement of his neck muscles; his face looked immovable, as if he were speaking to a stranger. "No," he said. "Either I own a property or I don't."
>
> "But . . . but you know that you can trust me. You don't have to worry about your supply of ore. We've made an agreement. You know that you can count on me."
>
> "I don't know it. I hope I can."
>
> "But I've given you my word."
>
> "I have never been at the mercy of anyone's word before."
>
> "Why . . . why do you say that? We're friends. I'll do anything you wish. You'll get my entire output. The mines are still yours—just as good as yours. You have nothing to fear. I'll . . . Hank, what's the matter?"
>
> "Don't talk."
>
> "But . . . but what's the matter?"
>
> "I don't like assurances. I don't want any pretense about how safe I am. I'm not. We have made an agreement which I can't enforce. I want you to know that I understand my position fully. If you intend to keep your word, don't talk about it, just *do* it." (222)

In the absence of objective law, if Larkin chooses not to fulfill these terms, Rearden has no recourse—other than *his* resorting to force to try to impose them. This chillingly illustrates the primitive conditions to which non-objective law thrusts us. As the legal system deteriorates in *Atlas*, we witness a regression to "each man for himself." Since the government cannot be counted on to pro-tect a man's rights, each must take matters into his own hands.

While a timeworn tactic of self-preservation is to cloak one's demands as those that serve "the public welfare," we have already seen how flimsy a shield this offers in the face of the subjective, constantly changing identity of "the public."[67] For stronger security, a person will need to adopt the more person-ally tailored methods of money and professional dealbrokers to exert influence

on his behalf. Once the government is run not as a principled protector of individual rights but as a favor-trading auction, a person needs resources to bid
and personal patrons to exploit them to his advantage. (Rearden, we observe, is
forced to buy his divorce and must employ Wesley Mouch as his "man in Washington," a cretin sufficiently adept at this corruption as to later assume one of
the highest government offices [933, 895, 50].) Long before "lobbying" became
a mainstay in our political vocabulary, Rand forecast its growth by recognizing
it as not the result of individuals' personal corruption (bad apples in office), but
as the inevitable consequence of a corrupt system. Non-objective law requires
manipulation by non-objective means; lobbyists are the result. When laws lack
objective criteria of enforcement, those charged with applying them are open to
non-objective criteria. That is what lobbyists specialize in supplying.[68]

At times, even these forms of influence prove inadequate. When the pretense of civil intercourse can no longer be manipulated to get what one wants,
people will resort to hiring "private guns," literally: not well-dressed lobbyists,
but gunmen. At their most desperate, the rulers in *Atlas* use armed goons to
try to have Galt do as they wish. And the heroes must respond with force, to
rescue him.

This is the Hobbesian state to which non-objective law reduces us.

THE DARKEST EVIL

A government is a tremendously powerful body. It is that institution within a
society that holds a monopoly on the legitimate use of force (apart from that
which is sometimes justified in a person's immediate self-defense). The reason
for its holding this power is to protect individual rights from the unjustified
imposition of force. It is precisely because the government is the agent "of re-
straining and combating the use of force," Rand writes, that its actions "have
to be rigidly defined, delimited and circumscribed; . . . If a society is to be free,
its government has to be controlled."[69]

The objectivity of laws is a crucial means by which we confine a government's exercise of power to its proper boundaries. Non-objective law represents the unjustified use of force. Whether it is non-objective in design or in
application, deliberately or not, any non-objective law infringes individual
rights. This infringement will be more or less flagrant, depending on the particular law in question. But all non-objective law, in the end, either punishes
a man for doing something that he is rightfully entitled to do or, by failing
to prohibit actions that would violate his rights (either private actions or the
government's own), it assists in their violation. As such, non-objective law
defeats the point of having a government. Instead of the law's serving as a firm
safeguard against the initiation of force (including by government itself), law
that is non-objective grants rulers a blank check (1063). As Peikoff observes,

it "represents a monopoly on the use of force granted to an agency ruled by whim."[70]

Notice the implications of this. The problem with non-objective law is not simply that it fails to fulfill its function (grave a failing as that is, given the vital importance of protecting individual freedom). Non-objective law allows and authorizes the unjustified use of force—which is the most destructive, deadly enemy known to human existence. The use of force, we have seen, paralyzes its victim's mind. It thus prevents the possibility of rational action, which is what human life depends on. If men cannot reason, men cannot survive. This, I think, is why Narragansett characterizes non-objective law as "humanity's darkest evil."

Non-objective law wipes out the fundamental precondition of human life. While a person under a government run by strictly objective law might still confront a good deal of irrationality in the people around him, that irrationality cannot destroy him unless it is imposed by force. When it is, however (as through non-objective law), the denial of his freedom disarms his capacity to act as human survival demands. He is rendered helpless, delivered to the mercy of those wielding brute force. Human beings cannot survive under such conditions. (The impotence of reliance on force is starkly exposed when Galt is being tortured for refusing to give his captors what they demand. Since they have renounced the use of reason, they can create no *values* to offer Galt in exchange. The bankruptcy of their venture is fully revealed in their inability to repair the torture device itself; they must rely on Galt's mind to do that for them.)

What makes non-objective law distinctively destructive is its pretense of offering protection. That is, a non-objective legal system is worse than worthless; it is an active (if disguised) agent of injustice and of death. For it provides men with a false sense of security. By fraudulently encouraging individuals' belief that their rights are being safeguarded, non-objective law disarms the innocent. If a man knows that he is on his own to protect his rights, he can (and usually will) take measures to do so. If, however, he mistakenly believes that government will protect his rights, he will unwittingly cooperate in his own immolation. He will respect the legal system on the premise that it is a just ally.

The façade of the rule of law that non-objective law maintains, in other words, readily recruits submissive victims because people do not realize that they *are* victims. (Indeed, it exploits people's desire to uphold justice by using that desire against them.) In this way, non-objective law's pretense of objective validity makes men uniquely vulnerable. Thinking that they are protected by a just government, those living under such a system are like the armed soldier who does not realize that his guns are loaded with blanks. Actually, it is worse: under non-objective law, a man's "guns" are turned against him, since the government enjoys a monopoly on the use of force. Having taken over the individual's authority to use defensive force himself, the government now directs force against him. This *is* a "horror machine," as Narragansett had seen.

Rearden recognizes the grotesque injustice of non-objective law when he refuses to mount a defense against his criminal prosecution, refusing to "simulate the illusion of dealing with a tribunal of justice" (477). Even a thief is less depraved, he observes, since a burglar, at least, "does not ask me to sanction his act" (477). Charged by a regime of non-objective law, Rearden names the charade for what it is: "I will not help you to pretend that I have a chance. I will not help you to preserve an appearance of righteousness where rights are not recognized. I will not help you to preserve an appearance of rationality by entering a debate in which a gun is the final argument. I will not help you to pretend that you are administering justice" (479).

The most corrupt kangaroo court is no worse, in principle, than a trial "governed" by non-objective law.

Over the course of *Atlas*, we witness the steady descent of a law-governed society into a state of anarchy. By the book's end, guns and gangs are in command. This is the inevitable result of non-objective law. Because its premise is untenable, it will eventually implode. When people realize that their government does not provide the rightful rule of law, they will no longer respect it as if it did and the resort to force will be more visible and more widespread. Open anarchy would be both more honest and more safe, however, since when the absence of law is forthrightly acknowledged, a person knows his vulnerabilities and can act accordingly. Non-objective law exterminates individual freedom far more effectively by providing false assurances of its security.

CONCLUSION

Given that the concept of objective law is hazy in many people's minds, it is easy, amid the numerous philosophical insights of *Atlas Shrugged*, to overlook Judge Narragansett's claim. The extreme character of his condemnation of non-objective law, however, should summon our attention. And examination of his claim does, indeed, reveal valuable lessons.

A proper legal system is constructed to serve the proper function of government. Objective law is validated by its service to that end: the protection of individual rights. Non-objectivity, whether in law's content or in its implementation, subverts the law's ability to fulfill that function and reflects the opposing dictum that might makes right. For any failure of objectivity means that government power is being used to serve alternative, illicit ends. As such, non-objective law converts the would-be guardian of man's freedom into an additional threat to it. Under the guise of protecting man's rights, law that is not objectively valid uses the government's monopoly on force to violate his rights. In this way, non-objective law represents evil of the most lethal sort: the unjustified use of force. Given that human life depends on reason and on the freedom that makes reason possible, the unjustified use of physical force, by paralyzing its victim's mind, cripples a man's means of survival; it attacks his *capacity* to live.[71] This is a dark evil, indeed.

If we were to treat Narragansett's verdict as a precise statement of Rand's considered philosophical conclusion about the relative depths of evil (as I have advised we not treat it), a full vindication of this verdict would require a systematic investigation of competing evils, which is beyond the scope of this paper. Even without that, however, our inquiry has illuminated the critical value of objectivity in law. Given the unique destructive power of physical force, whenever a person is authorized to use force, it is imperative that he use it justly. Similarly, insistence on objectivity in the law is our means of ensuring that government use *its* coercive power justly. When any aspect of a legal system is not objective, what suffers is individual freedom and, as a result, an individual's ability to live.[72]

NOTES

1. On hatred of the good, see Ayn Rand, "The Age of Envy," in *Return of the Primitive: The Anti-Industrial Revolution*, Peter Schwartz, ed. (New York: Meridian, 1999), 130–58.

2. I would stress that features of a fictional work, including lines of dialogue, cannot be treated as precise statements of an author's philosophy. The demands of plot, character, theme, and so on that are necessary for an integrated story militate against that. Moreover, Rand herself indicated that this was her view of fiction, in a 1965 letter. See Michael S. Berliner, ed., *Letters of Ayn Rand* (New York: Dutton, 1995), 631–32.

3. See, for instance, Lon Fuller, *The Morality of Law* (New Haven, Conn.: Yale University Press, 1964); Brian Z. Tamanaha, *On the Rule of Law: History, Politics, Theory* (New York: Cambridge University Press, 2004); Richard H. Fallon, Jr., "The Rule of Law as a Concept in Constitutional Discourse," *Columbia Law Review* 97 (1997): 1–56; Andrei Marmor, "The Rule of Law and its Limits," *Law and Philosophy* 23 (2004): 1–43; Joseph Raz, "The Rule of Law and its Virtue," *The Authority of Law* (Oxford: Clarendon Press, 1979), 210–29. Also see Aristotle, *Politics* Book III, 15.

4. See Tamanaha, 122; Aristotle, *Politics* III 15.1286a17-20, 16.1287a18-32.

5. Rand discusses this in "The Nature of Government," *Capitalism: The Unknown Ideal* (New York: Signet, 1967), 332. Also see Leonard Peikoff, *Objectivism: The Philosophy of Ayn Rand* (New York: Dutton, 1991), 368.

6. Notice that many of the formal elements of the rule of law are required because of their necessity to give individuals a fair chance to comply with the law. It is because people could not be reasonably expected to obey conflicting laws or laws whose provisions are so ambiguous as to be compatible with multiple competing interpretations, for instance, that we require clarity and consistency in form. The concern animating these formal requirements is a morally substantive one: treating people justly.

7. This is only a crude statement of the nature of objectivity. A conclusion is objective insofar as it is governed by a person's efforts to reach his conclusions by all and only the relevant facts, logically understood and evaluated. Peikoff characterizes objectivity as "volitional adherence to reality through the method of logic," *Objectivism*, 316. For more precise and detailed discussion, see *Objectivism*, 110–51; Ayn Rand, *Introduction to Objectivist Epistemology*, second edition (New York: New American Library, 1990), 46–47, 52–54, 82, 101–6; and Tara Smith, "'Social' Objectivity and the Objectivity of Value," in *Science, Values, and Objectivity*, eds. Peter Machamer and Gereon Walters (Pittsburgh: University of Pittsburgh Press, 2004), 143–71.

8. The specific laws are "necessitated" in the goal they seek to serve, not in every detail of the means by which they do so.

9. Rand, "Man's Rights," in *Capitalism*, 321–22.
10. Rand, "Nature of Government," and Peikoff, *Objectivism*, 363–69.
11. Rand, "Man's Rights," 322. Also see Galt's Speech in *Atlas*, 1012, and "Nature of Government," 330.
12. For more extensive explanation of reason as our means of survival, see Rand, "The Objectivist Ethics," in *The Virtue of Selfishness* (New York: New American Library, 1964), especially 19–27; Peikoff, *Objectivism*, 193–198; Tara Smith, *Ayn Rand's Normative Ethics—The Virtuous Egoist* (New York: Cambridge University Press, 2006), 56-61; and Tara Smith, *Moral Rights and Political Freedom* (Lanham, Md.: Rowman & Littlefield, 1995), 32–37. Rearden, after passage of the Equal Opportunity Bill, observes that thought is the motor of rational and productive action, and thus of life, 214.
13. Rand, answering a question after a speech given at Ford Hall Forum, Boston, 1973. *Ayn Rand Answers*, ed. Robert Mayhew (New York: New American Library, 2005), 5.
14. As John Locke observed, "it is one thing to persuade, another to command; one thing to press with arguments, another with penalties." *A Letter Concerning Toleration*, published 1689 (Indianapolis: Hackett, 1983), 27.
15. For a fuller explanation of the first part of this analysis, concerning the way in which physical coercion thrusts its victim into a "must lose" situation, see Smith, *Moral Rights and Political Freedom*, 123–39 and 141–63. And for more on the destructive power of physical force, see Peikoff, *Objectivism*, 318–20, and Rand, "Man's Rights," 323, and "Nature of Government," 330–34. For further explanation of the validation of man's rights, see Peikoff, *Objectivism*, 353–55, Rand, "Man's Rights," and Smith, *Moral Rights and Political Freedom*, 31–59.
16. Peikoff, *Objectivism*, 312, emphasis in original. Also see 311–15.
17. This phrase is from Darryl Wright. For an incisive analysis of force vis-à-vis reason to which some of the following is indebted, see Wright's lectures "Reason and Freedom," available at www.aynrandbookstore2.com/.
18. My mind does direct my physical actions, but *my* mind and body are physically linked.
19. Locke made a similar observation about the impotence of force to effect thought, writing: "such is the nature of the understanding, that it cannot be compelled to the belief of anything by outward force. Confiscation of estate, imprisonment, torments, nothing of that nature can have any such efficacy as to make men change the inward judgment that they have framed of things." Further: "It is only light and evidence that can work a change in men's opinions; which light can in no manner proceed from corporal sufferings, or any other outward penalties." Locke, *Letter Concerning Toleration*, 27.
20. Rand, "Nature of Government," 331, emphasis in original. Also see 330.
21. Emphasis in original; also see *Atlas*, 1062–66.
22. See "Man's Rights," 323.
23. Peikoff, *Objectivism*, 359.
24. I address the anticipated objection concerning those who are alive but unfree in *Moral Rights and Political Freedom*, 50–51.
25. "Nature of Government," 332, emphasis hers. Laws against murder would thus be objective in their aim insofar as they are grounded in the individual's right to his life; laws against theft would be objective insofar as they are grounded in the individual's right to property. (Obviously, all aspects of objectivity must be maintained, in order for a particular law to be fully objective, without qualification.)
26. Rand directly addressed the difference between anarchy and the gulch in a question period after a lecture given at Ford Hall Forum in 1972, observing that "Galt's Gulch is not a society; it's a private estate." See her full answer to the question in *Ayn Rand Answers*, 75–76.
27. The assertion of a moral claim obviously cannot prevent actual attacks on rights, as people can and do violate rights. Recognition that the initiation of force is a violation of rights, however, respects the moral barrier and conveys what types of action are inappropriate vis-à-vis a rightholder. For related discussion of purported conflicts between rights, see Smith, *Moral Rights and Political Freedom*, 195-199 and "Rights Conflicts: The Undoing of Rights," *Journal of Social Philosophy* 26, no. 2 (Fall 1995): 141–58.

28. For more on anarchy and on the idea of competing governments, see Rand, "Nature of Government," 330–35, and Peikoff, *Objectivism*, 371–73.

29. Transfats and sugary soft drinks are among recent dietary targets. As an example, see Kim Severson, "Effort to Limit Junk Food in Schools Faces Hurdles," *New York Times*, December 2, 2007, 22, national edition.

30. Admittedly, *he* chooses to limit his activities, but he does so only because of the government's threat to impose an even worse fate, if he does not. That threat is created by the lack of clarity or consistency in the relevant laws. He must conform his conduct to a law that means a *or* b, *or* c, rather than to a law that clearly tells him the relevant legal boundaries.

31. Bascom is but one of a number of figures in *Atlas* for whom the application of law by subjective preference is routine operating procedure.

32. For comments on the fear and anxiety that non-objective law generates, see Rand, "Vast Quicksands," *The Objectivist Newsletter*, 2, no. 7 (July 1963): 25, 28; and "Nature of Government," 336.

33. In a related development, businesses now sometimes *seek* regulations in order to pre-empt tougher laws that might otherwise be imposed. See Eric Lipton and Gardiner Harris, "In Turnaround, Industries Seek US Regulation," *New York Times*, September 16, 2007, 1, national edition.

34. For an example in *Atlas*, see Weatherby offering James Taggart "permission" to close the Rio Norte Line, 511.

35. After freezing the railroad bonds, Mouch's subsequent directive providing assorted escape routes from his measures is a similar showcase of subjectivism. The directive "ruled that people could get their bonds 'defrozen' upon a plea of 'essential need': the government would purchase the bonds, if it found the proof of the need satisfactory. There were three questions that no one answered or asked: 'What constituted proof? . . . What constituted need? . . . Essential—to whom?'" (352)

36. On the incompatibility of purported welfare rights with genuine rights, see my "On Deriving Rights to Goods from Rights to Freedom," *Law and Philosophy* 11 (Winter 1992): 217–34; "Why a Teleological Defense of Rights Needn't Yield Welfare Rights," *Journal of Social Philosophy* XXIII, 3 (Winter 1992): 35–50; and *Moral Rights and Political Freedom*, 194–206.

37. For some of the demands that were later enacted into laws in a society increasingly emulating the disastrous policy of the Starnesville factory, also see 299 and, on Starnesville, 323.

38. To use concepts that Rand employs in other contexts, objective law reflects the primacy of existence, while non-objective law reflects the primacy of consciousness. In this context, this essentially means that objective law is faithful to those facts that give rise to the existence of government while non-objective law elevates individuals' attitudes, desires, and other subjective irrelevancies above those facts. On the primacy of existence and the primacy of consciousness, see Rand, "The Metaphysical Versus the Man-Made," *Philosophy: Who Needs It* (New York: Bobbs-Merrill, 1982), 29 ff; *Introduction to Objectivist Epistemology*, 53–54 and 245–52; and Peikoff, *Objectivism*, 17–23.

39. Rearden also comes to realize that his accomplishments are being destroyed not by minds, but by whim. "By what right?" he wonders, as he confronts the fact that under non-objective law, right does not rule (214–15).

40. This is comparable to the way in which men must cheat on irrational moral principles. On that, see Peikoff, *Objectivism*, 309–10. For further commentary on the political point, see Rand, "The Pull Peddlers," *Capitalism*, 167–72.

41. For discussion of this in regard to the interpretation of law, see my lecture, "How 'Activist' Should Judges Be? Objectivity in Judicial Decisions," available at www.aynrandbookstore2.com/.

42. In the margins of Lowell Mason's *The Language of Dissent*, Rand remarks that "government controls *have to* grow, since they cannot and do not work, but merely create growing problems," Robert Mayhew, ed., *Ayn Rand's Marginalia* (New Milford, Conn.: Second Renaissance Books, 1995), 201, emphasis in original.

43. Rearden's family is aghast at his admission that he may actually be imprisoned, since they are accustomed to relying on his apparent omnipotence, 462. Also see Dagny contemplating the strange new experience of helplessness against a "fog without shapes or definitions," 298.

44. See Francisco's Money Speech, 410–15.

45. On the close relationship between independence and rationality, see Smith, *Ayn Rand's Normative Ethics*, 114–16 and 124–25, and Peikoff, *Objectivism*, 253–55.

46. Recall Dave Mitchum's dilemma of choosing between his children's well-being and that of the train passengers and calling his fellow workers out to die by their work, rather than to earn their living, 598–99.

47. Ragnar comments on the choice posed, in this society, between being a looter or a victim, 575.

48. Because the victims of non-objective law are forced to resort to the methods characteristic of crooks, the adoption of those methods does not reflect immorality (as it would, were they willingly adopted in a free society). As Galt says in his speech, "morality ends where a gun begins," 1023. While some of Ragnar's friends do not approve of his course, their objection is not moral; rather, they fear that his path is too dangerous. See 580. For description of Ragnar's project, also see 573. For much fuller explanation of the status of morality under force and in emergencies, see Rand, "The Ethics of Emergencies," *Virtue of Selfishness*, 49–56; Smith, *Ayn Rand's Normative Ethics*, 94–100; and Peikoff, *Objectivism*, 274–76 on the contextual character of morality.

49. The growing number of deserters eventually overwhelms the ability of the police to arrest them (567).

50. Hank observes that, if he were sent to jail by this government, he would feel no shame, but would regard it as comparable to an accident without any moral significance, 384. Knowing the corruption of the system, Dagny is similarly indifferent to the legality of her actions. See 628–29.

51. Rand identifies these seven (reason, productiveness, and the rest) as the fundamental moral virtues. See Galt's Speech, 1018–21; "Objectivist Ethics," 28–30; Peikoff, *Objectivism*, 220–29, and chapter 8, 250–324. Smith, *Ayn Rand's Normative Ethics* systematically examines each of these virtues.

52. On the relationship between independent thought and independent action, see Peikoff, *Objectivism*, 225–29, and Smith, *Ayn Rand's Normative Ethics*, 123–28.

53. For much further explanation of each of these virtues, see Peikoff, Objectivism, 220–29 and chapter 8, 250–310, and Smith, *Ayn Rand's Normative Ethics*.

54. This is obviously a large subject. For further explanation, see Peikoff, *Objectivism*, 310 and 314–15.

55. Most nations around the globe are in similar or worse situations.

56. For further information on the latter, see, for instance, www.pay-equity.org/info-leg.html.

57. Michael Pollan, "Weed It and Reap," *New York Times*, November 4, 2007, online at: www .nytimes.com/2007/11/04/opinion/04pollan.html?_r=1&oref=slogin.

58. A.D. Neale, *The Antitrust Laws of the U.S.A.*, Cambridge University Press, 1960, 20, quoted in Rand, "Antitrust: The Rule of Unreason," *The Voice of Reason*, Leonard Peikoff, ed. (New York: New American Library, 1988), 255.

59. Quoted in Gary Hull, ed., *The Abolition of Antitrust* (New Brunswick, NJ: Transaction, 2005), Appendix, 164. This Appendix offers a synopsis of major antitrust legislation.

60. Rand, "Antitrust: The Rule of Unreason," 255.

61. Hull, *Abolition of Antitrust*, 111.

62. For further comments of Rand's on antitrust, see "Antitrust: The Rule of Unreason," 254–59; *Ayn Rand Answers*, 6, 39; and *Ayn Rand's Marginalia*, 193–98.

63. See *Grutter v Bollinger*, 539 US 306 (2003) and Arthur L. Coleman and Scott R. Palmer, "A More Circuitous Path to Racial Diversity," *Chronicle of Higher Education*, July 13, 2007, B10.

64. Equal Employment Opportunity website: www.eeoc.gov/.

65. "Let the Blowhards Blow," *The Economist*, July 21, 2007, 36. The Fairness Doctrine was in effect from 1949 until 1987, and support for reinstating it has recently grown. See John Fund,

"'Fairness' is Foul—Liberals vs. the First Amendment," *Wall Street Journal*, Oct. 29, 2007, available online at www.opinionjournal.com/diary/?id=110010795. Legislation concerning hate speech and hate crime offers further examples of non-objective law.

66. For comments on preventive law, see *Ayn Rand's Marginalia*, 198, *Ayn Rand Answers*, 8–13, and for related discussion of the impropriety of laws banning obscenity, see Rand, "Censorship: Local and Express," *The Ayn Rand Letter*, 2, nos. 23-25 (3-part essay) (August and September, 1973): 229–42.

67. Dagny thinks of "the public welfare" as a "voodoo stamp" routinely treated as "superseding contract, property, justice, reason and lives," *Atlas*, 913.

68. Rand refers to "pull peddlers" on 913 of *Atlas*. For her analysis of the phenomenon, see "The Pull Peddlers," *Capitalism*, 167–72. This phenomenon is hardly confined to the United States. On the growth of European Union regulations spawning a proliferation of lobbyists in Belgium, where the EU is headquartered, see Carol Matlack, "Why Brussels is Abuzz with Lobbyists," *Business Week*, Oct. 29, 2007, 81–83.

69. "Nature of Government," 331.

70. Peikoff, *Objectivism*, 365.

71. Recall Galt's saying as much in his speech, 1023.

72. Thanks to Robert Mayhew for helpful comments on an earlier draft.

19

The Role of Galt's Speech in *Atlas Shrugged*

Onkar Ghate

Anyone who reads John Galt's radio broadcast and who has some familiarity with the ideas that have shaped and continue to shape Western culture, should recognize his speech as a statement overflowing with original ideas—the work of an enormously powerful mind, whether or not you happen to agree with the speech's content.

But as impressive as the speech is, many readers I think fail to appreciate the integral role the speech plays in the action and story of *Atlas Shrugged*. I've met more than a few readers who skipped over the speech on a first reading of the novel, treating it as an interruption in the action, impatient to see how Ayn Rand's dramatic story ends. The implicit premise of such fast-forwarding is that you can understand the story's ending without understanding the content of the speech. I don't think this is true.

Even many readers who don't skip the speech regard it as something of a digression or as a pause in the action, albeit a fascinating one. When I ask such readers why Galt gives his radio broadcast, they are almost always at a loss to answer. Often, their reply is that the speech is primarily a vehicle for Rand to disseminate her ideas and is only tenuously connected to the progression of the story. Again, I don't think this is true.

So, *why* does Galt give his speech? Who is he addressing? Why does he say what he says in his radio broadcast and why does he structure it the way that he does? Why does he give it when he does? What is he seeking to accomplish? How *is* his action of speaking to the world connected to the plot and its climax? More broadly, how does the speech contribute to the novel's theme?

There are I think interesting answers to all these questions, and in answering them we will see that Galt's Speech is crucial to the story and to the novel's characterization of its hero, John Galt.

The theme of *Atlas Shrugged*, it is important to keep in mind throughout this discussion, is (as Rand formulated it): "the role of the mind in man's existence—and, as corollary, the demonstration of a new moral philosophy: the morality of rational self-interest."[1] Equally important, the novel's plot-theme—a literary term coined by Rand and which she defined as "the central conflict or 'situation' of a story—a conflict in terms of action, corresponding to the theme and complex enough to create a purposeful progression of events"—is: "the men of the mind going on strike against an altruist-collectivist society."[2] *Atlas Shrugged* is a novel about a strike.

To understand the role that Galt's speech plays in the story, therefore, we must identify the speech's connection to the strike by the men of the mind. Considered as an action, I will argue, Galt's Speech is an aspect of the whole strike. Considered from the perspective of its content, Galt's Speech explains the precise nature of the strike and gives outward form to the mind of its leader. His speech, in other words, is intimately tied to both the novel's plot and theme.

When Galt goes on the radio, the world is near collapse. Galt tells the world that it is he who has brought it to this state:

> I am the man who has deprived you of victims and thus has destroyed your world .... Men do not live by the mind, you say? I have withdrawn those who do. The mind is impotent, you say? I have withdrawn those whose mind isn't. There are values higher than the mind, you say? I have withdrawn those for whom there aren't. ... We are on strike, we, the men of the mind. (1009–10)

But he also tells the world that unlike any other strike, the men of the mind have no claim to press and no desire to negotiate.

> There is a difference between our strike and all those you've practiced for centuries: our strike consists, not of making demands, but of granting them. We are evil, according to your morality. We have chosen not to harm you any longer. We are useless, according to your economics. We have chosen not to exploit you any longer. We are dangerous and to be shackled, according to your politics. We have chosen not to endanger you, nor to wear the shackles any longer. We are only an illusion, according to your philosophy. We have chosen not to blind you any longer and have left you free to face reality—the reality you wanted, the world as you see it now, a world without mind. ...
>
> We have no demands to present to you, no terms to bargain about, no compromise to reach. You have nothing to offer us. *We do not need you.* (1010–11)

But if the men of the mind have nothing to demand or to negotiate, why is Galt speaking on the radio?

It is primarily an issue of justice. Galt *has* stopped the motor of the world and hastened the world's destruction. He owes the world an explanation: to explain how he has done it and why he was *right* to do it. In the name of justice, he will demonstrate to the people of the world that they are not innocent victims: they are not suffering because of their virtues but, properly, paying for their sins. And particularly in the name of anything good and human remaining in them, Galt will explain to them the cause of their plight and the only path to a solution.

As Galt says near the end of his speech:

> If in the chaos of the motives that have made you listen to the radio tonight, there was an honest, *rational* desire to learn what is wrong with the world, you are the man whom I wished to address. By the rules and terms of my code, one owes a rational statement to those whom it does concern and who're making an effort to know. Those who're making an effort to fail to understand me, are not a concern of mine. (1066)

It is illuminating to compare Galt's motivation here to that of a real-life case: that of America's Founding Fathers in the Declaration of Independence. The Founding Fathers' act of rebellion turned the political landscape of their world upside down. Against what seemed to the rest of the world like an equitable arrangement between crown and colony—and the American colonies were certainly not severely oppressed when compared to many millions of people throughout the world then or since—the Founding Fathers declared that it would no longer be business as usual, that rule by the divine right of a king was illegitimate and tyrannical and would be brought to an end. The people of the world, confronted with this enormous upheaval in their way of life, had a right to an explanation. "When in the Course of human Events," the Declaration begins,

> it becomes necessary for one People to dissolve the Political Bands which have connected them with another, and to assume among the Powers of the Earth, the separate and equal Station to which the Laws of Nature and of Nature's God entitle them, a decent Respect to the Opinions of Mankind requires that they should declare the causes which impel them to the Separation.

The Declaration then goes on to name the political principles that guide the rebels and the reason for their rebellion: the outrages committed by Great Britain against the colonies.

As America's Founding Fathers did, so John Galt does. He names to the world the principles—this time moral and philosophical—that govern the strikers and caused them to strike, and he names the opposite principles, accepted by most of the people in the world and responsible for all their vicious actions, against which the strikers had every right to rebel. Galt names the reasons which, in reason, every person should accept as valid: the people of the world should agree that the men of the mind had ample cause to strike and to let the world be consumed by its own irrationality.

And to all those individuals who see that he is right, Galt offers the knowledge and the course of action necessary for them to avoid their destruction and to speed the return of the strikers: he urges them to go on strike. This is Galt's other purpose in announcing the strike and its justice.

> I am speaking to those who desire to live and to recapture the honor of their soul. Now that you know the truth about your world, stop supporting your own destroyers. . . . Withdraw your sanction. Withdraw your support. . . . Go on strike— in the manner I did. Use your mind and skill in private, extend your knowledge, develop your ability, but do not share your achievements . . . .
>
> If you find a chance to vanish into some wilderness out of their reach, do so, but not to exist as a bandit or to create a gang competing with their racket: build a productive life on your own with those who accept your moral code and are willing to struggle for a human existence. You have no chance to win on the Morality of Death. . . . When the looters' state collapses, deprived of its best slaves . . . when the advocates of the morality of sacrifice perish with their final ideal—then and on that day we will return.
>
> We will open the gates of our city to those who deserve to enter . . . . We will act as the rallying center for such hidden outposts as you'll build. . . . Those who join us, will join us; those who don't, will not have the power to stop us; hordes of savages have never been an obstacle to men who carried the banner of the mind. (1066–67)

In order to get the better people left in the world to choose the side of the strike, Galt has to convince them that there is no chance to win on the Morality of Death. He must show them, as he does in his radio broadcast, the true nature and consequences of the Morality of Death. He must show them that there is another mode of existence: the Morality of Life. And he must show them that their choice is: either-or.

Given the basic purpose of his speech, I think it is clear who Galt is above all addressing in his radio broadcast. He is not addressing the looters—the advocates of the Morality of Death; throughout the speech he refers to them as "your teachers," "the mystics," "your moralists," and so on. Galt has no reason to speak to them directly, as he makes clear during his capture (to speak to them directly would sanction their irrationality and evil by granting that they were actually struggling to understand and to live). Nor is Galt addressing Dagny or anyone else like her who may remain in the world: "The last of my words," he says near the very end of his speech, "will be addressed to those heroes who might still be hidden in the world" (1068). The first of Galt's words, in contrast, were addressed to the people of the world, the majority of whom Galt regards as part victims and part perpetrators of the looters' creed. Near the start of his broadcast he says "if you wish to know why you are perishing—you who dread knowledge—I am the man who will now tell you" (1009)—and later: "Yes, you *are* bearing punishment for your evil. . . . And if you wish to go on living, what you now need is not to *return* to morality—you who have never known any—but to *discover* it" (1011)—and later: "Whoever you are, you who are hearing me now, I am speaking to whatever living remnant is left uncorrupted within you, to the remnant of the human, to your *mind*, and I say: There *is* a morality of reason" (1013–14)—and still later: "You, who are half-rational, half-coward, have been playing a con game with reality, but the victim you have conned is yourself" (1054).

As to the question of why Galt chooses to address the world at the moment he does, observe that it would undermine the strike to announce it any earlier. Part of what the Morality of Death teaches the world, Galt knows, is to ignore the existence of the men of the mind, even as the world exploits these men. When Galt quits the Twentieth Century Motor Company, he realizes no one will yet care that the men of the mind are beginning to strike. But when Galt chooses to announce the existence of the strike, people care. The world is disintegrating and its people have a nameless sense, which they often try to evade, that there are no minds left in their world. All around them, whether at work or walking the streets of their cities, they sense that competent men are being replaced by the responsibility avoiders. They now worry when another industrialist deserts. They see the looters trying to chain men like Hank Rearden to their jobs, and yet these men still vanish. They've seen Francisco dynamite his business empire—and have sensed the reason why. The people of the nation—at least the better of them—are now ready to listen to a report on the world crisis. "That," says Galt at the beginning of his broadcast, "is what you are going to hear" (1009).

Galt knows, moreover, that the looters and all those sympathetic to them will try to find, chain, and kill the men of the mind. He can only address the world when the strikers are out of reach, which they aren't earlier in the strike; the valley becomes self-supporting only years after being established by Midas Mulligan. At earlier stages in the strike, too many strikers and soon-to-be strikers remained in the world, in danger if the strike were made public. Galt addresses the nation only after he gets his last and greatest catch: Hank Rearden. At that point, only Dagny remains in the looters' world, but she has chosen to remain.

Once we understand the basic purpose and intended audience of Galt's broadcast, we can see that those factors dictate its structure. The strike, as I've said, represents a complete break with the existing order of society. Galt and the other strikers are not demanding, say, that some of their taxes be lowered or that some of the regulations strangling them be loosened. The men of the mind have rejected the entire terms of their society and have no interest in discussion, negotiation, or compromise with its leaders. This is what Galt explains in what I term the introduction of the speech, which I locate from the paragraph beginning with Galt's sentence: "'Ladies and gentlemen,' said a voice that came from the radio receiver—a man's clear, calm, implacable voice, the kind of voice that had not been heard on the airwaves for years— 'Mr. Thompson will not speak to you tonight'"—to the paragraph beginning with the sentence: "Whatever else they fought about, it was against man's mind that all your moralists have stood united" and ending with the sentence: "Now choose to perish or to learn that the anti-mind is the anti-life" (1009–12).

After Galt discloses to the world the strike and its radical nature—namely, that the misery the world is experiencing is the consequence of its moral ideal brought into full reality for the first time, and that this has happened because the men of the mind have consciously rejected that ideal and are no longer willing to be sacrificed in its name—the rest of Galt's radio broadcast then divides into three major sections. First, to the world's people he explains in the name of what new moral ideal the strikers have broken with existing society. Second, he explains the exact nature and source of the ideal the men of the mind have broken with—and why no alternative action and no compromise on their part would have been proper. Third, he explains to the world's better people why their choices have reduced to one: either choose the Morality of Life and therefore a chance at life—or choose the Morality of Death and therefore imminent destruction.

In the first section of his speech, Galt begins with the positive. The strike is a rejection of the mystics' whole view of existence and the corrupt moral code it requires, in favor of the strikers' view of existence and the moral code it demands. Galt begins by presenting to the world his new Morality of Life and, crucially, explains the view of existence, the metaphysics, which generates it: the universe as an absolute, governed by the law of identity; man's life as conditional, requiring a definite course if it is to endure; man's reasoning mind as his only key to unlocking the identity of the universe; and therefore, as a corollary in the field of morality, the essence of virtue as the embrace of existence through the use of your mind and its power of logical thought. When he declares to the world that "We, the men of the mind, are now on strike against you in the name of a single axiom, which is the root of our moral code, just as the root of yours is the wish to escape it: the axiom that existence exists"—Galt means it (1015).

This first section on the Morality of Life I locate from the paragraph beginning with Galt's sentence: "Man's mind is his basic tool of survival"—to the paragraph beginning with the sentence: "You seek escape from pain" and ending with the sentence: "It is not death that we wish to avoid, but life that we wish to live" (1012-24).

In the second section, Galt shows the people of the world the full and exact nature of the code they have been taught and have (partially) accepted—a code that begins by damning man's nature as evil, that proclaims as virtue the sacrifice of your values, and that declares the passkey to the moral elite to be a lack of intelligence, of ability, and of mind—a code that, in actual fact, holds emptiness—the zero—death—as its standard. And Galt shows the people of the world the view of existence that has spawned the Morality of Death: the view held by the world's teachers, the mystics of spirit and the mystics of muscle. The universe of these mystics' dreams is a nightmare universe in which a zero is superior to a something, the causeless is superior to the caused, the unearned is superior to the earned, and their wishes can supersede the basic law of existence, the law of identity.

This second section on the Morality of Death I place from the paragraph beginning with Galt's sentence: "You, who have lost the concept of the difference, you who claim that fear and joy are incentives of equal power—and secretly add that fear is the more 'practical'—you do not wish to live, and only fear of death still holds you to the existence you have damned"—to the paragraph beginning with the sentence: "It is a conspiracy of all those who seek, not to live, but to *get away with living*, those who seek to cut just one small corner of reality and are drawn, by feeling, to all the others who are busy cutting other corners—a conspiracy that unites by links of evasion all those who pursue a *zero* as a value . . ." and ending with the sentence: "*Death* is the premise at the root of their theories, *death* is the goal of their actions in practice—and *you* are the last of their victims" (1024–47).

In the speech's third and final section, Galt tells the world's people that they must now choose. Either choose the strikers' view of existence, the morality of life that this view entails and, armed with the new philosophical knowledge Galt has taught them, the joy and happiness that they could achieve. Or continue to choose their teachers' view of existence, the Morality of Death it requires, and the destruction that can no longer be postponed. "We, who were the living buffers between you and the nature of your creed," Galt tells them at the beginning of this section, "are no longer there to save you from the effects of your chosen beliefs. We are no longer willing to pay with our lives for the debts you incurred in yours or the moral deficit piled up by all the generations behind you. You had been living on borrowed time—and I am the man who has called in the loan" (1047).

But even those people of the world who have retained some good element within their souls, and who have now heard Galt's identification of the Morality of Life and the Morality of Death, are afraid to take sides. So in this third section, Galt explains to them the sources of their fear, why their fear is misplaced, and what they must gather the courage to do: to embrace the Morality of Life and join the strike. It is the Morality of Death, Galt shows them, that has made them look at morality—*any* morality—as a necessary evil, that has made them avoid every extreme and seek the middle of any road, that has turned their own need of morality and of self-esteem into their enemy, and that has made them regard any man of the mind as their exploiter.

This third and final section I place from the paragraph beginning with Galt's sentence: "We, who were the living buffers between you and the nature of your creed, are no longer there to save you from the effects of your chosen beliefs"—to the paragraph beginning with the sentence: "Such is the future you are capable of winning" and ending with the sentence: "Let your mind and your love of existence decide" (1047–68).[3]

You could, therefore, summarize the speech's structure as follows: (1) We, the men of the mind, are on strike against your moral ideal and in the name of ours. (2) Our ideal is the Morality of Life. (3) Your ideal is the Morality of Death. (4) You must now choose: it is either-or.[4]

And when you understand the purpose, intended audience, and basic structure of Galt's Speech, I think you can see that his radio broadcast is a logical and crucial element in the story's action. Galt *must* deliver his speech. He, the most rational and objective of men, would be acting non-objectively if he did not present his stand to the world and the reasons behind it.

Notice how crucial the speech is to the climax of the story. The looters torture Galt to force him to become Economic Dictator of the nation. They know their lives depend on him starting to produce—and they visit *pain* on him for the privilege of sustaining them. They must resort to physically torturing him, because he "refuses to play his historical part" (1104): he will not voluntarily hand his mind to them. "It is not your wealth that they're after," Galt said in his speech. "Theirs is a conspiracy against the mind" (1046–47)—and now the full nature of this deeper conspiracy is being exposed.

It *must* be Galt, the preeminent man of the mind, whom the looters want to tell them what to do. And when Galt refuses to play his part, the full futility and evil of the mystics' course of action is exposed. It is the futility of the mindless, who must resort to force to try to extract ideas from Galt's mind—ideas which he himself knows and has told them to be impossible. But to them the realm of thought is a magical domain: *somehow*, Galt could generate the ideas to save their system, if only he would choose to do so. "We want you to rule," Ferris declares to the naked, shackled figure of John Galt. "Understand? We want you to give orders and to figure out the right orders to give. . . . Speeches, logic, arguments or passive obedience won't save you now. We want ideas—or else" (1140). A few moments later Ferris shouts to Mouch: "I want him to *believe*! To accept! To *want* to accept! We've got to have him work for us *voluntarily*!" (1142). Their impotence is such, however, that they cannot even torture Galt without his aid—it is he who must tell them how to fix the generator.

By his knowingly being a pawn in a demonstration to win Dagny, Galt reveals to her—and to the looters—the full meaning of the mystics' cult of zero-worship: the looters want to kill Galt, knowing that their own deaths will follow.

But why is it *Galt* on the looters' torture rack? The looters had been desperately trying to chain industrialists like Hank Rearden to their jobs and to punish deserters, but they didn't even know of John Galt's existence—until the speech. It is his radio broadcast that announces the strike and the fact that Galt is its leader. And more: Galt is not just the leader of the strike, he is the preeminent man of the mind, a fact which the looters, in their habitual way, half evade—"It wasn't real, was it?" are Mr. Thompson's first words after hearing Galt's broadcast (1070)—and half grasp: they want to find Galt because, as Mr. Thompson says just a few moments later, "He knows what to do" (1074). How do the looters know that Galt is the preeminent man of the mind? They've heard his speech. Without this fact, the climax doesn't make sense. But with this fact, the looters' public pleas for Galt to contact Washington, to negotiate and join the leaders of the nation in this time of crisis, alongside their secretive attempts to capture him, are to be expected.[5]

Galt's Speech, therefore, is crucial to the characterization of John Galt: of establishing who he is and why he is the leader of the strike. He is the foremost man of ability, of intelligence, of mind, of genius. Certainly part of this fact about Galt is conveyed by Galt's actions and words in the valley when Dagny crash-lands there. Part of it is conveyed by the respect, admiration, and loyalty that Francisco and the other strikers show Galt. And part of it is conveyed by Galt being the inventor of the motor. But the motor, obviously, is science fiction; we as readers can project the kind of thought its invention would require, but not its specifics. But we can do precisely this for Galt's Speech. The speech *is* a work of genius. This I think is an incredible literary achievement on Rand's part: her plot requires that Galt be a man of genius, and she then proceeds to put in her novel, as his actual statement, a product that could only come from the mind of a genius. And not only does this product make vivid and real Galt's genius, it also contributes crucially to the plot: when the looters hear Galt's radio broadcast, they set out to find and to torture him—as given the logic of their premises, they must.

Since Galt's Speech is indispensible to the story's climax, it also serves, unsurprisingly, as a powerful way of conveying the theme of the novel: the role of the mind in man's existence. What enables the men of the mind to free themselves from their society's shackles? Only an act of the mind—Galt's mind.

The content of Galt's Speech conveys what Galt has come to grasp about the men of the mind and their enemies. Galt has *identified* the view of existence and the code of morality that his fellow strikers had been acting on, but had been unable to put into words and therefore consistently practice. "They were men who had lived by my code, but had not known how great a virtue it represented. I made them see it. I brought them, not a re-evaluation, but only an identification of their values" (1015). He also has *identified* the opposite code, the code of their enemies, a code whose nature and origins are so monstrously evil that the strikers were too clean to understand them. And Galt has *identified* why, despite their power, the men of the mind have been continuously losing to the zero-worshippers: the sanction of the victim. This sanction, Galt grasps, is much more than a political sanction of the looters' laws: it is a moral, and deeper, a metaphysical sanction. The men of the mind—and this is what Hank and Dagny must each learn (and do learn)— have sanctioned the looters' entire view of existence, the view of existence on which the looters' corrupt morality and political system are built. The men of the mind have sanctioned the *metaphysical* idea that wishes trump facts and that the irrational supersedes the rational. (For this reason, Galt's Speech deals heavily with metaphysics.)

This new knowledge, discovered by Galt's mind, drives the entire story.

It explains why Galt quits the Twentieth Century Motor Company and tells all those who voted for the Starnes plan that he will stop the motor of the world. It explains why, when Francisco and Ragnar learn what Galt has discovered, Francisco takes the disguise of a playboy and destroys his copper empire and Ragnar becomes a pirate. It explains why, when Akston and Mulligan and Wyatt and Halley learn what Galt has discovered, they quit and vanish. It explains, as a result, why America is disintegrating. It explains why Dagny senses there is a destroyer loose in the world, whom she must stop. It explains why she found an abandoned motor. It explains why there is someone in Dannager's office before Dagny gets there and why she has to chase a plane across the skies of Colorado, hoping not to lose Quentin Daniels forever.

The content that is Galt's Speech drives all the essential action of the story. This content had to be made explicit somewhere in the novel, because learning this content is what causes the men of the mind to strike. The story would be unsatisfying and the novel's theme unconvincing without Galt's Speech; as readers, we would know *that* the men of the mind go on strike but not *why* they do.

Given that the story is a mystery, it is natural that this content would be revealed only near the end. As Dagny observes, a mind has to reach a certain point to be ready to hear what the "destroyer" has to say. The two minds—the two potential strikers—whose inner thoughts we as readers are privilege to, namely Hank and Dagny, are for most of the story not yet at that point. Hank reaches that point first, at the looters' conference where they propose to him their Steel Unification Plan. And it is immediately after Hank quits—and Francisco has come to tell him the rest of what he has to learn, and he then meets Galt—that the full content of what Galt has been teaching the strikers is revealed in *Atlas Shrugged*.

Observe too that Galt's subsequent actions are explained by the fact that his *mind* fully understands what he has said in his speech. It's not just that the looters' desperate attempt to find and coerce Galt would be inexplicable without them having heard his radio broadcast. Galt's actions when captured would not be entirely convincing either.

Why is Galt immune to the looters' pleas—when all the other men of the mind had in one way or another swallowed some aspect of the looters' creed? Because Galt's mind knows what it knows. Galt knows fully where he stands *and* where they stand.

Here's a flavor of Galt's exchanges with the looters in the Wayne-Falkland hotel room; in reading them, think how different they are from Dagny and Hank's interactions with the looters earlier in the book, prior to these two learning from Galt and Francisco some of the principles that Galt has discovered.

"I can't argue, Mr. Galt," Chick Morrison tells him. "I'm just begging for your pity. . . . I'm begging you to pity those who suffer. I'm . . . Mr. Galt . . . what's the matter? What are you thinking of?" "Hank Rearden," Galt answers. "Uh . . . why?" Galt's reply: "Did they feel any pity for Hank Rearden?" (1114).

"How can you be so sure you're right?" Jim Taggart cries to Galt. "How can you take it upon yourself, at a terrible time like this, to stick to your own ideas at the risk of destroying the whole world?" Galt replies: "Whose ideas should I consider it safer to follow?" "How can you be sure you're right?" Taggart continues. "How can you *know*? Nobody can be sure of his knowledge! You're no better than anyone else!" "Then why do you want me?" Galt replies (1112).

"It's the question of moral responsibility that you might not have studied sufficiently, Mr. Galt," Ferris tells him. "To fail to save a life is as immoral as to murder. The consequences are the same—and since we must judge actions by their consequences, the moral responsibility is the same. . . . For instance, in view of the desperate shortage of food, it has been suggested that it might become necessary to issue a directive ordering that every third one of all children under the age of ten and of all adults over the age of sixty be put to death, to secure the survival of the rest. You wouldn't want this to happen, would you?" "Don't believe him!" cries Mr. Thompson. "He doesn't mean it!" "Oh yes, he does," Galt answers. "Tell the bastard to look at me, then look in the mirror, then ask himself whether I would ever think that *my* moral stature is at the mercy of *his* actions" (1114).

"What I've got to offer you is your life," Mr. Thompson tells Galt. Galt answers, softly: "It's not yours to offer." Galt continues: "Now . . . do you see what I meant when I said [on the radio] that a zero can't hold a mortgage over life? It's I who would have to grant you that kind of mortgage—and I don't. The removal of a threat is not a payment . . . the offer not to murder me is not a value. . . .I'll tell you more: I know that I want to live much more intensely than you do. I know that that's what you're counting on. I know that you, in fact, do not want to live at all. I want it. And because I want it so much, I will accept no substitute" (1102).

Galt is immovable because of the knowledge *he* has discovered and possesses. He can even withstand physical torture at the looters' hands, because he is serene in the knowledge that he is in the right and has stayed true to his love of existence.

In contrast—but in further support of the novel's theme—Dagny has not yet fully learned what Galt says in his speech, particularly about the Morality of Death and the life-hating view of existence which generates it. And because of this error of knowledge—the failure of her mind to see fully the metaphysical evil she faces—she is the one who delivers Galt, the man she loves, to the looters. She gives them the idea to search for Galt and she then leads them to his apartment. The mind is the source of all the values of man's existence; but when it is placed in service of the mindless, whether through deliberate choice or through error, it becomes, as Dagny learns, the destroyer of all man's values.

Galt's radio broadcast and the subsequent action that builds to the novel's climax are indispensible in conveying the novel's theme.

Thus the overall conclusion is clear. What an analysis of Galt's Speech reveals—an analysis of its purpose, its content, its structure, its role in the story, and its contribution to the novel's theme—is that far from being "propaganda," a digression in the story's plot or even simply a pause in its action, the speech is integral to the novel. Without Galt's Speech, John Galt would not be John Galt—and *Atlas Shrugged* would not be *Atlas Shrugged*.

NOTES

1. Ayn Rand, *For the New Intellectual* (New York: Signet, 1963), 88.

2. Ayn Rand, "Basic Principles of Literature," in *The Romantic Manifesto: A Philosophy of Literature*, revised edition (New York: Signet, 1975), 85.

3. Or, if you want to include within the last section also the choice that confronts individuals like Dagny, then the third section would include the last five paragraphs of the speech and thus would end with the following: "You will win when you are ready to pronounce the oath I have taken at the start of my battle—and for those who wish to know the day of my return, I shall now repeat it to the hearing of the world: 'I swear—by my life and my love of it—that I will never live for the sake of another man, nor ask another man to live for mine.'" (1069)

4. I discuss the speech's structure at more length in a series of lectures entitled "A Study of Galt's Speech," the recording of which is published by and available for purchase from the Ayn Rand Bookstore (www.aynrandbook2.com) and also freely accessible online at atlasshrugged.com/book/a-study-of-galts-speech.html. Although there are some elements in those lectures that I now think are inaccurate, I still agree with the essence of what I said there; that earlier material formed the basis for this essay.

5. Turning his face away, Francisco says to Galt, thinking of Galt's torture at the hands of the looters, "'It's only that it was you . . .' he whispered, '*you* . . . if it were anyone but you . . .'" Galt replies: "'it had to be me, if they were to try their last, and they've tried, and'—he moved his hand, sweeping the room—and the meaning of those who had made it—into the wastelands of the past—'and that's that'" (1155).

20

Galt's Speech in Five Sentences (and Forty Questions)[1]

Allan Gotthelf

[T]he range of what man can hold in the focus of his conscious awareness at any given moment, is limited. The essence, therefore, of man's incomparable cognitive power is the ability to reduce a vast amount of information to a minimal number of units—which is the task performed by his conceptual faculty.

—Ayn Rand, *Introduction to Objectivist Epistemology*[2]

INTRODUCTION

John Galt's Speech, as Onkar Ghate well explains in the preceding essay, has an "integral role . . . in the action and story of *Atlas Shrugged*."[3] As Ghate relates, Galt announces to the world that he has taken the men of the mind on strike and explains the reasons and rightness of their strike.[4] Galt ascribes the collapse of the world to the dominance and implementation of a philosophy that is in all respects *anti-mind*, and ascribes the recent acceleration of that collapse to the withdrawal of the strikers. And, to all those in his audience "who desire to live and to recapture the honor of their soul" (1066), he presents a rational view of existence and morality that is pro-mind and pro-life, he identifies the destructive essence of the dominant moral code and its underlying view of existence, and he calls on these men to make an unequivocal and uncompromising choice between the pro-life and the anti-life codes. For those making the pro-life choice, he offers knowledge of how to implement it and inspiration to do so, and urges them, also, to withdraw from the world, thereby avoiding any further harm to themselves and speeding the return of the strikers.

The speech, as Ghate makes clear, is, on Galt's part, both an act of justice to those left in the world who still deserve a rational statement explaining his and the strikers' action, *and* a crucial way of serving the aims of the strike. Moreover, I would add, it is an act that brings the strike to a climax. As Galt says, referring first to his own and Francisco's and Ragnar's early withdrawal and then to the speech he is now giving: "It was the three of us who started *what I am now completing*" (1060, my emphasis).[5]

A close study of the speech is as integral to a full understanding of the novel as the speech itself is to the novel's action. Because of the speech's wide-ranging philosophical content, however, its close study is also an invaluable source for the understanding of Rand's philosophic thought.[6] But such a study is not easy. In this essay, then, I offer readers interested in embarking on a detailed exploration of the speech some methods for doing so, and some key results of my own application of these methods.

We need well-defined methods for approaching any complex text. Without them, a reader retains only a vague sense of the whole, or a collection of discrete points that he cannot connect to one another. (This is why many readers fail to appreciate the role of the speech in the plot and some find it repetitive.) The problem is one we face whenever we are confronted with a wealth of information: because there are only so many units that a person can hold in his conscious mind at any moment, we are unable to comprehend the whole. But, as Rand states in the epigraph I have chosen for this essay, we have a way to deal with such cases—a way which is in fact essential to all successful human cognition. This method of condensation—of "unit economizing," as Rand calls it— takes many forms; and because we can iterate it, condensing our condensations, there is no limit to what we can comprehend. The application of this method to a complex text is *outlining* or *summarizing*. The outline or summary makes it possible to see the structure of the whole and to relate any detail, no matter how fine, to it by relating it first to its proximate context, which we see then as playing a role in a wider context, and that in something yet wider, and so forth.[7]

So, in my first section, "Summarizing the Content, and Finding the Structure, of Galt's Speech" I introduce a method of successive condensation of the speech, via the production of a series of increasingly shorter outline-summaries. Eventually I reach a summary some 600 words in length. One result of taking such a concentrated overview will be the discovery of explicit *transitions* in the speech from one broad focus to another, transitions that are for the most part clearly marked by Galt (and Rand). We will find four main transitions, and thus five main parts to the speech.

In the next section, that division into five parts will, with the help of further condensation, enable the formulation of the "Five Sentences" of that section's—and this essay's—title. I will offer confirmation of that division of the speech into five parts, and of my choice of summary statements for each part, by providing a (relatively brief) overview of some of the content and structure of each part.

Both to reconfirm such an analysis of the speech's structure and to get a full mastery of its content, nothing of course can substitute for line-by-line study. In much of my teaching of philosophical and literary texts, I have long found it valuable, both for my students and for myself, to provide a series of *study questions* that isolate and highlight key features of the reading's content and structure at a very fine grain. Working through such questions is an invaluable way of grasping and (if the questions are properly formulated) integrating the content.

I prepared such a set of study questions for the teaching of Galt's Speech many years ago, grouped under the Five Sentences, and (with occasional revision) have used them time and again to great effect.[8] So, I provide here a slightly edited version of those questions, in my third section, titled "Galt's Speech in Forty Questions."

The techniques for studying the speech that we will have explored to this point do not—of course—exhaust all the different ones one might use in a close study of the speech. In a coda to this essay's presentation of the methods of condensation and study-question answering, I identify one more technique for focusing in on fundamental content of the speech, which my students and I have found both fascinating and rewarding to use, although in applying it I will leave John Galt to speak in his own words, and you to express the results of its use in yours.

SUMMARIZING THE CONTENT, AND FINDING THE STRUCTURE, OF GALT'S SPEECH

As a graduate student many years ago, I was struck by the value to readers, in certain older books, of the running capsule phrases in their margins, which capture the essential idea of a paragraph or two. So I decided to do the same for Galt's Speech in the (wide) margins of a hardback copy of *For the New Intellectual*. I then typed up, in continuous form, what I had written in my margins, converting phrases to summary sentences. Reading through the seven-page single-spaced summary that resulted, I found the structure and unity of the speech coming to life in my mind. So I did the same thing for those seven pages, and the resultant page and a half condensation of the speech was even more revealing. My next, and penultimate, stop was a half-page summary totaling 600 words (Galt's Speech is roughly 35,000 words).

Here is an example of the condensation process, applied to two consecutive paragraphs in the latter part of the speech, in which Galt is addressing those in the world who have not completely abandoned their desire to live (1052).

> But to those of you who still retain a remnant of the dignity and will to love one's life, I am offering the chance to make a choice. Choose whether you wish to perish for a morality you have never believed or practiced. Pause on the brink of

self-destruction and examine your values and your life. You had known how to take an inventory of your wealth. Now take an inventory of your mind.

Since childhood, you have been hiding the guilty secret that you feel no desire to be moral, no desire to seek self-immolation, that you dread and hate your code, but dare not say it even to yourself, that you're devoid of those moral "instincts" which others profess to feel. The less you felt, the louder you proclaimed your selfless love and servitude to others, in dread of ever letting them discover your own self, the self that you betrayed, the self that you kept in concealment, like a skeleton in the closet of your body. And they, who were at once your dupes and your deceivers, they listened and voiced their loud approval, in dread of ever letting you discover that they were harboring the same unspoken secret. Existence among you is a giant pretense, an act you all perform for one another, each feeling that he is the only guilty freak, each placing his moral authority in the unknowable known only to others, each faking the reality he feels they expect him to fake, some having the courage to break the vicious circle.

In the margin to the first paragraph, I wrote: You have never practiced or believed this morality.

In the margin to the second one, I wrote: You had no desire to be "moral"—but each of you faked it to the others.

Here is the full running summary I wrote for these two paragraphs and the ten that follow them:

You have never practiced or believed this morality. You had no desire to be 'moral'—but each of you faked it to the others. You now preserve the root of all your compromises: the belief that the moral and the practical are opposites; you see your choice as to be moral or to live. The result was to remove morality from life—and to view actual evils as practical. And when you are happy you feel guilt, and pain you view as normal, believing evil to be potent since the moral is the practical. And so you believe that morality is a necessary evil. As a result of this false dichotomy, life is torn by impossible conflicts. It began when you discarded your mind. Reality is final, A is A. To say that you don't have to go to extremes is to reject identity, reason, and morality, is to be responsible for all the blood that is spilled in the world. Reality is an absolute. There is no middle—in any compromise between good and evil it is only the evil that can profit.

In the next ten paragraphs, Galt identifies further consequences for those torn between their desire to live and the morality of sacrifice they've accepted, including the loss of self-esteem, and the sense of betrayal of self. In the five paragraphs that follow, Galt offers an alternative. Here's the summary I provided for those five:

In childhood you knew the radiance of an independent, rational consciousness facing an open universe. I am only the man who chose consistently to be and live that way. That choice is the dedication to one's highest potential, and is made by realizing that the noblest act is choosing to think. Accept the fact that your life depends on your mind and that the responsibility of a rational consciousness is not to be evaded.

The full running summary for these twenty-seven paragraphs, including the portions of the summary already given, would be about twenty-five sentences long. The next condensation (which I no longer have) would be about eight sentences long and look as follows:

> You don't practice or believe this morality, but you preserve its split between the moral and the practical, which is at the root of your doctrine of compromise. But compromise between good and evil, is an abandonment of the mind, in which only the evil can profit. Morality, to you, is duty, pain—a scarecrow waving away your pleasures. You abandon your mind, straddle every fence, surrender to mysticism, accept the muscle-mystics' claim to be the voice of reason. You blank out any evidence of the opposite, because you have tied your self-esteem to that mystic "unselfishness." Man's need of self-esteem is a volitional being's need to know his own value and his fitness for existence. It is your abandonment of your mind that has produced your fear and guilt, and a sense of self-betrayal. Reject your morality, reclaim your love of existence and of being a man. The choice is still open to you—the dedication to your highest potential, which requires grasping that thought is the noblest of acts.

In the final condensation, prior to the Five Sentences, the running summary of these twenty-seven paragraphs is *three* sentences long:

> You will perish unless you reject this morality and its split between the moral and the practical, a split which leads you to the doctrine of compromise. You have tied your self-esteem to sacrifice, and thereby made your life unbearable. A glorious existence comes from dedication to the highest: to thinking.

Although, of course, important detail is lost in these successive condensations, one gains an increasing grasp of the whole. And with that grasp one can then return to a close study of those details, able now to relate them to the whole, and to hold them as part of that whole.

Now that we have seen an example of the condensation process, let's turn to the 600 word summary of the entire speech, which I produced just prior to producing the Five Sentences.

Summary

The state of the world is due to its moral code, which is anti-mind, anti-life: the code of sacrifice. We, the men of the mind, are on strike against it.

A morality of reason rejects the self-sacrifice of mystical and social ethics, and holds *man's life* as the standard of value. This morality is based on the axioms of existence, consciousness, identity, and a view of man's consciousness as *volitional*. Man possesses the choice to think or not to think, that is his basic choice, and the exercise of this power to think is his means of survival. The ruling values of this morality are: Reason, Purpose, and Self-Esteem. Rationality is its basic virtue, the other virtues are all expressions of this one; they are: Independence, Integrity, Honesty, Justice, Productiveness, and Pride. Happiness is the result of achieving rational values. Human relationships must be based on trade, with the initiation of force banished.

The code of sacrifice is the Morality of Death: it is based on the doctrine of Original Sin and the soul-body dichotomy. It attacks the mind, it attacks selfishness— all in the name of full sacrifice. The good of others is the standard, but those who are to be served are those who cannot earn the values you give them—the standard is *need*, an absence, a lack. Your motive, according to this code, should be *love*, love for those who have no value, love of the zero.

The teachers of this doctrine attack you through your fear of relying on your own judgment. They attack even the Law of Identity, to make their irrational Wish supreme. Their desire is to achieve the unearned, they want to take over the products of the mind, even while denying that the mind exists. They want to reduce man's mind to the level of a savage, yet to have him continue to produce—all in order to gain power, power over those consciousnesses to whom they have surrendered their own. They cannot harness nature, so they try to harness the mind by making the men of the mind feel guilty for their minds, and thus willing to exist in servitude. Their hatred of themselves, and their resentment against those who can survive as they cannot, results in a hatred of all of existence, a hatred of the good for being the good—and a longing for destruction. They do not want to live; *death*—their own and that of their victims—is their ultimate motive.

You will perish unless you reject this morality and its split between the moral and the practical, a split which leads you to the doctrine of compromise. You have tied your self-esteem to sacrifice, and thereby made your life unbearable. A glorious existence comes from dedication to the highest: to thinking, it comes from a proper standard of perfection, it comes from the fight for your rational happiness, and from your rejection of the doctrine of sacrifice. On this morality America will become a country of *rights* again, with a government whose purpose is solely to *protect* those rights. In a society which leaves the men of superior intelligence free, everyone benefits. In the present society every rational man must and should go on strike, allowing it to collapse. Do not give up. Do not compromise. Fight for the value of your pride and your person, knowing that your code is the Morality of Life, and the source of every greatness that has ever existed. Reach the point where you can join us in the striker's oath, swearing by your life and your love of it, never to live for the sake of another man nor ask another man to live for yours.

Each of these sentences is the result of a separate condensation, and we can see that the sentences fall naturally into paragraphs. The paragraphing points to a structure.

In the first paragraph, the accelerating collapse of the world is attributed to a strike that Galt is leading of the men of the mind against the prevailing moral code of sacrifice with its damnation of the mind.

Then, in the second paragraph, the proper moral code, in the name of which the strikers are striking, a code which Galt calls "the Morality of Life," is presented. It is shown as resting on basic facts of man's nature, and certain axiomatic facts about reality and knowledge, which are explained. The code's standard of value is established, and its ruling values and basic virtues are identified. This presentation ends with a statement of the fundamental principles that should govern human interrelationships.

From there Galt moves, in the third paragraph, to an examination of the nature—and evil—of the morality the strikers are on strike against: the code of sacrifice. He identifies the view of man's nature—and of man's basic evil— that is at its base, and the contradictions inherent in that base. He analyzes the nature and shows the destructiveness of the code of sacrifice—its anti-mind, anti-life character—and condemns it as "the Morality of Death."

Galt then speaks, in the next paragraph of my summary, of the "teachers" (or "preachers") of this morality, identifying their deepest motives to be hatred and destruction, and not the love of man they sometimes profess. This section of the speech might be thought to be merely the culmination of the examination of the moral philosophy against which the strikers are on strike and not a part distinct from that examination. But that is a mistake. The distinction between the content of the code of sacrifice and the motivation of those who preach it (the mystics and the looters) is an important distinction within *Atlas Shrugged* as a whole, and because of this Galt (and Rand) intends the analysis of the content and inherent destructiveness of the code and the analysis of the psychology of its teachers as distinct parts of the speech.[9]

One way to underscore the difference of focus between the third and fourth parts of the speech is to consider the different status of their respective theses in Dagny's mind. Dagny is *never* tempted to accept a morality of sacrifice, but her fundamental conflict, and her refusal to go on strike, stem from the fact that she does *not* believe, until late in the novel, that the villains are motivated by death.[10]

Consider her exchange with Hugh Akston, when she explains her reason for leaving the valley:

> "If you want to know the one reason that's taking me back, I'll tell you: I cannot bring myself to abandon to destruction all the greatness of the world, all that which was mine and yours, which was made by us and is still ours by right— because I cannot believe that men can refuse to see, that they can remain blind and deaf to us forever, when the truth is ours and their lives depend on accepting it. They still love their lives—and *that* is the uncorrupted remnant of their minds. So long as men desire to live, I cannot lose my battle."
>
> "Do they?" said Hugh Akston softly. "Do they desire it? No, don't answer me now. I know that the answer was the hardest thing for any of us to grasp and to accept. Just take that question back with you, as the last premise left for you to check." (807)

We shall see further evidence for this division when we discuss shortly Galt's explicit transitions from one part of the speech to the next. Let's now continue with the summary, turning to its final paragraph.

Having identified hatred and destruction as the underlying motive of the mystics and looters, Galt is in a position to say to those in the world who still retain a desire to live that they must make a fundamental choice: either continue their acceptance of the teachings of those destroyers—and perish; or reassert their love of life, consistently accept the moral code he and his strikers live by. Having made this choice, he asks them to join the strikers by withdrawing from the world, thereby hastening the day of their return, and describes the kind of world that will now be possible—a world of reason, achievement, pride, and joy.

In short, then, the overall structure of the speech is as follows: The men of the mind are on strike against the morality of sacrifice. The proper morality is one of life and reason. The morality of sacrifice is a morality of death. Those who preach that morality are motivated by hatred and destruction. If you wish to go on living you must uncompromisingly reject those teachings and fully embrace the values of life and reason—the reward for which is a life of achievement and joy.

Transitions as a Guide to Structure

I said in the introduction that Galt (and Rand) for the most part clearly marks the transitions from one of these five parts of the speech to the next. Let us turn, then, to those transitions, for confirmation of this analysis into five parts (including the separation of the analysis of the morality of sacrifice from the analysis of the motivation of its teachers).

Galt opens the speech by attributing the collapse of the world to its practice of its moral ideal of sacrifice and its denial of the value of the mind, and he announces that he has accelerated that collapse by withdrawing the creative men of the mind. And then he says:

> Your moral code has reached its climax, the blind alley at the end of its course. And if you wish to go on living, what you now need is not to *return* to morality— you who have never known any—but to *discover* it. (1011)

The next three paragraphs support this by identifying the prevailing variants of the morality of sacrifice, the mystical and the social. The very next paragraph, which begins: "Man's mind is his basic tool of survival" (1012), starts listeners on that journey of discovery. Galt is now presenting the facts of human nature on which his analysis of the basis of the concept of *value* in the concept of *life*, and the content of the Morality of Life, depend. That, then, is our first transition.

Having completed his presentation of his new concept of *morality*, and of its content and basis, with an analysis of the evil of the initiation of force (1023–24), Galt distinguishes between the life- and happiness-affirming motivation of the practitioners of his code and the "zero-worshipping" motivation of those who would initiate force. The latter do not wish to live and, as he says to them, "only fear of death still holds you to the existence you have damned.

You dart in panic through the trap of your days . . ." trying to evade the fact that "yours is the Morality of Death."[11] Note what Galt says to them next:

> Death is the standard of your values, death is your chosen goal, and you have to keep running, since there is no escape from the pursuer who is out to destroy you or from the knowledge that that pursuer is yourself. Stop running, for once—there is no place to run—stand naked, as you dread to stand, but as I see you, and take a look at what you dared to call a moral code. (1025)

And with this the transition to the third part of the speech is complete.

Galt's analysis, through that third part, of the morality of sacrifice ends with a look at the attempt to justify sacrifice in the name of love:

> The justification of sacrifice, that your morality propounds, is more corrupt than the corruption it purports to justify. The motive of your sacrifice, it tells you, should be *love*—the love you ought to feel for every man. A morality that professes the belief that the values of the spirit are more precious than matter, a morality that teaches you to scorn a whore who gives her body indiscriminately to all men—this same morality demands that you surrender your soul to promiscuous love for all comers. (1033)

The analysis continues for three more paragraphs, in the course of which Galt presents his own view of love (1033–34). Galt's next two paragraphs begin, respectively, "Such is your morality of sacrifice" and "Such was your goal." And then he says:

> The degree of your ability to live was the degree to which you broke your moral code, yet you believe that those who preach it are friends of humanity, you damn yourself and dare not question their motives or their goals. Take a look at them now, when you face your last choice—and if you choose to perish, do so with full knowledge of how cheaply how small an enemy has claimed your life. (1034)

And from here on, for the next fourteen pages, the primary subject of Galt's statements is "they," not "you" as in the third part; he is now speaking of the teachers. The only exceptions are the places where Galt addresses those he has addressed in the third part in order to explain the errors and the evil of their teachers' attack on the senses, reason, axioms, and causality, and the places where Galt sees those he is addressing as having accepted and put into practice those teachings. This contrast of pronouns is brought out dramatically in what I take to be the last sentence of this fourth part of the speech:

> *Death* is the premise at the root of their theories, *death* is the goal of their actions in practice—and *you* are the last of their victims. (1047)

This sentence is followed with two paragraphs explaining that the strike has removed "the living buffers between you and the nature of your creed." Then, with the words, "Twelve years ago, when I worked in your world, I was an inventor," followed by a description of the motor he created, Galt initiates a narrative of the beginnings of the strike. He describes his discovery, "one night at a factory meeting," where he was told that, precisely because of his superlative achievement, he belongs to, and must serve, others, that "the enemy was an inverted morality—and that my sanction was its only power." He saw that all he had to do was to say "No"—and so he did. "I quit that factory. I quit your world. I made it my job to warn your victims" (1047–48).

From here on, Galt makes clear that his listeners must make an unequivocal choice between his Morality of Life and the prevailing Morality of Death, he speaks of the rewards of choosing the former, offers guidance in making and consistently carrying out that choice, speaks of the only social order in which life and achievement are possible, identifying the nature and foundation of *rights*, and urges those who make the choice to value their lives to withdraw from the world themselves, thereby hastening the return of the strikers. This part, starting with the narrative of the beginning of the strike, has an evident unity as the final part of the speech, clearly distinct from the fourth part on the motivation of the teachers of the Morality of Death.

FIVE SENTENCES

The final step in the series of condensations that began with the seven-page summary of the speech is to crystallize for each of the five parts a one-sentence statement of the essence of its content. Here, with some slight editing, are the formulations I arrived at by working from the five paragraphs of the 600 word summary.[12]

I. The world is perishing from the morality of sacrifice, and the men of the mind are on strike against this morality, which is speeding up the process of destruction (1009–11).

II. The proper, rational morality for man is one of *life* and *reason*, based on the axiom that *existence exists* (1011–24).

III. The morality of sacrifice is the morality of *death*, for it demands renunciation of that which makes life possible: the mind—and thus of any enjoyment of life on earth (1024–34).

IV. This code is taught by men who, having renounced their minds, seek power over the consciousnesses of other men, by attempting to convince them to renounce their own minds and accept the morality of sacrifice; the deepest motive of these teachers of sacrifice is hatred of existence, of life, of man, of themselves—and their goal is to destroy their victims and themselves (1034–47).

V. If all men who desire to live reject—as we the strikers have—these doctrines of mysticism and sacrifice, realizing that no compromise is possible, and refuse to support their destroyers, demanding instead a

society of rights and freedom, then the society of the mystics and looters will perish, and we will come to have a world of reason, freedom,
achievement, and joy (1047–69).

These five capsule statements, I submit, help one to see the overall structure
and the unity of Galt's Speech. By successive condensations of the speech we
have successively increased our comprehension of the whole, precisely in accordance with the epistemic principle Rand has described in our epitaph (375).

With this overview of the speech's structure in hand, we are ready to zoom
in for a fine-grained, line-by-line analysis of the speech. I mentioned earlier the
device I developed for this purpose: a focused set of study questions, grouped
under the Five Sentences. Here are those study questions, so grouped.

GALT'S SPEECH IN FORTY QUESTIONS

I recommend first just reading through the questions in order; that by itself
should illuminate the organization within each of the parts of the speech, and
the flow of the argument across the whole. It should also make a subsequent
effort of answering the questions one by one, ideally in writing, all the more
rewarding.

I. **The world is perishing from the morality of sacrifice, and the men
of the mind are on strike against this morality, which is speeding up
the process of destruction (1009–11).**
   1. The strike "granted you everything you demanded of us," yet it
   hastened the process of destruction of the society. What does that
   reveal about the moral code against which the strikers are on strike?
   (1009–11).

II. **The proper, rational morality for man is one of *life* and *reason*, based
on the axiom that *existence exists* (1011–24).**
   2. The exposition of the Morality of Life falls, roughly, into three parts:
   First (1012), certain basic facts about human nature are identified. Then (1012–15) the foundation of the morality is laid down,
   beginning with an analysis of the concept of *value*, showing it to rest
   on the concept of *life* (1012–13), then with a derivation of a standard of value from this (1013–15), and then with a statement of the
   metaphysical axioms and central epistemological tenets on which
   all this rests (1015–17). The third part or stage of the presentation
   is the specification of the content of the morality: the delineation
   of the "ruling values" and virtues (1017–21), the definition of happiness and its source (1021–22), and the identification of the basic
   social principle: the banishment of the initiation of force, or to put
   it positively, the acceptance of the principle of trade (1022–24).

This question and the next few questions follow that three-part structure. So, first: explain what Galt means by, and what his reasons are for asserting, the two statements that give the basic facts about human nature on which the Morality of Life depends: "Man's mind is his basic tool of survival"; and: "Man is a being of volitional consciousness" (1012).

3. The two facts just discussed are distinctive to man. But there is one other fact about human nature that is crucially relevant—and this man shares with all living things: man is a *living* being. What does Galt mean by the statement (1012) that "the existence of life is not [unconditional]"?

4. How are the previous facts relevant to the concept of *value*? Present, in logical progression, Galt's analysis of the concept of *value*, showing its dependence on the concept of *life*. Explain how it follows from this that for any living organism, its life is its standard of value. Then explain how the volitional character of man's consciousness gives rise to the concept of *moral* values, and necessitates for man a code of morality.

5. Galt starts the presentation of the metaphysical and epistemological basis of the Morality of Life with the statement "We, the men of the mind, are now on strike against you in the name of a single axiom, which is the root of our moral code, just as the root of yours is the wish to escape it: the axiom that *existence exists*" (1015). What does Galt mean by the statement "existence exists"? What is meant by the statements: "Existence is Identity, Consciousness is Identification"? What is his definition of "reason"? Of "logic"? Of "reality"? Of "truth"?

6. Skipping ahead in the speeach for a moment, what is an *axiom*? (1040) How is a statement which is an axiom shown actually to be an axiom? (1039–40). What is the fallacy of the "stolen concept"? (1039).

7. What is the law of causality? (1037). What is its relationship to the axiom of Identity?

8. Returning now to Galt's presentation of the Morality of Life, why is "thinking . . . man's only basic virtue"? (1017).

9. What is the meaning of the statement, "My morality . . . is contained in a single axiom: existence exists—and in a single choice: to live" (1018). How is it dependent on that axiom? How is it dependent on that choice?

10. Identify the "ruling values" of the Morality of Life, and describe each one in your own words (1018).

11. What does Galt mean, on p. 1018, when he says "all his virtues pertain to the relationship of existence and consciousness"? Let's approach this in stages, by examining each of the seven virtues Galt

identifies: rationality, independence, integrity, honesty, justice, productiveness, and pride, as follows.

   (i)   Define and summarize each of the virtues, as presented on pp. 1018–21.

   (ii) What is the significance of the fact that the account of each virtue begins with a sentence containing the words "is the recognition of the fact that"? To answer this, first (a) identify in each case what the relevant fact is, then (b) identify what all of these facts are facts *about*; then (c) identify how, as policies of action based on these recognitions, they *are* recognitions of those facts, then finally (d) return to the statement on p. 1018 with which this question began, and explain its meaning.

   (iii) With your answers to (i)–(ii) as background, explain *why* Galt holds that each of the seven virtues he lists *is in fact* a virtue. Focus especially on how their status as a virtue is entailed by the choice to *live*.

12. (i)   What is an emotion? What determines which emotion a person will experience in response to a situation? (1021–22).

   (ii) What is Galt's definition of "happiness"? (1014). What is its *source*, and what isn't? (1022).

   (iii) Discuss how the answers to (i) and (ii) are connected. In regard to this, explain the relationship between the successful pursuit of life (see again, Q. 10 above) and the achievement of happiness (Q. 12 [ii] just above).

   (iv) Make use of your answers to (i)–(iii) to explain the fundamental distinction Galt makes on p. 1024 between motivation by joy (or love of life) and motivation by fear (or the avoidance of pain or death). Note how this serves as the transition to the examination of the morality Galt and his strikers reject: the prevalent morality of *sacrifice*, and to the analysis of it as a morality of *death* (1024–25, and see Sentence III, just below).

13. Galt ends his presentation of the Morality of Life with the fundamental moral principles of human interaction. Why does he hold the principle of *trade* as the fundamental social principle, and the initiation of force as the fundamental evil in human interaction? (1022–24) In what way are they both—the advocacy of the *voluntary* in human relations and the condemnation of the initiation of force—an expression of the fundamental virtue of *rationality*? (1022).

III. **The morality of sacrifice is the morality of *death*, for it demands renunciation of that which makes life possible: the mind—and thus of any enjoyment of life on earth (1024–34).**

14. Galt maintains that the morality of sacrifice starts from a damnation of man as evil, then builds from there (1025). "The name of this monstrous absurdity is Original Sin." What is the doctrine of Original Sin? (1025). (Observe that Galt does not restrict the doctrine to the version of it taught by Catholicism.) What is its basic contradiction? (1025) What, according to Galt, is the actual moral status of that which it holds to be a sin? (1025–26).

15. What is the view of human nature that the morality of sacrifice is based upon? (Elsewhere it is called "the soul-body dichotomy") (1026). In what way does this doctrine "negate man's mind"?

16. What are the two doctrines that Galt ascribes to the "mystics of spirit" and "mystics of muscle"? In what way are they both advocates of the soul-body dichotomy (especially since the mystics of muscle deny the existence of mind)? Identify first the view of human nature of each, then the ethical view of each, then identify what these two doctrines have in common (1027). (Do you see in what way Christianity and Marxism are representatives of each, and in what way these categories extend beyond those particular teachings to label two broad *types* of view shared by various and sundry viewpoints?)

17. What is a "sacrifice"? Is *any* help to others a sacrifice? Why is actual sacrifice evil and fundamentally self-destructive? Why does it involve "sacrifice of the mind"? Can it rationally be maintained that one derives one's happiness from sacrifice, as advocates of that ethics sometimes maintain? (1027–31).

18. What is the standard of the good in an ethics of sacrifice? Why does it divide mankind into "two enemy camps"? If selfishness is evil and sacrifice is good, why—and when—is it moral for the receivers of sacrifices to accept them? What, according to Galt, is the deeper meaning of such a code? (1030–33).

19. According to the code Galt is attacking, the justification of sacrifice is *love*. What *is* love, in fact, and what, then, is the meaning of the idea that you should love all human beings equally and *disinterestedly*? (1033–34).

20. Summarize (a) the fundamental metaphysical dichotomy underlying the morality of sacrifice (return to the initial summary on pp. 1026–27, second paragraph, for a better perspective now on its meaning), and its view of human nature and the consequent ethics); and (b) why this is "the morality of death," according to Galt.

IV. **This code is taught by men who, having renounced their minds, seek power over the consciousnesses of other men, by attempting to convince them to renounce their own minds and accept the morality of sacrifice; the deepest motive of these teachers of sacrifice is hatred of** existence, of life, of man, of themselves—and their goal is to destroy their victims and themselves (1034–47).

21. What are the epistemological claims of the two schools of mystics? (1034–35). What are the metaphysical claims—that is what is it that they claim to perceive by higher means? (1035–36). What philosophical objections does Galt make to these epistemological and metaphysical claims? (1034–35). What does he say is the *motive* for which they make such claims? (1035–36). Why is it ultimately "a desire not to be"?

22. "The nature of an action is caused and determined by the nature of the entities that act." (1037) Explain. How is this formulation of the law of causality validated? In what way is the code of sacrifice—both the doctrine that one should give one's wealth sacrificially and the doctrine that one should give one's love sacrificially—an attempt to deny or evade the law of causality? (Compare Francisco's analysis of the motivation behind the practitioners of promiscuous sex, in *Atlas* pp. 489–92.)

23. After reviewing your answer to Q. 6 above, identify each of the concepts or principles listed on pp. 1039–40 which cannot be rejected without violating the axioms, explaining why they cannot. Summarize Galt's explanation of the validity of the senses (1040–41).

24. Summarize (a) Galt's refutation of the mystics' attack on (i) objective reality, (ii) the senses, (iii) reason; (b) his view of the consequences of accepting these attacks; and (c) his refutation of the denial of the existence and efficacy of the mind by the "mystics of muscle." Why might one think that Marxism and Behaviorism, although not mentioned by Galt, are versions of the doctrines held by the "mystics of muscle"?

25. Summarize Galt's analysis of the psychology of a mystic: how it develops, the nature of his psychological dependence on other consciousnesses, his need to dominate them, his consequent resentment and hatred of them, his desire to destroy them. (I've just given you a summary of the steps in the analysis; explain how each step follows from the preceding one) (1044–47).

V. If all men who desire to live reject—as we the strikers have—the doctrines of mysticism and sacrifice, realizing that no compromise is possible, and withdraw from the world, demanding instead a society of rights and freedom, then the society of the mystics and looters will perish, and we will come to have a world of reason, freedom, achievement, and joy (1047–69).

26. What role does Galt's account of the beginnings of the strike (1047–48) play in his transition from part IV to part V of the speech?

27. What, according to Galt, is the role of the mind in production and survival (1047–49), and what does he mean when he says "I am the first man of ability who refused to regard it as guilt."? (1050). In what way has society regarded productive ability as a measure of guilt? (1049–50).

28. In what way does the morality of sacrifice lead to a split between the "moral" and the "practical"? How has this split led to a general cultural *a*morality (and a consequent *im*morality in practice)? (1053–54). Why do so many people "live without dignity, love without fire, and die without resistance"? State exactly what Galt means by each part of this statement, and then explain why he holds it to be true.

29. "There are two sides to every issue: one side is right and the other is wrong, but the middle is always evil." Explain this statement, making use of the entire discussion of the philosophy of "compromise," of "uncertainty," and of "non-absolutes," spawned by the absence of self-esteem (1054–55). Why does Galt hold that "The man who refuses to judge, who neither agrees nor disagrees, who declares that there are no absolutes and believes that he escapes responsibility, is the man responsible for all the blood that is now spilled in the world." What is Galt's answer to the claim that "there are no absolutes"? (1054).

30. Galt explains that even though people see that the morality of sacrifice is responsible for the devastation and destruction around us, still they refuse to challenge and reject it. His explanation of this refusal is: "You blank it out, because your self-esteem is tied to that mystic 'unselfishness'" (1056). Explain:
    (i)   why man needs self-esteem (showing how this derives from man's "free will");
    (ii) what self-esteem is and how it is acquired (making use also of the definition given on p. 1018, and the discussion of Pride, the virtue by which one acquires self-esteem, on pp. 1020–21);
    (iii) what effect the lack of self-esteem has on a person's general emotional state and perspective on the world;
    (iv) what the consequences are of tying one's self-esteem to living by a moral code which is in fact impossible to practice (1057–58).
    Having answered (i)–(iv), go on now to give a unified explanation of Galt's statement quoted at the beginning of this question.

31. One's reaction to the first full paragraph on p.1058 is a very private matter, and I will not ask anything specific about it, though I will ask you to explain each sentence of it to yourself.

32. Why, according to Galt, is it that "the noblest act you have ever performed is the act of your mind in the process of grasping that two

and two make four"? Why is accepting this fact—if it is fully and consistently understood and accepted—"the dedication to one's highest potential"? (1058).

33. What is Galt's answer to the following statements?
    (i)   "I'm afraid to trust my mind, I know so little" (1058).
    (ii) "Man is imperfect" (l059—explain how he understands "moral perfection"; in this connection explain clearly the distinction between "errors of knowledge" and "breaches of morality").

34. And what is Galt's answer to these two statements?
    (i)   "I can live without happiness" (1059).
    (ii) "The morality you present is too hard to practice" (1060).

35. What, according to Galt, is a "right"? What is the meaning of the statement, "The source of man's rights is not divine law or congressional law, but the law of identity"? For example, explain what rights does man have, according to Galt, and how Galt proves that we have such rights (1061–62).

36. Explain clearly Galt's derivation of the right to property (1062).

37. What contribution to survival is made by the industrialist, and by any productive person of superior intelligence? Is the return such a person receives in a free society commensurate with his contribution? Explain (1063–65).

38. What is the nature of the betrayal that Galt attributes to people such as Robert Stadler? (1066).

39. What (i) practical and (ii) inspirational advice does Galt give to "those who desire to live"? In what other ways does Galt characterize these individuals? What future does he offer? (1066–68).

40. To whom is Galt addressing "the last of my words" (1068), and what is distinctive about what he says to them? To whom has he been speaking throughout the rest of the speech? (Review the entire speech to answer this. Is it the identical audience throughout? Compare Ghate's answer, 366 above, with your own.) To whom are the final four paragraphs of the speech addressed? Sum up in your own words what he says in those final paragraphs (1068–69).

CODA

Who is John Galt?—The Speech's Own Answer

Atlas Shrugged opens with the question "Who is John Galt?" In a sense, the entire novel is an answer to that question, and if Galt's Speech is a summation of that answer, it is perhaps fitting for us to close our study of the speech with the speech's own, explicit multipart answer to that question. Note that immediately after Galt announces that he has taken over the airwaves, he begins the body of the speech with the words: "For twelve years, you have been asking: Who is John Galt? This is John Galt speaking." His next sentence begins: "I am the man who . . ."—and thus begins his first statement of his own answer to that question. Across the speech, Galt refers to that question some five times, and provides some sixteen statements that begin with "I am the man who . . ." or something similar. The sixteen answers overlap in content, but are never fully identical, serving as they do in their specific contexts. But they are certainly consistent, providing us with different *facets* both of a deeply integrated speech and of a profoundly integrated person. These passages, then, need to be studied, first one at a time, identifying the precise meaning conveyed—and then as a whole, condensing the sequence of identified meanings into a single statement, much as, at the start of this essay, we discussed doing via successive condensations of the speech. This is a very difficult assignment, but the rewards are significant: a deeper understanding of the content of the speech, of the thought and the character of John Galt, of the role in *Atlas Shrugged* both of John Galt and of his speech, and of the thought and soul of the novel's author.

As I mentioned in the introduction, however, I shall leave it to Galt to present his multifaceted answer to the question Who Is John Galt? in his own words, and to you, my reader, to produce a single, unified formulation of it in yours. (The emphases are my own.)

For twelve years, you have been asking: **Who is John Galt?** This is John Galt speaking. **I am the man who** loves his life. **I am the man who** does not sacrifice his love or his values. **I am the man who** has deprived you of victims and thus has destroyed your world, and if you wish to know why you are perishing—you who dread knowledge—**I am the man who** will now tell you. (1009)

You have destroyed all that which you held to be evil and achieved all that which you held to be good. Why, then, do you shrink in horror from the sight of the world around you? That world is not the product of your sins, it is the product and the image of your virtues. It is your moral ideal brought into reality in its full and final perfection. You have fought for it, you have dreamed of it, and you have wished it, and I—**I am the man who** has granted you your wish. (1010)

Through centuries of scourges and disasters, brought about by your code of morality, you have cried that your code had been broken, that the scourges were punishment for breaking it, that men were too weak and too selfish to spill all the blood it required. You damned man, you damned existence, you damned this earth, but never dared to question your code. Your victims took the blame and struggled on, with your curses as reward for their martyrdom—while you went on crying that your code was noble, but human nature was not good enough to practice it. And no one rose to ask the question: Good?—by what standard?

You wanted to know **John Galt's identity. I am the man who** has asked that question. (1011)

Are you beginning to see **who is John Galt?** I am the man who has earned the thing you did not fight for, the thing you have renounced, betrayed, corrupted, yet were unable fully to destroy and are now hiding as your guilty secret, spending your life in apologies to every professional cannibal, lest it be discovered that somewhere within you, you still long to say what I am now saying to the hearing of the whole of mankind: I am proud of my own value and of the fact that I wish to live. (1021)

We, who were the living buffers between you and the nature of your creed, are no longer there to save you from the effects of your chosen beliefs. We are no longer willing to pay with our lives the debts you incurred in yours or the moral deficit piled up by all the generations behind you. You had been living on borrowed time—and **I am the man who** has called in the loan.

I am the man whose existence your blank-outs were intended to permit you to ignore. **I am the man whom** you did not want either to live or to die. You did not want me to live, because you were afraid of knowing that I carried the responsibility you dropped and that your lives depended upon me; you did not want me to die, because you knew it. (1047)

Did you want to know **who is John Galt?** I am the first man of ability who refused to regard it as guilt. **I am the first man who** would not do penance for my virtues or let them be used as the tools of my destruction. **I am the first man who** would not suffer martyrdom at the hands of those who wished me to perish for the privilege of keeping them alive. **I am the first man who** told them that I did not need them, and until they learned to deal with me as traders, giving value for value, they would have to exist without me, as I would exist without them; then I would let them learn whose is the need and whose the ability—and if human survival is the standard, whose terms would set the way to survive. (1050)

Some of you will never know **who is John Galt.** But those of you who have known a single moment of love for existence and of pride in being its worthy lover, a moment of looking at this earth and letting your glance be its sanction, have known the state of being a man, and I—**I am only the man who** knew that that state is not to be betrayed. **I am the man who** knew what made it possible and who chose consistently to practice and to be what you had practiced and been in that one moment. (1058)

NOTES

1. With the kind permission of Wiley-Blackwell, this essay draws on material from my chapter "Galt's Speech and the Philosophy of Objectivism" that will appear in *Ayn Rand: A Companion to Her Works and Thought*, Allan Gotthelf and Gregory Salmieri, eds. (Oxford: Wiley-Blackwell, forthcoming). A good deal of the material in the present essay goes back to my preparation for a workshop on the Objectivist ethics I gave in New York City in 1967 (on which see further in n. 12 below); and a portion was developed in connection with my frequent teaching of the novel in

courses at The College of New Jersey (formerly Trenton State College). Most of this teaching was done in an honors course on "Human Love in Philosophy and Literature" that I cotaught biennially, across some twenty years, with James Brazell of the college's English department. I offer my deep gratitude to Jim and to our many students, for the wonderful teaching (and learning) experiences the course provided me; it was truly one of the long-term personal highlights of my teaching career. (One of our former students, Gregory Salmieri, as it happens, is a contributor to this volume.) In this essay I have made good use of other essays in the present volume, and recorded lectures, by Onkar Ghate, Shoshana Milgram, and Greg Salmieri. I also thank Greg and Mary Ann Sures for extensive and valuable comments on a previous draft.

2. Expanded second edition, ed. H. Binswanger and L. Peikoff (New York: Meridian, 1990), 63.

3. "The Role of Galt's Speech in *Atlas Shrugged*," above, 363.

4. For the meaning in *Atlas Shrugged* of the phrase "the men of the mind," see Gregory Salmieri's essay above, "*Atlas Shrugged* on The Role of the Mind in Man's Existence," 219–21.

5. Ghate also discusses, with great insight, why, for such a strike to be possible, Galt must be a man of genius, and how only an achievement such as the speech can show that, and thus, from the standpoint of the success of the novel in creating both a convincing story line and in exemplifying its basic theme, why the speech, in full, must be present. It is arguable whether Ghate's argument by itself establishes a need for a speech of this length (viz. some three hours [1071, 1100] and some sixty pages). But that argument, together with the sort of close analysis of the speech's content and progression we are about to embark on, in my view certainly does.

6. On the relationship between Galt's Speech and Rand's philosophic system, which she came to call "Objectivism," see her preface to *For the New Intellectual: The Philosophy of Ayn Rand* (New York: Random House, 1960), vii–viii, and my discussion in the chapter on Galt's Speech in *Ayn Rand: A Companion to Her Works and Thought* (above, n. 1). Also useful in this connection are Onkar Ghate's essay on Galt's Speech just above and Gregory Salmieri's discussion of *Atlas Shrugged*'s particular character as a *philosophical* novel, in his "Discovering Atlantis," esp. 399–403 and 442–43 below. (Salmieri's other contribution, on the wide-ranging character of the novel's theme, "*Atlas Shrugged* on the Role of the Mind in Man's Existence," is relevant as well, as are several other contributions to this volume.)

7. My gratitude to Greg Salmieri, who helped me to formulate the connection between this essay's epigraph and the method of condensation I am recommending here. For further discussion of the epistemic significance of the principle of unit-economy, see Rand, *Introduction to Objectivist Epistemology*, chapter 7; Gotthelf, "Ayn Rand on Concepts: Another Approach to Abstraction and Essence," unpublished; and Salmieri, "The Objectivist Epistemology," in *Ayn Rand: A Companion to Her Works and Thought* (above, n. 1).

8. See n. 1 above.

9. Here I take issue with Onkar Ghate's analysis of this part of the speech (above, 1, 363).

10. For an excellent discussion of this issue, see Salmieri, "Discovering Atlantis," 435–49 below.

11. Witness the life of James Taggart—and recall what Galt says to him, in the torture room, when this fact about himself breaks into Taggart's consciousness, and Taggart moans "No . . . No . . ." (1146):

"Yes," said Galt.

He saw Galt's eyes looking straight at his, as if Galt were seeing the things he was seeing.

"I told you that on the radio, didn't I?"

12. The draft typescript for my presentation on Galt's Speech in my 1967 workshop on the Objectivist Ethics (n. 1, above) included a five statement outline (very close to the Five Sentences I use in this essay). Ayn Rand kindly agreed to read and comment on the entire draft before the class met. In a memorable meeting in her apartment that summer, she read through the typescript, marking with her typical backwards-checkmarks places where she had comments to make. When she was done, she looked up with a smile and said, "You've got it." To the five statement summary of Galt's Speech she had one correction, to the fourth statement, the validity of which I could see immediately and incorporated into my typescript. (I no longer recall the precise point she made.)

With the rest, she was in agreement. In recounting this, I do not mean to imply that the five-part structure I identify in this essay, and the way I formulate the essential content of each part, is the way Rand herself identified the structure and content when she prepared the speech or the way she would have done so had she herself taken on in 1967 the task of reoutlining the published speech. But I do want to report, for the historical record, my recollection of her approval, for public presentation, of my account of the basic structure and content of the speech. Readers should in any case work through my account on their own, comparing it, and the evidence in the speech I provide for it, with the speech itself—and should ideally prepare their own outline, as I have done mine. In the essay on which the present one is based (above n. 1), I briefly discuss the evidence for the content of Rand's own outline(s) during the writing of the speech, as that is available in her journal notes; meanwhile, see Shoshana Milgram's discussion of this topic (above, 53), and the passages she refers to in David Harriman, ed., *Journals of Ayn Rand* (New York: Dutton, 1997). Readers can also compare the full outline of the speech that Gregory Salmieri—building in part as he says (467) on my analysis of the speech and in part on lectures by Onkar Ghate—provides in an appendix to the present volume.

21

Discovering Atlantis

Atlas Shrugged's Demonstration of a New Moral Philosophy

Gregory Salmieri

I think I'm discovering a new continent. . . . A continent that should have been discovered along with America, but wasn't. (438)

Hank Rearden has just had Floyd Ferris ejected from his office, refusing to succumb to his attempt at blackmail, and he has seen a connection between this blackmail attempt and the manner in which his wife Lillian is attempting to punish him for his adultery. This is an important step in what he will later describe as his "liberation from guilt." Rearden's description of what he's discovering as a "new continent" is an allusion to Atlantis, which had been associated with America earlier in the novel (153–54), by an old spinster who claimed that the mysterious John Galt had found the lost island. Atlantis becomes a recurring symbol in parts II and III, and, in his radio speech, Galt describes it (along with several similar legends) as representing "a radiant state of existence" (1058) which most men experience only in early childhood or isolated moments of their adult life. To maintain this state, Galt explains, requires a moral philosophy which is implicit in America's founding and in the lives of men such as Hank Rearden, but which Galt himself was the first to define and implement consistently.

For some time prior to his encounter with Ferris, Rearden feels "a strange excitement . . . as if he were on the trail of some discovery still too distant to know, except that it had the most immense importance he had ever glimpsed" (366), and in the present scene he "discovers another step along his half-glimpsed trail" (435). The trail leads to Galt's philosophy; and, unbeknownst to Rearden, Galt is facilitating his progress. He does this in part through his agent, Francisco d'Anconia, and in part by creating a social and economic circumstance in which the nature and consequences of the prevailing moral code are increasingly obvious, the contrast between it and Rearden's own code of values is increasingly stark.[1]

Galt has called a secret strike of the men of the mind against this prevailing moral code and in the name of his new philosophy. *Atlas Shrugged* opens in the tenth year of this strike and follows Dagny Taggart and Hank Rearden, the last significant scabs, over the course of three years, as they learn of and are won over to Galt's cause. Their joining the strike precipitates the full collapse of society and clears the road for the men of the mind to return to the world and rebuild it on the right philosophical foundation (1168). But before Dagny or Rearden can be ready to join the strike they must discover the truth of Galt's philosophy and why it requires this drastic action. And the reader must discover this too, if he is to understand the characters' motivations and the logic of the plot. It is for this reason that Rand includes "the demonstration of a new moral philosophy" in her statement of the novel's theme.[2]

In philosophical contexts especially, "to demonstrate" means to *prove;* and since a theme is an essentialized statement of "a novel's abstract meaning,"[3] to say that demonstrating a moral philosophy is part of *Atlas Shrugged*'s theme is to say that proving this philosophy is essential to the novel. This is a striking thing for Rand to hold, since she argued in other contexts that, though art often does prove or teach philosophical principles, this is a consequence, rather than a part of, its purpose: "since every art work has a theme, it will necessarily convey some conclusion, some 'message,' to its audience. But that influence and that 'message' are only secondary consequences. *Art is not the means to any didactic end.*"[4] The demonstration of a moral code is essential to *Atlas Shrugged*, however, because of the role it plays in the novel's plot. *Atlas* dramatizes "the role of the mind in man's existence" by showing Galt's strike—an action that is explicitly motivated by a philosophy and accomplished by convincing the other men of the mind of its truth.

Dagny and Rearden in particular are convinced by a complex train of reasoning extended over the years in which the novel is set—a chain of reasoning that both arises from and gives rise to the actions that constitute the novel's plot.[5] This train of reasoning is *Atlas Shrugged*'s demonstration of a new moral philosophy, and one needs to follow it in order to fully appreciate the novel, either as a work of literature or as a work of philosophy. My project here is to outline this progression and to highlight some of its most important developments, bringing out the order in which the principles are established and some of the relations between them. In doing so, I hope to give readers a sense of the whole and to introduce them to a way of reading and thinking about the novel that will enable them to better appreciate, enjoy, and learn from it. In particular, I will discuss: how Rearden grasps and applies the principle of the sanction of the victim; Dagny's sharpening identification of the premise that ties her to the looters' world; and the final realizations that lead Dagny and Rearden to join the strike. Before taking up these topics it will be instructive to discuss some preliminaries concerning the way in which *Atlas Shrugged* demonstrates principles and, more generally, how it is possible for a novel to demonstrate anything at all.

ATLAS SHRUGGED AS A WORK OF PHILOSOPHY

I have already indicated that Rearden and Dagny reach their conclusions on the basis of the events that constitute the novel's plot: they observe and reflect on the effects of the strike and the differences made stark by it between themselves and the villains and between their own values and the prevailing moral code. It is on the basis of these same observations that the reader too is supposed to become convinced of Galt's philosophy. However, since the events of the novel are fictitious, the reader—unlike the characters living in the universe of the novel—cannot take these events as facts and assume that generalizations reached from them will apply in the real world. Novelists routinely depict events or situations that could not occur. For example, one finds in fiction many socialist utopias replete with ever-improving technology and happy citizens—something that Rand argues is impossible. Of course, the existence of these societies in fiction does not prove Rand wrong on this point, and, by the same token, the mere fact that socialism fails in her novels does not prove that it must fail in reality.

How then can a novel prove anything? Novels—or at least Romantic novels, such as Rand's—do not simply portray situations and events haphazardly. They show some events as *following* from others and from facts about the circumstances and characters—especially from the characters' choices.[6] As readers we can assess whether these events do in fact follow from such causes, and we can consider whether the causes—the kinds of characters and circumstances presented in the novel—actually exist.

Of course we rarely if ever encounter in the real world people or situations exactly like those in novels. This is true even of Naturalistic novels, which aim to mirror real-life circumstances, and it is all the more true of Romantic novels, which aim to project a world grander than that of day-to-day life. However, if the characters, circumstances, and events in a work of fiction are not journalistic reproductions of real things, neither are they entirely divorced from them. As Rand observed, an artist *stylizes* reality by "isolating and stressing" those elements of it that he regards as significant and "omitting the insignificant and accidental."[7] As a result of this stylization, a work of fiction can make salient causal connections that, though not obvious in the real world, can be easily observed there once our attention has been called to them.[8] It is in this way that fiction can demonstrate, for example, that socialism cannot succeed. By depicting a world in which the facts that lead to this conclusion stand in sharper relief than they do amidst the train of accidental minutiae that constitutes so much of daily life, *Atlas Shrugged* helps us to notice these facts and their implications.

We can, then, draw conclusions from the events in a novel, just as the characters do, and apply these conclusions to our world and our lives, when we can identify in our world the facts from which these conclusions follow. But we cannot apply conclusions about the world of a novel to our own without doing this. We would not, for example, decide based on the events of *Atlas Shrugged* that we ought to buy or sell shares of Taggart Transcontinental, when in fact there is no such company. Similarly, we should not conclude from the novel that the proper course of action in America today is to go on strike.

In interviews, Rand said that it would not be proper or necessary to withdraw from the world until a dictatorship was established that banned free speech, because after this point it would be impossible to fight a battle of ideas within society. Certainly such a dictatorship was in power by the end of *Atlas Shrugged*, but this was not yet the case when Galt initiated his strike.[9] Galt calls for a strike before there is a dictatorship because the universe in which he lives is different from ours in some respects. In her early notes for the novel, Rand described the strike as an element of "fantasy."[10] It would not be possible for one man to recruit and organize all the productive men as Galt does—much less for him to do it secretly and within a single generation.

There are too many such people in the real world, and, whereas, in the novel, most characters are either black or white—producers or parasites—in reality, there are many more shades of grey. Consider, for example, Warren Buffet and Bill Gates, both of whom produced fortunes in innovative and honest ways but also advocated for welfare-statist measures. Again, the founders of Google created major values with their search engine and other services, but they also used antitrust legislation to persecute Microsoft, and they collaborated with the Chinese government's censors. Such mixed people can be analyzed in terms of black and white elements: their productive actions have the same sorts of motivations and consequences as do Rearden's, though they sometimes act in the manner of Orren Boyle.[11] In a world where so many of the great producers are mixed in this way, a strike such as Galt's is not possible, even if it were otherwise logistically feasible.

Thus, the specific conclusion that Dagny and Rearden reach—that they should go on strike—is not applicable in our world. What *Atlas Shrugged* demonstrates is not this conclusion, but rather a philosophy that necessitates a strike in the world of the novel but different actions in our world. Rand went on to write many nonfiction articles and books concerning the application of her philosophy to actual events, and I will make occasional reference to such real-world applications later in this essay. For the most part, however, I will confine myself to the world and events of the novel and the conclusions that the heroes draw from them. Before turning to these heroes and tracing their development, it will be instructive to consider holistically the nature of what they learn and the structure of the novel.

What Rearden and Dagny (and the reader) discover over the course of the novel is not a collection of isolated points, but a philosophy—a complex system of abstract principles by which one can guide one's life. The novel progresses from comparatively concrete points to increasingly abstract principles that integrate and explain them. I alluded earlier to the novel's demonstration that socialism cannot work. This is not a point that any of the heroes need to learn; it is one of a number of moral and political convictions that they share from the beginning of the novel. Such convictions motivate Dagny and Rearden's actions across part I, during which the reader is given several demonstrations of their truth. In part II, Dagny and Rearden come to see these convictions as components of a *moral code* that makes life possible. The events, premises, and characters from part I are reconceived in part II in terms of the alternative between this moral code and its antithesis—thus the part's title, "Either-Or."[12] This new, integrative perspective gives Dagny and Rearden a deeper understanding of themselves and of the villains, it motivates them to actions they could not have taken in part I, and it enables them to interpret the results of their actions in ways that lead to further realizations. As a result of this, in part III, they come to see the opposite moral codes as expressions of opposite attitudes towards existence as such; and it is grasping this and everything that follows from it that motivates them to join the strike. Recall how Galt describes the strikers' position: "We, the men of the mind, are now on strike against you in the name of a single axiom, which is the root of our moral code, just as the root of yours is the wish to escape it: the axiom that *existence exists*" (1015). Thus, while part II is essentially *moral*, part III is essentially *metaphysical*, which is why it has as its name the "formula" that Galt tells us "defines the concept of existence": "A is A" (1015).[13]

The difference between the three parts is especially clear when one compares the way the same issues are treated across them. For example: in part I, we see numerous examples of Rearden and Dagny acting (both in business and in their personal lives) as traders to mutual advantage, and we see how the villains' demands for sacrifice lead to destruction. Already in part I, Rearden opposes many of the calls for sacrifice, but he does something markedly different during his courtroom speech in part II, when, after arguing that "nobody's good can be achieved at the price of human sacrifices," he concludes:

> It is not your particular policy that I challenge, but your moral premise. If it were true that men could achieve their good by means of turning some men into sacrificial animals, and I were asked to immolate myself for the sake of creatures who wanted to survive at the price of my blood, if I were asked to serve the interests of society apart from, above and against my own—I would refuse. I would reject it as the most contemptible evil, I would fight it with every power I possess, I would fight the whole of mankind, if one minute were all I could last before I were murdered, I would fight in the full confidence of the justice of my battle and of a living being's right to exist. Let there be no misunderstanding about me. If

it is now the belief of my fellow men, who call themselves the public, that their good requires victims, then I say: The public good be damned, I will have no part of it! (481)

Rearden rejects sacrifice as such as impractical and evil, and he sees it as the consequence of an evil *moral premise*. As we will see in greater detail later, this is not something that he would have been able to do earlier in the novel. Now contrast this with Galt's discussion of conflicts of interest early in part III of the novel:

> Did it ever occur to you, Miss Taggart, that there is no conflict of interests among men, neither in business nor in trade nor in their most personal desires—if they omit the irrational from their view of the possible and destruction from their view of the practical? There is no conflict, and no call for sacrifice, and no man is a threat to the aims of another—if men understand that reality is an absolute not to be faked, that lies do not work, that the unearned cannot be had, that the undeserved cannot be given, that the destruction of a value which is, will not bring value to that which isn't. The businessman who wishes to gain a market by throttling a superior competitor, the worker who wants a share of his employer's wealth, the artist who envies a rival's higher talent—they're all wishing facts out of existence, and destruction is the only means of their wish. If they pursue it, they will not achieve a market, a fortune or an immortal fame—they will merely destroy production, employment and art. A wish for the irrational is not to be achieved, whether the sacrificial victims are willing or not. But men will not cease to desire the impossible and will not lose their longing to destroy—so long as self-destruction and self-sacrifice are preached to them as the practical means of achieving the happiness of the recipients. (798)

Here conflicts of interest are seen as arising not simply from a false moral premise, but, more deeply, from the denial that reality is absolute—that is, from a false metaphysical premise.

We will see further evidence of the progression between the three parts later, when we turn to the details of Rearden and Dagny's development. For now, as a further indication, we can note that the frequency of the words "moral" and "evil" more than triples between parts I and II, and that between parts II and III, the frequency of metaphysical terms such as "reality" and "existence" triples.[14]

Since it is primarily in the last two parts of the novel that the philosophical principles are articulated, my focus will be there. It will be helpful at the outset, however, to comment briefly on Part I, which provides the context for what follows. It is the story of Dagny Taggart's greatest achievement and its consequences. We see in great detail how the John Galt Line is the product of her and Rearden's virtue, and we see why the Line is necessary to save the Colorado industrialists and, with them, Taggart Transcontinental and the nation. We also see how the Line, in fact, serves to hasten the destruction of these very industrialists: the bonds they invest in it are "frozen," thus depriving them of crucially needed assets, and regulations on the size, speed, and frequency of trains prevent them from getting the transportation their businesses need to survive (333–35). The fate of the Line is a paradox—an apparent contradiction—which Dagny and Rearden must come to understand in parts II and III of the novel. In order to do so they will need, in the words of Akston and Francisco, to "check their premises" (199, 331, 489, 618, 737, 807).[15]

REARDEN'S LIBERATION FROM GUILT

Rearden first feels the excitement of being "on the trail of some discovery still too distant to know" at the beginning of part II, during his interview with the nameless bureaucrat who looks like a "traffic cop" and tries to intimidate him into selling Rearden Metal to the State Science Institute. The bureaucrat keeps up the pretense that the interview is "an amicable discussion," and reacts with a mixture of bewilderment and fear when Rearden, refusing to maintain this pretense, states that he only granted the interview under the threat of arrest, which is the traffic cop's "ultimate argument against" him and is "implied by every sentence in this discussion." It is in observing this reaction that Rearden first glimpses the trail, and he pursues it by challenging the bureaucrat to seize his metal openly by force, as he would have to without Rearden's help pretending that the transaction is a sale. The result is an "instinctive, involuntary cry"— "Good God, Mr. Rearden, what would the public think!"—and Rearden knows that he has taken "the right steps down the trail he had glimpsed" (366).

Shortly after the event, Rearden has a discussion with Dagny from which we can learn what he does and does not understand at this point. He describes the bureaucrat as "scared way deep":

> Of what? I don't know—public opinion was just his name for it, but it's not the full name. Why should he have been scared? He has the guns, the jails, the laws—he could have seized the whole of my mills, if he wished, and nobody would have risen to defend me, and he knew it—so why should he have cared what I thought? But he did. It was I who had to tell him that he wasn't a looter, but my customer and friend. That's what he needed from me. (377)

Rearden is a victim of the State Science Institute, and the bureaucrat needs his help to pretend that this is not the case.

Rearden immediately recognizes this same phenomenon at work when Dagny describes her unexplained feeling that she should not have called Robert Stadler (377, cf. 353). Stadler, Rearden says, wanted a "recognition" from her "that he was still the Dr. Robert Stadler he should have been but wasn't and knew he wasn't."

> He wanted you to grant him your respect, in spite of and in contradiction to his actions. He wanted you to juggle reality for him, so that his greatness would

remain, but the State Science Institute would be wiped out, as if it had never existed—and you're the only one who could do it for him. . . . Because you're the victim. (377)

The State Science Institute was created "as a personal present" from the nation to Stadler, who had used his prestige to advocate for it (186). In part I, it issued a slanderous statement about Rearden Metal that made it impossible for Taggart Transcontinental to complete the Rio Norte Line, which was to be made out of Rearden Metal rails. Dagny was able to complete the line only by leaving the job that had been her life's goal and forming an independent company, finding independent investors (whose investment was eventually seized by order of Wesley Mouch), and running herself ragged for months. Stadler knew that the Institute's statement was false and unscientific, but refused to repudiate it when Dagny confronted him. The call she felt she should not make occurred a year later. Though she did not know this, it came moments after he declined to repudiate a book, published under the auspices of the Institute, that distorted his own scientific work into a profane attack on the mind. As a result he felt, "in the fog of a pain that he would not define," "the desperate feeling that no one—of those he valued—would ever wish to see him again"; and he realized that he had to wish that Galt, "the man he longed to see more than any other being in the world," was dead and so unable to learn of his shameful action (348). This is the context in which he eagerly accepted Dagny's invitation for a meeting; these are the facts that he wanted Dagny to juggle out of existence for him.

Rearden's identification of what Stadler and the bureaucrat want begins to sum up and explain these events and numerous smaller episodes in the novel; and this is why, when making the identification, he feels "a sudden, violent clarity of perception, as if a surge of energy were rushing into the activity of sight, fusing the half-seen and half-grasped into a single shape and direction." He identifies his present state of understanding as follows:

> Dagny, they're doing something that we've never understood. They know something which we don't, but should discover. I can't see it fully yet, but I'm beginning to see parts of it. . . . I don't know what it is that they think they accomplish—but they want us to pretend that we see the world as they pretend they see it. They need some sort of sanction from us. I don't know the nature of that sanction—but, Dagny, I know that if we value our lives, we must not give it to them. If they put you on a torture rack, don't give it to them. Let them destroy your railroad and my mills, but don't give it to them. Because I know this much: I know that that's our only chance. (377–78)

Dagny agrees: "I can't understand their game, but this much is right: We must not see the world as they want us to see it. It's some sort of fraud, very ancient and very vast—and the key to break it is to check every premise they teach us, to question every precept, to—" (378) She stops because "her next words would have been the ones she did not want to say to him"; she has realized the connection between the issue at hand and another path of discovery along which Rearden is traveling—his "struggle for deliverance" with which she must "help him in every way except in words" (376). We will come to this struggle and its relation to Rearden's present discovery shortly. For now, we can observe that he is struggling against "some sort of perversion in what we're taught, some error that's vicious and very important" (372, 373). Dagny understands the nature of this error more fully than does Rearden, and it is her observation of his struggle against it, along with the principle of premise-checking taught to her by Francisco and Akston, that enables her to identify the way in which she and Rearden must proceed on the present issue.

Let's take stock, now, of what Rearden does and does not understand. He knows that the looters keep up a pretense to themselves about their own nature and actions; that for some reason they need their victims' complicity in this pretense; and that by giving it, the victims grant the looters some sort of sanction. He does not know why the looters need this or the nature of the sanction involved. These answers will come as he progresses further down his trail.

Rearden makes his next significant discovery in the following chapter, when he grasps the point that Dagny refrained from telling him: that there is a connection between his conflict with the looters and his personal conflict over his affair. This occurs during his illegal sale of Rearden Metal to Ken Danagger:

> He thought that he had been made to hide, as a guilty secret, the only business transaction he had enjoyed in a year's work—and that he was hiding, as a guilty secret, his nights with Dagny, the only hours that kept him alive. He felt that there was some connection between the two secrets, some essential connection which he had to discover. He could not grasp it, he could not find the words to name it, but he felt that the day when he would find them, he would answer every question of his life. (384)

Now aware that there is an essential connection between the conflicts in his professional and personal lives, Rearden begins increasingly to apply things he learns in one sphere to the other, and even when Rearden doesn't draw the connections himself, the reader's attention is called to them. Thus, before we proceed further in our discussion of his conflict with the looters, we need to look at Rearden's personal life.

The family he supports trivializes the productive achievements that are Rearden's central purpose in life and subjects him to constant moral censure for his selfishness and lack of nonmaterial values. In part I, he regards their views about business, and those of the whole world, as "tripe" and remains guiltlessly committed to his business; but they nonetheless influence his conception of himself. Most notably he agrees with the accusation that he is evil and describes himself and Dagny as "a couple of blackguards" who "haven't any spiritual goals or qualities" and care only for "material things" (147, 87).

The worst insults come from his wife Lillian, who shows distain not only for his work, but also for his sexual appetite, to which she acquiesces with a condescending indifference. Rearden cannot understand what she sought from the marriage: she shows no affection for him but has not tried to exploit him materially. He concludes that she must be motivated by a love that he cannot comprehend. Thus, though he has come to despise her, he can find no grounds on which to condemn her. Because of this, and because he himself thinks that sex is depraved, he accepts the torture of their marriage as his own fault and cannot justify leaving her (159–60).

Through his relationship with Dagny, for which he initially damns himself, Rearden discovers by degrees the spiritual meaning of sexual desire, learns that the enjoyment of sensual pleasures has its root in spiritual values, and comes to see the connections between his desires for such pleasures and the qualities on which he prides himself in his professional life. Throughout this process his contempt for Lillian grows. Already at the end of part I, we see an anticipation in his dealings with her of the method he employs with the traffic cop. In response to a belittling remark about his manufacturing plumbing pipes, he asks: "[W]hy do you keep making those cracks? I know that you feel contempt for the plumbing pipes. You've made that clear long ago. Your contempt means nothing to me. Why keep repeating it?" (308). Noticing that this "hit her" in some manner that he does not understand, he wonders "why he felt with absolute certainty that *that* had been the right thing to say" (308).

Lillian's next appearance occurs early in part II, moments after Rearden sees the connection between his two guilty secrets. She arrives unannounced at his hotel room and demands that he escort her to Jim Taggart's wedding, though she knows that he despises such occasions:

> I've asked nothing of you. I've let you live your life as you pleased. Can't you give me one evening? Oh, I know you hate parties and you'll be bored. But it means a great deal to me. Call it empty, social vanity—I want to appear, for once, with my husband. I suppose you never think of it in such terms, but you're an important man, you're envied, hated, respected and feared, you're a man whom any woman would be proud to show off as her husband. You may say it's a low form of feminine ostentation, but that's the form of any woman's happiness. You don't live by such standards, but I do. Can't you give me this much, at the price of a few hours of boredom? Can't you be strong enough to fulfill your obligation and to perform a husband's duty? Can't you go there, not for your own sake, but mine, not because *you* want to go, but only because I want it? (386)

The cost to Rearden is higher than Lillian realizes. Rearden knows that Dagny will be at the wedding and he would rather die than "let her see him as the husband proudly being shown off," but "because he had accepted his secret as guilt and promised himself to take its consequences" and "because he granted that the right was with Lillian" he agrees to go (386).[16] He has made a contract with Lillian and he is duty bound to honor it—though, now sensitive to the parallels between his professional and personal life, it occurs to him "that in business transactions the courts of law did not recognize a contract wherein no valuable consideration had been given by one party to the other" (398).

Rearden recalls Lillian's demand later that evening, when Dagny explains why she does not resent his marriage and was not hurt by his attendance at the wedding:

> Hank, I knew you were married. I knew what I was doing. I chose to do it. There's nothing you owe me, no duty you have to consider. . . . I want nothing from you except what you wish to give me. Do you remember that you called me a trader once? I want you to come to me seeking nothing but your own enjoyment. So long as you wish to remain married, whatever your reason, I have no right to resent it. My way of trading is to know that the joy you give me is paid for by the joy you get from me—not by your suffering or mine. I don't accept sacrifices and I don't make them. . . . If ever the pleasure of one has to be bought by the pain of the other, there better be no trade at all. A trade by which one gains and the other looses is a fraud. You don't do it in business, Hank. Don't do it in your own life. (425)

Reflecting on the difference between Dagny's words and Lillian's, he begins to see "the distance between the two, the difference in what they sought from him and from life" (426), though he will not fully grasp what Lillian wants from life until well into part III, and he continues to wonder what Lillian wants from him throughout part II.

The connection between the conflicts in Rearden's personal and professional lives is drawn explicitly in his conversation with Dagny after the wedding, and indeed Dagny's discussion of trade in personal relationships recalls a point that has just been made about financial trade by Francisco, at the wedding that they both attended:

> Money demands of you the recognition that men must work for their own benefit, not for their own injury, for their gain, not their loss—the recognition that they are not beasts of burden, born to carry the weight of your misery—that you must offer them values, not wounds—that the common bond among men is not the exchange of suffering, but the exchange of *goods*. (411)

The quote comes from the novel's first great philosophical speech: Francisco's hymn to the meaning of money (410–15). In it, Francisco gives an abstract statement of the central philosophical principle that has been dramatized by the novel up to this point: *moral virtue*—rationality in particular—is the source of wealth (and, therefore, of survival) and is required to maintain and enjoy it.[17] The speech and Francisco's subsequent conversation with Rearden is a turning point in the novel. The two had met before, but this encounter marks the beginning of their friendship and of Francisco's role as Rearden's teacher. Their first meeting was at the Reardens' anniversary party—an occasion at which all the guests were united in their scorn for Rearden and their support for a piece of legislation (the Equalization of Opportunity Bill) that would soon "slash away part of his life" (214). Francisco offered Rearden gratitude, pointing out that none of the other guests would; and he asked why Rearden was willing to support them. Rearden's unhappiness, he suggested, was evidence of a battle in which these people were using a "terrible weapon" against him (147–48). At the time Rearden damns Francisco, but at Taggart's wedding, he recalls the offer:

> When I met you, do you remember that you said you wanted to offer me your gratitude? . . . I told you that I didn't need it and I insulted you for it. All right, you've won. That speech you've made tonight—that was what you were offering me, wasn't it? . . . It was more than gratitude, and I needed the gratitude; it was more than admiration, and I needed that too; it was much more than any word I can find, it will take me days to think of all that it's given me—but one thing I do know: I needed it. (417)

Months later, Francisco explains to Rearden what he gave him in that speech and why Rearden needed it. We will come to this in due course; for the present let's turn to Francisco's first lesson: "There are no evil thoughts except one, the refusal to think" (418). He explains that Rearden is making the same error, though "in a nobler form," as a woman who dismissed Francisco's speech because she didn't *feel* that it was true (415). Both are "refusing to recognize reality," though for opposite reasons. The woman, and those like her, "keep evading thoughts that they know to be good . . . because they want to avoid effort."

> You keep pushing out of your mind thoughts which you believe to be evil . . . because you won't permit yourself to consider anything that would spare you. They indulge their emotions at any cost. You sacrifice your emotions as the first cost of any problem. They are willing to bear nothing. You are willing to bear anything. They keep evading responsibility, you keep assuming it. But don't you see that the essential error is the same? (418)

Thus, Francisco councils Rearden to examine his desires rather than sacrificing them.

We have seen already how Rearden sacrifices his desires in connection with his marriage and his passion for Dagny. His attendance at the wedding is an example of this; amongst his reasons for consenting to Lillian's demand was that "he heard the pleading cry in his mind: 'Oh God, Lillian, anything but that party!' and he did not allow himself to beg for mercy" (386). Later that evening, reflecting on the pain he (mistakenly) thinks he has inflicted on Dagny, he says of his own pain, "I wish it were worse," and adds, "At least

I'm not letting myself get away with it" (425). When, as a response to these and similar statements, Dagny points out to Rearden that his "only real guilt" is that he's "always rejected [his] own pleasure too easily" and "been willing to bear too much," Rearden recognizes this as the same point Francisco made earlier in the evening (427). But, as Rearden points out, he and Francisco were "talking about quite a different subject": in connection with his professional life also, Rearden has been sacrificing his desires and suppressing thoughts that might alleviate his burdens. Consider how he reacted to the news of Ellis Wyatt's disappearance:

> He tried to avoid these thoughts [that the world is devolving into a Dark Age and that his struggle against it is hopeless]. He had to stand on guard against his own feeling—as if some part of him had become a stranger that had to be kept numb, and his will had to be its constant, watchful anesthetic. That part was an unknown of which he knew only that he must never see its root and never give it voice. He had lived through one dangerous moment which he could not allow to return.
>
> It was the moment when—alone in his office, on a winter evening, held paralyzed by a newspaper spread on his desk with a long column of directives on the front page—he had heard on the radio the news of Ellis Wyatt's flaming oil fields. Then, his first reaction—before any thought of the future, any sense of disaster, any shock, terror or protest—had been to burst out laughing. He had laughed in triumph, in deliverance, in a spurting, living exultation—and the words which he had not pronounced, but felt, were: God bless you, Ellis, whatever you're doing!
>
> When he had grasped the implications of his laughter, he had known that he was now condemned to constant vigilance against himself. Like the survivor of a heart attack, he knew that he had had a warning and that he carried within him a danger that could strike him at any moment. (363)

Rearden bursts into triumphant laughter again at the wedding when Francisco precipitates a run on d'Anconia Copper stock thus ruining many of the looters who profited from the regulations crippling Rearden's mills. Though Rearden suppresses the feeling and repeats his earlier condemnation of Francisco, later that evening he admits that he is "certain of nothing about him—except that I like him" (427), and he agrees with Dagny's assessment that he has "fallen for" Francisco. He now faces directly his thoughts about the state of the world and about what Dagny and Francisco mean to him:

> all that's left for us ahead is to keep the ship afloat as long as we can and then go down with it. . . . I look at people and they seem to be made of nothing but pain. He's not. You're not. That terrible hopelessness that's all around us, I lose it only in his presence and here. Nowhere else. (428)

And, as Rearden acknowledges that he cannot damn Francisco, he acknowledges too that he cannot damn himself and Dagny for their relationship: "the things I said to you that morning in Ellis Wyatt's house . . . I think I was lying to myself" (428).

On the night of Taggart's wedding, then, Rearden hears a moral defense of trade that explains how proper human relationships are based on mutual advantage; he recognizes that his relationship with Dagny is of this nature, whereas his relationship with Lillian is not; he grasps that he has been suppressing as evil thoughts that would alleviate his suffering; and he faces some of these thoughts directly. All of this sets the context for his reaction the following morning when Lillian discovers his adultery.

Lillian's response is revolting. She seems to delight in Rearden's hypocrisy, likening him, "the man who wanted to hold himself as perfect," to Icarus, who "wanted to reach the sun on wings made of wax"; and the punishment she proposes for him targets his "vaunted self-esteem":

> I want you to face, in your own home, the one person who despises you and has the right to do so. I want you to look at me whenever you build another furnace, or pour another recordbreaking load of steel, or hear applause and admiration, whenever you feel proud of yourself, whenever you feel clean, whenever you feel drunk on the sense of your own greatness. I want you to look at me whenever you hear of some act of depravity, or feel anger at human corruption, or feel contempt for someone's knavery, or are the victim of a new governmental extortion—to look and to know that you're no better, that you're superior to no one, that there's nothing you have the right to condemn. (431)

Rearden feels "so overwhelming a tide of revulsion that it swamped Lillian out of human form," but he can account for her ugliness only as an attempt to hide the pain of a betrayed lover, and though he despises Lillian and no longer condemns his passion for Dagny, he does still feel responsible for breaking his marriage vows and hurting Lillian, so he accedes to her wishes. Nevertheless, as Lillian passes sentence on him, he has "the thought that there was some flaw in the scheme of the punishment she wanted him to bear, something wrong by its own terms, aside from its propriety or justice, some practical miscalculation that would demolish it all if discovered" (431).

In the next scene, Rearden, who is now on the premise of noticing parallels between the problems in his personal and professional lives, discovers this same flaw in Floyd Ferris' attempt to pressure him into selling Rearden Metal to the State Science Institute. When Ferris threatens to arrest him for the sale of Rearden Metal to Ken Danagger, Rearden names the act as blackmail, but notes "a peculiar difference between the manner of a plain blackmailer and that of Dr. Ferris." Whereas the former would "show signs of gloating over his victim's sin" and convey a sense of danger to both parties, Ferris' "manner was that of dealing with the normal and the natural, it suggested a sense of safety, it held no tone of condemnation, but a hint of comradeship, a comradeship based—for both of them—on self-contempt" (435).

This had been true of Lillian's manner as well. Seized by a feeling of eager attentiveness, Rearden feels that "he is about to discover another step along his half-glimpsed trail," and he points out that Ferris seems "pleased" that

Rearden had broken one of his laws. When Ferris explains that the laws are made to be broken, so that power-lusting bureaucrats can "cash in on the guilt," Rearden's face takes on the "look of luminous serenity that comes from the sudden answer to an old dark problem." He explains: "There is a flaw in your system, Dr. Ferris, a practical flaw which you will discover when you put me on trial for selling four thousand tons of Rearden Metal to Ken Danagger" (437). Though we are not told this until later, what Rearden realizes is that his trial depends on the pretense, which requires his complicity, that the laws on which he will be tried are legitimate and that his action is a crime. Something analogous is true for Lillian's scheme of punishment, but before Rearden can be in a position to articulate it, there is a crucial lesson that he must learn.

He learns it from his "young teacher," who visits his office two days after his indictment. Francisco has come to make the argument that the strikers use to recruit new members—the argument that we hear in a more complete form from Galt in part III—and he gets a considerable distance into it. The crucial points, and the ones that have the biggest impact on Rearden, are that *morality is man's motive power* and that there are *two opposite moral codes*, one of which makes life possible. Francisco explains that Rearden is "one of the last moral men left to the world," and his morality consists in the manner in which he runs his mills, where every detail is ruthlessly selected so as to be best for his purpose, which is his standard of value. If he has been made to suffer rather than being rewarded for this achievement, it is because he has not exercised this same selectivity when dealing with people.

> You take pride in setting no limit to your endurance, Mr. Rearden, because you think that you are doing right. What if you aren't? What if you're placing your virtue in the service of evil and letting it become a tool for the destruction of everything you love, respect and admire? Why don't you uphold your own code of values among men as you do among iron smelters? You who won't allow one per cent of impurity into an alloy of metal—what have you allowed into your moral code? (453–54)

Rearden had already grasped that the looters needed something from him. Now he begins to see what it is. As Francisco speaks, he hears in his mind, "like the beat of steps down the trail he had been seeking," the words "the sanction of the victim." Francisco goes on to deliver two of the most important paragraphs in the novel, which answer the questions he raised for Rearden in their previous encounters:

> You, who would not submit to the hardships of nature, but set out to conquer it and placed it in the service of your joy and your comfort—to what have you submitted at the hands of men? You, who know from your work that one bears punishment only for being wrong—what have you been willing to bear and for what reason? All your life, you have heard yourself denounced, not for your faults,

but for your greatest virtues. You have been hated, not for your mistakes, but for your achievements. You have been scorned for all those qualities of character which are your highest pride. You have been called selfish for the courage of acting on your own judgment and bearing sole responsibility for your own life. You have been called arrogant for your independent mind. You have been called cruel for your unyielding integrity. You have been called antisocial for the vision that made you venture upon undiscovered roads. You have been called ruthless for the strength and self-discipline of your drive to your purpose. You have been called greedy for the magnificence of your power to create wealth. You, who've expended an inconceivable flow of energy, have been called a parasite. You, who've created abundance where there had been nothing but wastelands and helpless, starving men before you, have been called a robber. You, who've kept them all alive, have been called an exploiter. You, the purest and most moral man among them, have been sneered at as a "vulgar materialist." Have you stopped to ask them: by what right?—by what code?—by what standard? No, you have borne it all and kept silent. You bowed to their code and you never upheld your own. You knew what exacting morality was needed to produce a single metal nail, but you let them brand you as immoral. You knew that man needs the strictest code of values to deal with nature, but you thought that you needed no such code to deal with men. You left the deadliest weapon in the hands of your enemies, a weapon you never suspected or understood. Their moral code is their weapon. Ask yourself how deeply and in how many terrible ways you have accepted it. Ask yourself what it is that a code of moral values does to a man's life, and why he can't exist without it, and what happens to him if he accepts the wrong standard, by which the evil is the good. Shall I tell you why you're drawn to me, even though you think you ought to damn me? It's because I'm the first man who has given you what the whole world owes you and what you should have demanded of all men before you dealt with them: a moral sanction.

You're guilty of a great sin, Mr. Rearden, much guiltier than they tell you, but not in the way they preach. The worst guilt is to accept an undeserved guilt—and that is what you have been doing all your life. You have been paying blackmail, not for your vices, but for your virtues. You have been willing to carry the load of an unearned punishment—and to let it grow the heavier the greater the virtues you practiced. But your virtues were those which keep men alive. Your own moral code—the one you lived by, but never stated, acknowledged or defended—was the code that preserves man's existence. If you were punished for it, what was the nature of those who punished you? Yours was the code of life. What, then, is theirs? What standard of value lies at its root? What is its ultimate purpose? Do you think that what you're facing is merely a conspiracy to seize your wealth? You, who know the source of wealth, should know it's much more and much worse than that. Did you ask me to name man's motive power? Man's motive power is his moral code. Ask yourself where their code is leading you and what it offers you as your final goal. A viler evil than to murder a man, is to sell him suicide as an act of virtue. A viler evil than to throw a man into a sacrificial furnace, is to demand that he leap in, of his own will, and that he build the furnace, besides. By their own statement, it is *they* who need you and have nothing to offer you in return. By their own statement, you must support them because they cannot survive without you. Consider the obscenity of offering their impotence and their need—their need of *you*—as a justification for your torture. Are you willing to accept it? Do you care to purchase—at the price of your great endurance, at the price of your agony—the satisfaction of the needs of your own destroyers? (454–55)

Rearden had been unable to explain what Francisco gave him in his speech at Taggart's wedding and what it was that the looters needed from him and Dagny. Now he knows: it is a moral sanction. Francisco had told him at their first meeting that his unhappiness was evidence that a horrible weapon was being used against him, and that he was wrong to "permit anyone to call [his attitude toward his work] evil" (147). Now Rearden can see why. The weapon is a moral code antithetical to the one by which he lives. His code—his virtues—is the one that makes life possible and is the source of all efficacy. The looters need his acceptance of their code in order to give it power, and he grants this acceptance when he permits himself to be branded as evil.

Francisco's words echo through his mind at Thanksgiving dinner as his family damns him and Lillian tries to manipulate him through a guilt that he no longer feels. He can now name "the flaw in her scheme of punishment":

She wanted to force upon him the suffering of dishonor—but his own sense of honor was her only weapon of enforcement. She wanted to wrest from him an acknowledgment of his moral depravity—but only his own moral rectitude could attach significance to such a verdict. She wanted to injure him by her contempt—but he could not be injured, unless he respected her judgment. She wanted to punish him for the pain he had caused her and she held her pain as a gun aimed at him, as if she wished to extort his agony at the point of his pity. But her only tool was his own benevolence, his concern for her, his compassion. Her only power was the power of his own virtues. What if he chose to withdraw it?

An issue of guilt, he thought, had to rest on his own acceptance of the code of justice that pronounced him guilty. He did not accept it; he never had. His virtues, all the virtues she needed to achieve his punishment, came from another code and lived by another standard. He felt no guilt, no shame, no regret, no dishonor. He felt no concern for any verdict she chose to pass upon him: he had lost respect for her judgment long ago. And the sole chain still holding him was only a last remnant of pity.

But what was the code on which she acted? What sort of code permitted the concept of a punishment that required the victim's own virtue as the fuel to make it work? A code—he thought—which would destroy only those who tried to observe it; a punishment, from which only the honest would suffer, while the dishonest would escape unhurt. Could one conceive of an infamy lower than to equate virtue with pain, to make virtue, not vice, the source and motive power of suffering? If he were the kind of rotter she was struggling to make him believe he was, then no issue of his honor and his moral worth would matter to him. If he wasn't then what was the nature of her attempt?

To count upon his virtue and use it as an instrument of torture, to practice blackmail with the victim's generosity as sole means of extortion, to accept the gift of a man's good will and turn it into a tool for the giver's destruction . . . he sat very still, contemplating the formula of so monstrous an evil that he was able to name it, but not to believe it possible. (464–65)

Though he too generously concludes that Lillian does not understand what she is doing, he knows that he has "discovered a secret much greater than the problem of his marriage, that he had grasped the formula of a policy practiced more widely throughout the world than he dared to contemplate at the moment" (466), and he immediately acts on this knowledge. When Lillian says that the government targets him because he's been difficult to deal with, he responds that he's been too easy. When his mother tries to manipulate him into backing down on the grounds of the disgrace his trial will bring to the family, he responds that he doesn't "know or care" what it will do to them. When his brother, Philip, speaking "with the assurance of a man who knows that the moral ground of his stand is not open to question," declares that he is guilty and his actions contemptible, Rearden recalls Francisco's questions, "By what right?—by what code?—by what standard?" and announces that he will throw Philip out on the street if he ever expresses such opinions again. His family is immediately deflated. Philip has gone too far, his mother pleads, but Rearden shouldn't be hard on him: it would prey on his conscience; he has to be kind and to have pity; and he wouldn't want to be thought selfish. When Rearden responds that it wouldn't prey on his conscience, that he isn't kind, has no pity, and is selfish, she has nothing further to say. Whereas "his consideration for them" over the years "had brought him nothing but their maliciously righteous reproaches," they are now unable to "throw at him all those accusations of cruelty and selfishness, which he had come to accept as the eternal chorus to his life." It was his sanction—his acceptance of their standards as legitimate—that had permitted it (467–70).

The following day he takes the same approach at his trial, where he refuses to help disguise the nature of the proceeding and denies the legitimacy of the court and of the laws on which he is being tried.

That is the flaw in your theory, gentlemen, and I will not help you out of it. If you choose to deal with men by means of compulsion, do so. But you will discover that you need the voluntary co-operation of your victims, in many more ways than you can see at present. And your victims should discover that it is their own volition—which you cannot force—that makes you possible. I choose to be consistent and I will obey you in the manner you demand. Whatever you wish me to do, I will do it at the point of a gun. If you sentence me to jail, you will have to send armed men to carry me there—I will not volunteer to move. If you fine me, you will have to seize my property to collect the fine—I will not volunteer to pay it. If you believe that you have the right to force me—use your guns openly. I will not help you to disguise the nature of your action. (479)

In response to the judges' questions, as to those of his mother, he adheres ruthlessly to his moral code, and repeatedly rejects their attempts to intimidate him into making concessions to theirs. When the eldest judge, for example, says that he wouldn't want to be "misunderstood" and "give support to the widespread impression" that he is "a man devoid of social conscience" who "works for nothing but his own profit," Rearden affirms that this impression is correct and speaks eloquently about the virtue of selfishness. After this, when the judge, no longer in a posture of authority, tries to cast all the blame for the illegal sale on Danagger (who has since vanished), Rearden insists that it was made by "equal, mutual, voluntary agreement"; and, when another judge tries to justify the action on the grounds that Rearden "was prompted to disregard the legal technicalities by the critical situation of the coal mines and crucial importance of fuel to the public welfare," Rearden responds that he was prompted only by his own profit and interests (482). As a result, Rearden is given only a small fine, which is suspended, and the audience applauds him.

The actions Rearden takes on Thanksgiving and at his trial are made possible by what he has learned, and this knowledge is the result—for Rearden and for the reader—of reflection on events earlier in the novel. Though some of the key principles are articulated by Francisco, they are only convincing because of the evidence provided by these earlier events. And indeed, during the crucial discussion in Rearden's office, Francisco makes continual reference to the consequences of Rearden's creation of his Metal and to the results of its use on the John Galt Line.

The actions Rearden takes based on his new-found knowledge confirms it, raises new questions, and forms a basis for further conclusions. Looking at the judges who folded so easily, Rearden contemplates "with a bitter wonder that was almost fear . . . the enormity of the smallness of the enemy who was destroying the world," and he recognizes that if men such as himself were defeated by such an enemy, it can only be through their own fault. Such an impotent evil can only triumph when good men are "willing to let the brand of evil be stamped upon us and silently to bear punishment for our virtues" (483). This observation gives rise to a question: In what ways that they do not yet realize are Rearden and Dagny still giving their moral sanction to evil? Francisco poses this question to Rearden by suggesting that he read a transcript of the speech he made at his trial and consider whether he "is practicing it consistently—or not" (487).

The results of the trial give rise to another question as well. Looking over the crowd, Rearden observes that "they had cheered him today" as he had been cheered during the first run of the John Galt Line, but that these same people would "clamor" for more of the statist measures that shackled him and that were driving the country to ruin, "because they would be told to forget, as a sin, that which had made them cheer Hank Rearden."

Why were they ready to renounce their highest moments as a sin? Why were they willing to betray the best within them? What made them believe that this earth was a realm of evil where despair was their natural fate? He could not name the reason, but he knew that it had to be named. He felt it as a huge question mark within the courtroom, which it was now his duty to answer.

This was the real sentence imposed upon him, he thought—to discover what idea, what simple idea available to the simplest man, had made mankind accept the doctrines that led it to self-destruction. (483–84)

Over the course of the next six months Rearden will identify this "simple idea"—"the worst of our enemies' creed"—as "the one tenet by which they destroy a man before he's started, the killer-tenet: the breach between his mind and body" (857–58).[18] We have already seen that it is because of this dichotomy that Rearden initially damns himself and Dagny for their affair, and we have seen how he comes by degrees to recognize that there is something wrong in the traditional views of sex and pleasure and how he admits that, in his initial condemnation of the affair, he was "lying to himself." By the time of his trial, he no longer regards his feeling for Dagny as evil and even takes a sort of pride in it and in his newfound enjoyment of sensuous pleasures. He has not, however, identified the nature or moral character of this enjoyment. In short, at the time of his trial, Rearden's attitude toward sex is equivalent to his attitude toward his work earlier in the novel: he loves it unreservedly, but without an understanding of its nature or the conviction that he is morally right to do so.

As Francisco's speeches at Taggart's wedding and in Rearden's office help Rearden to understand the meaning of money and the moral nature of his work, so Francisco's speech on "The Meaning of Sex" (486–93), shortly after Rearden's trial, gives him the words he needs to understand the cause and moral significance of his passion for Dagny and to identify for the first time the error he made in damning sex. Francisco identifies the mind-body dichotomy explicitly and explains how both promiscuity and Platonic love are variants of the same error made by the people who denounce wealth.

We can see the consequences of this new knowledge in Rearden's next encounter with Lillian, when she learns the identity of his mistress. Rearden does not show any sign of guilt, as he did when Lillian first discovered that he was having an affair. In the earlier scene, he acknowledged to Lillian that she had "the right to condemn me in any way you wish" and "to decide what you wish me to do" (430). Though he said that he would not comply with a demand that he give up the affair, he acknowledged that she had the right to make such a demand. However, in the present scene, when Lillian asserts this right, he responds that "no human being can hold on another a claim demanding that he wipe himself out of existence," and he tells her that he would continue his affair with Dagny "even if it took your life" (529). Moreover, when Lillian damns Dagny for her sexuality, just as Rearden himself had "in the sun-striped bedroom of Ellis Wyatt's house," he fully appreciates the moral difference between the two women's attitudes toward sex and sees "the obscenity of letting impotence hold itself as virtue and damn the power of living as a sin": "he saw, with the clarity of direct perception, in the shock of a single instant, the terrible ugliness of that which had once been his own belief" (530). When Lillian leaves he feels a wondrous sense of freedom and deliverance in "the shining, guiltless knowledge" that it "did not matter" and "did not have to matter" "what Lillian felt, what she discovered, or what became of her" (531).

Rearden could not have achieved this deliverance prior to coming to understand the meaning of sex, nor could he have appreciated Francisco's speech on this topic prior either to his relationship with Dagny or to his coming to understand the morality of the principles on which he conducts his business and the relation of these principles to his private life. However, he has not yet reached the end of his trail. Though he no longer feels guilty for his passion for Dagny and he finds Lillian despicable, he still believes that Lillian is motivated by some incomprehensible form of love for him, and he feels responsible for breaking his word to her. Because of this, he is willing to "atone" for his infidelity by remaining in a marriage that by his standards is "a vicious fraud": "my standards are not yours. I do not understand yours, I never have, but I will accept them. If this is the manner of your love for me, if bearing the name of my wife will give you some form of contentment, I won't take it away from you" (530). Furthermore, though he grasps the nature and ugliness of Lillian's belief about sex, he does so only in the form of a "feeling, left unsealed by his mind" (530). As a consequence of this, he is unable to appreciate all the consequences of this knowledge, and its connections with what he has learned about the sanction of the victim, and so he is unable to deal existentially with Lillian. When she insults Dagny, he responds with a threat and the demand that "Neither you nor anyone else is to discuss her," which lets Lillian know that he is susceptible to blackmail (431).

It is when Ferris uses Lillian's discovery to blackmail him into signing the Gift Certificate for his Metal that Rearden comprehends the connection between the mind-body dichotomy, the sanction of the victim, and the opposing moral codes. Ferris' extortion depends on the fact that Rearden is virtuous. The metal is an effect of his virtue, as is his affair with Dagny. He creates life-sustaining values because he loves them—because he loves life. This is the essence of his code, but Ferris and the other looters live by an opposite code. They extort their living from men like Rearden by holding their values hostage. Ferris, who calls Rearden's loyalty to values "impractical," represents a moral code that

> hooks a man's love of existence to a circuit of torture, so that only the man who had nothing to offer would have nothing to fear, so that the virtues that made life possible and the values which gave it meaning become the agents of its destruction, so that one's best became a tool of one's agony and man's life on earth became impractical. (561)

Rearden has learned that the practice of such a code requires the acceptance and sanction of the victims, in myriad ways. Chief among these is the victims' acceptance of their own virtue as guilt for which they are willing to bear punishment—"a punishment that requires the victim's own virtue as the fuel to make it work" (561). When he asks himself what could make the victims accept this, he sees the answer:

> Hadn't he done it also? Hadn't he given his sanction to the code of self-damnation? Dagny—he thought—and the depth of their feeling for each other . . . the blackmail from which the depraved would be immune . . . hadn't he, too, once called it depravity? Hadn't he been first to throw at her all the insults which the human scum was now threatening to throw at her in public? Hadn't he accepted as guilt the highest happiness he had ever found? (561)

And he recalls Francisco's question: "You, who won't allow one percent impurity into an alloy of metal, what have you allowed into your moral code?" In that same conversation Francisco told Rearden that he was guilty of the great sin of accepting an unearned guilt and paying blackmail to the impotent for the virtues that kept men alive (455). Rearden grasps now for the first time how he was guilty of "damning as guilt that which was my best":

> I broke their code, but I fell into the trap they intended, the trap of a code devised to be broken. I took no pride in my rebellion, I took it as guilt, I did not damn them, I damned myself, I did not damn their code, I damned existence—and I hid my happiness as a shameful secret. . . .
>
> I did it—in the name of pity for the most contemptible woman I know. That, too, was their code, and I accepted it. I believed that one person owes a duty to another with no payment for it in return. . . . I believed that love is some static gift which, once granted, need no longer be deserved—just as they believe that wealth is a static possession which can be seized and held without further effort. . . . I placed pity above my own conscience, and *this* is the core of my guilt. My crime was committed when I said to her, "By every standard of mine, to maintain our marriage will be a vicious fraud. But my standards are not yours. I do not understand yours, I never have, but I will accept them."
>
> Here they are, lying on my desk, those standards I accepted without understanding, here is the manner of her love for me, that love which I never believed, but tried to spare. . . .
>
> It was not the cheap little looters of wealth who have beaten me—it was I. They did not disarm me—I threw away my weapon. This is a battle that cannot be fought except with clean hands—because the enemy's sole power is in the sores of one's conscience—and I accepted a code that made me regard the strength of my hands as a sin and a stain. (564–65)

At their first meeting, Francisco told Rearden that the impotent guests who damned him while eating his food and surviving by dint of his productive genius, were using a "terrible weapon" against him. Rearden now grasps for the first time how this is the case. As he later explains to Dagny, "I took pride in my ability to think, to act, to work for the satisfaction of my desires. But I did not know that this was virtue." As a result, he "accepted punishment for it . . . at the hands of an arrogant evil, made arrogant solely by my ignorance and my submission" (858).

In that first encounter Francisco described Rearden as working for his enemies, and now Rearden can see that he was correct. Since it is morality that determines one's purposes, in conceding the realm of morality to his enemies, Rearden delivered his ability into their hands.

> I, who knew that wealth is only a means to an end, created the means and let them prescribe my ends. I, who took pride in my ability to achieve the satisfaction of my desires, let them prescribe the code of values by which I judged my desires. I, who shaped matter to serve my purpose, was left with a pile of steel and gold, but with my every purpose defeated, my every desire betrayed, my every attempt at happiness frustrated.
>
> I had cut myself in two, as the mystics preached, and I ran my business by one code of rules, but my own life by another. I rebelled against the looter's attempt to set the price and value of my steel—but I let them set the moral values of my life. I rebelled against demands for an unearned wealth—but I thought it was my duty to grant an unearned love to a wife I despised, an unearned respect to a mother who hated me, an unearned support to a brother who plotted for my destruction. I rebelled against undeserved financial injury—but I accepted a life of undeserved pain. I rebelled against the doctrine that my productive ability was guilt—but I accepted, as guilt, my capacity for happiness. I rebelled against the creed that virtue is some disembodied unknowable of the spirit—but I damned you, *you*, my dearest one, for the desire of your body and mine. But if the body is evil, then so are those who provide the means of its survival, so is material wealth and those who produce it—and if moral values are set in contradiction to our physical existence, then it's right that rewards should be unearned, that virtue should consist of the undone, that there should be no tie between achievement and profit, that the inferior animals who're able to produce should serve those superior beings whose superiority in spirit consists of incompetence in the flesh. (858–59)

Rearden's liberation from guilt—the progression we have been following—is a *philosophical* development, which consists in drawing abstract and evaluative conclusions from his observations of the world and integrating them into more and more abstract principles—of checking progressively deeper and more abstract premises about the way in which he and others live, when he finds that these premises contradict one another or his experience. Thus, though at the beginning of the novel, if "some man like Hugh Akston" told him that there was a connection between his view of sex and his economic exploitation, he would have "laughed in his face," by the beginning of part III he has grasped the connection. His mills have come to be "ruled by human scum," he sees "the achievement of my life serving to enrich the worst of my enemies," and he understands *why* this is the case (859).

He has not yet reached Atlantis, however: rather than a sense of radiant joy, "He felt nothing—nothing but the sense of an even restful twilight like a spread of slag over a molten metal, when it crusts and swallows the last brilliant spurt of the white glow within" (571). He is not ready to go on strike; his acceptance of the mind-body dichotomy was not the only chain holding Rearden to the looters' world. Like Dagny, who never accepted the dichotomy and "was completely incapable of experiencing a feeling of fundamental guilt" (87), he will not be able to break with the looters wholly and achieve happiness until he understands their basic motivation and just how his sanction has enabled them. In the final section of this paper I will trace the final steps that lead to this understanding. I turn now to the earlier stages of Dagny's progression.

DAGNY'S DESPERATE QUEST

The immediate context for Dagny's development across parts II and III of *Atlas Shrugged* is the paradox of the John Galt Line—her greatest achievement, which has served to undermine the very values for the sake of which she created it. But this paradox is only the most dramatic case of a contradiction that Dagny has faced her whole life. She tells Galt that she started her life with "a single absolute: that the world was mine to shape in the image of my highest values and never to be given up to a lesser standard, no matter how long or hard the struggle" (812). Dagny knows that her values are rational, and therefore that they can be achieved and are not to be given up. But though she takes all the actions required to achieve them, they inexplicably remain forever beyond her reach. This contradiction intensifies over the course of part II, and in the valley is resolved into a single question, which is her last premise left to check when she returns to the world in part III (807).

We can see this paradox from her childhood onward. At nine years old, bored with the people around her and having "caught a glimpse of another world . . . that created trains, bridges, telegraph wires, and signal lights winking in the night," she decides that she will grow up into that world and run Taggart Transcontinental. In pursuit of this goal, she hangs "around the tracks and the roundhouses like a humble student" with "a hint of future pride" (51). At the age of sixteen, as she begins her first job on the railroad and prepares for her first ball, she thinks that she has "entered her kind of world," but she soon learns that she has not (51).

The world she seeks is the "luminously rational" one of science and mathematics, a world where one can feel the "joy of admiration and of one's own ability growing together" and where one is tried against worthy adversaries (50). It is a world in which she will meet the man who she imagines beyond the horizon holding the railroad tracks in his hand at the point where they converge—the man who represents the sort of ability that creates railroads (220). By contrast, at the ball she meets only "helpless young men" for whom she feels contempt (104). And, in her first few years at Taggart Transcontinental, she finds herself "screaming silently, at times, for a glimpse of human ability, a single glimpse of clean, hard, radiant competence" and has "fits of tortured longing for a friend or an enemy with a mind better than her own." The adversary she is "forced to fight" is "not worth matching or beating": rather than "a superior ability which she would have found honor in challenging," it is "ineptitude—a gray spread of cotton that seemed soft and shapeless, that could offer no resistance to anything or anybody, yet managed to be a barrier in her way. She stood, disarmed, before the riddle of what made this possible. She could find no answer" (52). Later, as Vice-President in Charge of Operation, when walking through Manhattan surrounded by buildings that "rise to such heights that her glance [cannot] find the sky," she thinks, "It has taken so much to build this city, it should have so much to offer" (66). But she can find little to admire and nothing to inspire her. Her work consists in fighting incompetence and arguing with cowards who cry despairingly: "Who is John Galt?"

The railroad is her highest value, and in order to preserve it, she must complete the Rio Norte Line. When, as the result of a series of senseless evils, it becomes impossible for her to do this except by taking a leave of absence and forming an independent company, she names the company "John Galt, Inc." in defiance of the idea represented by the question invoking that name—the idea that one's highest values are "unattainable" (201). But consider what she then feels, sitting in her new office "on the ground floor of a half collapsed structure":

> She knew she was alone in the ruins of a building. It seemed as if she were alone in the city. She felt an emotion held back for years: a loneliness much beyond this moment, beyond the silence of the room and the wet, glistening emptiness of the street; the loneliness of a gray wasteland where nothing was worth reaching; the loneliness of her childhood.
>
> She rose and walked to the window. By pressing her face to the pane, she could see the whole of the Taggart Building, its lines converging abruptly to its distant pinnacle in the sky. She looked up at the dark window of the room that had been her office. She felt as if she were in exile, never to return, as if she were separated from the building by much more than a sheet of glass, a curtain of rain and the span of a few months.
>
> She stood, in a room of crumbling plaster, pressed to the windowpane, looking up at the unattainable form of everything she loved. She did not know the nature of her loneliness. The only words that named it were: This is not the world I expected. (219–20)

Dagny does not doubt that she will succeed in completing the Line or saving the Railroad or that she will resume her position as Vice-President. It is not these concretes that she sees as unattainable, but her world—the world the railroad represents. "She would never find it. Her own thought of what life could be like, was all she would ever have of the world she had wanted. Only the thought of it—and a few rare moments, like a few lights reflected from it on her way—to know, to hold, to follow to the end" (220). Here we see Dagny's contradiction. She is building the John Galt Line in defiance of the premise that one's highest values cannot be attained—a premise which is the antithesis of the single conviction that is central to her character. And yet, she herself feels that her ideal—her world—is unattainable.

During the first run of the John Galt Line and in its immediate aftermath the contradiction seems to be resolved. Dagny has achieved her values, she is in her world. She disembarks the train into the company of the Colorado industrialists who are the bondholders of John Galt, Inc., all men she admires. Moreover, her triumph has brought out the most admirable traits in all the people around her: all of the Taggart engineers volunteer for the run (232); the crew performs excellently, enjoying their competence; the crowds are enthusiastic and even the reporters shed their cynicism (238); "sons of Taggart employees" and "old railroad men" assemble into an honor-guard (242); people gather on hills and at porches and windows to watch the train pass, greeting it with flowers and fireworks (243). This is Dagny's world—a benevolent universe in which ambitious values can be achieved and such achievements unite men in good will.[19] That evening she fully expects that after a year of running trains on the Line, she will be able to rebuild the whole Taggart system and "offer three-day freight service across the continent, on a Rearden Metal Track from ocean to ocean!" (250), and waking up the next morning beside Rearden, she likens the pattern of sunlight and shadow cast by the Venetian blinds to

> the cracks of a wall which the John Galt Line had broken, the advance notice of what awaited them outside—she thought of the trip back, on the new rail, with the first train from Wyatt Junction—the trip back to her office in the Taggart Building and to all the things now open for her to win. (254)

It is not long, however, before her achievement is threatened by a new variant of the "grey spread of cotton" that has always inexplicably managed to bar her way:

> this was a fog without shapes or definitions, in which something kept forming and shifting before it could be seen, like semi-clots in a not-quite-liquid—it was as if her eyes were reduced to side-vision and she were sensing blurs of disaster coiling toward her, but she could not move her glance, she had no glance to move and focus. (299)

Back in Colorado four months after the first run, Dagny looks "for a moment's relief in the sight of a victorious achievement" at a train about to start down the track of the Line. Noticing how the passengers now take the Line for granted, she thinks "We've done it—this much, at least, is done" (333). But, she is wrong. Moments later she learns that the blurs of disaster have coiled into a set of directives issued by Wesley Mouch nullifying her achievement. The number and speed of trains on the Line is severely restricted and railroad bonds are frozen.

[T]here would be no trains and no life-blood of freight, the John Galt Line had been only a drainpipe that had permitted Jim Taggart to make a deal and to drain [the Colorado industrialists'] wealth, unearned, into his pocket, in exchange for letting others drain his railroad—the bonds of the John Galt Line, which, this morning, had been the proud guardians of their owners' security and future, had become in the space of an hour, scraps of paper that no one would buy, with no value, no future, no power, save the power to close the doors and stop the wheels of the last hope of the country—and Taggart Transcontinental was not a living plant, fed by blood it had worked to produce, but a cannibal of the moment, devouring the unborn children of greatness. (335)

Ellis Wyatt, who was the prime mover of the Colorado boom on which Dagny counted to save the railroad and the country, sets fire to his oil wells and disappears.

Part II of the novel picks up six months later, by which time Dagny's job consists in canceling trains to dying Colorado towns and struggling against senseless regulations to maintain some sort of service in the few remaining productive areas (351). Instead of the "brilliant pride" she used to feel at the sight of Taggart rail, she now feels "a foggy, guilty shame, as if some foul kind of rust had grown on the metal, and worse: as if the rust had a tinge of blood." The rail remains a superlative achievement that she loves and will not "surrender to the men of blood and rust," but the nature of her work and her attitude toward it is now fundamentally different (352).

In part I, Dagny had a plan to save the railroad; there was an ambitious positive value she was pursuing; but with Colorado dying, she no longer sees any way forward. As part II progresses, it seems increasingly inevitable that industrial civilization will vanish from the face of the earth—a prospect that has been made all too vivid by her experience in Starnesville (282–86). Her work is a war of attrition in which she tries to delay this outcome—to hold out a little longer. In doing so she is sometimes motivated by a hope that political conditions will improve, making it possible to rebuild (645). More often, however, she goes on out of dedication to a cause she believes is lost (632). Throughout, she lacks any positive long-range goal. "I have stopped thinking of a future, or of a railroad system," she says at the meeting at which the Board of Taggart Transcontinental decides to close the John Galt Line, "I intend to continue running trains so long as it is still possible to run them. I don't think that it will be much longer" (509).

"The only goal in sight that gave meaning to her struggle"—"the only part of her work that made her able to bear the rest"—is her inquiry concerning the motor, that she and Rearden discovered in the abandoned factory of the Twentieth Century Motor Company (352, cf. 381). Initially she wants to rebuild the motor as a means of running trains on a reinvigorated Taggart Transcontinental, but already by the beginning of part II there is little hope of this, and it becomes increasingly clear that the motor is needed "not to move trains, but to keep her moving" (672). The motor and the man who made it supplant Taggart Transcontinental as the emblem of human achievement and of the world that Dagny wants.

As a result, her inquiry concerning the motor becomes disconnected from her job, and sometimes conflicts with it (300, 688–89). Thus, in part II, the values that give meaning to Dagny's life are detached from her work, which is increasingly a senseless burden. In part I, when she was still pursuing a plan to rebuild the system, she could take pleasure and pride in her work, despite the loathing she sometimes felt for the grey cotton that was her adversary. By the beginning of part II, however, "The only pride of her workday was not that it had been lived, but that it had been survived. It was wrong, she thought, it was viciously wrong that one should ever be forced to say that about any hour of one's life." (367)

"Stretched in an armchair of her living room" after a particularly senseless and ugly workday, her thoughts turn from this topic to Rearden and his development over the course of their relationship. Reflecting on both his efficacy and his capacity for enjoyment, Dagny thinks of him as "a man who belong[s] on earth," or more exactly as "a man to whom the earth belong[s]":

> Why, then—she wondered—should he have had to carry a burden of tragedy which, in silent endurance, he had accepted so completely that he had barely known he carried it? She knew part of the answer; she felt as if the whole answer were close and she would grasp it on some approaching day. (370)

The part of the answer that Dagny knows is that Rearden has accepted the false dichotomy between spirit and body. She has always rejected it, and during the first run of the John Galt Line she found the words to formulate her premise that the mind and body are a unity and grasped how this premise lies behind her conviction that one can and must bring one's highest values into reality (240–41).[20]

Rearden, like Dagny, has always taken pride in achieving his values—in "shaping matter to his wishes by the power of his brain" (158). By the beginning of part III, he has come to celebrate his affair with Dagny and his new-found ability to enjoy luxury, as an expression of this same conviction:

> Dagny, if some artist painted you as you are now, men would come to look at the painting to experience a moment that nothing could give them in their own lives. They would call it great art. . . . Dagny, they'd feel it and go away and sleep with the first barmaid in sight—and they'd never try to reach what they had felt. I wouldn't want to seek it from a painting. I'd want it real. I'd take no pride in any hopeless longing. I wouldn't hold a stillborn aspiration. I'd want to have it, to make it, to live it. Do you understand? (368)

Dagny's emphatic response ("Oh yes, Hank, I understand!") underscores the centrality to her character of rejecting "hopeless longings" and of making and *living* her values. Yet, she too is carrying a "burden of tragedy"; and, in her career at least, she is no longer living her values. Though she has achieved every concrete goal she set for herself, she has not succeeded at making *her world*: the achievements have slipped away and her professional life has been reduced to an increasingly hopeless drudgery. This suggests that she suffers from some form of the same error as does Rearden; and Dagny recognizes this herself, "as she lay in an armchair of her living room on a dismal evening of spring, waiting for him to come" and reflecting on his remark that there is a "vicious and very important error" in "what we're taught":

> Just a little farther, my darling—she thought—look a little farther and you'll be free of that error and of all the wasted pain you never should have had to carry. . . . But she felt that she, too, had not seen the whole of the distance, and she wondered what were the steps left for her to discover. . . . (373)

Dagny needs to discover the way in which she is the cause of her own suffering. She needs to understand why her creation of the John Galt Line led to the results it did, and more generally how her work is undermining rather than promoting her values. It is Francisco who articulates these questions for her. Consider the first exchange between them after the Line has been completed and the Colorado-destroying directives passed. When he asks, "Don't you want to tell me what a brilliant achievement the John Galt Line turned out to be?" she accuses him of despising achievement, and he responds:

> "Yes, don't I? I despise that Line so much that I didn't want to see it reach the kind of end it has reached."
> He saw her look of sudden attentiveness, the look of thought rushing into a breach torn open upon a new direction. He watched her for a moment, as if he knew every step she would find along that road, then chuckled and said, "Don't you want to ask me now: Who is John Galt? . . . Don't you remember that you dared him to come and claim your Line? Well, he has."
> He walked on, not waiting to see the look in her eyes—a look that held anger, bewilderment and the first faint gleam of a question mark. (408–9)

She now realizes that Francisco, who had predicted that John Galt would claim her Line (201), foresaw its fate from the beginning. In addition to providing an insight into Francisco's character, which has perplexed Dagny for years, this realization implies that the fate of the Line was predictable—that it *had* to end as it did and, therefore, that she was wrong to create it. These thoughts, not yet named in words, are the "first faint gleam of a question mark" in Dagny's mind—her first inkling that the premises that lead her to build the Line need to be checked.

Francisco begins to challenge the premises explicitly in their next meeting. It occurs on the evening when Taggart Transcontinental's Board of Directors, a body composed of the "gray cotton" that has always inexplicably barred

Dagny's way, votes to close the John Galt Line (509, cf. 518). Thinking of her great-grandfather Nat Taggart, who created the railroad in the face of tremendous obstacles and great pain, Dagny rededicates herself to the fight to preserve the railroad for as long as possible (510). If she let the railroad perish, she tells Francisco, she would be betraying Nat Taggart and "any man living now and capable of knowing" what he felt in his most difficult hour (514). He responds:

> Dagny, the men of your Board of Directors are no match for Nat Taggart, are they? There's no form of contest in which they could beat him, there's nothing he'd have to fear from them, there's no mind, no will, no power in the bunch of them to equal one thousandth of his. . . . Then why is it that throughout man's history the Nat Taggarts, who make the world, have always won—and always lost it to the men of the Board? . . . How could men who're afraid to hold an unqualified opinion about the weather, fight Nat Taggart? How could they seize his achievement, if he chose to defend it? Dagny, he fought with every weapon he possessed, except the most important one. They could not have won, if we—he and the rest of us—had not given the world away to them. (514)

When Dagny responds that it is men like Francisco and the vanished industrialists who have given the world to the men of the Board, Francisco asks "Who built the John Galt Line for them?"

> He saw only the faintest contraction of her mouth, but he knew that the question was like a blow across an open wound. Yet she answered quietly, "I did."
> "For this kind of end?"
> "For the men who did not hold out, would not fight and gave up."
> "Don't you see that no other end was possible?" (514)

She answers that she does not and resolves to go on taking as "much injustice" as she is "able to fight," but now the premise on which she has been acting is explicit for the first time. *The Line could have succeeded but failed because the Colorado industrialists gave up.* They could have held out, like Dagny, struggling to remain in business and to preserve an industrial society, despite the destructive injustice of the frozen bonds and rationed trains. Had they done so, Colorado and the Line would have lasted for a little longer at least.

When she learns of Directive 10-289, Dagny does quit, because she is unwilling to "work as a slave or a slave driver" and to do so would be to betray Nat Taggart (552). However, she still does not see that the John Galt Line and her career at Taggart Transcontinental *had* to end as they did. As a result, sequestered in her cabin in Woodstock, she faces a paralyzing confusion:

> There were long stretches of calm, when she was able to face her problem with the dispassionate clarity of weighing a problem in engineering. But she could find no answer. She knew that her desperate longing for the railroad would vanish, were

she to convince herself that it was impossible or improper. But the longing came from the certainty that the truth and the right were hers—that the enemy was the irrational and the unreal—that she could not set herself another goal or summon the love to achieve it, while her rightful achievement had been lost, not to some superior power, but to a loathsome evil that conquered by means of impotence. (611)

But it is not true . . . that there is no place in the future for a superlative achievement of man's mind; it can never be true. No matter what her problem, this would always remain to her—this immovable conviction that evil was unnatural and temporary. She felt it more clearly than ever this morning: the certainty that the ugliness of the men in the city and the ugliness of her suffering were transient accidents—while the smiling sense of hope within her at the sight of a sun-flooded forest, the sense of an unlimited promise, was the permanent and the real. (612)

We see here, in a newly intense form, the contradiction that Dagny has faced her entire life: her values are possible and proper and the world is hers to shape in their image; and yet, incomprehensibly, they remain forever out of reach. Whatever she creates is seized, destroyed, or somehow negated by men who, in logic, should be powerless. Evil and ugliness are unnecessary, yet they are somehow pervasive and co-opt her achievements.

Earlier she had resolved to remain at her job rather than to surrender Nat Taggart's achievement to the "men of blood and rust" (352, 510, 514); now she has quit because "I couldn't let his achievement, and mine, end up with the looters as our final goal" (616). Either course of action, however, offends against the conviction that her world is achievable and not to be given up.

It seems monstrously wrong to surrender the world to the looters, and monstrously wrong to live under their rule. I can neither give up nor go back. I can neither exist without work nor work as a serf. I had always thought that any sort of battle was proper, anything, except renunciation. I'm not sure we're right to quit, you and I, when we should have fought them. But there is no way to fight. It's surrender, if we leave—and surrender, if we remain. I don't know what is right any longer. (618)

Danny is speaking here to Francisco who has come to recruit her to the strike, as he came to Rearden in his office, two days after his indictment. That conversation was cut short by a breakout in the mills, and Rearden's response to the emergency made it clear that he was not yet ready to be told of the strike. At the sound of the alarm both men sprang into action, as if by instinct, to avert the crisis (456–58). Rearden saw the episode as illustrating why good men will defeat the looters: "We're able to act" and "They're not" (460). And this answers the question Francisco had been about to ask him when the alarm sounded: How can you continue your work, understanding the nature of the burden you are carrying? (460). Rearden loves his ability to act and is unwilling to stand idly by while his values are threatened. In order to preserve them, he will be willing to bear any burden, no matter how unjust, until he comes to understand that his mills are not a value in the context of a society built on the looter's moral and metaphysical premises. The same applies to Dagny with the railroad. We have seen, however, that Francisco did accomplish something in that conversation with Rearden: he gave him a conceptual framework for his development going forward. The same is true of the present conversation with Dagny. It is interrupted by the news of the Winston Tunnel collapse, and she runs back to Taggart Transcontinental "as he had run at the sound of the alarm siren in Rearden's mills" (622). Prior to this, he introduces two crucial ideas.

As he did with Rearden, Francisco explains that the virtuous are responsible for the destruction of their own values because they "produced the wealth of the world" while "letting our enemies write its moral code." Dagny answers, as Rearden could not have, that "we never accepted their code" but "lived by our own standards." Francisco's response is significant:

> Yes—and paid ransoms for it! Ransoms in matter and in spirit—in money, which our enemies received, but did not deserve, and in honor, which we deserved, but did not receive. *That* was our guilt—that we were willing to pay. We kept mankind alive, yet we allowed men to despise us and to worship our destroyers. We allowed them to worship incompetence and brutality, the recipients and the dispensers of the unearned. By accepting punishment, not for any sins, but for our virtues, we betrayed our code and made theirs possible. Dagny, theirs is the morality of kidnappers. They use your love of virtue as a hostage. They know that you'll bear anything in order to work and produce, because you know that achievement is man's highest moral purpose, that he can't exist without it, and your love of virtue is your love of life. They count on you to assume any burden. They count on you to feel that no effort is too great in the service of your love. (619)

Two weeks earlier, when contemplating the Gift Certificate for his Metal, Rearden reached this same identification of the world's morality as a "hostage system" (561), but the point is new to Dagny, and it has an immediate impact on her understanding of her own actions. When she returns to the world she is self-consciously paying ransoms: she instructs Eddie to give certain Taggart employees the authority to bribe "stooges of the Unification Board" with her own money ("I'll pay it"), and she challenges the "stooges" to sue her personally (628). Moreover, consider what she says to Rearden upon her return:

> Hank, I don't think they care whether there's a train or a blast furnace left on earth. We do. They're holding us by our love of it, and we'll go on paying so long as there's still one chance left to keep one single wheel alive and moving in token of human intelligence. We'll go on holding it afloat, like our drowning child, and when the flood swallows it, we'll go down with the last wheel and the last syllogism. I know what we're paying, but—price is no object any longer. (632)

Francisco's second crucial point to Dagny is that her tie to the looters is related to the spirit-body dichotomy. He is destroying d'Anconia Copper, he explains, out of love for the "spirit of which it was the shape" (617). When she describes Taggart Transcontinental as "almost like a living person" (619), he says that it is not any longer. Her belief that to abandon it would be "renouncing and giving up" is a result of her failure to grasp fully the relation between mind and body:

> Dagny, we who've been called "materialists" by the killers of the human spirit, we're the only ones who know how little value or meaning there is in material objects as such, because we're the ones who create their value and meaning. We can afford to give them up, for a short while, in order to redeem something much more precious. We are the soul, of which railroads, copper mines, steel mills and oil wells are the body—and they are living entities that beat day and night, like our hearts, in the sacred function of supporting human life, but only so long as they remain our body, only so long as they remain the expression, the reward and the property of achievement. Without us, they are corpses and their sole product is poison, not wealth or food, the poison of disintegration that turns men into hordes of scavengers. Dagny, learn to understand the nature of your own power and you'll understand the paradox you now see around you. You do not have to depend on any material possessions, they depend on you, you create them, you own the one and only tool of production. Wherever you are, you will always be able to produce. But the looters—by their own stated theory—are in desperate, permanent, congenital need and at the blind mercy of matter. Why don't you take them at their word? They need railroads, factories, mines, motors, which they cannot make or run. Of what use will your railroad be to them without you? Who held it together? Who kept it alive? Who saved it, time and time again? Was it your brother James? Who fed him? Who fed the looters? Who produced their weapons? Who gave them the means to enslave you? The impossible spectacle of shabby little incompetents holding control over the products of genius—who made it possible? Who supported your enemies, who forged your chains, who destroyed your achievement? . . . Leave them the carcass of that railroad, leave them all the rusted rails and rotted ties and gutted engines—but don't leave them your mind! Don't leave them your mind! The fate of the world rests on that decision! (620)

During the first run of the John Galt Line, Dagny grasped that machines are animated by the men of the mind and would be still and worthless without them (245–56), and she understands that the railroad would be of no value to the looters without her; what she must "learn to understand" is that it cannot be of any value *to her* so long as it is not "the reward and the property of achievement."

We will see shortly how Francisco elaborates this point that evening, when he next sees Dagny. Notice first, that between these two conversations, when she returns to work, there is strong evidence of a breach between her mind and her body. Her voice has "the sound of a business machine"; her manner conveys to Eddie the sentiment that she would feel compassion and gratitude "if we were alive and free to feel, but we're not"; and while "reciting a list of figures without a break," she sweeps a display of propaganda magazines off her table with an "abrupt explosive movement of sheer physical brutality," "as if there were no connection between her mind and the violence of her body" (627, 631). That evening, looking out at the city from her apartment, what she feels is not "the joy of working; it was only the clear, cold peace of a decision reached—and the stillness of unadmitted pain" (633). The city seems to be sinking into coils of "gray-blue fog," and she likens it to the sinking of Atlantis "and all the other kingdoms that had vanished, leaving the same legend in all the languages of men, and the same longing."

> She felt—as she had felt it one spring night, slumped across her desk in the crumbling office of the John Galt Line, by a window facing a dark alley—the sense and vision of her own world, which she would never reach. . . . You—she thought—whoever you are, whom I have always loved and never found, you whom I expected to see at the end of the rails beyond the horizon, you whose presence I had always felt in the streets of the city and whose world I had wanted to build, it is my love for you that had kept me moving, my love and my hope to reach you and my wish to be worthy of you on the day when I would stand before you face to face. Now I know that I shall never find you—that it is not to be reached or lived—but what is left of my life is still yours, and I will go on in your name, even though it is a name I'll never learn, I will go on serving you, even though I'm never to win, I will go on, to be worthy of you on the day when I would have met you, even though I won't. . . . She had never accepted hopelessness, but she stood at the window and, addressed to the shape of a fogbound city, it was her self-dedication to unrequited love. (633–34)

She returns to work because she cannot "stand by and watch what they did at that tunnel" and "accept what they're all accepting," "that disasters are one's natural fate, to be borne, not fought. I can't accept submission. I can't accept helplessness. I can't accept renunciation. So long as there's a railroad left to run, I'll run it" (635). But in her determination to keep fighting, she has resigned herself to the view that her highest values are not to be attained. She tells Francisco that she is fighting not "in order to maintain the looters' world," but "to maintain the last strip of" hers. But it is only the last strip, and she does not have hope of maintaining even this for long; she expects to go down "with the last wheel and the last syllogism" (632).

Francisco pursues the line of thought we saw him introduce that morning, pushing her to identify why the railroad remains of value to her:

> "I know why one loves one's work. I know what it means to you, the job of running trains. But you would not run them if they were empty. Dagny, what is it you see when you think of a moving train?"
> She glanced at the city. "The life of a man of ability who might have perished in that catastrophe, but will escape the next one, which I'll prevent—a man who has an intransigent mind and an unlimited ambition, and is in love with his own

life . . . the kind of man who is what we were when we started, you and I. You gave him up. I can't."

"Do you think that you can still serve him—that kind of man—by running the railroad? . . . You will stop on the day when you'll discover that your work has been placed in the service, not of that man's life, but of his destruction. . . . You said that we were of his kind once, you and I. We still are. But one of us has betrayed him."

"Yes," she said sternly, "one of us has. We cannot serve him by renunciation."

"We cannot serve him by making terms with his destroyers."

"I'm not making terms with them. They need me. They know it. It's my terms that I'll make them accept."

"By playing a game in which they gain benefits in exchange for harming you?"

"If I can keep Taggart Transcontinental in existence, it's the only benefit I want. What do I care if they make me pay ransoms? Let them have what they want. I'll have the railroad."

"He smiled. "Do you think so? Do you think that their need of you is your protection? Do you think that you can give them what they want? No, you won't quit until you see, of your own sight and judgment, what it is that they really want. You know, Dagny, we were taught that some things belong to God and others to Caesar. Perhaps their God would permit it. But the man you say we're serving—he does not permit it. He permits no divided allegiance, no war between your mind and your body, no gulf between your values and your actions, no tributes to Caesar. He permits no Caesars." (635–36)

Dagny is, of course, thinking of the man at the end of the railroad tracks— her romantic ideal and the representative of her highest values, who she will later identify as John Galt. Francisco is thinking concretely of Galt, the man to whom he has given his life (517). The dialogue focuses the question of whether Dagny is right to return to work on the relation between her work and the idea personified in Galt. Dagny thinks she is serving him, but Francisco argues that the man who loves his life cannot be served by her acceptance of a joyless existence in which she must surrender the values she creates as ransom to vicious men for the privilege of having created them. Later, in part III, Galt himself characterizes this policy as one of "carrying unchosen burdens, taking undeserved punishment, and believing that justice can be served by the offer of your own spirit to the most unjust of torturers" (813); and Dagny conceives of herself as accepting the role of a "victim" because "there's still a chance to win" (1001).

Throughout, Dagny is willing to immolate herself in order to save the Taggart Transcontinental, which is her top value; but already, in part II, we have seen that she no longer finds any joy in the railroad, which has served to cannibalize rather than sustain the sorts of men she admires. She is in this impossible position because she cannot understand why this is the case—why the John Galt Line met the end that it did. Francisco now tells her that what she needs to understand is what the looters really want. When she does, she will see that her work on the railroad is not in the service of Galt but of his destroyers and that this is why her values have always been inexplicably out of reach.

For the present, she is not yet free of the contradiction that has intensified over the course of her life. She reflects on it at the end of part II, looking down from her airplane as she flies to Utah in a desperate attempt to prevent Quenton Daniels from disappearing.

> When she saw the lights of a town, like a handful of gold coins flung upon the prairie, the brightly violent lights fed by an electric current, they seemed as distant as the stars and now as unattainable. The energy that had lighted them was gone, the power that created power stations in empty prairies had vanished, and she knew of no journey to recapture it. Yet these had been her stars—she thought, looking down—these had been her goal, her beacon, the aspiration drawing her upon her upward course. That which others claimed to feel at the sight of the stars—stars safely distant by millions of years and thus imposing no obligation to act, but serving as the tinsel of futility—she had felt at the sight of electric bulbs lighting the streets of a town. It was this earth below that had been the height she wanted to reach, and she wondered how she had come to lose it, who had made of it a convict's ball to drag through muck, who had turned its promise of greatness into a vision never to be reached. (691)

Watching the sunlight struggle to break through the clouds, she hears in her mind a piece of music that is emblematic of her contradiction, "the cry of a tortured struggle, with the chords of its theme breaking through, like a distant vision to be reached" (692)—Halley's Fourth Concerto, which earlier in the novel is described as "a great cry of rebellion"

> It was a "No" flung at some vast process of torture, a denial of suffering, a denial that held the agony of the struggle to break free. The sounds were like a voice saying: There is no necessity for pain—why, then, is the worst pain reserved for those who will not accept its necessity?—we who hold the love and the secret of joy, to what punishment have we been sentenced for it, and by whom? . . . The sounds of torture became defiance, the statement of agony became a hymn to a distant vision for whose sake anything was worth enduring, even this. It was the song of rebellion—and of a desperate quest. (67)

When Dagny opens her eyes after crashing the plane, she sees "sunlight, green leaves" and the face of John Galt, and she hears the triumphant theme of Halley's Fifth Concerto—"The Concerto of Deliverance" which "swept space clean" in the "joy of an unobstructed effort" and "spoke in laughing astonishment at the discovery that there was no ugliness or pain, and there never had had to be." "This was the world as she had expected to see it at sixteen—and now she had reached it" (701, 13).

The valley is Atlantis—the world she has been seeking her whole life—"her goal, the end of track, the point beyond the curve of the earth where the two straight lines of rail met and vanished" (748, cf. 765)—and Galt is the man who holds the rails in his hand; he is the worthy adversary she could never find, the inventor of the motor that had kept her going in her darkest hours, and the "consciousness like her own who would be the meaning of her world as she would be of his" (220). However, Dagny is not ready to join Galt's strike:

> the pull of the outer world [. . .] was the vision of Hank Rearden's courage and the courage of all those still fighting to stay alive. He would not give up the search for her plane, when all others had long since despaired, as he would not give up his mills, as he would not give up any goal he had chosen if a single chance was left. Was she certain that no chance remained for the world of Taggart Transcontinental? Was she certain that the terms of the battle were such that she could not care to win? They were right, the men of Atlantis, they were right to vanish if they knew that they left no value behind them—but until and unless she saw that no chance was untaken and no battle unfought, she had *no right* to remain among them. This was the question that had lashed her for weeks, but had not driven her to a glimpse of the answer. (801–2)

During her month in the valley, no less than in Woodstock over the previous month, she cannot renounce the railroad without being convinced that it is "impossible or improper" to preserve it. To do so would be to commit treason against all of her values, indeed against values as such. Taggart Transcontinental is the central value around which she has organized her life and to simply walk away from it would be to adopt the attitude that even the things one thinks of as most important are not worth fighting for. This casual attitude is the opposite of the principle on which Dagny has lived her life. Were she to accept it by abandoning the railroad, she would be betraying everything that she has lived by and cared about—the very things that make the valley and Galt so important to her. Thus she must return to the world: "So long as I choose to go on living, I can't desert a battle which I think is mine to fight" (807).

In Woodstock, she was trying to find a purpose for her life without the railroad, and she found that any project she could undertake would lead her back to the railroad and its world. This is true concretely in the case of projects like reclaiming the local apple orchards, because the produce would need to be shipped by rail (610). But even in cases where she would not need to have direct dealings with Taggart Transcontinental, any purpose she could conceive for herself would eventually take her back into the world where Directive 10-289 was law, the world in which her office of Vice-President in Charge of Operation was turned into that of a slave and a slave driver.

> She could renounce the railroad, she thought; she could find contentment here, in this forest; but she would build the path, then reach the road below, then rebuild the road—and then she would reach the storekeeper of Woodstock and that would be the end, and the empty white face staring at the universe in stagnant apathy would be the limit placed on her effort. Why?—she heard herself screaming aloud. There was no answer. (611)

She was tortured because acting on anything more than a trivial scale required making contact with the world she was trying to renounce.

In the valley, though there are more interesting and larger projects to undertake, the problem remains essentially the same. After a moment of excitement over the possibility of building a small railroad to service Francisco's copper mine, she cries in despair, "Oh, what for? To build three miles of railroad and abandon a transcontinental system!" (794). The apathetic stare of the storekeeper is still placing a limit on Dagny's effort; her sphere of action can now extend through the valley, but no further. She sees the valley, like the cabin in Woodstock, as a small and remote place where she can take refuge from the wider world in which she is inexplicably unable to achieve her values. Thus, she sees the decision to go on strike as giving up the world to the looters and letting them limit the sphere of one's action to an isolated "underground." And she cannot accept this because her basic conviction is that *the world* is "mine to shape in the image of my highest values and never to be given up to a lesser standard, no matter how hard or long the struggle." Thus she tells Galt:

> It was this valley that I saw as possible and would exchange for nothing less and would not give up to a mindless evil. I am going back to fight for this valley—to release it from its underground, to regain for it its full and rightful realm, to let the earth belong to you in fact, as it does in spirit—and to meet you again on the day when I'm able to deliver to you the whole of the world. (812)

In Atlantis she finds the sort of life that she has always known is possible, but she is not content to let it remain exiled in an underground valley, and so she resolves to fight for it in the outside world.

In fact, the strikers have not given up the world. They are waiting for the collapse of society—"the day when the looters will perish, but we won't" (635)—at which point they will return to "rebuild the world" (748). They now think this day will come within their own lifetimes, but Galt did not think this when he began the strike, and he did not yet have (or anticipate) a valley where the strikers could create a society of their own. Nevertheless, he did not conceive of himself as giving up the world to the looters. Rather he recognized that his work as an inventor was but undermining his own values, and he realized *why* this was happening and why it *had* to happen, given the sort of people with whom he was dealing; so he resolved to "put an end [. . .] once and for all" to the sort of society geared to such people and to create for the first time the conditions under which it would be possible to achieve one's highest values (671). Values *cannot* be attained in the looters' world, so by dropping out of it the strikers are not *giving up* anything; rather they are undertaking

> a struggle that consists of rising from ledge to ledge in a steady ascent to the top, a struggle where the hardships are investments in your future, and the victories bring you irreversibly closer to the world of your moral ideal, and should you die without reaching full sunlight, you will die on a level touched by its rays. (1068)

The strikers see the valley as a ledge reached in this struggle—not a retreat from the world, but the beginning of a new one.

Dagny cannot see it this way because she does not yet understand what is wrong with the existing society and why it cannot be redeemed. She still does not see why the John Galt Line *had* to end as it did and, more generally, why any productive work in the looters' society necessarily undermines one's values. Consequently she still thinks she can serve Galt by returning to the railroad. When she returned from Woodstock, Francisco attributed this view to a mistake about the looters' motivation—to her not knowing "what they really want." When she decides to return from the valley, she gives is explicit about what she thinks they want and about what role this plays in her decision.

> If you want to know the one reason that's taking me back, I'll tell you: I cannot bring myself to abandon to destruction all the greatness of the world, all that which was mine and yours, which was made by us and is still ours by right—because I cannot believe that men can refuse to see, that they can remain blind and deaf to us forever, when the truth is ours and their lives depend on accepting it. They still love their lives—and that is the uncorrupted remnant of their minds. So long as men desire to live, I cannot lose my battle.

"Do they desire it?" asks Akston softly, inviting her to "take that question back with you as the last premise left for you to check" (807).

During her stay in the valley, Dagny's tie to the looters is essentialized into this single premise, and Akston's question sets the context for her thoughts across the remainder of Part III, in which she checks and ultimately rejects it. With this premise in mind, and reinvigorated by the spirit of the valley, Dagny returns to the world with the conviction that victory is possible. She had returned from Woodstock convinced that her highest values were "not to be reached or lived," and resolved to fight for the world represented by the man at the end of the railroad tracks though she would never learn his name—to serve him "even though I'm never to win." When she leaves the valley, she has met that man and she is determined to win the world for him.

Concretely, she thinks that, because of the rapid deterioration of the economy, the looters will have to relinquish power in order to avert total collapse: they will eventually listen to reason and repeal their controls, just as they were anxious to make any "special exceptions" she might request in the immediate aftermath of the Winston Tunnel catastrophe (630). Shortly after Galt gives his speech, she tells Eddie:

> There will be no looters' government within ten days. Then men like Cuffy Meigs will devour the last of our rails and engines. Should I lose the battle by failing to wait one more moment? How can I let it go—Taggart Transcontinental, Eddie—go forever, when one last effort can still keep it in existence? . . . I'm not helping the looters. Nothing can help them now. (1078)[21]

By saving the railroad, she thinks she will make it possible for the strikers to
return to an industrial nation, with infrastructure and institutions that can
be restored, rather than to a country in anarchy, composed of "starving robber gangs fighting to rob one another" and "hidden outposts" of civilization
(1067).

Of course, Dagny knows that the world is collapsing as quickly as it is precisely because of the strike. Her position would be a straightforward form of
hypocrisy if she did not think that there is some way that the strikers could
have achieved their aims without going on strike. She never expresses this
view after Galt tells her of the strike, but immediately before he tells her she
comments that Akston's book on ethics could "save the world" if it were published outside of the valley (738). Presumably she continues to think that if
the strikers had remained in the world, they could have reversed the course of
the nation by advocating for the right philosophy and taking actions such as
Rearden did at his trial. This is not an unreasonable view: such actions are precisely what Rand herself advocated in the actual world, and, even within the
world of the novel, Francisco says that Rearden "could have saved the world"
three generations earlier (487). In the course of those generations, however,
the America of the novel has reached a point of no return; its soul has become
fully infected by a mystical morality that is driven by and fosters a hatred of
existence (1061). Dagny has yet to understand its nature or motivation—she
has yet to understand the villains. When she does, she will see why it is impossible to make terms with them, and why their world must be utterly destroyed
in order for hers to be realized.

DELIVERANCE

I wrote earlier that part III of the novel is essentially metaphysical. In part II,
the heroes' actions are characterized in predominantly moral terms; part III
recasts them in terms of their relation to reality as such. Galt, for example, is
described as having "that look of respectful severity with which a man stands
before the fact that the truth is the truth" (725), and both he and Rearden talk
about the disastrous consequences of "faking reality" (795, 859–60). Likewise,
the villains, who were earlier shown to evade particular facts or responsibilities, are now portrayed as attempting to escape the law of identity and to reverse the relation between consciousness and existence (1035–36). Across part
III, what Dagny and Rearden come to understand is the way the villains view
reality, the motivation associated with this, and their own responsibility for
making this way of existence possible.

Dagny returns to a world approaching final collapse, in which everyone
is struggling to avoid the knowledge of what is happening and why. On her
flight to New York, she notices the other passengers listening as though they

comprehend it the broadcast of an unintelligible speech: "these people pretend to themselves that they are not pretending; they know no other state of existence" (833). Having returned to the world with the mission (from Akston) to understand the looters and to check her premise that they want to survive, she is keenly alert to how deeply different the people she encounters are from herself. This is especially the case with villains such as Jim. Back in the office, she learns of the Railroad Unification Plan, which will obviously destroy the railroad industry in a matter of months:

> Jim had always managed to switch the weight of his failures upon the strongest plants around him and to survive by destroying them to pay for his errors, as he had done with Dan Conway, as he had done with the industries of Colorado; but this did not have even the rationality of a looter—this pouncing upon the drained carcass of a weaker, a half-bankrupt competitor for a moment's delay, with nothing but a cracking bone between the pouncer and the abyss.
>
> The impulse of the habit of reason almost pushed her to speak, to argue, to demonstrate the self-evident—but she looked at their faces and she saw that they knew it. In some terms different from hers, in some inconceivable manner of consciousness, they knew all that she could tell them, it was useless to prove to them the irrational horror of their course and of its consequences, both Meigs and Taggart knew it—and the secret of their consciousness was the means by which they escaped the finality of their knowledge. (842)

She has returned on the premise that men value their lives and so cannot remain blind and deaf forever when the truth is hers and their lives depend on accepting it. But Jim and Meigs are not open to reason, though they face "the abyss." She sees now that the villains have some other manner of consciousness of which she cannot conceive. She comes a step closer to understanding how they escape the finality of their knowledge when she connects this issue to the question of moral sanction. Jim and the other looters are desperate for her to make a statement reassuring the public that "it isn't true that Directive 10-289 is destroying industry, that it's a sound piece of legislation devised for everybody's good, and that if they'll just be patient a little longer, things will improve and prosperity will return" (844). She realizes that they need "her sanction, not to reassure their victims, but to reassure themselves" (846). It is significant that in sanctioning the plan Dagny would be giving them her assurance that it *could work*, that it could save them.

The Plan's inevitable result is destruction: the railroad is consumed by maggots such as Meigs, an "undisguised gangster" who loots its assets and sells them in other countries. With mass starvation imminent, Dagny wonders what the looters are "counting on." As if in answer to her question Jim demands: "You must do something! . . . It's *your* job, it's your province, it's your duty! . . . To act. To do. . . . How should I know [what]? It's *your* special talent. You're the doer." It is Dagny that he's counting on, though he is not counting on any *specific* action from her; he knows of no action that would save him, and he evades the growing realization that no such action is possible.

> She chuckled. *There* was the form of the formless, she thought, *there* was the method of his consciousness: he wanted her to protect him from Cuffy Meigs without acknowledging Meigs' existence, to fight it without admitting its reality, to defeat it without disturbing its game. (915)

The sanction Jim wants from her is the acceptance of this role, and the pretense that there is a solution; she refuses to grant it: "You're asking for reassurance, Jim. You're not going to get it. [. . .] I'm not going to help you pretend—by arguing with you—that the reality you're talking about is not what it is, that there's still a way to make it work and to save your neck. There isn't" (916).

As when Rearden refused to grant the sanction of the victim to his family at Thanksgiving or to the government at his trial, the response Dagny gets is not anger or reprisal but retreat. Jim asks in "the feebly uncertain voice of a man on the verge of abdication" what *she* would do, and we have the first real test of her theory that the villains cannot remain blind forever. Without her help, Jim can no longer pretend that the Unification Plan can work and he is ready to listen to her alternative. She gives it: "Give up—all of you, you and your Washington friends and your looting planners and the whole of your cannibal philosophy. Give up and get out of the way and let those of us who can, start from scratch out of the ruins." His response is telling:

> "No!" The explosion came, oddly, now; it was the scream of a man who would die rather than betray his idea, and it came from a man who had spent his life evading the existence of ideas, acting with the expediency of a criminal. She wondered whether she had ever understood the essence of criminals. She wondered about the nature of the loyalty to the idea of denying ideas.
>
> "No!" he cried, his voice lower, hoarser and more normal, sinking from the tone of a zealot to the tone of an overbearing executive. "That's impossible! That's out of the question! . . . Why do you always think of the impractical? Why don't you accept reality as it *is* and do something about it? You're the realist, you're the doer, the mover, the producer, the Nat Taggart, you're the person who's able to achieve any goal she chooses! You could save us now, you could find a way to make things work—if you *wanted* to!" (916–17)

Notice that Jim would rather *die* than betray his idea. The fact that life depends on rejecting it will not prevent him being blind and deaf to Dagny when she presents an alternative. She begins to realize that there is something about his motivation—about the motivation of criminals—that she has never understood. Jim is not an idealist willing to die for some principle, he has spent his life evading the need to act on principle, and Dagny recognizes that the idea to which he is clinging is a means of evasion. It is a mechanism by which the looters attempt to avert the responsibility of thinking by inducing the producers to accept "the will of Cuffy Meigs as a *fact* of nature, irrevocable and absolute like steel, rails and gravitation"—to "accept the Meigs-made world as an objective, unchangeable reality"—and to "continue producing abundance in that world" (917).[22] But she still does not understand how Jim can cling to this evasion in the face of all the facts when his life is on the line. She still does not understand his motivation, but she is coming to see that there is a question.

Rearden grasps the answer before she does. The crucial step comes when his brother Philip alleges, in the course of demanding a job from him, that he has never had any feelings: "You've never felt anything at all. You've never *suffered!*"

> It was as if a sum of years hit Rearden in the face, by means of a sensation and a sight: the exact sensation of what he had felt in the cab of the first train's engine on the John Galt Line—and the sight of Philip's eyes, the pale; half-liquid eyes presenting the uttermost of human degradation: an uncontested pain, and, with the obscene insolence of a skeleton toward a living being, demanding that this pain be held as the highest of values. You've never suffered, the eyes were saying to him accusingly—while he was seeing the night in his office when his ore mines were taken away from him—the moment when he had signed the Gift Certificate surrendering Rearden Metal—the month of days inside a plane that searched for the remains of Dagny's body. You've never suffered, the eyes were saying with self-righteous scorn—while he remembered the sensation of proud chastity with which he had fought through those moments, refusing to surrender to pain, a sensation made of his love, of his loyalty, of his knowledge that joy is the goal of existence, and joy is not to be stumbled upon, but to be achieved, and the act of treason is to let its vision drown in the swamp of the moment's torture. You've never suffered, the dead stare of the eyes was saying, you've never felt anything, because only to suffer is to feel—there's no such thing as joy, there's only pain and the absence of pain, only pain and the zero, when one feels nothing—I suffer, I'm twisted by suffering, I'm made of undiluted suffering, that's my purity, that's my virtue—and yours, you the untwisted one, you the uncomplaining, yours is to relieve me of my pain—cut your unsuffering body to patch up mine, cut your un-feeling soul to stop mine from feeling—and we'll achieve the ultimate ideal, the triumph over life, the zero! He was seeing the nature of those who, for centuries, had not recoiled from the preachers of annihilation—he was seeing the nature of the enemies he had been fighting all his life. (931–32)

As I discuss in my other contribution to this volume, joy and positive desires result from setting values and achieving them.[23] Because the villains in *Atlas Shrugged* do not do this, they do not experience the sorts of feelings that motivate the heroes. They experience only negative emotions such as fear and pain, which they seek to alleviate. This is the only a form of motivation possible to men who do not use their minds. The state they seek to achieve is not a positive but the removal of a negative. This is a significant theme in Galt's speech, where he describes this "zero worship" as the "secret core" of the Morality of Death, and points out that death is the only state that fulfills the zero-worshipers ideal (1031–32). Rearden doesn't yet grasp these implications. His immediate identification of the point is that there are men who "worship pain." During his next encounter with his family, when they beg his forgiveness and beseech him to continue to immolate himself to save them, he grasps one of the crucial implications that Galt will draw in his speech. "Henry, don't abandon us!" cries his mother, "Don't sentence us to perish! Whatever we are, we're human! We want to live!" He responds, passing from astonishment to horror as the thought strikes him: "Why, no, I don't think you do. If you did, you would have known how to value me" (973).

For Dagny, this is the final premise left to check, and when she comes to the same conclusion, four chapters later, she immediately goes on strike. Rearden's context is slightly different. Since identifying the worship of pain, he has come to feel progressively detached from and disinterested in a society comprised of beings he can no longer regard as people. He could not "grant any anger, indignation or moral concern to the senseless motions of the un-living; no, worse, he thought—the anti-living" (932). He takes the realization that his family and, in general, villains, do not want to live in this same spirit. Whereas Dagny's central error is a misunderstanding of the motives of evil people, this realization on Rearden's part comes as a mere coda to what he had realized about them when confronted with the Gift Certificate. Having made these realizations he feels divorced from the world in which he has lived, a feeling that extends even to the mills—"no, he was not indifferent to his mills; but the feeling which had once been passion for a living entity was now like the wistful tenderness one feels for the memory of the loved and dead. The special quality of what one feels for the dead, he thought, is that no action is possible any longer" (964).

What ties him to the world is a failure to realize the role he is still playing in supporting the looters. He grasps now that there is something left to see and is going through his days "as if some final knowledge were in the process of unraveling before him, a process not to be hastened or stopped" (964). The process reaches its culmination a few hours after his realization about his family, at a meeting of bureaucrats who present him with the blatantly irrational Steel Unification Plan. It is modeled after the Railroad Unification Plan and will destroy Rearden Steel and the industry as a whole in a matter of months. In the ensuing discussion three "tumblers" click in Rearden's mind, the last of which is described as "completing the sum and releasing the intricate lock, the answer uniting all the pieces, the questions and the unsolved wounds of his life" (986).

The first tumbler is Dr. Ferris' statement: "You won't go bankrupt. You'll always produce. You can't help it. It's in your blood. Or, to be more scientific: you're conditioned that way" (984–85). As Jim had wanted Dagny to accept Meigs' edicts as natural laws, so Ferris treats it as a law of nature that Rearden will always create values, no matter what the conditions. The second tumbler concerns these conditions. When Rearden says that there is nothing possible ahead except starvation, Lawson responds: "Well, after all, you businessmen have kept predicting disasters for years, you've cried catastrophe at every progressive measure and told us that we'll perish—but we haven't" (985). They haven't perished because Rearden, Dagny and others had saved them, which brings us to the third tumbler—Jim Taggart's cry, "Oh, you'll do something!"

> Then—even though it was only a sentence he had heard all his life—he felt a deafening crash within him, as of a steel door dropping open at the touch of the final tumbler. . . . In the moment of silence after the crash, it seemed to him that he heard Francisco's voice, asking him quietly in the ballroom of this building, yet asking it also here and now: "Who is the guiltiest man in this room?" He heard his own answer of the past: "I suppose—James Taggart?" and Francisco's voice saying without reproach: "No, Mr. Rearden, it's not James Taggart,"—but here, in this room and this moment, his mind answered: "I am."
>
> He had cursed these looters for their stubborn blindness? It was he who had made it possible. From the first extortion he had accepted, from the first directive he had obeyed, he had given them cause to believe that reality was a thing to be cheated, that one could demand the irrational and someone somehow would provide it. If he had accepted the Equalization of Opportunity Bill, if he had accepted Directive 10-289, if he had accepted the law that those who could not equal his ability had the right to dispose of it, that those who had not earned were to profit, but he who had was to lose, that those who could not think were to command, but he who could was to obey them—then were they illogical in believing that they existed in an irrational universe? He had made it for them, he had provided it. Were they illogical in believing that theirs was only *to wish*, to wish with no concern for the possible—and that *his* was to fulfill their wishes, by means they did not have to know or name? They, the impotent mystics, struggling to escape the responsibility of reason, had known that he, the rationalist, had undertaken to serve their whims. They had known that he had given them a blank check on reality—his was not to ask *why?*—*theirs* was not to ask *how?*—let them demand that he give them a share of his wealth, then all that he owns, then more than he owns—impossible?—no, *he'll do something!* . . . He was seeing the progression of the years, the monstrous extortions, the impossible demands, the inexplicable victories of evil, the preposterous plans and unintelligible goals proclaimed in volumes of muddy philosophy, the desperate wonder of the victims who thought that some complex, malevolent wisdom was moving the powers destroying the world—and all of it had rested on one tenet behind the shifty eyes of the victors: *he'll do something!* . . . We'll get away with it—he'll let us—*he'll do something!* . . .
>
> You businessmen kept predicting that we'd perish, but we haven't. . . . It was true, he thought. They had not been blind to reality, *he* had—blind to the reality he himself had created. No, they had not perished, but who had? Who had perished to pay for their manner of survival? Ellis Wyatt . . . Ken Danagger . . . Francisco d'Anconia. (986–87)

With the clicking of this tumbler Rearden has come to the end of the trail, and we can see how what he learns in this moment depends on and integrates earlier steps down the road he has traveled. It is worth recalling some of these to indicate the pattern. When initially visited by the bureaucrat from the State Science Institute who looked like a traffic cop, he grasped that the looters need some sort of sanction from him. By degrees he grasped that the productive activity on which human life depends and on which he always prided himself is the essence of morality and that the sanction the looters need from him is his acceptance of their alien moral standard. He learned how this acceptance fed on and contributed to a gulf between his mind and his body, his ideals and his actions, his ends and his means. How it amounted to allowing them to specify the ends to which his virtue would be the means. Now he sees that in always finding a way to continue producing despite the irrational, unjust, and increasingly onerous burdens placed on him, he was sanctioning and making possible a way of life in which the whims of the vicious, who have no genuine values, are fulfilled at the expense of the virtuous, whose values can, as a consequence, never be realized.

This is the final step for Rearden of the road that all the strikers must travel "to Atlantis" (637), and we can see that he has reached the destination in the way he looks at his mills, when he sees them again hours later:

> He had never loved his mills as he did in that moment, for—seeing them by an act of his own vision, cleared of all but his own code of values, in a luminous reality that held no contradictions—he was seeing the reason of his love: the mills were an achievement of his mind, devoted to his enjoyment of existence, erected in a rational world to deal with rational men. If those men had vanished, if that world was gone, if his mills had ceased to serve his values—then the mills were only a pile of dead scrap, to be left to crumble, the sooner the better—to be left, not as an act of treason, but as an act of loyalty to their actual meaning. (988)

He grasps here what Francisco had earlier tried to convey to Dagny about Taggart Transcontinental. It is a corpse, of no value, except when it is able to serve the lives of the rational men who produce and sustain it. And Rearden sees now why his mills cannot serve his life, because he sees now what social context is required for them to do so. As a result, his feeling of detachment is gone: the pain that he had had to bear because of the mills is passed and he can now love them without contradiction for everything they were to him. But the mills are only a remnant or promise of the world in which such values can be achieved without contradictions and serve their proper purpose. Rearden has now reached that world, and the mills are to be left behind.

Rearden's progression to this point is a complex series of inductions from the events in the novel, which culminates in a changed perspective on the world—a new moral philosophy—that leads him to join the strike. Only when this progression is completed, do we find a systematic exposition of this philosophy in Galt's Speech. The speech contains few ideas which have not been made explicit earlier in the novel.[24] Its primary function is to bring order to what has been learned so far, and completes the novel's presentation of its philosophy.

There remains, however, one plot conflict to resolve. Dagny must come to understand the villains' motivation. Rearden has grasped that they do not value their lives, and Galt has made this point in his speech. But she continues not to see it. The point is essential, because so long as she believes that they value their lives, she thinks that she has some common ground with them and that it will be possible to come to terms: in loyalty to their love of their lives the looters will eventually have to renounce their irrational way of life when they can no longer evade that the alternative is death. That Dagny expects it is evident from what she says to Mr. Thompson in the immediate aftermath of Galt's Speech:

> You're through. Don't you see that you're through? What else do you need, after what you've heard? Give up and get out of the way. Leave men free to exist. . . . You're still alive, you're using a human language, you're asking for answers, you're counting on reason—you're still counting on reason, God damn you! You're able to understand. It isn't possible that you haven't understood. There's nothing you can now pretend to hope, to want or gain or grab or reach. There's nothing but destruction ahead, the world's and your own. Give up and get out. . . . You wish to live, don't you? Get out of the way, if you want a chance. Let those who can, take over. He knows what to do. You don't. He is able to create the means of human survival. You aren't. . . . You know the truth, all of you, and so do I, and so does every man who's heard John Galt! What else are you waiting for? For proof? He's given it to you. For facts? They're all around you. How many corpses do you intend to pile up before you renounce it—your guns, your power, your controls and the whole of your miserable altruistic creed? Give it up, if you want to live. Give it up, if there's anything left in your mind that's still able to want human beings to remain alive on this earth! (1073)

Since her return from the valley she has been gradually coming to understand the villains' way of life, but she has not yet reached the end of the trail. We have already discussed her initial steps along it. There is one more significant development prior to Galt's Speech. It occurs during a dinner meeting between Dagny, Jim, Mouch, Lawson, Ferris, Weatherby, and Meigs to discuss the future of the railroad system, which has been destroyed by the Unification Plan and cannot continue to run in its present condition. Dagny takes her invitation to the meeting as "an acknowledgement of the fact that they needed her and, perhaps, the first step of their surrender" (944). During the meeting it becomes clear that this is not the case. She is asked questions but is "interrupted before she had completed the first sentence of the answer" and her name is "tossed into the conversation at half-hour intervals, tossed perfunctorily with the speakers eyes never glancing in her direction." It becomes clear that they want her there only in order to "delude themselves into believing that she had agreed" with the decisions they reached; so by being present she grants just the sort of sanction or reassurance that she earlier refused Jim (945–46).

The decision that needs to be reached is whether to discontinue transcontinental traffic or the Minnesota branch line. Closing the former would cut off "our lines of communication over a third of the continent," but that third consists of "empty miles of westerns sands, of scraggly pastures and abandoned fields," whereas the Minnesota line services "the Mesabi Range, the last of the major sources of iron ore" and "the Minnesota farmers, . . . the best producers of wheat in the country. . . . [T]he end of Minnesota would end Wisconsin, then Michigan, then Illinois"; it would mean "the red breath of the factories dying out over the industrial East." Thus Dagny argues for preserving the Minnesota line:

> give us leeway to save the Eastern states. That's all that's left of the country—and of the world. If you let us save that, we'll have a chance to rebuild the rest. If not, it's the end. . . . Let us shrink back to the start of this country, but let us hold that start. We'll run no trains west of the Missouri. We'll become a local railroad—the local of the industrial East. Let us save our industries. There's nothing left to save in the West. You can run agriculture for centuries by manual labor and ox-carts. But destroy the last of this country's industrial plant—and centuries of effort won't be able to rebuild it or to gather the economic strength to make a start. How do you expect our industries—or railroads—to survive without steel? How do you expect any steel to be produced if you cut off the supply of iron ore? Save Minnesota, whatever's left of it. The country? You have no country to save, if its industries perish. You can sacrifice a leg or an arm. You can't save a body by sacrificing its heart and brain. Save our industries. Save Minnesota. Save the Eastern Seaboard. (946–47)

The planners are unmoved. Meigs in particular insists that the "transcontinental dragnet" must be preserved: "you won't be able to keep people in line unless you have transportation—troop transportation." Lawson's "soft lips twist into a smile" when he speaks of having the "courage" to sacrifice thousands of people. Ferris, citing the example of nonindustrial India, muses that "the importance of industry to a civilization has been grossly overemphasized" (947).

> Then she saw the answer; she saw the secret premise behind their words. . . . [T]hese men were moved forward, not by the image of an industrial skyline, but by the vision of that form of existence which the industrialists had swept away— the vision of a fat, unhygienic rajah of India, with vacant eyes staring in indolent stupor out of stagnant layers of flesh, with nothing to do but run precious gems through his fingers and, once in a while, stick a knife into the body of a starved, toil-dazed, germ-eaten creature, as a claim to a few grains of the creature's rice, then claim it from hundreds of millions of such creatures and thus let the rice grains gather into gems.

She had thought that industrial production was a value not to be questioned by anyone; she had thought that these men's urge to expropriate the factories of others was their acknowledgment of the factories' value. She, born of the industrial revolution, had not held as conceivable, had forgotten along with the tales of astrology and alchemy, what these men knew in their secret, furtive souls, knew not by means of thought, but by means of that nameless muck which they called their instincts and emotions: that so long as men struggle to stay alive, they'll never produce so little but that the man with the club won't be able to seize it and leave them still less, provided millions of them are willing to submit . . . —that the feudal baron did not need electronic factories in order to drink his brains away out of jeweled goblets, and neither did the rajahs of the People's State of India.

She saw what they wanted and to what goal their "instincts," which they called unaccountable, were leading them. She saw that Eugene Lawson, the humanitarian, took pleasure at the prospect of human starvation—and Dr. Ferris, the scientist, was dreaming of the day when men would return to the hand-plow.

Incredulity and indifference were her only reaction: incredulity, because she could not conceive of what would bring human beings to such a state—indifference, because she could not regard those who reached it, as human any longer. They went on talking, but she was unable to speak or to listen. She caught herself feeling that her only desire was now to get home and fall asleep. (948)

Dagny's realization here is parallel to Rearden's realization (in the same chapter) that certain men worship pain. Both are recognitions of a difference between the ultimate motivations of the heroes and the villains—a difference deep enough to make the heroes question whether the villains are human at all. Notice, though, that this is not a recognition that the villains do not want to live—the unhygienic rajah is, after all, alive. What Dagny does see is that there can be no real community of values with such creatures, no basis for interaction. This is why, for both Dagny and Rearden, the realization engenders a sense of detachment from a world populated by such people. Rearden, as we saw, moves from this stage quickly to the realization that the villains (in particular, his family) do not want to live, when he reflects on the fact that they do not "know how to value him." But to Dagny the state of a consciousness that does not love life remains inconceivable. When, after Rearden has gone on strike, the looters bemoan his loss, she wonders, "If they see Hank Rearden's value now, why didn't they see it sooner? Why hadn't they averted their own doom and spared him years of torture? She found no answer" (1002). Convinced that they want to live, she cannot understand why they did not value him, and for the same reason she thinks that they must reverse course eventually. This is why she is bewildered by their response to Galt's Speech (1074).

Dagny comes to understand the villains only through the episode of Galt's capture. He tells her, after she has inadvertently led them to him: "You haven't seen the nature of our enemies. You'll see it now. If I have to be the pawn in the demonstration that will convince you, I'm willing to be—and to win you from them, once and for all" (1091). This is what happens. In order to save Galt she must pretend to take his enemies' side, which requires her to emulate them in action; and in doing this, she approximates their mode of consciousness which had until now been unreal to her. We can see her beginning to understand it in the narration of her thoughts as she denounces Galt to Thompson:

> It was easy, she thought. It would have been difficult in that distant time when she had regarded language as a tool of honor, always to be used as if one were under oath—an oath of allegiance to reality and to respect for human beings. Now it was only a matter of making sounds, inarticulate sounds addressed to inanimate objects unrelated to such concepts as reality, human or honor. . . . It had been easy, because she had felt as if she were in some dreary non-world, where her words and actions were not facts any longer—not reflections of reality, but only distorted postures in one of those side-show mirrors that project deformity for the perception of beings whose consciousness is not to be treated as consciousness. Thin, single and hot, like the burning pressure of a wire within her, like a needle selecting her course, was her only concern: the thought of his safety. The rest was a blur of shapeless dissolution, half-acid, half-fog.
> But this—she thought with a shudder—was the state in which they lived, all those people whom she had never understood, this was the state they desired, this rubber reality, this task of pretending, distorting, deceiving, with the credulous stare of some Mr. Thompson's panic-bleary eyes as one's only purpose and reward. Those who desired this state—she wondered—did they want to live? (1109)

Here we see Dagny asking for the first time in her own voice whether the villains want to live. We will see shortly how she answers the question.

The final steps of Dagny's decision to go on strike are complicated somewhat by the existential circumstance that Galt, the love of her life, is in immediate danger. As a result her immediate concern is not running the railroad, as it would be if she were not on strike, but she cannot abandon the railroad and her old life as she would if she were on strike. She is in a kind of limbo. From the moment of Galt's capture, there is no question in her mind that she will join the strike. Eddie tells her that he knows she will quit as soon as Galt is free and she does not disagree; indeed she tries to discourage him from flying to San Francisco to reinitiate the halted transcontinental traffic: "It doesn't matter now. There's nothing to save" (1116). However, she does not yet have the perspective on the world that is characteristic of the strikers—the perspective with which we saw Rearden look on his mills for the last time. Her state is similar to Rearden's earlier that morning, when he was waiting for the final knowledge to unravel before him. The dominant emotion she feels now, as she begins to question whether the villains want to live, is still a form of indifference:

> Were she able to feel—she thought as she walked through the concourse of the Terminal—she would know that the heavy indifference she now felt for her railroad was hatred. She could not get rid of the feeling that she was running

nothing but freight trains: the passengers, to her, were not living or human. It seemed senseless to waste such enormous effort on preventing catastrophes, on protecting the safety of trains carrying nothing but inanimate objects. She looked at the faces in the Terminal: if he were to die, she thought, to be murdered by the rulers of their system, that these might continue to eat, sleep and travel—would she work to provide them with trains? If she were to scream for their help, would one of them rise to his defense? Did they want him to live, they who had heard him?

The check for five hundred thousand dollars was delivered to her office, that afternoon; it was delivered with a bouquet of flowers from Mr. Thompson. She looked at the check and let it flutter down to her desk: it meant nothing and made her feel nothing, not even a suggestion of guilt. It was a scrap of paper, of no greater significance than the ones in the office wastebasket. Whether it could buy a diamond necklace or the city dump or the last of her food, made no difference. It would never be spent. It was not a token of value and nothing it purchased could be of value. But this—she thought—this inanimate indifference was the permanent state of the people around her, of men who had no purpose and no passion. This was the state of a non-valuing soul; those who chose it—she wondered—did they want to live? (1109)

It is this experience of indifference that enables her to understand the villains' psychology, and when she fully understands it the indifference vanishes. Running to a phone booth to call Francisco, after her final realization, she has "the sense of freedom of a world that had never had to be obstructed" (1136). "It did not make her feel estranged from the city: it made her feel, for the first time, that she owned the city and that she loved it, that she had never loved it before as she did in this moment, with so personal, solemn and confident a sense of possession" (1133).

We witness Dagny's progression from indifference to the strikers' perspective during and immediately after the banquet to announce the "John Galt Plan." As she looks at the faces of the different attendees, connecting what she notices about them with points from Galt's Speech, she continues to ask whether they desire to live. Increasingly the question takes on a rhetorical character, as she grasps that they do not.

Don't they see the hallmark of death in those faces, and the hallmark of life in his? Which state do they wish to choose? Which state do they seek for mankind? . . . She looked at the faces in the ballroom. They were nervously blank; they showed nothing but the sagging weight of lethargy and the staleness of a chronic fear. They were looking at Galt and at Mouch, as if unable to perceive any difference between them or to feel concern if a difference existed, their empty, uncritical, unvaluing stare declaring: "Who am I to know?" She shuddered, remembering his sentence: "The man who declares, 'Who am I to know?' is declaring, 'Who am I to live?'" Did they care to live?—she thought. They did not seem to care even for the effort of raising that question. . . . She saw a few faces who seemed to care. They were looking at Galt with a desperate plea, with a wistfully tragic admiration— and with hands lying limply on the tables before them. These were the men who saw what he was, who lived in frustrated longing for his world—but tomorrow, if they saw him being murdered before them, their hands would hang as limply and their eyes would look away, saying, "Who am I to act?" . . . .

Dagny observed some faces—it took her an effort fully to believe it—who were looking at Galt with hatred. Jim was one of them, she noted. When the image of Mouch held the screen, these faces were relaxed in bored contentment, which was not pleasure, but the comfort of license, of knowing that nothing was demanded of them and nothing was firm or certain. When the camera flashed the image of Galt, their lips grew tight and their features were sharpened by a look of peculiar caution. She felt with sudden certainty that they feared the precision of his face, the unyielding clarity of his features, the look of being an entity, a look of asserting existence. They hate him for being himself—she thought, feeling a touch of cold horror, as the nature of their souls became real to her—they hate him for his capacity to live. Do *they* want to live?—she thought in self-mockery. Through the stunned numbness of her mind, she remembered the sound of his sentence: "The desire not to be anything, is the desire not to be." (1124)

Dagny's development culminates when, after the banquet, she hears Jim and others plotting to torture Galt:

She knew. She knew what they intended doing and what it was within them that made it possible. They did not think that this would succeed. They did not think that Galt would give in; they did not want him to give in. They did not think that anything could save them now; they did not want to be saved. Moved by the panic of their nameless emotions, they had fought against reality all their lives—and now they had reached a moment when at last they felt at home. They did not have to know why they felt it, they who had chosen never to know what they felt— they merely experienced a sense of recognition, since *this* was what they had been seeking, *this* was the kind of reality that had been implied in all of their feelings, their actions, their desires, their choices, their dreams. This was the nature and the method of the rebellion against existence and of the undefined quest for an unnamed Nirvana. They did not want to live; they wanted *him* to die.

The horror she felt was only a brief stab, like the wrench of a switching perspective: she grasped that the objects she had thought to be human were not. She was left with a sense of clarity, of a final answer and of the need to act. He was in danger; there was no time and no room in her consciousness to waste emotion on the actions of the subhuman. (1135)

From this moment on Dagny is in Atlantis. She runs, with her feeling of "weightless freedom," to call Francisco. There is a moment of "blinding pain" in her office when she learns of the destruction of the Taggart Bridge (the very event that she had returned to the world to prevent) and as if by instinct seizes the telephone receiver. Placing the receiver back in its cradle is her first concrete action as a striker, and in taking it she gives up Taggart Transcontinental. Minutes later she stands "solemnly straight" and with Francisco and "the buildings of the greatest city in the world, as the kind of witnesses she wanted" takes the oath of Galt's new moral philosophy: "I swear—by my life and my love of it—that I will never live for the sake of another man, nor ask another man to live for the sake of mine" (1138).

This had always been Dagny's "own rule of living" (732), and *Atlas Shrugged* demonstrates that it is the rule each of us follows in "whatever living moments [we] have known" (1060). But few recognize that this is virtue, or understand how to implement it consistently. This is what Galt is the first to grasp and what Rearden and Dagny come to understand over the course of the novel. Only by coming to see the world in a new way—by learning a new philosophy—can they pronounce those words with the meaning Galt intended. Through the story of how these heroes discover Atlantis, the novel demonstrates this philosophy to us, its readers. In reading *Atlas Shrugged* we can ourselves follow the same complex process of reasoning and rethinking as do its heroes, moving from concretes to progressively broader, deeper, and more tightly integrated philosophical principles, which make it possible to understand that much of the pain, boredom, and despair felt by so many people is unnecessary and to achieve the "radiant state of existence" epitomized by Galt.

My aim in this essay was to call attention to this progression. Focusing on it enables one to better enjoy and appreciate the novel's plot, to better learn from it, and to better understand its impact. Following this progression—working through the demonstration the novel gives of its philosophy and understanding how its conclusions apply to our own lives in a world where a strike of Galt's sort would be impossible and improper—is too large a task for a single essay. Ultimately, it is something each of us must do for himself. I hope only to have provided some leads.

I leave you with Ayn Rand's own advice, given during a question period in 1961, on how to implement Galt's philosophical discovery in our social context:

> Never take things literally when they are inapplicable; or rather, take them literally only when they apply literally. What do I mean by that? Well, in *Atlas Shrugged*, I show that men go on strike. So long as we have not yet reached the state of censorship of ideas, one does not have to leave a society in the way the characters did in *Atlas Shrugged*. One does not have to yet break relationships to a society. But you know what one has to do? One has to break relationships with the culture. Meaning, while you live in this society, break all cultural relationships—meaning, withdraw your sanction from those people, groups, schools, or theories which preach the ideas that are destroying you. . . . If you've read *Atlas Shrugged*, you will understand what I mean by the situation of the sanction of the victim. . . .
>
> Now, what we have to do today: anyone who is serious about saving the world would have to first discard all the ideas—the entire cultural philosophy which is dominant today. Do not accept any of their ideas. Stand on your own as much as if you had to go into a separate valley, like in *Atlas Shrugged*. Stand on your own—your own mind. Check your premises. Define your convictions—define them rationally. Do not take anyone on faith, and do not believe that your elders know what they're doing, because they don't. You have to be the responsible creators of

a new culture, if there is to be any culture. That is the sense in which *Atlas Shrugged* is applicable to our period. . . .

You may observe in the history of philosophy that all ideas change in various periods, but morality is the one realm that did not change; only its superficial forms changed. Men have always been taught that they have to live for others, and they have to be sacrificial animals. . . . Break with the morality of altruism. Don't be afraid to assert *your* right to exist, but don't assert it as an arbitrary whim. [To succeed] you would have to know how to justify it, rationally and philosophically; and why you have that right. . . . When men drop all [the] ramifications of altruism, then you will see what a benevolent ideal society one could have; and America almost had it. The world came near to it at the end of the 19th century. . . .

You do not even know what a magnificent world America had. Now, it isn't fully gone, and it's in your power to build it again. But the retirement [into] which you have to go is cultural. Break with altruism and with every idea that is based on it. At least make the effort to think it out, very carefully. You'll be surprised how easy that revolution will be and how difficult it appears now [though] it isn't. Just give it one day's thought, and you'll have a different view. Now, I don't mean that that's all it will take. I mean, just give that to consider whether it's possible, after which you will have to do harder thinking than you've ever attempted before, because it will have to be totally on your own—totally relying on your own judgment and the logic of the arguments you hear or consider, rejecting all authorities, rejecting all bromides, and taking nothing on faith. But if you try it, you'll be surprised how close the Renaissance is to us, and it's up to each human being to work for it.[25]

In another context, Rand wrote that she did not know whether we would see a Renaissance in our time. "What I do know is this: anyone who fights for the future, lives in it today."[26]

NOTES

1. In this way Galt drives the action of the novel, and this is why Rand identifies him, rather than Rearden or Dagny Taggart, as the protagonist.

2. Ayn Rand, *For the New Intellectual* (New York: Random House, 1961; Signet paperback edition, 1963), 88. The full statement is: "The role of the mind in man's existence—and, as corollary, the demonstration of a new moral philosophy: the morality of rational self-interest." I discuss the novel's conception of the role of the mind in my other contribution to this volume, "*Atlas Shrugged* on the Role of the Mind in Man's Existence." The demonstration of a new moral philosophy is corollary to this in that the philosophy consists in *recognizing* the mind's role along with its presuppositions and consequences.

3. Ayn Rand, "Basic Principles of Literature," in *The Romantic Manifesto: A Philosophy of Literature* (New York: Signet, 1975), 81.

4. Ayn Rand, "Psycho-Epistemology of Art," in *Romantic Manifesto*, 22.

5. Rand defined "plot" as "a purposeful progression of logically connected events leading to the resolution of a climax" ("Basic Principles of Literature," 82). This sort of relationship exists only when the characters' later actions are motivated by their understanding and evaluation of earlier events. In her lectures on fiction writing, Rand takes *Les Misérables* as the paradigm of a well-plotted novel because "everything [Jean Valjean] does is always conditioned by what he

concluded (or misconcluded) from a previous event," and similarly for the antagonists (Tore Boeckmann, ed., *The Art of Fiction* [New York: Plume, 2000], 24).

6. See Tore Boeckmann's "What Might Be and Ought to Be: Aristotle's *Poetics* and *The Fountainhead*" in Robert Mayhew, ed. *Essays on Ayn Rand's* The Fountainhead.

7. Ayn Rand, "Art and Sense of Life," in *Romantic Manifesto*, 36.

8. Fiction functions as an extended hypothetical example or thought experiment.

9. When Directive 10-287 is being planned, twelve years into the strike, the bureaucrats are worried that they might encounter resistance because of a provision that would end freedom of the press (532–34, 545–46). This suggests that no such provision was in effect prior to this point.

10. David Harriman, ed., *Journals of Ayn Rand* (New York: Dutton, 1997), 398.

11. See Ayn Rand, "The Cult of Moral Grayness," in *The Virtue of Selfishness: A New Concept of Egoism* (New York: New American Library, 1964).

12. The three parts, of course, are named for the three axioms of traditional logic, but there are reasons why each part has the name it does. For a more detailed discussion, see Onkar Ghate's "The Part and Chapter Headings of *Atlas Shrugged*" in the present volume.

13. Strictly speaking, on Rand's view, "existence," as an axiomatic concept, does not have a definition. See Ayn Rand, *Introduction to Objectivist Epistemology*, second edition, Harry Binswanger and Leonard Peikoff, eds. (New York: Meridian, 1990), 40–41. Whether she had formulated this position at the time of writing Galt's Speech is unclear.

14. These shifts remain dramatic even if one factors out the novel's main philosophical speeches (i.e., those reproduced in *For the New Intellectual*) all of which occur in parts II and III. The statistics are as follows: in part I, there are on average 0.11 occurrences of "Moral" or "Evil" per page. In Part II they average is 0.38 occurrences per page (or 0.28 if the speeches are factored out), and in Part III the average is 0.83 (0.26 without the speeches). Unambiguously metaphysical words ("reality," "existence," "real," and "unreal") average 0.14 occurrences per page in Part I, 0.22 occurrences per page in part II (whether the speeches are included or not), and 0.67 occurrences per page in part III (0.34 if the speeches are removed).

15. This is not the only paradox introduced in part I, which is aptly named "Non-Contradiction": Francisco d'Anconia, a boy who could not have become a worthless playboy, has nevertheless become one (116), and yet he does not act like one (199); Lillian, who clearly despises Rearden, nevertheless "wants him" in some inexplicable "non-material" sense (309); an invention of genius which is of immeasurable financial value, is abandoned to rust in the closed factory of a bankrupt motor company (289, 331); and, people who love their jobs and excel at them are abandoning them for menial positions (25, 64, 331). These paradoxes set the context for parts II and III of the novel. See Ghate, "Part and Chapter Headings."

16. There are also costs that Lillian knows and Rearden does not. As Francisco explains, Rearden's attendance constitutes a dangerous sanction of Taggart (415), and this is Lillian's actual motive for insisting that he escort her (398–99).

17. I discuss *Atlas Shrugged*'s view of the nobility of material production in "*Atlas Shrugged* on the Role of the Mind in Man's Existence," 229–36. See also Debi Ghate's contribution to this volume, "The Businessmen's Crucial Role: Material Men of the Mind."

18. On the evil of this doctrine, see "*Atlas Shrugged* on the Role of the Mind in Man's Existence," 242–46.

19. Rand spoke often of what she called "the benevolent universe premise" (Harriman, *Journals of Ayn Rand*, 425, 555, 557, 673, 710; Michael S. Berliner ed., *Letters of Ayn Rand* [New York: Dutton, 1995], 643), though she never used the phrase in the writings she intended for publication. For discussion see Peikoff, *Objectivism*, 342–44 and Allan Gotthelf, *On Ayn Rand* (Belmont, Calif.: Wadsworth), 4–6, 94–96. Gotthelf discusses the premise as it bears on Dagny's characterization in particular in his "A Note on Dagny's 'Final Choice'" in the present volume, and in his chapter "The Benevolent Universe and the Heroic View of Man," in Allan Gotthelf and Gregory Salmieri, eds., *Ayn Rand: A Companion to Her Works and Thought* (Oxford: Blackwell, forthcoming).

20. Cf. "*Atlas Shrugged* on the Role of the Mind in Man's Existence," 242–44.

21. Eddie's response shows that, at this point in the novel, he understands the looters' motivation better than does Dagny. Galt ends his speech with a beautiful coda, directed primarily to Dagny, in which he explains how the depth of her own love of life makes it especially difficult for her to comprehend the nature and magnitude of villains' evil (1068).

22. In her essay "The Metaphysical vs. the Man-made," in *Philosophy: Who Needs It* (New York: Signet, 1984), Rand discusses the widespread error of confusing unchangeable facts of reality with things made (and changeable) by men, and notes that often in political debates people proceed on the implicit premise that "men's decisions are an absolute" and "reality's demands are not" (45).

23. "*Atlas Shrugged* on the Role of the Mind in Man's Existence" 236–39.

24. Those which it does are comparatively technical points concerning the nature of knowledge and the relations between the key concepts in ethics.

25. This material comes from the question period following Rand's presentation of "Faith and the Force: The Destroyers of the Modern World" at the Ford Hall Forum in 1961. It has been printed, in an edited form, in Robert Mayhew, ed., *Ayn Rand Answers: The Best of Her Q&A* (New York: New American Library, 2005), 54. I quote here from a transcript of the event, rather than from the more polished published version, so as to retain the more personal and advice-giving character of Rand's extemporaneous remarks. A recording of the event can be found online at www.aynrand.org/site/PageServer?pagename=reg_ar_faith_and_force as part of the *Ayn Rand Multimedia Library*, a project of the Ayn Rand Institute. The relevant remarks are made in response to the first question, and I recommend listening to Rand's answer in full.

26. *Romantic Manifesto*, viii.

This essay is based on my 2007 course, *Atlas Shrugged as a Work of Philosophy*, and I'd like to thank Allan Gotthelf and Karen Shoebotham for their input while I was planning those lectures. Karen also made helpful editorial comments as did Jennifer Scricco and Charlotte Jarrett. Like my other contribution to this volume, this essay benefited from discussion at the January 2008 workshop on *Atlas Shrugged* sponsored by the Anthem Fellowship for the Study of Objectivism at the University of Texas at Austin and the Ayn Rand Institute. I'd like to thank Robert Mayhew and Yaron Brook in particular for suggestions they made at the workshop about how best to refocus the material for presentation in written form.

22

A Note on Dagny's "Final Choice"

Allan Gotthelf

> Now I'll tell you what it was that you wanted to tell me—because, you see,
> I know it and I accept: somewhere within the past month, you have met the
> man you love, and if love means one's final, irreplaceable choice, then he is
> the only man you've ever loved."
>
> —Rearden to Dagny, *Atlas Shrugged* (860)

Rearden is right. Dagny has met the man she loves. His name is John Galt.
Our question is why is Galt, and not Rearden or Francisco, is Dagny's "final,
irreplaceable choice."

This is a complex question, but a large part of its answer becomes very clear
once one collects the relevant passages. The focus in what follows, then, is on
a selection of texts, which I take the liberty of quoting at some length.

The extended passage at the start of part III describing Dagny's first encounter with Galt, when she awakens from the crash of her plane in the valley,
will turn out to be one of our richest single sources of information, so I begin
with it:

> When she opened her eyes, she saw sunlight, green leaves and a man's face.
> This was the world as she had expected to see it at sixteen—and now she had
> reached it—and it seemed so simple, so unastonishing, that the thing she felt
> was like a blessing pronounced upon the universe by means of three words: But
> of course.
>
> She was looking up at the face of a man who knelt by her side, and she knew that
> in all the years behind her, *this* was what she would have given her life to see: a face
> that bore no mark of pain or fear or guilt. The shape of his mouth was pride, and
> more: it was as if he took pride in being proud. The angular planes of his cheeks
> made her think of arrogance, of tension, of scorn—yet the face had none of these
> qualities, it had their final sum: a look of serene determination and of certainty,

and the look of a ruthless innocence which would not seek forgiveness or grant it. It was a face that had nothing to hide or to escape, a face with no fear of being seen or of seeing, so that the first thing she grasped about him was the intense perceptiveness of his eyes—he looked as if his faculty of sight were his best-loved tool and its exercise were a limitless, joyous adventure, as if his eyes imparted a superlative value to himself and to the world—to himself for his ability to see, to the world for being a place so eagerly worth seeing. It seemed to her for a moment that she was in the presence of a being who was pure consciousness—yet she had never been so aware of a man's body. . . .

This was her world, she thought, this was the way men were meant to be and to face their existence—and all the rest of it, all the years of ugliness and struggle were only someone's senseless joke. She smiled at him, as at a fellow conspirator, in relief, in deliverance, in radiant mockery of all the things she would never have to consider important again. He smiled in answer, it was the same smile as her own, as if he felt what she felt and knew what she meant.

"We never had to take any of it seriously, did we?" she whispered.

"No, we never had to." (701–2)

After her return from the valley, in response to the remark that serves as the epigraph of this essay, Dagny says to Rearden:

It's true. I've met the man I love and will always love. . . . What you meant to me can never be changed. But the man I met—he is the love I had wanted to reach long before I knew that he existed. . . . (861)

Readers of the novel have already been introduced to the love Dagny had wanted to reach long before she knew that he existed, in the scene in part I when she was in the dilapidated office of the John Galt Line, exhausted and lonely:

She stood, in a room of crumbling plaster, pressed to the windowpane, looking up at the unattainable form of everything she loved. She did not know the nature of her loneliness. The only words that named it were: This is not the world I expected.[1]

Once, when she was sixteen, looking at a long stretch of Taggart track, at the rails that converged—like the lines of a skyscraper—to a single point in the distance, she had told Eddie Willers that she had always felt as if the rails were held in the hand of a man beyond the horizon—no, not her father or any of the men in the office—and some day she would meet him.

She shook her head and turned away from the window.

She went back to her desk. She tried to reach for the reports. But suddenly she was slumped across the desk, her head on her arm.

Don't, she thought; but she did not move to rise, it made no difference, there was no one to see her.

This was a longing she had never permitted herself to acknowledge. She faced it now. She thought: If emotion is one's response to the things the world has to offer, if she loved the rails, the building, and more: if she loved her love for them—there was still one response, the greatest, that she had missed. She thought: To find a feeling that would hold, as their sum, as their final expression, the purpose of all the things she loved on earth . . . To find a consciousness like her own, who would be the meaning of her world, as she would be of his . . . No, not Francisco d'Anconia, not Hank Rearden, not any man she had ever met or admired . . . A man who existed only in her knowledge of her capacity for an emotion she had never felt, but would have given her life to experience. (220)[2]

John Galt is that man—the love she has always wanted to meet—the consciousness like her own in a way that not even Francisco or Rearden is.

We see signs of this in Dagny's first response to Galt's face, quoted above, which echoes some of the last line of the passage we have just examined. Compare:

A man who existed only in her knowledge of her capacity for an emotion she had never felt, but would give her life to experience. (220)

with:

She was looking up at the face of a man who knelt by her side, and she knew that in all the years behind her, *this* was what she would have given her life to see: (701)

Dagny's initial emotional response to Galt's face, and then to his person and his body, anticipates the full response she comes to have, across the early scenes in the valley, as she comes to learn more about, and to experience more of, him. To understand the nature and source of her full feeling for Galt—what Dagny means by "a consciousness like her own" and why she has found this in Galt, and only Galt—it will be useful to step back and examine a key nonfiction text in which Ayn Rand presents her (and Dagny's) view of the nature of (romantic) love.

Love is a response to values. It is with a person's sense of life that one falls in love—with that essential sum, that fundamental stand or way of facing existence, which is the essence of a personality. One falls in love with the embodiment of the values that formed a person's character, which are reflected in his widest goals or smallest gestures, which create the *style* of his soul—the individual style of a unique, unrepeatable, irreplaceable consciousness. It is one's own sense of life that acts as the selector, and responds to what it recognizes as one's own basic values in the person of another. It is not a matter of professed convictions (though these are not irrelevant); it is a matter of much more profound, conscious *and subconscious* harmony.[3]

Our question, then, is this: What is Dagny's "essential sum," her "fundamental stand or way of facing existence"? What are those basic values of hers that she recognizes in the person of Galt, values that are also his and which "are reflected in his widest goals [and] smallest gestures," which create the very "*style* of his soul."

For an answer, consider the following passages:

Dagny Taggart was nine years old when she decided that she would run the Taggart Transcontinental Railroad some day. She stated it to herself when she stood alone between the rails, looking at the two straight lines of steel that went off into the distance and met in a single point. What she felt was an arrogant pleasure at the way the track cut through the woods: it did not belong in the midst of ancient trees, among green branches that hung down to meet green brush and the lonely spears of wild flowers—but there it was. The two steel lines were brilliant in the sun, and the black ties were like the rungs of a ladder which she had to climb.

It was not a sudden decision, but only the final seal of words upon something she had known long ago. In unspoken understanding, as if bound by a vow it had never been necessary to take, she and Eddie Willers had given themselves to the railroad from the first conscious days of their childhood. . . .

She never tried to explain why she liked the railroad. Whatever it was that others felt, she knew that this was one emotion for which they had no equivalent and no response. She felt the same emotion in school, in classes of mathematics, the only lessons she liked. She felt the excitement of solving problems, the insolent delight of taking up a challenge and disposing of it without effort, the eagerness to meet another, harder test. She felt, at the same time, a growing respect for the adversary, for a science that was so clean, so strict, so luminously rational. Studying mathematics, she felt, quite simply and at once: "How great that men have done this" and "How wonderful that I'm so good at it." It was the joy of admiration and of one's own ability, growing together. Her feeling for the railroad was the same: worship of the skill that had gone to make it, of the ingenuity of someone's clean, reasoning mind, worship with a secret smile that said she would know how to make it better some day. She hung around the tracks and the round-houses like a humble student, but the humility had a touch of future pride, a pride to be earned. (50–51)

Note the excitement of using her mind to solve problems, to confront as an adversary something so demanding, "so luminously rational." Note the worship of the skill, the ingenuity of someone's clean, reasoning mind, that had gone to create mathematics—and the railroad. Note the pleasure in her future pride that she would do it even better some day. Note her startling independence (and self-esteem) in the next passage:

She was twelve years old when she told Eddie Willers that she would run the railroad when they grew up. She was fifteen when it occurred to her for the first time that women did not run railroads and that people might object. To hell with that, she thought—and never worried about it again. (51)

In the following passage, we get our first clear signs that the world around Dagny is not turning out as she had expected it to (and we will return to this); but note that reference is made again to the value to her of the joy of facing a worthy adversary, of superior ability:

At sixteen, sitting at her operator's desk, watching the lighted windows of Taggart trains roll past, she had thought that she had entered her kind of world. In the years since, she learned that she hadn't. The adversary she found herself forced to fight was not worth matching or beating; it was not a superior ability which she would have found honor in challenging; it was ineptitude—a gray spread of cotton that seemed soft and shapeless, that could offer no resistance to anything or anybody, yet managed to be a barrier in her way. She stood, disarmed, before the riddle of what made this possible. She could find no answer.

It was only in the first few years that she felt herself screaming silently, at times, for a glimpse of human ability, a single glimpse of clean, hard, radiant competence. She had fits of tortured longing for a friend or an enemy with a mind better than her own. (52)

Francisco d'Anconia was the one exception in her life then: her summers with him were a wonder of exploration, excitement, and passionate talk of their future plans, his for d'Anconia Copper and hers for Taggart Transcontinental. Their first sexual experience was with each other. Afterwards,

[w]hen she came home, when she lay in bed, naked because her body had become an unfamiliar possession, too precious for the touch of a nightgown, because it gave her pleasure to feel naked and to feel as if the white sheets of her bed were touched by Francisco's body—when she thought that she would not sleep, because she did not want to rest and lose the most wonderful exhaustion she had ever known—her last thought was of the times when she had wanted to express, but found no way to do it, an instant's knowledge of a feeling greater than happiness, the feeling of one's blessing upon the whole of the earth, the feeling of being in love with the fact that one exists and in this kind of world; she thought that the act she had learned was the way one expressed it. (108)[4]

The feeling just described, which she learned the sexual act enabled her to express, embodies one aspect of her "fundamental stand or way of facing existence": she faces it as one who loves the world in which she lives and the fact that she lives in it.

Related aspects are revealed in a pivotal scene, years later, in Rearden's office, while he and Dagny are discussing his new metal, which will revive her railroad:

"Did I tell you that I'm having tests made of communications wire of Rearden Metal?"

"I'm making so many tests that I'll never get through showing people what can be done with it and how to do it."

They spoke of the metal and of the possibilities which they could not exhaust. It was as if they were standing on a mountain top, seeing a limitless plain below and roads open in all directions. But they merely spoke of mathematical figures, of weights, pressures, resistances, costs.

She had forgotten her brother and his National Alliance. She had forgotten every problem, person and event behind her; they had always been clouded in her sight, to be hurried past, to be brushed aside, never final, never quite real. *This* was reality, she thought, this sense of clear outlines, of purpose, of lightness, of hope.

This was the way she had expected to live—she had wanted to spend no hour and take no action that would mean less than this.

She looked at him in the exact moment when he turned to look at her. They stood very close to each other. She saw, in his eyes, that he felt as she did. If joy is the aim and the core of existence, she thought, and if that which has the power to give one joy is always guarded as one's deepest secret, then they had seen each other naked in that moment. (87)

What has the power to give Dagny joy, is a world of great minds and achievements, of limitless possibilities, a world "of clear outlines, of purpose, of lightness, of hope," a world in which every moment is *important*. This is the world as she had expected it, and the only world in which she is at home. But we can say more than that: this is Dagny's view of *reality*, as she herself thinks. What she is referring to is an aspect of what Rand calls a person's "implicit metaphysics," expressed in his *sense of life* (see note 4 below). Rand explains further:

Long before he is old enough to grasp such a concept as metaphysics, man makes choices, forms value-judgments, experiences emotions and acquires a certain *implicit* view of life. Every choice and value-judgment implies some estimate of himself and of the world around him—most particularly, of his capacity to deal with the world. He may draw conscious conclusions, which may be true or false; or he may remain mentally passive and merely react to events (i.e., merely feel). Whatever the case may be, his subconscious mechanism sums up his psychological activities, integrating his conclusions, reactions or evasions into an emotional sum that establishes a habitual pattern and becomes his automatic response to the world around him. What began as a series of single, discrete conclusions (or evasions) about his own particular problems, becomes a generalized feeling about existence, an implicit *metaphysics* with the compelling motivational power of a constant, basic emotion—an emotion which is part of all his other emotions and underlies all his experiences. *This* is a sense of life.[5]

The view of reality Dagny is experiencing is what Rand elsewhere calls "the benevolent universe premise" and its corresponding sense of life "a benevolent sense of life." The benevolent universe premise is the view that this is a world open to man, in which great things are possible, in which success is the norm, and pain or suffering the accidental.[6] Here is the clearest statement of Dagny's form of this premise, notably expressed at a time when Dagny is under great duress and the possibility of future success seems hopeless:

But it is not true . . . that there is no place in the future for a superlative achievement of man's mind; it can never be true. No matter what her problem, this would always remain to her—this immovable conviction that evil was unnatural and temporary. She felt it more clearly than ever this morning: the certainty that the ugliness of the men in the city and the ugliness of her suffering were transient accidents—while the smiling sense of hope within her at the sight of a sun-flooded forest, the sense of an unlimited promise, was the permanent and the real. (612)[7]

Understanding the deepening challenges to this premise that Dagny experiences throughout her life and her resulting internal conflict,[8] helps us to understand the first two sentences Dagny and Galt say to each other, and what they portend for the depth and finality of her love for him. We will return to this shortly.

As a way of crystallizing the distinctive nature of Dagny's love for Galt, let us return to the exchange between Rearden and Dagny with which we began, to see the limitations of her (authentic) love for Rearden as compared to her love for Galt. In response to Rearden's report of his inference from the past tenses in the radio speech she has just returned from giving, Dagny confirms that she *has* met the man she "had wanted to reach long before she knew that he existed." Consider Rearden's reply and Dagny's response:

> "I think I've always known that you would find him. I knew what you felt for me, I knew how much it was, but I knew that I was not your final choice. What you'll give him is not taken away from me, it's what I've never had. I can't rebel against it. What I've had means too much to me—and that I've had it, can never be changed."
>
> "Do you want me to say it, Hank? Will you understand it, if I say that I'll always love you? . . . I've always seen you as you are now. That greatness of yours which you are just beginning to allow yourself to know—I've always known it and I've watched your struggle to discover it. Don't speak of atonement, you have not hurt me, your mistakes came from your magnificent integrity under the torture of an impossible code—and your fight against it did not bring me suffering, it brought me the feeling I've found too seldom: admiration. If you will accept it, it will always be yours. What you meant to me can never be changed." (861)

We have, in parts I and II of the novel, seen ample evidence of the intensity of Dagny's feeling for Rearden. It comes out most dramatically during their ride together in the locomotive of the first run of the John Galt Line, which is well described in Greg Salmieri's first essay (above, 242–43), and in the description of their first sexual encounter, as it takes place in Ellis Wyatt's house:

> Through all the steps of the years behind them, the steps down a course chosen in the courage of a single loyalty: their love of existence—chosen in the knowledge that nothing will be given, that one must make one's own desire and every shape of its fulfillment—through the steps of shaping metal, rails and motors—they had moved by the power of the thought that one remakes the earth for one's enjoyment, that man's spirit gives meaning to insentient matter by molding it to serve one's chosen goal. The course led them to the moment when, in answer to the highest of one's values, in an admiration not to be expressed by any other form of tribute, one's spirit makes one's body become the tribute, recasting it—as proof,

as sanction, as reward—into a single sensation of such intensity of joy that no other sanction of one's existence is necessary. He heard the moan of her breath, she felt the shudder of his body, in the same instant. (252)

Why, then, is her feeling for him not total, why is he not her "final choice"? Clearly the first thing is the conflicts Rearden experiences, due to his philosophical errors. Though Dagny, as she says, has always seen him as he is at the time of her return from the valley, and greatly admires his struggle, and the virtues that characterize it, notice her first response to Galt's face:

She was looking up at the face of a man who knelt by her side, and she knew that in all the years behind her, *this* was what she would have given her life to see: a face that bore no mark of pain or fear or guilt. The shape of his mouth was pride, and more: it was as if he took pride in being proud. (701)

Rearden, because of his conflicts, cannot be free of pain or fear or guilt in that way. Rearden also, for much of the time of their relationship, has not fully shared Dagny's clean, holy view of sex. That perspective on sex is obviously a central value of Dagny's: we see it as central to each of her sexual encounters that is narrated in the novel. (See, e.g., *Atlas*, 108, 252 [just quoted], and 956–57.) Rearden, by contrast, had developed a view of sexual desire as degrading, as a result of which he not only fails to share Dagny's conscious valuation of sex, but condemns her for her desire for him (254). Furthermore, Rearden's view of sexual desire as degrading and outside his volitional control results in a feeling (however mixed) of *self*-contempt (158–59, 254). Dagny, by contrast, "was completely incapable of experiencing a feeling of fundamental guilt" (87). Contrast that with Galt, who is unadulteratedly proud of everything about himself, and even—as his face projects to Dagny—takes pride in being proud. This is an analogue of Dagny's loving her love of her values (220). The unalloyed character of the qualities she loves is central to the man at the end of the tracks, and to her response to Galt.

Francisco, though, does not suffer from philosophical errors in that way, and he shares Dagny's view of sex:

"Isn't it wonderful that our bodies can give us so much pleasure?" he said to her once, quite simply. They were happy and radiantly innocent. They were both incapable of the conception that joy is sin. (108–9) [9]

But throughout most of the novel he is a paradox to Dagny, and the part she doesn't understand prevents the sort of response she might well have given him, had they reached full adulthood in a rational world. More fundamental than that, though, is an insight Dagny reaches about her earlier response to Francisco. It occurs to her when she is with Francisco in the valley, at his house,

sitting together on the floor, bending over the sheets of paper he spread before her, studying the intricate sections of the smelter—with the same joyous earnestness they had once brought to the study of scraps in a junk yard.

She leaned forward just as he moved to reach for another sheet, and she found herself leaning against his shoulder. Involuntarily, she held still for one instant, no longer than for a small break in the flow of a single motion, while her eyes rose to his. He was looking down at her, neither hiding what he felt nor implying any further demand. She drew back, knowing that she had felt the same desire as his.

Then, still holding the recaptured sensation of what she had felt for him in the past, she grasped a quality that had always been part of it, now suddenly clear to her for the first time: if that desire was a celebration of one's life, then what she had felt for Francisco had always been a celebration of her future, like a moment of splendor gained in part payment of an unknown total, affirming some promise to come. In the instant when she grasped it, she knew also the only desire she had ever experienced not in token of the future but of the full and final present. She knew it by means of an image—the image of a man's figure standing at the door of a small granite structure. The final form of the promise that had kept her moving, she thought, was the man who would, perhaps, remain a promise never to be reached. (772)

This image has been a constant presence in Dagny's mind since she experienced that man's figure standing at the door of that structure.[10] It will be worth quoting the narration of that experience of Dagny's at length. The structure is, of course, the powerhouse that serves the valley, containing Galt's motor, in operation.

She stood looking up at the structure, her consciousness surrendered to a single sight and a single, wordless emotion—but she had always known that an emotion was a sum totaled by an adding machine of the mind, and what she now felt was the instantaneous total of the thoughts she did not have to name, the final sum of a long progression, like a voice telling her by means of a feeling: If she had held onto Quentin Daniels, with no hope of a chance to use the motor, for the sole sake of knowing that achievement had not died on earth—if, like a weighted diver sinking in an ocean of mediocrity, under the pressure of men with gelatin eyes, rubber voices, spiral-shaped convictions, non-committal souls and non-committing hands, she had held, as her life line and oxygen tube, the thought of a superlative achievement of the human mind—if, at the sight of the motor's remnant, in a sudden gasp of suffocation, as a last protest from his corruption-eaten lungs, Dr. Stadler had cried for something, not to look down at, but up to, and *this* had been the cry, the longing and the fuel of her life—if she had moved, drawn by the hunger of her youth for a sight of clean, hard, radiant competence—then here it was before her, reached and done, the power of an incomparable mind given shape in a net of wires sparkling peacefully under a summer sky, drawing an incalculable power out of space into the secret interior of a small stone hovel.

She thought of this structure, half the size of a boxcar, replacing the power plants of the country, the enormous conglomerations of steel, fuel and effort— she thought of the current flowing from this structure, lifting ounces, pounds, tons of strain from the shoulders of those who would make it or use it, adding hours, days and years of liberated time to their lives, be it an extra moment to lift one's head from one's task and glance at the sunlight, or an extra pack of cigarettes bought with the money saved from one's electric bill, or an hour cut from the work-day of every factory using power, or a month's journey through the whole, open width of the world, on a ticket paid for by one day of one's labor, on a train pulled by the power of this motor—with all the energy of that weight, that strain, that time replaced and paid for by the energy of a single mind who had known how to make connections of wire follow the connections of his thought. But she knew that there was no meaning in motors or factories or trains, that their only meaning was in man's enjoyment of his life, which they served—and that her swelling admiration at the sight of an achievement was for the man from whom it came, for the power and the radiant vision within him which had seen the earth as a place of enjoyment and had known that the work of achieving one's happiness was the purpose, the sanction and the meaning of life.

The door of the structure was a straight, smooth sheet of stainless steel, softly lustrous and bluish in the sun. Above it, cut in the granite, as the only feature of the building's rectangular austerity, there stood an inscription:

I SWEAR BY MY LIFE AND MY LOVE OF IT THAT I
WILL NEVER LIVE FOR THE SAKE OF ANOTHER MAN,
NOR ASK ANOTHER MAN TO LIVE FOR MINE.

She turned to Galt. He stood beside her; he had followed her, he had known that this salute was his. She was looking at the inventor of the motor, but what she saw was the easy, casual figure of a workman in his natural setting and function—she noted the uncommon lightness of his posture, a weightless way of standing that showed an expert control of the use of his body—a tall body in simple garments: a thin shirt, light slacks, a belt about a slender waistline—and loose hair made to glitter like metal by the current of a sluggish wind. She looked at him as she had looked at his structure.

Then she knew that the first two sentences they had said to each other still hung between them, filling the silence—that everything said since, had been said over the sound of those words, that he had known it, had held it, had not let her forget it. (730–31)

Galt's incomparable mind, the scope and wonder of the material achievement of his motor, its power to expand life, to contribute so much to the joy which is man's birthright—all of this is real, in the present, before her, all captured in that effortlessness of posture that reflects his command of existence, his immense at-homeness in reality. All this is embodied in what Dagny sees at the powerhouse.

But there is one more thing she sees—which Galt, since their meeting, "had not let her forget." It pertains to the conflict she could not resolve between the world she had expected to find at sixteen and the world in which she had been living—the "ocean of mediocrity" with their "non-committal souls" and their inexplicable ability to thwart or destroy great achievements such as the John Galt Line. The man she sees at the powerhouse is also the man whose superlative intelligence—philosophical as well as technological—has swept away that conflict. It is Galt who confirms what she knew in her deepest soul, that she never had to take any of those obstacles seriously. And it is Galt alone.

Even Francisco says: "I saw no way to fight it. John found the way" (766). Galt identified the full Morality of Life, Galt identified the principle of the sanction of the victim, Galt created the strike, and Galt made it possible—made real— the valley, the world Dagny has expected, her Taggart Terminal (748). He is in every way the man at the end of the tracks.

To sum up our portrait of Dagny's basic values and way of facing existence, we must say that: The world for Dagny is a place in which joy is the natural state, in which man is at home, in which great things are possible. She is in love with the fact that she exists and in such a world. She loves man's ability to view that world from a height, to set important goals, to pursue them in a straight-line direction, to achieve them— and to take joy both in that achievement and in that which makes that achievement possible. She takes joy—and pride—in her own ability to understand a world so "luminously rational," to take up ever growing challenges, against worthy adversaries, and to meet them, and to move on to more. In particular, she loves the ability to master the material realm, to bring one's spirit and one's vision of the joy—the glory—of shaping matter into the tools of man's life and pleasure—the rail and motors and "signal lights winking in the night" (51). Her symbol of all this was the man beyond the horizon, who held the rails in his hand, who, like the Taggart Terminal, was both a symbol and a destination—the man whose world she wanted to build and whom she expected to find when she had. Dagny is tortured by the contradiction between her conviction that this world is possible and the mounting evidence that it is not. Her search for the inventor of the motor and her worship of the mind that had created it were a manifestation both of her love of this world and her desperation for a solution. Galt, as we have seen, is the man who invented that motor, the man who held the rails in his hand, and the mind who found the solution and showed how her world was indeed possible, real, hers. He is the workman "with a weightless way of standing that showed an expert control of the use of his body—a tall body in simple garments: a thin shirt, light slacks, a belt about a slender waistline—and loose hair made to glitter like metal by the current of a sluggish wind." He is the man who confirmed to her that "we never had to take any of it seriously."[11]

In the office of the John Galt Line, Dagny had longed "to find a consciousness like her own, who would be the meaning of her world, as she would be of his" (220). She found such a consciousness, in Galt. The joyous is the natural for Galt as well; he loves material achievement; he takes joy in his intellectual and technological powers. He has an unsurpassable love for existence and "pride in being its worthy lover" (1058, and see the coda to my other essay, above pp. 391–93). And there is of course much more as one explores the concrete forms in which these values of Galt are expressed. (That there is much more in part explains the title of this essay.)

But until she learned that Galt's is the way to practice the rule by which they have both always lived (732 and 813), they could not fully be "travelers . . . in the same direction" (1020) and therefore could not yet build a life together. At the end of the novel, as Dagny is riding on the plane, back to the valley, following the rescue of Galt,

> [s]he felt the whole struggle of her past rising before her and dropping away, leaving her here, on the height of this moment. She smiled—and the words in her mind, appraising and sealing the past, were the words of courage, pride and dedication, which most men had never understood, the words of a businessman's language: "Price no object." . . .
> Then they lay still, leaning back in their chairs, silently looking at each other. Then their persons filled each other's awareness, as the sum and meaning of the future—but the sum included the knowledge of all that had had to be earned, before the person of another being could come to embody the value of one's existence. (1159)[12]

NOTES

1. Notice the contrast with Dagny's first thought, after she opened her eyes in the valley, in the passage just quoted.
2. Though Dagny is not here said to *love* the man at the end of the tracks, notice the following, from part II:

> She felt—as she had felt it one spring night, slumped across her desk in the crumbling office of the John Galt Line, by a window facing a dark alley—the sense and vision of her own world, which she would never reach. . . . You—she thought—whoever you are, whom I have always loved and never found, you whom I expected to see at the end of the rails beyond the horizon, you whose presence I had always felt in the streets of the city and whose world I had wanted to build, it is my love for you that had kept me moving, my love and my hope to reach you and my wish to be worthy of you on the day when I would stand before you face to face. (633–34)

3. "Philosophy and Sense of Life," in *The Romantic Manifesto: A Philosophy of Literature* (New York: Signet, 1975), 32. At the start of that essay Rand defines a sense of life as "a pre-conceptual equivalent of metaphysics, an emotional, subconsciously integrated appraisal of man and of existence. It sets the nature of a man's emotional responses and the essence of his character" (25). For further explanation of a *sense of life*, see below, 458.
4. This is the first appearance in *Atlas Shrugged* of Rand's view of the meaning of sex. For a fuller picture, see (among other passages) the sex scene between Rearden and Dagny at Ellis Wyatt's house, after the first run of the John Galt Line (252), and the conversation between Francisco and Rearden in Francisco's suite (489–92) (a passage which is reprinted, under the heading "The Meaning of Sex," in *For the New Intellectual* (New York: Signet, 1963), (98–101). See also, in Gregory Salmieri's first essay above, 240–41.
5. "Philosophy and Sense of Life," 25–26.
6. For more on this, see my *On Ayn Rand* (Belmont, Calif.: Wadsworth, 2000), chapters 1 and 11, and my chapter on the topic in Gotthelf and Salmieri, *Ayn Rand: A Companion to Her Works and Thought*. See also the passages from Leonard Peikoff, *Objectivism: The Philosophy of Ayn Rand* (New York: Dutton, 1991), and David Harriman, ed., *Journals of Ayn Rand* (New York: Dutton, 1997) cited by Salmieri in "Discovering Atlantis" (above, 451 n. 19). See also the next note.
7. Dagny experiences the same feeling during and immediately after her ride on the first run of the John Galt Line. See above, in Salmieri, "Discovering Atlantis," 422. Galt shares this premise, and expresses it himself, to Dagny, at 959–60.

8. See, for example, the passages cited above, 457, 459; these challenges and the conflict which results are brilliantly traced by Greg Salmieri in his essay "Discovering Atlantis."

9. In the passage I have quoted from "Philosophy and Sense of Life," Rand speaks of "the *style* of a soul." This is a very subtle issue, and part of the full picture of Dagny's preference for Galt, which I cannot get into here. It has to do, as Rand indicates, with the way a sense of life gets expressed. I mention only a teaser, which can serve as a lead to this issue. Back in the 1960s, during a brief conversation I had with Ayn Rand about the sense of life affinities between Dagny and Galt, she remarked that in sense of life, Dagny was closer to Rearden than to Francisco. For now, I leave it to you to consider what she meant.

10. Later that day:

> She kept seeing his figure in her mind—his figure as he had stood at the door of the structure—she felt nothing else, no wish, no hope, no estimate of her feeling, no name for it, no relation to herself—there was no entity such as herself, she was not a person, only a function, the function of seeing him, and the sight was its own meaning and purpose, with no further end to reach. (733)

In this connection, recall, in Rand's nonfiction remarks on love quoted above (455–56), the words "smallest gesture": "One falls in love with the embodiment of the values that formed a person's character, which are reflected in his widest goals or smallest gestures, which create the *style* of his soul—the individual style of a unique, unrepeatable, irreplaceable consciousness." Galt's way of standing, and his entire physical presence, including of course his face, reflect for Dagny his unique, unrepeatable consciousness. Her response to him, from the moment she opens her eyes in the valley, is both to his body and to his soul—it is to the unified entity of body and soul which he is, and neither aspect should be underemphasized. See the long excerpt from that first meeting above, 453–54; for the full passage, worth comparing with the image she responds to at the powerhouse, see 730–31. See, too, the way the physical and the spiritual are merged in the characterization of what is embodied in Dagny's response to Galt's touch in their first sexual encounter, in the Taggart Terminal tunnel (956–57).

11. "Then she knew that the first two sentences they had said to each other still hung between them, filling the silence—that everything said since had been said over the sound of those words" (731).

12. With the kind permission of Wiley-Blackwell, this essay draws on material in two of my chapters in *Ayn Rand: A Companion to Her Works and Thought* (Wiley-Blackwell, forthcoming). It has grown in depth and in the aptness of many of its formulations from discussion with Greg Salmieri, whose profound understanding of *Atlas Shrugged* has been a great help. Mary Ann Sures has also given me valuable editorial advice. A special thanks to Cassandra Brazié Love, who brought to my attention some thirty years ago the significance of the first two sentences said between Dagny and Galt for understanding why he is her "final choice."

Appendix A

Outline of *Atlas Shrugged*

Gregory Salmieri

This outline was produced in conjunction with my 2007 lecture course "*Atlas Shrugged* as a Work of Philosophy." The relative detail in which events are summarized is due in part to my concerns in that course, but I think that the outline should be of more general use in studying the novel, and I present it here in that hope. In preparing the outline, I made use of on an earlier summary by Allan Gotthelf, and the present version reflects the feedback of Tore Boeckmann and Robert Mayhew. I'd like to thank all three for their contributions.

Ayn Rand divided *Atlas Shrugged* into three parts, each part into ten chapters, and most of the chapters into sequences (separated from one another by three asterisks). I have assigned each sequence an Arabic numeral for ease of reference, and represented all of Rand's divisions in the left side of the outline. The right side contains my own further divisions of the novel into scenes or events; adjacent scenes are grouped together when the main character(s) is the same or there is some other obvious continuity.

PART I: NON-CONTRADICTION

I.	**THE THEME**	1.	Eddie	Reflections en route to Taggart Building	3
				Confrontation with Jim about Rio Norte Line	7
				Conversation with Pop Harper	11
		2.	Dagny	Response to hearing Halley's Fifth Concerto	12
				Orders re stopped train; plan to promote Owen Kellogg	15
		3.		Attitude toward tunnels in the Taggart Terminal (TT)	17
		4.		Meeting w/ Jim re Rearden Metal (RM) rails for Rio Norte Line	18
				Phone call to publisher re Richard Halley	24
				Meeting with Owen Kellogg who quits	24
II.	**THE CHAIN**		Rearden's work life	Train passengers' attitudes toward him	27
				Response to pouring the first heat of RM	28
				Reflections on his life while walking home from the mills	29
			Rearden's home life	His family's condescension toward him & his work	32
				Lillian's trapping him into agreeing to an anniversary party	35
				His gift of the bracelet to Lillian	36
				Conversation with Larkin re political situation	38

VII.	**THE EXPLOITERS AND THE EXPLOITED**	1.	Dagny in Colorado	Overcoming obstacles caused by people's discomfort with RM	162
				Her relationship with Wyatt & with Nealy (the subpar contractor)	165
				Rearden's visit: their attitudes to Colorado & each other; idea for RM bridge; his lie to avoid flying her to NY.	167
		2.	Dagny in car w/ Jim	Jim's fear of the public reaction to RM	172
				His attempt to trick her into debating Scudder; she leaves his car	175
			Dagny in slum diner	Bum's opinions re morality & the spirit-body opposition	176
				Tramp's Galt legend (discoverer of the Fountain of Youth)	178
		3.	The State Science Institute	Dr. Potter's attempts to make Rearden withdraw RM	178
		4.	(SSI) vs. RM	Mowen's cancellation of Dagny's order for RM switches	182
				Dagny reads SSI's smear of RM & decides to see Dr. Stadler	183
		5.		History of Stadler & SSI	185
				Dagny & Stadler's discussion (his attitude toward technology, people, the efficacy of reason—his three students)	186

		6.	Formation of John Galt, Inc.	Jim's panic & Dagny's decision to complete the Rio Norte independently of TT as The John Galt Line (JGL)	193
		7.		Attempt to sell JGL bonds to Francisco	197
		8.		Dagny's meeting with Rearden re JGL; their feelings for one another.	201
		9.	Rearden at office	Response to copper emergency (including decision to buy mine)	205
				Rejection of mother's demand for a job for Philip	207
				Mr. Ward's respectful appeal for metal & Rearden's reaction	209
				Passage of EOB	212
				Despondent reflection on his own motivation; new idea for bridge	214
VIII.	THE JOHN GALT LINE	1.	Eddie's conversation with Galt re JGL & Dagny's reliance on Sanders for diesels		217
		2.	Dagny's metaphysical loneliness in office (after Sanders quits); the tortured shadow		219
		3.	Rearden's Compliance with EOB	Sale of ore mines to Larkin; reflection on the situation	221
				Sale of coal mines to Danagger	224
				Mouch's bureaucratic position; progress on JGL bridge	224
				Meeting with Eddie: moratorium on TT's bill; their attitudes re EOB	225

3.	Dagny	Choice between fighting for Colorado and keeping appointment with Lawson re motor	298
		The various restrictions demanded by various parties that would cumulatively kill Colorado	298
		Discussion w/ Jim re the situation	299
		Decision to see Lawson	300
4.	Rearden	Larkin's betrayal: shipping his ore to Boyle (also using TT rather than lake boats); the search for ore	301
		Conversation w/ purchasing manager re political situation & character	302
		Morally disarmed in fight against looters	303
		Lillian re love, the change in Rearden, & his obligation to her happiness; his reaction; her lack of purpose	304
5.	Dagny's inquires	Conversation with Lawson	309
6.		Conversation with Hunsacker: his suit against Mulligan (whose story Dagny recalls); appeal of Narragansett's decision	313
7.		The three Starnes heirs; Ivy's explanation of the noble plan; mention of Hastings as chief engineer	321

		Meeting with Stadler re motor: he suggests Daniels to reconstruct it; mentions having known a John Galt	354
3.	Rearden	Refusal to sell RM to SSI for Project X	360
		Attempts to comply with the regulations; the results	361
		The Wet Nurse	362
		Reaction to Wyatt fire; reaction to his reaction	363
		Wet Nurse re refusal to sell to SSI	364
		Visit from "traffic cop": his fearful reaction when Rearden refuses to pretend that he's not being coerced	364
4.	Rearden & Dagny over the past six months	The contrast between her unfulfilling days & "his nights"	367
		His gift of the ruby; how a painting of her would be inspiring art, but he would "want it real"	367
		Other expensive gifts; his attitude toward luxuries	368
		The blue fox cape; the ride to NJ; her reflection on why he, to whom the earth belongs, should have to suffer	369
		His selfish motive in gift-giving; confusion as to whether this is good or bad	369

		His previous inability to enjoy his wealth and new determination to do so; how he's paid for Dagny	371
		How the image of a playboy as the enjoyer of material pleasures represents a vicious and important error	371
		How the night in the NJ restaurant is a reward he anticipated in his youth but never found	372
		Her reflection on the vicious error and on what she has yet to discover about it	373
	Rearden & Dagny that night	En route from copper conference to Dagny's apartment: his metaphysical revulsion & lack of sexual desire	373
		At apartment: their estimate of those who want them sexually	375
		Discussion of SSI issue & of motor, which restores his sense of the world	376
		Discussion of the issue of sanction	377
		The return of his sexual desire & his implicit recognition of the cause & of its moral implications	378
II. THE ARISTOCRACY OF PULL	1. Dagny	The progressive disappearance of the Colorado industrialists; her idea that it is due to a "destroyer"	379

		TT train delayed by storm b/c of regulation & absence of the CO industrialists; resulting factory closures	497
		Cultural response to these events	498
		Collapse of Atlantic Southern Bridge (due to Boyle) leaving Taggart Bridge as only link across continent	499
		Copper shortage, due to Ragnar: top floors of buildings abandoned; no RM rails for TT; consequent wrecks	500
		Illegal mining of ore	501
	Dagny	Board of Directors Meeting: vote to close JGL; TT now beholden to Weatherby (representing Mouch)	501
		Drink w/Francisco: her attitude re the line & TT; his love of her & of Rearden; his Galt legend (Prometheus)	511
2.		Visit to Marshville & last run of Rio Norte Line	517
3.	Lillian	Lunch w/Jim: her failure re Rearden's trial; her continued intention to deliver him	521
		Discovery that Rearden must be traveling with a mistress	524
4.		Realization that Dagny is Rearden's mistress; exchange with her re JGL closing	525

			Confrontation w/ Rearden re the affair: Rearden's acceptance of her desire to remain his wife, but rejection of her request to terminate the affair; his reflection on her and Dagny	527
VI.	MIRACLE METAL	1.	Washington meeting re 10-289: attitudes toward it; Mouch's history; Taggart can make Rearden sign the "Gift Certificate"	532
		2.	Dagny resigns in response to 10-289 and goes to the cabin in Woodstock	549
		3.	Rearden — Resignation of the head of Rearden Steel Workers Union in response to 10-289	554
			Wet Nurse offers to cover up anything Rearden does and asks him to refuse to sign Certificate on principle	555
			Lillian goes on vacation	556
			Ferris's blackmail; Rearden's reflection on morality, his errors, his love of Dagny; he signs the Certificate	557
VII.	THE MORATORIUM ON BRAINS	1.	Eddie & Galt: the best men are quitting; Kip's special; Dagny's location	567
		2.	Ragnar & Rearden	571
		3.	The tunnel catastrophe	584
VIII.	BY OUR LOVE	1.	Dagny at her cabin in Woodstock — Her goals; building the path; reflection re purpose; how every purpose integrates to TT; her conflict	608

			Alone w/ Rearden: Rearden's regret; Dagny tells him that Franciso was her first lover; Rearden takes Dagny; discussion of his feeling for Francisco	641
			Resignation letter from Daniels; Dagny calls him, decides to head for Utah at once	643
		2.	Eddie	In Dagny's apartment: notices Rearden's robe in and realizes she's having an affair with him	648
				w/ Galt re Daniels & the motor; Dagny's trip to Utah ; the affair— Galt rushes out	651
X.	THE SIGN OF THE DOLLAR	1.	Dagny on the Comet	Thoughts about the deteriorating world; desperate loneliness	654
				Jeff Allen: she saves his life; invites him for dinner; their conversation	656
				The story of John Galt and the 20th Century Motors	660
			Frozen train	Dagny's reflections on her goals	672
		2.		The situation; the attitudes of the passengers	673
				Dagny and Kellogg walk to track phone: discussion of people & Ivy Starnes; job offer; $ cigarettes	678

		Annual reunion at Akston's house: reminiscences; Stadler; the power of logic in human life; Akston's treatment of Dagny as Galt's wife	785
5.	Dagny's visit w/ Galt to Francisco's Mine	Francisco & Galt's friendship; Francisco doesn't guess about her and Galt; might Galt give her up to Francisco?	791
		Her short-lived enthusiasm for the prospect of building a railroad in the valley	793
		She might stay if she didn't have to hear about TT; Galt responds that no one stays by faking reality	794
		Story of how Galt sent Francisco to cabin (fuels Dagny's worries); Galt explains that he couldn't have a chance until Francisco had had every chance	795
		Francisco's invitation for her to stay with him for the last week: she asks Galt to decide; he says no	796
		Her relief; egoism vs. altruism; Galt on the lack of conflicts of interest; application to the present situation	797
	Dagny's decision to return to the world	Sighting of Rearden's plane: the pull of the world; she can't give up on her values while they are possible	799

		6.	Final conference: She initially asks for one more day to decide; discussion of the principles by which she should decide, Galt too is uncertain about whether he'll return; Mulligan concretizes dangers; she decides to return to hold Taggart Bridge—people love their lives and can't refuse to see forever.	802
			Dagny, Galt, & Francisco: Galt says he's returning; Francisco realizes why; gives them his blessing	808
			Dagny & Galt: She wants to win the world for him; he says that she is seeking justice by submitting to the unjust; his advice not to "damn existence" if she fails	810
III.	**ANTI-GREED**	1.	Demonstration of Project X: Stadler's compliance with Ferris's orders to give a speech	816
		2.	Dagny's return: the senseless unhappiness and the meaningless speeches; call to Rearden	831
			Dagny at office	w/Eddie re Meigs: the crony-driven schedules under the Railroad Unification Plan (RUP); no repairs to lines	836

			w/Jim & Meigs: her refusal to reassure them or country; the RUP; how they avoid their knowledge	838
			Lillian's blackmail	847
	3.	Dagny at the Radio station	Dagny (on Scudder's program) reveals that Rearden was blackmailed	850
			Cab ride: reflection on Galt; cab driver's gratitude; her response	854
		Dagny in her apartment with Rearden	His love for her; the soul-body dichotomy; honesty vs. faking reality; how she's found her love	854
			Discussion: Galt; their plan to fight until they win or learn it's hopeless	861
IV. **ANTI-LIFE**	1.	Jim	Alone in evening: his indifference to values, desire to celebrate, fear of self-knowledge	864
			Reflection on his day: parties at which plans were finalized for the nationalization of dAC	864
			At home: conversation w/Cherryl re his deal, Dagny's broadcast, his character, and the marriage	868
		Cherryl's year as Jim's wife	Attributes her impression that Jim is a weak coward to her ignorance; tries to learn & rise; his resentment of this	873

		Doubts about his character & role at TT; learns from Eddie; Jim explains that he *"feels"* & married her out of need for "understanding"	875
		Confrontation between Jim and Cherryl: he wants unearned love and to be great w/o the necessity of *being*; he evades this; he enjoys dCA's destruction; she leaves	883
2.	Dagny	Her first month back: no achievements, only averted catastrophes; loneliness for valley & Galt	886
		Cherryl: apology & bonding; "unfeeling"; non-identity; lack of moral guidance; independence; hatred of the good	887
3.	Jim	Destruction of vase: satisfied by thoughts of those who prized it & of the desperate people it could have fed	892
		Lillian: he can't help her avert her divorce; their bond; hatred of Rearden; sex "in celebration of the triumph of impotence"	893
4.	Cherryl	At home: her horror at Jim's act; why he married her; he's "a killer for the sake of killing"; he hits her; she runs out	900

			Horror: achievements seized; b/c of inverted morality people know only pain & are concerned only for the guilty	904
			Suicide: her rejection of this world as all that's left of hers; the social worker; she runs off the pier	907
V. THEIR BROTHERS' KEEPERS	1.	Dagny	Scarcity of copper; Meigs' thievery; supplies spread thinly across the system; lack of initiative among workers	909
			w/Jim: RUP is irrational; demand that she make it work b/c she's the doer & he has the right of weakness	910
			dCA nationalized but it's been totally destroyed; Jim's reaction	918
			Dinner w/ Rearden: his attitude toward Francisco & work; plans to bootleg metal for machines for MN farmers	921
			Francisco's parting message to the world; Rearden's reaction	925
	2.		Dagny sends copper wire from MN to MO, which is one of the few remaining suppliers of copper	925
		Rearden	Government officials suddenly solicitous toward him	926

		Phillip's request for a job: he needs it, he's R's brother, and unlike R he feels; R grasps the idea of zero-worship	927
		Divorce court: reflections on the nature of the proceedings; it goes too easily; he feels divorced from the society	932
		Wet Nurse asks Rearden for a job	934
3.	Minnesota catastrophe	Deteriorating state of TT: wire sent from terminal to MN; Dagny learns about system from anonymous tips	937
		Tip that cars haven't been sent for MN harvest (they were sent to Kip's Ma); last-ditch effort to get them	939
		The grain rots, MN descends into violence; the soybeans are moldy	943
4.	Dagny	Broken wire in terminal puts signal system out of commission	943
		Dagny had been at dinner meeting w/ leaders: they're indifferent to industry and want only power & loot	944
		En route to TT she reflects on waning motivation, but orders herself onward	949

		At TT: she calls for engineer from other railroad and decides to signal trains manually	949
		Galt: among the track workers; follows her into the tunnels, where he takes her; how he has watched her for ten years; now he has knowingly endangered himself	954
VI.	**THE CONCERTO OF DELIVERANCE**	The set-up	Controversy re steel workers' wages	963
			"Accidental" attachment on Rearden's property	964
			Holloway's request for a meeting	965
			Slagenhop & Philip	966
			Rearden's mother's insistence on seeing him	967
		Rearden goes on strike	His family: They plead for his sacrificial help; he sees that they don't want to live & grasps what Lillian is after	968
			Leaders: they expect him to make the irrational work; "three tumblers" click into place, setting him free	977
			Driving back to his mills he grasps fully the nature of their value; the context that makes them a value is gone	987

			The attack on the mills	Wet Nurse's death (just after learning what it is to be alive); Rearden's reflection on education	989
				The fighting at the mills; Rearden is knocked unconscious	995
				Rearden and Francisco's reunion	998
VII.	"THIS IS JOHN GALT SPEAKING"		Jim tells Dagny that Rearden has quit, appeals to her to bring him back; her reaction to the news; Rearden's note; her anxiety re Galt.	1001
			Dagny is tricked into being in the audience for Mr. Thompson's speech, which he cannot give because the frequencies are blocked	1004
			Galt's speech: the strike; the morality of life; the morality of death; the mystics; the nature of one's choice	1009
VIII.	THE EGOIST	1.	Thompson et al. & Dagny: they try to evade the speech; she says if they want to live they must decontrol; Thompson suggests a deal	1070
		2.	Dagny & Eddie re Galt and her view that the looters will give up b/c they value their lives and know they're through (which Eddie questions)	1076
		3.	Effects of speech: best men quitting all over the country; government claims Galt will solve problems & broadcasts appeals to him	1078
			Dagny & Thompson: his attempt to reach Galt through her; her advice to decontrol; his suggestion that Galt may be dead	1084
		4.	Dagny & Galt: she comes to his house; he welcomes her; tells her that police will come and she'll have to take their side to save him	1086
			Galt's arrest	1094

5.	Galt and Thompson: Thompson tries to make a deal but has nothing to offer; a zero can't hold a mortgage over life		1097
6.	Thompson & advisors: their fear of Galt		1105
	Dagny	w/Thompson: lying to him, wonders if fakers want to live; puts Galt's safety before ending regime & saving TT	1108
		At her office: indifference to reward check; wonders whether "non-valuing people" want to live; Francisco's note	1111
	Galt's visitors	Thompson & Jim	1111
		Thompson &Morrison	1113
		Thompson & Ferris; Galt requests Stadler	1114
	Thompson & Mouch: shortages of staples		1115
	Dagny and Eddie: he says she'll quit as soon as she can; he decides to go to CA in effort to save TT; she says there's nothing to save		1116
	Galt & Stadler: Stadler, brought by force, denies that he wants to use force against the mind but ends by saying Galt must be killed		1116
7.	Banquet	Galt brought there by force	1119
		Dagny, in audience, noticing different people's responses to Galt, challenges the premise that they want to live	1120

				Galt maneuvers so that gun is visible on cameras and says "Get the hell out of my way!"	1125
IX.	**THE GENERATOR**	1.	Stadler's attempt to seize Project X: Meigs beats him to it; the mechanism goes off, killing many and destroying the Taggart Bridge		1126
		2.	Dagny goes on strike	Having overheard the villains' plans to torture Galt and understood the motivation, she calls Francisco	1133
				Home & office: she collects a few items, hesitates only momentarily over news of the Bridge's collapse	1137
				Meets Francisco; takes oath	1138
		3.	Project F: torture of Galt; Jim's breakdown		1139
X.	**IN THE NAME OF THE BEST WITHIN US**	1.	Rescue of Galt	Dagny and guard: she shoots him because he will not decide	1147
				Francisco, Rearden, and Ragnar extract Galt from Project F	1148
				Plane ride to the valley	1156
		2.	Eddie's uncertain fate		1160
		3.	Strikers in valley prepare to return		1167
			Galt, in mountains w/ Dagny, declares an end to the strike		1168

Appendix B

Outline of Galt's Speech

Gregory Salmieri[1]

NOTE

1. In preparing this outline, I drew heavily on earlier outlines and analyses of the speech by Allan Gotthelf and Onkar Ghate. The present version of the outline incorporates some further revisions suggested by Gotthelf.

Select Bibliography

This bibliography is limited to books by Ayn Rand—and books about Ayn Rand and her philosophy, Objectivism—cited in this collection.

Berliner, Michael S., ed. *Letters of Ayn Rand.* New York: Dutton, 1995; paperback edition, Plume, 1997.

Binswanger, Harry. *The Biological Basis of Teleological Concepts.* Marina del Rey, Calif.: Ayn Rand Institute Press, 1990.

Branden, Nathaniel. *Who Is Ayn Rand? An Analysis of Ayn Rand's Works,* with a Biographical Study by Barbara Branden (New York: Random House, 1962).

Britting, Jeff. *Ayn Rand.* New York: Overlook Press. 2005.

Gotthelf, Allan, and Gregory Salmieri, eds. *Ayn Rand: A Companion to Her Works and Thought.* Oxford: Wiley-Blackwell, forthcoming.

Harriman, David, ed. *Journals of Ayn Rand.* New York: Dutton, 1997; paperback edition, Plume, 1999.

Mayhew, Robert, ed. *Ayn Rand Answers: The Best of Her Q&A.* New York: New American Library, 2005.

——, ed. *Ayn Rand's Marginalia.* New Milford, Conn.: Second Renaissance Books, 1995.

——, ed. *Essays on Ayn Rand's* Anthem. Lanham, Md.: Lexington Books, 2005.

——, ed. *Essays on Ayn Rand's* The Fountainhead. Lanham, Md.: Lexington Books, 2007.

——, ed. *Essays on Ayn Rand's* We the Living. Lanham, Md.: Lexington Books, 2004.

McConnell, Scott. *One Hundred Voices: An Oral History of Ayn Rand.* Irvine, Calif.: Ayn Rand Institute Press, forthcoming.

Peikoff, Leonard, ed. *The Early Ayn Rand: A Selection from Her Unpublished Fiction.* New York: New American Library, 1984; paperback edition, Signet, 1986; revised version, Signet, 2005.

——. *Objectivism: The Philosophy of Ayn Rand.* New York: Dutton, 1991; paperback edition, New Meridian, 1993.

Rand, Ayn. *Anthem.* Fiftieth anniversary paperback edition. Introduction by Leonard Peikoff. New York: Signet, 1995.

——. *The Art of Fiction: A Guide for Writers and Readers.* Edited by Tore Boeckmann. Introduction by Leonard Peikoff. New York: Plume, 2000.

——. *Atlas Shrugged.* New York: Random House, 1957; Signet thirty-fifth anniversary paperback edition, 1992.

———. *Capitalism: The Unknown Ideal.* New York: New American Library, 1966; expanded paperback edition, Signet, 1967.

———. *For the New Intellectual.* New York: Random House, 1961; Signet paperback edition, 1963.

———. *The Fountainhead.* New York: Bobbs-Merrill, 1943; Signet fiftieth anniversary paperback edition, 1993.

———. *Introduction to Objectivist Epistemology.* Expanded second edition. Edited by Harry Binswanger and Leonard Peikoff. New York: New American Library, 1990.

———. *Philosophy: Who Needs It.* New York: Bobbs-Merrill, 1982; Signet paperback edition, 1984.

———. *Return of the Primitive: the Anti-Industrial Revolution.* Edited by Peter Schwartz. New York: Meridian, 1999.

———. *The Romantic Manifesto: A Philosophy of Literature.* Revised edition. New York: Signet, 1975.

———. *The Virtue of Selfishness: A New Concept of Egoism.* New York: New American Library, 1964.

———. *The Voice of Reason: Essays in Objectivist Thought.* Leonard Peikoff, ed. New York: New American Library, 1989; paperback edition, Meridian, 1990.

———. *We the Living.* Sixtieth anniversary paperback edition. Introduction by Leonard Peikoff. New York: Signet, 1996.

Smith, Tara. *Ayn Rand's Normative Ethics—The Virtuous Egoist.* New York: Cambridge University Press, 2006.

———. *Viable Values—A Study of Life as the Root and Reward of Morality.* Lanham, Md.: Rowman & Littlefield, 2000.

Sures, Mary Ann and Charles. *Facets of Ayn Rand: Memoirs by Mary Ann Sures and Charles Sures.* Irvine, Calif.: Ayn Rand Institute Press, 2001.

Index

About the Contributors

Michael S. Berliner holds a Ph.D. in philosophy from Boston University. He was executive director of the Ayn Rand Institute for its first fifteen years and previously taught philosophy of education and philosophy at California State University, Northridge. He created the first two catalogs of the Ayn Rand Papers at the Ayn Rand Archives and is currently compiling a definitive inventory. He is editor of *Letters of Ayn Rand* and Ayn Rand's *Russian Writings on Hollywood*. He has lectured throughout the United States and in Europe, Australia, and Israel on Ayn Rand's life.

Andrew Bernstein holds a Ph.D. in philosophy from the Graduate School of the City University of New York and teaches at Marist College and SUNY Purchase. He is the author of *The Capitalist Manifesto: The Historic, Economic, and Philosophic Case for Laissez-Faire* (2005) and, most recently, *Objectivism in One Lesson: An Introduction to the Philosophy of Ayn Rand* (2008). His website is: www.andrewbernstein.net.

Harry Binswanger, a longtime associate of Ayn Rand, taught philosophy at Hunter College (City University of New York) from 1972 to 1979, and at the University of Texas, Austin, in Spring 2002. During the 1980s, he was editor of *The Objectivist Forum*, a journal devoted to Rand's philosophy. Since 1994, he has been professor of philosophy at the Objectivist Academic Center of the Ayn Rand Institute. He is the author of *The Biological Basis of Teleological Concepts* and editor of *The Ayn Rand Lexicon* and of the second edition of Rand's *Introduction to Objectivist Epistemology*. Dr. Binswanger is currently writing a book on consciousness and cognition.

Tore Boeckmann writes and lectures on the nature and origins of romanticism in literature and painting. Recent publications include *"Anthem* as a Psychological Fantasy" (in *Essays on Ayn Rand's* Anthem), *"The Fountainhead* as a Romantic Novel" and "What Might Be and Ought to Be: Aristotle's *Poetics* and *The Fountainhead"* (in *Essays on Ayn Rand's* The Fountainhead), and "Caspar David Friedrich and Visual Romanticism" (in *The Objective Standard,* Spring 2008). He edited Ayn Rand's *The Art of Fiction: A Guide for Writers and Readers.* His mystery short stories have been published and anthologized in several languages.

Jeff Britting is archivist of the Ayn Rand Archives, a collection of the Ayn Rand Institute. He is author of the short illustrated biography *Ayn Rand.* He developed and associate produced the Academy Award© nominated documentary *Ayn Rand: A Sense of Life* and the feature film *Take Two,* as well as the first stage productions of Ayn Rand's play *Ideal* and her novella *Anthem.* As a composer, he has written incidental music for eleven stage productions and three films, and is currently writing an opera based on an original libretto set in the Middle Ages.

Debi Ghate is vice president of academic programs at the Ayn Rand Institute. Mrs. Ghate has a BSc in Psychology and Biology from the University of Toronto, and a LLB in Law from the University of Calgary. She is also general manager and corporate secretary for ARI Canada, a Canadian charitable organization. Her writing has been published in newspapers such as the *Philadelphia Inquirer,* the *San Francisco Chronicle,* the *Providence Journal, Education Update* and the *U.K. Daily Express.* Mrs. Ghate is also the senior director of the Anthem Foundation for Objectivist Scholarship, a separate organization from ARI that supports scholarly work based on Ayn Rand's corpus.

Onkar Ghate holds a Ph.D. in philosophy from the University of Calgary. He is a senior fellow at the Ayn Rand Institute, where he specializes in Ayn Rand's philosophy of Objectivism and teaches philosophy in the Institute's Objectivist Academic Center. Recent publications include "Objectivism: The Proper Alternative to Postmodernism" (in *Postmodernism and Management: Pros, Cons and the Alternative*), an entry on Ayn Rand in the *Encyclopedia of Science, Technology, and Ethics,* and "The Basic Motivation of the Creators and the Masses in *The Fountainhead"* in *Essays on Ayn Rand's* The Fountainhead.

Allan Gotthelf is multiyear visiting professor of history and philosophy of science at the University of Pittsburgh, where he holds the University's fellowship for the study of Objectivism. He is a distinguished Aristotelian scholar, whose collected Aristotle papers is slated for publication in 2010. He is also the author of *On Ayn Rand* (2000) and coeditor of *Ayn Rand: A Companion to Her Works and Thought,* forthcoming in early 2010. He knew Ayn Rand and studied with her, and has lectured on her writings and her philosophy of Objectivism throughout the United States and in Canada, Europe, and Japan.

Edwin A. Locke is Dean's Professor of Motivation and Leadership (Emeritus) at the R. H. Smith School of Business at the University of Maryland, College Park. He has published over 270 books, chapters, notes, and articles. He is internationally known for his research and writings on work motivation, leadership, wealth creation, job satisfaction, and the philosophy of science, including the application of Objectivism to psychology and management. He is a fellow of the American Psychological Association, the Association for Psychological Science, and the Academy of Management, and has received numerous scholarly awards. He has lectured and given courses at numerous Objectivist conferences.

Robert Mayhew is professor of philosophy at Seton Hall University. He is the author of *Aristotle's Criticism of Plato's* Republic, *The Female in Aristotle's Biology*, *Ayn Rand and* Song of Russia, and *Plato: Laws 10* (a translation with commentary). He has translated a play of Aristophanes (*Assembly of Women*), and edited three volumes of unpublished material of Ayn Rand: *Ayn Rand's Marginalia*, *The Art of Nonfiction*, and *Ayn Rand Answers*. He is currently preparing an edition of the Greek text, with translation, of the Aristotelian *Problemata*.

Shoshana Milgram [Knapp] holds a Ph.D. in comparative literature from Stanford University, and is associate professor of English at Virginia Tech. She has published articles on a variety of nineteenth- and twentieth-century figures in French, Russian, and English/American literature, including Napoleon Bonaparte, Victor Hugo, George Sand, Anton Chekhov, Fyodor Dostoevsky, Leo Tolstoi, Victoria Cross, George Eliot, John Fowles, W. S. Gilbert, Henry James, Ursula K. LeGuin, Vladimir Nabokov, Herbert Spencer, W. T. Stead, E. L. Voynich—and Ayn Rand. She is also the author of introductions to editions of *Toilers of the Sea* and *The Man Who Laughs*, by Victor Hugo, and *The Seafarers*, by Nevil Shute. Her current project is a study of Ayn Rand's life up to 1957.

Leonard Peikoff holds a Ph.D. in philosophy from New York University, and is the preeminent Rand scholar writing today. He worked closely with Ayn Rand for thirty years and was designated by her as heir to her estate. He has taught philosophy at Hunter College, Long Island University, and New York University, and has lectured on Rand's philosophy throughout the country. He is the author of *The Ominous Parallels* and *Objectivism: The Philosophy of Ayn Rand*, and is currently writing a book entitled *The DIM Hypothesis*.

Richard E. Ralston received a B.A. in history from the University of Maryland after serving seven years in the U.S. Army. He then completed an M.A. in international relations at the University of Southern California. He has been the managing director of the Ayn Rand Institute, and circulation director and publishing director of the *Christian Science Monitor*. He is the editor of two books, *Communism: Its Rise and Fall in the 20th Century* and *Why Businessmen Need Philosophy*. He is presently the executive director of Americans for Free Choice in Medicine, and publishing director of the Ayn Rand Institute.

Gregory Salmieri holds a Ph.D. in philosophy from the University of Pittsburgh and is currently teaching at the University of North Carolina, Chapel Hill. His research centers on ancient philosophy and issues at the foundations of epistemology and ethics. He lectures regularly on Ayn Rand's philosophy and novels, and is coeditor (with Allan Gotthelf) of *Ayn Rand: A Companion to Her Works and Thought* (forthcoming).

Tara Smith is professor of philosophy at the University of Texas at Austin, where she holds the BB&T Chair for the Study of Objectivism and is the Anthem Foundation Fellow. She is the author of *Ayn Rand's Normative Ethics: The Virtuous Egoist* (2006), *Viable Values: A Study of Life as the Root and Reward of Morality* (2000), and *Moral Rights and Political Freedom* (1995), as well as numerous articles, primarily focused in moral, legal, and political philosophy.

Mary Ann Sures taught art history at New York University (Washington Square College) and at Hunter College. Her lectures on esthetics include a ten-lecture course ("Esthetics of the Visual Arts") in which she applied Objectivist esthetics to painting and sculpture, and which was written in consultation with Ayn Rand. She is coauthor with her late husband Charles of *Facets of Ayn Rand*, memoirs of their longtime friendship with Ayn Rand and her husband, Frank O'Connor.

Darryl Wright is professor of philosophy at Harvey Mudd College. He received his B.A. from Princeton University and his Ph.D. from the University of Michigan. He has written and lectured on a variety of topics in ethics, the history of ethics, and political philosophy. His scholarly publications include two previous articles on the ethical thought of Ayn Rand.